Eroticism

Oxford History of Art

Alyce Mahon was educated at Trinity College Dublin and the Courtauld Institute in London. She is Senior Lecturer in Modern Art at the University of Cambridge and a Fellow of Trinity College Cambridge. She specializes in twentieth century art and critical theory, with a particular research emphasis on Surrealism, French art and politics, and performance art. Her other publications include *Surrealism and the Politics of Eros, 1938–1968* (2005).

Oxford History of Art

Titles in the Oxford History of Art series are up-to-date, fully illustrated introductions to a wide variety of subjects written by leading experts in their field. They will appear regularly, building into an interlocking and comprehensive series. In the list below, published titles appear in bold.

WESTERN ART

Archaic and Classical Greek Art
Robin Osborne

Classical Art From Greece to Rome
Mary Beard & John Henderson

Imperial Rome and Christian Triumph
Jas Elsner

Early Medieval Art
Lawrence Nees

Medieval Art
Veronica Sekules

Art in Renaissance Italy
Evelyn Welch

Northern Renaissance Art
Susie Nash

Art in Europe 1700–1830
Matthew Craske

Modern Art 1851–1929
Richard Brettell

After Modern Art 1945–2000
David Hopkins

WESTERN ARCHITECTURE

Roman Architecture
Janet Delaine

Early Medieval Architecture
Roger Stalley

Medieval Architecture
Nicola Coldstream

Renaissance Architecture
Christy Anderson

Baroque and Rococo Architecture
Hilary Ballon

European Architecture 1750–1890
Barry Bergdoll

Modern Architecture
Alan Colquhoun

Contemporary Architecture
Anthony Vidler

Architecture in the United States
Dell Upton

WORLD ART

Aegean Art and Architecture
Donald Preziosi & Louise Hitchcock

Early Art and Architecture of Africa
Peter Garlake

African-American Art
Sharon F. Patton

Nineteenth-Century American Art
Barbara Groseclose

Twentieth-Century American Art
Erika Doss

Australian Art
Andrew Sayers

Byzantine Art
Robin Cormack

Art in China
Craig Clunas

East European Art
Jeremy Howard

Indian Art
Partha Mitter

Islamic Art
Irene Bierman

Japanese Art
Karen Brock

Native North American Art
Janet Berlo & Ruth Phillips

Polynesian and Micronesian Art
Adrienne Kaeppler

WESTERN DESIGN

Twentieth-Century Design
Jonathan Woodham

Design in the USA
Jeffrey L. Meikle

Fashion
Christopher Breward

PHOTOGRAPHY

The Photograph
Graham Clarke

American Photography
Miles Orvell

WESTERN SCULPTURE

Sculpture 1900–1945
Penelope Curtis

Sculpture Since 1945
Andrew Causey

THEMES AND GENRES

Landscape and Western Art
Malcolm Andrews

Portraiture
Shearer West

Eroticism and Art
Alyce Mahon

Beauty and Art
Elizabeth Prettejohn

REFERENCE BOOKS

The Art of Art History: A Critical Anthology
Donald Preziosi (ed.)

Oxford History of Art

Eroticism and Art

Alyce Mahon

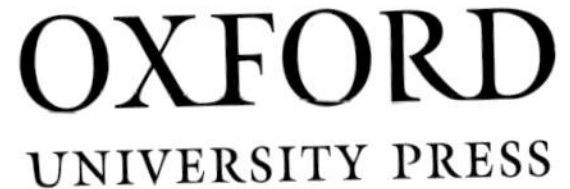
OXFORD
UNIVERSITY PRESS

OXFORD
UNIVERSITY PRESS

Great Clarendon Street, Oxford OX2 6DP

Oxford New York

Auckland Bangkok Buenos Aires Cape Town
Chennai Dar es Salaam Delhi Hong Kong Istanbul Karachi
Kolkata Kuala Lumpur Madrid Melbourne Mexico City Mumbai
Nairobi São Paulo Shanghai Taipei Tokyo Toronto

and associated companies in Berlin Ibadan

Oxford is a registered trade mark of Oxford University Press
in the UK and in certain other countries

First published 2005 by Oxford University Press

British Library Cataloguing in Publication Data
Data available

Library of Congress Cataloging-in-Publication Data
Data to follow
ISBN 978 0 19 280733 5
1 3 5 7 9 10 8 6 4 2

Picture research by Elisabeth Agate
Printed in China on acid-free paper by C&C Offset Printing Co. Ltd

To Mark

Contents

Acknowledgements

I would like to thank Katharine Reeve of Oxford University Press for commissioning this book and Matthew Cotton who later took over from her and saw it through to completion. I am warmly grateful for the generosity of the artists, galleries, museums, and collectors who have helped to make this such a handsomely illustrated publication. I thank my picture researcher, Elisabeth Agate, who liaised with them industriously on my behalf; and David Williams, who skilfully copy-edited the manuscript and laid out the pages. I also gratefully acknowledge the constructive criticism and insightful comments provided by my anonymous readers.

At the University of Cambridge, I thank my colleagues in the Department of History of Art who have encouraged and supported my research: especially Jean Michel Massing, with whom I have enjoyed so many discussions on art, erotic and not erotic; Paul Joannides, for sharing his thoughts on nineteenth-century painting; and my facilitating and sponsoring Head of Department, Deborah Howard. I am also grateful to the Master and Fellows of Trinity College and the University of Cambridge for providing funding towards the costs of my primary research.

Two dear friends offered scholarly feedback on sections of the book: Aya Soika, especially on Vienna, Weimar, and German Expressionism in Chapters 3 and 4; and Nebahat Avcioglu, on Orientalism and Ingres in Chapter 1. As friends, their *joie de vivre* always lifted my spirits. My father, Joseph Mahon, provided comments on an early draft which helped me fine-tune aspects of my argument. My mother Evelyn, my brother James, and my sister Amy were always there with encouragement and kindness as I worked through what often seemed a mammoth project. I dedicate this book with love to my constant intellectual and emotional companion, Mark Shiel.

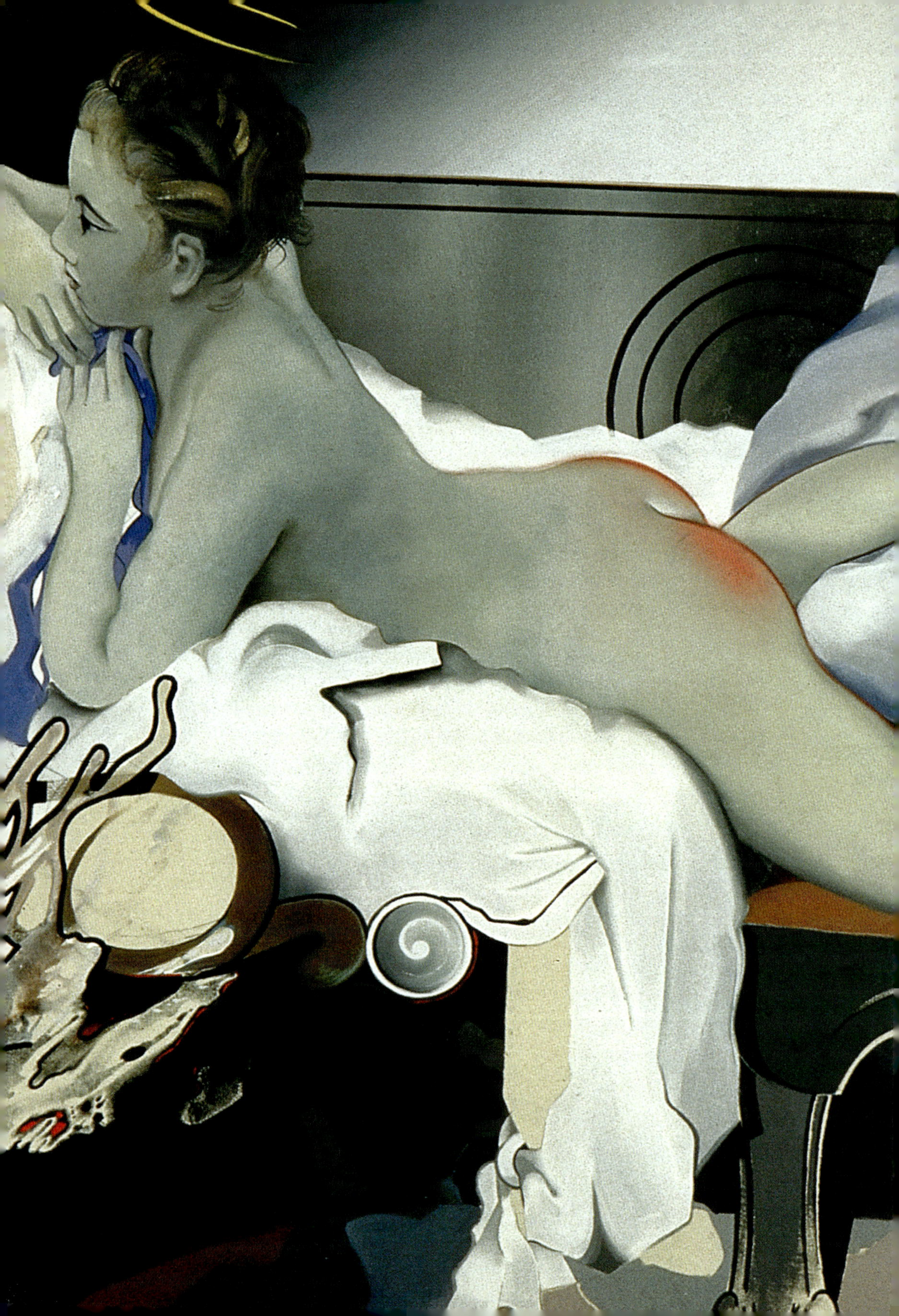

Introduction

Erotic desire is a fundamental part of our private and public lives. It permeates every aspect of our popular culture—cinema, television, publishing, advertising, music. Irrespective of how we choose to express or repress erotic desire, and irrespective even of our differences of opinion over what forms of eroticism are permissible, representations of the erotic inevitably speak to us all. The power of eroticism is perhaps never so challenging, however, as when given visual form in art. Then we can both indulge and confront our fantasies. Erotic art brings us face to face with love and sexual desire, titillation and carnal attraction, as well as the desires of others which we may find repulsive. It tests our individual and collective idea not only of what is 'pleasing' but also of what is 'decent' or 'proper'.

The erotic is defined in the *Oxford English Dictionary* as 'of or pertaining to the passion of love; concerned with or treating love' and in the *Collins Dictionary* as 'of, concerning, or arousing, sexual desire or giving sexual pleasure'.[1] The origin of the word lies in the Greek *eros*—sexual desire or passionate love, the life drive itself. The Greek notion of Eros encompasses a range of expression, from thoughts of desire and their representations in art and literature to the sexual act itself. These origins immediately alert us to the complexity and potency of the erotic and its psychological—as well as physical—dimension, which often drives the individual to act and think differently in his/her pursuit of passion, life, and fulfilment. Eros is not merely about sexual procreation, it is about the production of pleasure and, most importantly, is often expressed in opposition to Thanatos (its opposite, the death drive), and in the name of an ideology of choice, unfettered by social and moral norms. In the dominant Western philosophical tradition from the Greek philosopher Plato (427–347 BC) to the Enlightenment philosopher Immanuel Kant (1724–1804), Eros was contained and subjugated because of its association with the baser, sensuous faculties and appetites of the individual, and because of the privileging of a much 'higher' faculty—reason. Where Eros and love were recognized within this tradition it was not to indulge in sexual desire but to attain greater knowledge; Eros became ennobled. Thus in Plato's *Symposium* love, which is 'powerful and treacherous', is explained as 'every type of desire

Detail of 11

for good things or happiness'. Knowledge is all; the pleasures and desires of the flesh are only a distraction, and sexuality an obstacle to the spirit. Those concerned with 'making money or athletics or philosophy' are not said to be 'loving' or 'lovers'.[2] The greatest desire within the Platonic tradition is not for the flesh but for knowledge, a purified knowledge spoken of in abstracted, contemplative terms that liberates it both from the body and from sexuality and the erotic, carnal dimension of Eros. This is the idealizing, ascetic philosophical tradition that largely dominated Western thought up until the twentieth century, against which the history of erotic art must be viewed. Occasional voices went against this tradition, of course. The English philosopher David Hume (1711–76), for example, argued in *A Treatise of Human Nature* (1739–40) against the view in philosophy and common life that 'men are only so far virtuous as they conform themselves to [reason's] dictates', endeavouring to prove instead that it is the passions, not reason, that motivate us.[3] For Hume, rather than be perceived as dangerous, the passions should be recognized for the positive effects they can have on human nature and actions. Thus he saw lust in virtuous terms, as Simon Blackburn has argued.[4] Hume reasoned there was no opposition between reason and passion because reason was the slave of the passions, and obliged to obey them, and passion was a 'virtue', defined by Hume as any quality of mind 'useful or agreeable to the person himself or to others'.[5] However, Hume's more influential contemporary Kant confidently wrote in his *Lectures on Ethics*:

> Sexual love makes of the loved person an Object of appetite; as soon as that appetite has been stilled, the person is cast aside as one casts away a lemon which has been sucked dry . . . Taken by itself it is a degradation of human nature . . . that is why we are ashamed of [sexual desire], and why all strict moralists, and those who had pretensions to be regarded as saints, sought to suppress and extirpate it.[6]

Not only is erotic desire and sensuous feeling removed from the dominant philosophical tradition with which Kant is associated—and (by extension) from aesthetic pleasure—but sexuality, sexual desire, and the body are all proposed as a *threat* to rational, civilized society. Eroticism, because it is linked to the emotions (from sexual arousal to fear and anger), has the power to agitate the mind, the soul, and to disrupt order. This struggle—between Eros and knowledge, emotions and reason, the flesh and the spirit, sexual expression and repression—is at the heart of erotic art and its power to reinforce dominant ideology, or to assault it.

It is the field of erotic expression in art, especially modern and contemporary art, that is the concern of this book: how the marriage of eroticism and art transforms both, how the sexual and visual are tested in this partnership. When incorporated in art, eroticism is not only about sexual desire and pleasure, it is something more. It draws on the Western metaphysical tradition, the battle between the body and the mind; it also speaks to our desire for a communion with others, our passion for life, our fear of mortality. As the French philosopher and writer Georges Bataille wrote in 1957, 'Eroticism, unlike simple sexual activity, is a psychological quest independent of the natural goal: reproduction and the desire for children . . . eroticism is assenting to life even in death.'[7] Sexual desire is an intrinsic part of human nature, but social and moral limits are imposed on it by society as the body is regulated and codes of appropriate sexual behaviour laid down. Unlike the sexuality of other animals, human sexuality is restricted by social custom, by taboos that deem certain acts forbidden or unlawful (including menstruation, nakedness, incest). The essence of eroticism lies in the transgression of these taboos, drawing on the sacred and forbidden origins of the very term 'taboo', such that, as Bataille puts it, eroticism 'presupposes man in conflict with himself'.[8] The Bataillean understanding of eroticism—that man's erotic urges terrify him—informs this book. For it is the frisson of the narrow divide between erotic desire and erotic excess, between acceptable representations of eroticism and ones that cause outrage, that exposes not just the true nature of eroticism but our human trepidation when the erotic is given representational form.

This broader philosophical and sociological significance of the erotic has figured in many Francophone theorists' writings, including the historian and philosopher Michel Foucault and the semiotician and psychoanalyst Julia Kristeva. Foucault's investigation of the conflict between desire and power, carnality and subjectivity, and Kristeva's exploration of the abject body both bring the body into the discourse of the social sciences and have expanded our understanding of the socialization of the sexual body. Foucault's writings allow us to see how desire and eroticism can be viewed as a site not only of knowledge–power but also of resistance, and Kristeva's help us to appreciate that sexuality is not an innate quality in women or men but is developed through family and social nurture.[9] Both recognize libidinal pleasure as a powerful aspect of individual and collective life, Kristeva in particular emphasizing the subversive potential of *jouissance*—a term which may be understood as pleasure but also as sexual climax and the bliss of enjoyment without fear of the costs.[10] Erotic art is all about *jouissance*, shifting from visual pleasure to the pursuit of pleasure without concerns about rules, ends, or closure. These perspectives on the body and erotic pleasure also underpin this book's understanding of erotic art.

Unsurprisingly, given the life-enhancing, pleasurable dimension of the erotic and its potential to challenge rules and defy social and moral boundaries, many artists have been drawn to it for its aesthetic and ideological power. Throughout the history of erotic representations in Western art, artists have been able to use the erotic to address the classical ideal, the beautiful, and the sublimation of our basic sexual desires for a greater moral good. In the nineteenth and twentieth centuries, however, artists increasingly employed the erotic for its subversive significance, for the danger it could pose to art and society. Like Plato and Kant, they recognized that eroticism has the power to threaten the orderly balance between the flesh and the spirit, individual desire and the common good. But they tended to revel in it rather than seek to control it.

Eroticism's Intent

Erotic art is usually acknowledged as such when it speaks to the individual's notion of sexual desire but also to the general consensus on aesthetic value. It is to be distinguished from pornography, which historically has been defined as 'a description of prostitutes or of prostitution, as a matter of public hygiene' (1857) and which is today described as 'writings, pictures, films, etc., designed to stimulate sexual excitement'.[11] While pornography has expanded in meaning to embrace both the acts of prostitutes and their patrons and the representation of those acts, the vital difference between the erotic and the pornographic lies in the intent. Pornography's sole intent is to stimulate sexually; it is an aid to sex or masturbation. Coming from the Greek *porne* (a harlot, prostitute), and *graphos* (describing or writing), pornography involves an imbalance of financial power: a pornographic magazine or film intended to act as a sexual aid usually only exists for the purpose of making money. Furthermore, with pornography, the purchaser is oblivious to the individuality of the sexual performer, whether that performer is in a fantasy position of submission or domination. Thus while pornography draws on an individual's desires and fantasies—often deriving from childhood memories and fantasies, long repressed by social conditioning—the element of dehumanization and sexual objectification in that individual's fantasy relationship with an other or others is key to pornography's fundamental relationship with power, not with sex or Eros. By extension, *consent* remains a key distinction between the erotic and the pornographic: consent allows for sexual diversity (for example a preference for heterosexual, gay, and lesbian S/M) in eroticism. It also ensures a sexual ethics that proscribes the pornographic description, staging, or enactment of rape or paedophilia fantasies (for example) characteristic of hardcore pornography, in which there is a graphic connection between 'sex and violence, hatred, pain, and humiliation'.[12] Unlike pornography, erotic art is about equality between members of the opposite and same sexes. This distinction was crucial to radical feminists' critique of pornography in the 1970s and 1980s. As Gloria Steinem wrote in her 1977 essay 'Erotica vs. Pornography', 'pornography is not about sex. It's about an imbalance of male–female power that allows and even requires sex to be used as a form of aggression. Erotica may be the word that can differentiate sex from violence and rescue sexual pleasure.'[13] She continues: 'Though both erotica and pornography refer to verbal or pictorial representations of sexual behaviour, they are as different as a room with doors open and one with doors locked.'[14] The 'open door' metaphor reminds us that erotic art goes beyond the physical, sexual act itself, insofar as the sense of illusion that is key to pornography derives either from the pretence that the sexual act is being witnessed unbeknownst to the actors or from the knowledge that we would never normally be allowed to see it at all. Erotic art may draw on aspects of pornography, notably the depiction of sexual organs and sexual practices, but it does not do so for sexual arousal alone. It also plays on the aesthetic imagination, usually employing sexual imagery as a shocking means to express social, religious, and political criticism or defy bourgeois taste and its preconceptions of 'good' and 'bad' art.

Much of the erotic art discussed in this book has been denounced as an 'outrage to morality', as 'obscene'. For art that focuses on the depiction of the sexual organs is often taken as an indicator of the 'obscene', since it appears to deny any erotic sentiment and to focus on the genitals, which are in themselves often deemed to be offensive to the eye. Some of the works of art discussed might fall under Andrea Dworkin and Catharine A. MacKinnon's 1988 radical feminist definition of pornography as 'graphic sexually explicit materials that subordinate women through pictures and words', notably where 'women's body parts—including but not limited to, vaginas, breasts, or buttocks—are exhibited such that women are reduced to those parts'.[15] But Dworkin and MacKinnon's definition would outlaw much art and literature, as their many feminist critics recognized at the time and continue to recognize now. Indeed, much erotic art in the 1980s which engaged in sexually explicit material such as gay and lesbian S/M was deemed obscene, especially in the United States, where it was attacked by critics from both the Left and the Right. It was at this time, for example, that the ex-prostitute, female performance artist Annie Sprinkle (b. 1954) invited the public to look into her vagina with a speculum, in art she described as 'post porn modernism'. Sexually explicit imagery, often where women (and men) seemed to be reduced to their body parts, was increasingly used by minority groups as a way of insisting that their human sexual rights *not* be thrown in with the very different issues of sexual slavery, prostitution, and hardcore pornography, as Dworkin and MacKinnon's definition tended to do.

It is one of the arguments of this book that our understanding of eroticism has been too blinkered. It has been restricted both by conservative and libertarian sexual politics and debates. By extension erotic art has either been too quickly dismissed as pleasurable for the sake of pleasure alone or it has been torn apart for being politically incorrect. If we are to assess sexually explicit art critically—rather than merely react to it—then we must look to its social, historical, and political contexts, its artistic intent, and its popular and critical reception. The traditional image of the erotic work of art as a pink and fanciful representation of voluptuous female nudes is only a tiny fraction of our visual past and present. Eroticism has *always* been one of the most important protagonists in the story of Western art. With the Enlightenment and the birth of modern art which followed, however, a shift occurred in which the body, sexuality, and erotic art were gradually liberated from the controlling powers of the Church and State. Between the emergence of the 'painter of modern life' (in the nineteenth-century poet and critic Charles Baudelaire's oft-cited terms) and today's postmodernism in which erotic transgression seems to have no limits, erotic art has been particularly challenging and exciting, a place for artists to explore the issue of power. From the mid-nineteenth century, erotic art began to challenge openly the acceptable limits of sexual representation. As Michel Foucault argued in volume one of *The History of Sexuality* (1976), the nineteenth century saw a new complication of sexuality and individuality, as the body became increasingly regulated (for example through the family and the control of the female body with the monitoring of the birth rate, prostitution, and sexual disease), and increasingly repressed through social custom (taboo) and legislation. The bourgeois anxiety over sexuality of which Foucault speaks coincided with a rapidly changing social environment which saw the rise of mass culture and sexually explicit images which entered into high culture, threatening its aesthetic principles—its 'civilizing' mission—in the process. Many artists drew inspiration from the culture of the masses, the popular press, advertising, and cheap pornography, and from new technological means of expression, especially photography and film. Through the embrace of low culture, the aspirations of high culture could be challenged, the concept of good taste questioned, and taboos transgressed. From the mid-nineteenth century, traditional erotic art and its timeless, heroic and/or moralizing depiction of the erotic body began to be replaced with a new erotic art that spoke to contemporary reality. The viewer of art was put into a new, often awkward, position. The majority of the artists discussed in this book not only turned to the erotic as a theme and a strategy to question the history and aesthetic traditions of art itself but to affect society radically and advance political agendas.

Seeing Sexual Desire

Art allows erotic fantasy to become reality. Eroticism in art may be knowingly arousing and titillating, designed to please the erotic tastes of the viewer—whether the dominant erotic tastes of society or its avant-garde alternatives. One only has to think of the beauty of a reclining female nude by Titian (1485–1576) **[1]** or a heroic male nude by Michelangelo Buonarroti (1475–1564) **[2]** to appreciate the dominant erotic tradition in Western art. Yet these works are more than the sum of their parts, they reflect very specific notions of beauty and taste promoted in their day; they use the perfect body, female and male, as a reminder of greater truths, greater beauties. We find more than pearly flesh in Titian, we also find moral codes, notably the expression of virginity, chastity, and fidelity expressed largely through prudish gesture, a veiled sex, and the presence of a pet animal (a symbol of loyalty). Equally

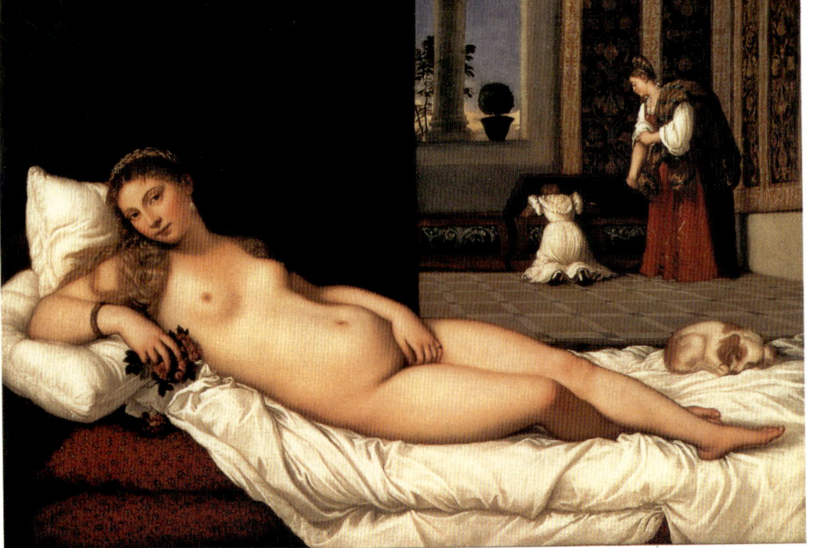

1 Titian
Venus of Urbino, before 1538

Painted for the Duke of Camerino, Guidobaldo della Rovere, this is one of the many reclining Venuses Titian painted. In pose it is indebted to Giorgione's *Sleeping Venus* (*c.*1510). However, where Giorgione's nude is asleep and in nature, Titian's is awake in a splendid palatial interior. She holds a small bouquet of flowers and is accompanied by her sleeping dog, while a maid and lady are visible in the chamber behind. Like Giorgione's Venus, she coyly covers her sex, enticing the viewer towards it—a pose to which Manet's *Olympia* (1863) **[4]** later paid homage.

2 Michelangelo
David, 1501–4

David was initially intended for one of the buttresses of Florence Cathedral, but the herald of the Republic of Florence decided it should stand in front of the main entrance to the Palazzo Vecchio as a proud symbol of Florentine political and humanist values. While the statue's heroic nudity was central to its symbolism, it was not put in place until its sex and what Vasari called its 'divine flanks' were discreetly camouflaged by a 'girdle' of 28 copper leaves.

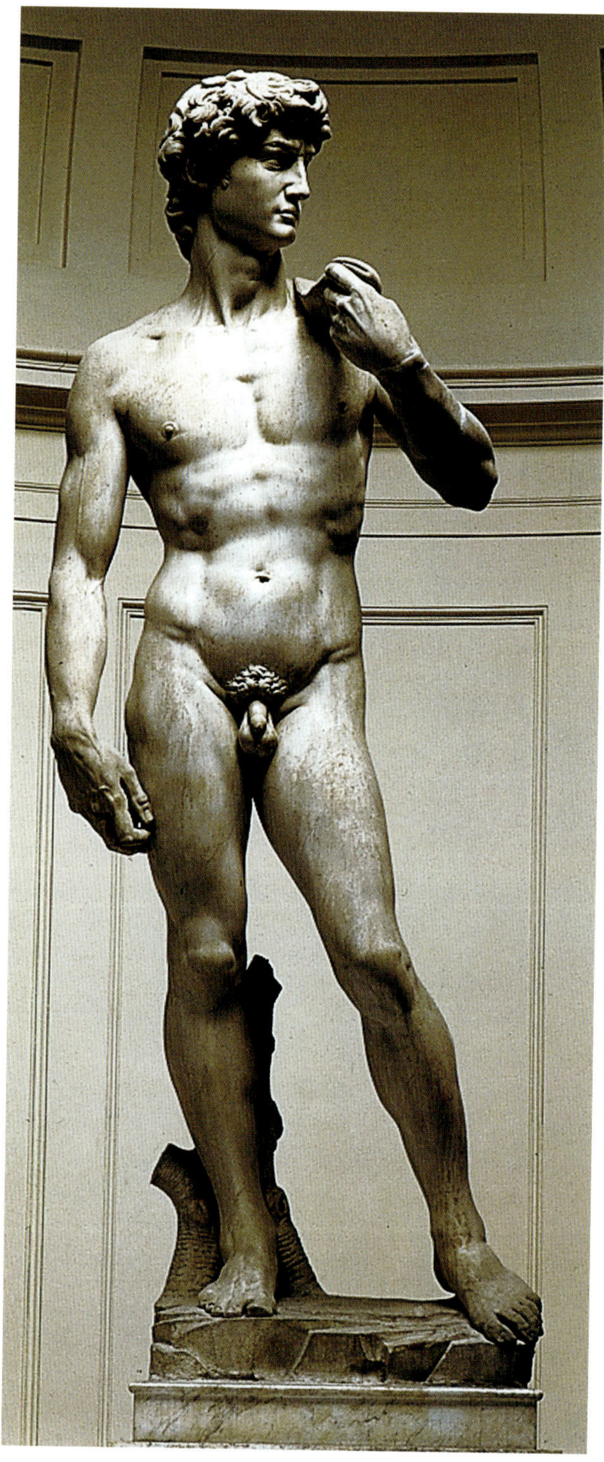

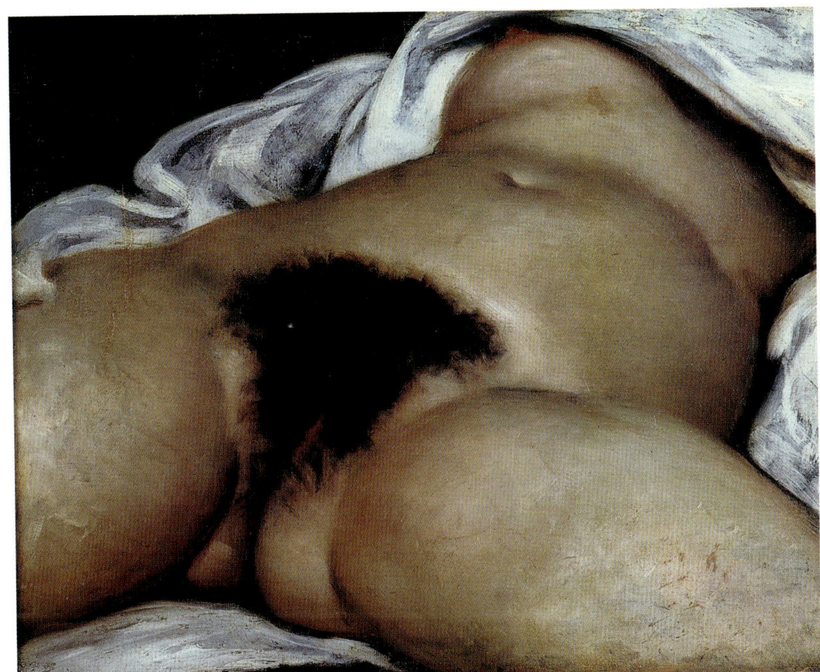

3 Gustave Courbet
The Origin of the World,
1866

Rejecting the classicism and Romanticism of his academic masters, Courbet's audacious foreshortening, brushwork, and use of the palette-knife to portray the luminosity of a white sheet, flesh, and hair lend this painting of the female sex a startling and palpable realism.

Michelangelo's perfectly sculpted male suggests the attributes of inner beauty and knowledge, grace and modesty, as well as glorifying the perfectly 'sculpted' State and its particular ideological vision.

When this 'contained' erotic tradition is not respected we find the boundaries of the visible and aesthetically acceptable challenged. Purity gives way to danger, beauty is replaced with obscenity, grace with abjection, and modesty with the explicit. Sexual desire is no longer simply staged between the viewer and the object in the image so that the former may be elevated, his/her mind raised above the flesh to ponder on the spirit. The viewer is no longer seduced, he/she is shocked, the eye is affronted and moral certainty disturbed. Artists who pursue this provocative erotic path include the French painter Gustave Courbet (1819–77), whose *The Origin of the World* (1866) **[3]** replaced traditional erotic purity with impure explicit sexuality in boldly presenting a painting of what the philosopher Roger Scruton has bashfully described as a woman's 'lower portrait'. For Scruton, a painting such as Courbet's 'which conceals the face but exposes the genitals must inevitably verge on the obscene'.[16] Certainly the very act of 'making visible' the female sex lends this painting its continued controversial erotic force, as we shall see. But while Scruton rightly acknowledges the drama of desire this particular painting stages, it is Courbet's powerful rendition of the dynamics and politics of desire—between the artist, model and

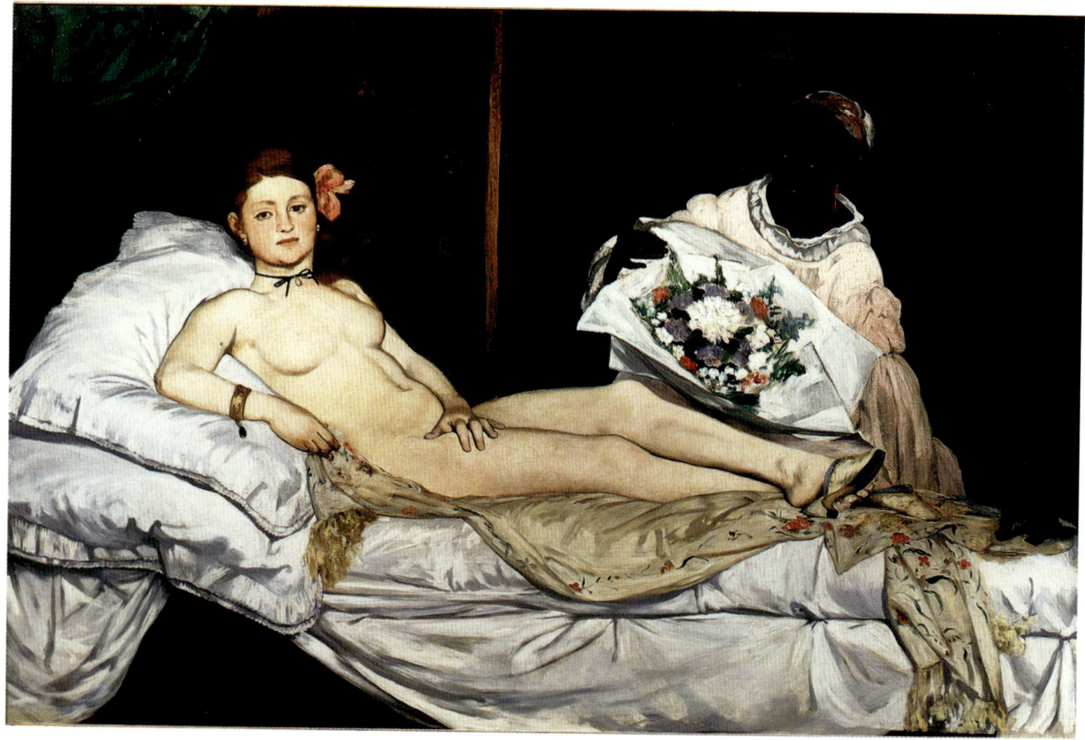

4 Édouard Manet
Olympia, 1863
Decried at the Paris Art Salon of 1865 as a 'yellow-bellied Odalisque' and a 'sort of female gorilla', Olympia adopts the pose of classical Venuses by Giorgione and Titian—Manet copied Titian's *Venus of Urbino* in 1856. Yet she also embodies a startlingly frank modernity, expressed not just in loose daubs of colour but in her bold return of the gaze.

spectator—that begs further attention. Herein lies the key to its erotic defiance of both traditional beauty and the fear of the forbidden and the obscene—the latter deemed by Scruton and others to be too great a threat to the moral good to be permissibly erotic.

Erotic art both challenges and produces power. Artists turn to eroticism as a means of exploring the nature and role in society of both sexual desire and art itself. They also turn to eroticism as a means of pushing back the boundaries of art practice and aesthetic 'norms', and by extension, as a means of challenging, if not breaking, socially accepted codes of sexual behaviour too: in *Olympia* (1863) **[4]**, a painting of a modern-day prostitute by Édouard Manet (1832–83), we find an assault on the French academic art tradition and a heralding of a new art practice independent of court or Church patronage; in *Helmut* (1978) **[82]** by Robert Mapplethorpe (1946–89), we see a homoerotic close-up photograph of a man's buttocks in leather, work of a kind which led to calls for censorship from the Christian Right in the United States in the late 1980s. To appreciate how art is inscribed with ideology we need to go beyond the two- or three-dimensional object and consider art as a social product. We need to consider the relationship between the work of art (the product), its producer (the artist), and its consumer (the

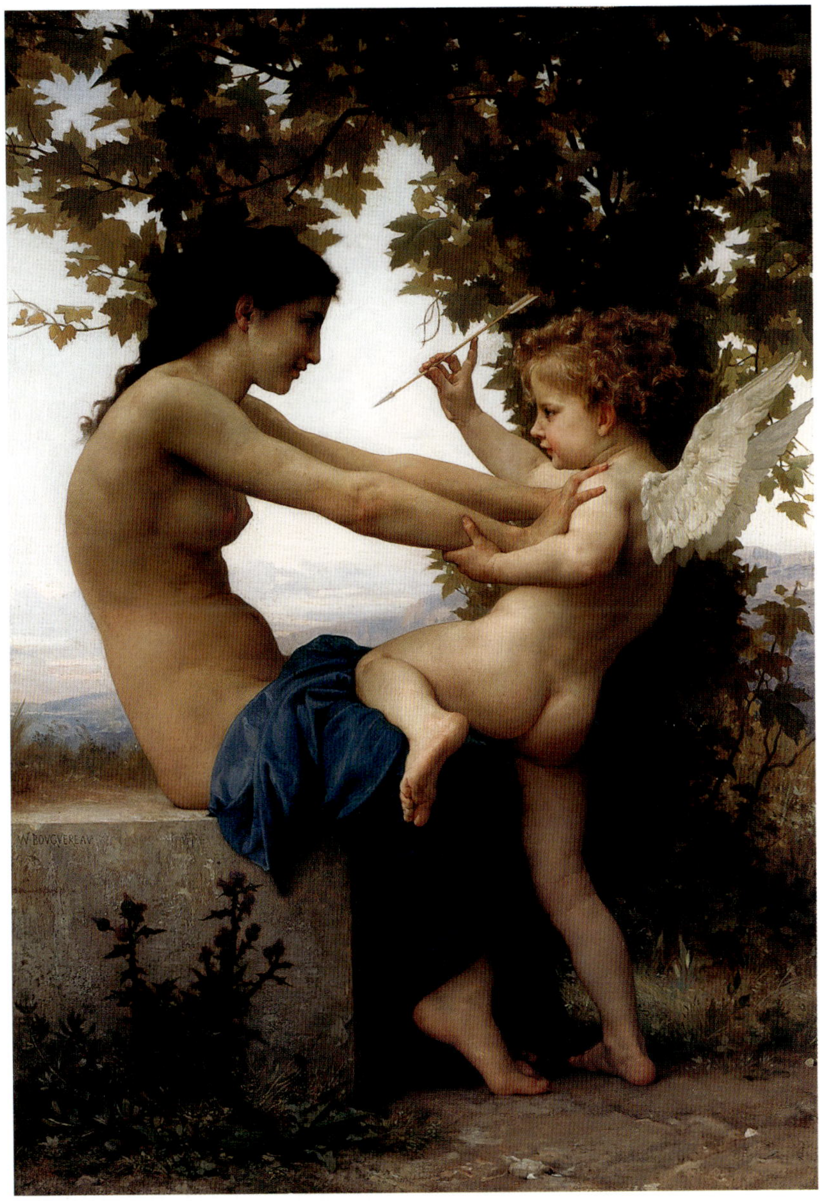

5 William Adolphe Bouguereau
A Young Girl Defending Herself against Eros, *c.*1880

Bouguereau's young girl fends off Eros, who wields a golden arrow plumed with dove feathers to incite love. The artist stages his nude to allow the viewer to appreciate her nubile form in profile, her flesh dramatically offset by the cold plinth and the vibrant blue cloth.

public). *A Young Girl Defending Herself against Eros* (*c.*1880) **[5]**, by William Adolphe Bouguereau (1825–1905), reminds us of the complexity of an image, its many layers of meaning, especially when it pertains to the erotic. It is a painting we might not immediately date as late nineteenth century given its mythological subject-matter, classical technique, and timeless message at a time when Impressionist painters were wreaking havoc on such highly finished academic style. It exemplifies the

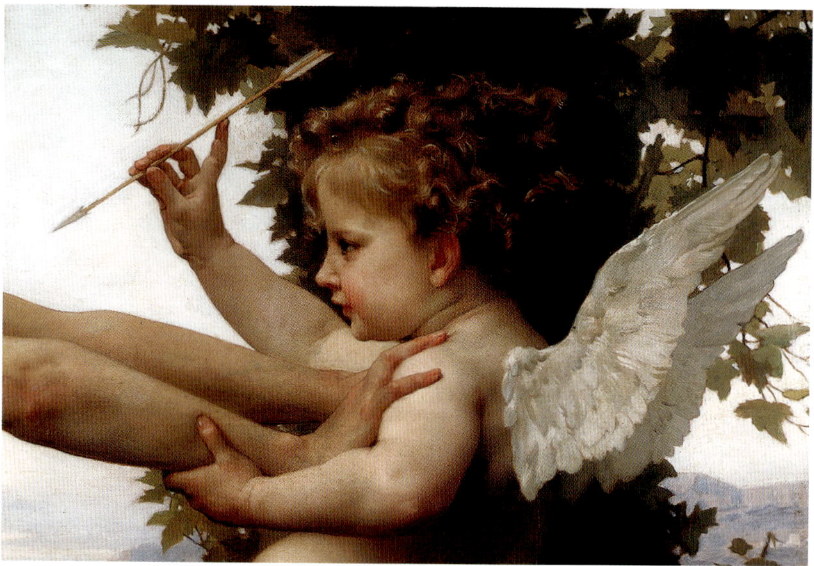

Detail of 5

dominant taste for classical, controlled eroticism among the bourgeoisie even in the last decades of the nineteenth century. Like his Venetian models, Titian and Veronese (*c.*1528–88), Bouguereau turned to myth for his erotic sources. He also warned of the danger of unleashed eroticism in his title and depiction of *A Young Girl Defending Herself against Eros.* At a time when rapid modernization in French industry and in social and sexual attitudes was occurring, Bouguereau chose to present an erotic image of a nude in a style which had been timeless but now began to seem outmoded, although the painting was warmly received when exhibited in 1880 at the official annual exhibition of the Paris Salon.

If we look closely at the painting we see that Bouguereau depicts a beautiful nude woman playing with a curly-haired boy in an Arcadian landscape. She smiles, but we are told she is 'defending' herself against him. While he strikes us as an angelic, chubby creature, a nostalgic reminder of Renaissance *putti*, his wings and plumed arrow reveal him to be the Greek god Eros, the son of Aphrodite (the goddess of love, beauty, and sexual rapture), and Ares (the god of war), or in Roman mythology, Cupid (from the Latin *cupere*, to desire), the son of Venus and Mars. As the offspring of love and war, Eros/Cupid is the god of love and sexual desire and the primordial life force of the universe. Despite his baby face, one shot from his arrow could lead Bouguereau's young woman to dangerous heights of sexual arousal. According to myth, Eros is charming and beautiful and typically carries two types of arrows: golden ones plumed with dove feathers to incite love, and leaden arrows with owl's feathers to incite indifference. There are many tales about him, both as Eros in Greek myth and as Cupid in later accounts. One the most popular dates from the second century AD, from Lucius Apuleius's *Golden Ass* or *Metamorphoses*, in which, as Cupid, he becomes involved with a beautiful mortal woman, Psyche. Sent by his jealous mother Venus to shoot the beautiful Psyche with one of his arrows—to make her fall in love with the ugliest man on earth—he instead was so taken by Psyche's beauty that he fell in love with her, secretly visiting her every night in the safety of darkness, forbidding her to see him. One night, Psyche's curiosity got the better of her and with the aid of an oil lamp she stole a look at her mysterious lover; a drop of hot oil fell on him, awakening him and causing him to flee in anger. She roamed the earth trying to find him again until Jupiter, the ruler of gods and mortals (known as Zeus in Greek mythology), took pity on her and reunited her with her lover, giving consent for god and mortal to marry. A tale of mad, irrepressible love, it reinforced the individual's need for, and fulfilment through, Eros. Thus Eros was often portrayed by the Greeks as a passionate young man, with a perfect athlete's body but a tempestuous spirit and in later times, in the guise of Cupid, as proof that love conquers all; throughout the ages his power lies not only in the arousal of sexual excitement but also the potential threat of that excitement to the social order.

In this painting, Bouguereau chooses not to depict Eros as the Greeks did—as a virile, passionate man—but as the Romans did, as a young, curly-haired boy. Bouguereau portrays Eros in de-eroticized terms as Cupid. Yet he does remind us of the danger of sexual longing. As we look at the painting we are privy to the temptation of a young woman's nude body, perched precariously on a cold stone plinth, her sex coyly covered by a brilliant blue cloth that strategically enhances both the pinkness of her skin and that of Cupid's buttocks. Her gesture allows us to appreciate her nude form in profile, while the methodical application of paint reminds us of the tradition of Renaissance nudes, especially the luscious nudes of Titian, whom Bouguereau believed presented the eye with perfection itself.[17]

The Erotic Tradition

Bouguereau's return to the classical tradition in 1880 not only involved a re-working of Greek myth. Neoclassical art of the late nineteenth century also drew upon more than two thousand years of figurative and erotic art. In Greek visual culture the worship of gods and goddesses often took the form of the celebration of erotic and fertile prowess in

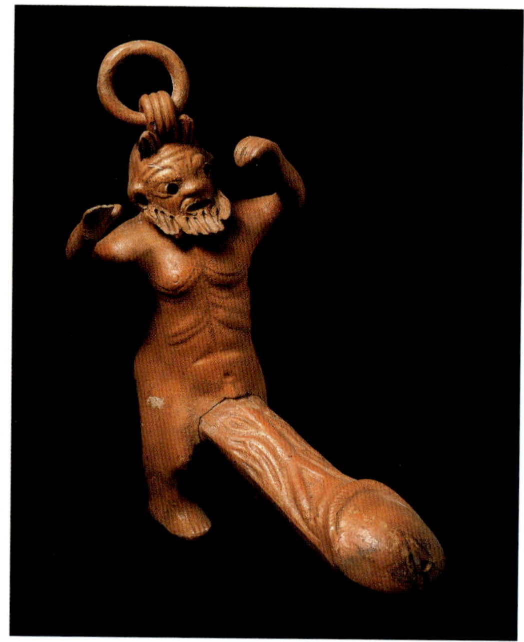

6 Anonymous
Priapus, first century AD, from Pompeii

The god of fertility and protector of horticulture and viticulture, Priapus was identified by his large phallus, a symbol of potency as well as a talisman against evil.

explicitly sexual imagery. The orgiastic cult of Dionysus, the Greek god of wine and revelry, is perhaps the most renowned example, revealed in artefacts and architectural detail from Classical Greece to the late Roman Empire (although to the Romans Dionysus was Bacchus).[18] In ancient Rome the fertility god Priapus **[6]**, the offspring of Venus and Bacchus, was another popular erotic subject. Images of Priapus with his mighty phallus were common on the walls of public baths. Phallic amulets were also popular as simple good-luck charms because Priapus was seen as the bearer of happiness and as the protector of gardens, vines, bees, and flocks. He was a figure of superstitious myth or even religious devotion.

It was not until the Renaissance in Italy from the fourteenth to the sixteenth centuries that the sexual connotations of Priapus' erect phallus became a subject of concern, notably for the Catholic Church. Then we find that his large phallus was usually concealed, its erectness only suggested by the folds of his garments, as in Giovanni Bellini's bacchanal painting, *The Feast of the Gods* (*c.*1514/1529). Here, the Venetian painter depicts a scene from Ovid's *Fasti* in which the gods revel in a pastoral setting while Bacchus tries to steal up on the sleeping nymph Lotis only to be caught out by a braying ass and laughed at by his fellow deities. Then as now the erect male organ, the privilege of male desire, was taboo.[19] Of course the beautiful irony of erotic art is that it developed within the art patronized by the Church and good Christians, and that such camouflaging or censorship of sexual desire in art only added to the erotic suspense. To preach morality and goodness one needed to be able to conceive of immorality and evil: earthly delights needed to be given form if the demise of the soul and an afterlife in purgatory were to be truly appreciated in all their terrifying detail. In the Middle Ages, sexual temptation had been deemed to be the work of the devil. Woodcuts and drawings, cathedral carvings and books of prayer, clearly linked the pleasures of the flesh with damnation and the fall from godly grace. The writings of Saint Augustine, born in 354, became influential in the Middle Ages, notably his *Confessions*, written after his conversion to Christianity at the age of 43. Here he confesses to his own youthful indulgences in the flesh and the flames of desire (with his conversion he abandoned his partner and son), and in a very human—and moderate for its day—manner admitted to the temptations that face even a man who has chosen the path of chastity. Thus while warning against the gratification of the senses he begged God to help him restrain himself 'from the lust of the flesh, the lust of the eyes, and the ambition of the world', a lust that particularly taunted him in his sleep when he feared that reason seemed to sleep too.[20]

As the Italian Renaissance resurrected the body in all its earthly glory, a shift occurred. Art still instructed, but the wooden, tormented forms of much medieval art gave way to full-blooded, fleshy forms. The Florentine painter and architect Giotto di Bondone (1267–1337) revolutionized art in drawing from nature, liberating form, and introducing realistic perspective. For Giorgio Vasari, in his *Lives of the Artists* (1568), Giotto breathed life into Italian painting by abandoning the 'crude tradition' of the Greek East; for this, Giotto deserved to be praised as 'a pupil of Nature'.[21] Giotto's fresco cycle (*c.*1303–10) for the Arena Chapel, dedicated to the Virgin of Charity, in the university town of Padua, brought realistic figures, animals, architecture, and landscape together, linking scenes in a heavenly blue in a perspectival scheme that not only vividly instructed the public on the life of the Virgin but also allowed them to empathize and identify with characters, and 'to step into' the time and space Giotto depicts, just as we so easily do today when watching a film. The entrance wall depicting *The Last Judgement* brought the temptations of the flesh into pulsating form in a powerful presentation of the sacred and profane, with Christ at the centre averting his gaze from the damned to one side below him. *The Last Judgement* presents an explicit warning to all pilgrims to lead ascetic lives, as the dead are either welcomed into Heaven by Christ or condemned to a torturous eternity in Hell. Among those closest to the fire of Hell are a damned couple, surrounded by other naked bestial creatures. They

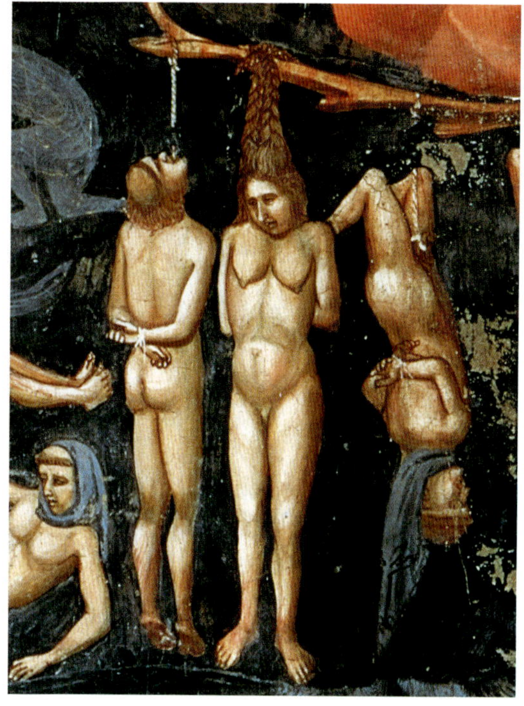

7 Giotto
The Last Judgement (detail), *c.*1303–10

While the virtuous are welcomed into Heaven in Giotto's depiction of the Last Judgement, the damned suffer in Hell.

have overindulged in the flesh, as has another who may be seen hung up, literally, by his genitals **[7]**. The traces of medieval fear and Saint Augustine's plea to the Lord to help him quell his sensual fire are here commandingly rendered in Giotto's natural style.

The Renaissance thus continued the humanist ideal and emphasis on the weaknesses of the flesh and the purity of the soul, albeit in increasingly realistic, earthy figures portrayed in such natural styles as to make their pleasures and pains all the more impressive for the devout. The phallic glory of Priapus could not be worshipped but forms of veiled eroticism emerged, with religious iconography tending to take one of two paths when it came to the erotic: the ecstasy of martyrdom or heavenly beauty. Martyrdom, with all its bloody narratives of pain, flagellation, and mutilations, signified the embrace of purification and purging of the flesh *in extremis*. Here the sexual body was literally punished and ultimately killed, and the taboo of murder transgressed: Saint Agatha's torment, for example, involves the crushing and cutting off of her breasts; Saint Sebastian is bound and then pierced with arrow after arrow. This was a de-eroticized pleasure and yet in Platonic terms one far richer and more satisfying than any delight of the weak flesh. *St Sebastian* **[8]** by Andrea Mantegna (1431–1506) seems to revel in the contrast of cold marble and hot skin, archaic knowledge and bodily

8 Andrea Mantegna
St Sebastian, 1481

St Sebastian's torture was slow and cruel: due to his loyalty to God, Imperial Rome ordered that he be tied up and fired upon with arrows. Having survived this torment he was then flogged to death and his body thrown into the Roman sewers. Mantegna portrays him on the brink of death, blood dripping from his pierced flesh, and augments his vulnerability by juxtaposing him with a cold, classical column and arch which stand as symbols of Rome.

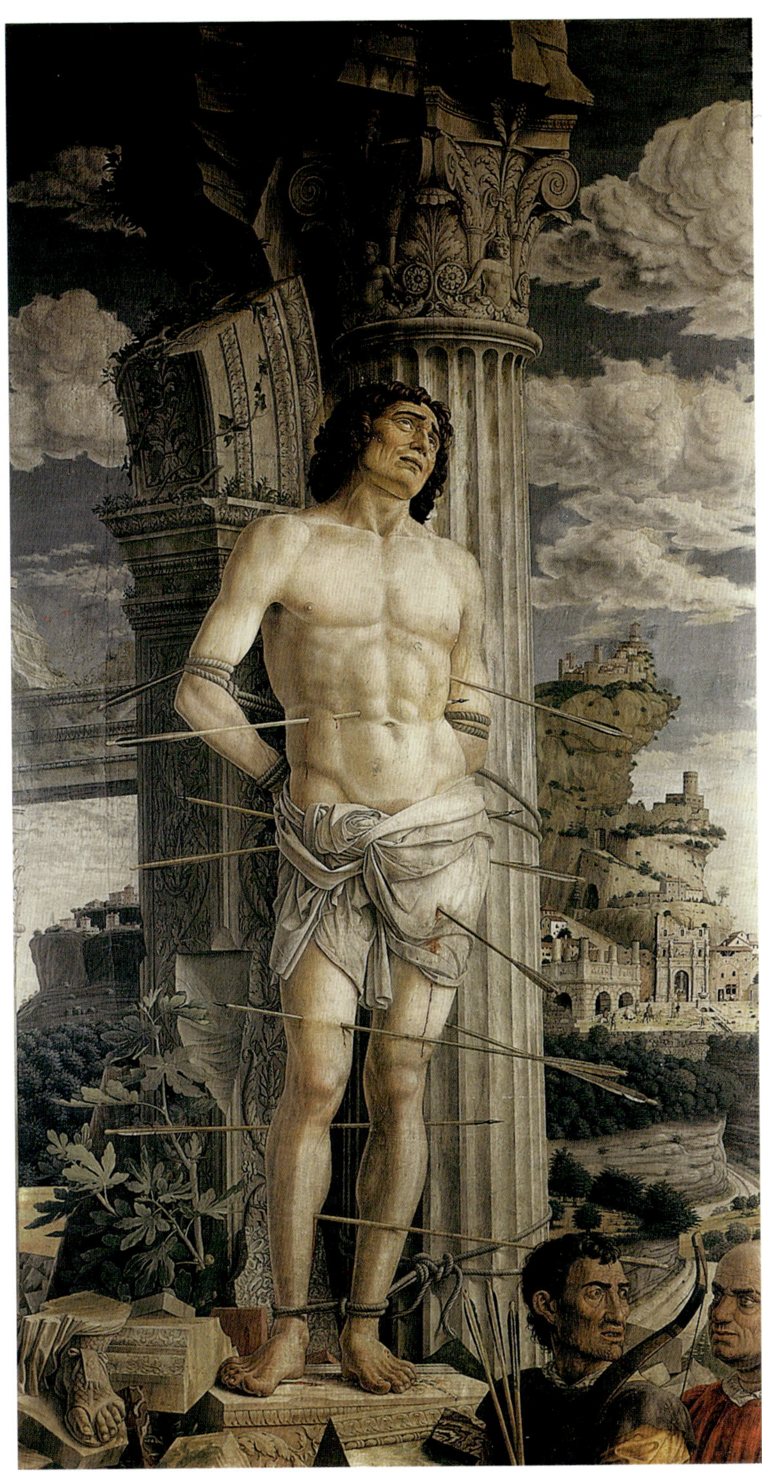

pain, reminding us of the ultimate pleasure good Christians aspired to—the purity of the soul. Mantegna produced three paintings of Saint Sebastian, from 1459 to 1490; the second version, seen here, is the most elaborate. A Roman column and arch lends a cruelly cold backdrop to his bleeding flesh as blood drips from every arrow wound and as his eyes search the skies for divine strength. Saint Sebastian's story is one of great devotion, but its homoerotic potential has not been lost on artists of the present day, especially those raised in Catholicism, such as the London-based Italian artist Franko B (b. 1960) **[91]**. In what might be viewed as a postmodern version of Saint Sebastian's martyrdom, in his performance art Franko ritualistically sacrifices his own flesh, letting his own blood, to express his homosexuality and society's fascination with and fear of the wounded body. This fascination was as strong in the fifteenth century as it is today, as demonstrated by the popularity of Sebastian's tragic death as an artistic subject-matter (a young man is tied up and pierced by male soldiers under orders from Imperial Rome because of his loyalty to God; he is then flogged to death and his body thrown into the sewers) during the Renaissance. But while the conflation of the erotic and the wound today often connotes society's fear of sexual disease, most notably AIDS, during the Renaissance wounded, latently erotic bodies spoke not just of temptation, and its possible consequences, but of redemption. To suffer and die as Sebastian did entailed the purging of the flesh but it also ensured the purity of his soul.

The Ecstasy of Saint Teresa (1647–52), by Gianlorenzo Bernini (1598–1680) is another remarkably erotic exploration of saintliness, again indicating the greater pleasure that was possible when one abandoned the body and physically suffered and devoted all to the soul. The marble statue, housed in the Chapel of Santa Maria della Vittoria in Rome, is a fantastic Baroque display of the mortification of the flesh for a greater sacred pleasure. It depicts that orgasmic moment when an angelic boy (now representing God rather than Eros) penetrates Teresa with his arrow. As she recounts in her autobiography (written 1562–5):

> Beside me, on the left hand, appeared an angel in bodily form . . . He was not tall but short, and very beautiful; and his face was so aflame that he appeared to be one of the highest ranks of angels, who seem to be all on fire . . . In his hands I saw a great golden spear, and at the iron tip there appeared to be a point of fire. This he plunged into my heart several times so that it penetrated to my entrails. When he pulled it out, I felt that he took them with it, and left me utterly consumed by the great love of God. The pain was so severe that it made me utter several moans. The sweetness caused by this intense pain is so extreme that one can not possibly

> wish it to cease, nor is one's soul content with anything but God. This is not a physical, but a spiritual pain, though the body has some share in it—even a considerable share.[22]

But religious art was not all focused on torment. Religious iconography of the Virgin Mary during the Renaissance offered examples of perfect grace through wholesome images of fecund female beauty. The Virgin's untainted body augmented her status as ideal mother and, paradoxically, lent her a glorious, womanly sexual potency. As Irish writer W. B. Yeats acknowledged in 1928, there emerged from Giotto and the trecento on for over three centuries 'an art of the body, an especial glory of the Catholic Church' in which 'the likeness of the Virgin [changed] from that of a sour ascetic to that of a woman so natural nobody complained when Andrea del Sarto chose for his model his wife, or Raphael his mistress, and represented her with all the patience of his "sexual passion"'.[23] The Madonnas of the High Renaissance painter Raphael (1483–1520) are certainly famed for their lifelike beauty. From the *Cowper Madonna* (1504) to the *Madonna of the Chair* (1518), his Madonnas share common features, from deep-set eyes to sculpturesque, voluptuous bodies, their attractiveness and gentle demeanour made all the more tactile by the chubby baby Jesus they usually hold in their arms. An atheist and ladies' man, according to Vasari, Raphael depicts Virgins who speak of a female ideal but embody a sensuality and 'sexual passion' that Yeats rightly recognized as a vital component of their iconographic power.

Unlike religious art, civic art in Renaissance Italy did not have to deny the body and its baser desires; yet we find it, too, was ideologically encoded such that the represented body, however erotic, indicated a state of mind albeit if attained through the emotions. One only has to think of the freestanding bronze adolescent *David* (1444–6) by the Florentine sculptor Donatello (*c.*1386–1466), standing triumphantly on the severed head of Goliath. The sculpture is a 158 cm-high nude who is almost disarmingly real and boyish in comparison to the gargantuan Goliath. His casual but seductive stance is further enhanced by a feather from Goliath's helmet which tantalizingly edges up his inner leg. Yet *David*'s particular boyish eroticism (his femininity, his delicate limbs) speaks of a particular narrative: the triumph of the brave and intelligent over the monstrous. Michelangelo's marble sculpture of *David* (1501–4) **[2]** is erotic in a much more explicitly heroic way: it is symbolic of Florentine rule in its composed balance of body and mind, musculature, and thoughtful expression. Vasari described *David* in ideal terms, proposing that Michelangelo had perfected nature with such success that its grace and serenity 'have never been surpassed'.[24] Michelangelo's *David* was true to the discipline of *designo*, the foundation of sound art in the Renaissance: namely, the artist perfects nature because he is inspired by the divine Idea of the object he is reproducing. For Vasari, in his marble masterpiece Michelangelo achieved the Neoplatonic ideal of the perfect male figure. Kenneth Clark, in his seminal study *The Nude* (1956), shares Vasari's sentiment despite the gap of some four hundred years. Clark claims: 'Since the Greeks of the 4th century [BC] no man felt so certain of the godlike character of the male body as Michelangelo.'[25] Yet the possibility of 'a hidden love' adds a further erotic dimension to many canonical Renaissance male nudes. Michelangelo's later marble *Victory* (1532–4) has been read by Dominique Fernandez as 'an image of masochism in love', a rendition of the Greek relationship between an older master (*erastes*) and young male student (*eromenos*). For Fernandez, the contemporary pencil drawing of *Ganymede* (1532), in which an eagle (Zeus in disguise) lifts the young mortal Ganymede into the air, prising his legs open with ferocious claws in so doing, is a powerful rendition of homoerotic desire.[26] Fernandez's reading of *Ganymede* is all the more persuasive since Michelangelo gave the drawing to the beautiful young Roman Tommaso dei Cavalieri. While it would be naive to reduce the image solely to a homoerotic reading, especially given that Neoplatonic philosophers present the story of young Ganymede in terms of *furor amatorius* (the intellect seized by contemplative ecstasy), it is still a dimension that augments our appreciation of the work rather than undermines it. Michelangelo was hailed as a 'genius' but the sexual explicitness of some of his art did lead to cries for censorship at the time. The representation of numerous naked genitals in his fresco of *The Last Judgement* (completed in 1541), for the altar wall of the Sistine Chapel in the Vatican, incited a censorship campaign by Cardinal Carafa and Monsignor Sernini. Pope Julius III did not give in to their pressure, but a law was issued at the time of Michelangelo's death to conceal genitals in art; the painter Daniele da Volterra had to design suitable cloth 'briefs' to drape the more explicit parts of the fresco.

If Renaissance art in the West attests to the frequent idealizing of the sexual body and an elevation of the flesh so that it becomes sign and symbol for something greater than mortal man, namely God, by the time of the Enlightenment no such premise was necessary. In eighteenth-century British culture the erotic misdeeds of secret masonic societies of the period, such as the Hellfire Club, and loose-living debauched men, known as 'rakes', became key subjects for the prints of the satirist William Hogarth (1697–1764). The author of *Analysis of*

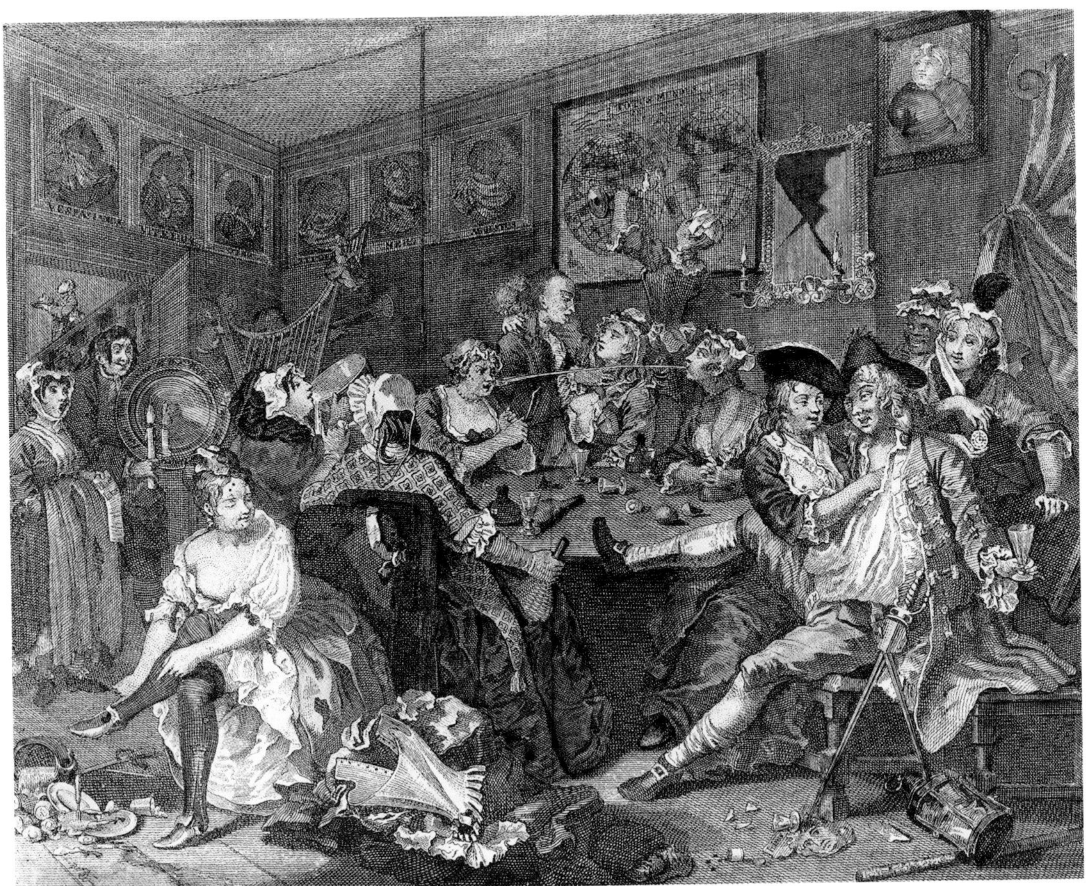

9 William Hogarth
The Rake's Progress
('The Orgy'), 1735
This is the third plate (of eight) in the story of Tom Rakewell, a young aristocrat whose rakish ways lead to his financial misfortune and eventual end in Bedlam, the madhouse. It depicts an orgy in a dishevelled private room, the drunken Tom seen in the right foreground with a prostitute who cleverly amuses him while stealing his pocket watch.

Beauty (1753), Hogarth was concerned with the ideal, with the sublime symbolism of 'serpentine' form, and also with physiognomy. It is not surprising that his satirical works present social caricatures (or 'characters', as he called them) amidst their everyday activities, exposing the underbelly of his society and often using sexual symbolism to denote political, economic, and moral corruption. His popular print series included *The Harlot's Progress* (1732), depicting the sexual downfall of a poor country girl in the corrupt city of London, and *The Rake's Progress* (1735) **[9]**, documenting the rake's 'successful' marriage to an old, wealthy maid, to his gambling away of his riches, to his demise in the madhouse of Bedlam.

Yet the eighteenth century also produced one of the great libertines of all times, Donatien Alphonse François de Sade (1740–1814), whose novels not only shed a perverse light on the violent era of the French Revolution but whose perversion gave rise to the term *sadism*—the enjoyment of cruelty—a word which first made it into a dictionary in

1834. The author of *Justine, or The Misfortunes of Virtue* (1791), *Juliette, or The Prosperities of Vice* (1798) and *120 Days of Sodom* (written 1782–5, lost 1789 and first published 1904), and a powerful philosophical treatise woven amidst a fantastic tale of a young girl's sexual re-education, *Philosophy in the Boudoir* (1795), Sade's writings have been seen as explorations of sexual and political freedom in their encyclopedic cataloguing of every possible form of sexual perversion. His lifestyle, on the other hand, led to condemnation and imprisonment; as he was accused of being a multiple rapist, torturer, and proto-murderer, most notoriously in the case of the 36-year-old widow, Rose Keller, whom he wooed to his country house in Arcueil with the promise of housekeeping work only to hold her captive there and force his particular erotic desires upon her. Keller was made to strip, tied to a bed, whipped, and cut with a penknife before the Marquis dripped molten sealing wax on her wounds. She later managed to escape by using bedcovers as a rope and climbing out a small window. The case, which became the subject of a criminal investigation and much press reportage, was held up as an example of aristocratic decadence. His self-defence—in which he insisted that he believed Keller to be a prostitute as he had met her near the church of the Petits-Pères, a common haunt for prostitutes, and was thus his sexual property as long as he was paying—was very much in keeping with the sexual codes of the Ancien Régime. Imprisoned for some thirty years of his life in the Bastille prison in Paris and subsequently housed in a madhouse at Charenton, his writings are those of an unfettered imagination and are addressed to 'voluptuaries of all ages, of every sex' in the hope that they will find nourishment in its libertine principles.[27] As French writer Maurice Blanchot wrote, 'Sade's eroticism is dream eroticism', but it is also steeped in a counter-Enlightenment logic.[28] His importance to the modern history of eroticism lies in his total liberation of sexual desire, his exploration of male and female sexual fantasies, his furious dialogue between desire and death. In Sade's world, the greatest pleasure is derived from the violation of taboos and laws, the greatest logic is thus to remove morality and law and allow man to follow his nature. His legacy is art that explores erotic excess and refuses to separate sex and power, desire and social relations.

Sade's was an era of cultural decadence perhaps most commonly associated with the erotic courtly paintings of French artists François Boucher (1703–70), Jean-Honoré Fragonard (1732–1806), and Antoine Watteau (1684–1721) with their Rococo depiction of lovers, boating parties, and boudoir nudes in predominantly pink palettes. Boucher continued to use myth as an erotic decoy, but also indulged in flagrant images of sexual consumption. His painting of *Mademoiselle O'Murphy*

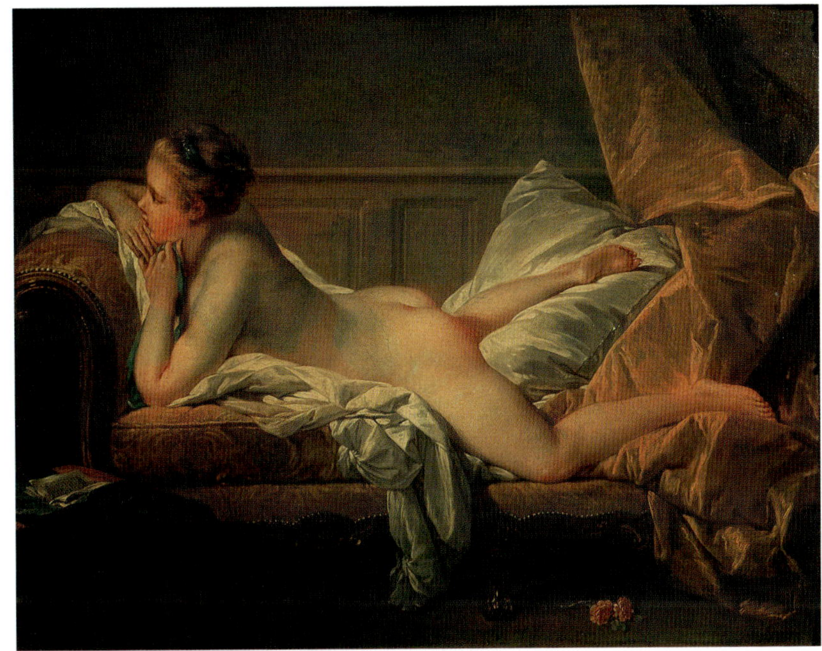

10 François Boucher
Reclining Nude (Mademoiselle O'Murphy), 1751

Boucher's portrait of Mademoiselle O'Murphy, one of Louis XV's mistresses, portrays an intimate boudoir scene, the young woman's distinctive pose emphasizing not only her youth and beauty but her role as sexual *provocateuse*.

(1751) **[10]**, the young mistress of Louis XV, has been described by Kenneth Clark as the delicate expression of the 'freshness of desire'.[29] While Clark was quick to balance his admiration of her 'freshness' with the historical note that Boucher's chief patron was a woman, the King's mistress Madame de Pompadour, Miss O'Murphy's round, young, pink limbs express the fantasy that she is a 'fresh' pubescent girl, just as her pose—propped up on her stomach on cushions on a sofa—emphasizes her childish manners. This was also the age of the political philosopher, educationist, and essayist, Jean-Jacques Rousseau (1712–78), whose writings were the very antithesis of Sade's philosophy. Rousseau defended the need for a liberal education and the rights of children (while handing, allegedly, his own five illegitimate children to a foundling institution). His novel *Émile* (1762) offered an example of his new vision of child rearing where the child is kept free from books until the age of 12 on the basis that so-called civilization corrupts man's natural goodness. *Mademoiselle O'Murphy* may be held up as an example of Sade's or Rousseau's vision of human nature: she is either unfettered by notions of morality and indulging her natural desire for sexual gratification; or, as a young girl not much older than 12, she is an example of society's perversion of the individual's natural goodness.

That she was also reputedly an Irish girl led Irish artist Micheal Farrell (1940–2000) to adapt her erotic status for his own modern, political

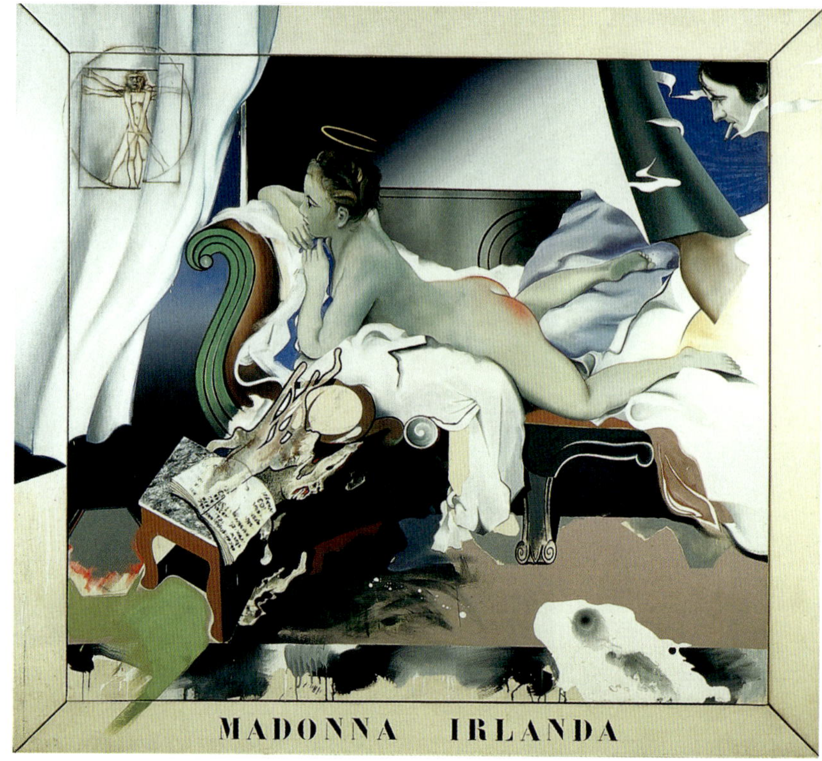

11 Micheal Farrell
Madonna Irlanda, 1977

One of a series of paintings by Farrell devoted to 'Mademoiselle O'Murphy', mistress of Louis XV, and popular model for Boucher, Farrell updates Boucher's original painting of O'Murphy, who was the daughter of an Irishman, in order to make a political point about Ireland's 'whoring' of herself to Britain and her oppression by the Catholic Church. The artist includes a self-portrait, to the right, and a modified version of Leonardo's famous Vitruvian man, with his genitals covered, to the left.

end. In *Madonna Irlanda or The Very First Real Irish Political Picture* (1977) **[11]**, one of a series of works based on Boucher's original, Farrell replaces Boucher's Rococo sensuality with a flagrant erotic violence. He reddens the girl's buttocks so that they seem to smart under our gaze and under that of the artist (seen to the right of the composition, a cigarette in his mouth) and Leonardo da Vinci's Vitruvian man (to the left of the composition), who is either protecting his genitals or masturbating. Farrell seizes the connotations of sexual consumption and exchange in Boucher's original to address the historical conflict in Northern Ireland between Britain and Ireland known as the 'Troubles' (1969–94) and to suggest the downfall or hypocrisy of the Republic of Ireland, a modern country still clinging to her identity as an island of saints and scholars. His pastiche of Boucher's portrait suggests that Ireland has whored her body and soul to the British colonizer, as she happily bares all despite her halo. It also reflects his belief that 'Catholicism is the strangler', that the Catholic Church has too much power in Ireland, not least in oppressing sexuality through its moral force.[30] Traditionally represented in poetry, song, and painting as a woman, whether as Roisín Dubh or Caitlín Ní Houlihan, Ireland here is presented as a whore. As Farrell stated, 'Miss O'Murphy was for me a Caitlín Ní Houlihan figure. I used this as a metaphor to attack the political system in another way.'[31] Farrell's painting demonstrates the political appropriation of the classical erotic tradition by contemporary artists; revealingly while the painting was purchased by the municipal gallery in Dublin, the Hugh Lane Gallery, it was kept from public view for ten years—testament to the subversive power of its eroticism.

Taboo and Transgression

Micheal Farrell, like Boucher before him, uses erotic art as a means of offering new and subversive insights into the social and political context of his day. However, the eroticism of Farrell's painting is more knowing than that of Boucher's insofar as, as Michel Foucault explains in his *History of Sexuality*, since Boucher's day a veritable discursive explosion has occurred around the subject of sex. The eighteenth century through which Boucher lived was marked by an increasing appreciation of the scientific realities of sexual desire—preoccupations with population, birth and death rates, marriage, sexual disease, and contraception.[32] These preoccupations led to an increasing investigation, categorization, and regulation of sexuality. By the nineteenth century 'an analytics of sexuality' was in place, and sexuality was inscribed in every aspect of society from law to racism (the taboo of mixed racial blood, for example) as the control of sexuality became a vital tool in the techniques and infrastructures of power.[33] The fear of sexual perversion, and its pathologization, coincided with European imperialism, the rise of museums, ethnography, and the infiltration of Europe by non-Western cultures, each with its own sexual practices and iconographies. The role of phallic worship and vulvic worship in Hindu India, Shinto Japan, and other so-called pagan cultures became the subject of many late nineteenth-century publications arguing that the refinement and repression of erotic urges was a fundamental good which led to the civilized Christian religions. In addition, unbridled sexual desire became associated with primitivism, especially in the psychoanalytic doctrine of Sigmund Freud. He claimed that the repression of primitive, uncontrolled erotic urges through socially agreed taboos was necessary for the success of civilization. But the increasingly independent outlook of modern art found itself more and more at odds with Freud's arguments in favour of necessary repression. Visual representation, especially where concerned with issues of sexuality and gender, arrived at an artistic crisis, a crisis intensified by the challenge posed to traditional figuration in art by the new technologies of photography and motion pictures. Artists began to look outside museums and official Salon exhibitions for inspiration, convinced that to be modern, art must be of its day ('il faut être de son temps').[34]

As the twentieth century began, sexual transgression in art became an increasingly common motif. Artists turned to the erotic body as a means of addressing a whole gamut of personal and political questions. In Paris, Vienna, and New York, artists such as Pablo Picasso (1881–1973), Egon Schiele (1890–1918), and Marcel Duchamp (1887–1968) seized the erotic as a means of challenging and transgressing the accepted categories of high art, particularly the tradition of the nude. Artists replaced the ideal body with the real body in their art practice. A burgeoning avant-garde defied bourgeois conservatism in Europe between the two World Wars by using sexual obscenity as a metaphor for political obscenity. Dada artists, including George Grosz (1893–1959) and Hannah Höch (1889–1978) in Weimar Germany, were key players in this political use of the erotic body, though their 'degenerate' art would soon fall victim to the classicized, controlled eroticism used to propagate racial stereotypes and the image of a fertile nation race under Adolf Hitler. Surrealist artists also represented the explicitly erotic body in scandalizing new ways, from the explorations of Sadean desire by André Masson (1896–1987) to oral and anal desire in Salvador Dalí (1904–89).

The trauma of World War II inevitably affected artists' depiction of the erotic body, leading to what I will describe as an 'existential eroticism' after the war as artists, including Willem de Kooning (1904–97) and Jean Dubuffet (1901–85), assaulted the female nude in (respectively) Abstract Expressionist daubs of paint and Art Brut muddy canvas surfaces. While New York supposedly 'stole' modern art from Paris during the World War II, we find that post-war Surrealism, exemplified in the art of Roberto Matta (1911–2002) and Jean Benoît (b. 1922), continued to call for sexual and political revolution through the erotic. The Surrealists anticipated a new post-war generation of performance artists who were equally steadfast in their faith in the radical power of Eros. Artists such as Carolee Schneemann (b. 1939) and Jean-Jacques Lebel (b. 1936) staged emphatically erotic '*Happenings*' in the 1960s in which the explicit body was used as a symbol for and an agent of political dissent. Eroticism was also used to expose commodity capitalism as Pop artists such as Andy Warhol (1928–87) and Tom Wesselmann (1931–2004) parodied the blatant sexualization of advertising campaigns.

In the aftermath of the events of May 1968, feminist, gay, and race politics entered the mainstream, often with 'terrorizing' erotic imagery. The 'Cunt Art' of Judy Chicago (b. 1939) and Mapplethorpe's photographs of the black male nude foregrounded the potent effect of the unruly female sex and the homoerotic gaze, respectively. The taboo around lesbian desire became a subject in the photography of Catherine Opie (b. 1961), as did the repression of inter-sexual existence in the art of Della Grace (b. 1957), sado-masochism in the performances of Bob Flanagan (1952–96), and the carnal art performances of Orlan (b. 1947). Such artists explore and celebrate 'deviant' sexual desire, drawing on eroticism's other half—Thanatos, the violent, death drive—as the most powerful polemical strategy for making society look at itself through new eyes. And yet in this apparent pursuit of transgression above all else, some of these artists look back to or recall that age-old Christian fascination with martyrdom, with the ecstatic, spiritual potential of corporeal pain when the flesh is sacrificed for enlightenment.

Each of these artists will be explored in turn through the chapters of this book. In exploring the intentions, production, and reception of a wide range of works of art I hope to begin a questioning of our own desires and fears when faced with erotic art and to argue that eroticism has not been marginal but central to the history of art as a whole. My intention is not to be encyclopedic—my focus is primarily on European and American art since the mid-nineteenth century. Nor do I attempt to regulate the erotic in art by categorizing artists and works according to iconography and theme, as other have done.[35] Such categorizations lose the sense of the historical and political trajectory and agency of the erotic in art. Instead, I begin this book with the premise that eroticism is a site of power, in which power is produced and challenged. I assess eroticism as a subversive strategy in modern and postmodern art, showing how artists of the past 150 years, associated with the predominantly progressive and oppositional politics of modernism, turned to the erotic as a provocative means of undermining social, political, sexual, gender, and racial stereotypes and orthodoxies. In the artworks I examine in detail, eroticism is not just about the pleasures of the flesh, it concerns the fear of sexual desire and the return of repressed desires. As we shall see, erotic art reveals the tensions between the individual's artistic and sexual freedom on the one hand, and the ambitions and anxieties of society on the other. Erotic desire is celebrated in this book for its own sake, but eroticism—notably the erotic body—is also presented as a disputed terrain that allows artists to ask some of the most difficult questions at critical moments in our history. I hope this book will not only present a survey of erotic art but will remind us of its power to unsettle us, to make us think, and even to act differently.

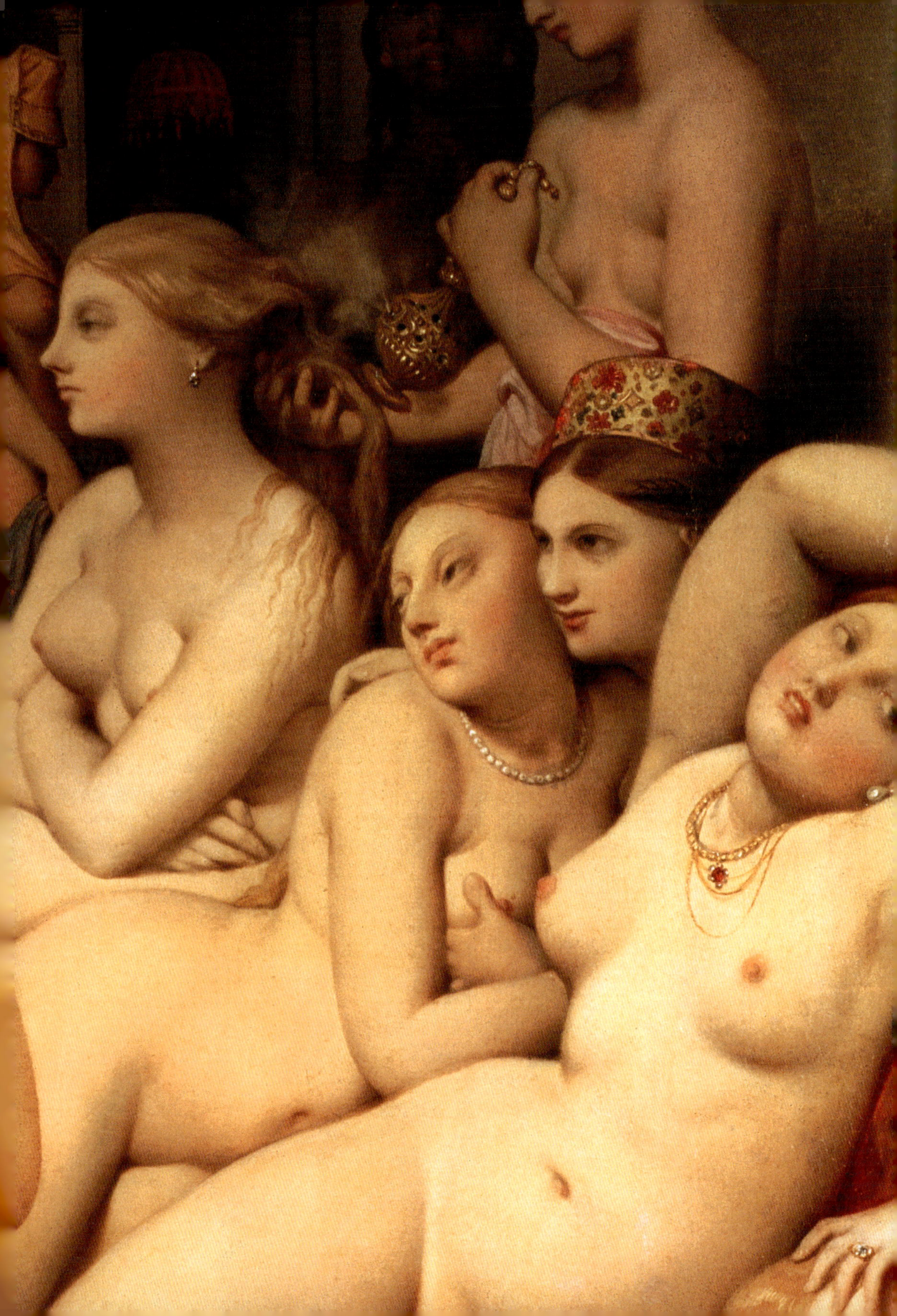

1

The Rhetoric of the Nude

The female nude is not a *subject* of art but a *form* of art. The manner and style in which the nude is represented is indicative of the dominant idea of art and its role in society at a particular moment in history. It is invariably framed in acceptable terms in art; a woman is presented as beautiful, virginal, and blissfully unaware that she wears no clothes. The viewer is to enjoy her body but is also helped refrain from lewd, lustful thoughts through this very particular idealizing moral 'frame'. Beauty is one of the key elements which allows the female body to be mapped as an ideal nude. While beauty is an elusive category, in art it is usually discussed in terms of form and expression; these are in turn inevitably subject to a greater distinguishing feature—*mimesis*. Mimesis is the imitation or representation of nature in its most harmonious state in the work of art. An understanding of mimesis helps clarify the distinctive role of the nude as an ideal form of art.

The view that art is imitation dates back to Plato and his account in Book 10 of his treatise *The Republic*. Here Socrates discusses poetry and the subject of imitation; he sets out a clear distinction between the real and the imitation, insisting that the art of poets and painters, as imitation, is far removed from the truth.

He gives the example of a piece of furniture—a couch or a table—to explain this hierarchy:

1 There is the perfect unique Form of a couch, made by God.
2 There is the couch made by the carpenter, a craftsman, which we can use.
3 There is the copy of the couch, produced by the artist, which is an imitation of 2.

For Plato, there exist ideal forms of which the artist in the real world can only produce copies. He is an 'imitator', the 'maker of the product two removes from nature'.[1] The artist only holds a mirror to nature and then

Detail of 13

only produces an imitation of an imitation, a deceptive illusion of reality. Given this hierarchy it is not surprising that for Plato art was a 'kind of play'.[2] Plato and his protégé Aristotle, and later the Neoplatonists of the Renaissance, agreed on one important thing: that nature in all its unruly reality was in need of ideal 'completion', while art, like science and reason, had the mastery to carry out this act of completion. As Aristotle wrote, 'one should surpass the model'.[3] If we replace Plato's couch with the representation of the figure, or the female nude, it is twice removed from the divine, however idealized it is, and thus more likely to tempt and distract the viewer from the divine than to lead to self-improvement.

In Western art from ancient times a series of polar opposites were set up that reinforced the concept of the artist as mediator between the ideal and nature. Within this system of polarities, man was typically grouped with the ideal; masculine characteristics were deemed to include logic, rationality, linearity, solidity, contemplation. Woman, in contrast, was viewed in terms of nature; feminine characteristics included emotionality, irrationality, fluidity, and sensorial pleasure. This system of polarities had its own erotic frisson: feminine characteristics were deemed natural, sensual, and attractive; therefore they needed to be controlled by man and masculine reason in the name of civilization. This bias against the feminine was reflected in a general gendered discourse of art analysis and appreciation, and lies behind our understanding of the nude. The privileging of reason over emotion, control over loss of control, calls for a *contemplative* visual experience even when faced with a representation of a desirable erotic female: the flesh might enjoy but the mind must always have the last word. When facing a male nude we must not indulge in lustful thoughts either: it is to be appreciated as a sign and advertisement for controlled form, of authority, rationality, balance. The female nude was more threatening, however, as it was closer to nature than to art. It had to be kept in check as it had the power to arouse but also to overindulge immorality and base desires. It had to be made to demonstrate the command of art over nature, mind over body, turning woman and nature into a cultural artefact.[4] Otherwise the female nude could wreak havoc on the Western metaphysical tradition and on art itself.[5]

The Dynamics of Desire

The balance between art and nature in depiction of both the male and female nude was usually maintained by artists through recourse to traditional symbolism—that is, through a particular erotic *iconography* appropriate to a particular mythological, religious or historical narrative. This allowed for the display of nudity but in the name of a specific story and greater truth. As a result, when we face a representation of the nude body in an art museum, we are looking at something much more than the flesh perfected—we are faced with a particular form of artistic rhetoric, one that conforms to an ideal body type and reveals as much about society as it does about the art work. Typically, the female is represented in her nude state as an object, there to be passively framed and erotically enjoyed by the (male) artist and (male) viewer; within this scenario the male, as viewer or artist, stands as the active subject. She may be pictured loitering innocently in nature or in her bedchamber, half-covered in satin sheets, and often wearing pearl earrings to remind us of her sexual purity and ruby jewels to remind us of her sensual skin tone, lips, and concealed sex. We see this erotic game in many of Titian's nudes, as in his famous *Venus of Urbino* (before 1538) **[1]**. We continue to see this rhetoric over three hundred years later, as in Auguste Renoir's *Blonde Bather* (1881). Painted in Impressionist Paris, where many country girls migrated with the dream of prosperity and romance only to end up working as life models or prostitutes, Renoir's painting still remains true to the pursuit of purity within the erotic. With Titian and Renoir we find particular dynamics of desire at play, dynamics which reveal the role of sexuality in art, how it is controlled and mapped out to portray clear social and political messages to the viewer. Both artists express the traditional power relationship in the visual arts which flatters a pre-defined male viewer and insists that men see and women are seen.[6] This dominant dynamics of desire, or the 'play of desire within and generated by looking at images',[7] which occurs both within the work of art and in the spectator's looking at it, lies at the heart of our appreciation of canonical and contemporary erotic art. Psychoanalytic theory has been influential in offering a discourse of *the gaze*, or *the look* within which this dynamics of desire, this 'play', can be discussed. Fuelled by film theory from the 1970s, notably by Laura Mulvey's seminal article of 1975 on the male gaze (which will be discussed in Chapter 8), art historians now discuss the power relationship within a work of art and between the work of art and the spectator in terms of the politics of looking, recognizing that there is no such thing as visual indifference. They also retrace the steps of art's history to see where and how this politics of looking was played out and how it might enhance our appreciation of the relationship between art and society at a given moment.

Let us look at the period of the Enlightenment to assess how and why aesthetics have been dominated by a set of values which privilege the male viewer—and by extension the all-powerful male gaze—and the mind over the female and matter, and how modern and contemporary artists have engaged with these values. Following the political upheavals of the French Revolution of 1789, a new direction in European art emerged, fuelled by Enlightenment ideas and public spirit. This period saw an entrenchment of traditional, patriarchal aesthetics, but it also marked the start of a new and unsettling direction in art. It saw the beginning of the end of the classical nude and the first steps towards modernism, as contemporary life, social anxieties, and political ambitions became increasingly visible in art, albeit in latent, coded form. The Enlightenment, as a historical movement, believed that human reason could be used to combat ignorance, superstition, and tyranny. Enlightened thinkers stood against the monarchy and institutionalized religion —a stance that was a result of wars of religion, absolutism, and tyranny. *Sapere aude* (dare to know): this was Kant's motto for an Age of Reason driven by critique, to which everything had to submit, including the dark side of the human psyche. Philosophers such as Jean-Jacques Rousseau, John Locke, David Hume, and Immanuel Kant believed that intellectual enlightenment would lead to a growth of toleration and, by extension, political and social reform. They attempted to develop what Hume called 'the science of man', hoping to do for human psychical and social life what Isaac Newton had done for the understanding of the physical universe.

The art of the Spanish court painter Francisco Goya (1746–1828) exemplifies Enlightenment thinking in its exposé of society, from the decadent aristocracy to the peasantry burdened by religion and ignorance. In his portrayals of majas he challenges issues of class and race as well as the power of the gaze itself. According to J. F. de Bourgoing, the French Ambassador to Spain writing in 1788, the maja was of the lower class but, for the bewitched male, she was 'the most seducing priestess that ever presided at the altars of Venus'.[8] Majism was the imitation of real majas, a subcultural style of life and way of dress and would be an important aspect of the revolutionary call for democracy in the nineteenth century.[9] Goya's *The Naked Maja* (1798–1805) **[12]** and her counterpart *The Clothed Maja* (*c.*1800–3), represent the power of majism at the time. In both images, the maja brazenly confronts the viewer, her hands poised for best erotic effect, her fashionably coquettish shoes, shimmering dress, and lace bolero in the latter appearing all the more tantalizing than her bare flesh in the former. She is not idealized, or innocent of her charms; rather, she is a daringly erotic portrait in an era when nudes were banned in Spain by the all-powerful Church. In this way Goya's majas should be seen within the context of his 1796–7 *Caprichos*. The term *capricho* originates in the Italian *capriccio*, meaning a caprice or *jeu*

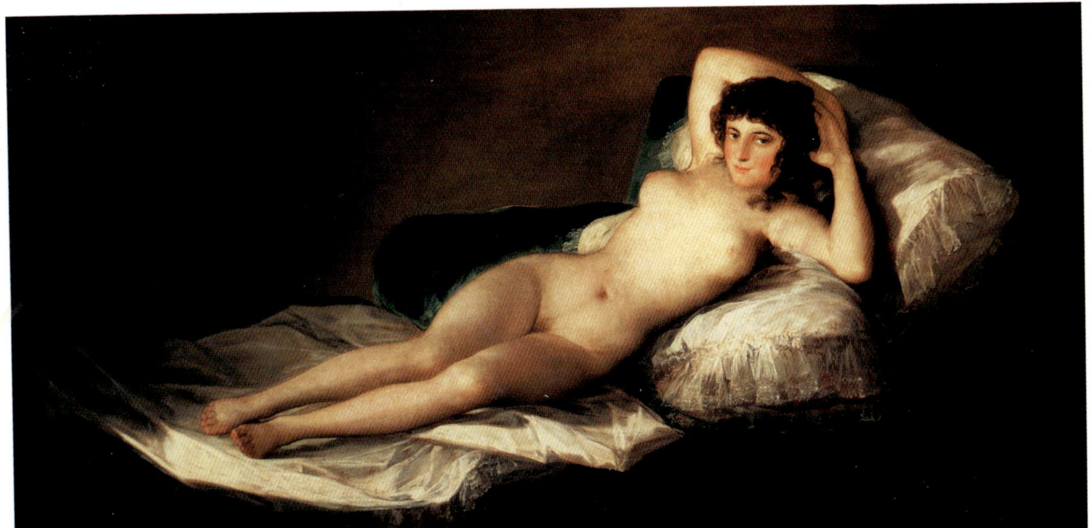

12 Francisco de Goya *The Naked Maja*, *c.*1800

Goya painted *The Naked Maja* and *The Clothed Maja* for Manuel Godoy, the Queen's minister and lover, who chose to show one or the other to his guests. Described in 1788 by J.-F. de Bourgoing, the French Ambassador to Spain, as 'the most seducing priestess that ever presided at the altars of Venus', the maja woman was of the lower class of society but a popular figure in artistic circles.

d'esprit outside the usual rules. By the 1790s it referred specifically to the arts and to the power of creative ingenuity rather than adherence to norm or custom. Locally, the term was also used to describe moral points made in Spanish comedies, and as Goya was a keen theatre-goer it is this understanding of the term that critics often use when reading his art.[10] The paintings of the majas are part of this *capricho* spirit too, as they refer to the personal and the political; Goya may parody his patron the Duchess of Alba and her courtly lifestyle (the Duchess was rumoured to be the model for the *Naked Maja*, both having rich black hair), but his *Caprichos* also show his faith in the power of fantasy not just to lead art into a brave new world but to help expose the hidden desires and fears of a politically corrupt society, and so to enlighten it too.

Orientalism

The nudes of Jean-Auguste-Dominique Ingres (1780–1867) reveal a more coded, subconscious engagement with socio-politics through their timeless and antique style. Ingres painted the female nude throughout his life, including studies of erotic sixteenth-century prints by Marco da Ravenna, Rosso, and Bonasone. It is Ingres's images of the Orient (the hot desert lands of north Africa and the Middle East) that reveal the Western erotic imagination unleashed, however. At the same time, his exotic odalisques reveal his desire to control matter, from the female body to the very paint he works with, in the name of high art, and at the service of imperialist ideology in a century of extensive colonial expansion, led by France and Britain. While this was an exciting period

13 Jean-August-Dominique Ingres
The Turkish Bath, 1863

Using an Oriental theme as a pretext for grouping voluptuous female nudes in a harem, the erotic force of Ingres's painting lies not only in its voyeuristic staging but in the fantasy of control, exercised over so many women by one man, the Sultan. The painter's attention to detail gives a sense of Orientalist authenticity—for example, the costume of the woman holding a coffee cup and the woman with the golden, outdoor headdress.

of travel, ethnographic exploration, and cultural tourism, Rome was the furthest Ingres had ever travelled and his odalisques were far from ethnographically correct. Rather, they were staged in studios, with European models and Turkish props, and presented an 'Oriental mirage'.[11]

For *The Grand Odalisque* (1814) Ingres claimed to have used a 10-year-old model in Rome, but the painting also alludes to another Roman beauty: Raphael's *The Madonna of the Chair*, supposedly a portrait of his mistress 'La Fornarina' in a turban.[12] John Berger has compared this odalisque to a modern pin-up, as her expression responds 'with calculating charm to the man she imagines looking at her—although she doesn't know him. She is offering up her femininity as the surveyed.'[13] While Berger's reading may be supported by the École de Nice painter Martial Raysse (b. 1936), whose painting *Made in Japan—La grande odalisque* (1964) uses neon colour to turn Ingres's Odalisque into a kitsch green giantess with one eye boldly staring at us, it is a little too quick for our purposes. Ingres's painting draws on an erotic tradition while also adding a new dimension to that tradition. It is an image about sexual desire but its erotic strategy is much more subtle than that of a 'girlie magazine'. With Ingres we do not find sexual desire in excessive terms, we find displacement; the fantasy of the pursuit is far more thrilling than any real sexual satisfaction.[14] Desire, in pin-up terms, is never made explicit. Ingres's *The Grand Odalisque* draws on Renaissance precedents and is quite Mannerist in her elongated form with her unnaturally long spine and right arm. But it is the use of colour to carefully delineate the narrative around her nudity that is so telling. The half-glimpsed right breast and buttock are made all the more seductive by their staging: luscious silk sheets and satin drapes, the exotic plumed fan and hookah, her turban and jewellery which cleverly lead our eye from her eyes to her wrist. These carefully chosen and placed details are sufficiently exotic to ensure that she remains a figure of the imagination—the very opposite of a real, palpable pin-up woman. Through exoticization lust is not overindulged in, and the viewer is kept at a safe distance from the object of titillating delight. Her exotic sexuality can be enjoyed from afar, for, thanks to her props, she is shown to be a creature of *foreign* sexual practices. As an odalisque, she is a concubine, a sexual slave whose life in a harem is hedonistic and morally alien to the Western eye.

When considered alongside Ingres's *The Turkish Bath* (1863) **[13]** we appreciate this majestic controlling gaze all the more. While drawing on the 1763 *Letters* of Lady Mary Wortley Montagu (1689–1762), written during her travels in Europe, Asia, and Africa, and recounting (among other episodes) her visits to harems, Ingres again indulges in his Orien-

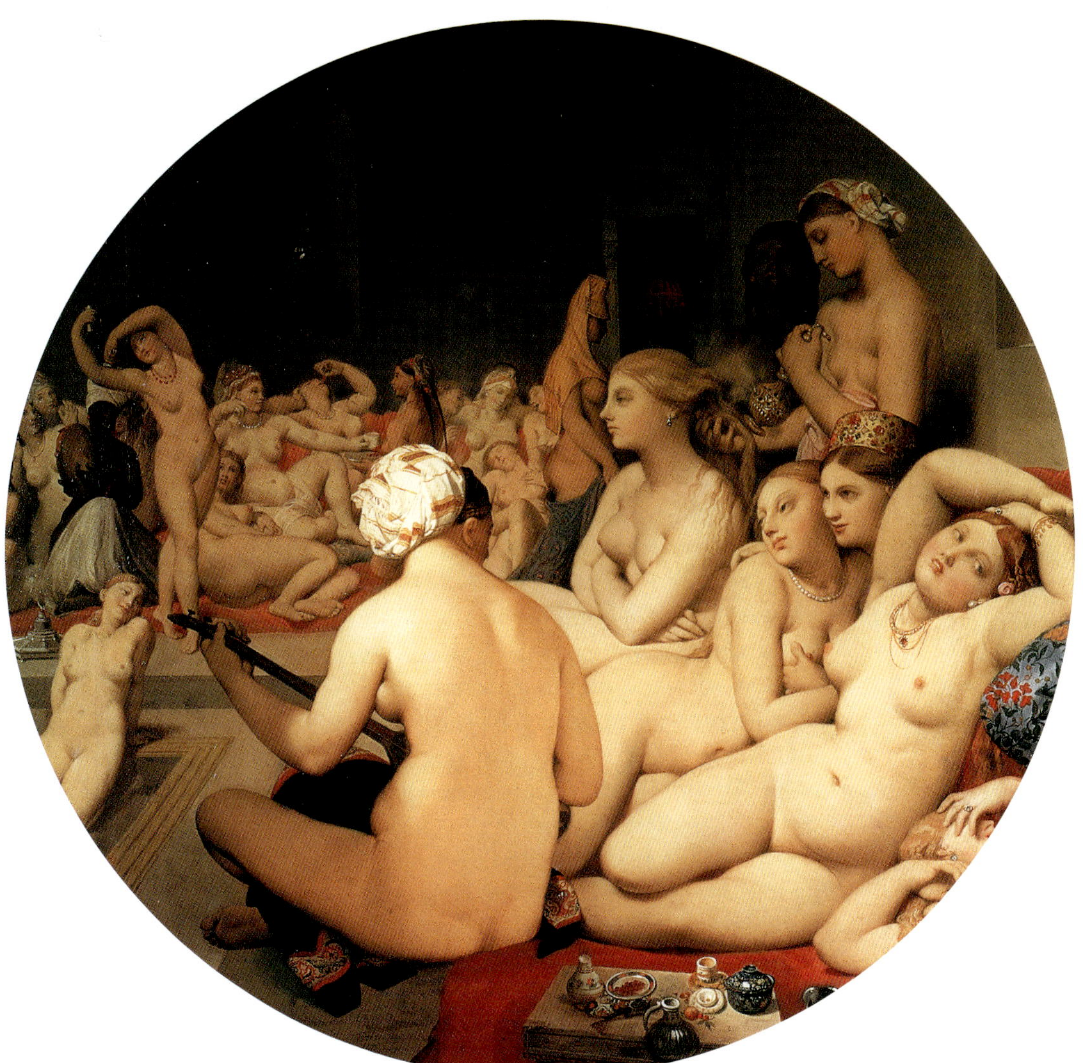

tal fantasies. We see a veritable orgy of female nudes from every angle and with every skin colour and erotic expression. Their reclining and orgasmic postures, and the lesbian overtones of some pairings, suggest their sexual appetites are insatiable. Again some are attended by slaves and some wear splendid headdresses, notably the woman who marks the central axis of the painting. These details lend an Oriental 'realism', the central, walking nude's headdress recalling one documented in an image of a mistress and her slave on the way to the *hammam*, or bath, in Nicolas de Nicolay's *Les Quatre Premiers Livres des navigations, pérégrinations et voyages* (1567).[15] Ingres thus succeeds in fusing erotic romance with historical document, allowing the viewer's eye to dance from the nape of one woman to the curve of the breast of another, all the time paying particular attention to every detail, whether Ottoman in origin or a simple still life, as in the foreground. The words of the contemporary critic Théophile Gautier certainly suggest it was greatly appreciated as an erotic feast in its day, describing it as

> a marvellous pretext for grouping unveiled, in a circular frame, all the variety of types that the harem sends to such a rendezvous of Oriental coquetry . . . It is an important and singular moment in the work of Ingres, a canvas lovingly caressed with his suavest brush, twenty times left and taken up, like a woman with whom one cannot decide to break.[16]

The circular frame emphasizes that the women's space of this foreign fantasia is mapped out quite differently from that of the viewer. The women do not seem to interact with each other, even though one nude in the right foreground squeezes another's breast and a woman in a turban behind her is in the midst of putting an ornate comb in a blonde woman's hair. They strike us as a collage of male-fantasy women, glued together but not coming together as one unified coherent image. This distancing technique is in keeping with the nineteenth-century fascination with the harem as a forbidden, segregated space for women, from which all men, except the Sultan, were banned. The paintings make manifest the Orientalist gaze Edward Said described as 'a Western style for dominating, restructuring and having authority over the orient'.[17] Representations of the Orient cannot be appreciated without a consideration of the power relationship between the West and the East as a tension between the familiar and the unfamiliar, identity and difference. In the language of postcolonial and postmodern theory, we have here a power relationship between the 'Self' and the 'Other', the male viewer and the framed female.[18] The East is framed, codified to reinforce difference, 'Otherness', but also to flatter the Western colonial eye. Within this relationship, the Orient is represented in feminine terms, as a land and peoples in need of control; by extension, the Occident is depicted in knowledgeable, controlling, powerful masculine terms. Thus the erotic power of Ingres's *The Turkish Bath* lies not only in the voyeuristic fantasy of seeing these women, but in the fantasy of control, specifically *one* man's sexual control and enjoyment of them.[19] The painting is about the displacement and control of female sexuality on the one hand, and, on the other, the ultimate colonial fantasy for Ingres (by now a 72-year-old *grand maître* of the French art world) and the male viewer—the fantasy of stepping into a Sultan's shoes.

The paintings of Eugène Delacroix (1798–1863) are at odds with the classicism of Ingres but many continue this Orientalist tradition of

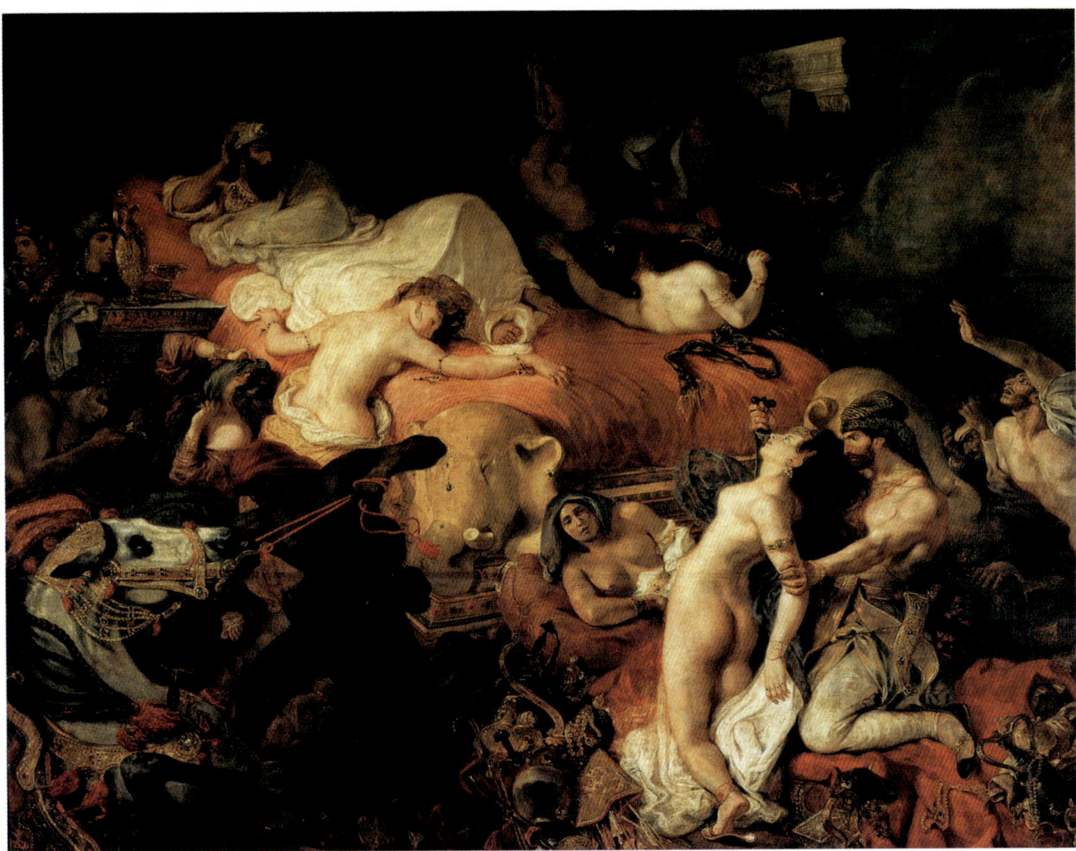

14 Eugène Delacroix
The Death of Sardanapalus, 1827

Causing an outcry when it was exhibited at the Salon in Paris in 1828, this painting's baroque sadism lies not only in its anarchic composition and red palette but its seemingly amoral depiction of King Sardanapalus of Nineveh destroying all his earthly possessions, including his concubines, before his imminent death at the hands of his enemies.

eroticism. Delacroix unleashed havoc on the Art Salon tradition with his *The Death of Sardanapalus* (1827) **[14]**. Painted before the artist visited Morocco in 1832, and inspired by Lord Byron's 1821 tragedy of the same name, it presents the Orient as a hotbed of sexuality, lust, despotism, and irrationality. We see King Sardanapalus of Nineveh, seventh century BC, as his Assyrian city is destroyed by the Babylonians. He is preparing for his imminent death at the hands of his enemies by destroying all his earthly possessions, including his concubines, in a final act of self-sacrifice. Delacroix emphasizes the impending bloody, fleshy slaughter through deep-red hues and an orgiastic composition of nudes. The composition is centred round Sardanapalus, who lies back calmly enjoying this final sacrificial rite and act of male potency. Sardanapalus, like Delacroix, and like the male viewer, is privy to the expanse of sexual flesh and violence but not threatened by it. *The Death of Sardanapalus*, with all its Romantic, baroque sadism, caused an outcry when it went on show at the Salon in Paris in 1828.[20] This was not just due to its unruly composition, loose brushstrokes, and violent representation of the subject, it lacked moral clarity and brought the spectator into a world of hedonism rather than keeping him safely at a distance. Thus it went against the typical sublimated eroticization of the Orient as seen in Ingres. However, the Orient is again feminized: it is shown to be morally inferior and in need of Western control; sexual and imperial politics are fused, and the colonial expansion of France and of Christian Europe in general legitimized.

Where Delacroix brings the viewer dangerously close to his exotic subject-matter, Jean-Léon Gérome (1824–1904) frames the Orient as if he were an ethnographer. He offers a paradigmatic image of the Orient which most flattered French imperialism. In *The Slave Market* (early 1860s), we find that a 'dispassionate empiricism' is employed as tidy brushstrokes and a balanced composition deflate the sexual subject-matter and contrive to present a 'sociological', rational image of authentic life in the Near East.[21] Yet under the guise of documentary realism the artist has justified the ideology behind political imperialism (West over East, Occident over Orient), religion (Christian over Muslim), and sexual politics (man over woman) by portraying the Orient as an amoral, lustful world where women are bought and sold by men, as commodities—a world that needs Western 'civilizing'. In contrast, Gérome's conflation of eroticism and colonial politics is less apparent in professional women's paintings of the Orient. *A Visit (Harem Interior, Constantinople, 1860)* and *Flute Player* (*Harem Interior, Constantinople, 1860)*—both dated 1861, by the French painter Sophie de Boutailler (1829–1901), who exhibited under the name Henriette Browne—deny the male 'Sultan fantasy' in showing *clothed* women meeting and chatting. Browne travelled in the East and actually visited a harem in Constantinople (a privilege male painters were clearly denied). Her paintings may be seen as privileging a female gaze by means of an ethnographic perspective that frames the harem in terms of a European, domestic, and familial space.[22] Browne and other women Orientalists (including women travel diarists) render the harem a subject suitable for a female painter and a female audience, even if they exploit their position of privilege as females in a female-only space. The harem allowed the woman artist or writer to be both spectator and participant, allowing for the successful balance of ethnography and fantasy.[23] That said, Browne's paintings' lack of explicit titillation did not go unnoticed by some contemporary male critics. In 1861 Olivier Merson described Browne's paintings of harems as showing 'silent and bored women . . . chaste in the muslin of their long dresses', admitting 'these paintings somewhat disrupt our dreams of the Orient'.[24]

New Masculinities

Masculinity, like femininity, is socially constructed, not fixed. But in that time of imperialist expansion masculinity was conceived of with clear moralizing, patriotic, heroic, and virtuous overtones. Accordingly, masculinity is visualized in the nineteenth century through recourse to classical and chivalrous narratives, male sexuality and desire always being kept subservient to the great moral truth. In addition, while Freud aligns phallic power with the male sexual organ, we find that images of the male nude in the nineteenth century do not tend to show males who are well endowed, let alone sexually aroused. Instead, the 'modest size' of male genitals in art seems standard practice, continuing the standard size of the penis set up in the fifth century BC, honoured by Michelangelo and by such neoclassical painters as Jacques-Louis David.[25] In nineteenth-century paintings and sculptures of men we find sexual decorum abounds: the penis is either concealed, or coyly suggested by drapery, swords, and scabbard; when visible, it is limp. This is in keeping with our series of opposites discussed above: the female body is aligned with nature, disorder, the flesh, lust; the male with art, order, the mind and control. The male nude demonstrated his classical perfection and heroism through his modesty and control of his baser urges.

However, a powerful male sensuality is evident in the art of the painters Frederic Leighton (1830–96) and Simeon Solomon (1840–1905). In both cases, we come closer to phallic power through the depiction of male friendship, battle, or mentorship. Their images of male homosociality reflect a society and time in which there was no name for homosexual desire: 'homo-sexuality' did not enter the *Oxford English Dictionary* until 1892, and 'heterosexuality' until 1900. Leighton was a classicist in subject-matter and technique, and president of the Royal Academy from 1878 to his death in 1896. His knowledge of Greek and Latin and his passion for Greco-Roman art was in keeping with the classical revivalism of the critic Walter Pater (1839–94) and poet and critic Matthew Arnold (1822–88), and was demonstrated in his elevation of the male nude to the highest form of physical and moral beauty. In *Greek Studies* (published posthumously in 1895), Pater lauds Greek sculpture as it addressed 'the deepest elements of man's nature and destiny, to command and express these'.[26] Leighton's private life aside—Leonée and Richard Ormond discuss the fact that his male models were all handsome and his circle, including Henry Greville, homosexual in leaning; Peter Webb notes the artist's interest in Wilhelm von Gloeden's 1893 photos of nude Sicilian youths—there is certainly an interest in what the Victorians called 'Greek love' in his art.[27] This is the erotic relationship

15 Frederic Leighton *Athlete Wrestling with a Python*, 1877

Described by the novelist Henry James as 'a noble and beautiful work', this sculpture celebrates the male body and may be read as demonstrating an Apollonian homoeroticism, insofar as it recalls Apollo's killing of the female serpent Python.

between the older, wise male mentor, the *erastes* (lover) and the younger male pupil, the *eromenos* (beloved), as formulated in Plato's *Symposium*. Leighton's *Daedalus and Icarus* (1869) explores this *erastes–eromenos* relationship through the story of a brilliant father and his naive son. Daedalus, with his dark skin and wrinkled face, acts as a visual foil to the beautiful subject of his gaze: the marmoreal body of Icarus who stands upright and nude apart from a scarf of silk which coyly covers his sex. It will be lost when he leaps into the air. He looks to the sun, which will lure him to his death, and to another greater master—Apollo, the sun god and more powerful male heroic ideal.

Leighton's compositions were often influenced by the reclining figures of the Elgin Marbles, and his technique reflects the rather stilted style in which he depicted drapery: he would paint the body and then 'append' the drapery, often resulting in unnatural swags and folds and a monumental air that again allowed eroticism to be safely controlled. However, we find little restraint in his bronze sculpture *Athlete Struggling with a Python* (1877) **[15]**, a dramatic work referencing both the head of Michelangelo's *David* and the monumental *contrapposto* of *The Death of Laocoön and His Sons*, a sculpture (*c.*150 BC, unearthed in 1506) of a heavily muscled, heroic father and his young sons twisting as they struggle with serpents. The model for the athlete, Angelo Colarossi, was an Italian who sat for many of the leading Victorian painters (including John Singer Sargent, John Everett Millais, and George Frederic Watts). The sculpture's physical beauty, enhanced by the play of light on the surface of the dark metal, was not lost on the novelist Henry James who saw it exhibited at the Royal Academy in 1877 and wrote: 'it is a noble and beautiful work . . . Whenever I have been to the Academy I have found a certain relief in looking for a while at this representation of the naked human body, the whole story of which begins and ends with beautiful play of its muscles and limbs.'[28] His admiration was shared by critics who applauded Leighton's success at capturing motion and musculature in the rather unwieldy medium of bronze—a medium he had never worked with before. There is an eroticism in this choice of medium too, a 'sensualized aesthetic': we might compare the athlete wrestling with his python to Leighton wrestling with the medium of bronze and struggling to find a balance between ancient, academic classicism of Greek bronze sculptures (though Greek statuary was only known to the nineteenth century through marble copies), and erotic, tactile modernism.[29] Furthermore, since pleasure is allowed in this representation of the male, an alternative masculine model is presented, one which allows for male pleasure in looking at male bodies. Joseph Kestner goes further in his analysis of Leighton's representations of the

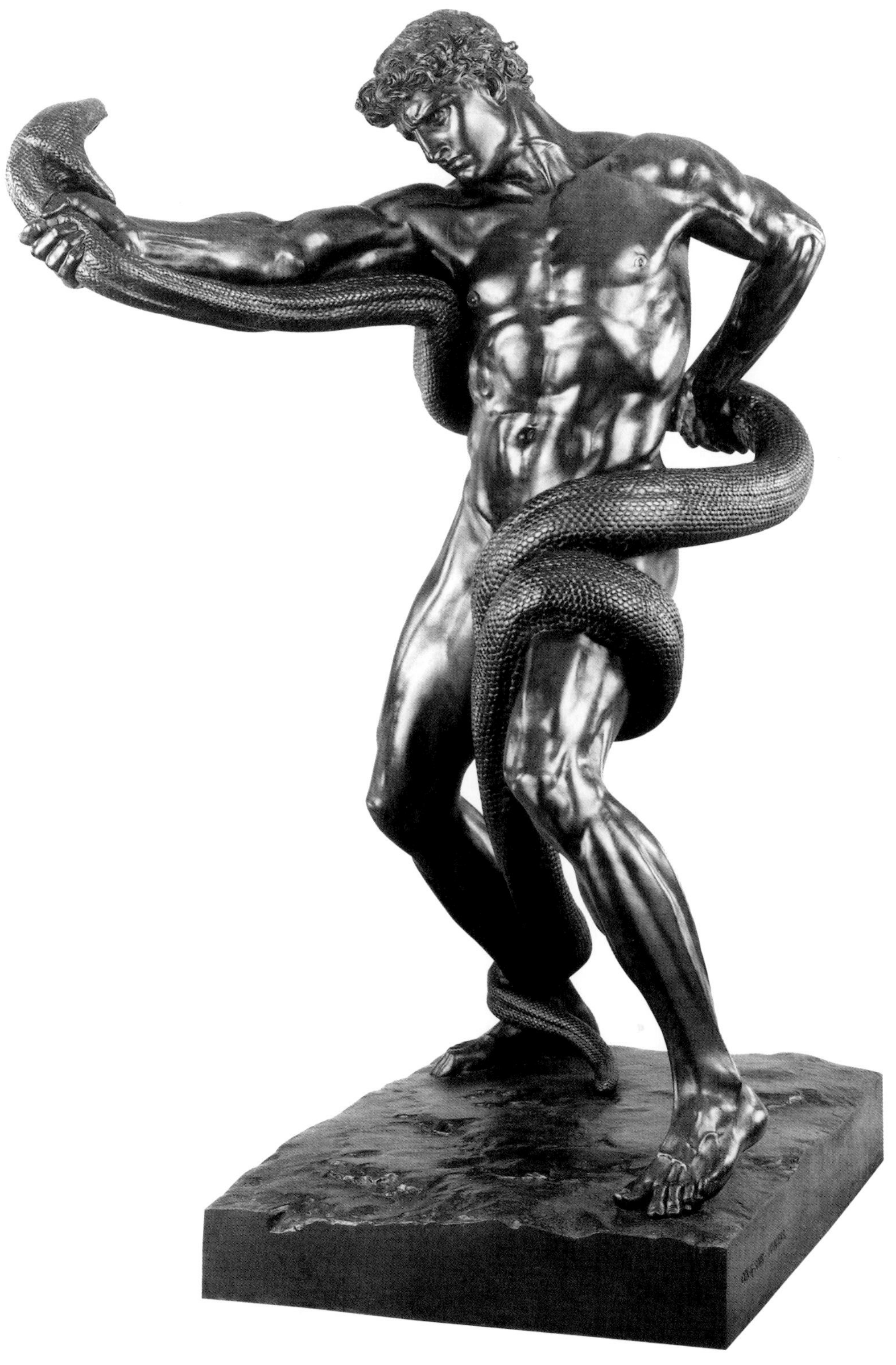

athlete, finding a homoerotic phallic play in the sculpture, contrasting the large serpent to the small penis of the athlete, and writing: 'The fact that the serpent nearly crushes the genitals may represent the guilt Leighton associated with sexuality. The snake itself is the gigantic phallus that is part of some homoerotic fantasies.'[30] Again, as in Leighton's *Daedalus and Icarus*, Apollonian homoeroticism is to be found, as we can link the python to the sun god. In mythology, Apollo killed the female serpent Python and condemned her to rot (*pytho* is the Greek for rot). Thus Leighton's brave athlete embodies the triumph of the masculine, of the sun god, and a castration anxiety that the female might appropriate his phallus.[31] The eroticism of the sculpture lies not only in its immediate perfection but in a homoerotic subtext too.

Colin Cruise offers a comparable reading of the male figures of the Pre-Raphaelite painter Simeon Solomon. He suggests that Solomon's effeminate male studies should be read within the tradition of beauty inspired by Leonardo, Botticelli, Titian, and the Sienese artist Sodoma, as well as alongside the writings of Pater, who was a friend, given Pater 'proposes a new kind of masculinity: an aesthete who enjoys the spectacle of male beauty and who can discern a subtle masculinity perhaps invisible to observers'.[32] In general terms, Pater's essay 'The Age of Athletic Prizemen' (1894) might be taken as an example of this new masculinity as Pater clearly aligns masculinity and perfection. In 'A Study of Dionysus' (1876) Pater actually refers to Solomon's painting of *Bacchus* (1867) and 'perceives Solomon as depicting a masculinity alternative to that of Christ, whose sexuality was perceived as heterosexual, unchanging and moral'.[33] Bacchus, the god of wine and revelry, may strike us as an odd example of the new male but it is his half-human side that seems to appeal to the artist and critic as a male figure who is half god, half man; half male, half female; half sacred, half profane; half sensual, half chaste. Solomon's *Bacchus* is a young beauty with effeminate ruby lips, long hair, and a noble brow. The viewer of this painting is to experience not only a sensual but also a spiritual pleasure as he or she reflects on these binary qualities.

Female Loveliness

A more languid, ethereal form of female beauty coincided with these representations of new masculinity. In 1882, in *The Aesthetic Movement in England*, Walter Hamilton wrote:

> it is in the portrayal of female beauty that Aesthetic art is most peculiar, both in conceptions as to what constitute female loveliness, and in the treatment of it. The type usually found is that of a pale distraught lady

> with matted auburn hair falling in masses over the brow, and shading eyes full of lovelorn languor, or feverish despair, emaciated cheeks and somewhat heavy jaws; protruding upper lip, the lower being withdrawn, long crane neck, flat breasts, and long thin nervous hands.[34]

This is the lady who stares out at us from the canvases of the Pre-Raphaelites, the artistic 'brotherhood'. The group was formed in 1848, the year of revolutions in Europe, by the painters James Collinson (1821–81, then engaged to the Pre-Raphaelite 'sister', Christina Rossetti), William Holman Hunt (1827–1910), John Everett Millais (1829–96), Dante Gabriel Rossetti (1828–82), Frederic George Stephens (1828–1907), the sculptor Thomas Woolner (1825–92), and the critic William M. Rossetti, who kept the group's *Journal* from 1849 to 1853 and published *Some Reminiscences* in 1906.[35] As their chosen name indicated, the Pre-Raphaelites were inspired by the art before Raphael, before 1500, an era undoubtedly very much at odds with Victorian England, its representative democracy, large-scale industrialization and increased urbanization. They were championed by the influential critic John Ruskin, who proclaimed in his *Modern Painters* (5 vols, 1843–60) that the paintings of northern Flemish artist Rembrandt (1606–69) and Spanish artist Bartolomé Murillo (1617–82) were disgusting and the Victorian social system wicked. Ruskin favoured the Venetian Gothic in architecture, the Greek and Florentine in sculpture, and the paintings of English Romantic painter J. M. W. Turner (1775–1851), which, in his view, were as beautiful as they were true. Ruskin found the picturesque in the Pre-Raphaelites; in 1851, when they were under severe attack from other critics, he defended them in a letter to the Editor of *The Times* and in a pamphlet on *Pre-Raphaelitism*. He believed that their art continued the great Renaissance tradition of religious art even in its exploration of the theme of desire and females displaying 'feverish despair'.

Dante Gabriel Rossetti's *Bocca baciata* (1859) **[16]** exemplifies the sensuality of the Pre-Raphaelite muse. The title, which translates as 'The mouth that has been kissed', refers to the fourteenth-century Italian writer Boccaccio and his *Decameron*, specifically the phrase 'Bocca baciata non perda ventura, anzi rinova come fa la luna' (The mouth that has been kissed loses not its freshness; still it renews itself even as does the moon), which is written on the back of the painting. It alludes to the tale of the daughter of the Sultan of Babylon, Alatiel, who is betrothed to the King of Algarve but is shipwrecked en route to marry him. She is rescued by a noblemen who then seduces her, she becomes involved with his brother who commits fratricide to have her, and soon her great beauty leads to another affair. Her beauty is famed and her sexual

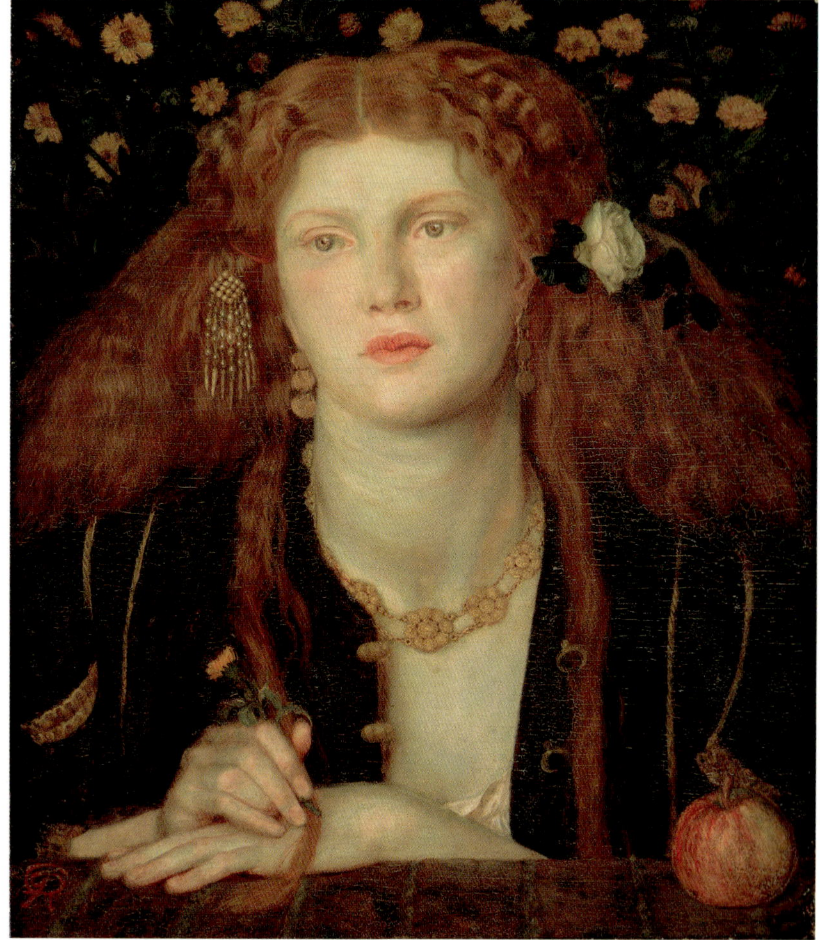

16 Dante Gabriel Rossetti
Bocca baciata, 1859
This painting of 'the mouth that has been kissed' refers to Boccaccio's *Decameron*, and the story of Alatiel. Rossetti lingers over the luscious mouth and flame-red hair of his model and lover, Fanny Cornforth, enhancing her ethereal beauty and its potency with the inclusion of flowers and an apple.

knowledge ever increasing such that men love her and kill for her, until she finally returns to her father and persuades him she has spent her years of exile in a convent. Her marriage to the King of Algarve is finally organized; on her wedding night, despite having had some eight lovers, she persuades her husband that she is a virgin bride, and they live happily ever after. Hence the expression underpinning the work: Alatiel's mouth may have been kissed many a time but never lost its freshness. Hers is a story of passion, but it plays out at the expense of a woman who is passive before men and Fortune. The erotic tale is evident in details of the painting. As Griselda Pollock has observed, the mouth in the painting, in all its ruby glory, can function as 'a displaced sign of female sexuality, her genitals', but it also suggests regression to the oral phase, of being suckled, and so offers up a maternal fantasy too.[36] J. B. Bullen notes the flowers in her hair suggest 'her continuing life of passion'; he reminds us that Rossetti's friends all knew the sitter, Fanny Cornforth, was a 'woman of easy virtue'.[37] Of course a more obvious set of symbols are visible in the painting too, and refer to the Renaissance iconography of female sexuality: the flower symbolizes 'deflowering', reminding us of the crux of Alatiel's story; the apple is an attribute to Venus but also alludes to Eve's Fall, thus continuing the theme of chastity and the fallen woman whose fate is rarely that of Alatiel. In English culture at the time, long flowing hair also suggested improper sensuality—an emotionality we see too in Millais's *Ophelia* (1851–2), where Shakespeare's heroine's fall from rationality is symbolized by her wild hair and the flowers she scattered and holds.[38] With all this in mind we better appreciate the eroticism of Rossetti and how the poet Algernon Swinburne could appreciatively describe *Bocca baciata* as 'more stunning than can decently be expressed'.[39]

Edward Coley Burne-Jones's (1833–98) *Pygmalion Cycle* (1868–79), with four panels *The Heart Desires*, *The Hand Refrains*, *The Godhead Fires*, and *The Soul Attains*, also speaks to contemporary English mores and acceptable codes of eroticism. A pupil and friend of Rossetti, he painted the cycle twice, first in 1868–70, then a larger set from 1869–79. Though married to Georgiana Macdonald since 1860, both sets reflect his affair with Maria Zambaco which began in 1866. The first set was painted for Zambaco's mother, Euphrosyne Cassavetti; the second was painted after a 1868 rupture with her.[40] Given his illicit relationship it is curious to see both erotic desire and fear at work in both sets, notably the second. Pygmalion's story is of the search for perfection in a woman. As recounted by Ovid, he is the King of Cyprus who rejects the real women of Cyprus and carves his own ivory beauty instead. He prays to Aphrodite to give him a wife as beautiful as his statue; she gives his statue life, turning ivory into the fair Galatea. The story allowed Burne-Jones to address his own torn attitude to woman or, more specifically, his mistress.[41] It also reflects Victorian society's anxiety over the weaker sex. Let us not forget that in 1871 Charles Darwin claimed in *The Descent of Man* that through natural selection man had become superior to woman, and the faculties females often outshone in—intuition, perception, and imitation—only confirmed the inferiority as they were 'characteristic of the lower races, and therefore of a past and lower state of civilisation'.[42] In the second version of the cycle, Burne-Jones certainly seems to dwell on the imperfections of real women and the unattainability of the perfect woman. In *The Heart Desires* we find Pygmalion pontificating on womankind (real women in the street are visible to the left of the image, through an archway) and his ideal (sculpted graces, positioned to the right of our protagonist, their perfect forms highlighted by rays of sun). In *The Hand*

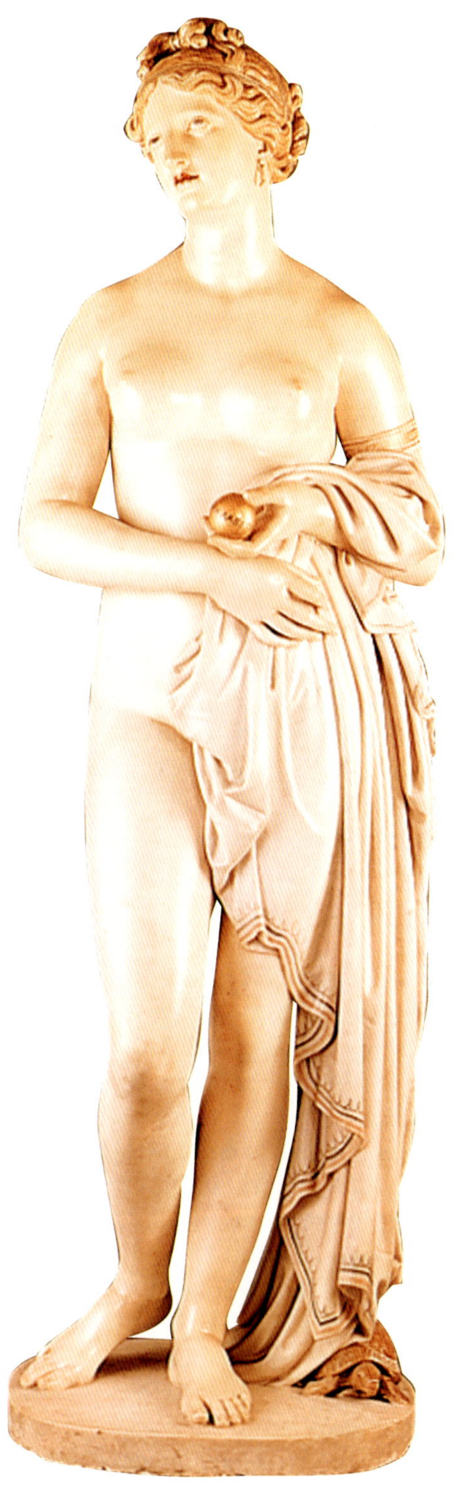

17 John Gibson
Tinted Venus, 1851

Venus holds her prize from Paris, a golden apple, having competed alongside Juno and Minerva in his beauty contest. In her polychrome surface, the British sculptor Gibson departs from the convention of the white statue and its association with purity, lending a 'blush' to her curvaceous form that critics were quick to admire.

Refrains he looks rather fearful before the perfect Venus he has sculpted, and in *The Godhead Fires* he is banished as Aphrodite gives life to the sculpture. Finally the story ends with a tremulous Pygmalion in *The Soul Attains* as he kneels before his ideal turned to flesh, his Galatea, who is certainly of ideal proportions but who looks beyond him as if oblivious to this lesser creature and his adoration. Neither body nor soul seems to find resolution here.

The pursuit of the ideal was very much in vogue in England by the 1860s, with artists increasingly influenced by Joshua Reynolds's (1723–92) *Discourses on Art* in which he urged artists to look to the antique, transcend the model (from the 1850s on female models were being increasingly used in art schools), and present an ideal type.[43] Two celebrated nude, marble sensations at London's Crystal Palace exhibition in 1851 certainly reflect this dominant desire that the nude continue to elevate the mind. The first was the *Tinted Venus* **[17]** one of the first polychrome—coloured—sculptures of the day, by the Royal Academician John Gibson (1790–1866); the second was the *The Greek Slave* by the American sculptor, Hiram Powers (1805–73). Gibson's *Tinted Venus* not only evoked ancient myth but also the morals we should learn from them. She holds a golden apple—her prize from Paris, having competed in his beauty contest alongside Juno and Minerva. Her polychrome surface evokes another erotic tale: Pliny's story in his *Natural History* of the Aphrodite of Cnidus (Knidos) by Praxiteles, the first monumental female nude in classical sculpture, which was so beautiful that one admirer left a 'stain' on the marble. In addition, while the tortoise at her feet has the inscription 'Gibson made me in Rome', this sculpture looks back to the Greeks, when sculptures were painted, and so to its idealizing classical tradition. Powers had a similar intent in his *The Greek Slave*. It took pride of place in the American section of the Exhibition, and again spoke of purity despite the nude's blatant sensual appeal. The context for her nudity was indicated by her Orientalist accessories: her chains and the Turkish carpet on which she stands. Ostensibly contemporary in subject-matter—a Christian captured by the Turks in the Greek War of Independence (1822–30)—its reification of the female form and promotion of chastity is age-old. Her lack of shame, despite her sexual fate, indicates her moral superiority. *The Greek Slave* was so popular at the exhibition and when it toured towns across the United Sates that six full-size and many small-size replicas of it were made. This virtuous reading of her nudity was somewhat undercut by the fact that in some of these exhibitions women and children viewed the statue on different days to men. Clearly there was a tension between morality and lust over this sensuous sculpture, as indicated in an engraving published in the

Cosmopolitan Art Journal at the time. It depicts a mixed audience looking at the sculpture: the womenfolk are shown to be instructing their male companions on how to read her erotic form respectfully, as indicated by the fact the men have taken off their hats and are looking intently at their female companions rather than the majestic nude form on a pedestal which dominates the room.[44]

By 1870, however, we find a new direction for the nude in England, a shift marked by John Everett Millais's *The Knight Errant* (1870) **[18]**. Here we are presented with a naked woman bound to a tree as a chivalrous knight comes to rescue her from her distress. There is no obvious mytho-

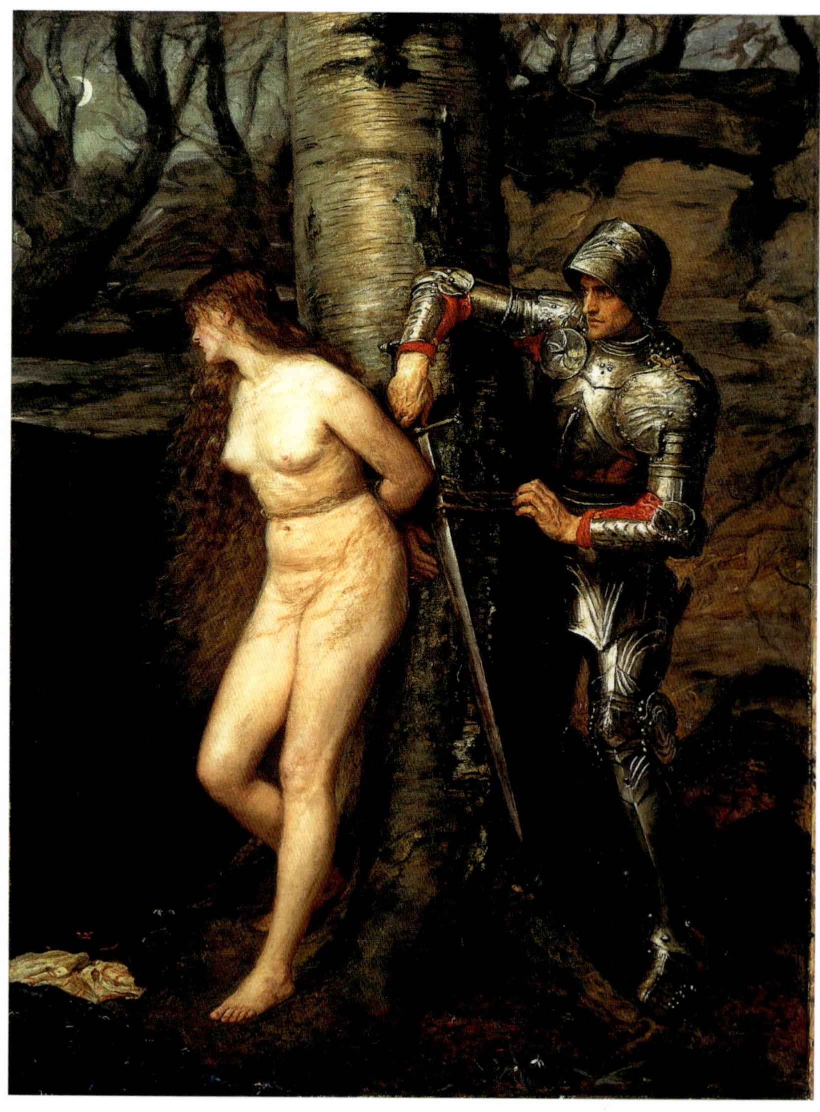

18 Sir John Everett Millais
The Knight Errant, 1870
One of the founding members of the Pre-Raphaelite Brotherhood and championed by the critic John Ruskin, Millais here turns to the nude, a form favoured by Queen Victoria and Prince Albert. He depicts an Arthurian romance in which a noble knight cuts the cords that bind a naked damsel. The first version of the painting caused a furore, leading Millais to adjust the damsel's head and shoulders so that she looks away from the knight in shame rather than into his eyes with gratitude.

logical subject, though the knight evokes medieval England; there is no obvious literary source, and—despite the accompanying quotation, 'The order of the Knight Errant was instituted to protect widows and orphans and to succour maidens in distress'—there is no obvious source of distress. The maiden's realistic naked body, her full breasts, and wild hair scandalized the public and critics when it was first exhibited at the Royal Academy in 1870. J. B. Atkinson wrote in the *Saturday Review* that she had been 'denuded' so successfully by Millais that 'it is scarcely surprising that the spectators called for clothes'.[45] It was the model's natural form and gaze that undoubtedly scandalized so, as revealed by the fact that Millais, after the 1870 exhibition, repainted her head, changing her gaze from a frontal one, looking out at the viewer, to one of modesty, looking into the canvas, as we see in the final version we know today. This 'censorship' reveals the sheer sexual power of the represented female gaze and the economics of art too—for only by changing her expression to one of modesty and shame did Millais ensure that his painting sold. For Alison Smith, Millais's *Knight Errant* may even be a 'rearguard gesture, promoting the protection of women to counter the ambitions of the middle-class woman outside the home', or a reminder that only a working-class woman would bare herself to the public so.[46] The knight would thus be protecting this fair damsel from the immorality of modernity itself. This was a very real concern at the time, as signalled by the passing of the Contagious Diseases Acts in 1862, 1866, and 1869, and by increased concern over the use of naked models for life class in art colleges like the Slade (which opened in 1871).[47] This concern was especially for female art students: thanks to the Slade, and indeed the Académie Julian in Paris (the independent art school that opened in 1868 and welcomed women, unlike the state-funded École des Beaux-Arts, which excluded them until 1897), female students were now drawing from the human figure.[48] The fact that women were no longer restricted to the lower genres they had hitherto been expected to focus on—flower painting, animals, botanical illustration, stitchery, tapestry—signalled the beginning of their long battle for artistic and social liberation but made society fearful of their 'corruption' too.

The End of the Age of Innocence

The demise of the classical nude was also affected by the rise of a new art form, photography. Beginning in 1839 in France with Louis Jacques Daguerre's (1787–1851) *daguerreotype*—a method of receiving, on a prepared plate, an image produced by the camera obscura and thus allowing nature to 'reproduce herself'—this new scientific process had immense repercussions for representations of the body, especially the erotic body. The camera was a machine, bringing art into the industrial age and promising simplicity, speed, and accuracy for all, not just artists. It would also pave the way for the representation of the naked body and the sexual act itself.

Nude photographs began with the *académies*: the academic studies used by Parisian artists, which removed the expense of hiring a real life model. Inevitably, however, these photographs began to be collected by the voyeuristic public such that a new popular culture of pornography emerged in French and other societies. Charles Baudelaire wrote of the potential of the stereoscope in 1862:

> It was not long before thousands of pairs of greedy eyes were glued to the peep holes of the stereoscope, as though they were the skylights of the infinite. The love of obscenity, which is as vigorous a growth in the heart of natural man as self-love, could not let slip such a glorious opportunity for its own satisfaction . . .[49]

Photographic nudes tended to adopt the style of the canonical high art tradition, with models classically posed with antique, Oriental or simply erotic props (jewellery, fans, stockings) and rather theatrical settings (velvet curtains, luxurious couches, or beds). In their erotic display these photographs further distanced the nude from the Platonic ideal while subjecting it more than ever to the harsh reality of sexual consumption.

The economic reality behind Victorian nudes was particularly acute when it came to photographs of children. Before the mid-eighteenth century, pictures of children were effectively pictures of small adults: children were dressed, staged, and framed within the orthodox tradition of portraiture. Also, those children who were pictured were the children of nobility or future leaders of state. When Jean-Baptiste Greuze (1725–1805) painted *The Broken Pitcher* (1773) or Sir Joshua Reynolds *The Age of Innocence* (1788), they were catering to a taste for innocence and for an ideal of childhood that had hitherto been neglected in fine art and that emerged with Enlightenment concern for childrearing and education, notably in the philosophical writings of Locke and Rousseau. *The Broken Pitcher* alludes to the loss of virginity by means of the broken pitcher the girl carries; this is reinforced by her sad expression and hands that awkwardly grapple with flowers and frame her sex. *The Age of Innocence* shows a girl whose innocence is intact, her carefree life indicated by her clean feet and pretty dress. The introduction of photography to the art world added a new dimension to the

Romantic representation of the child, however, as photography contributed to the rise of the *concept* of childhood. As Carol Mavor states, 'The child and the photograph were commodified, fetishized, developed alongside each other: they were laminated and framed as one.'[50] Unlike painting or sculpture, photography demands the performance of a body or object before the photographic lens. As a result, where the photograph is of a child, not to mention an erotically staged child, it forces the viewer into a new, compromising experience where they realize that the image before them is real, having been 'snapped' from life. We enter into a fictitious dialogue with the represented person. As the act of photographing is itself an act of appropriation and capturing, it inevitably invokes the erotic in a new way.

The writer, clergyman, mathematician, and photographer Lewis Carroll (Charles Lutwidge Dodgson, 1832–98), photographed young girls clothed and unclothed from 1856 to 1880 to capture their innocence and 'unspoiled beauty'.[51] Four nude photographs of children taken by Carroll have been discovered; one in particular, the image of *Evelyn Hatch* (*c.*1878) **[19]**, echoes the Western tradition of the elongated nude (such as Titian's *Venus of Urbino*) in posture, as well as the vogue of Orientalism in the emphatic contrast between her gypsy-like dark face and her pale body. In the photograph, Evelyn brazenly and confidently stares at the camera, as if she is aware of the viewer's fascination with her and her body. Accordingly, one could say that erotic passion is presented as belonging to the child; the artist merely understands and captures it.[52] However, this reading denies the sheer fact that we are looking at an image of a child, staged for sexual pleasure. It demands

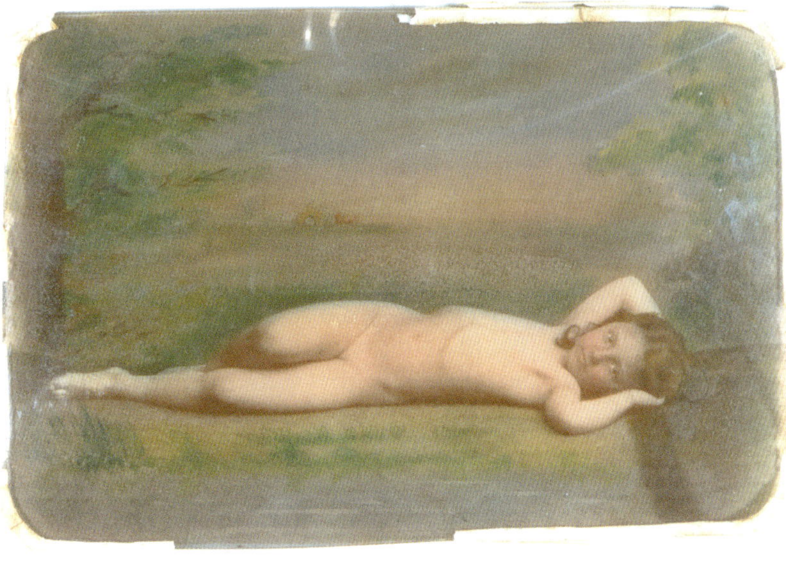

19 Lewis Carroll (Charles Lutwidge Dodgson)
Evelyn Hatch, *c.*1878

Famous as the author of *Alice's Adventures in Wonderland* (1865) and *Through the Looking Glass* (1872), Carroll also took numerous photographs of children, including Beatrice and Evelyn Hatch, and Edith, Lorina, and Alice Liddell, the daughters of Henry George Liddell, the Dean of Christ Church, Oxford. Where photography was tending towards a new realism in the representation of the nude, here Carroll makes his photograph 'painterly'. The image of Evelyn, who is only about 6 years old, is printed on emulsion on a curved piece of glass and backed with another piece of painted glass so that her naked form takes on a flesh-like hue, while the painted landscape around her allows the whole image to radiate.

that little Evelyn (who is probably only 6 years old) has some sexual agency within this photographic image. We may be suspicious of Carroll's desire or perhaps be tempted to go so far as to agree with the contemporary critic Joris-Karl Huysmans, who wrote in 1881 that 'only a woman is qualified to paint childhood' (albeit in a review of the American Mary Cassatt's (1844–1926) Impressionist paintings of bourgeois interiors, including her *A Mother Kissing Her Baby on the Cheeks*).[53] As a child and urchin staged for the camera Evelyn is certainly Carroll's foil, his 'Other', and so as part of that Orientalizing tradition that exoticizes the erotic, as indicated by Carroll's allusion to immorality through Evelyn's darkened skin and seemingly brazen sexuality. Certainly this allows the eroticism of the child to remain safely within the confines of a Victorian sensibility.

Carroll's photograph must be seen alongside the rise of photography as a medium for raising funds for charity work at the time, as in the case of Dr Barnardo, who began in 1870 to publish and sell photographs of urchins to raise money for his institutions. But it also coincides with the vogue for paintings of gypsy girls, street urchins, and beggars in art, as we have already seen in Greuze, and the general concern with a child's innocence. So, for example, John Everett Millais's *Cherry Ripe* (1880), where fruit acts as sexual metaphor for the 'ripe' young urchin girl, is contemporaneous with *Evelyn Hatch*. In a similar fashion to Millais, Evelyn is fetishized by Carroll, as both child and soon-to-be-woman. Her erotic pose reminds us too of the contemporary Victorian obsession with the ideal of childhood and how it was at odds with the problematic rise of child prostitution and a white slave trade in virgins in England. This problem was revealed by William Thomas Stead in the *Pall Mall Gazette* from 6–10 July 1885, when he published *The Maiden Tribute of Modern Babylon*, his investigation into the white slave trade in England and the Continent. The exposé led to the Criminal Law Amendment Act in which the age of consent for girls was raised from the age of 13 to 16.

Ultimately, to understand the nude during the period from the Enlightenment to the late nineteenth century, one must remember the ongoing conflict in art between the ideal and the real, the chaste and the sinful, classicism and contemporaneity. One must also recognize that this reflected the larger economic, political, and sexual conflicts of changing industrial societies. For example, in England, the period witnessed the start of the suffragette movement and the publication of John Stuart Mill's *The Subjection of Women* (1869), which demanded equality between the sexes; yet Victorian society also clung to a patriarchal and authoritarian vision of the home and family where women were shut away from the public gaze, and continued to profess prudery in an age when pornography was becoming rampant. Of course, as mentioned in the Introduction, it was in 1857 that the word 'pornography' entered the *Oxford English Dictionary* where it was explained as a 'matter of public hygiene', thus aligning the private and the public through a concern with contamination. This fear of contamination led to an increasingly desperate academic defence of the classical tradition. However, those Realist, Impressionist, and Expressionist artists who reacted against classicism's glorification of myth, purity, and the ideal body, and who turned instead to the naked truth, would soon sound the death knell of the old regime and bring about the birth of modern art. In very different ways, from the seemingly style-less to the most individualistic expressive art, artists began to overthrow Plato's neat divide between imitation and the real by questioning reality itself. And of course, that couch we began this chapter with would now become the perfect site for transgression as artists wantonly displayed the female body stretched out on a bed or chaise longue in an erotic knowingness.

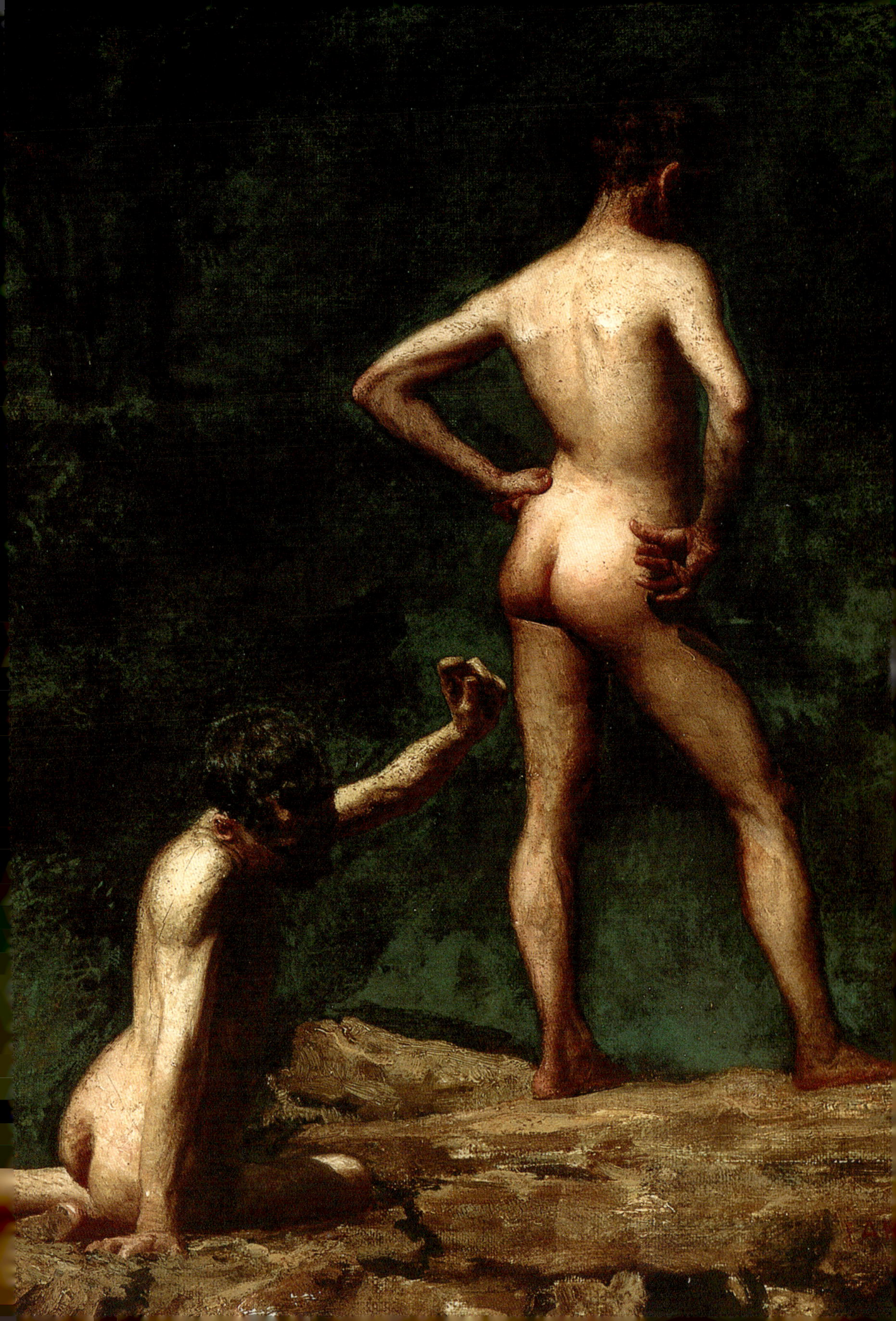

2 The Naked Truth

The demand that art be 'of the moment' was one of the central tenets of modern art and coincided with a new sense of the agency of modernity itself, such that artists and critics strove not only to represent their changing world but to contribute to that change. This new value placed on contemporaneity was reflected in new artistic styles and subject-matter. Realism and Impressionism often focused on the modern metropolis and the activities of its working-class and bourgeois inhabitants. There was an increased concern with the very stuff of art—evidenced in unorthodox perspectival views, collage, gestural brush-strokes, and brash, unnatural palettes—which has led some critics to view these new modern art movements as pursuing formal concerns above and beyond all else. For example, in 1939 the influential American critic Clement Greenberg in his essay 'Avant-garde and Kitsch' interpreted the exciting formal innovations in modern art as a desire for autonomy from society, as an 'art for art's sake'.[1] However, the rise of the modernist art critic, from Charles Baudelaire to Greenberg, was in itself central to the advances and interpretations of modern art. Critics' interpretations of the major movements in modern art tended to set up an *opposition* between sociopolitical and formal concerns.

Yet, as we shall see, representations of the erotic body began to test that opposition, exposing it as an impossible divide; and, at the same time, a number of themes emerged in the first decades of modern art, many of which pertained to the erotic potential of the modern body. We find one type of woman, the prostitute, taking on a special relevance, becoming a cipher for modernity itself. In the figure of the prostitute, whether working on the street or as a high-class courtesan, art drew closer and closer to the key themes of the age: modern urban society, changing sexual mores, the place of women in the public arena, the economics of sexuality, and class tensions. Most importantly, the *naked* erotic body now supplants the *nude*, acting as a mirror for a rapidly changing and increasingly depersonalized urban society and the artist's role within it.

Detail of 24

The pursuit of 'honest truth'—to borrow the definition of 'Realist' given by Gustave Courbet in 1851—through eroticism is not peculiar to the dawn of the twentieth century. It runs counter to the return to classicism discussed in the previous chapter. Courbet, we recall, produced *The Origin of the World* **[3]** in 1866—one of the most scandalous erotic paintings of the day. An audacious painting of a foreshortened female nude, it does not resort to myth or moralism as pretext but luxuriates instead in the sexual subject-matter and medium of paint. We see no head, no feet, only the shadow of a woman's left breast and the curve and nipple of her right breast from under a loosely painted white sheet, and her stomach, thighs, and vaginal lips, peeping through behind thick black pubic hair. The site of self-pleasure and shared pleasure, the symbol of birth, both literal and artistic—and, for Freud, of castration—is here deemed a worthy and beautiful subject-matter.

Eleven years earlier Courbet published a manifesto in which he defined his artistic aim as wanting to create a 'living art'; perhaps this is the best route to appreciating his powerful image of a living woman. He rejected the classicism and Romanticism of his academic masters, replacing it with a socially orientated style that many see as the birth of modern art itself. He painted working-class people as a subject-matter in their own right—as in *The Stone Breakers* (1850), in which a nameless old man and a young man are portrayed with heroism as they break stones by the mountain side, and *A Burial at Ornans* (1849), a massive painting standing 3 metres high and 6 metres wide, where nameless people were painted with the solemnity and on the scale of history painting. Courbet brought the banal and the bleak into the realm of high art, presenting in a noble light the working class and the everyday in paintings exhibited for the middle and upper classes.

He applied the same stark realism to erotic subject-matter. *The Origin of the World* continues the daring vantage point adopted in *The White Stockings* (1861), a woman pulling on her stockings in a position that allows us full view of her naked sex, and the contemporary *The Sleepers* (1866), an image of two naked lesbians, one fair, one dark. While the lady with the white stockings sits by the waterside, thus suggesting a narrative of bathing, and while the lesbian couple wallow in a life of 'idleness and luxury' (*paresse et luxure*, the subtitle of the painting[2]), as indicated by the symbolic details (the pearls and goblet), there is no obvious frame, no context, for this close study of the site where all life begins. *The Origin of the World* was commissioned by Khalil Bey, the Ottoman Ambassador to Paris and a major art collector, who also owned Ingres's *Turkish Bath* (1862). Thereafter its owners included Sylvie Bataille Lacan, the former wife of Georges Bataille and wife of psychoanalyst Jacques Lacan; she kept it concealed in a wooden hiding device constructed and painted by the Surrealist painter André Masson, which slid off—adding to the voyeuristic thrill—to reveal the delights within.[3] Though aware of Ingres, Courbet does not lead fantasy abroad as he does; rather, Courbet stages it smack in the middle of any bedroom.[4]

The erotic legacy of *The Origin of the World*, both in terms of erotic iconography and manipulation of artistic medium to enhance it, continues in contemporary art today, as proved by the recent video piece by the Yugoslav artists Zoran Naskovski (b. 1960) and Vesna Pavlovic (b. 1970). Their collaborative *L'Origine du monde* (1997) translates Courbet's tactile use of paint and his daring composition into an 11-minute-long video piece showing a real, breathing woman (Pavlovic) in Courbet's pose. Were we to see Courbet's original as a voyeuristic image of a passive female, splayed for the lusty male, this work causes us to think differently, to consider the model, not the artist, and to enter the frame from a female perspective. We see Pavlovic touching herself, caressing her own breasts, against the music of Mozart's Andante from his *Piano Concerto No. 21 in C Major*. As a *tableau vivant* of Courbet's original this video-film cleverly offers a very different, feminist, reading of Courbet's eroticism: it not only reclaims the female body, it suggests that rather than viewing Courbet's painting as an image designed solely for male pleasure, we should see it as an image of auto-eroticism, one that stimulates the fantasy of the male and female spectator.

Painting Modern Life

In his essay 'The Painter of Modern Life' (1863), Charles Baudelaire defined modernity as 'the ephemeral, the fugitive, the contingent, the half of art whose other half is the eternal and the immutable'.[5] For Baudelaire, a contemporary of Courbet, the modern painter is an observer, a *flâneur*—the male who strolls aimlessly around the streets of the modern city, anonymous among the city crowds. Baudelaire wrote that one of the objects of the modern painter's observation is the quintessential creature of wanton beauty: the prostitute. She is the woman of artifice, the woman who is 'in revolt against society', and 'the perfect image of the savagery that lurks in the midst of civilization'.[6] In the same year as Baudelaire's essay, the young painter Édouard Manet painted a controversial painting of the red-haired model, artist, and supposed lesbian, Victorine Meurent (1844–1927) as a prostitute—*Olympia* (1863) **[4]**.[7] The painting was exhibited at the Paris Art Salon of 1865, where it was decried as a 'yellow-bellied Odalisque'.[8] Manet's painting not

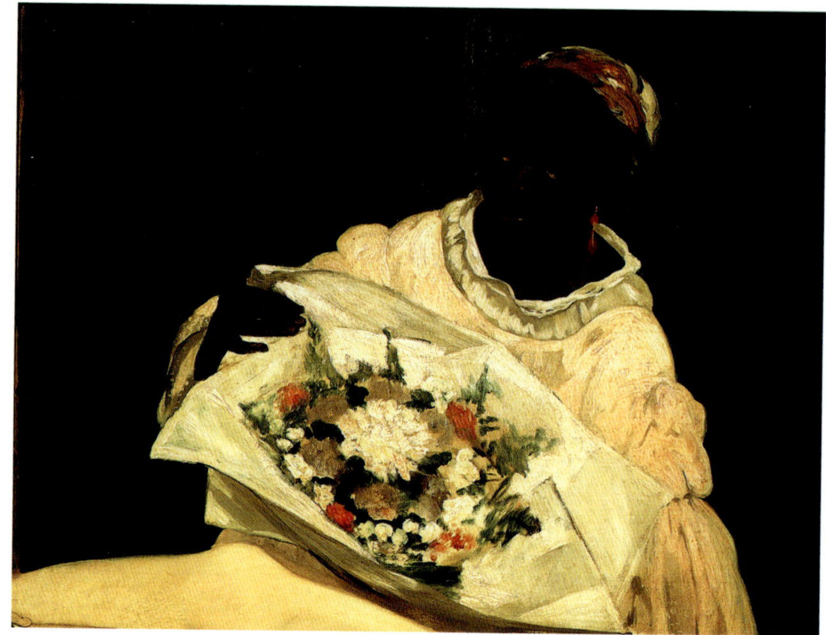

Detail of 4
The black maid in this controversial painting, modelled by a woman known to us as Laura, alludes both to classical tradition in which black 'primitive' skin offered an erotic foil to white 'virginal' skin, but also to Charles Baudelaire's *Vénus noire*.

only destroyed the erotic mirage presented in Orientalist odalisques, it mocked the Western tradition of the elongated nude, blatantly inviting comparison with Titian's *Venus of Urbino* (before 1538) **[1]**, which Manet had copied in 1856. Indeed, one critic, Amédée Cantaloube, described *Olympia* in terms that remind us of the sexual and racial hierarchy promoted by the dominant art tradition: a 'sort of female gorilla, grotesque indiarubber surrounded by black, apes on a bed, in a complete nudity, the horizontal attitude of the Venus of Titian, the right arm rests on the body in the same way, except for the hand which is flexed in a sort of shameless contraction'.[9] There were clear allusions to that tradition—the staging of the female on a luxurious bed, the inclusion of a maidservant (see picture detail above), and a pet animal (Manet chooses a black cat). Yet Manet used these accessories to his own modern end as a means of replacing a coy, timeless nude with a brazen, shabby, naked prostitute. Where the classical Salon tradition in France believed in an absolute of beauty and an ideal to which all artists must aspire, Manet believed in humanity, in flesh and blood, and, in the words of the novelist and critic Émile Zola, 'a new and personal vision of Nature'.[10] *Olympia* is presented to us as a sexual, material reality, in her working boudoir and in the process of receiving flowers from a paying guest. Her name both mocks mythological nudes and is true to the day—Olympia was a popular choice among prostitutes who had to choose a working pseudonym on entering a *maison de tolérance*.[11] Of course Olympia is a high-class prostitute of the type clearly associated with the Second Empire, a *femme galante*, who worked from her own town-house and was protected from the police by her rich, powerful Parisian patrons. That said, the reality of her life is not hidden from the viewer: her feet are dirty, her pubic hair visible, her sheets soiled. Worse still, her right hand, as noted by Cantaloube, does not indicate modesty and conceal her sex—it flaunts it in the eyes of her wealthy client.

Olympia's black maidservant, known to us only as 'Laura', completes the assault on the classical tradition wherein skin tones of the young and old, white and black, were contrasted for erotic effect. She symbolizes deviant sexuality, in a manner reminiscent of black servants painted by William Hogarth in his popular prints *A Rake's Progress* (1733–4) and *A Harlot's Progress* (1731). She might also be viewed as the ultimate sign of woman's servitude and sexuality, magnified through race. So she is Mammy and Jezebel.[12] She may even be a symbolic homage to Baudelaire's 'Black Venus' section of *Les Fleurs du mal* (1861), a publication that had been the object of an obscenity trial in 1857. Undoubtedly, like her mistress Olympia, she is a symbol of modern society and woman's role within it. However, it should be noted that slavery had not long been abolished in France at this time: while it had been abolished in 1794, it was restored in 1802 and only re-abolished in 1848. Even when this liberation was commemorated in art, race and eroticism were all-too-often conflated. Finally, Manet's inclusion of a cat in his portrait of Olympia also has a loaded symbolic significance in terms of the Western art tradition and the new modern world: it replaces the traditional dog that usually accompanied the classical nude as a symbol of loyalty, and suggests its opposite—promiscuity. Cats also appear in Baudelaire's *Les Fleurs du mal*, and of course everyone in Paris in the 1860s knew that one of the slang words for the female genitalia was *chatte*. Even Manet's painterly technique was emphatically crude as he abandoned academic training (anatomical accuracy, high finish, chiaroscuro) for rough painterly brushstrokes, daubs of pure colour, and blurred contours.

Manet's later image of another high-class prostitute, the courtesan *Nana* (1877), was a further, if less controversial, example of his approach to eroticism. This painting also has literary connotations as Nana was the subject of Zola's 1877 novel *L'Assommoir*, the tale of a 'fallen woman', the daughter of an alcoholic couple who ends up running off with an older man. Three years after Manet's painting, Zola would also publish his own novel entitled *Nana* (1880), again the tale of a pretty girl who uses her sexuality as her only weapon for social and economic escape from the dire poverty of the Paris slums. The model for *Nana* was Henriette Hauser, known as Citron, and the mistress of the Prince of

Orange. In Zola's novel, Nana is a shallow, greedy woman but also a very successful modern-day courtesan who dreams of being as successful an actress. Her attempts at performance outside of the boudoir fail miserably, however, and when she finds herself being mocked on stage she resorts to the one weapon she has—her body. Having failed in her attempt to sing and dance, she returns in the second scene stark naked. As Zola writes:

> Nana was naked, flaunting her nakedness with a cool audacity, sure of the sovereign power of her flesh. She was wearing nothing but a veil of gauze; and her round shoulders, her Amazon breasts, the rosy point of which stood up stiff and straight as spears, her broad hips which swayed to and fro voluptuously, her thighs—the thighs of a buxom blonde—her whole body, in fact, could be divined, indeed clearly discerned, in all its foam-like whiteness, beneath the filmy fabric.[13]

Given the boldly erotic style and subject-matter it is little wonder that instalments of the novel in *Voltaire* in October 1879 whetted appetites for more: when the first print run of the novel was finally published on 15 February 1880 all 55,000 copies printed sold out on the same day.[14]

Even though Manet's painting does not show a woman who is naked, her attire and coquettish pose clearly mark her as a courtesan. We are in no doubt that she stands before us as an object to be consumed: in the background of the portrait there is a painting of a bird, a Japanese crane, known as *grue* in French—a slang term for a prostitute. Once again, Manet takes a taboo subject and street vulgarism into the public domain, threatening the traditional decorum of art and the social codes of contemporary France. The thrill and threat of women like Nana is vital to their erotic charge. In Zola's novel, when Nana stands on stage in all her 'foam-like whiteness' her presence quells any laughter and leaves men's mouths parched. She stands as 'a disturbing woman with all the impulsive madness of her sex, opening the gates of the unknown world of desire.'[15] Manet's homage to the courtesan remains one of the quintessential erotic turning-points for art.

Bathing Beauties

Despite the rise of the prostitute as a popular genre in art, the female nude in an idealized, Arcadian setting did not go away with the birth of modernism: rather, she resurfaces throughout the story of modern art, often as the embodiment of a nostalgic hankering for past or ancient times. Some artists effectively reacted to the modern industrialized world by retreating into paintings of rosy nudes caught unaware as they bathed or dried themselves in sunny landscapes. (Pierre) Auguste Renoir

(1841–1919) is perhaps the best-known Impressionist painter of voluptuous female nudes in the same joyful spirit of his images of boating parties and *bals populaires*. These nudes are modern in that they have no allegorical or mythological frameworks, but they still retain a classicism in their monumentality and titillating poses; they also hark back to the more recent decadent fun of Boucher, Fragonard, and Watteau's paintings of the *fête galante*—young lovers courting in parks. Indeed, in the 1850s Renoir earned his living as a porcelain painter, often reproducing such amorous images. However, he is better known for exposing the unspoken desire behind Rococo images of lovers picnicking. In his paintings of the voluptuous female nude he went beyond Courbet's erotic realism, both promoting a sense of modern happiness and continuing the Renaissance tradition of the heroic nude. Having visited Italy in the autumn of 1881 he was particularly impressed by Raphael, whose nudes in the Villa Farnesina in Rome he greatly admired. Renoir's heroic aspect would influence Picasso and his monumental nudes of the 1920s.

Renoir's *Nude in Sunlight* (1875–6) portrays woman as nature, as fertile, and comfortable in her earthy surroundings; light and colour are used to amplify her curvaceous, wide-hipped form. Building on numerous nude sources—from the luscious nudes of Rembrandt to the images of nude bathers by Watteau and Boucher—here Renoir clearly takes a stand against the modernizing tendencies of France and the city girls of Paris and instead offers a nostalgic escape into woman and nature. And yet details of the painting reveal that it is not just her flesh that is caressed in sunlight, her accessories also gleam—a ring, a bracelet, and gold earrings. As Tamar Garb points out in her reading of Renoir's nudes, these adornments remind us that she is a Parisian model and that her world is one of sexual exchange.[16] That said, Renoir strove to keep the female body as sign and symbol of nature and desire; in this way, his paintings are not unlike Aristide Maillol's (1861–1944) classicizing sculptures, such as his *Female Bather Standing* (1899) and *The Mediterranean* (1900–2). Renoir's nudes met with mixed reaction in their day, however. When *Nude in Sunlight* was exhibited (along with 17 of his other works) in the second exhibition of Impressionism at the Galerie Durand-Ruel in 1876, the respected *Figaro* critic Albert Wolf felt the loose brushstrokes and predominant use of green suggested putrefaction. In contrast, Zola found its luminosity comparable to the genius of the Spanish painter Diego Velázquez (1599–1660) and admitted to being intrigued by her half-smile, while the Impressionist painter Gustave Caillebotte (1848–94) purchased it.[17] Certainly Renoir's nudes became increasingly popular in the following decades, when he was seen as an example of good 'French' art. In 1900 he exhibited 11 paintings at the Exposition Universelle in Paris and was awarded a Chevalier de la Légion d'Honneur; some 35 canvases by Renoir hung in the Salon d'Automne in Paris in 1904; and in the aftermath of World War I he enjoyed further success as his images of feminine plenty were appreciated anew as fertile symbols of the reconstruction and renewal of the French nation.[18]

While Renoir's nude bathers may have been celebrated for their acceptable eroticism and their nudity staged in the safety of a *plein air* ruralism, bathing had clear sexual and social associations at the time. Public hygiene was important for the prevention of disease, and levels of personal hygiene were a key indicator of class. This reflects the public concern over moral and sexual contamination—the prostitute was not just the bearer of immoral desire, she also acted as a harsh reminder of the rise in syphilis at the time. Edgar Degas (1834–1917) also depicted bathing beauties but (like Manet) brought sexual desire back into the modern-day interior and so engaged with this social fear. Unlike Renoir, Degas does not remove his nudes from their urban lives, however; unlike Manet, his models do not return our gaze. Rather, with Degas we are given access to moments of great privacy and thus erotic potential, whether he is depicting *Dancers at Their Toilette* (*c.*1879), or a brothel scene like *The Name of the Madam* (1876–7). His unusual pictorial vantage point is usually referred to as his 'keyhole' perspective.

Degas's images of women at their toilette are particularly intimate and unconventional in pose, a combination that led at the time to the suspicion of misogyny. In his pastel drawing *The Tub* (1886) **[20]** we see a woman crouched in her small metal tub, her rather classical pose (the serpentine curve of her back) offset by the contemporaneity and bleakness of her setting: the proximity of the hairbrush, ribbon, and water jug to the right and her towel or bed sheet to the left suggest she lives in a small attic room. In *Woman Bathing in a Shallow Tub* (1885), the model's pose is less graceful as she stiffly bends to wash her left foot. These were two of the pastels of women bathing Degas exhibited at the Impressionist Exhibition in Paris in 1886, and they received harsh criticism. The critic Joris-Karl Huysmans decried Degas's replacement of the 'nude goddess' with 'real living denuded flesh'—an act Huysmans read as indicative of 'an attentive cruelty and as patient hatred'.[19] Another review of the exhibition mocked the rise of the all-too-realist nude too, aligning Degas's *intimiste* art to Zola and Manet's courtesan, *Nana*: 'No! Nana washing herself, sponging herself, grooming herself, arming herself for combat, that's the Impressionist ideal! Don't forget that the Exhibition is two steps from the corner of the boulevard.'[20]

However, artistic style and temperament were clearly being confused

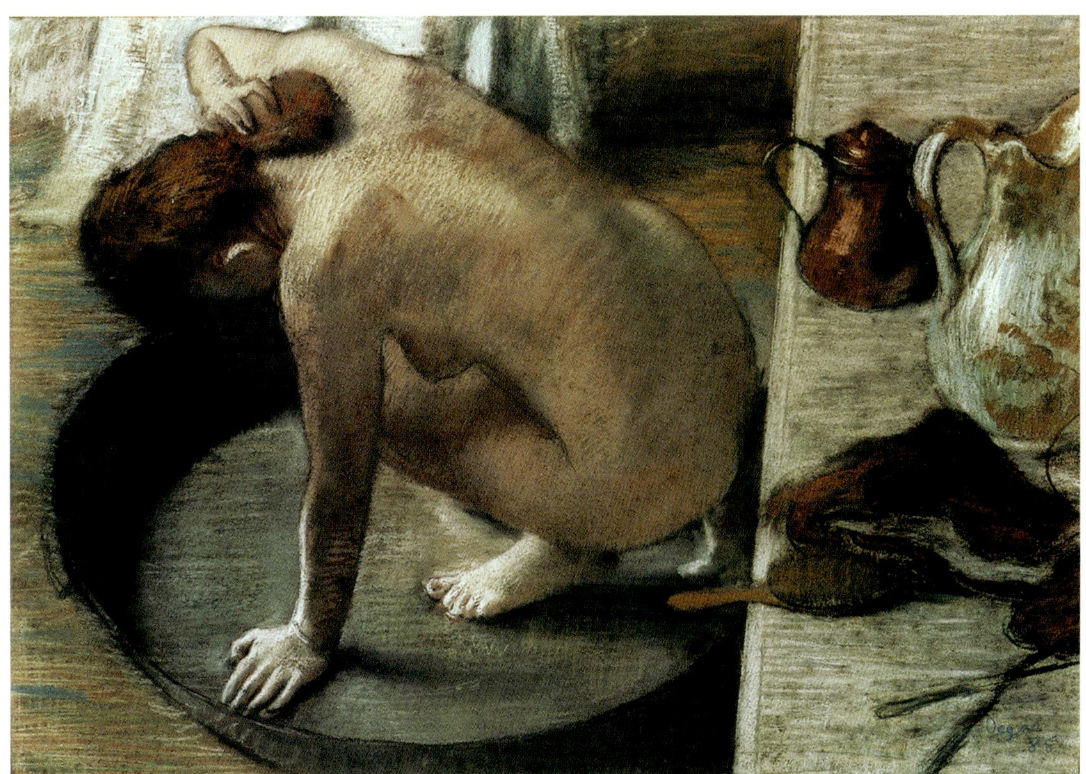

20 Edgar Degas
The Tub, 1886

In this study of a bathing female, Degas may be seen to draw on classical prototype, notably the Hellenistic *Crouching Aphrodite*, but placing her in a contemporary interior setting. Abandoning oil paint for pastels, Degas enhances the tactile eroticism of the image in his sensitive use of the medium, while demonstrating the Impressionists' concern to capture the effects and motion of light and their preference for unconventional points of view.

here. As Norma Broude argues, Degas's stripping away of idealized conventions led to the presumption of misogyny, in Degas's day and in much art-historical analysis up until the 1970s. Indeed, Degas's contemporary Georges Rivière, who met the artist in 1875, was surprised to find 'Degas enjoyed the company of women!' Interestingly he compares Degas with Renoir, famed for his sensitive nudes: 'This attitude presented a curious contrast to that of Renoir. The latter, though he painted women seductively, endowing with charm even those who did not possess it, generally experiences little pleasure from the things they valued. He was interested in women, with few exceptions, only if they were likely to become models.'[21]

While Degas was not a champion of women's rights—in her memoir 'Degas et son modèle' (1919), Alice Michel recounts the exhausting experience of modelling for the very exacting Degas (and for a mere 5 francs a session)—his art challenged the ideologies of modesty and virtue which had hitherto dominated the nude.[22] Far from representing a hatred of women, Degas's art demonstrates a sympathetic eye, albeit from a 'Peeping Tom' point of view, but it still shows woman as real, as noble, whether she is a poor art model or prostitute, a female friend

(*Portrait of Mary Cassatt*, *c.*1880–4), or a mythological heroine (*Petites filles spartiates provoquant des garçons*, *c.*1860). Given that Mary Cassatt exchanged one of her pictures for Degas's *Woman Bathing in a Shallow Tub* we might deduce, as Heather Dawkins does, that she found in it the kind of disruption of bourgeois taste that she strove for in her own art.[23] Indeed, Huysmans reading of Degas's pastels as representing woman 'debased in her tub, in the humiliating posture of intimate care' not only ignores classical precedent, notably the Hellenistic *Crouching Aphrodite* (*c.*250–240) which the artist could have seen in the Louvre collection, but it also reminds us that it is not the pose of the nude that was so upsetting but the banal signs (tub, brush, jug) of her contemporaneity.[24] Impressionist advances in technique were one thing but Degas's democratizing portrait of the fleshy body of the working woman was quite another: it did not just challenge the erotic ideal of the female nude, it boldly engaged with class and sexual reality.

Male Bathers

Bathtub subjects were paradigmatically feminine by the 1880s and were identified with heterosexual eroticism.[25] However, we find erotic images of male bathers at this period in French art too, especially in the art of Caillebotte and the post-Impressionist Paul Cézanne (1839–1906). In *Man Drying His Leg* (*c.*1884) **[21]** and *Man at His Bath* (*c.*1884), Caillebotte presents us with images of modern masculinity. In both he depicts a man vigorously drying himself after a bath, within a domestic setting, oblivious to the viewer's gaze and yet attractive in his confident and casual nakedness. In *Masculinity and Male Codes of Honor in Modern France* (1993), Robert A. Nye offers a fitting contextualization for Caillebotte's males. He documents how the military defeat of France in the Prussian war of 1870 and the civil conflicts that followed led to a crisis in masculinity in France as well as a drastic slump in the national birth rate. A virile appearance, lifestyle, and disposition were encouraged in the name of national reconstruction. As a result, acts of male vigour —for example such sports as boxing—were promoted as a means of reinvigorating French masculinity and reminding men of their reproductive duties. In *Man Drying His Leg*, the man's muscular torso with ruddy hands, face, and neck indicate he is athletic, fond of outdoor sports like rowing, perhaps. The bare functionality of the bathroom suggest he is hygienic rather than vain. His vigorous rubbing defies any idea that he might be preening himself, while the very fact that he has an indoor bathroom indicates his class. However, when compared to *Man at His Bath* we might find a further—homoerotic—dimension to

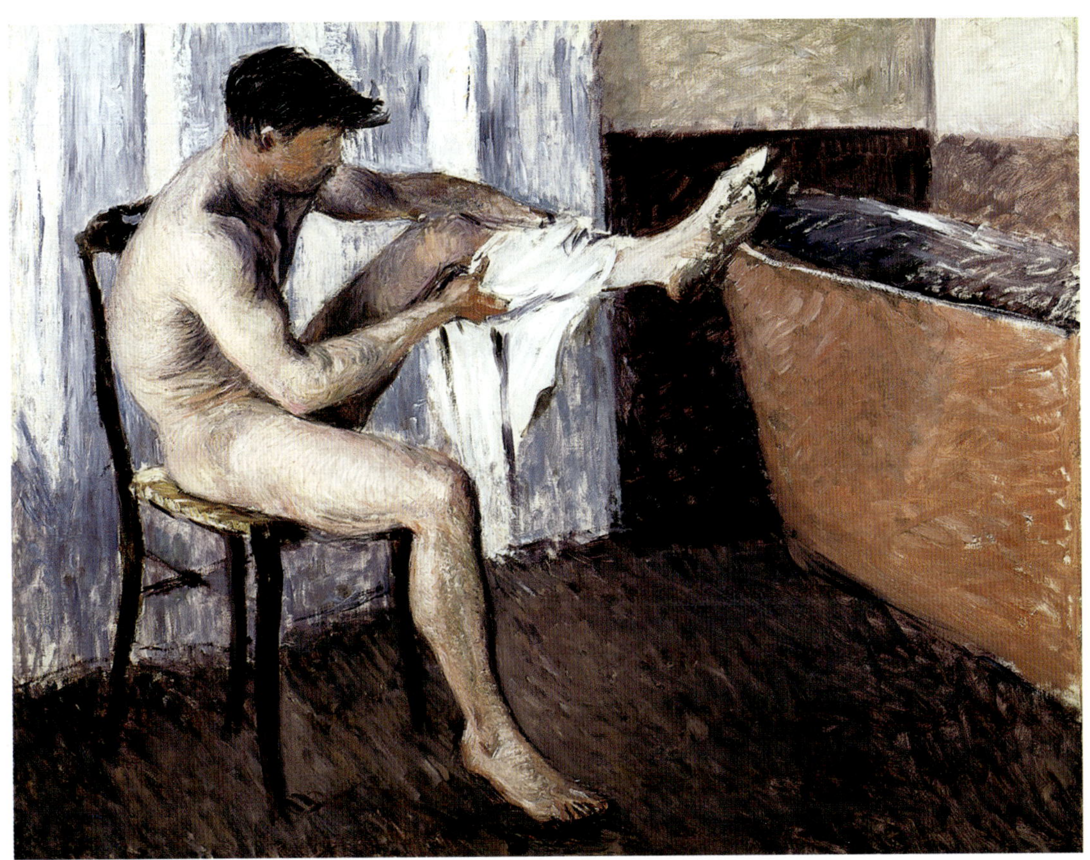

21 Gustave Caillebotte
Man Drying His Leg, c.1884
Caillebotte's male bather might be viewed as emphatically masculine in his ruddy complexion, muscular arms, and vigorous rubbing of his legs. Coupled with the spare functionality of his bathroom and his obliviousness to the viewer, the painting keeps a safe distance from the erotic tradition of female bathers. The combination of virility and intimacy in the man's image is potentially homoerotic.

these paintings of male bathers. As Tamar Garb has argued in her reading of *Man at His Bath*, the naked male's bare, clenched buttocks are painted in flesh-pink brushstrokes that take on the seductive texture typical of one of Renoir's female bathers. His stance (legs apart), his firm but rouged buttocks, the way the natural light falls on his front so as to cast a shadow on his testicles, allow us to consider the painting as an image of 'forbidden' sexual desire at a time when masculinity and heterosexual procreation were being promoted.[26] Thus alongside a promotion of sporting virility, these two paintings perhaps stage a homoerotic fantasy, a framing of the male body which is considerably more erotic in its indulgence in the banal than we first appreciate.

In 1945, the philosopher Maurice Merleau-Ponty viewed Cézanne as an artist who saw painting as 'the exact study of appearance' and so strove 'to make visible how the world touches us'.[27] This phenomenological dimension is certainly fundamental to Cézanne's peculiar erotic style and his important role for twentieth-century erotic art. Cézanne's *A Modern Olympia* (1873) pushed back the boundaries of artistic subject-matter and form in its exaggeration of all the sexual details of Manet's original. In loose brushstrokes the black maid now dramatically unveils Olympia for an eager male customer who sits on a couch before her, the angle of his cane and the excited little dog on the floor (who replaces the black cat)—as well as a huge flower arrangement and wine and fruit on a nearby table—all making explicit the erotic subtext of Manet's painting. Since the male customer is a bald gentleman not unlike Cézanne himself, the artist also pokes a finger in the eye of modern art as well as modern society. Like Manet and Zola, Cézanne was negative about the French state, the Empire of Louis Napoleon, the Parisian art establishment, and the continued power of classical aesthetics. In 1866, when the Salon rejected Cézanne's art, his comrade Zola defended it in his publication of collected reviews entitled *Mon Salon*, in which he described the two rebels from Aix-en-Provence as follows: 'In the midst of the complaisant and superficial crowd we felt lost . . . Do you realise that we were revolutionary without knowing it? . . . Do you remember our long conversations? We agreed that even the smallest new truth could not see the light of day without exciting fury and jeers . . .'[28] Cézanne rejected the techniques established by the École des Beaux-Arts: rather than working from line to chiaroscuro to colour, he based his art practice around colour from the start. Inevitably this had powerful resonance when it came to the representation of the naked body, Cézanne believing that the artist should 'master' nature.

Cézanne's series of female and male bathers depict the body as heavy-limbed, set in a space that lacks illusionism and against trees that are as fleshy as the bodies are wooden. His bathers are totemic in form: the bodies seem to signify something greater than the sum of their body parts. His *Male Bathers at Rest* (one of four images in a series, 1876–7), depicts an idyllic scene of male camaraderie, as does his *Male Bathers* (1875–7) **[22]**, which would eventually be the subject of some twenty paintings. Cézanne presents naked masculinity in frieze-like compositions that enhance the sense of virile activity. We see male bathers from every angle: frontal, outstretched on the grass in a pose traditionally reserved for the female nude, and even flexing muscles. In choosing to represent the male bather Cézanne may have been nostalgically recalling his youth in Provence when he and his friends, including Zola, spent summer days swimming and sunbathing by the river.[29] Or he may have been drawing on more recent memories, as his later letters refer to young soldiers he had watched and sketched swimming in the River Arc, south of Aix.[30] If the latter, we might also draw a comparison with Michelangelo's 1504 *Battle of Cascina* cartoon depicting Florentine soldiers surprised by the enemy while bathing. In this way we find a

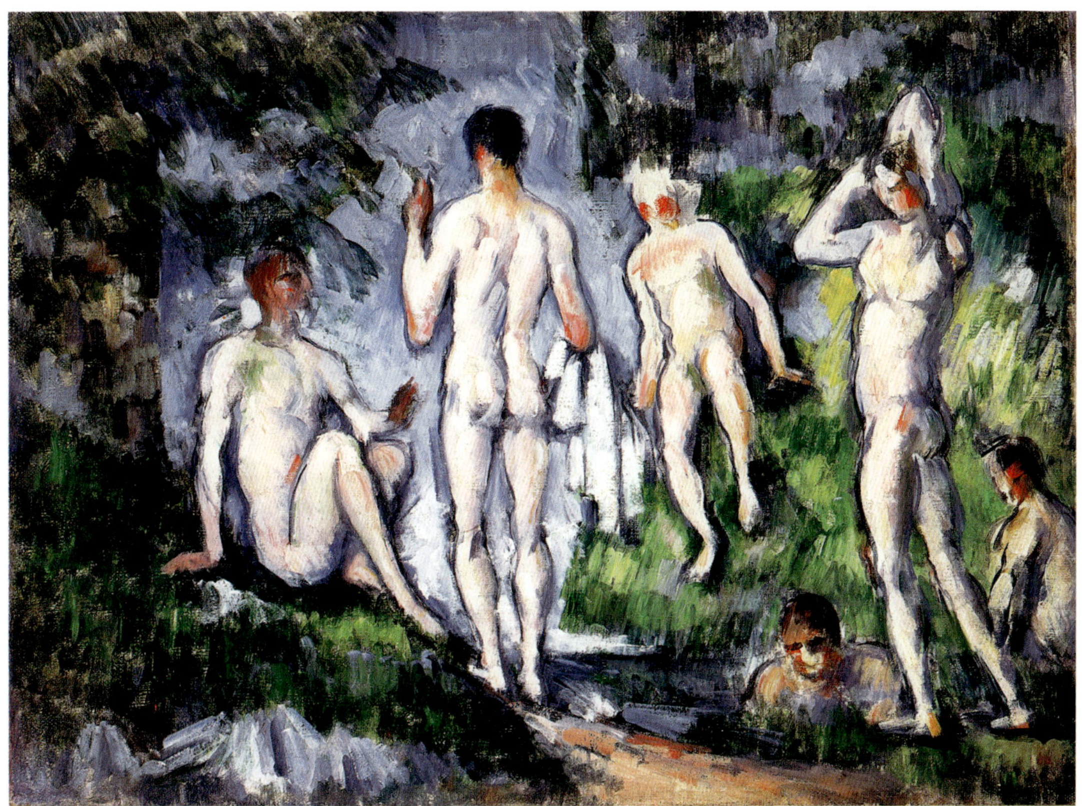

22 Paul Cézanne
Male Bathers, 1875–7
While abandoning classical anatomy and modelling and moving beyond Impressionism in his rather rough and loose handling of paint and form, Cézanne's image of male bathers retains a totemic heroism. By not finishing the detailing of the bodies or of the painted landscape around them, the artist introduces a new expressionism to art in the last decades of the nineteenth century.

nostalgia for the heroic in Cézanne's bathers, a monumentalization of the male nude which looked back to the Renaissance, though never achieving the fleshy sensuality of Renoir. And yet these are young modern men, portrayed in a style that draws our attention to the medium and process of painting as much as to the subject-matter portrayed. Theirs is a veiled eroticism, the artist demonstrating a faith in natural, *plein air* virility at a time of urbanization and social change.

Of course, Paris was not the only city in which erotic bodies reflected both anxieties over the birth rate and nostalgia for happier times. We find equally erotic images of male bathers in the paintings of northern European and American artists, many of whom were influenced by the progressive approach to the body of Manet; like him, they were searching for a new naturalism in their art practice. There was a certain romance, a return to nature quite unlike the bathing scene of French art, however. For example, the German artist Max Liebermann (1847–1935), one of the founder members of the Berlin Secession (one of the many forums for disaffected artists that were formed in German and Austrian cities in the 1890s), produced images of boys bathing in the sea in the years before and after 1900, as in his well-known painting of *Boys Bathing* of 1898. While Liebermann was influenced by French art, having visited Barbizon in 1874 and 1875, and was even awarded the Légion d'honneur in 1896, his critics were quick to defend him against French 'femininity', insisting instead that his portrayal of the nude reinforced a Germanic 'masculinity'.[31] Certainly his realist style was highly controlled and in keeping with the earthy realism of the school of Berlin, though his looser brushstrokes and attention to light aligned him with French Impressionism too. In *Boys Bathing* this fusion is apparent as he depicts young boys swimming under a blue sky in a manner that pays as much attention to sunlight skimming a wave as a little boy's tentative stepping into the sea. In Anglo-American art, examples of artists who produced paintings of male bathers include the British Impressionist artist Henry Scott Tuke (1858–1929), also renowned for his paintings of nude or half-clothed boys in the open air, as in his *Noonday Heat* (1902) **[23]**. Tuke painted direct from nature, and in the late 1880s befriended the Uranian circle of poets, known for their celebration of the beauty and heroism of the male youth.[32] In a sonnet penned by Tuke this glorification of the male—and its latent homoeroticism—is quite apparent. He writes:

> Youth standing sweet, triumphant by the sea
> All freshness of the day and all the light
> Of morn on thy white limbs, firm, bared and bright

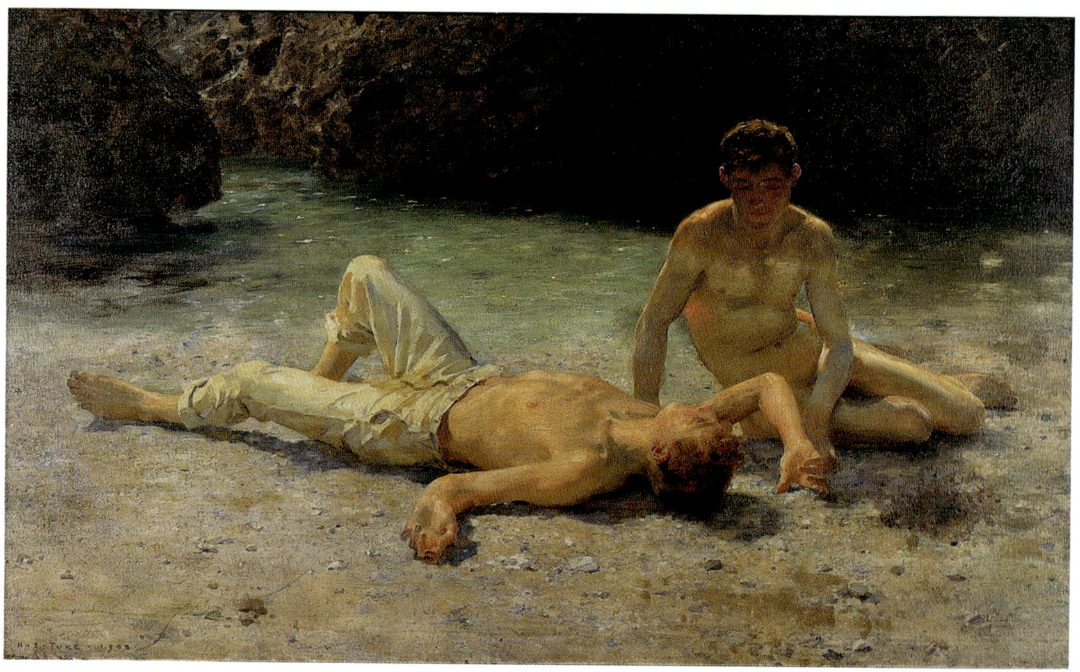

23 Henry Scott Tuke
Noonday Heat, 1902

One of the best known of the naturalistic images of male nudes by Tuke, this painting exemplifies his sensitive depiction of the body and landscape, working directly from nature. While he also portrayed male nudes in classical themes, he earned his reputation as a British Impressionist for his images of contemporary relaxed male camaraderie. Tuke produced a later, smaller, watercolour version of this painting in 1911 in which both young men are naked.

For conflict and assured of victory,
Youth, make one conquest more, and take again
Thy rightful crown, in lover's hearts to reign![33]

Noonday Heat displays such 'firm, bared and bright' young limbs as two young men loiter by the sea, enjoying a moment of friendship and intimacy. The models, Georgie Fouracre and Bert White, regularly posed for Tuke, especially White, an apprentice fitter at a Docks Foundry, whom the artist described as *kalos*, a Greek word that not only meant 'the good' but connoted a goodness inscribed on the body in the form of beauty.[34]

In the United States, Thomas Eakins (1844–1916) produced some of the most striking images of the male body of their era, their erotic potential lying in their rugged athleticism and comradeship, not unlike Caillebotte's or Tuke's paintings. Eakins studied with Jean-Léon Gérome at the École des Beaux-Arts in Paris in the mid-1860s and was also influenced by the realist style of the paintings of Velázquez and Jusepe de Ribera (1591–1652) which he saw on his travels in Spain in 1869. Eakins drew from life, especially the sports he practised and followed, notably rowing, boxing, and baseball. He taught at the Pennsylvania Academy and was made Director of the Academy in 1882. However, he was dismissed from this post over his desire for anatomical accuracy: in a class of male and female art students, he lifted the loincloth of a male life-model in order to point out a muscle. This was seen as scandalous behaviour, especially in front of young women. In the 1880s, Eakins increasingly used photography as an artistic tool; this is central to our appreciation of his paintings, especially his sporting and bathing images. For example, in *Swimming* (1885) **[24]** he used photographs of his art students swimming at Mill Creek near Bryn Mawr, Pennsylvania, for his informal composition.[35] Eakins presents what might be described as a modern adaptation of the Greek male nude: an image of camaraderie and athletic poise on the one hand, and of the banal pleasures of modern life and athletic fun on the other. We note that the models are posed in a way that is modest—that is, largely from the rear, so that the penis is removed from visible sight—and which connotes the male ideal. Thus the male lying on the rock alludes to the antique statue of *The Dying Gaul*.[36] However, there is an erotic—or more specifically a homoerotic—dimension in this idealized image of masculinity.[37] Yet we find that comparison can be drawn between Caillebotte's man who dries himself after his bath and the central male in this painting. The composition of *Swimming* draws our eye, male or female, to his buttocks, which are not simply classical but painted with colour and

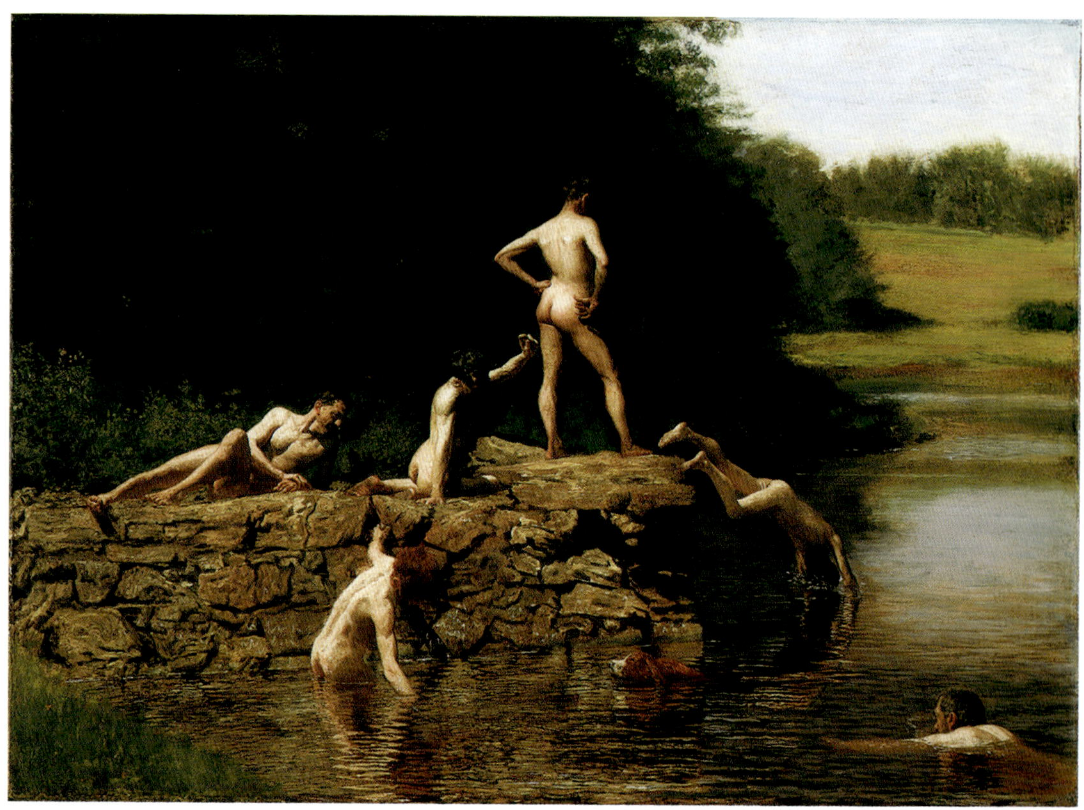

24 Thomas Eakins
Swimming, 1885

Eakins pays homage to male beauty and friendship, portraying young men at ease in their nakedness as they swim in a river. Both the central standing figure and the male lying on the rock allude to the antique, while the artist includes a self-portrait too—the man swimming in the right corner of the painting.

light in such a way as to seem palpable, while the man standing in the pond, reaching into a crack in the rock, may be read as a further sexual *double entendre*, just as a 'penetrative' gaze is suggested by the central standing figure who looks down at the young male diving into the water.[38] The men are staged to be viewed, they enjoy their freedom of movement and ease at their own nakedness without the artist turning to any narrative to justify that state of undress. The realist style adds a tangibility not felt in Cézanne's bathers. The painting goes beyond the safe confines of the classical, and the viewing field is opened up such that any man within the painting is at liberty to see and think as he wishes. Eakins, who appears as the man swimming in the bottom right of the painting, looks to his fellow men, and invites the male viewer to enjoy the male body.

While Eakins presents us with an image of homoerotic desire, his image of male bathers does not shock the viewer: he keeps a safe distance between the viewer and the human subject. He recapitulates the classical tradition of landscape painting in his division of the image into foreground, middleground, and background, and into areas of bright light and heavy shade. In this way, the threat of the painting's eroticism is somewhat camouflaged. Artists soon after would do away with such classicism and realism by presenting the *primitive* body and its unruly desires in brash new styles that would shock modern art into the twentieth century. In doing so, these new 'modernists' would come to form some of the most dynamic and influential avant-gardes, revolutionizing both artists' and audiences' conception and understanding not only of the body in art but of art itself.

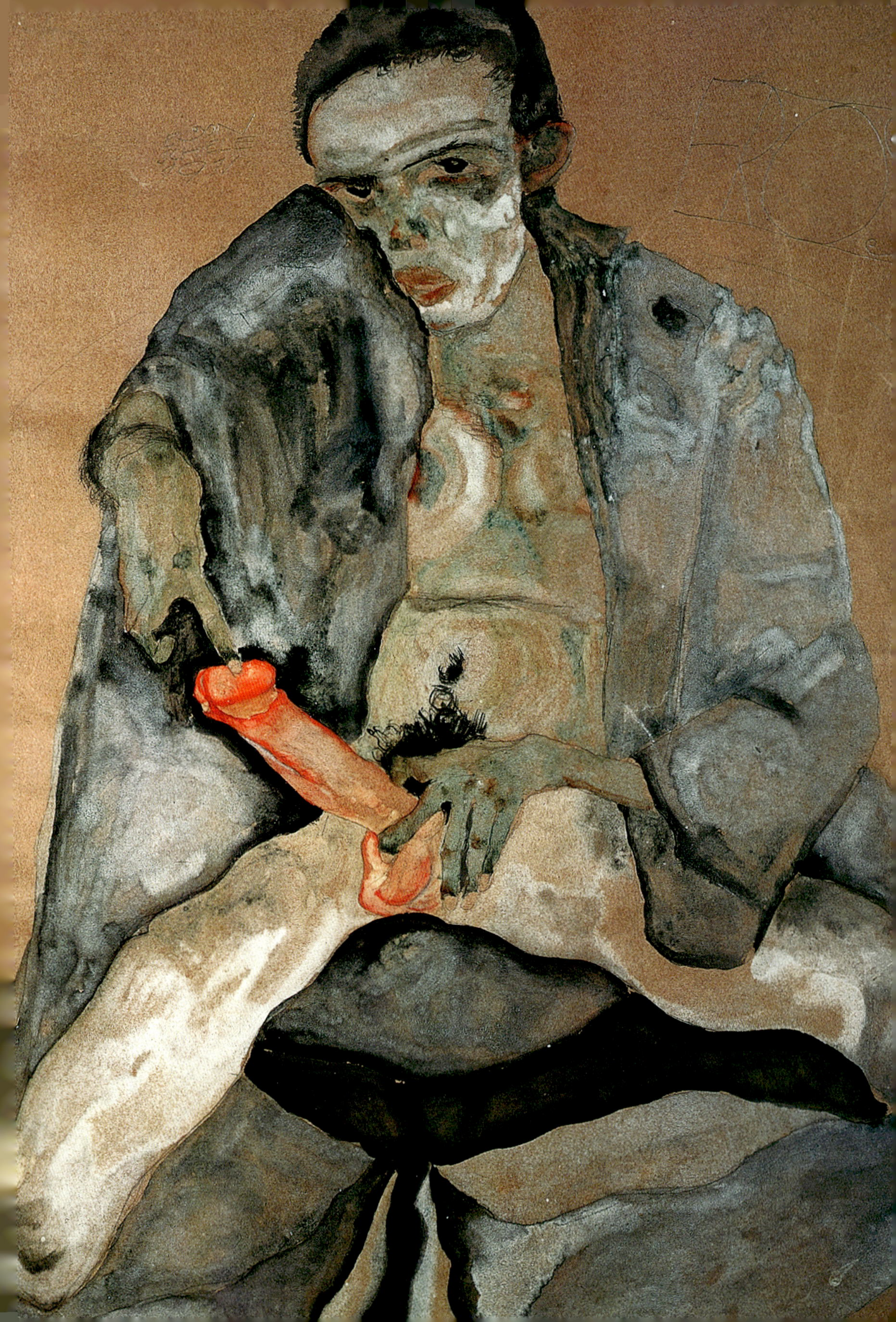

3 Primitive Drives

25 Egon Schiele
Self-Portrait Masturbating (Eros), 1911

Schiele's subjects, male and female, were often united in angst, their grimacing expressions mirrored in their contorted, exposed bodies. His self-portraits varied from images of himself as a dandy, as a cardinal, as Saint Sebastian, and, in this powerful painting, as a masturbator whose manic expression, twisted limbs, and throbbing phallus are intensified by the fluidity of the medium of watercolour. The year after Schiele produced this work he was investigated for 'pornographic' art and imprisoned on charges of paedophilia, the judge even burning one of his drawings in the courtroom.

Modernism, in Greenberg's terms, should be understood as 'the use of the characteristic methods of a discipline to criticize the discipline itself—not in order to subvert it, but to entrench it more firmly in its area of competence'.[1] He sees modernism as art calling attention to art, as art that privileges painting over sculpture, rejects Renaissance illusionism, and presents art the spectator clearly sees as painted surface in all its materiality. Of course, Greenberg's important observation that modern art draws attention to its media—the matter, the lumpy paint on the two-dimensional canvas, the attempt to represent a three-dimensional image on a two-dimensional surface—leads us to consider the effect this has on the spectator. If we look at a modern painting and find we are not seduced into a historical or mythological mirage, but instead find our eye focusing on a crude lump of paint, a child-like composition, or a portrait painted in garish green and blue, then inevitably we begin to ask questions. We wonder why an artist would knowingly reject his academic training and the academic tradition in favour of new child-like techniques that seem to threaten the progress and reputation of art itself. Why replace ideal forms with disquieting real forms that present sexual desire in all its crude, economic, and lustful terms? Why look to art in an ethnographic museum when one has a wealth of 'masterpieces' at the Louvre to draw from?

It is the affinity between the primitive and the modern which now begins to lead modernism and eroticism in a radical new direction, resulting in what art historians call 'Primitivism'. This label is used to express 'the interest of modern artists in tribal art and culture, as revealed in their thought and their work', to cite William Rubin's definition in his highly influential exhibition and catalogue, *'Primitivism' in 20th-Century Art: Affinity of the Tribal and Modern*, held at the Museum of Modern Art, New York, in 1984.[2] 'Primitive' as an art-historical term emerges in the late nineteenth century defined in the illustrated *Larousse* dictionary (1897–1904), though the generic use of the word 'primitive' was used by artists much earlier, and to cover a broad spectrum of periods and cultures, for instance for work pre-dating the Renaissance to the art of Peru. Its association with Africa and Oceania is a twentieth-century and Eurocentric phenomenon, however, and was fortified by the 'discovery' of African and Oceanic artefacts by Henri Matisse (1869–1954), Pablo Picasso (1881–1973), and others.[3]

Gauguin the 'Barbarian'

Modern artists did not only look to Africa and Oceania, of course. Post-Impressionists were influenced by non-Western art, though their fascination lay largely with the art of Japan. For example, Vincent Van Gogh (1853–90) admired the Japanese for their 'savage' style. But his *Japonisme* is largely about form rather than content, as is demonstrated in his paintings by his flat use of colour, unusual viewing angles, and decorative use of landscape. Paul Gauguin (1848–1903) used the words 'primitive' and 'savage' for Brittany as well as for the artistic styles of Persia, India, Egypt, Cambodia, and Peru. Polynesia would later be added to the list and became the heart of his vision of the primitive. Though born in Paris, Gauguin spent his childhood years (1851–5) in Lima, Peru, and proudly characterized himself as 'a barbarian' and as 'an Indian from Peru'. He also worked as a merchant mariner from 1865 to 1871, which allowed him to travel in the tropics. Gauguin exhibited with the Impressionists between 1879 and 1886, befriended Degas in 1885 and Van Gogh the following year, but he felt that Impressionism had overindulged the eye and led to scientific reasoning, neglecting the emotions and the spirit—what he termed 'the mysterious centre of thought'.[4] He sought new means of expression and new lands for inspiration. He travelled to Panama and Martinique in 1887, and in 1891 he left France for Tahiti. Tahiti had changed from a protectorate of France to a colony in 1881 and had a particular reputation as a land of sexual people and pleasure ever since its discovery in 1767. It had been described by Louis-Antoine de Bougainville (1729–1811), the first European to see several islands in the Pacific, in mythological terms laced with erotic titillation in his journal *Voyage round the World* (1771): 'These people breathe only repose and the pleasures of the senses. Venus is the goddess one feels ever-present. The softness of the climate, the beauty of the landscape, the fertility of the soil . . . everything inspires voluptuousness.'[5] Little wonder that Gauguin hoped to immerse himself in a land where people 'experience only the sweet things of life'.[6] Gauguin's appreciation of Tahiti should be interpreted as erotic in itself, then, and certainly cannot be separated from his search for his own savage self amidst a people he viewed as noble savages. His paintings depict heavy-limbed peoples who are beautiful and proud, but who are also exoticized as a people obsessed with folklore and ritual. In 1892, prior to his brief return to Paris (1893–5), he painted two of his most famous works, both representative of his vision and its latent eroticism.

Mana'o Tupapa'u (The Specter Watches Over Her) of 1892, began, by Gauguin's own account, as a 'slightly indecent' nude, and shows his lover Teha'amana lying on her front on a bed, frightened as she looks out of the frame. The apparent source of her fear, a spirit (*tupapau*), sits dressed in black behind her. The title, the artist explained, could be 'either she thinks of the spirit, or the spirit thinks of her', though she may be interpreted as Gauguin's commentary on Manet's *Olympia*, since he had made sketches of it.[7] Yet the painting seems more loving than Manet's caustic commentary on the *bonne bourgeoisie*. While her boyish figure and alluring buttocks may invite a penetrative gaze, the model does not indicate her sexual availability and she does not draw our eye to her sex as Olympia does; her white sheet only offsets the richly decorated bedding, the fuchsia tones of the room itself, and the deadly blackness of the spirit's hooded cloak. The painting is also based on a real scenario, drawn from Gauguin's illustrated part-journal, part-fictional account of Tahiti, *Noa Noa* of 1893–7 (*noa* meaning secular, worldly, the opposite of the spirit world, though the title is usually translated as 'very fragrant'). In this text, which was intended to expose the Parisian public to his experiences there, the artist recounts how he returned home from Papeete very late one night and startles Teha'amana, who did not seem to recognize him and looked at him with wide-open, frightened eyes as if he were a demon or spectre. The account of this experience was possibly aided by his reading of J. A. Moerenhout's 1837 two-volume study of the religious beliefs, customs, literature, and social and political life of Tahiti, *Voyages aux Îles du Grand Océan*, which he was lent by a French colonial, Auguste Goupil, in March 1892.[8] Equally, Gauguin's sense that he came across as a demonic threat to the exposed woman is undoubtedly a sexually charged sensation built on racial and sexual stereotypes and was part of an increase in studies of non-Western peoples and colonies.[9] However, his conflation of Western colonialism and Polynesian spirituality might lead us to see the artist as also exploring his own position within those two worlds in trying to marry both his experience of European painting and his knowledge of local philosophy. His 'failure' to do so may be suggested by the eyes of both woman and spirit, who seem to alienate the artist/spectator further—if we are to imagine Gauguin stumbling upon this scene then he must stand at the opposite side of

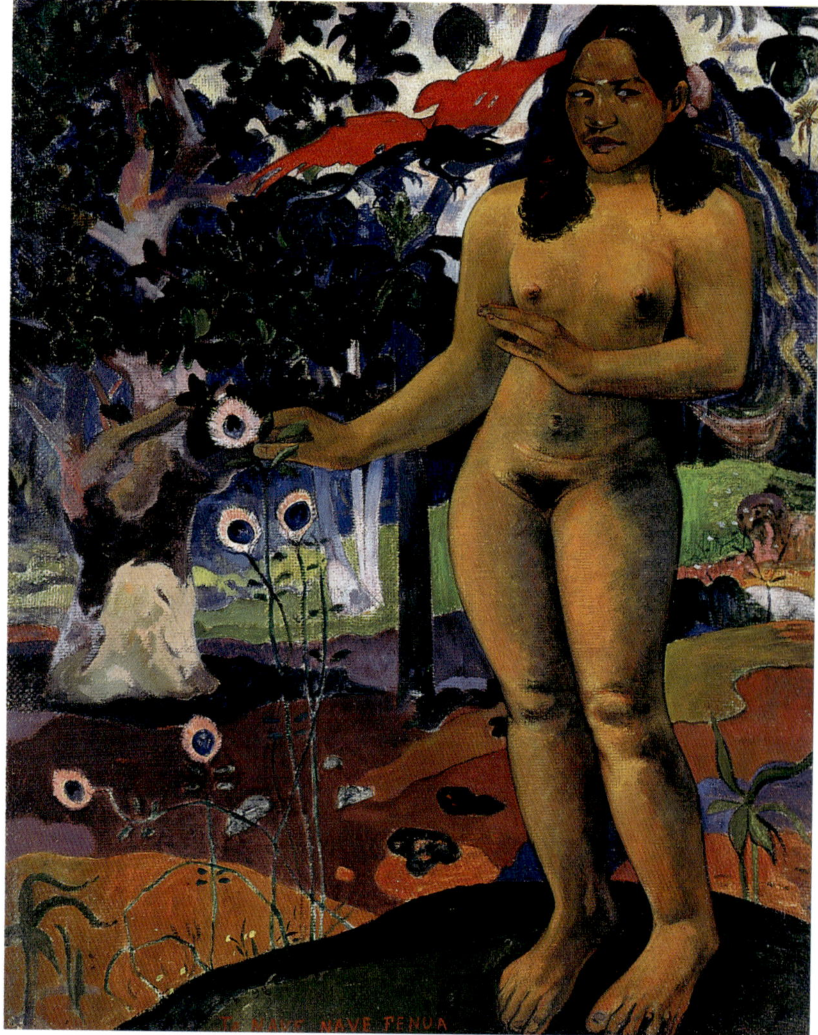

26 Paul Gauguin
Te Nave Nave Fenua (The Delightful Land), 1892

Abandoning his life as a family man and banker in Paris, Gauguin's search for a new artistic style and subject-matter led him first to Arles and to Pont Aven, from 1888–91, and then to the South Pacific. From 1892, Teha'amana, the Tahitian woman whom the artist married that year, appears in his paintings. Here she is presented in an idyllic, exotically coloured landscape as an 'Edenic Eve', as Achille Delaroche described her in 1894.

the canvas as a sexual and colonial Other in their eyes. While Gauguin mythologized Teha'amana's fear in his account in *Noa Noa*, her greater erotic force than his (in this perspective) is further corroborated by a local legend that asserts that Teha'amana enjoyed an autonomous sexual life and did not limit herself to old Gauguin.[10]

Te Nave Nave Fenua (The Delightful Land) **[26]** dates from the same year; again it represents Gauguin's South Seas style and how it is as much indebted to European symbolism as Polynesian art. A young woman, probably his lover Teha'amana again, symbolizes a fusion of the artist's European heritage and the model's Tahitian one: she is oblivious of her nudity but does not conform to any of the traditional Western notions of classical beauty, with her dark skin, dense pubic hair, strong features, and thick-set body. Yet her beauty is undeniable in its difference, and specific local details reinforce this alternative appreciation. As Stephen Eisenman points out, her posture refers to a sculpted figure of a Buddha in Gauguin's collection, her body seems to sway as she reaches to pick a flower with one hand and positions her other hand just beneath her right breast. The theme of temptation seems to lie behind her distracted gaze as a plumed serpent with vivid red wings flies towards her face. Eisenman concludes that she is both 'a child of nature and the product of culture'.[11] This view is reinforced by Gauguin's flat style and the lack of three-dimensional depth, which makes his canvases seem like Egyptian friezes.

Given Gauguin's bold use of colour, his flattening of the figure, and his creative and spiritual fascination with primitive cultures, it is not surprising that a retrospective of Gauguin in Paris at the Salon d'Automne in 1906 would dramatically influence a new generation of artists. One group to whom his work particularly appealed was the Fauvists, who included the French painters André Derain (1880–1954), Henri Matisse, and Maurice Vlaminck (1876–1958). They introduced glaring, unnatural colours to art—colours that resonated with symbolism and that complemented the often Bacchanalian subject-matter of their paintings. The 'wild' violent nature of their art lies behind their collective label, 'wild beasts' (*fauves*), coined by critic Louis Vauxcelles when their art created a furore at the Salon d'Automne in Paris in 1905. Matisse is perhaps the best known of the Fauves and undoubtedly an artist whose approach to the primitive would in turn influence further generations of artists. Like Vlaminck and Derain, he collected non-Western art; in 1906 he travelled to northern Africa, where he was impressed by Negro sculpture and its truth to materials. On his return a series of nudes he painted show this influence. He distorts the body so that it displays some of the physical characteristics typifying the art of so-called primitive cultures—an elongated neck, flattened buttocks, protruding breasts, and a disproportionately large head. Matisse was influenced by Gauguin's nudes, though his *Two Negresses* (1908), exhibited at the Salon d'Automne two years after Gauguin's retrospective there, suggests he remained distant from his subject-matter, unlike Gauguin. Though it was exhibited under the title *Groupe de deux jeunes filles*, it was clearly a study of African form, immediately recognizable to the French eye with the large breasts and protruding 'shelf' buttocks typical of the wooden figurines, especially those produced by the Baul and Fang peoples, then popular among collectors.[12] The colour of the bronze added to their blackness, while the composition—two young girls' confident embrace—was very similar to a photograph published in *L'Humanité féminine* in January 1907, as James Herbert has shown, of two naked 'Tuareg Girls' embracing in the same poses so that we see one from the front, the other from the rear.[13] Like Matisse's 'negresses', these two women were also labelled under the generic term 'Tuareg' that is used to identify diverse groups of people from northern Africa. Finally, Matisse's *Two Negresses* evoke the iconic black woman who was a subject of sexual fascination for ethnologists and public alike at the height of European colonial expansion—the Hottentot Venus. This woman, Saartje ('Little Sarah') Baartman (1789–1815), from the Khoisan tribe in South Africa, was brought from Cape Town to London in 1810 to be displayed as a sexual freak due to her steatopygia (fat on and around the buttocks). Presented as a black 'Venus', she was then shipped to France where she was subjected to further humiliation and abuse at the hands of scientists and medical researchers. Her story is a bitter reminder of the implications of the equation of blackness with the erotic—and not just in days of old: the Musée de l'Homme in Paris exhibited Baartman's sexual organs and brain up until 1986. Matisse's ethnic nudes may be seen to cater to the colonial imagination, fetishizing the non-white and keeping the black Other safely within the parameters of the Western art canon.

Les Demoiselles d'Avignon

According to Freud's understanding, the fetish is an object of blind reverence. In practical terms it is an object or body part (for example a woman's stiletto, shoe, or foot) that substitutes for the desired woman's (the mother's) penis that the little boy believes she has lost. It also serves as 'a token of triumph over the threat of castration', given that the male has a penis.[14] With this in mind, the primitive or ethnic nude is *doubly* fetishized. It stands for the simultaneous fascination with and disavowal of woman and her phallic lack, for both the difference of sex and of race. Thus it has even greater potential to disturb the status quo. Where Ingres, Gérôme, Matisse, and others played with that fetishizing thrill, it is the Spanish painter Pablo Picasso who makes visible the unspoken fear of the exotic 'Other' in his famous brothel scene, *Les Demoiselles d'Avignon* (1907) **[27]**. Perhaps the most notorious combination of primitivism and eroticism in art in the first years of the twentieth century, it drew on the advances of Gauguin and Matisse—Gertrude Stein, in her autobiography *The Autobiography of Alice B. Toklas* (1933), claimed that Matisse introduced Picasso to primitive art—and his keen interest in Iberian sculpture. It also sprang from his exposure to African artefacts.

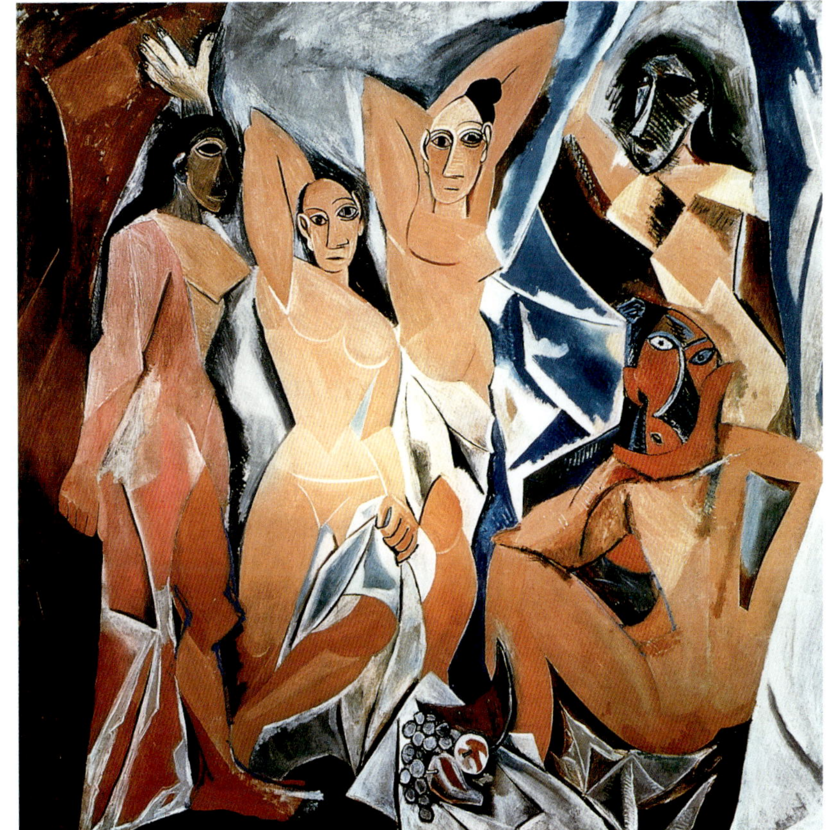

27 Pablo Picasso
Les Demoiselles d'Avignon, 1907

With an Iberian nude to the far left, classical, European nudes in the centre, and startling, Africanized nudes to the right, Picasso's brothel scene disturbs the tradition of the female nude in its bold conflation of eroticism and primitivism. According to the writer Gertrude Stein, who befriended the artist in 1906 and published a study on him in 1934, the painting was 'too awful' for many. The Russian merchant Tschoukine, who had purchased several paintings by Picasso, tearfully proclaimed the 'loss' for French art it announced when he visited her after seeing it.

Though he claimed he did not visit the Ethnographic Museum in Paris in 1907—a collection he found revelatory when he did—he had seen tribal artefacts at the studios of Matisse and Derain. But this is a painting that goes further than the Orientalists or the Fauves, as it explicitly conflates primitive form with primitive sexuality and stages a confrontation between the classical and the modern nude. It is a veritable 'erotic theatre' in which fantasy is unveiled by the women themselves and prudery banished; it is Picasso's response, perhaps, to the Louvre's decision in January 1907 to hang two provocative images of female flesh, Manet's *Olympia* and Ingres's *The Grand Odalisque*, side by side.[15]

In his variation on an age-old theme, Picasso assaults the classicizing tradition. We see an Iberian nude (to the far left) and European nudes (centre and centre left), and their confrontation in turn with the two further nudes to the right who are related to African and Oceanic models of femininity and have startling Africanized heads.[16] There is also a stylistic three-way clash in the painting between the classicism of the pose of the central nudes (the taller of whom recalls the central nude of Cézanne's female *Four Bathers*, 1888–90), the Gauguin-like woman with her solid, frieze-like form to the far left, and the Cubism of the two nudes to the right, whose unfinished bodies demonstrate the fracturing of form and the attempt to capture multiple perspectives that would become central to that style.[17] We find a conflation of eroticism, primitivism, and politics in Picasso's use of Africanized masks for the nudes on the right too. For Picasso does not merely exploit the exotic potential of African masks, he also alludes to the 'civilizing mission' of France in her colonies. As Patricia Leighten has persuasively argued, here Picasso draws on French popular notions of Africa as the site of the grotesque and attacks French policies in the Congo at a time when many were voicing their anticolonialism in political debate in Paris.[18] Thus Picasso celebrates African culture and criticizes French colonial brutality through an exposition of erotic tastes and fears, in keeping with the political position of his anarchist circle in Paris at the time. The political significance is augmented by his composition, his framing of the scene. The viewer of the canvas effectively stands like a bidder in a sexual sale, surveying a range of erotic possibilities. Indeed, for some feminist scholars this painting epitomizes the inherent misogyny of modernism itself in its framing of five women in a confined space and its depiction of them as savage, sexualized creatures who are the bearers of disease and avarice.[19] Picasso had in fact included two males in the composition in early studies for the painting: a medical student holding a skull (suggesting sexual disease) and a sailor (suggesting sexual promiscuity). In deciding to get rid of them, Picasso effectively removed any clear moral connotations from the work and instead allowed the power of female sexuality to dominate. Woman seems to be staged as both the bearer of sexual delight and of vice, of life (Eros) and death (Thanatos).[20] Through recourse to the erotic, Picasso offers us a 'philosophy in the boudoir', just as the Marquis de Sade did before him and many of the Surrealists would after him.[21] He simultaneously subverts Western attitudes to *l'Afrique noir* and to prostitution and the belief that both needed to be controlled.

Of course Picasso also revelled in all things erotic and enjoyed the female body regardless of any overt political agendas. He always delighted in passion itself and in the tension between sacred and profane love. To visualize Picasso's attitude to the erotic, we need only look at his oil painting *The Kiss* (1931) **[28]**, in which two lovers devour each other; Picasso offers a violent interpretation of a much-loved theme in modern art also taken up by Rodin's *The Kiss* (1886), Munch's painting *The Kiss* (1897), and Brancusi's *The Kiss* of both 1908 and 1912. Or we might look at his many erotic engravings, like *Scène bacchique au*

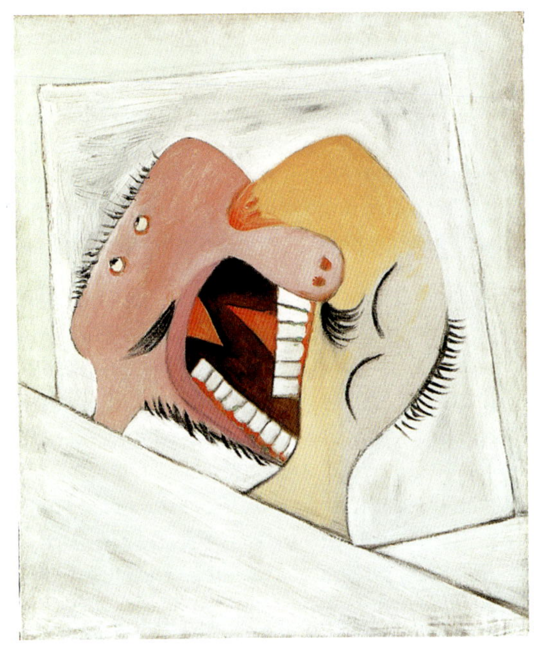

28 Pablo Picasso
The Kiss, 1931

Picasso produced several images of lovers devouring each other in a passionate kiss throughout his long career. Their near-cannibalistic desire, darting, phallic tongues, and round, sculptural forms remind us of Picasso's obsessive return to eroticism, specifically to the theme of violent attraction.

Minotaure (1933), in which he depicts man as God and Beast—both sides of Picasso's persona perhaps—revelling in lust. Picasso's erotic art always explores the fine line between controlled eroticism, culture, and civilization, and unleashed eroticism, nature, and taboo.

German Expressionism

Western society's Manichaean distinction between the civilized and the primitive was also contested by the German Expressionists, many of whom were influenced by Gauguin in their travels and style. Max Pechstein (1881–1955) travelled to the Palau Islands in the Pacific, Emil Nolde (1867–1956) joined the Imperial Colonial Office expedition to New Guinea in 1913–14, while the painted nudes of Paula Modersohn-Becker (1876–1907) and the woodcuts of Ernst Ludwig Kirchner (1880–1938) share Gauguin's naive solidity. They were members of or influenced by the Brücke (Bridge), a group formed in 1905 in Dresden and led by Kirchner and others. Nolde and Pechstein joined in 1906, and Otto Müller (1874–1930) in 1910, helping to create a new German art up until the group's dissolution in 1913.[22]

Kirchner and his Brücke friends were influenced by a Romantic, turn-of-the-century notion of the peasant and nature cults. Reacting to modernization with its industrialization and urbanization, they took spiritual refuge in a very particular utopian notion of the 'primitive'. In his unfinished book *Artistic Expression of Primitive Peoples* (begun in 1912), Nolde wrote:

> Primitive people begin making things with their fingers, with material in their hands. Their work expresses the pleasure of making. What we enjoy, probably, is the intense and often grotesque expression of energy, of life . . . There is enough art around that is over-bred, pale and decadent. This may be why young artists have taken their cue from the aborigines.[23]

The primeval force of non-Western art (and of early primitive European art too) attracted the young artist. While travelling with a state-sponsored group to New Guinea he was critical of colonial expansion, writing in a letter of 1914 to his friend Hans Fehr: 'The undermining and zealous cultural annihilation of weaker peoples is painful to experience first hand.'[24]

When it came to the erotic, however, the German Expressionists' vision was Dionysian, influenced by the writings of German philosopher Friedrich Nietzsche, notably by his understanding of the relationship between the Apollonian and Dionysian. As Nietzsche outlined in his *The Birth of Tragedy* (1871), the Apollonian was a conceptualization of life and the world based on order, rationality, knowledge; the Dionysian was based on violence and ecstasy. Nietzsche also related the 'genesis' of art to the sexual experience, proclaiming in *The Will to Power* (1901): 'The demand for art and beauty is an indirect demand for the ecstasies of sexuality communicated to the brain.'[25] As a result, these artists' understanding of the erotic was not confined to their subject-matter, it was lived. They invited circus performers, dancers, and models (both Caucasian and Negro) into their studios and communal homes, they went bathing naked at the lakes, and insisted that their studio/home/bedroom were one and the same space for inspiration and action. Theirs was a youthful, spirited attempt to liberate themselves from the moral oppression of the Wilhemine era (1871–1914).

Kirchner's nudes are full of this willful energy. The female forms he depicts in his 1909–11 art, as in his painting of *Bathers in a Room* (1908, repainted 1920) **[29]**, are totemic in their angular shapes and squat proportions (a style influenced by woodcut technique). His bathers are a good example of this hard style, while their brash non-naturalistic coloured flesh in the busily decorated room gives a sense of energy. And, as Donald Gordon reminds us, Kirchner emphasizes their life force by exaggerating their eyes, mouths, breasts, and genitalia.[26] Decorative motifs in the painting allow us to locate it in history too: the brightly coloured curtains, rug, and primitive figures on the door jambs are influenced by the African and Oceanic artefacts in the Dresden Ethno-

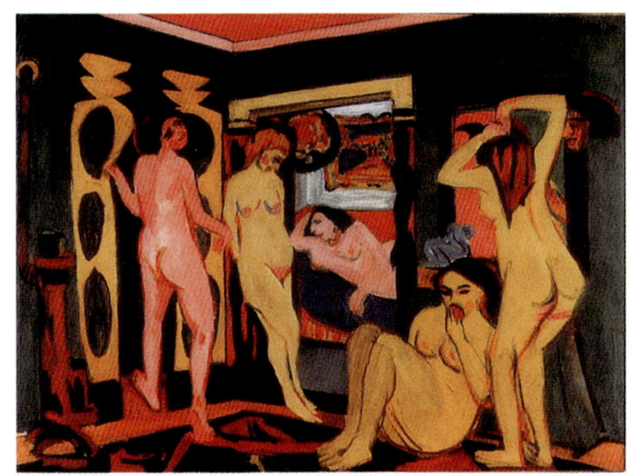

29 Ernst Ludwig Kirchner
Bathers in a Room, 1908

The German Expressionists believed modern man needed to be liberated from his inhibitions and to rebel against bourgeois society and academic culture. Kirchner, the son of an engineer, evokes this spirit in his palette, his debt to African and Oceanic art, and his celebration of unrestrained sexuality in this image of women in a room, painted three years after he formed *Die Brücke* group. Kirchner's bathers do not merely symbolize an equation of woman with nature but a celebration of Mother Nature herself as a guide for new spiritual communion.

graphical Museum (notably the erotically decorated beams of the Palau Islanders Kirchner first saw in the museum in 1903). They also relate to the vogue for ethnography itself, as evidenced by the shows of 'exotic' cultures which began in Dresden in 1909.[27] But the staging of this room also suggests sexual decadence, leading us to fantasize about the lover the nude on the left is going to, the lover the nude in the rear bedroom has just been satiated by, and why—in stark contrast to Picasso's *Demoiselles*—these women's poses seem to imply that we are part of their erotic world. Kirchner brings pagan revelry to his exotic room but in a manner that plays to an idea of 'authenticity'. He drew inspiration from the Negro model at this time in his career, notably from two black circus performers, Sam and Milli, who were the subject of his 1911 painting *Negro Couple* in which the emphasis on Sam's penis and Milli's buttocks expose the artist's perpetuation of racial stereotypes. The blatant voyeurism of his photographs and lithographs of them engaging in sex further problematizes his declared ambition for 'immediacy and authenticity' in his art.[28]

With his move to Berlin in 1911, Kirchner became increasingly fascinated with city life and its protagonists, especially with the prostitute. In 1913–15 he produced numerous images on this theme, including *Five Women in the Street* (1913), most of which were initially sketched, appropriately enough, from the street. Influenced by George Simmel's *Philosophy of Money* (1900) and his essay 'The Metropolis and Modern Life' (1903), in which Simmel argued that modern society's idolization of money led to a loss of community and increased alienation, Kirchner presents the female prostitute as the symbol of this alienation and/or identifies with her. Yet the women's elongated, angular crow-like forms, their sultry lips and blood-red nails, suggest he may also have been erotically intrigued by these new, emphatically urban, erotic creatures.[29] Kirchner's prostitutes may also be seen as a commentary on the debate that raged in the press in the winter of 1913–14 over the moral implications of sexualized advertising and the issue of the artistic nude. This debate would be taken up by the German Parliament and the Prussian House of Deputies, leading to a resolution in which the government was required to take all possible legal measures to suppress metropolitan vice and to protect youth from its influence.[30] His prostitute may be a response to this call for censorship, a vital part of his vision of art as a bridge between the present-day and the art and society of the future. However, as we shall see in the next chapter, it is not until the Weimar period (1919–33) and the art of the Dadaists that we find the prostitute, city, and advertising come into their scandalously erotic own and wielded as weapons against the establishment. But first we must turn to Vienna, where new theory and art would pave the way for this erotic turn.

Sigmund Freud, Vienna, and Egon Schiele

The writings of Sigmund Freud (1856–1939) gave a new psychological insight to the subject of sexual desire and repression and offered a new discourse to modern artists. In 1900, Freud published *The Interpretation of Dreams*, recognizing that there was as yet no 'sexual theory' and that the analysis of dreams allowed for a more profound understanding of man's sexual neuroses and desires. Here, and in subsequent publications such as *Totem and Taboo* (1913) and *Civilization and Its Discontents* (1930), Freud offered a radical redefinition of the erotic in terms of social anthropology. He interpreted desire in terms of the life drive (Eros) and the death drive (Thanatos), recognizing the drive to procreate, on the one hand, and the dark side of desire and man's tendency to sexual violence, on the other. Civilization is a battle between both drives, the instinct of life and the instinct of destruction.

For Freud our animalistic sexual drives are linked to our primitive ancestry and must be controlled for the good of civilization. This correlates with his division of the human psyche into three parts, the id, ego, and superego, which he explains in 'The Ego and the Id' (1923). The id is the source of Eros and represents our instinctive emotions, which are illogical and driven by the pleasure principle; the ego is the conscious part of the mind and keeps the id in check; and the superego is our moral conscience, nurtured by parental standards and societal values. Our desires, kept in check by the ego and superego, resurface in our subconscious, thus providing fascinating insight into our repressed, baser desires. Our dreams reveal these desires, as they represent 'wish-fulfilment'. However, they often present us with a whole series of bizarre symbols that make no immediate sense. Many can be unravelled by analysing a person's childhood, when their sexual urges are first experienced and then repressed. Herein lies the significance of Freud's other major contribution to our comprehension of erotic urges: the Oedipus complex, where the boy desires to possess the mother and exclude the father. Desires and fears reveal themselves in symbols in our dreams: stairs or a tunnel come to symbolize fear of impotence; tall, erect objects or machines (umbrella, chimney stack, cannon) or particular creatures (fish or snake) symbolize the phallus; and vessels or cavities (cup, spoon, cave, open door) or particularly tactile materials (fur, velvet) represent the female sexual organ. Freud's pioneering work led to the development of an extraordinary array of sexual symbols that have now become part of our vocabulary when we look at images; these would be increasingly exploited by artists in the twentieth century. And yet given that he viewed the artist as a near-neurotic who channels his desires in his art, it is perhaps surprising that artists were intrigued, if not flattered, by his libidinous image of them. As he famously wrote in 1917:

> An artist is once more in rudiments an introvert, not far removed from neurosis. He is oppressed by excessively powerful instinctual needs. He desires to win honour, power, wealth, fame, and the love of women; but he lacks the means for achieving these satisfactions. Consequently, like any other unsatisfied man, he turns away from reality and transfers all his interest, and his libido too, to the wishful constructions of his life of phantasy, whence the path might lead to neurosis.[31]

Even though he was writing at a time when women artists abounded, Freud always privileged the male in his writings and theories. He claimed in his lecture on the topic, 'Femininity', that woman was a 'riddle', and that she could resolve her disgust at her inferior sexual make-up (she bears no penis/phallus), and compensate for this lack, by replacing her wish for a penis by one for a baby, or a 'baby-penis'. In finding a husband and producing a child she finds fulfilment. As Freud admits, 'that is all I have to say to you about femininity'.[32] Little wonder artists, especially women artists, would take inspiration from Freud but want to go deeper into the relationship between sexual function, social conditioning, and gender politics.

In the decades before and after the turn of the century, Freud's Vienna saw the birth of a particularly cosmopolitan form of art. Cultural and political changes were reflected in a desire for 'truth' in artistic expression, and a near-obsessive fascination with the psychology of the artist, such as in the music of Gustav Mahler, the architecture of Otto

Wagner, and the paintings of Gustav Klimt (1862–1918). Their revolutionary ideas were later developed by such figures as Arnold Schönberg and his atonal music, Adolf Loos and his purist architecture, and Oskar Kokoschka (1886–1980) and Egon Schiele's (1890–1918) brutally erotic canvases. Like Paris in the latter half of the nineteenth century, Vienna had been transformed into a modern city with bold new architectural design and public spaces supported by unprecedented economic growth. Gustav Klimt made his reputation decorating new buildings in a modern *Art Nouveau* style. Through his presidency of the Vienna Secession (assumed in 1897), which promoted the 'total work of art' (*Gesamtkunstwerk*) and subsequently the Vienna Workshop (*Wiener Werkstätte*), he insisted that art should promote a public spirit and defy old-Empire academicism. However, his style was too erotically suggestive for his Viennese audience: his commissioned series of allegorical ceiling panels, depicting the faculties of philosophy, medicine, and jurisprudence for the University of Vienna, created a public uproar when exhibited in 1900 and 1901 at the Vienna Secession, and were ultimately refused by the university. Klimt had depicted the three faculties as naked figures embodying desire and angst in a dark, macabre style displaying none of the glory typical of public monuments. Klimt's allegorical eroticism and sexualized ornament tacitly critiqued the bourgeois audience who commissioned him. He rejected neoclassicism and exposed society's neuroses at a time when the old order was crumbling (the Austro-Hungarian Empire did not survive World War I).[33]

The Secessionists' critique (with Klimt as a spokesperson, until he left the group in 1905) of the old order was taken over by a new generation of painters. In 1913 the Vienna Secession displayed the paintings of Egon Schiele for the first time. Schiele was similar to Klimt in his exploration of sexual desire, but where Klimt's representation of the human body was symbolist and sensual, Schiele's was raw and naked.[34] One might say that the introspection of Klimt's generation evolved into a more anxious, self-analytical exploration in the next; Schiele rejected art for art's sake in favour of introspective, non-allegorical images of the body. Their fascination with the body and with self-expression also involved a critique of the moral and cultural demands of society where the individual was constantly being repressed in favour of the common good. For Schiele, the sexual only served as a reminder of mortality, and the erotic as a reminder of psychological anxiety. Indeed, his art displayed an almost neurotic concern with the subject of tortured sexuality and the direct conflict of Eros and Thanatos. Although trained in the Academy of Fine Art in Vienna (and thus in the classical tradition of the nude), by 1910 Schiele's nudes—especially his series of nude self-portraits—reveal a disturbing eroticism where sexual repression is unleashed in images of thwarted desire or contorted naked limbs. The fierce Romantic and sensual mannerism of Klimt's representations of literary lovers (Judith, Dana, and Salome) is not repudiated by Schiele but is simply advanced in his angst-ridden exploration of naked models, including the 17-year-old Wally Neuzil whom he met in 1911 and who became a favourite model and his lover.

Schiele portrays the sexual body in angular lines and sketchy strokes of violent colour and explicit detail, as in *Self-Portrait Masturbating (Eros)* (1911) **[25]** or *Male Nude* (1912), in which he portrays the male genitalia in daubs of blood-like ochre paint. His nudes were typically elongated, emaciated, and distraught in expression and are often portrayed from a height (with the artist looking down on them) as if the models were unaware of the artist's presence. His figures seem removed from desire and even desperate in their attempts to achieve some physical pleasure in bleak interior settings. In 1912, Schiele was sentenced to 24 days in prison in Neulengbach and St Pölten on charges that his work was pornographic. A local judge not only accused Schiele of pornography (police had seized several 'pornographic' drawings) and paedophilia (due to his affair with Wally Neuzil), he actually burnt one of Schiele's drawings in the courtroom. In prison, Schiele produced letters and drawings that depicted his inner turmoil and the sheer existential trauma of having to live in a cell, unshaven and cold, with his own excrement. It was an experience that he described, almost masochistically, as somehow purifying.[35] His self-analysis while incarcerated affected his art: it displayed an anguished self-exploration where the soul seemed imprisoned in the flesh. This was true both of his self-portraits (for example as St Sebastian in his poster for an Arnot Gallery exhibition in 1914, or his *Self Portrait Standing* of 1910) and his depiction of women, including his younger sister Gerti. The contorted poses of his nudes reveal not only an inner angst but also a performativity that echoed the psychoanalytic explorations of the day: their awkward gestures and poses and the unflattering angles from which they were drawn literally reflects the psychological drama of the sitter. By 1915, Schiele was conscripted and married, and his life seemed to be emerging out of a 'blue' period; however, he caught Spanish flu in 1918 and died at the age of 28. His career was short lived, but Schiele had revealed the nude to be a privileged site of 'a deep-seated falseness'.[36] Through recourse to the erotic the brutal reality of life had been exposed. This exposure would reach even more shocking heights in the aftermath of World War I.

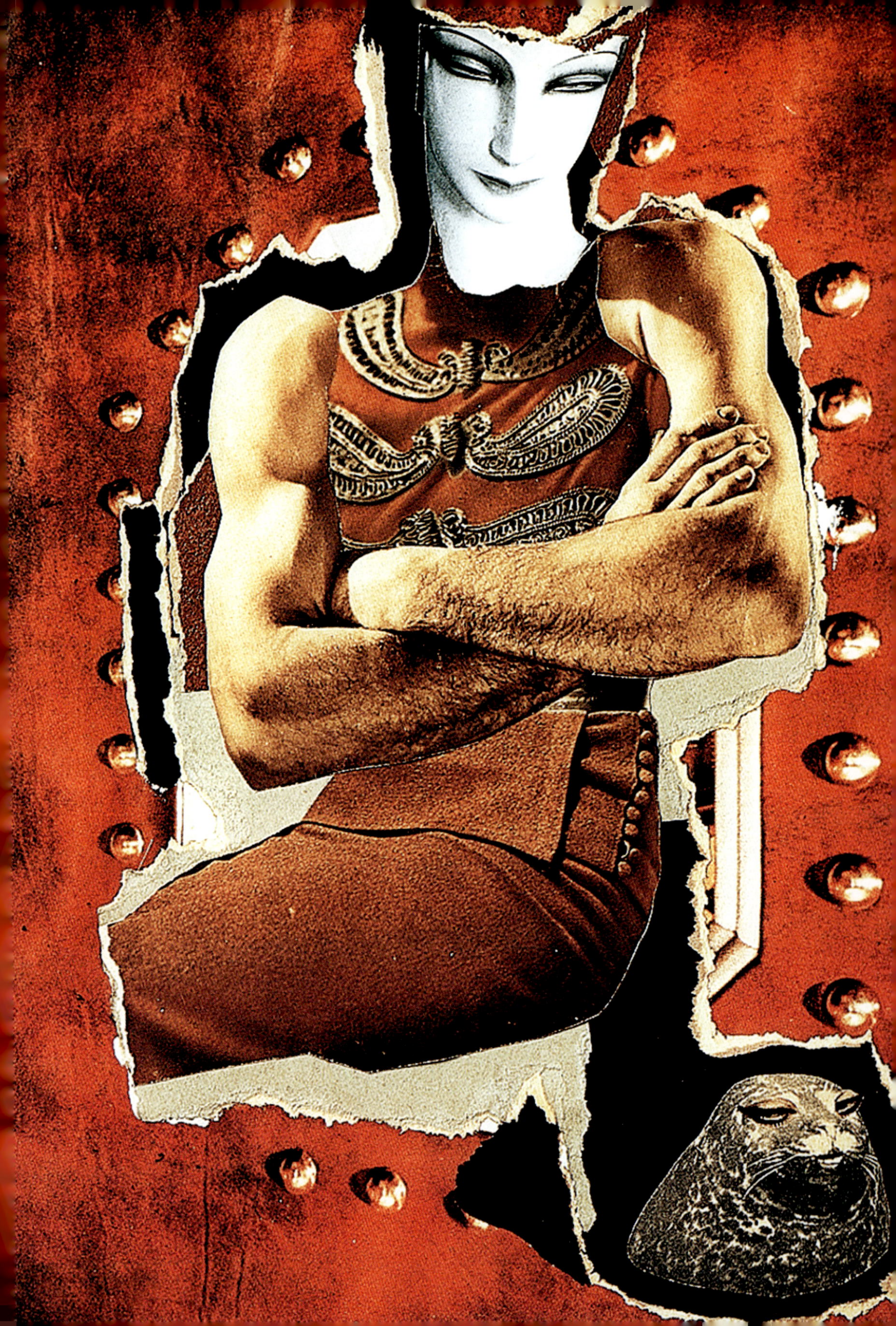

4 The Erotic Body between the Wars

30 Hannah Höch
Tamer, *c.*1930
Höch's collage—juxtaposing athletic male arms with a fashion model's torso, a mannequin head and a sea-lion—challenges the viewer in its defiance of the gender stereotypes and body perfection of Weimar Germany as well as in the unfinished quality of its ripped paper surfaces.

Artists in the inter-war period increasingly turned to eroticism as an explicit means of shocking their bourgeois audiences, rejecting the institutions of Family, Church, and State, and transgressing the taboos that society enforced on the individual. The influence of Sigmund Freud and the advances in psychology and the science of sexuality in general became increasingly evident not only in artists' symbolism and subject-matter but also in their manipulation of the findings of psychoanalysis to probe the psychosexual aspects of society. This was particularly true of the avant-garde, namely insurgent artists, writers, thinkers, and musicians whose ideas and techniques were ahead of their time and who strove to liberate art from academic tradition as well as from moral conventions. As the origin of the term 'avant-garde' indicates—a military term for the 'advance guard', those soldiers at the front of the battle line who bravely lead the way—these artists were determined not only to lead art in new directions but to lead society in new directions too. The first non-military use of the term is credited to Henri de Saint-Simon, who wrote of the emancipatory potential of the artist in his 1825 book *Literary, Philosophical, Industrial Opinion*, claiming 'the power of the Arts is the swiftest and most expeditious'.[1] Gabriel-Désiré Laverdant also wrote of avant-garde art in 1845, three years before the revolutions of 1848, as 'the most advanced social tendencies: it is the forerunner and the revealer', and aligned it to the exposure of 'all the brutalities, all the filth, which are at the base of our society'.[2] This dialectical relationship with society—indeed an *antagonistic* dialectical relationship with society—was key to the concept of avant-gardism and to the rise of '*the* avant-garde': those new artistic groups who identified themselves through manifestos, who advanced art in provocative directions but who also self-consciously battled to make art part of society rather than autonomous to it. Impressionism, Expressionism, Cubism were among those avant-garde movements fighting for new modern means of formal expression and embracing new modern subject-matter. Following World War I, however, Dadaism and Surrealism map out the historical avant-garde par excellence in their assault on traditional art and politics.[3] Unsurprisingly, eroticism offered the perfect means of exposing the subconscious desires and fears of society during the inter-war years, as fascism and its peculiar 'virile' discourse became a burgeoning threat. Moreover, an increased Freudian appreciation of eroticism and of society's need to repress erotic desire for its 'civilizing' mission and control of the masses meant that the Dadists and Surrealists developed sophisticated erotic shock tactics to challenge issues of nationalism, morality, and taste, to attack Right-wing thought and practice, and to try to shake liberal audiences into self-recognition and ultimately incite resistance.

Dada Beginnings

Dada art forced a whole new way of thinking on the public through both an assault on academic technique and the introduction of 'base' eroticism. In *Paroxysm of Pain* (1915), by the French Dadaist Francis Picabia (1879–1953), machine parts seem to pirouette and the artist exotically toys with the relationship between sexual pleasure and pain. Made of ink and metallic paint on cardboard, it is an image whose erotic significance is not immediately appreciated. It is only through the psychoanalytic lens of Freud that an erotic anthropomorphism begins, one that allows inanimate machine objects to take on human, sexual (notably phallic and feminine) forms. Picabia claimed in the *New York Tribune* at the time that he wanted to capture the American machine spirit as a new means of expression. But of course he perverts the machine age, as he transforms inanimate efficiency into animate eroticism. His choice of title, *Paroxysm of Pain*, begins the process by encouraging us to look afresh at the seemingly banal and invest it with sexual energy and to draw on our own cultural baggage, notably images of ecstatic pain from Western visual culture. He alludes to Catholic iconography, to traumatic images of martyrdom and spiritual ecstasy. He continues this theme in *Girl Born without a Mother* (1916–18), where again sexual dynamism becomes central to our reading of banal industrial objects as the artist literally paints over a found image of a railway wheel, piston, and cylinder. Looking at the painting again through Freudian eyes, a round machine part morphs into a female form, and the shaft and piston 'she' is attached to becomes distinctly phallic. The smooth motion of the latter thrusting in and out leads the former to rotate, rhythmically and with pleasure, we presume. Of course the title adds a further nuance: it mocks the more famous son born without a

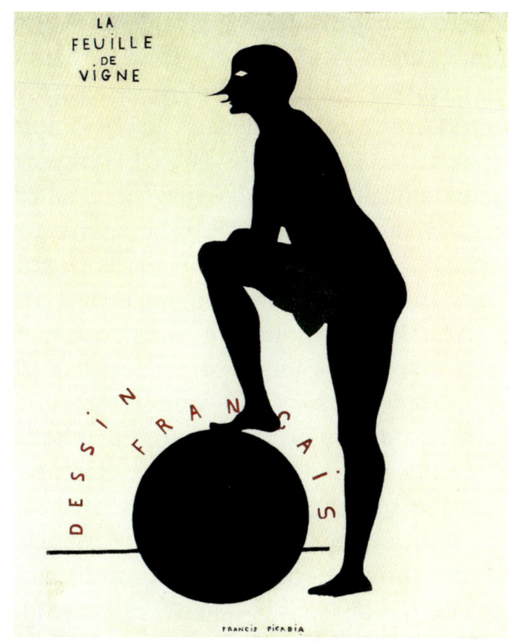

31 Francis Picabia
The Fig-Leaf, 1922

Picabia's painting alludes to the profile of Ingres's nude Oedipus in *Oedipus and the Sphinx* (1808) and challenges the oppressive reign of the Academy in its inclusion of a vine leaf and tongue-in-cheek inscription, DESSIN FRANÇAIS (French drawing). It is painted over Picabia's earlier painting *Les Yeux chauds* whose mechanomorphic form had caused a scandal when presented by him to the Salon d'Automne in 1921.

father—Jesus Christ. In a similarly blasphemous fashion, *The Holy Virgin* (1920), an explosion of black ink on paper with the title scrawled at the top, evokes the erotic through abstract formlessness—an unruly blot that suggests either a blood stain (symbol of virginity) or ejaculate (symbol of satisfaction). The artist wrote of the Virgin as the 'patron of prostitutes'; his profanation of the sacred expresses the same sentiment.[4] Picabia's *The Fig-Leaf* (1922) **[31]** again uses the machine to attack the Church as he draws attention to the call for the fig leaf (*la feuille de vigne*) to conceal the male sex and preserve decency when gazing at the nude. Once more he fuses traditional and mechanized erotic symbolism as he paints a male nude over an image of a turbine brake in shiny industrial paint (Ripolin). He adds insult to injury in alluding to the French 'master' Ingres and his *Oedipus and the Sphinx* (1808) in his choice of composition, as well as in attacking the vogue for conservative, academic art in Paris at the time through the ironic inscription DESSIN FRANÇAIS—French drawing. Sexual and artistic repression are one for Picabia, and he calls for their liberation.

Picabia's recourse to the erotic always had a subversive edge, however subtle. His many kitsch images from the 1920s of Spanish ladies—*Espagnoles*, with mantillas and sexy eyelashes—parody erotic tourism; he also satirizes Western man's fascination with the exotic Latin lady, as well as the Western obsession, fuelled by religion, with the Virgin and whore. Many of his paintings parody Catholic icons of the Virgin Mary.

The nudes he painted during World War II again initially strike one as example of erotic kitsch, but they also harbour their own assault on the all-too-passive viewer. In these paintings, produced while living on the Côte d'Azur, Picabia translates 'low' soft-pornographic photographs, many from 1936–7 editions of such soft-pornography magazines as *Mon Paris* and *Paris Sex Appeal*, into 'high' oil paintings with a knowing smile. In *Woman with Idol* (1940–2), based on an illustration from *Mon Paris* (no. 15, January 1937), Picabia adds a macabre twist to the original: he keeps the desirable woman (wearing French knickers, stockings, stilettos) but has her mounting a large African idol with gargantuan feet instead of the doctor in the original scenario. In the process he again refers to academic art's use—and abuse—of the primitive for erotic effect while at the same time exploiting its fetishistic power himself, to startle the viewer and take the erotic into a base direction not usually toyed with in soft pornography.[5]

Picabia was a Dadaist, a member of the Dada art movement that had a powerful international impact up until around 1923, spreading to many international cities—New York, Berlin, Barcelona, Hannover, Paris, Rome, Cologne, Budapest, and Tokyo. Launched in 1916 in Zurich, where many political refugees had fled with the outbreak of World War I, Dada began with the founding of the Cabaret Voltaire by German poets Hugo Ball and Emmy Hennings. Dada was 'anti-art': it entered into a dialectical dialogue with high art, it exposed the aesthetic prejudices that traditional art had tried to conceal. Dada never defined itself in the traditional sense of an art 'movement' but is best understood in the sense of a riotous action or spirit that manifested itself in the arts. The name was accordingly nonsensical and taken at random from a dictionary; but it also had many irrational, infantile, and primitive connotations that reveal the subversion behind its 'madness'. Dada was reminiscent of the first sound or word a child makes (*dada* for father or *da*, the German for there). It is also child-speak for hobby horse in French; in parts of Italy both mothers and dice are called dada; and, apparently, the tail of a holy cow is called a dada by the Kru Africans. Dada, as its chosen name suggests, was founded on the nihilistic principles of irrationality, incongruity, and irreverence towards accepted aesthetic criteria, Dadaists believing that respectable, bourgeois society was responsible for the horrors of war and in need of self-awareness—this could only be achieved through shocking anti-art tactics, typically using improvisation and transgressing taboo. The negation of art promoted by the Dadaists led to radical new means of producing art, typically involving violence and/or chance and the unconscious. For example, the artist Hans Arp (1887–1966) created a new 'automatic' art form when he tore up pieces of paper and discovered abstract compositions in the fallen torn shreds.

In New York, there were two main Dada centres: one around the poet and collector Walter Conrad Arensberg, the second around the photographer Alfred Stieglitz (1864–1946), who founded the quarterly publication *Camera Work* in 1903 and ran the 291 Gallery on 291 Fifth Avenue. Stieglitz helped promote photography as art and was instrumental in launching the careers of many young artists, including that of his future wife, the artist Georgia O'Keeffe (1887–1986), to whom he gave a show at 291 in 1916, eight years before they were married. Their relationship is documented in over five hundred photographs Stieglitz took of O'Keeffe. His sophisticated but unconventional framing of the female form in his photographs influenced younger photographers, notably the young American Man Ray (1890–1976). Stieglitz's early nude photographs of O'Keeffe—such as *Georgia O'Keeffe, Squeezing Breasts* (1918) and *Georgia O'Keeffe—Hand and Breasts* (1919), emphasize O'Keeffe's long hands and young breasts—squeezing them in the former, delicately touching them in the latter. Stieglitz presents her eroticism 'free of anecdote and cheap sentiment', as Man Ray said of the older photographer's art.[6] Stieglitz's choice of composition in both works may also have had social significance, however, in keeping with his Dada milieu in New York. It may have been a conscious teasing out of the classical association between the hand and modesty. For Stieglitz was an admirer of the writings of the English psychologist Henry Havelock Ellis, whose *Studies in the Psychology of Sex* (1897–1928) adopted a scientific approach to sex that pre-dated the investigations into sexual practices by the American professor of entomology and zoology Dr Alfred C. Kinsey in assessing sexual relations from a multicultural perspective. While Ellis's analysis of homosexuality in *Sexual Inversion* was highly controversial and censored in Britain, Stieglitz was particularly interested by Ellis's *The Evolution of Modesty*.[7] In this volume, Ellis argued that the gesture of a hand covering the breast, as seen in many ancient sculptures such as the *Medici Venus*, where the goddess touches her left breast with her right hand, was initially meant to symbolize the extraction of milk and thus to symbolize fecundity—the reading of the gesture as one of modesty, as a coy attempt to cover the breast, was a later projection.[8] Given Stieglitz's fascination with sexual psychology and erotic symbolism, it is not surprising that he welcomed two French Dadaists when they arrived in New York in 1915—the aforementioned Picabia and Marcel Duchamp (1887–1968).

Duchamp saw eroticism as 'a way to bring out in the daylight things that are constantly hidden—and aren't necessarily erotic—because of the Catholic religion, because of social rules . . . [Eroticism] kept me from being obligated to return to already existing theories, aesthetic or otherwise.'[9] Though never officially a member of a Dada group, he was pure Dada in his iconoclasm. His oil painting *Nude Descending a Staircase* (1912) had caused a storm at the 1913 New York Armory Show. It depicted a nude figure (of uncertain sex) in motion in an art style that combined Cubist fragmentation and Futurist movement. However, where Cubism tended to align the nude form with nature (not the machine, speed, etc.), and where the Futurists loathed anything feminine—their leader F. T. Marinetti famously stating in the Futurist Manifesto of 1909 that their glorification of war included 'scorn for women' and an assault on morality and feminism—this painting aligned the modern material world with nudity, and possibly with the female nude rather than the virile, machine-like, male nude.[10] Kinetic motion was captured in traditional oil paint, thus undermining the stability and 'truth' of the viewing experience itself. In capturing motion in the two-dimensional image Duchamp was undoubtedly influenced by the photography of Eadweard Muybridge (1830–1904) and his innovative motion photographs of figures, notably his images of a naked woman descending stairs, from 1887.

The Bride Stripped Bare by Her Bachelors, Even (The Large Glass) of 1915–23 **[33]** continued Duchamp's fascination with sexual codes and gender stereotypes in society, expressed through a Dada sense of erotic humour. It is a work Duchamp began before his ready-made *Fountain* (1917) **[32]**—an inverted urinal signed R. Mutt which challenged the aesthetic and economic value society places on an art object and artist's signature—and which he continued to work on until 1923. Constructed of oil paint, varnish, lead foil, lead wire, and two glass panels, *The Large Glass* pushed the boundaries of the art object and aesthetic appreciation to extremes in parodying the theme of desire and marriage in a 'mechanico erotic language'—essentially, an erotic language which parodied the language of science and the doctrines of the Catholic Church.[11] It is an exploration of sexual desire but from a highly clinical, scientific perspective. The work has two principal elements: the virginal bride of the title, who occupies the upper half of the 3-metre-high transparent glass panel, and nine moulds/bachelors who strive in vain to reach her, in the panel below. The Bride is like a cross between a preying mantis and a motor suspended in space. In Duchamp's own notes on the work, she is a 'sex cylinder' in a state of disrobing, and the bachelors are like machine bits 'grinding their chocolate' (masturbating) and 'dazzling' (shooting) their sperm up at her in the hope that she will be penetrated and will experience a 'cinematic blossoming'

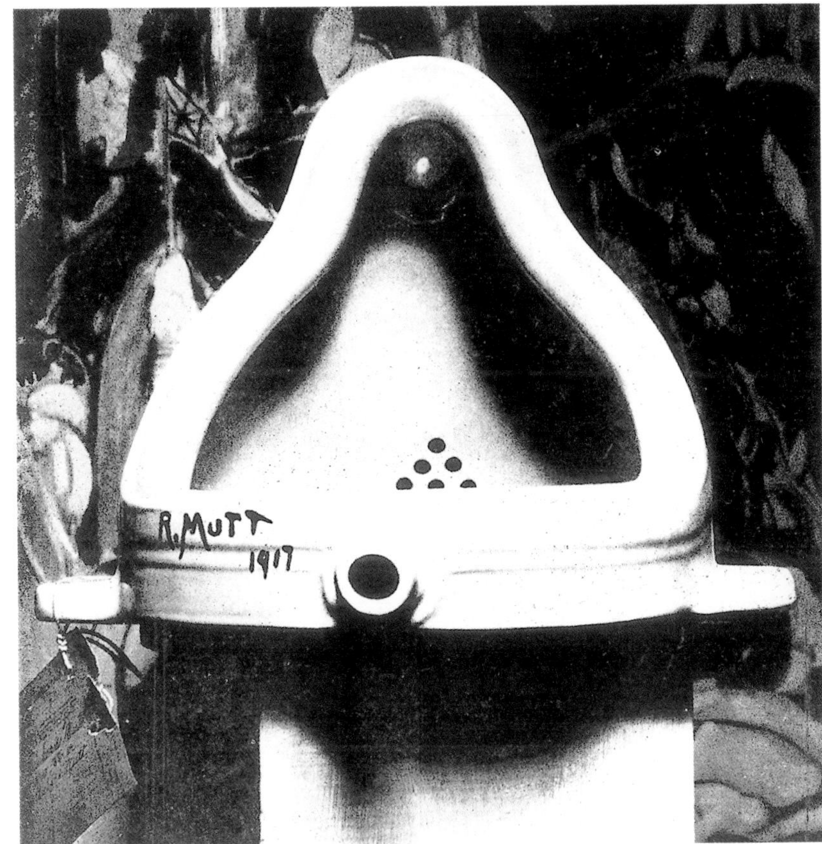

32 Marcel Duchamp
Fountain, 1917

Submitted under the pseudonym 'R. Mutt' to the first annual exhibition of the Society of Independent Artists in New York in 1917, Duchamp's ready-made *Fountain* revolutionized modern art by doing away with traditional notions of authorship, technique, skill, and aesthetic beauty. The work was rejected by the exhibition's organizing committee. This famous photograph of it by Stieglitz accompanied an anonymous article in *The Blind Man* defending the work: 'Whether Mr. Mutt with his own hands made the fountain or not has no importance. He CHOSE it. He took an ordinary article of life, placed it so that its useful significance disappeared under the new title and point of view—created a new thought for that object.'

(orgasm).[12] One might describe the work as a homage to unrequited love or, as the leader of the Surrealist movement, André Breton, saw it, as 'a mechanistic and cynical interpretation of the phenomena of love'.[13] It is this suspicion of cynicism in Duchamp's erotic play that continues to perplex and even outrage critics today. In 2000, Jean Clair, the Director of the Musée Picasso in Paris, wrote that Duchamp and his ready-made objects of this time, with all their lewd, base connotations, had led to the 'end of art'.[14] Certainly, Duchamp introduced a new erotic aesthetic to modern art which rejected bourgeois taste and niceties, but he also introduced what might be seen as a 'proto-feminist' element to the avant-garde's use of the erotic in his clever exposure of patriarchal and Catholic gender stereotypes. This subversive attitude extended into his personal life, or at least his public persona too. For, in a series of photographs taken by Man Ray in 1921 and 1924, Duchamp cross-dressed as a female alter-ego called Rrose Sélavy. His choice of female name indicated both his chess-playing sense of humour and the eroticism that inspired all his oeuvre, in punning on the expression

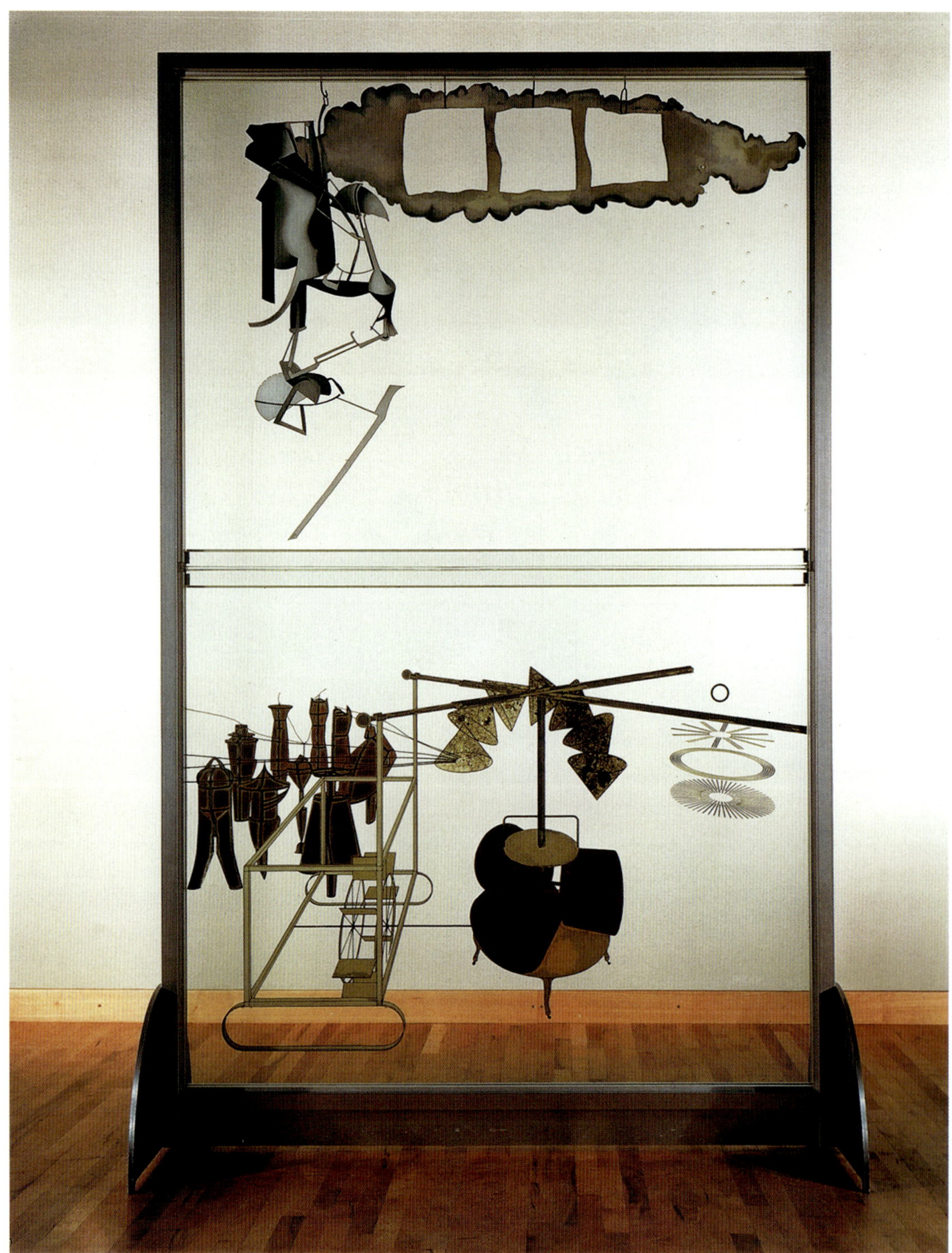

33 Marcel Duchamp and Richard Hamilton (left)
The Bride Stripped Bare by Her Bachelors, Even (The Large Glass), 1915–23 (replica 1965–6)

Described by André Breton as 'a kind of great modern legend' (*Minotaure*, no. 6, Winter 1935), this work presents an intriguing theatre of erotic fustration and play, fusing Catholic, alchemical, and Dada ideas: the 'bachelors' (9 Malic Moulds) 'grind' away in the lower glass panel as the 'bride', her Milky Way veil billowing behind her, hovers out of reach in the panel above. According to Duchamp's notes, if the bride achieves a 'blossoming' she may achieve orgasm that will bring about her 'fall'.

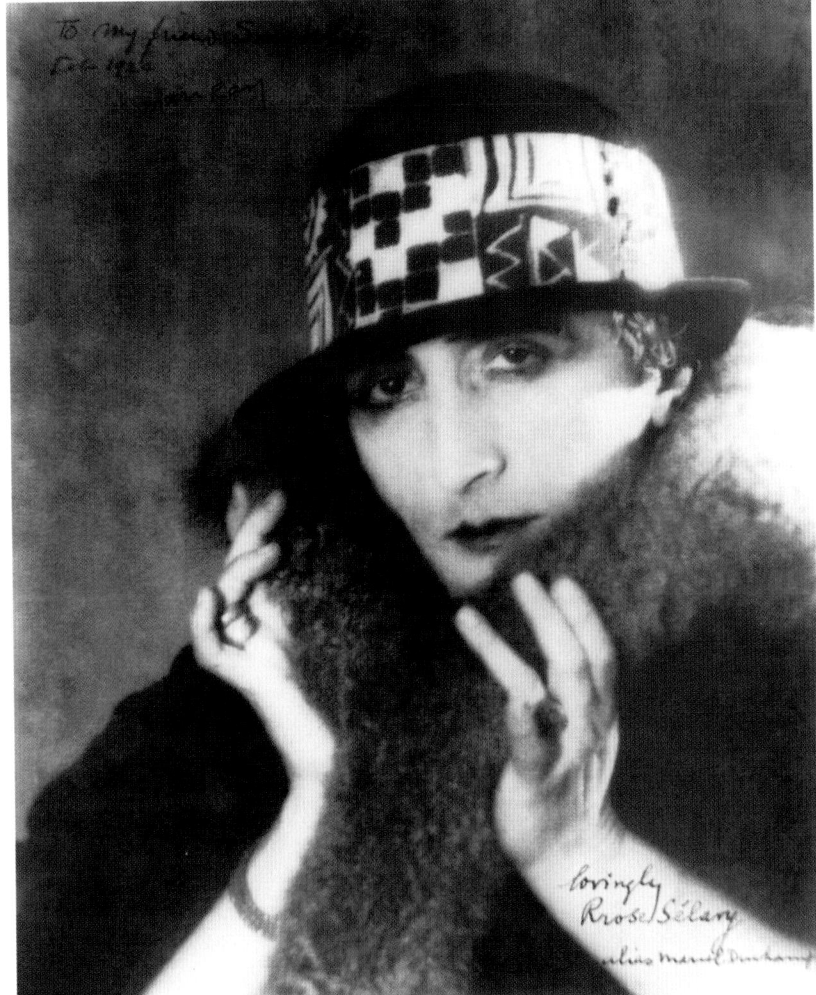

34 Man Ray (right)
Rrose Sélavy (with hands of Germaine Everling), 1924

Duchamp's female alter-ego, Rrose Sélavy, whose name puns on the expression 'Éros c'est la vie' (Eros, that's life), defies gender categories and pays homage to the new independent woman of the 1920s, who was the subject of a bestselling novel by Victor Margueritte, *La Garçonne* (1922).

'Eros c'est la vie' (Eros, that's life). In one photograph **[34]**, probably taken in 1924, we see Duchamp dressed as a coquettish woman, turning up her fur collar and wearing a fashionable hat, not unlike those designed at the time by the artist Sonia Delaunay. We take a second look at the photograph and notice the size of the hands—they seem more feminine than the face. The hands, like the hat, in fact belong to the wife of Picabia, Germaine Everling; Duchamp and Man Ray had cleverly staged a portrait of a person who defied gender categories. Rrose is a mannish woman who challenges the erotic 'norm', perhaps, and pays homage to the rise of the new independent woman in the 1920s, the *garçonne*, or the flapper, who cropped her hair, wore trousers and hats, smoked cigarettes with flair, and frequented jazz clubs.[15]

Weimar Eroticism

As Duchamp teased out gender roles and paid homage to the dandy woman of the 1920s, so Dadaists in Weimar Germany were exploring sexual consumerism and the rise of the 'New Woman' in both her dandy and femme fatale guises. By the 1920s, American expressions like 'sex appeal' and 'flirt' were being used in Germany, and jazz was associated with the new female flapper type in America and in Europe. The armistice of 1918 had brought peace to Europe but had left Germany a divided and traumatized nation. During the Weimar Republic (1919–33) the country initially witnessed a phase of economic prosperity and stability, marked by the rise of consumerism and the growth of mass print media. These gradually gave way to hyper-inflation and massive unemployment through the 1920s, however, leading to the Republic's collapse. The increasing economic uncertainty fuelled Germany's peculiarly antagonistic conflicts between the Left and the Right: the period began with the ultimately unsuccessful but symbolically important Spartacist revolt in Berlin in 1919, led by Rosa Luxemburg and Karl Liebknecht, and ended with the accession to power of Adolf Hitler and the Nazi Party in 1933. The Dadaists were part of the 'erotic revolution' witnessed during the Weimar era, a revolution wherein female eroticism was no longer directed towards child-bearing, and she was free to be 'sexually stimulated' and could 'move around freely for hours in an alcohol and a nicotine haze', as one writer worded it in 1924.[16] But the Dadaists were also among the first to undermine the aesthetic associated with this new liberated woman—'New Objectivity'. New Objectivity was the dominant visual style of Weimar Germany's dynamic consumer culture and was based upon the principles of efficiency and function. Art, architecture, design, and photography became non-decorative and streamlined, celebrating the modern city and its consuming masses as signifiers of the modern nation-state. Influenced by American 'objectivity'—as seen in the success story of the production model of car manufacturer Henry Ford, whose autobiography was published in German in 1923 and who opened a Ford plant in Cologne in 1924—it came under suspicion by many thinkers. Notably, in his *History and Class Consciousness* (1923), the Marxist Georg Lukács criticized New Objectivity and Ford's rationalization of the work environment as having grave repercussions for the personality and psyche of the worker. On a popular level, Fritz Lang's film *Metropolis* (1926) also offered a futuristic critique of the machine and the mechanization of the individual. The Dadaists' assault came through their representations of inhuman sexual practices and erotic politics: the mass production of whores to meet capitalist males' sexual needs. These women were portrayed as pitiless wretches, their ugly naked bodies and repulsive smiles reflecting the bestiality of their customers. *Three Women* (1926) **[35]** by Dadaist Otto Dix (1891–1969) is the perfect example. Dix mocks classical erotic precedent: the 'Three Graces', whom Paris famously had to decide between, are here presented in all their frank 1920s baseness in a seedy brothel. The emaciated body of one only adds to the fleshy sloth of another, while a third plays on the floor, on all fours, with a female dog—her position and well-pummelled breasts clearly compare her with it.

When Dada arrived in Berlin from Zurich in 1918, it quickly began to subvert mainstream visual culture. Led by Dix, George Grosz (1893–1958), Raoul Hausmann (1886–1970), Hannah Höch (1889–1978), Wieland Herzfelde (1896–1988), John Heartfield (1891–1968), and the self-appointed 'OberDada' architect and artist Johannes Baader (1875–1956), the Dadaists mocked Weimar consumer culture, its fantastic shop window displays, its environment of spectacle. Together they organized what might be understood as countercultural activities to assault dominant cultural practices. They held cabaret performances, anti-art exhibitions and published Dada magazines such as *Der Dada* (*The Dada*), and the more contentiously titled reviews *Deadly Earnest, Rose-coloured Spectacles of a Lavatory* and *Everyman His Own Football*. Their activities were anarchic, as evidenced in their numerous attacks on the art market, including one performance by Grosz in February 1918 in which he pretended to relieve himself—shouting 'art is shit'—against a painting by an important contemporary artist Lovis Corinth, who had trained with William-Adolphe Bouguereau at the Academie Julian in Paris and was President of the Berlin Secession at the time.

George Grosz's art was characterized by a perversion of popular erotic iconography, exposing society's underbelly, like Dix. Grosz had been conscripted to fight in World War I and spent much of 1917 in a military mental hospital where he began to sketch 'the beastly faces of my comrades, the malicious cripples, arrogant officers, lecherous nurses, etc. There was no particular point to these drawings; at first I made them . . . simply to record the laughable and grotesque world of the busy, deadly little ants around me . . .'[17] This experience placed an awareness of the body at the centre of his aesthetics and led to his radicalization as an artist as he became increasingly dedicated to artistic and social revolution. This revolutionary ambition found expression in brutal depictions of individuals subjected to sexual assault. In *Sex Murder in the Ackerstrasse* (1916) **[36]**, *John, the Lady Killer* (1918), and *Sexual Murder* (1922), Grosz depicts Jack the Ripper-like characters engrossed

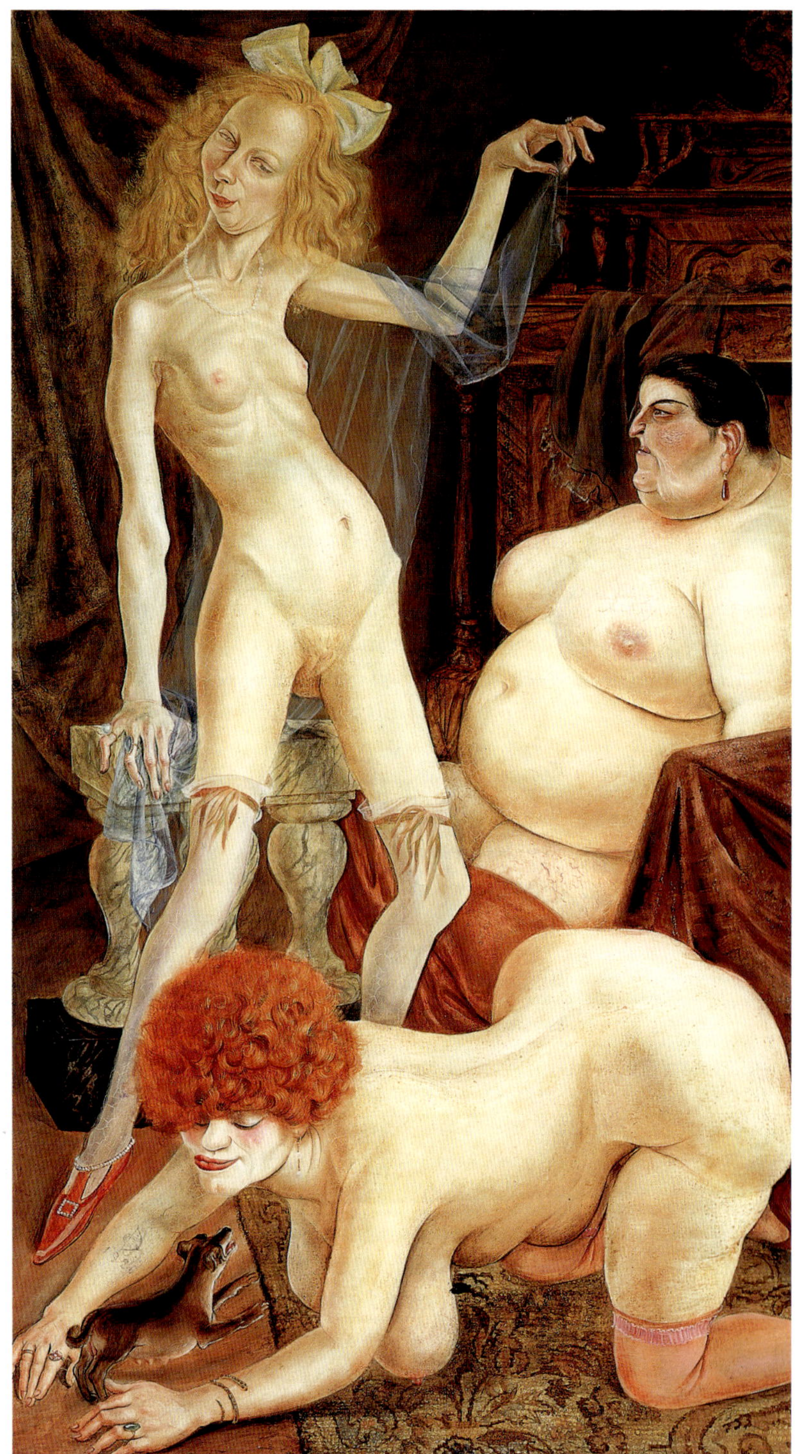

35 Otto Dix
Three Women, 1926

Though awarded the Iron Cross for valour in 1918, Dix's etchings voiced a strong condemnation of World War I in documenting images of dead, wounded, and crippled soldiers. He included a collection of fifty etchings, *Der Krieg* (*War*, 1924) in the anti-war exhibition *No More War!* in 1924. His painting of three whores in *Three Women* continues his assault on the warped values of society by exposing in scathing detail the spaces and activities of seedy urban brothels.

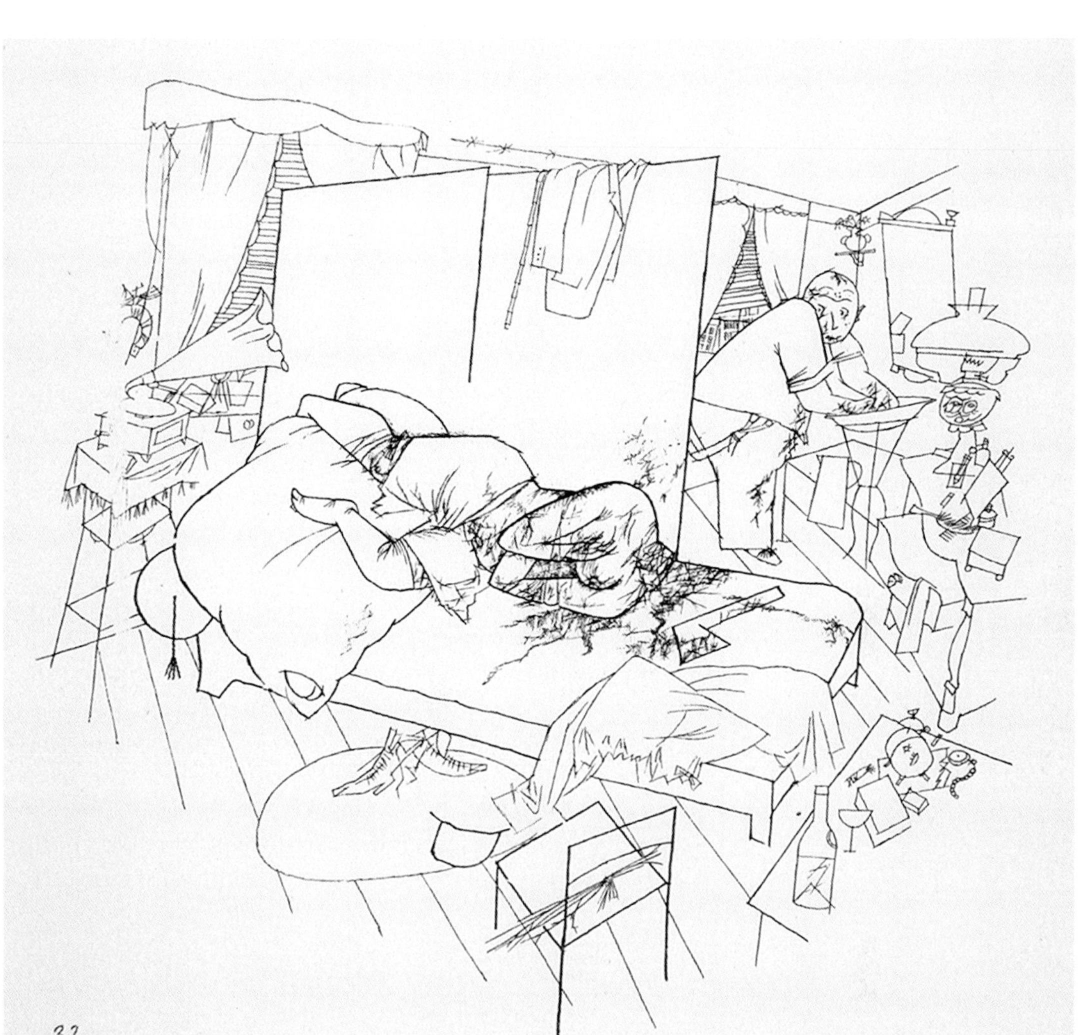

36 George Grosz
Sex Murder in the Ackerstrasse, 1916–17
In 1917 Grosz published a collection of images of murder, rape, and assault in the modern city, exposing the dehumanization of man and society. This lithograph draws on the modern world's insatiable appetite for horror while insisting on a need for new values in life and art.

in the mutilation of nameless female victims, parodying in his choice of titles the sensational captions of typical newspaper headlines. In *Sex Murder in the Ackerstrasse* we see the remains of a sexual encounter (wine, the lucky-in-love horseshoe, and the gramophone) as well as macabre details (a bundle of twigs on a chair), while the banal details of city life (a man's cane and bowler hat) are juxtaposed with a hideous image of a bloody headless female body and the guilty face of her killer, who washes her blood from his hands. Beneath the image, the artist wrote 'Jack the Killer—drawing by Dr William King Thomas', referring both to the notorious killer, Jack the Ripper, who fascinated Grosz, and one of his many signatory alter-egos, Dr Thomas, a nineteenth-century shipowner, famous for having destroyed one of his own vessels in an attempt at insurance fraud, killing hundreds in the process. Behind Grosz's apparent glorification of sexual violence and the erotic thrill of taboo lay political subversion, however. Grosz was a communist, a political radical whose art parodied the bourgeoisie and the burgeoning corruption in Weimar society—political, economic and sexual corruption. Through sexual analogy, Grosz depicts the new Germany, with its modern urban efficiency, as a futuristic nightmare where people—in this case working-class prostitutes—are disposable.

Hannah Höch also produced disconcerting images of the erotic body in her reworking of images from contemporary women's magazines. Höch and other Berlin Dadaists such as Heartfield invented the technique of *photomontage*—the hand-made combination of 'found' photographs and fragments of photographs in a composite two-dimensional image—and used it to subvert the streamlined mass production of images and publications in the culture of New Objectivity. By the mid-1920s over 4,000 titles were being published in Germany, from daily newspapers to illustrated magazines, with 45 morning and 14 evening newspapers being published every day in Berlin alone.[18] Within these publications pictures took an increasingly important role, not just to advertise products but to narrate feature stories. The photomontages of the Dadaists (for example those by John Heartfield for the illustrated workers' paper *Arbeiter Illustrierte Zeitung* (AIZ) in the 1920s) drew on this mass reproduction of images but twisted them to make political statements. Höch was particularly concerned with the ideal female type promoted in magazines and presented her own erotic versions of the images she found. She worked from 1916 to 1926 for Berlin's major newspaper and magazine publisher, Ullstein Verlag, producing knitting catalogues and other publications for the female market. In using the 'craft' of photomontage against the mechanized media industry, her art questioned media associations between woman, domesticity, and handicraft at a time when the New Woman was supposedly gaining liberation from the home. Höch retaliated by depicting the most threatening New Woman—the femme fatale. In her photomontage *Marlene* (1930), Höch uses the eroticism of the most famous femme fatale of the day, the actress Marlene Dietrich, to draw male and female spectator in alike. Erotic spectacle is staged through Dietrich's fetishized parts: her famous legs (inverted, on a classical pedestal, dominating the central plane) and lips (in the top right corner). The male spectator, represented by two men in the lower right corner whistling at her from their auditorium seats, enjoys a lingering shot of Dietrich's gargantuan stockinged legs, her signature 'Marlene' written across the middle ground as if autographing her own stage curtain, and her luscious red lips further up again, continuing the voyeuristic fantasy such that one almost hears the actress huskily whispering her own name. The female viewer could also enter this erotic fantasy, however, not only because Dietrich had a certain androgynous eroticism but also because she was a cult figure among lesbians in Berlin at the time, many of whom would try to look like her and even call themselves Marlene.[19] Höch's homage to Dietrich enjoys the tension between the erotic desire and fear that the femme fatale embodies, as the sexual object who does not just return the look but does so through heavily painted eyes.

As *Marlene* demonstrates, Höch was particularly concerned with the representation of the modern, emancipated woman in the mass media and popular culture. She subverted the media's construction of an ideal femininity through the procedure of montage itself—the cutting up, or mutilation, of ideal female types constituting an aggressive rejection of imposed gendered cultural norms. Her art also spoke to contemporary discussion and publications on bisexuality and the 'third sex', as well as the near-cult publication *Sex and Character* (1903) by the Austrian philosopher and sexologist Otto Weininger, a book now predominantly viewed as anti-Semitic and misogynistic. In the Weimar period homosexuals such as German physician and sexologist Magnus Hirschfeld and his Scientific Humanitarian Committee were campaigning for legal reform.[20] Hirschfeld, through his Berlin Institute for Sexology (which operated from 1919 to 1933), also promoted the theory of the 'third sex' as natural, rather than as a social deviation, and battled against Germany's penal law against male homosexuality. The Institute was devoted to the study of sexuality, including medical and legal research on sexuality, with a library for premarital consultation and instruction. On 10 May 1933 the Institute was ransacked and closed down by the Nazis. All its books were burnt.

Höch never identified herself as a bisexual although she had relationships both with men and a woman, the Dutch writer Til Brugman, from 1926 to 1935, but her open attitude to sexuality and critique of socially enforced gender roles—as well as her role as a Dada 'dandy', usually dressed in *garçonne* garb—emerges in a second photomontage of 1930, *Tamer* **[30]**. Here androgyny is more overt, while a scathing irony acts as a distancing technique to repel the traditional male gaze and invoke a new 'third' way of seeing through the corruption of gender norms. For female and male forms are fused: a female mannequin's body has muscular male arms, her mask-like face made of porcelain with doe eyes is mirrored in the face of a sea lion below. Voyeuristic pleasure is denied due to the similarity between the female's and the animal's eyes and the trans-sexualism of the mannequin's body, which is monstrous despite its ideal female and male parts. Höch's disruptive view of the modern 'new woman' reminds us of the contradictions of her existence: although enjoying new social and economic liberty in the Weimar Republic, the 'new woman' remained oppressed in terms of gender stereotypes and was all too easily politically pacified and socially constructed by consumer culture and the feminine ideals it promoted. Höch also points to the easy slippage between sexual liberation and sexual decadence which Nazi ideology would soon exploit. The sexually liberated culture of Weimar Germany would become one of the Nazis' main targets, not only as expressed in Dada art—singled out by Hitler for its 'degeneracy'—but also in film, including Fritz Lang's *M* (1928) and Josef von Sternberg's *The Blue Angel* (1930). The latter was based on the cabaret 'Tingeltangel' by the popular Weimar songwriter and composer Friedrich Hollaender. It starred Marlene Dietrich as a cabaret singer, Lola, a beautiful femme fatale who leads to the sexual, moral, and finally mental collapse of Professor Immanuel Rath. The Nazis would take a firm stance against such 'decadent' cabarets and turn the clock back on women's liberation too, beginning with the League of German Women's Association, formed in 1894 and formally dissolved by the Nazis in 1933.

Male Fantasies

While avant-garde artists between the wars explicitly used the erotic body to expose repressive political regimes and social stereotypes, state-sponsored artists in fascist regimes indulged in a different form of erotic 'coding'. Fascism adopted a particular male fantasy and rhetoric of virility wherein any political or racial threat was figured as a sexual threat.[21] This psychosexual fantasy (which had real political manifestations, needless to say) propounded a classical, fertile sexuality; politics itself were aestheticized, and the controlled male and female body became symbols of national and racial potency and pride.[22] If the avant-garde focused on the whore, the fragmented, the monstrous body, then fascist art portrayed the pure, the wholesome, and the classical body ideal, developing a new, controlled eroticism, one that mirrored a very particular body politic.

In Italy from 1922 to 1943, the National Fascist Party exercised considerable influence over aesthetic debates and artistic practice, promoting virility in all aspects of society and cultural representation. Benito Mussolini himself stood as the model of masculinity Italian fascism aspired to—his heroism, sportsmanship, strength, and vigour were perceived as the very embodiment of the New Man or 'Superman' the country needed.[23] Accordingly, his image in the media, notably in press photography and broadcasting, presented him as *the* iconic male, while representations of the virile male in art in general were equally if not more heroic. Notably male beauty, an athletic build, and a vigorous disposition were promoted as signifiers of a fertile, robust political regime. In the Foro Mussolini in Rome, an architectural complex planned by Enrico del Debbio in 1927, a Stadium of Marble was built with sixty 4-metre-tall, heroic male naked athletes, each adopting poses and courageous expressions emphasizing their Roman 'spirit'. While comparable to Michelangelo's *David* **[2]** in their ideal classical beauty, these sculptures' sexual vigour, signified in their firm, muscled youthful bodies, was in keeping with Il Duce's vision of the New Italy led by virile youths. Their impressive eroticism was perhaps best acknowledged by the Catholic Church: as with Michelangelo several centuries previously, the Church had to be appeased by the addition of fig leaves to hide the sex of the Foro sculptures.[24] Such monumentalized sculpture played a key role in Mussolini's Fascist vision as it lent antique authority to his many architectural projects and reinforced the theme of national 'construction'. While the Church feared the erotic thrill of such strident virile sculpture, one might describe art under Mussolini as striving to embody Eros as the procreative life drive, rather than sexual desire. Mussolini's Italy opposed individualism, liberalism, communism, socialism, but still presented an emphatically modern, procreative vision of man as citizen-soldier dedicated in his perfectly sculpted body to his Leader and State.

The monumental sculpture seen in Mussolini's architectural schemes, which invoked classical antiquity while promoting a new future, was paralleled if not outdone by German National Socialist male fantasies of power and the racialized and anti-Bolshevik rhetoric of male volunteer soldiers, the *Freikorps*, which fuelled its political success in the 1920s. On 23 March 1933, when Adolf Hitler became Chancellor he announced that his new government would ensure a thorough 'moral purging' of people, public life, the education system, the media, and the arts. Culture was a vital weapon, and special cultural conferences were held as part of the annual Nuremberg rallies. Along with the Great German Art Exhibitions, held annually in Munich between 1937 and 1944, Hitler ensured that art supported and encouraged the ambitions of National Socialism. Within this culture, the ideal German body was to act as a metaphor and model for the superiority and integrity of the German people as a race. Anyone that did not conform—communists, Jews, homosexuals, and the mentally and physically ill—were deemed outsiders and a threat to social stability, sexual morality, and racial purity. According to Hitler, the greatest threats to his Germany (as he claimed in *Mein Kampf*, written while he was imprisoned in Landsberg after the failed military coup of 9 November 1923, and published in 1925) were the Jews, who had a 'sham culture'. The Aryan race had to redeem culture by returning to Greek classicism and bringing Hellenism and Germanism together. The Weimar era was deemed to have led to the corruption of the German people in endorsing modernism and its corrupt trappings. Its objectivity had to be replaced with 'will, power and strength', based on a devotion to the Führer by the masses. Joseph Goebbels, the Minister of Propaganda, ensured that the collective virile image of the German race dominated and any effeminate threat to that image was ousted. Just as Mussolini promoted athleticism both in his self-image and in the image of his Fascist Italy, so too did Hitler encourage new sports complexes, fitness programmes, and film images of the Aryan race to impress national and international audiences. Of course the cult of the body and the promotion of nudity was not new to Germany and had been encouraged by both the Right and the Left. Most controversially during the Weimar period in 1923, Adolf Koch had begun teaching gymnastics in the working-class district of Berlin in the nude, claiming nakedness made everyone equal; he traced this practice, as the Nazis later did, back to Hellenism. But an even more rigorously applied rhetoric of the body was adopted under Hitler, one that was given cinematic form by Leni Riefenstahl's *Olympia—Feast of Nations*. A film of the Olympic Games in Berlin in 1936, it elevated the athletic and body programmes of the National Socialists to mythological heights by drawing on the postures and sculptures of ancient Greek gods in its representation of German athletes. As with Fascist Italy, the cult of the body was vital to the cult of the Nazi regime and its shaping of the Aryan Superman (and Superwoman). Riefenstahl's film not only set up the German Olympics as the continuation of the ancient Olympics, it drew on the perfection of ancient art to reiterate the perfection of the German body ideal by dramatically metamorphosing a sculpture of a discus thrower by the Greek sculptor Myron (active *c.*470–450 BC) into a live athlete adopting the same classical athletic pose. Sculpture was a powerful force for visual propaganda, literally taking the ideal male and female to monumental heights and offering totemic images of political power; these borrowed an erotic energy through their heavily 'armoured' musculature and upright stature. Images of the naked, controlled muscular male body were a constant reminder of the militant power of the State.

Thus sculpture as a medium not only reinforced Germany's link with the ancient past in adapting the Greek model to a Nordic tradition, it also played a key role in the public staging of political ideology by the Nazi regime. Sculptors like Fritz Klimsch (1870–1960), Richard Scheibe (1879–1964), and Georg Kolbe (1877–1947) were successful in the Weimar period but gained new status under the Nazis as artists who had stayed true to German realism and had not embraced modern, decadent styles. Their sculptures of male nudes with perfectly toned muscles and intense expressions were based on the classical ideal where mind and body are one, while their sleekly carved female nudes with broad hips and small breasts were reminiscent of the Renaissance ideal of fertile womanhood. The many architectural schemes of Albert Speer, Hitler's official architect, who designed everything from stadia to official buildings—most notably the Zeppelintribune (the parade ground at Nuremberg for the annual Nazi party rally) and the new Reich's Chancellery—provided the perfect spaces for such dramatic, monumental sculpture. The Nazis even passed a law in 1934 demanding that at least 2 per cent of all budgets for buildings had to go towards artistic embellishment.[25] Arno Breker (1900–91) was Hitler's favourite sculptor and in 1937 was awarded the prestigious title of Official State Sculptor. His sculpture *Readiness* **[37]**, exhibited at the Great German Art Exhibition of 1939, exemplifies both the controlled eroticism of Nazi art and the powerful role of sculpture within the political machine. It presents us with the German warrior, drawing his sword, staring his enemy in the eye, firmly rooted in German soil and ready to sacrifice himself in battling mercilessly for a greater Aryan good. His perfect, muscular torso proves his purity of race; the idealized, armouring of the nude makes the sculpture seem iconic rather than naturalistic. The sculpture was a symbol of the readiness of Germany itself as World War II began. While the male body is undeniably passionate, sexuality is sublimated for politics, and sexual energy and pleasure are channelled into the battlefield.

The Nazi female ideal complemented this virile male and continued art's indoctrination of the people: as bearer of the Aryan race her devotion was to her family and the State. As Klaus Theweleit has shown in *Male Fantasies* (1977), since the 1920s this vision of woman was intrinsic to the 'male fantasy' of the Right (notably the *Freikorps*) in Germany. The sexual, erotic woman had to be wiped out as a threat to the masculine regime, and by the 1930s all that the 'new woman' of the 1920s had achieved was quickly and brutally undone. Woman, like the masses, was subjugated—her potential for production had to be taken in charge, erotic unproductivity squashed. Indeed, Theweleit argues that the Fascist male battled with his own erotic drives as he battled against all

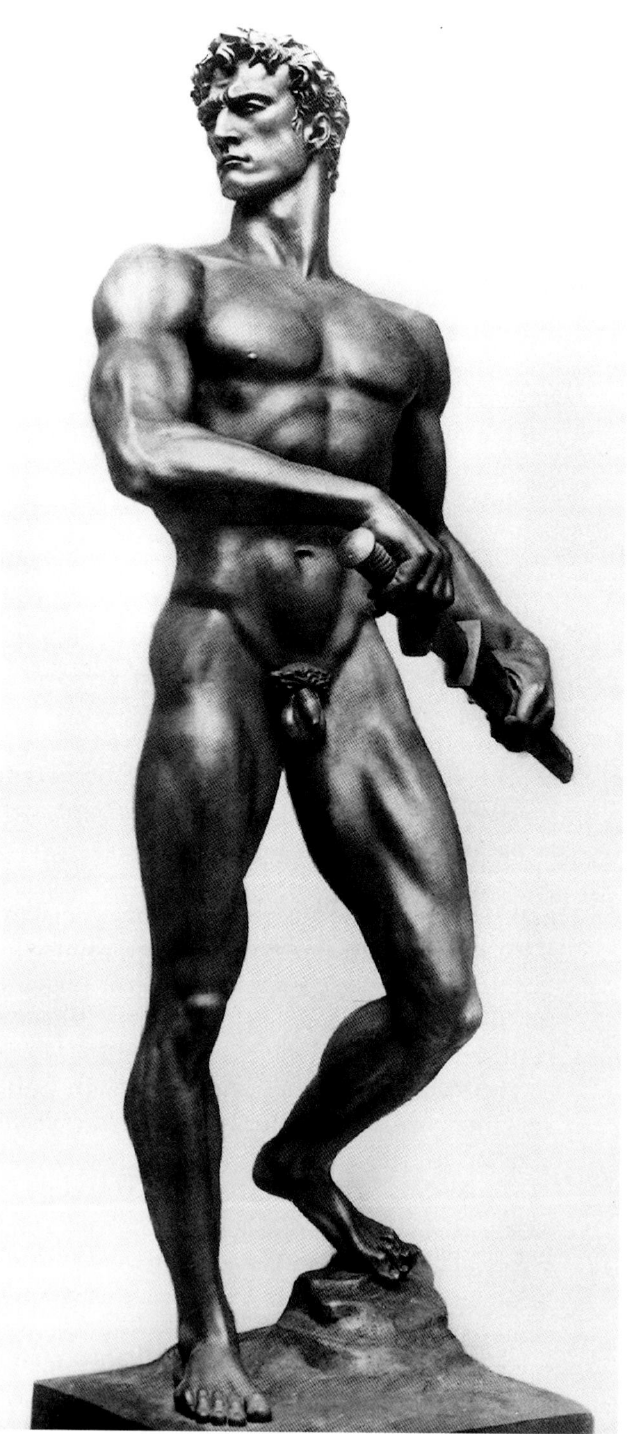

37 Arno Breker
Readiness, 1939

Bringing the symbolic heroism of Michelangelo's *David* into a whole new Aryan dimension, Breker's monumental sculpture celebrates the fascist 'armoured' body in its idealized physique, intense expression, and readiness to bear arms for the nation state.

that was 'feminine' (the prostitute, the outsider, the primitive, the Jew, the insane) and erotic, seeing both as a kind of 'menstruating threat' to the State. Thus the fear of woman and of the erotic in proto-fascist groupings in the 1920s became part of a burgeoning phenomenon wherein a particular form of male fantasy for a new people and era was linked to a violent racism and anti-communism. The nudes of Austrian painter Ivo Saliger (1894–1987) were regularly shown at the Great German Art exhibitions and typified the female ideal for the Third Reich in her cold, controlled, sanitized sexuality. Saliger's nudes were the antithesis of the *garçonne*, flapper, or Dietrichesque femme fatale. As in Saliger's *Diana's Rest* (1940), she was a Hellenic beauty, the sacred mother of a future divine race. Her sexual purity was displayed by her frank nakedness and firm limbs, suggesting a healthy, athletic attitude to the body rather than any libidinous 'degeneracy'. Her heroic 'ancestry' might typically be indicated by allusions to mythology, Leda and Diana for example. Of course Fascists and Nazis recognized the power of myth to influence mass psychology, as well as the latent sexual energy behind the fascist cult of authority and control, as the Austrian psychiatrist and psychoanalyst Wilhelm Reich (1897–1957) recognized in his 1933 *Mass Psychology of Fascism*, a book the Nazis quickly banned. The Fascist body ideal also emphasized the pure healthy blood of the *Volk* and feared its contamination. A clear polarity arose in images of the sexual, female body: the good, asexual, maternal nurturer, on the one hand, and the evil, erotic, threatening woman, on the other—the women painted by Saliger clearly came from the former camp. The nudes of Adolf Ziegler (1892–1959), the President of the Reich Culture Chamber who became known as the 'Master of Curly Pubic Hair', were equally marmoreal in form and mythological in subject-matter. *The Judgement of Paris* and *Female Nude*, both of 1939, clearly presented woman as a controlled and fair-skinned classical—never realist—beauty who flattered the virile Aryan gaze.[26] Ziegler's triptych, *The Four Elements* **[38]**, exhibited at the Great German Art Exhibition in 1937, took pride of place over the living-room fireplace in Hitler's apartment in Munich. It is an allegorical work depicting earth, air, fire, and water as four young nubile females whose eroticism lies not in sexual titillation but in a very particular erotic fantasy of the pure, unsullied female with Aryan features and healthy, gymnast-like bodies. Sexuality was about responsibility to the race, about procreation for the good of the body politic, about the thrill of power and superiority.

The Nazi fear of uncontrolled eroticism and the corruption of blood and race becomes apparent in their *Degenerate Art* (*Entartete Kunst*) exhibition in Munich 19 July to 30 November 1937. Ziegler and a committee

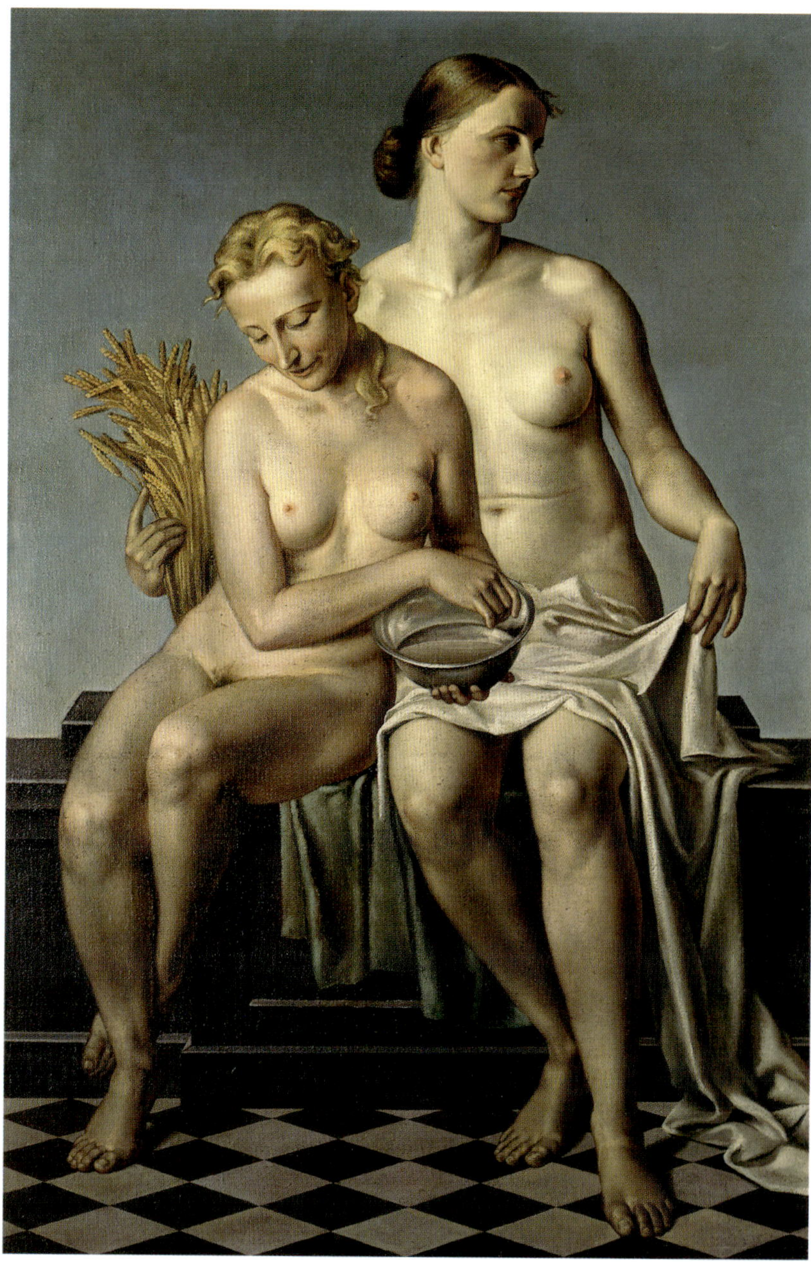

38 Adolf Ziegler
'Earth and Water', central panel from the triptych *The Four Elements*, 1936

Ziegler was one of Adolf Hitler's favourite artists and the president of the Reich Culture Chamber. This painting hung over the fireplace in Hitler's apartment in Munich. In their perfected, marmoreal form and passive expressions Ziegler's nudes symbolized the ideal women and girls of the Third Reich, catering to the Führer's demand that German art express German character.

of art historians seized art from public and private collections and presented them in an old gallery in the Hofgarten as an example of what Ziegler described (in a vitriolic speech at the opening which was broadcast nationally) as 'the crippled products of madness, impertinence and lack of talent'. 'Degenerate' artists were largely German modernists but also included some of those artists we have already discussed, such as Paul Gauguin, Henri Matisse, and Pablo Picasso. Artistic 'degeneracy' was linked to insanity, Bolshevism, and the Jews and was deemed a diseased threat in need of purging. For example, the element of the primitive in modern art was explained as an example of the 'niggerizing' of the visual arts in an attempt to 'uproot the racial instinct of the *Volk*'. Avant-garde images of nakedness and prostitutes (including a Dada image by the German artist Max Ernst (1891–1976) of a mechanized nude, her sex covered by a bird), were attacked as 'insults to German womanhood'.[27] For the Nazis, German womanhood could only be represented through a very particular erotic physiognomy: firm breasts and athletic bodies; she was only to be surrounded by clear signs of her purity: nature, the soil, and water. Their reconfiguration of woman effectively destroyed not only the 'new woman' of the Weimar Republic but also the advances of the avant-garde since the turn of the century.

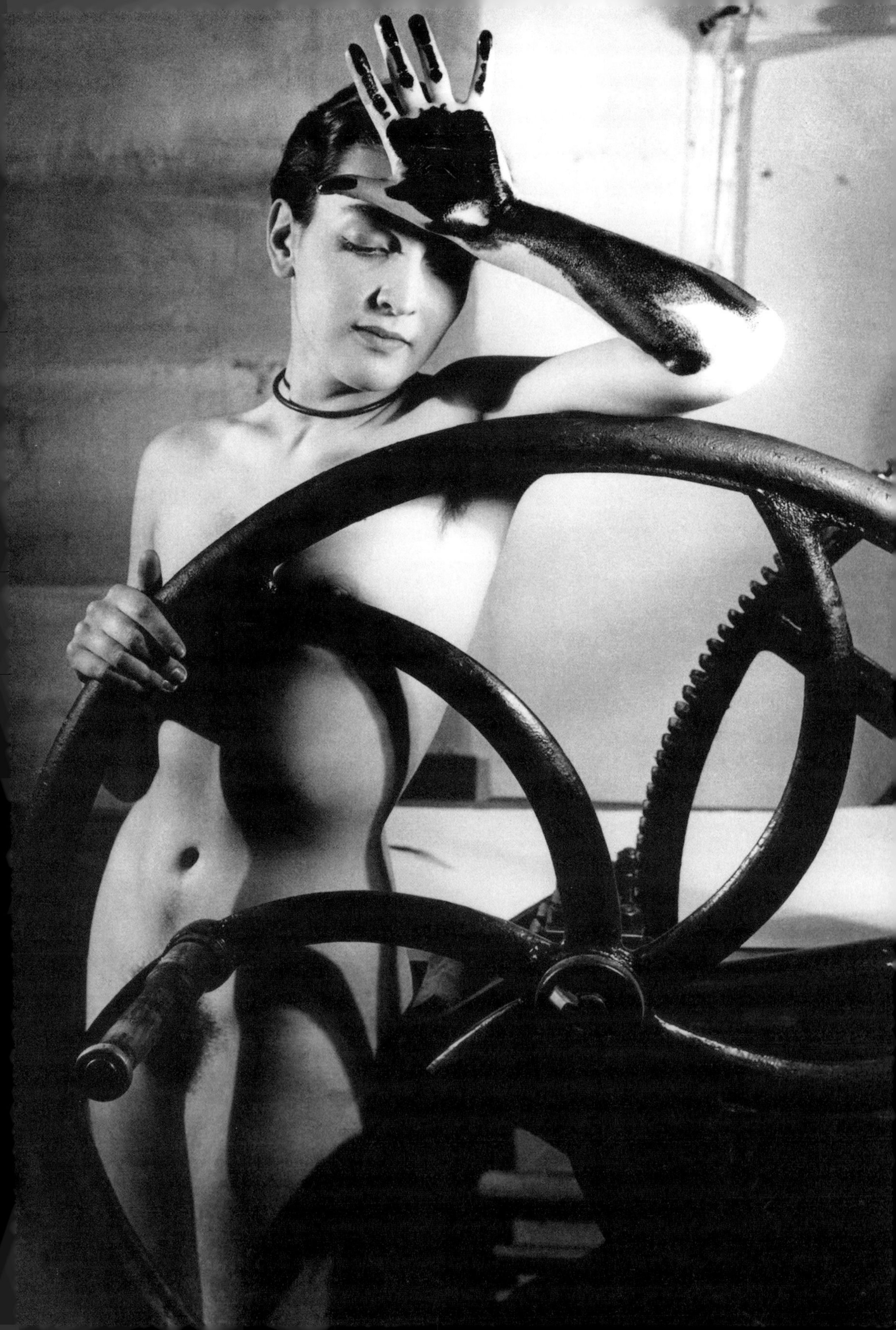

5 Surrealism's Erotic Politics

Despite the horrendous political and cultural purges under the Nazis, the avant-garde continued to exist in Germany, albeit in hiding and eventually in exile. In the same year that Hitler became Chancellor (1933), the Polish-German artist Hans Bellmer (1902–75) produced *The Doll* **[40]**, a macabre object about a metre high, made of papier mâché and plaster over an armature of wood and metal, with movable limbs. Bellmer was influenced by Dada in his art's violent approach to eroticism, befriending George Grosz and John Heartfield in the early 1920s as a young student in Berlin. Bellmer's particular fascination with the doll as an erotic object may also be linked to the Viennese Expressionist Oscar Kokoschka who, in 1918, had a life-sized doll made by the Munich doll-maker Hermineas as a substitute for his love, the Vienna femme fatale, Alma Mahler. Kokoschka's relationship with this doll was notorious, becoming the subject of his paintings such as *Self Portrait with Doll* (*c.*1922). Other aspects of Bellmer's psychosexual make-up which inspired his art included his own childhood fascination with little girls, his desire for his younger cousin Ursula, as well as his fear of his father—emotions triggered when his mother returned a trunk of childhood objects to him in 1931.[1] Jacques Offenbach's contemporary operetta, *The Tales of Hoffmann*, in which a doll (Olympia) is constructed, also influenced his decision to produce a doll-fetish.

39 Man Ray
Veiled Erotic, 1933
André Breton cropped this photograph of Meret Oppenheim at an iron printing press, editing out her sex, when he reproduced it in his article on 'convulsive beauty' in the Surrealist journal *Minotaure* in 1934. However, it is the strategic placement of the phallic handle of the press at Oppenheim's bare sex that lends Man Ray's photograph of his then-lover its subversive edge. This is further enhanced by the fact that her breasts are partially concealed, augmenting her androgynous look.

Having begun his artistic career illustrating works of popular fiction and designing advertisements for large industrial firms, Bellmer had benefited from the economic prosperity and mass media advances of the Weimar period. A Dadaist critique of that New Objectivity culture also infiltrated his graphic work of the 1920s, though: his book illustrations often involved the violent depiction of women while his advertising designs sometimes made use of photomontage. His particular concern with unconscious sexual desires is vital both to our appreciation of his doll and his embrace by the Surrealists in Paris, who published in their review *Minotaure* (no. 6, Winter 1934–5) 18 black and white

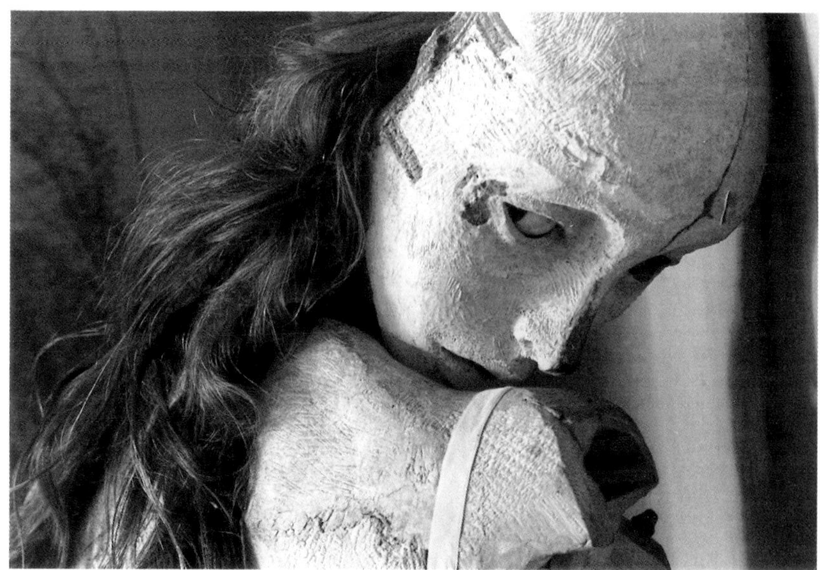

40 Hans Bellmer
The Doll, c.1934
Bellmer's first doll, created near the time that Hitler became Chancellor of Germany, is psychologically powerful. It confronts the viewer with a macabre image of a fragmented young girl, constructed of papier maché, contesting both the 'new woman' body ideal of the 1920s and the burgeoning fascist vision of woman as the bearer of the Aryan race.

photographs Bellmer took of the doll. The provocative title given to the photo spread, 'Variations on the Assemblage of an Articulated Minor', pointed to the threat of child sexual abuse or murder suggested by Bellmer's photographs. For the doll appeared as a dishevelled creature, her pubescent body, girlish hair ribbon, and Mary-Jane shoes indicating a childhood innocence that her fragmented, largely naked papier maché body denied. She was the *femme-enfant* (child-woman) of male fantasy, a kind of Lolita figure who knows her sexual allure and yet is still legally untouchable. Yet there was more afoot in Bellmer's frightening configuration of a minor: just as Nazi art at the time used sexuality as political analogy, so too did Bellmer. In an interview in 1972 Bellmer explained: 'I tried to rearrange the sexual elements of a girl's body like a sort of plastic anagram . . . I wanted to reveal what is usually kept hidden—it was no game—I tried to open people's eyes to new realities.'[2] His erotic doll with her dishevelled appearance, manipulated into every possible sexual angle, was the very opposite of a Ziegler female nude or of an Arno Breker sculpture, with its perfect musculature and balanced form, braced to fight. In addition, Bellmer's choice of medium (photography, where an image is literally taken from life) firmly placed the erotic in the here-and-now, not in the Hellenic past.

The 'new realities' of Germany were assaulted even further in Bellmer's second, more malleable doll with ball-joints, constructed in 1936. This second doll became the subject of a book collaboration between Bellmer and the Surrealist poet and writer Paul Éluard, entitled *The Games of the Doll* **[41]**. Here the doll's 'games' involved various erotic

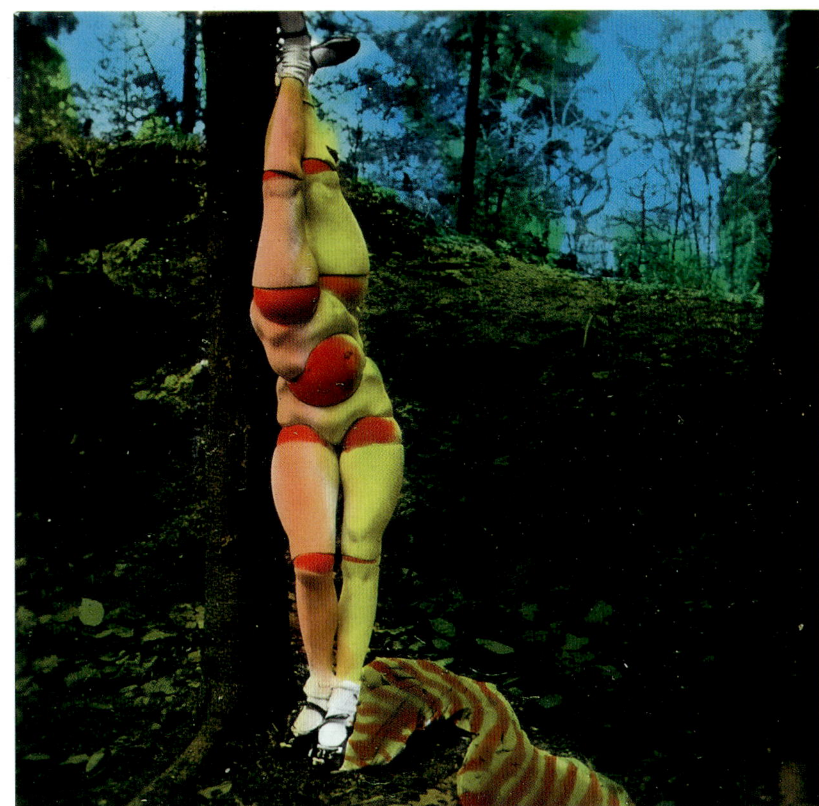

41 Hans Bellmer
The Doll, 1936
Bellmer's second doll, constructed round a ball-joint that allowed for greater manipulation, has here been staged out of doors, her clothing discarded apart from her Mary Jane shoes and ankle socks. Her missing head and arms and 'mirrored' sex and legs reinforce her monstrosity.

manipulations of her multiple buttocks and limbs as she is propped against a tree, bed, or stairs with several orifices visible. Bellmer added colour, predominantly shades of pink, to the developed photographs, giving the surface of the doll (who was already more shiny—and so more fetish-like—in appearance than her papier maché sister) a bruised appearance, reinforcing the element of sexual violence in the images. This fragmented, multi-orificed, baby-pink, naked doll assaulted bourgeois sensibilities in true avant-garde fashion, but it also assaulted the earthy, rural, and maternal ideal of Hitler's regime. Bellmer's doll embodied all that the Nazis loathed: the fragmented, the explicit, the feminine, the Other. It had to be kept hidden from the State and so could only be reproduced and later exhibited in Surrealist exhibitions in Paris in 1936 and 1938.

In Paris Bellmer found an ally in André Breton and the Surrealist movement. Launched in 1924, the movement took a stand against the love of God and love of the fatherland, believing in the revolutionary power of art and of dreams to change the world and to overhaul bourgeois morality: it wanted to lead the world in a radical new social and political revolution that would go beyond the Marxist quest for a new material order. The Surrealists believed 'we must all learn to read with and look through the eyes of Eros', and in their writings, painting, drawings, photography, film, performance art, and collective exhibitions they tried to initiate the public into this world view.[3] Between 1928 and 1932 the Surrealists organized 12 sessions to 'investigate' sexuality. Despite conflicting opinions, the discussions demonstrate a frank fascination with sexual practice and erotic desire (from clitoral stimulation to sodomy, fetishism, exhibitionism, and masturbation), an eagerness to explore the subject of sexual taboo (although it must be said that homosexuality remained a subject Breton did not like to address), and an insistence on the life-affirming power of love.[4] Indeed, love is the new religion of Surrealism, replacing the Church, and offering an absolute principle that leads to convulsive, marvellous, life-altering encounters with the opposite sex.

Surrealism, like the Dada movement from which it emerged, was both a philosophy and a way of life. The Surrealists believed in the power of art to revolutionize society, consciously using eroticism as a weapon to shock and change their public. The 1924 Surrealist manifesto made their rejection of traditional bourgeois aesthetic and moral values clear, defining Surrealism as 'Psychic automatism in its pure state, by which one proposes to express—verbally, by means of the written word, or in any other manner—the actual functioning of thought. Dictated by thought, in the absence of any control by reason, exempt from any aesthetic or moral concern.'[5] In the two styles of Surrealism which dominated its pre-World War II history—automatism and academic illusionism—eroticism is evident in expression and theme. Catalan Surrealist Joan Miró was described by Breton as devoted to 'pure automatism' and could 'perhaps pass for the most "surrealist" of us all'.[6] Beginning his automatist experiments in the summer of 1924, Miró would discover images in his drawings, seemingly abstract patterns and shapes giving birth to compositions whose chance—rather than academic—process was itself deemed erotic or chemical and indicative of unconscious mental activity. This experimentation occurred in Surrealist word and image play, both of which come together in Miró's painting, *A Star Caresses the Breast of a Negress* (1938). Here bold colour (pure black, white, red, yellow), fluid abstracted forms, and text (the words that give the painting its name) create an erotic rhythm of its own. In this painting-poem the Surrealists' assault on traditional technique is evident in the poetic use of figuration and the figurative use of poetry. Words literally trace and caress the black background, and figurative elements of the composition augment the power of the erotic

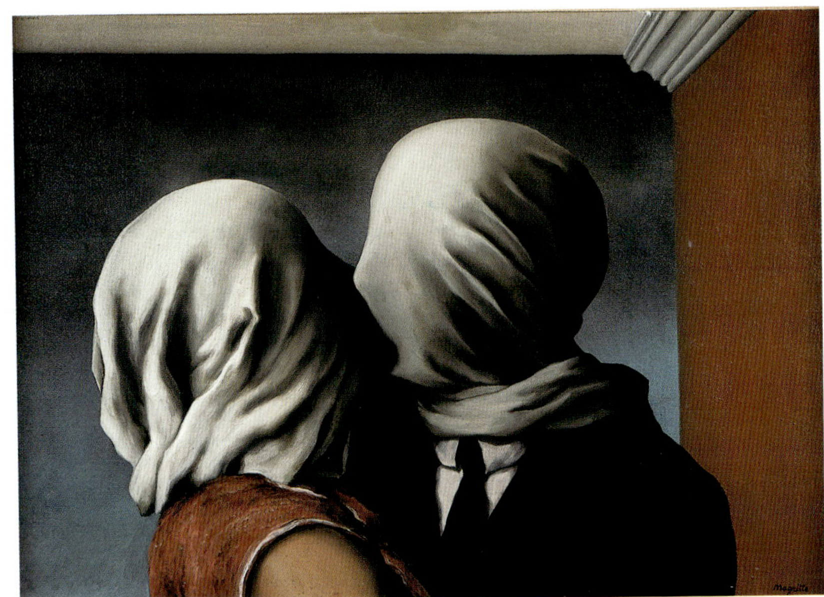

42 René Magritte
The Lovers, 1928
The bourgeois clothing of Magritte's lovers stands in dramatic contrast to their shrouded heads, the sheet suggesting perhaps an illicit relationship or orgasmic pleasure (when one experiences *la petite mort*, or little death).

imagination. The second style is perhaps better known and has a more immediate erotic appeal—the fantastic illusionism of the Catalan artist Salvador Dalí and Belgian René Magritte. In Magritte's *The Lovers* (1928) **[42]** we see an apparently respectable bourgeois couple, their heads wrapped and joined by a heavy white sheet. The sheet may symbolize the violence of the desire, suggesting in their threatening position the orgasmic 'little death' (*la petite mort*) of love-making, or perhaps secrecy and the taboo of illicit or incestuous desire. The architecture of the room in which the lovers are framed indicates this is a dream world of uncanny potential. Despite Magritte's relatively neutral, realistic style we are presented with an erotic picture puzzle, one that has an infinite number of solutions. As Magritte explained: 'My painting is a thought that sees without naming what it sees. What it sees in an object is another, hidden object.'[7] The psychological dimension of the erotic image is further magnified when we consider the life of Magritte. His mother committed suicide in 1912 by drowning herself in the River Sambre; the artist dramatized his recollection of this trauma by claiming that those who discovered her dead body found her nightgown wrapped around her face—he would dwell on the fact that no one ever knew whether she had veiled herself before death or whether the currents had simply washed her up in this manner. While this account of the nightdress was Magritte's, it still reminds us of the Surrealists' recognition of the importance of repressed memories and fears and how they were often revealed through sexual symbolism. And, more importantly,

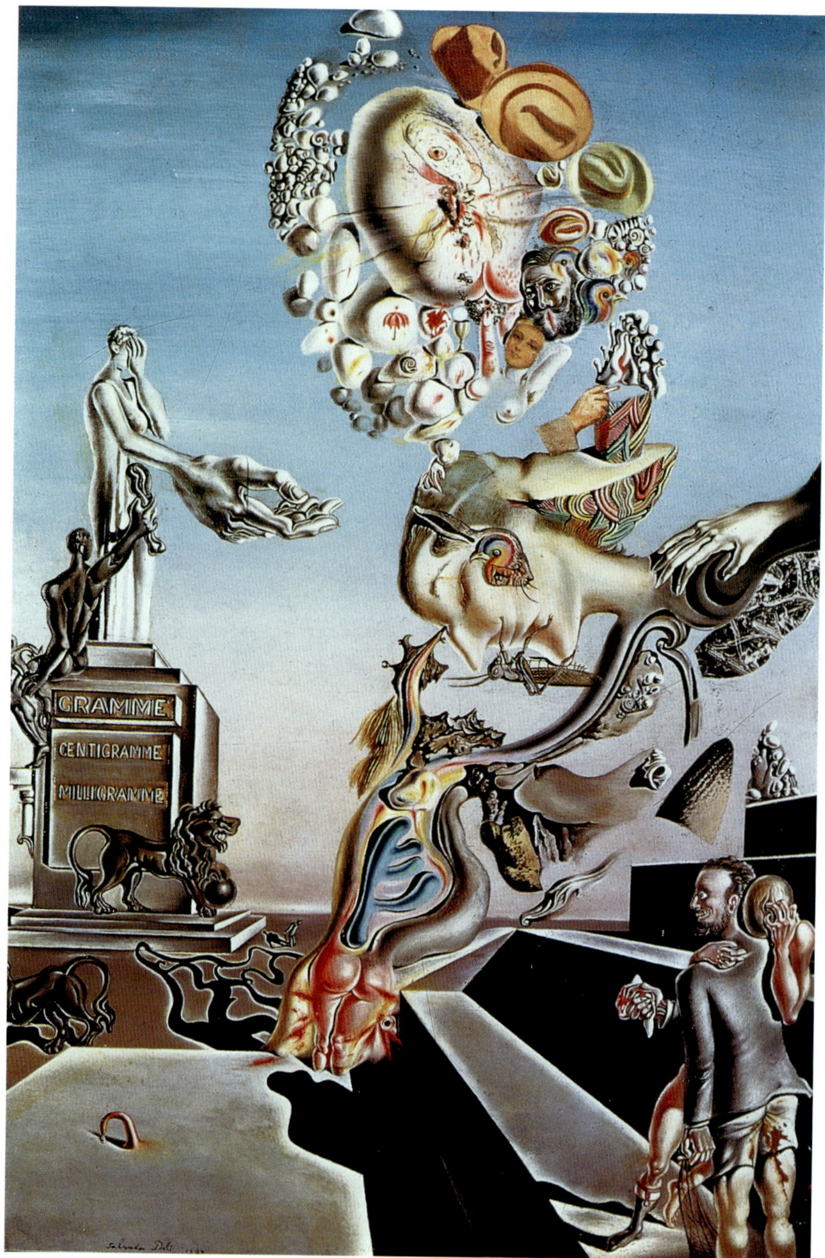

43 Salvador Dalí
The Lugubrious Game, 1929

Dalí's painting presents a theatre of uncanny desires and 'perversions' in fantastic detail, from the shameful masturbating monument with outstretched hand, to the ascending explosion where a chalice and anus are juxtaposed, to the grasshopper at the mouth of the profiled face, to the self-portrait with soiled schoolboy pants in the lower right corner.

it tells us that Surrealist art not only reveals the artist's desires and fears but the spectator's too, which come to light as we are forced to work out the meaning of an image.

In Dalí's small painting *The Lugubrious Game* (1929) **[43]** we find the marriage of personal memory and sexual taboo again. The painting depicts a veritable orgy of sexual signs and symbols: masturbation (the outstretched hand of the statue), coprophilia (the soiled pants of the young male in the right corner, possibly a self-portrait), Oedipal desire (in the form of the languid female head in the top centre), oral phobias (the grasshopper nibbling at the female's mouth), and metamorphosis (the whole central configuration—from the violently red buttocks at the foot of the steps to the head in profile and hand behind it—takes on the shape of an ass's head). Even the smallest details abound with sexual symbolism, such as the ear of the rabbit (above the eye of the head in profile and beside the colourful parrot), which morphs into a vaginal slit; while others blasphemously juxtapose the sacred and the profane, notably the chalice and host with an anus in the dream-like swirl to the top of the composition. The painting also relates to the return of repressed memory too. In the lower right corner we see a naked figure burying his head—which has a disturbing vaginal slit into which he sticks a finger—on the shoulder of a man in schoolboy trousers. The man's trousers are soiled and in his hand we see a bloody rag. A perfect Oedipal scenario is here staged: the child-man fears castration (symbolized by the bloody rag he holds and by the vaginal slit in the naked figure's head) while his fear and loathing for the father-figure—who must be overcome within the Oedipal scenario due to the boy's sexual desire for the mother—is indicated in his defecation. The symbolism may be traced to Dalí's childhood too. For his boyhood vision of his father was disturbingly tarnished one day when his father arrived home in a taxi and proclaimed to his family, who had rushed out to greet him, 'I've crapped'![8] His father's lack of shame only augmented the young Dalí's. This multifaceted painting is all the more impressive and erotic when we consider its small, intimate size (44 × 30 cm), which demands a close inspection from the spectator. His painting won Dalí a place in the Surrealist movement in 1929.

Sade Is 'Surrealist in Sadism'

Dalí's *The Lugubrious Game* also enflamed a debate about eroticism between Breton and the writer Georges Bataille, who described himself as 'Surrealism's old enemy from within'. In an essay of December 1929, Bataille wrote that he admired the 'terrible ugliness' of Dalí's painting, and compared it to the brutal despair of the Marquis de Sade as he screamed to rioters from his cell in the Bastille.[9] In contrast, Breton preferred to think of taboo in terms of its transgression, accusing Bataille in the 'Second Manifesto of Surrealism' in 1930 of being an 'excremental' philosopher, and insisting that Sade and his taboo-ridden sexual tracts were not about the body but the mind. Sade had to be understood as a revolutionary, one who strove 'to try to make the human mind get rid of its chains'.[10]

Sadean desire was key to Surrealism's radical use of eroticism, as indicated in the first manifesto's assertion that the Marquis de Sade was 'Surrealist in sadism'. In his novel *Liberty or Love* (1927), the French Surrealist writer Robert Desnos describes Sade as a 'hero of love, of generosity and of liberty'.[11] Equally, André Masson, a fellow Frenchman who is often referred to as a dissident or vagabond Surrealist, was particularly fascinated by the themes of Sadean transgression. In 1928, he illustrated a luxury edition of Sade's *Justine* (1791), a notorious novel that graphically recounts the sexual education of a young convent girl. Sade wrote an early version of the novel while imprisoned in the Bastille and completed it in 1791 while free. In Sade's philosophy God is evil and the sexual violence suffered by the virtuous Justine is a result of denying this truth. In the sequel *Juliette* (1798), the heroine is Justine's sister, who has no virtue and so enjoys the delights of sexual evil. Masson does not spare the viewer in his drawings for *Justine*: in one, a naked female hangs from the ceiling, her hands bound and her neck broken; in another a heroic, naked male with engorged penis beats several naked women with his bloody whip. Their cutout forms rotate around him adding an almost filmic motion, and certainly a Sadean syntax of breathless excess, to the image **[44]**. It is not surprising that these images of *Justine* were deemed by the commissioning publisher, Pascal Pia, to be too great a legal risk for publication. Masson's graphic interpretation of Sade was not published until 1961, when he illustrated a German edition of Sade's work, *Im Namen der Republik*. Masson's focus on the theme of sexual torture and sacrifice (he also did a series of images on the theme of *Massacres* from 1930 to 1934, in which men kill women and sometimes young boys with orgiastic pleasure), also related to his involvement with Bataille's more extreme projects, such as the journal *Acéphale*, published by a secret society of the same name between 1936 and 1939, which exhibited a fascination with sacrificial desire and castration—fascinations which were predominantly played out on the female object.

Sade's writings provided a catalogue of sexual abnormalities for Surrealist artists to try to visualize; just as Sade thought of the unthinkable—not to mention often the physically impossible—when it came to orgies, giving form to his Sadean world was a challenge to the imagination and brush. Yet they also recognized that Sade presaged many of Freud's theories in presenting sexual desire as determined from childhood practice, and all familial relationships as having a sexual compo-

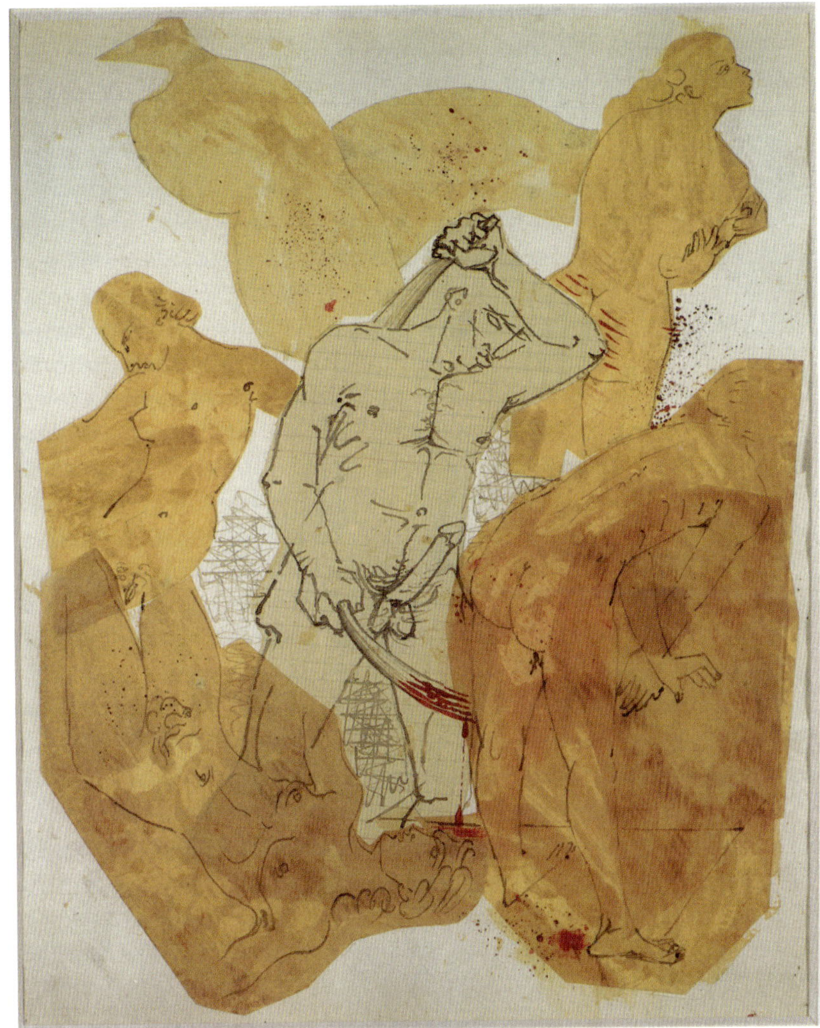

44 André Masson
Justine, 1928

Masson joined the Surrealist movement in 1925, and his art frequently displayed his fascination not just with erotic metamorphosis but also with Sadean terror. His images for an edition of the Marquis de Sade's novel *Justine* (1791) were deemed by the editor Pascal Pia to be too great a legal risk for publication.

nent. Their appreciation of Sade was ultimately philosophical and similar to that of contemporary writer Maurice Blanchot:

> We do not claim that [Sade's] thought can be lived out. But it shows us one thing: of the two, the normal person, who confines the Sadic person to a dead-end, and the Sadic individual, who converts that dead-end into a route of escape, it is the latter who grasps the [truth and] logic of his situation and possesses the deeper insights into it, and these enable him to help the normal person understand himself by assisting him in altering the conditions of all understanding.[12]

Dalí had a particular fascination with erotic, Sadean taboo. In his erotic text *The Visible Woman* (1930), he wrote that he considered perversion and vice as the most revolutionary forms of thought and activity; in another, *Reverie* (1931), a fantastic tale of sex and sodomy involving the 11-year-old Dulita, her mother, and an old prostitute (based on one of his own particularly impressive masturbation experiences), he again promoted the Sadean belief in the revolutionary potential of perverse desire. His films *Un Chien Andalou* (1929) and *L'Age d'or* (1930), made with fellow Spaniard Luis Buñuel, also explored passion, *amour fou* (mad love), and taboo with Sade-inspired flair, all the time recognizing the dream-like potential and structure of the moving image. The former, a 16-minute silent film, opens with an assault on the viewer and the genre of romantic films in showing a young man slicing his lover's eye—a close-up of a cut and subsequent oozing of gelatinous liquid brutally symbolizes castration while traumatizing the viewer.[13] The later film, 63 minutes long with sound, also 'documents' the story of two lovers, showing their transgressive battle against the institutions of State, Family, and Church. Buñuel and Dalí ensure the audience in a dark movie theatre are kept on the edge of their seats by juxtaposing bizarre images of the lovers wrestling in mud with a flushing toilet, the Pope with a plough (both of which are thrown out a window), a female servant on fire with aristocrats sipping sherry, and a young woman with a classical statue whose toe she lustfully sucks.[14] *L'Age d'or* was sponsored by the aristocratic patron Charles de Noailles (whose wife Marie Laure was a descendant of Sade), and the film's epilogue paid homage to Sade in a series of shots of a snowy chateau where four godless libertines have come for 120 days of orgies. The chateau is a replica of Sade's chateau at Silling in his erotic novel *120 Days of Sodom* but Dalí lends a particularly Catholic flavour to his homage—the film ends with the image of the remnants of a martyr's tortured body, Sade's libertine Duke de Blangis appearing as a white-robed Jesus Christ, and a cross with victims' scalps blowing in the wind. It is little wonder that the film caused havoc when it was shown at Studio 28 in Paris in November 1930. Six days after it opened, the film's screening was sabotaged by Right-wing protesters: the Camelots du Roi, the Jeunesses Patriotiques, and the Right-wing press stampeded the cinema, threw ink at the screen, fired guns, and slashed the Surrealist canvases by Yves Tanguy, Dali, Miró, and Man Ray that hung in the foyer. The Chief of Police, Monsieur Chiappe, decided to withdraw the film's licence as a result. For fifty years *L'Age d'or* could only be viewed in private screenings and cinemas. It would only go on public release in New York in 1980 and in Paris in 1981. Buñuel and Dalí, like the Surrealists, had deliberately provoked scandal, seeing it as a potent agent for revelation and revolution.

For Freud, man had a natural inclination towards sadism, a natural

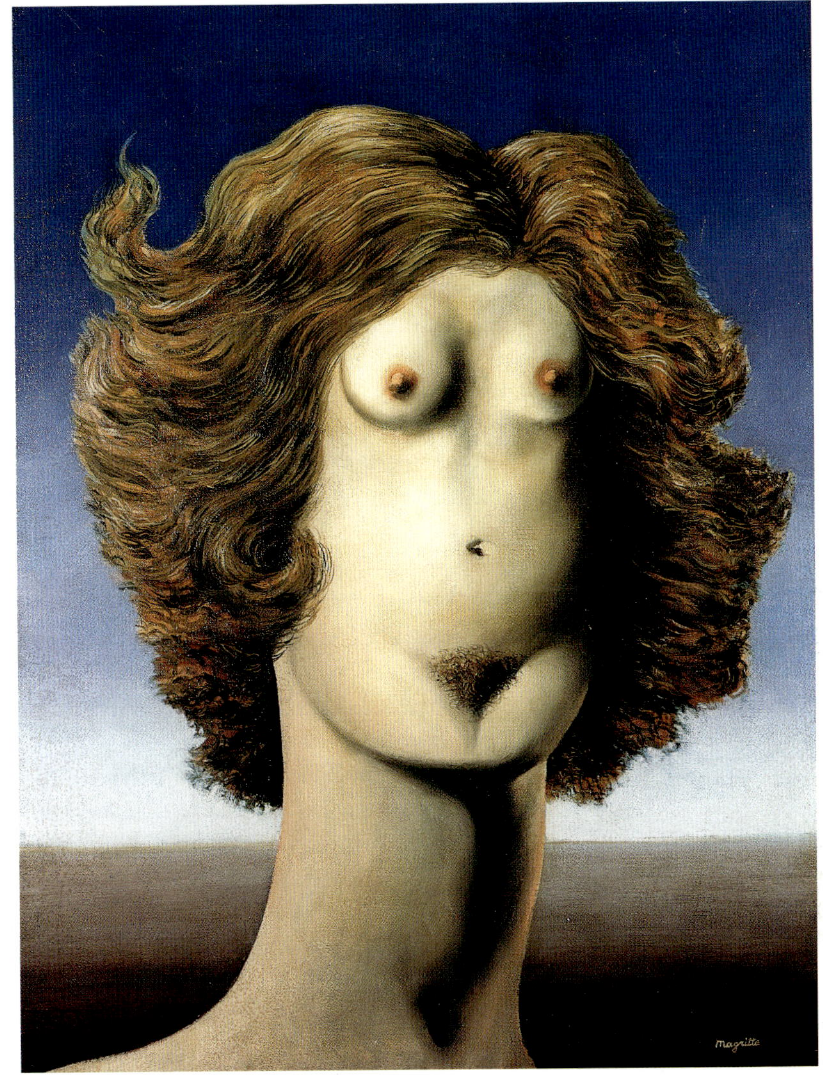

45 René Magritte
The Rape, 1934
The French title of this painting, *Le Viol*, reveals its many layers: punning on *viol* (rape) and *viole* (the viol), and *jouer au violon* (to play the fiddle, a euphemism for masturbation). André Breton indicated it was exemplary of Surrealism's assault on bourgeois art and society when he chose Magritte's drawing of it for the cover of the 1934 pamphlet *What Is Surrealism?*

desire to subjugate women (and by extension he claimed all women were natural masochists). Magritte's *The Rape* (1934) **[45]** gives form to this psychology as he literally projects male violent desire on to the face of a woman, conflating her facial and sexual features. The French title of this painting, *Le Viol*, puns on *viol* (rape) and *viole* (the viol), teasing out the idea that woman can be sexually 'played'. as well as the French expression for masturbation, *jouer au violon* (to play the fiddle).[15] It may also allude to the contemporary case of Violette Nozières who, having suffered her father's incestuous desires, poisoned him. In December 1933, the Surrealists published a collection of poems and illustrations in support of Violette Nozières's parricide. They perceived her revolt as one against bourgeois conformity and restrictions: Éluard, for example, hailed her as a girl dreaming of 'beautiful dresses of pure blood' (*belles robes de sang pur*), free from the father-figure.[16] A comparison might be drawn between Magritte's *The Rape* and Balthus's (Balthazar, the Comte de Rola, 1908–2001) painting *The Guitar Lesson*, also of 1934 and in a similar academic style. In this painting, a female music tutor seated by a piano simultaneously punishes and fondles a young girl who is stretched out on her lap so that her dress is lifted, exposing her prepubescent, naked sex. The tutor pulls her hair and touches her inner thigh, suggesting she is tuning and strumming the girl as if a guitar. The girl in turn tweaks her tutor's right nipple, her guitar fallen to the floor. Balthus here also puns on the idea of the female body as musical instrument while exploiting the thrill of erotic violence done to woman, in this case a young girl. Yet Balthus also updates and perverts a religious image in this work, notably the *Pietà of Villeneuve-les-Avignons* (*c.*1470), where the Madonna and dead Christ adopt a similar position. Balthus liked to borrow compositions from art history and erotically update them for ultimate scandalous effect. There is something 'cruel' about Balthus's art, as Antonin Artaud recognized in his 1934 review of Balthus's first solo exhibition at the Galerie Pierre in Paris: 'It makes sex inviting, but does not disguise its dangers.'[17] The power of such cruel eroticism disturbs even today. Balthus's addition of two further taboos—lesbianism and paedophilia—to his image of violent eroticism, caused alarm then, no doubt drawing the attention of many a Surrealist. Furthermore, when it was exhibited at the Galerie Pierre it was displayed in a room of its own, augmenting its erotic potential and the theme of aggressive sexual initiation for the spectator. Magritte's *The Rape* revels in a similar cruel frisson through shock. His depiction of the female nude is not only startling, it also fuses sexual parts: he portrays the female's neck in an elongated, shadowed manner so that it takes on a phallic nature while also allowing her pubic hair to suggest a goatee beard. In this way he seems to refer again to Freudian psychoanalysis, alluding to the fear of castration behind the fetish. Magritte's provocative externalization of unconscious desire was so appreciated by Breton that he used Magritte's drawing of *The Rape* as the cover of his 1934 pamphlet *What Is Surrealism?*

Negrophilia and Surrealist Photography

A different form of eroticism—a veiled, 'primitive' eroticism—emerged in Surrealist photography, notably in the art of Man Ray. Man Ray, who had befriended Duchamp in New York, came to Paris in 1921 and was particularly influenced by the 'negrophilia' (from the French, *negrophilie,* a love of black culture) then burgeoning in Parisian art circles due to the presence and influence of the ideas, art, and music of self-exiled African-Americans. They brought to Paris aspects of the African-American cultural movement that became known as 'The New Negro Movement' (later as the 'Harlem Renaissance') that started in the major cities of the United States (Chicago, New York, Washington DC) from *c.*1926–30. This was a cultural and political movement founded on a celebration of what sociologist and critic Alain LeRoy Locke termed, in his anthology of fiction, poetry, drama, and essays of the same name published in 1925, 'The New Negro'. Prominent Harlem Renaissance figures included the writers Zora Neale Hurston and Nella Larsen, the musician Duke Ellington, and the painters Aaron Douglas (1898–1979), William H. Johnson (1901–70), and Loïs Mailou Jones (b. 1905). Loïs Mailou Jones spent many years in Paris where she succeeded in marrying African 'authenticity' with Parisian 'negritude' in many of her works, as in her Surrealist-like oil painting *The Fetishes* (1938), where tribal masks take on a ritualistic, magical power. Perhaps the most famous Harlem Renaissance figure in Paris, however, was the singer and performer Josephine Baker. She drew crowds to the jazz spots of Montmartre and Montparnasse, and her performances—including such acts as the *Danse Sauvage* and the *Revue Nègre* in the Théâtre des Champs-Elysées (acts which travelled to London and Berlin too)—led to her erotic nicknames 'Black Venus', 'Black Pearl', and 'Creole Goddess'. Indeed, the impact of Baker in Europe was perhaps best expressed by a German correspondent's report on the *Revue Nègre* in 1926:

> The negroes are conquering Paris. They are conquering Berlin. They have already filled the whole continent with their howls, with their laughter . . . All of Europe is Dancing to their banjo. It cannot help itself . . . There are eight beautiful girls whose figures conjure up a stylized purity, reminiscent of deer and Greek youths. And at their head, the star, Josephine Baker. They have all oiled their curly hair smooth with a process just invented in New York . . . They dance a dance one might expect in a lunatic asylum.[18]

The correspondent fantasizes that these girls might be out of a New York ghetto or might be drawing on their family memories of slave labour; certainly their challenge to the sexual morality of Europe thrills him.

The Surrealists were undoubtedly equally thrilled but they were also artistically inspired by such performances when it came to their own erotic tactics. Their exposure to black culture came through their mentor, the poet and critic Guillaume Apollinaire (who first coined the term 'surreal' in his play *Les Mamelles de Tirésias*, 1917, set in a fictitious town called Zanzibar) and through Jacques Doucet, the fashion mogul and collector of art (including African art and 'black deco'), who would support Breton in his first years as a poet in Paris. Of course the Surrealists were also friendly with Pablo Picasso, whose *Les Demoiselles d'Avignon* (1907) **[27]** had been purchased by Doucet in the early 1920s and who allowed them reproduce the painting in their review *La Révolution Surréaliste* in 1925.

Man Ray's 1920s series of photographs of his lover Kiki indicate how the Surrealists were influenced by the 'negritude' movement of 1920s Paris. For Kiki was an exotic model known as 'Kiki de Montparnasse' (*kiki* is slang for vagina) and effectively a white Josephine Baker. In Man Ray's photographs of Kiki she is fashioned 'in a way both primitive and knowing', as Mary Ann Caws has said.[19] Born Alice Prin in 1901 in the Burgundy region, Kiki was 21 when she became Man Ray's lover and model. He photographed her as an exotic and erotic object of desire, either mirroring her mask-like face with a primitive mask, or photographing her naked in the 'wild' countryside. Artist and model also collaborated on a series of pornographic photographs, including one image of her cupid-bow lips on his erect penis. This image, and other explicitly sexual photographs, were published in *1929*, a collection of texts by Benjamin Péret and Louis Aragon, edited by André Breton. Photography offered the Surrealists a means to shock the public, whether through frank images of real sexual acts, or veiled or primitive eroticism. It allowed for what Rosalind Krauss has termed the 'fetishization of reality'—in other words, it was a means of stopping, framing, spacing society so that banal objects or body parts or a naked body took on a new poetic, erotic significance.[20] We see this more subtle fetishization in Man Ray's *Anatomies* (1929), where an outstretched woman's neck is photographed in such a way as to play with our sense of scale and so that a sexually neutral body part takes on the form of a majestic phallus.

This play with woman-as-phallus continued in Man Ray's series of photographs of the Swiss-born artist Meret Oppenheim, entitled *Veiled Erotic* (1933) **[39]**. Taken in the studio of painter Louis Marcoussis (who appears in some of the photographs wearing a bowler hat and false beard), we find Man Ray and Oppenheim collaborating on a series of erotic fantasies, each staged so that erotic roles—between woman as object and subject of the camera's gaze—are teased out. In one, we see Oppenheim framed as erotic object: her hands are smeared with black ink evoking tribal war paint, her boyish haircut and slim figure giving

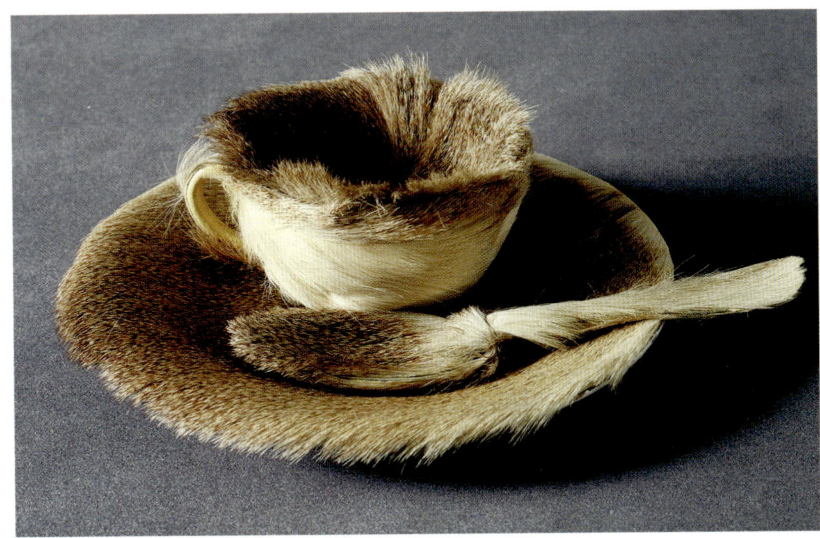

46 Meret Oppenheim
Object (Le Déjeuner en fourrure), 1936
The Swiss-born artist Oppenheim here transformed everyday household objects into exotic fetishes through the addition of fur, suggesting bestial sexuality and the sensual pleasure of the female sex (the open cup recalls Freud's description of the female sex as a vessel). The *Object* was first exhibited at the *Surrealist Exhibition of Objects* at the Galerie Charles Ratton, 14 rue Marignan, Paris, 22–29 May 1936, and purchased by Alfred H. Barr Jr for the Museum of Modern Art, New York, where it caused quite a scandal that year.

her a boyish or androgynous edge, while she stands in such a way that the handle of a printing press acts as a substitute phallus. In 1934, Breton cropped this image for an article on 'convulsive beauty' in the Surrealist journal *Minotaure*. Despite this, his very choice of the image, where woman as a naive primitive force is emphasized in her 'imprinted' hand and totemic presence, indicates the powerful role the primitive and photography had for the Surrealists' view of erotic desire. Interestingly, when Oppenheim herself later commented on this photographic collaboration with Man Ray, she insisted her role had always been as muse: 'He was the boss.'[21] Yet her Surrealist sculptures indicate her knowing subversion of traditional gender roles and her insistence on female erotic power too. In her 1936 *Object (Breakfast in Fur)* **[46]** she turns banal everyday things—a cup, saucer, and spoon—into an erotic object through the fetishistic association between fur and a woman's sex, and woman and the maternal breast (the taking of nourishment). It was inspired by a conversation in a café with Pablo Picasso and Dora Maar in which her friends admired her fur-covered bracelet, and by her own surreal response to their waiter when he offered her more coffee: she asked for a little more fur. Oppenheim's object merges the domestic and the erotic, and their compatibility, in woman. The once-neutral cup becomes a symbol of the female sex, and drinking from it a symbol of oral sex. André Breton named it, punning on Manet's *Déjeuner sur l'herbe* (1863) and Leopold von Sacher-Masoch's erotic novel *Venus in Furs* (1869). And yet one cannot help wanting to read the work as a teasing reproach to Breton's voiced opinion on the female orgasm in the Surrealist group discussions on sexuality a few years earlier, when he confidently asserted: 'I believe that it is very rare for women to have orgasms through the use of lips and tongue on the clitoris. It's a very uncertain method unless other techniques are also used.'[22] *Breakfast in Fur* was exhibited at the 1936 exhibition of Surrealist objects at the Galerie Charles Ratton in Paris and became an icon of Surrealist audacity and women Surrealists' important role in the movement when it was purchased by Alfred H. Barr Jr. for the Museum of Modern Art, New York, that year.

Women Surrealists

While Surrealism has often been accused of misogyny due to its obsession with woman as erotic muse and object, it is important to realize that women Surrealists were equally fascinated with all the aspects of Surrealist discourse already discussed, from the Marquis de Sade to photography and non-Western cultures.[23] The Czech woman Surrealist known as Toyen (1902–80; in 1926 she abandoned her birth name, Marie Čermínová, for this gender-neutral pseudonym), produced erotic imagery that is startling and yet wickedly funny in its sexual explicitness. She was a member of the Surrealist group in Prague founded by the poet Vítězslav Nezval in 1934. Other members of the group included Jindřich Heisler (1914–53) and Jindřich Štyrský (1899–1942), both of whom shared her penchant for the erotic.

Štyrský founded and published *Erotiká Revue* from 1930 to 1933. It brought a limited number of copies of European erotic texts to its subscribers, including extracts from Louis Aragon's *Le Con d'Irène* (1928) and Georges Bataille's *L'Histoire de l'œil* (1928). It could not be sold publicly or distributed as its contents broke with Czech obscenity laws due to its erotic drawings (including some by Aubrey Beardsley and Štyrský himself), erotic stories, essays on Freud's theories, and extracts from the Parisian Surrealist group's investigations into sexuality. Štyrský also founded a publishing house in 1931 to publish erotic texts, fittingly called *Edition 69* (each publication had a print run of 69 copies). Through their publishing house the Czech Surrealists promoted 'pansexuality' and 'pornophilia', believing that 'the artist emancipates the acts of the body from their biological purpose' and that 'Asceticism, any sort of renunciation of our sexuality, is indefensible.'[24] In 1932, Štyrský translated the Marquis de Sade's *Justine* for this luxury series of texts, and it was illustrated by Toyen.

In one of Toyen's illustrations for *Justine* (1930) she depicts a bound naked torso with whipped bleeding flanks from behind, juxtaposed with the face of a man with bright-red lips. Toyen's image is strong in its

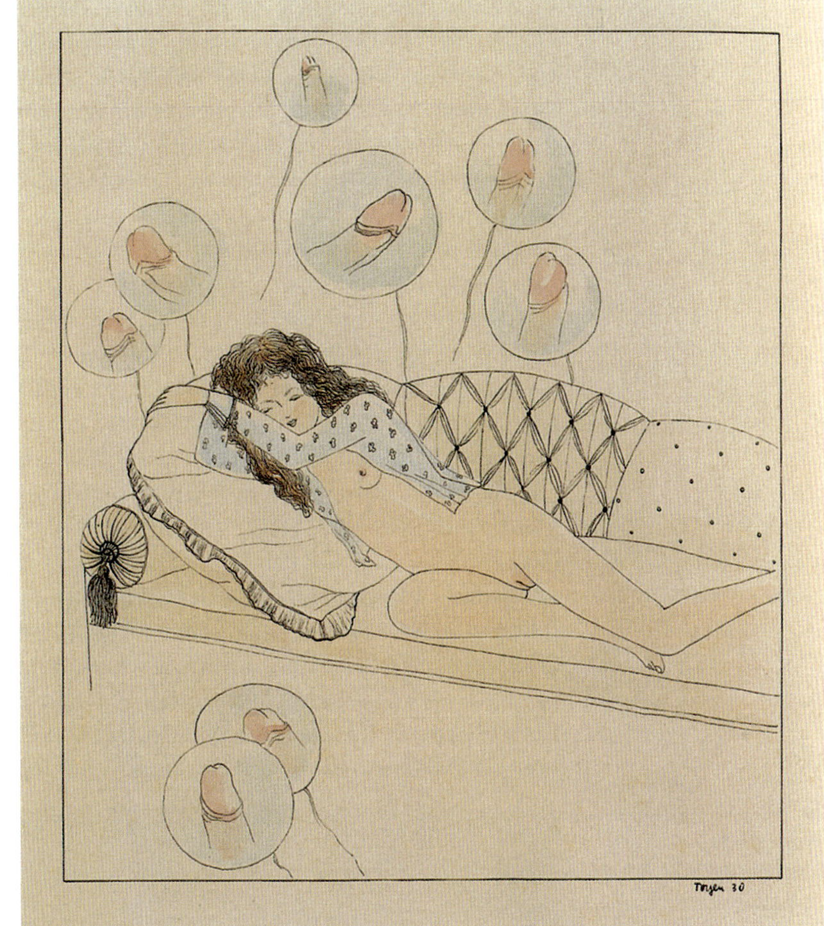

47 Toyen (Marie Čermínová)
Young Girl Who Dreams, 1930

From 1929 on, Toyen's art became increasingly erotic in subject-matter. In 1930 she began producing erotic drawings for her fellow Czech Surrealist Jindřich Štyrský's *Revue érotique*, and in 1932 she illustrated Sade's novel *Justine*. This work exemplifies her sense of erotic humour and fantasy, offering a wonderfully Sadean vision of the emancipated young woman.

controlled violence; it is the antithesis of Masson's manic illustrations for the same text. A second illustration by Toyen for *Justine* is equally simple in form and yet complex in message: a female blocks her eyes as a mammoth penis projects into the central space of the picture. Both drawings are calm renderings of the orgies described in *Justine*. In both images the eyes of the victim are blocked, so that the viewer cannot indulge in her fearful expression, nor in her masochistic pleasure. When viewed alongside another watercolour drawing from 1930, entitled *Young Girl Who Dreams* **[47]**, we see that Toyen was keen to represent female erotic fantasy in her art. She depicts a young girl stretched out on her chaise longue, asleep and smiling, as she dreams of sex, as indicated by the disembodied erect penises that float around her. Toyen also turned to eroticism as a means of voicing her political dissent during the war. Her painting *Rest* (1943) shows a young girl hanging upside-down on a beam, her frilly blue dress falling to reveal her equally pretty knickers, her feet dissolving into a rusty, stained wall, as one hand clings to a rail. A riding crop and a black bag in the foreground lend the image a particularly macabre air, as if symbolizing a beating and the muffling of cries or suffocation. Painted during the war and never shown since Surrealism was one of the degenerate art movements attacked by the Nazis, this painting might be interpreted as a symbolic representation of the abuse of power at a time when the artist's country was being victimized by a brutal war machine.

Other women artists to turn to erotic symbolism as a means of addressing the subject of power included English-born artist Leonora Carrington (b. 1917). She met Max Ernst at an exhibition of his paintings in London in 1937 and soon became his lover (albeit briefly, as the outbreak of the war led to Ernst's arrest as a German 'alien' in France in 1939 and her subsequent move to Spain and mental collapse).[25] One painting in particular, *Self-Portrait (The Inn of the Dawn Horse)* (1937) **[48]**, reminds us of Carrington's independent artistic and sexual spirit. Carrington portrays her erotic force through animal symbolism. In the painting, Carrington is sitting on an elegant armchair in a large room, wearing white jodhpurs, a green jacket, and high-heeled boots. Behind her we see a rocking horse, through the window a galloping horse; to her side we see a hyena bitch with pronounced teats. Carrington's wild mane of hair links her to the two horses in the image, while her intense

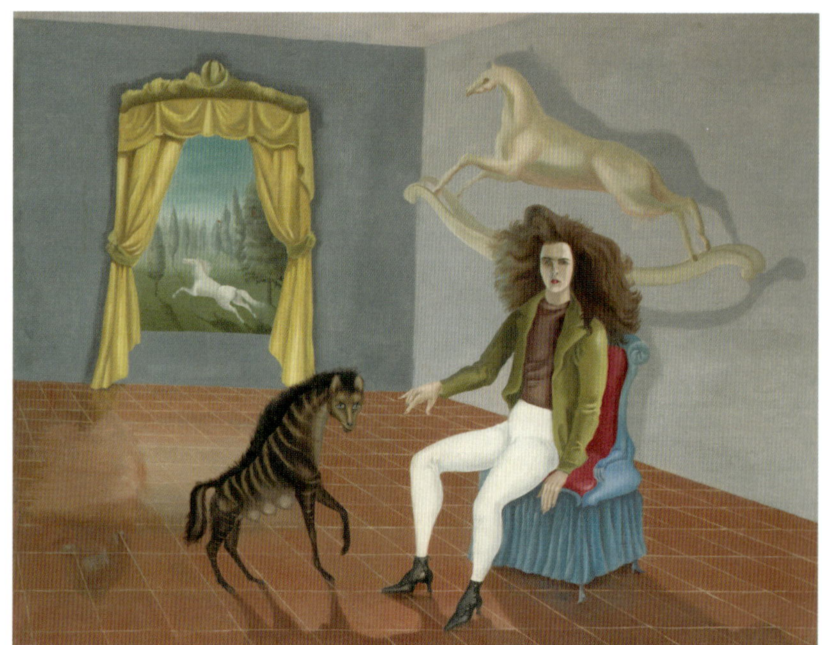

48 Leonora Carrington
Self-Portrait (The Inn of the Dawn Horse), 1937–8

Many women Surrealists turned to the self-portrait as a means of self-exploration. Carrington's self-portrait reveals aspects of her family background and her quest for artistic and sexual liberation: the Victorian chair on which she sits has begun to metamorphose into female legs, the ornate interior opens onto a garden of unbridled emotion (symbolized by the running horse), and her childhood rocking horse, suspended on the wall, seems to be about to take flight too.

expression links her to the bold hyena. The painting also relates to 'The Debutante' (1937–8), a short story by Carrington. In this story a young society girl befriends a hyena at the zoo and asks the hyena to take her place at a debutante ball her mother is organizing. The hyena agrees, returns home with the girl, and sets about disguising herself for the social event. She devours the girl's nursemaid, Mary, so that she can use her face as a mask at the ball. The debutante, happy that her hyena friend is taking her place at the ball, stays in her bedroom reading Swift's *Gulliver's Travels* and wallowing in her liberty. Her peace lasts only an hour, however, as her mother soon rushes to her room in a fury: the hyena not only filled the dining room with a strong stench, she tore off her borrowed face, wolfing it down in front of the startled guests before bounding out the window. The hyena symbolizes not only the young woman's desire for freedom but also her untamed, sexual self.[26]

A similar theme emerges in another story, 'The Oval Lady', shedding further light again on Carrington's animal symbolism in the painting as indicative of the threat untamed, bestial sexuality poses to 'civilized' society. In this story, a young girl, Lucretia, defies her nanny by playing with her rocking horse, Tartar, only to have it burnt by her father as punishment. She hides outside the nursery as he burns her horse; she hears 'the most frightful neighing . . . as if an animal were suffering extreme torture'.[27] Undoubtedly, the horse, like the hyena, is a symbol of Carrington's unbridled desire, her creative energy, and determination.

Women Surrealists often turned to animal symbolism in their art as a means of drawing on matriarchal, indigenous, or shamanic myth, and thus of empowering their self-image as woman and artist. Leonora Fini (1908–96) turned to the cat as her ideal leonine self and lover, often portraying herself—and woman in general—as a sphinx, as in *Little Hermit Sphinx* (1948), where a sphinx guards the entrance to an old ruin, the traces of her recent male victim (perhaps a male trying to solve the 'riddle of the sphinx'?) scattered around her—broken egg shells, a triangle, a bone. The sphinx's ultimate pleasure seems to lie in the kill. Frida Kahlo (1907–54), the Mexican artist claimed by Breton as a Surrealist when he met her in 1938 (though she always insisted it was her life—not her art—that was Surrealist), makes more subtle allusions to her sexual pleasures. In *Me and My Parrots* (1941), Kahlo depicts herself with four parrots, possibly alluding to Hindu imagery, where they are symbols of love. At the time Kahlo was enjoying a love affair with the portrait photographer Nickolas Murray despite having married Mexican muralist Diego Rivera for the second time the year before.

Finally, Claude Cahun (1894–1954), a writer, translator, actress, photographer, and lesbian, offers a remarkable final commentary on sex and society in the inter-war period, as well as making an interesting comparison with Duchamp's Rrose Sélavy, Bellmer's dolls, and Man Ray's Kiki. In her series of photographic self-portraits, Cahun not only 'masters' her own image through her rejection of gender stereotype, she forces us to rethink our very understanding of the fixed art image through her frequent superimpositions of image on image, suggesting a Baudrillardian precession of simulacra decades before postmodernism. Born Lucy Schwob into a literary family in Nantes, she enacted a textual cross-dressing by changing her name—adopted from the rabbinical class, as opposed to her father's similarly Jewish but more 'cultured' name—to Claude Cahun at the age of 23.[28] She continued to explore issues of gender identity in her photographs and photomontages, moving to Paris in 1922 where she lived in Montparnasse with her step-sister, lover, and sometimes collaborator Suzanne Malherbe. Malherbe was a successful graphic artist often publishing under the pseudonym Marcel Moore, and was described by Cahun as 'the other me'. In Paris, Cahun also performed in male and female roles in the avant-garde Theatre of Dramatic Research: this theatricality and fascination with performativity is evident in her art and writing. In *Self-Portrait* of 1928 **[49]**, she presents us with a double portrait in which she is both androgynous and assertive as she returns the gaze of the viewer. Here she not only advanced Duchamp's explorations of trans-gendering, she

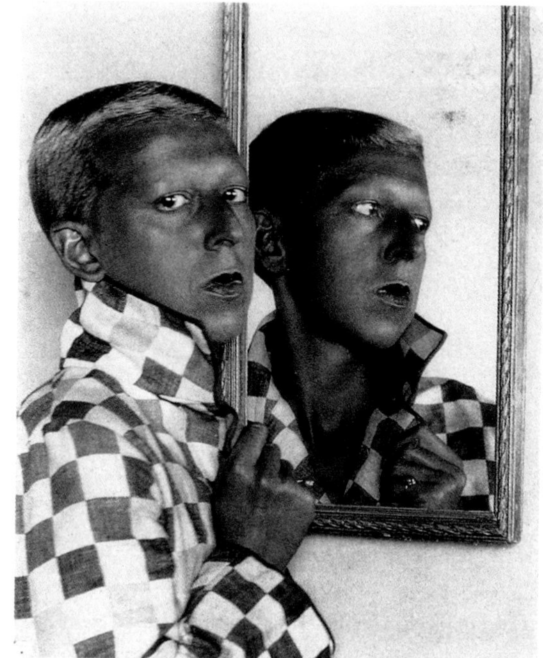

49 Claude Cahun (born Lucy Schwob)
Self-Portrait, *c.*1928

Cahun uses the medium of photography to explore gender as performance, her androgynous appearance and her position in front of a mirror creating a body 'double'. She questions the viewer's expectations of both gender codes and art as a mirror of nature while parodying Freud's equation of narcissism with homosexuality.

anticipates the art of contemporary American photographer Cindy Sherman in her subversive engagement with the feminine 'masquerade'. 'Womanliness as a Masquerade' was the subject of a highly influential essay of 1929 by British analyst and translator of Freud, Joan Riviere, in which Riviere argued that women—particularly highly successful, intellectual women—often adopted the 'mask of femininity' (wearing very feminine clothes, make-up, etc.) to 'hide the possession of masculinity' and the reprisals and fear discovery (by men) would lead to.[29] In her prose-poem *Aveux non avenus* (1930), illustrated with a series of photographs and photomontages, Cahun most fully explores the sophisticated personal and political implications of androgyny and masquerade. Here she draws again on a theme at the forefront of debate in the 1920s—the third sex. In her subversive play with metamorphosis, photographing her many selves in various male, female, and androgynous guises, Cahun presents not just a lesbian voice but also one that defies categorization. In her writings she rhetorically asks 'Masculine? feminine? But that depends on the situation. Neuter is the only gender which always suits me.'[30] The same year as Riviere's essay, Cahun translated Havelock Ellis into French (*L'Hygiène sociale—I—La Femme dans la Société*). Drawing on his idea of 'sexual inversion' as a congenital condition, biologically predetermined rather than a sexual 'deviancy' or crime, it is more than probable that Cahun knowingly troubles sexual and gender identities in her art, informed by the contemporary debates on gender. Cahun never lets the spectator/reader rest easily; her work 'queers' heterosexual and homosexual eroticism and opens up a third avenue for looking. As one photomontage in *Aveux non avenus* reads, 'Under this mask, another mask, I will never finish lifting up all of these masks . . .' Cahun defied erotic expectations, perhaps aligning herself to Sappho, of whom she writes in *Heroines* (1925); she never loses her sense of humour, of theatricality, or provocation—in *Heroines* she also writes of Cinderella's handsome prince as having a foot fetish.[31] Her defiance extended beyond her art: she was an active member of the Association of Revolutionary Writers and Artists, through whom she met Breton in 1932; of Counter Attack, the group of Left-wing intellectuals formed round Georges Bataille in 1935–6; and of the Resistance in Jersey (where she moved to in 1937 and stayed until her death in 1954), only escaping death at the hands of the Germans thanks to the commuting of a death sentence to six years in prison and the liberation of the island from the Nazis. If the avant-garde insisted that art had to be politically engaged, then Cahun stands as testimony to the realization of that ambition.

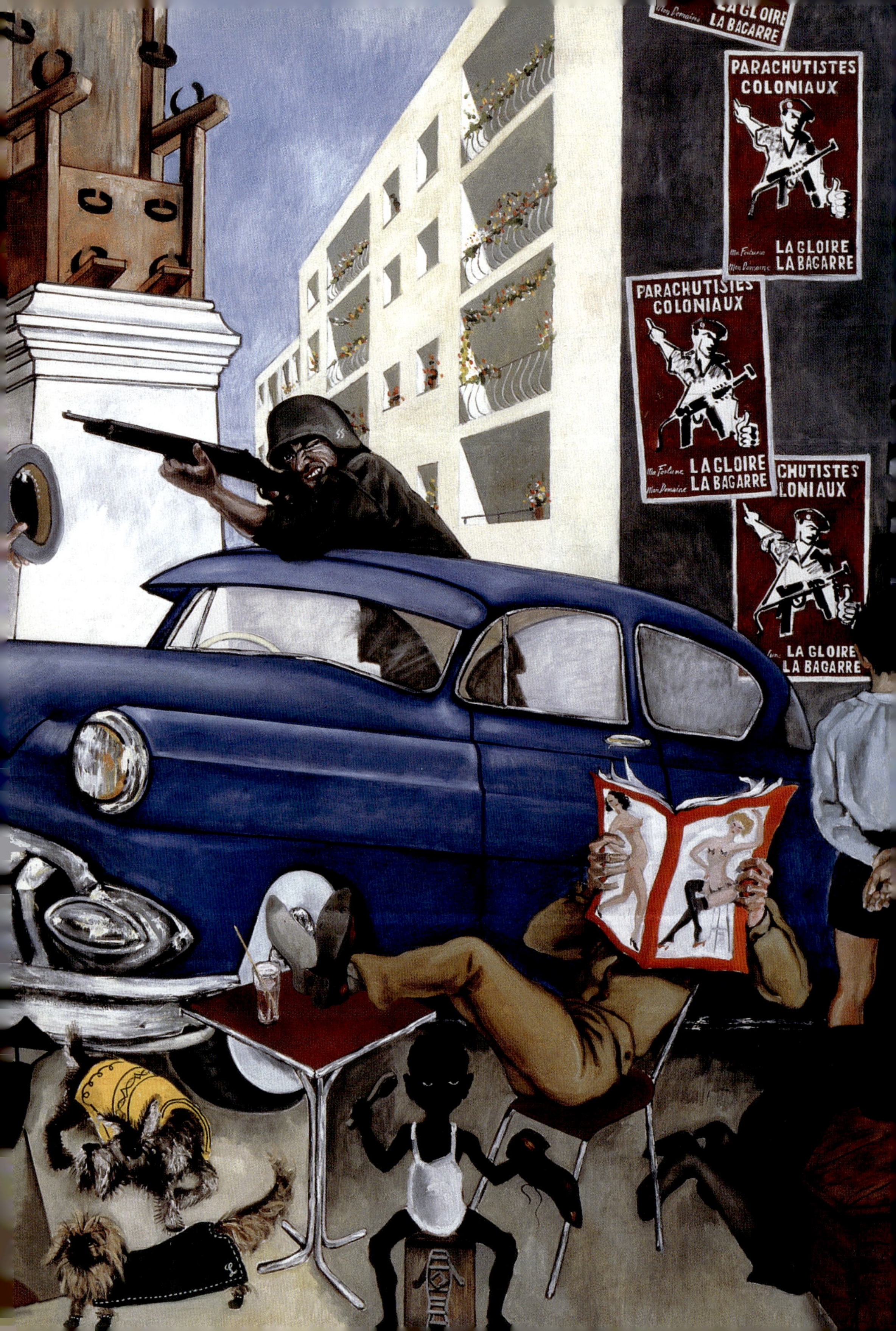
LA BAGARRE
PARACHUTISTES
COLONIAUX
LA GLOIRE
LA BAGARRE
PARACHUTISTES
COLONIAUX
LA GLOIRE
LA BAGARRE
CHUTISTES
LONIAUX
LA GLOIRE
LA BAGARRE

6

Erotic Art in Wartime and After

American artists flocked to Paris after World War I, but in 1939 European artists fled Europe for the United States. Among them were several of the artists already mentioned: George Grosz, John Heartfield, and Oskar Kokoschka, who fled Nazi Germany; and André Breton, André Masson, and Max Ernst, who quit Paris, via Marseilles, for New York. The Emergency Rescue Committee, which was set up under the patronage of Eleanor Roosevelt to rescue German refugees and Jewish and communist intellectuals from the Nazis, played an important role. The rescue was led by Varian Fry, a young American Quaker and ex-Harvard scholar in classics, who had travelled to Germany in 1935 and witnessed the Hitler regime first-hand. He led the rescue project from Marseilles from August 1940 to September 1941, organizing the escape of some 20,000 refugees.[1] The wealthy American art collector Peggy Guggenheim funded the safe passage for several of the Surrealists on Fry's list, notably Max Ernst, André Breton, his wife Jacqueline Lamba, and their daughter Aube. Surrealism's emigration to New York influenced generations of younger American artists and brought eroticism into the limelight in a country hitherto suffering from a veritable dearth of erotic art.

If Dada and Surrealism in Europe used eroticism as a critique or attack on society, especially on rising fascism, inter-war American art was far less erotic and controversial in tone and content. New York Dada did not affect Middle America; given that Picabia, Duchamp, and Man Ray were in Paris by the mid-1920s its impact was short-lived on the inter-war generation. It was of greater importance for post-war art thanks to individual artists' 'neo-Dadaist' styles, Robert Motherwell's 1951 anthology *The Dada Painters and Poets*, and Sidney Janis's 1953 'Dada 1916–23' exhibition in New York. Thus while Wisconsin-born Georgia O'Keeffe was part of the Dada milieu, not least thanks to her husband Alfred Stieglitz, she steered away from it to develop a highly individual style that was the very antithesis of Duchamp and Picabia's

Detail of 55

erotic humour. In her early work of the mid- to late 1920s she produced architectural and botanical paintings. In the former we find a stark rendition of modernist architecture in a series of cityscapes carried out in a Precisionist style that was also known as Cubist Realism. Yet given our, and O'Keeffe's, knowledge of Dada mechanico-erotics it is tempting to interpret geometric form as sexually symbolic. *City Night* (1926), where two black skyscrapers dominate the composition, soaring up to a blue sky, might be seen as a sexual landscape with male solids and female voids, and, by extension, as an ultimate celebration of a female gaze in an emphatically male environment.[2] This sexually symbolic reading of O'Keeffe's rendition of the architectural void may be extended to the more famous flower paintings she produced throughout her long and successful career, beginning with her first exhibition of them in New York in 1925. While they are undeniably captivating paintings when viewed as flowers, there is a latent erotic dimension to these works too. Open petals in luscious colours may be read as evocative of the male or female sex organ—as in *Iris* (1929) with its upright form, or *Grey Line with Black, Blue and Yellow* (1923) with its folding layers of pale colour which centre on a blue-black opening. Even if the latter is not read in terms of labial creases then it might be interpreted, more spiritually, as the symbolic expression of female sexuality and power. While O'Keeffe has denied such symbolism, stating 'Eroticism! That's something people themselves put in the paintings. They've found things that never entered my mind', in her art the flower is never just a flower: reality is not merely re-presented, it is heightened, magnified, given a pulsating quality through vibrant palettes, and is thus open to erotic interpretation.[3] There is something abstract about these flower studies due to the distortion of scale; something phenomenological, too, as they fill the frame. The sinuous lines of a flower opening out to the viewer may remind us of the beauty of nature in a modern and increasingly industrialized world, but to read it as a reminder of the beauty of the female sex—another gift of nature—may not be so far from the artist's original intent either.

As the effect of Dada wore off in New York, the rise of American Regionalism began, winning over popular opinion by the mid-1930s. The Regionalists promoted Midwestern rural America and revived landscape and portraiture as genres in their Social Realist style. The painter Thomas Hart Benton (1889–1975) is perhaps the best known of the Regionalists and serves as a useful reminder of mainstream America and why it was at odds with the avant-garde eroticism of Surrealism. Born in Missouri, Benton trained at the Art Institute of Chicago in 1907 before going to Paris to study for four years in 1908. By the late 1920s, his

Regionalist style was fully formed, his father's death in 1924 having rekindled his interest in rural America. He drew from the land and the people he saw as he travelled around the United States, documenting the rise of modernity and decline of old, communal ways. He also monumentalized everyday life and the nameless worker. Benton's *The Lord Is My Shepherd* (1926), a portrait of his elderly, deaf neighbours at Martha's Vineyard, George and Sabrina West, exemplifies his realist style in its celebration of rural America. While Benton initially had a leaning towards Marxism, by the mid-1930s his realist art would be denounced as Right-wing xenophobia by the artist Stuart Davis in the communist magazine *Art Front*. Davis claimed Benton's anti-modernist, anti-communist stance and his promotion of American nationalism, ruralism, and nostalgia in his art was fascist.[4] While Benton's art celebrates rural life and frequently resorts to stereotypes (racial as well as sexual), it cannot be compared to the fascist art we have seen, however. Davis's attack on him was largely in response to the cover story for the December 1934 (first-ever colour) edition of *Time* magazine, in which Benton and other Regionalists were hailed as a celebration of American life and an indication that American art need not look to Europe for innovative ideas and styles.[5] Benton was presented as quintessentially American—not unlike his most famous pupil, Jackson Pollock, whose Abstract Expressionist style would ironically not only be the very opposite of Benton's but would overshadow American Regionalism in the 1940s. While Benton's autobiography *An Artist in America* (1938) was a bestseller, it was his murals from the 1930s and early 1940s that won him such public attention at this period of American history. These included *America Today* (for the New School of Social Research in New York, 1930), *A Social History of Indiana* (for the State of Indiana's pavilion at the Chicago World's Fair, 1933) and *A Social History of Missouri* (for the House Lounge in the Missouri State Capitol Building, Jefferson City, 1935–6). His mural *America Today* exemplifies his monumental style: a rhythmic line allows heavily muscled men, machines, and modern women to be harmoniously linked and creates a sense of continuity between panels (the use of moulding in this mural also sets another rhythm and camouflages the boundaries between respective scenes). In the north wall section of the mural, *City Activities with Subway* (from *America Today*) (1930–1) **[50]**, we find every corner of modern American life portrayed in all its physical and erotic glory: from the music-hall girlies to the modern dame in a subway; from the sweaty bodies of two boxers to two young lovers kissing on a bench. A sign says 'God is love' but, unlike his earlier paintings, this religious wording is not genuine—this is a city, an 'America Today' of energy, lust, and technological

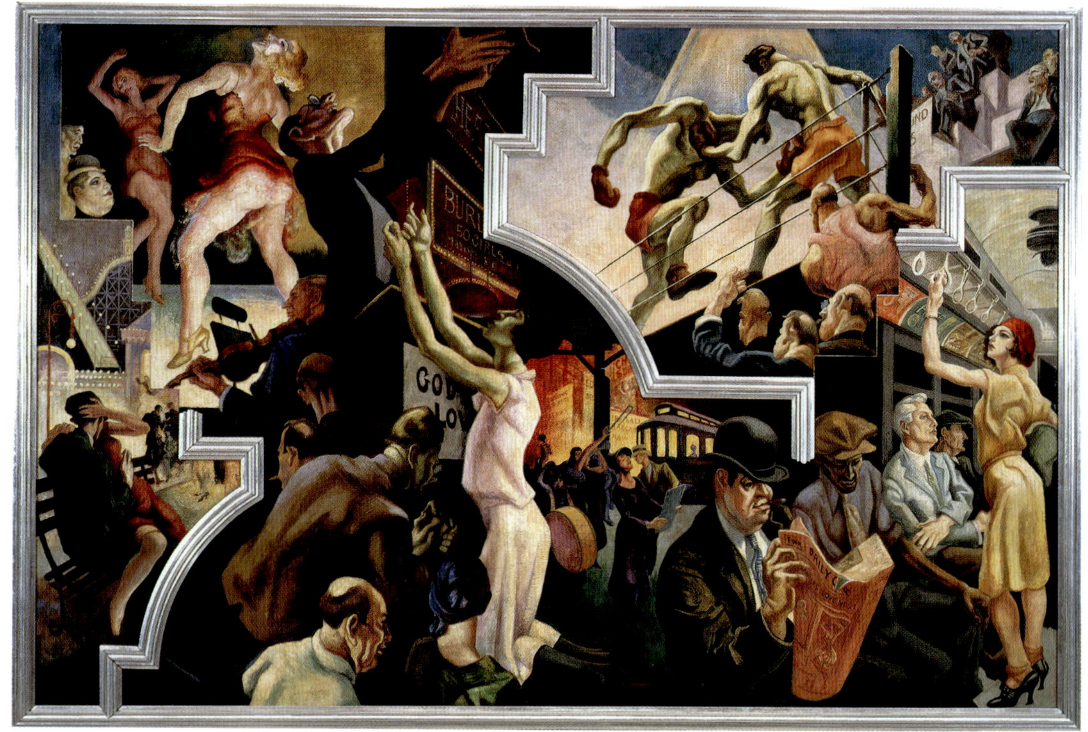

50 Thomas Hart Benton *City Activities with Subway* from *America Today*, 1930

Four years before he was celebrated in the first colour edition of *Time* magazine (December 1934), the Regionalist painter Benton portrays modern America in all its variety in this section of his monumental mural, *America Today*. From the urban sophisticate to the music hall performer and the pious wretch, Benton ingeniously interweaves vignettes of urban life through a sophisticated use of framing and moulding.

advance, albeit in caricature figures. When Benton applied his vernacular style to explicitly erotic subject-matter the board of Kansas City Art Institute (where he taught from 1935–41) were not so impressed, however. *Persephone* (1939), painted in egg tempera and oil on canvas, was a far cry from the heroic America of his monumental murals. It depicted a naked young woman reclining against a tree, her clothes and picnic basket discarded and a lecherous old man staring at her from behind the tree. While alluding to aspects of classical and modern art—most notably Renaissance images of the story of Susannah and the Elders (a theme he devoted a painting to in 1938) and Manet's controversial *Le Déjeuner sur l'herbe*, with its naked female picnicker in the foreground—Benton's caricature style was emphatically contemporaneous and thus somewhat shocking to Middle American audiences. His rendition of the old man, in particular, lent a humorous and everyday air to the painting, defying anyone to try to view the naked female in anything except lustful terms.

Angel's Flight (1931) by Californian artist Millard Sheets (1907–89) also represented the new modern America and the activities of its city dwellers. Los Angeles was the city to which many poor immigrants fled: Sheet's painting depicts the downtown working-class neighbourhood there known as Bunker Hill. Two young women stand on their balcony, looking down on a community below dominated by modern, impoverished women who gossip, hang out clothes, or climb the many steps of the stairway that runs alongside the Angel's Flight funicular railway. As Mike Davis describes them, they are 'streetwise but attractive "courtesans of the tenements" in casual conversation'. This is their 'erotic sanctuary' and as close 'to Montmartre as LA would ever get'.[6]

Sheets's painting was still a far cry from the glamour of the silver screen—the one place to find erotic escape in the 1930s. The public face of Los Angeles, notably Hollywood, displayed an abundance of visual beauty and decadence, free from toil, poverty, and rural life. Where fine art seemed to be striving for an authenticity and working-class nobility, Hollywood offered sex appeal and erotic allure in such stunning femme fatales as Joan Crawford and Greta Garbo. On the silver screen sexuality and visual pleasure could be indulged but always controlled. When the same—notably homoerotic—delights were expressed on American soil, consternation inevitably followed. *The Fleet's In!* (1934) **[51]** by Paul Cadmus (1904–99) caused a furore when it was exhibited at the Corcoran Gallery of Art in Washington in 1934. A New Yorker, Cadmus was employed by the Federal Art Project, specifically by the Public Works of Art Project (PWAP). The painting was meant to reflect the glory of American life. Instead it portrayed drunk and lecherous sailors having fun in Riverside Park in New York while on shore leave. The press delighted in the furore over the work (and its banishment from further public viewing due to the intervention of the Assistant Secretary to the Navy) and fuelled the fire by reproducing the work in its coverage. Cadmus not only presented five sailors and a marine in a debauched state, he showed them having their fun in front of eight civilians (seven females and one male); worse still, the sailors are shown grabbing the women. But it was not just their cavorting with women that seems to have insulted the

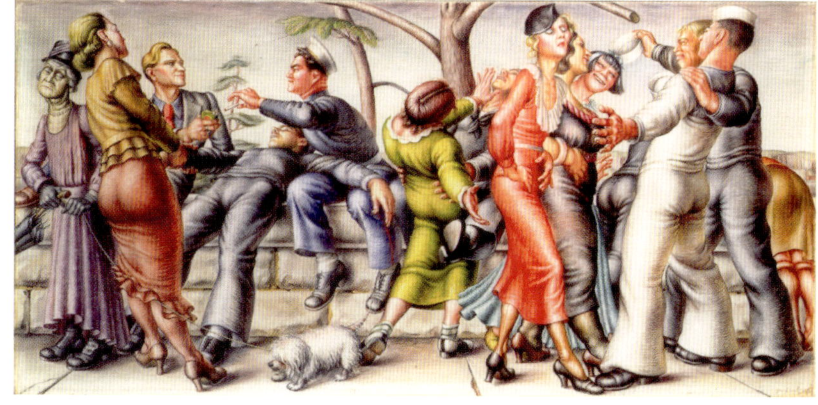

51 Paul Cadmus
The Fleet's In!, 1934

Cadmus's scene of five sailors and a marine enjoying their shore leave caused consternation when it was exhibited in Washington in 1934 due to its depiction of military men in a drunken, lecherous state. Cadmus's particular staging of his figures, which suggests anal desire by emphasizing their bulging buttocks, may also have led to the immediate censorship of the work.

navy. The men are all positioned in a composition that recalls a bas-relief in its horizontal, left-to-right framing device, with the men lined up in such a way that their tight trousers catch their firm buttocks; even the poses of the women emphasize 'an anal-erotic logic'.[7]

Cadmus was not alone in bringing homoeroticism into high art circles. He was a friend of the photographer George Platt Lynes (1907–55), who, along with Minor White (1908–77), played a major role in advancing homoerotic photography as art, influencing photographer Robert Mapplethorpe years later. For example, Lynes exhibited in the first exhibition to include photography at MoMA New York in 1932, and became a celebrated photographer of dancers and male nudes. In addition, a photo shoot taken in Lynes's New York apartment in 1938 sheds further light on our artist Cadmus and his daring depiction of the navy. The series of photographs includes one of Cadmus in only a ripped white T-shirt, his genitals subtly blocked from view; in others he poses in a similar fashion with his lover, Jared French, who is visibly naked in most. While the series was never published in Lynes's lifetime, they shed light on the composition and subject-matter of *The Fleet's In!* As Richard Meyer has observed, these photographs remind us of the social and sexual frame of the painting, as well as other satirical works Cadmus painted, indicating that we are being presented with 'a dialogue between that which has been depicted within the frame and that which has been excluded from it'.[8] Thus while no one *spoke* of the latent homoeroticism of *The Fleet's In!* its coded satire of navy life was undoubtedly at odds with the American nation's vision of its navy boys, and led to its quick censorship. The larger narrative again of course was the struggle between nostalgia and modernism, acceptable codes of visual culture and 'marginal' ones.

Over ten years later, in 1945, most of the iconography relating to the US navy was still firmly heroic, and homoeroticism driven underground. For example, Kenneth Anger's (b. 1927) film *Fireworks* (1947), shot in three days when he was 17, explores acceptable and unacceptable masculine codes of behaviour in imagined and brutally real terms. Given the film brings the subject of homoeroticism and the navy together, it also offers a further commentary on the America Cadmus had to negotiate with. Anger's film goes much further than Cadmus of course, depicting a young male's (Anger's) nightmare/reverie as he enjoys looking at a muscular sailor only to be then gang-raped by him and four others in a public restroom. Anger said of the film:

> It's a personal statement about my own feelings about violence and [a] certain kind of masculinity. Also a treatment of a kind of myth in Amer-

> ica which relates to the American sailor. That's part of history now, but the sailor then was a kind of sex symbol . . .[9]

The film's dream sequences and Anger's visualization of what he described, in very Surrealist terms, as 'inflammable desires dampened by a day under the cold water of consciousness are ignited at night by the libertarian matches of sleep, and burst forth in showers of shimmering incandescence' cannot but remind us of Dalí and Buñuel's film *Un Chien Andalou* (1929), not only in terms of visual assault but also in the exploitation of film as a medium that can powerfully represent the unconscious at work.

Surrealism in Exile

During and after World War II the exploration of desire—heterosexual or homosexual—struck most as particularly frivolous if not outrageous, given the political climate. To dwell in the unconscious mind and world seemed to indicate nothing more than an escapist attitude to art and life. Clement Greenberg, who favoured formal innovation above anything else, described Surrealism in 1944 as motivated to 'sin against decorum, violate all the rules, do the disreputable thing' and Dalí as 'not to be taken seriously as anything other than a symptom'.[10]

Salvador Dalí was the Surrealist most Americans knew. In 1939 he won the attention of the American press and public with his *Dream of Venus* pavilion in the Amusement area of the New York World's Fair. The pavilion was a bizarre funhouse described in the Official Guide Book as

> a thirty foot glass and steel tank filled with water, at the bottom of which is a room of a 'Dream House.' Lovely diving girls plunge into the tank and by their actions seem to reveal the secrets of some dreams. The representations include Dali's famous 'Soft Watches,' 'Piano-Women,' 'Anthropomorphic Sea-Weed,' 'Exploding Giraffes,' a cow at the bottom of the sea, a couch in the shape of Garbo's lips, and of course his 'Living Liquid Ladies.' Admission 25 cents.

His plan to include on the façade an image of a lady with the head of a fish was quashed by the organizing committee, leading Dalí to issue a 'Declaration of the Independence of the Imagination and the Rights of Man to His Own Madness' (a parody of the American Declaration of the Rights of Man), attacking the 'middlemen of culture'.[11] One entered the funhouse through a pair of women's legs, above which hung a gargantuan reproduction of Venus cut out from Botticelli's *Birth of Venus* (1485). Inside, topless females swam as erotic mermaids in a wet tank while a Hollywoodian Venus lay stretched out on a bed of pink satin.

She was packaged as a veritable feast for the senses: flowers were strewn around her as well as such luxury food stuffs as champagne and lobsters. Dalí's exotic pavilion struck a critic from *Time* as a shrewd combination of 'Surrealism and sex'.[12]

Yet the pavilion was at odds with the intense, *politicized* eroticism of the Surrealists in Paris. This is not surprising, for by 1939 Dalí had been ousted from the Surrealist group for his Right-wing political leanings and despairingly labelled 'Avida Dollars' (an anagram of Salvador Dalí) by André Breton for his blatant worship of money and fame. When Breton and other Surrealists fled France for New York their political engagement did not waver: Breton worked as an announcer for Voice of America radio broadcasts, his voice bringing hope to French listeners back home; the Surrealists also launched a review, *VVV*, whose title was a reference to Churchill's famous hand gesture and their battle 'over the forces of regression and of death unloosed at present on the earth'.[13] They also organized a 1942 Surrealist exhibition, *First Papers of Surrealism*, to raise funds for the Co-ordinating Council of French Relief Societies in the Council's premises, the Whitelaw Reid mansion on Madison Avenue. Breton's vision of the radical power of Eros was never as sure as during wartime. In the catalogue for the exhibition he wrote 'freedom must become flesh', and in a speech of 1944 insisted 'the world must come to look through the eyes of Eros'.[14]

This vision of Eros took different forms in individual Surrealists' art. In *The Vertigo of Eros* (1944) **[52]** the Chilean, Roberto Matta (1911–2002), who introduced himself to the Surrealist group in autumn 1937, is as apocryphal as Breton in his vision of Eros. Matta gives form to Sigmund Freud's description of Eros as vertiginous. Traditional perspective, with a single vanishing point, here gives way to futuristic, abstracted eroticism as floating forms keep the eye moving and receding into space. It is as if the artist paints the very sensation of losing oneself or of letting go, whether in orgasmic pleasure or in pontificating on the reality of death at a time of brutal war. The American Surrealist Dorothea Tanning (b. 1910) offers a striking contrast to Matta's abstracted forms in her paintings. She was born in Galesburg, Illinois, and studied at the Art Institute of Chicago in 1930 before moving to New York in 1936, where she earned a living as a commercial artist. Her exposure to Surrealist art there (notably at Alfred H. Barr's 'Fantastic Art, Dada, and Surrealism' exhibition at MoMA) and her 'discovery' by Max Ernst in 1942 and marriage to him in 1946 meant by the mid-1940s she was hailed as a Surrealist. Her art was Surrealist before she ever met Ernst, however, and is haunting and quite macabre in its erotic focus, all the time rejecting the puritan world and values of Midwestern America, where she had

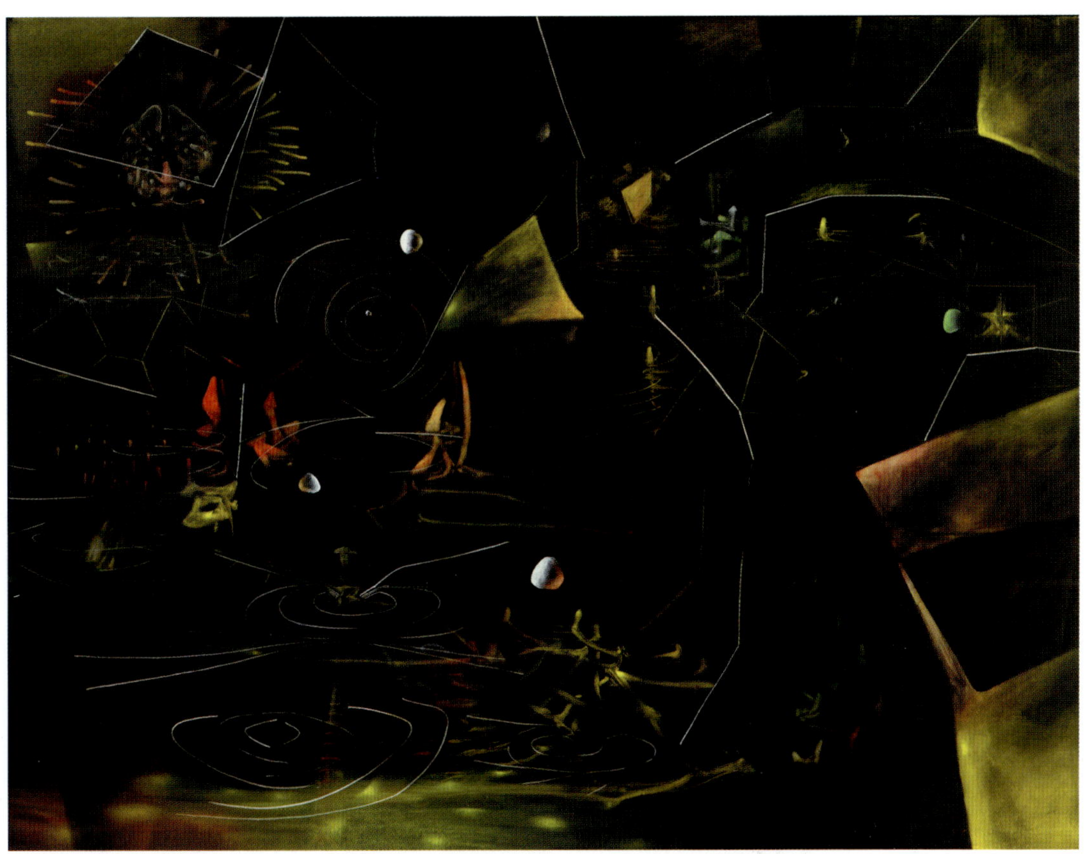

52 Roberto Sebastian Matta Echaurren
The Vertigo of Eros, 1944
The Chilean Surrealist Matta, who trained as an architect in Santiago before moving to Paris to work with Le Corbusier, joined the Surrealist movement in 1938, participating in their international exhibition and publishing in their journal *Minotaure* that year. In this painting he gives visual form to Freud's description of Eros (the life drive) as comparable with the sense of vertigo as one gazes down at Thanatos (the death drive).

been reared. In *Children's Games* (1942) Tanning does not depict typical childish make-belief but a nightmarish image of two girls in white Victorian-style nightdresses ripping wallpaper off the wall, a third child's legs and feet visible and seemingly lifeless in the foreground. As they rip the wallpaper it combusts, flames becoming the wild hair of one as well as consuming the image of a naked woman underneath the wallpaper. The power of the child-woman, so vital for many male Surrealists, is given a particularly violent edge as rippling cloth, hair, and paper shreds all evoke the electric power and thus erotic potential of the young girl. These girls are half Lewis Carroll's Alice in Wonderland, half the Marquis de Sade's re-educated Eugénie. In *Birthday* (1942) **[53]**, Tanning again creates an uncanny architectural space within which to stage female erotic power. A woman (Tanning) stands at an open door with numerous other open doors behind her. The bodice of her dress is ripped open to reveal her naked breasts; her skirt ripples furiously while morphing into green seaweed-like tendrils that are actually made up of writhing bodies. A chimera crouches at her bare feet—a fantastic

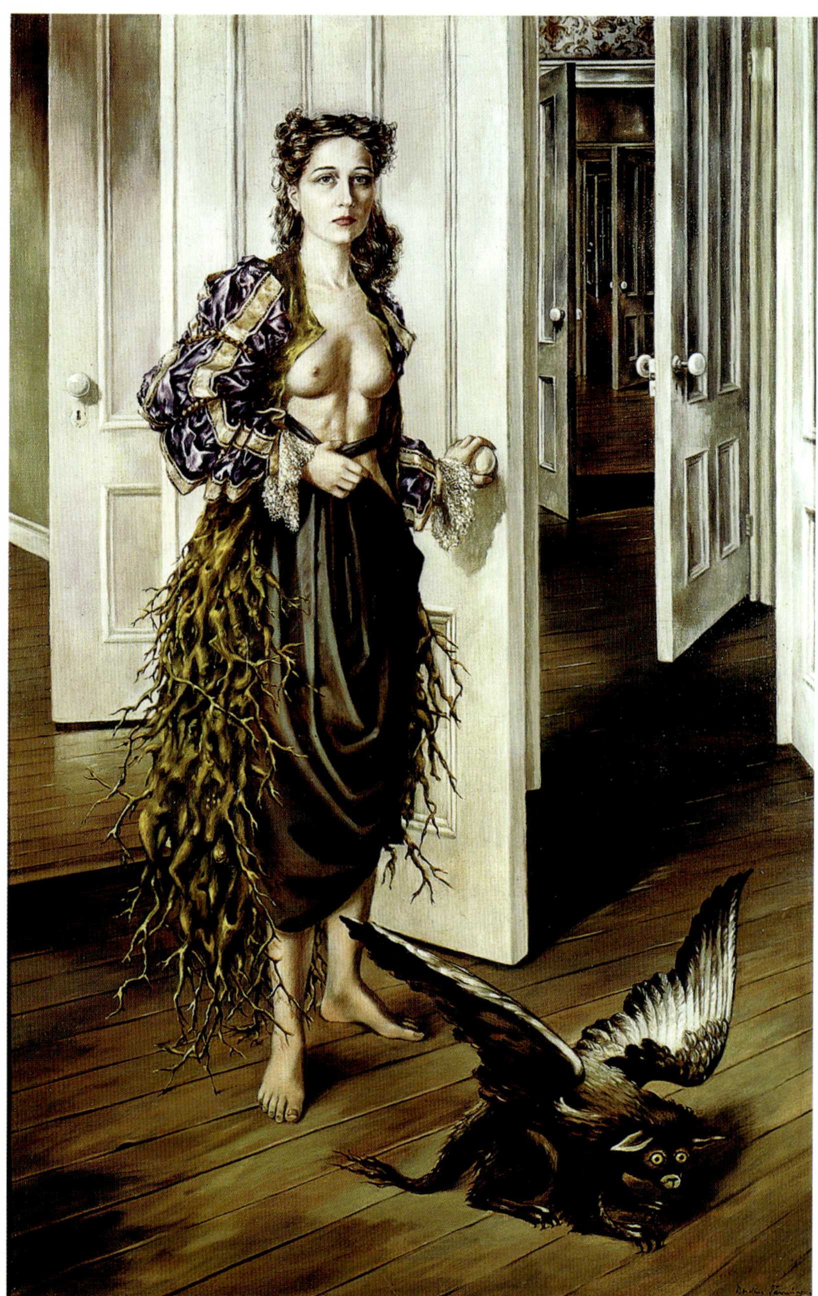

53 Dorothea Tanning
Birthday, 1942

Painted to mark her thirtieth birthday, this self-portrait portrays the power of dreams and the night, notably through the fantastic creature at her feet and her fine dress whose ripples comprise writhing male and female anthropomorphic forms. When the Surrealist artist Max Ernst saw the painting in Tanning's New York studio in the winter of 1942 he found it had no title and promptly christened it. A week later they were lovers. In her memoirs, *Between Lives* (2001), Tanning recounts how one day, when a collector expressed an interest in buying the painting, Ernst stated it was not for sale, proclaiming 'I love Dorothea. I want to spend the rest of my life with her. The picture is part of that life.'

creature that may be a variant of a lemur (a nocturnal creature associated with the spirits of the dead and with the continent called Lemuria by Theosophists, which was believed to have been inhabited by peoples with magic powers).[15] Here, despite the banal title (so given by Ernst as it was painted on the occasion of Tanning's thirtieth birthday), we are again presented with a never-ending world of dream and nightmare which hovers between pleasure and peril and where woman is the harbinger of erotic and magical adventure. Long corridors and open doors indicate the artist's challenge to the viewer to enter another realm where the mind and desire have no limits. If *Birthday* is to be considered in terms of birth then it is to the artist's own description of her birth that we must turn, and again appreciate it in terms of the dizzying, ecstatic power of Eros that Matta explored too: 'a day of high wind. A regular hurricane that blew down one of the three poplars in front of our house. My mother was terrified. So I was born.'[16]

Modernist Abstraction and Cold War Politics

By the post-war period America was no longer a province of European art. Rather, New York seemed to have succeeded in 'stealing' modern art from Paris.[17] It must be said though that the key aesthetic development in post-war American art—the break with representation and the move to modernist abstraction—was still strongly influenced by European avant-gardism. The Surrealists' rejection of the exterior visible world in favour of the interior world of the subconscious had already allowed for automatic means of creativity, but nonetheless the New York School was hailed as doing something quintessentially American. This was in keeping with the Cold War climate of 'us' versus 'them': while Europe was desperately trying to rebuild herself, America was enjoying economic prosperity and global power on the one hand and an increasing fear of Communist power and infiltration on the other, exacerbated by the Soviet Union's detonation of an atomic bomb in 1949 and Mao Tse-tung's Communist takeover of China. The execution of Julius and Ethel Rosenberg for espionage and conspiring with the Soviets in 1951 marked 1950s America as a decade of complacency and caution, one the writer Norman Mailer would call 'one of the worst decades in the history of man'.[18]

The American art—and celebration of the art—of this era must be viewed from an inter-war perspective of course. As Robert Rosenblum has argued, the notion of a peculiarly American quality to modern art emerged in the 1930s, arising out of the cultural inferiority complexes of the Roosevelt era (when the Museum of Modern Art in New York was hosting exhibition after exhibition of major European artists such as Picasso, Matisse, and Mondrian), and a general provincialism prior to the cultural migrations to New York of European artists as they fled the Nazi terror.[19] By the post-war era, cultural inferiority gave way to a new-found sense of superiority, helped by the rise of such prominent American critics as Clement Greenberg.

If the Paris of the Surrealists had long fascinated American imaginations, now Greenwich Village in New York took on a bohemian, Left Bank flavour, becoming a cosmopolitan, dynamic location for artists, writers, musicians, and others. More importantly, since the 1930s the America government had recognized the importance of the culture industry: a decade later we find American art gaining in public prominence and featuring in the national and international press and on television too. There was a desperate desire to find American cultural heroes. The New York School produced art that seemed to reflect this new-found pride, cultural confidence, and post-war economic prosperity: canvases were large in scale, dynamic in technique, and highly expressive and individualistic in subject-matter. They destroyed any sense of Cold War anxiety and spoke of the new, the audacious, the brave. Erotic expression was either latent or manifest in this new school of expression.

Jackson Pollock (1912–56) answered the call for an all-American artist-hero. While virtually unknown in 1944, by August 1949 he was the feature of a *Life* magazine spread that rhetorically asked if he was 'the greatest living painter in the United States?' The media exploited his Western image (Pollock was born in Wyoming and raised in California and Arizona) such that he became a cross between a John Wayne cowboy and a rebellious Marlon Brando. His death in a car crash at the age of 45 added to his mythic status in post-war America. He began to study painting in 1929 at the Art Students' League, New York, under Thomas Hart Benton. During the 1930s he worked in the manner of the Regionalists and Mexican muralist painters (Orozco, Rivera, Siqueiros), but by the mid-1940s he was painting in a dramatically different, non-figurative style. His 'drip' paintings of 1947–52, including *Autumn Rhythm Number 30* (1950)—which measures roughly 2.5 by 5 metres—marked a new direction for American modernism: he dripped and poured paint on to unprimed canvas on the floor, and used sticks, trowels, or knives to liberate his hand and mind from academic techniques. Pollock's art involved gesture and performance in his drip and splash style while all the time rejecting traditional technique in never actually touching the canvas with his brush. As the critic Harold Rosenberg wrote in his seminal 1952 essay, 'The American Action Painters', this was an art of action and revelation:

> In this gesturing with materials the esthetic, too, has been subordinated. Form, colour, composition, drawing, are auxiliaries, any of which—or

> practically all, as has been attempted logically, with unpainted canvases—can be dispensed with. What matters always is the revelation contained in the act.[20]

The textural play, the very painterly matter that creates crevices and pockets of paint, was lauded by Clement Greenberg, who found discipline and an American quality in Pollock's Abstract Expressionism despite his unruly drip technique. Greenberg enjoyed the light and shade created by this new formless technique, interpreting the paintings as non-corporeal despite the emphatic gestures involved: they were 'the most self-evidently corporeal means to deny [the paintings'] own corporeality'.[21] In looking at Pollock through a Duchampian lens one might find greater corporeal and erotic potential, however, especially if one thinks of Duchamp's small *Wayward Landscape* (1946), a semen stain on black satin he presented to his lover, the sculptor Maria Martins. Pollock's 'action' landscapes, as in *Lavender Mist No. 1* (1950), then seem to take on the form of a metaphoric ejaculate in process and finish. Such a reading would correlate with Pollock's emphatically male media image. In the *Life* magazine feature his photograph is quintessentially masculine: he stands with arms folded in paint-splattered jeans and a denim jacket, scowling and drooling on a cigarette. This image was present even when the artist was not, as indicated by the 1 March 1951 edition of *Vogue* magazine which used his drip paintings on show at Betty Parsons Gallery in New York as a backdrop for a four-page Cecil Beaton photo shoot. Here Pollock's presence was felt through his large unruly canvas, his persona and painting offering the perfect contrast to the models' classical and emphatically feminine poises in ball dresses. His sexual charisma was certainly behind *Time* magazine calling him 'Jack the Dripper' in 1956. This media image of the brooding loner amplified the somewhat tortured, abject quality of Pollock's painting technique as it defied boundaries, lines, and realistic forms. Yet it ironically also reinforced the latent erotic dimension too, as suggested by the Jack-the-[d]ripper tag and the artist's urination or ejaculation-like technique in defiance of traditional codes of artistic expression. Of course Pollock was also indebted to Surrealism, especially in such works as *The Moon-Woman Cuts the Circle* (1943), and is comparable to Masson and Miró in his ambition to liberate himself from traditional technique. He was looking to native American art too, notably to the sand-paintings of Navajo Indians—just as the Surrealists also took inspiration from shamanist rites and the technique of sand-painting, where art was never simply for art's sake. Thus while Greenberg appreciated the clean control and the prioritization of form in Pollock's art, the painter's technique and cultural references suggest that the critic's eagerness for order to be imposed upon disorder, form on formlessness, and 'masculine' rationality and intent on ever-threatening 'feminine' abjection belies the erotic potential of Pollock's art and exposes the repressed anxieties of post-war America as it embraced the new American artist hero.

A similarly explosive attitude to form occurred in the Abstract Expressionist art of the Dutch-born artist Willem de Kooning (1904–97). He came to the United States in 1926 and worked alongside Pollock on Works Progress Administrations (WPA) murals in the 1930s. In the post-war era, however, his art took a dramatic turn. In 1950 he began a series of 'Woman' paintings in which he assaulted the canvas and the figure while also expressing the element of spontaneity and fluidity typical of the New York School. In *Woman I* (1950–2) **[54]**, one of six paintings de Kooning produced on the theme of woman from 1951 to 1953, paint is applied in a laceration-like form, clearly showing a figure of a woman, and yet her monstrous, fragmented body suggests that same Jack the Ripper element of violence seen in Pollock. De Kooning's eroticism lies not just in the fleshy form he paints, it lies in his very application of paint, in the painting's rhythmic, excited, surface itself. When the paintings were first shown at the Sidney Janis Gallery in New York in 1953 de Kooning's emphatically figurative style, at odds with the abstraction typical of Abstract Expressionism and Pollock, received harsh criticism. Yet de Kooning's radical style may also be looked at from an art-historical perspective if we recall the association made by Greenberg between this new supposedly all-American Abstract Expressionism and European Cubism, specifically Synthetic Cubism.[22] De Kooning perhaps updates Picasso's innovations between 1912 and the 1920s in presenting multiple perspectives, exaggerated proportions, shallow pictorial space, and vibrant colour. While de Kooning's crude painterly style undoubtedly suggests an assault on form, it is not explicitly an assault on woman herself. Rather, he offers us an emphatically modern, post-war image of woman, updating images of woman from art's history. He also drew inspiration from Mesopotamian idols (notably two Sumerian statues which were on show at the Metropolitan Museum of Art in New York in the 1940s and 1950s), as well as from a wide source of paintings by the sixteenth-century French Le Nain brothers, Rembrandt (1606–69), and Ingres. Indeed, the arms of this woman and the blue daubs of colour (water) at the base of another in the series, *Woman IV* (1952–3), refer to Rembrandt's *A Woman Bathing in a Stream* (1654): a very beautiful, intimate portrait of his common-law wife, Hendrickje Stoffels, lifting her white shift as she wades in water. In this

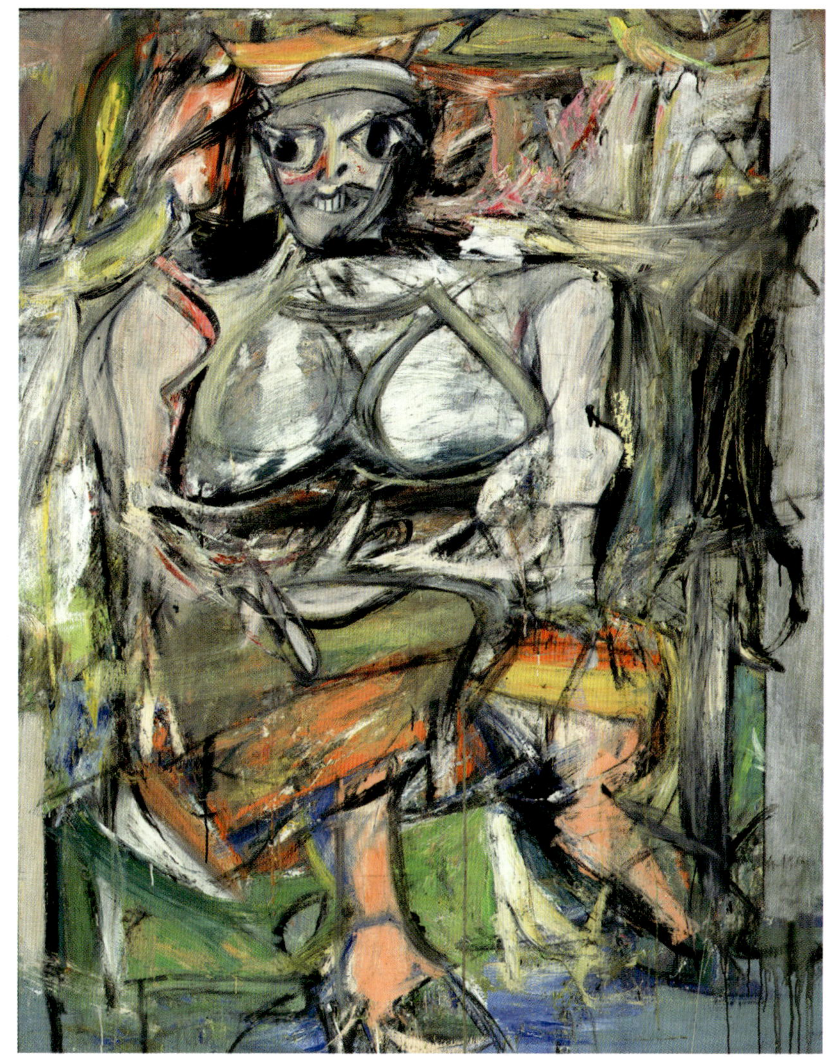

54 Willem de Kooning
Woman I, 1950–2
De Kooning's style and subject-matter are erotic in his 1951–3 series of painting based on 'Woman': his gestural strokes and heavy daubs of paint lend a fleshy, visceral quality to the surface of the canvas, while his emphatic outlining of the woman's eyes and breasts and rather frenzied rendition of her thighs and legs create a dramatic, and monumental, sense of expressive sexuality.

way, de Kooning's seemingly angry eroticism offers a critical commentary on an age-old tradition of erotic women in art.

While the USIA (the United States Information Agency, set up after the war to promote an international awareness and understanding of America, including American culture) were supporting exhibitions of Abstract Expressionism abroad, presenting it as indicative of American cultural energy and freedom of expression, conservative elements at home attempted to shut down the same exhibitions, often with the support of traditionalist artists' organizations such as the National Academy of Design. Conservative opinion insisted that realism was the only suitable aesthetic strategy for America, claiming modernism was communist (though ironically the Soviet Union was promoting Socialist Realism). Certain public figures, including Republican congressman George Dondero from Michigan, called for the banning of Abstract Expressionism, and withdrawal of all government support, deeming its 'distortion, grotesqueness and meaninglessness' to be 'un-American'.[23] Rumours even circulated that Abstract Expressionist paintings were, in fact, not art but elaborate Kremlin-inspired secret coded maps of American military installations and coded instructions to communist subversives. But by 1955, with the thawing in anti-communist anxieties, such intolerance was somewhat abated, and by the 1960s Abstract Expressionism was firmly canonized as a modernist style to be championed in the history of America's art.

By the mid-1950s America was an economic, military, political, and cultural power keen to preserve a very particular global image, and it was undergoing dramatic change. The 1950s saw a baby boom, a growth in education, and a new leisure industry and culture, with the suburban family spending more and more time shopping or occupied with indoor and outdoor leisure pastimes. In 1948 McDonald's opened, bringing in a new fast-food culture; Disneyland opened in 1955. Suburban romance, teen comics, drive-ins: this was the harmless fun of 1950s America. Television offered a window on the world and suggested new erotic attractions, though the golden hips of Elvis Presley were still too erotic for general consumption. Behind this apparent consumer happiness lay significant tensions, however, notably racial tensions, with increasing challenges to Southern segregation and the expansion of the Civil Rights movement. Cold War tensions were ever-present from 1949 to 1989, with the rise of a strident anti-communism and a shift of American politics and culture to the Right. Indeed, perhaps the pursuit of abstraction and individual expression in post-war American art might be viewed as the sublimation of Cold War anxieties—particularly the dread of the A-bomb. In addition, the emphasis on the individual rather than the collective in Abstract Expressionism signalled a distinct move away from inter-war avant-gardes towards an emphasis on self-achievement, again seeming to reflect the ethos of post-war American capitalism. The ascendancy of American painting, and of New York over Paris, was very much in keeping with the ascendancy of American ideology and economics in large parts of the Western world which accompanied the so-called *Pax Americana* of the late 1940s and 1950s. However, critics of the new post-war American way of life became increasingly numerous through the 1950s. John Kenneth Galbraith attacked laissez-faire economics and excessive consumption in his bestselling study *The Affluent Society* (1958), and the radical German-

American philosopher Herbert Marcuse profoundly critiqued capitalist society and its detrimental psychic effects in *Eros and Civilization* (1956) and *One-Dimensional Man* (1959), books that would influence the countercultural generation of the 1960s. In *Eros and Civilization* Marcuse argued that 'Art is perhaps the most visible "return of the repressed", not only on the individual but also on the generic-historical level.' He believed, as avant-garde and countercultural artists did, that the artistic imagination could stage and shape the freedom that civilized society denies.[24] Marcuse's writings would influence the 'class of '68' who were teenagers in the late 1950s and who began steadily forming a countercultural youth movement against middle-class, middle-aged domesticity. Even Hollywood recognized the growth of a teen culture, market, and spirit as Marlon Brando, James Dean, and Paul Newman starred in youth rebellion films like *A Streetcar Named Desire* (1951), *Rebel without a Cause* (1955), and *The Left-Handed Gun* (1958). Such films presented a different model of masculinity, one critical of white-collar, suburban married man, one more to do with the spirit of Abstract Expressionism in celebrating spontaneity, expression, and self-discovery.

The poetry and writings (as well as lifestyles) of the San Francisco-based Beats, such as Jack Kerouac, Allen Ginsberg, and Lawrence Ferlinghetti offered a further countercultural voice in the 1950s. Inaugurated by Allen Ginsberg's reading of *Howl*, in 6 Gallery, San Francisco, in October 1955, in which he exclaimed that 'The tongue and cock and hand and asshole are holy!', the Beats wreaked havoc on word and image and performance, as well as defeating obscenity charges.[25] Homosexual liberation was an important part of Beat culture—for example the openly gay lifestyles and declarations of the artist Jess Collins and poet Robert Duncan. Duncan published 'The Homosexual in Society' in *Politics* in 1944, a controversial article in which he called for sexual freedom and compared the situation of homosexuals to that of blacks or Jews. In its insistence on freedom from traditional expression Beat culture was also very much in keeping with Dadaism and Surrealism. Indeed, just as those two earlier avant-gardes had embraced African-American culture, so the Beats were influenced by and created alongside jazz musicians (Charlie Parker, Chet Baker), defying segregation.

If the 1950s is to be thought of as an era of suburban 'bliss' then it must also be thought of as the suburbia of twin beds as standard for married couples, and where families watching their brand-new television sets were censored from seeing Elvis's pelvis on each of his three appearances on the *Ed Sullivan Show* in 1956. Yet as Dr Alfred C. Kinsey would reveal, American men and women were living quite different lives to that advocated by religious and political leaders. Through the

Institute for Sex Research (since renamed the Kinsey Institute), set up in 1947 on the campus of Indiana University to research sexuality, gender, and reproduction, Kinsey was able to carry out and publish two major studies: *Sexual Behavior in the Human Male* (1948) and *Sexual Behavior in the Human Female* (1953). He found that 50 per cent of women in his survey had had pre-marital sex but up to 89 per cent disapproved of it on 'moral grounds', that over 33 per cent of married women had 'engaged in petting' with more than ten men, and that 37 per cent of men admitted to 'some homosexual experience'.[26] His findings led to widespread controversy, but *Sexual Behavior in the Human Male* became an immediate bestseller, selling over 200,000 copies that year. The revelations of *Sexual Behavior in the Human Female* were less well received, especially by the clergy, who claimed Kinsey's interviewees could not have been 'decent' American womenfolk. In addition, Cold War politics began to undermine his reputation and research funding. In 1954, the US Representative B. Carroll Reece and the 'House Committee to Investigate Tax-Exempt Foundations' began an investigation into Kinsey's financial backing for possible connections with the Communist Party, and as a result The Rockefeller Foundation's Board of Directors withdrew funding for his research.[27] However, sexuality and sexual desire were already a huge growth area for popular consumption, as Hugh Hefner recognized when he started his magazine *Playboy* for the average young suburban married man who worked hard to purchase the latest refrigerator model or a new family car. Launched in 1953 with an initial print run of 70,000, with articles about sex and photographs of naked women—whom Hefner saw as 'a symbol of disobedience, a triumph of sexuality, an end of Puritanism'—the magazine was intended as an attack on 'our ferocious anti-sexuality, our dark anti-eroticism'.[28] While *Playboy* clearly advocated a strongly heterosexual concept of sex and society, it signalled the dawn of a new sexualized America, shortly to become radicalized in the 1960s—as we shall see.

The Search for the Absolute

As America prospered so Europe struggled to reform itself in the aftermath of the war. It faced moral, political, economic crisis and also the burgeoning threat of Americanization. Despite the conferences organized by the Allies at Tehran (November–December 1943), Yalta (February 1945) and Potsdam (July–August 1945), Western democracies and the Soviet Union faced a period of immense estrangement after the end of World War II. In March 1946, Winston Churchill spoke of an 'Iron

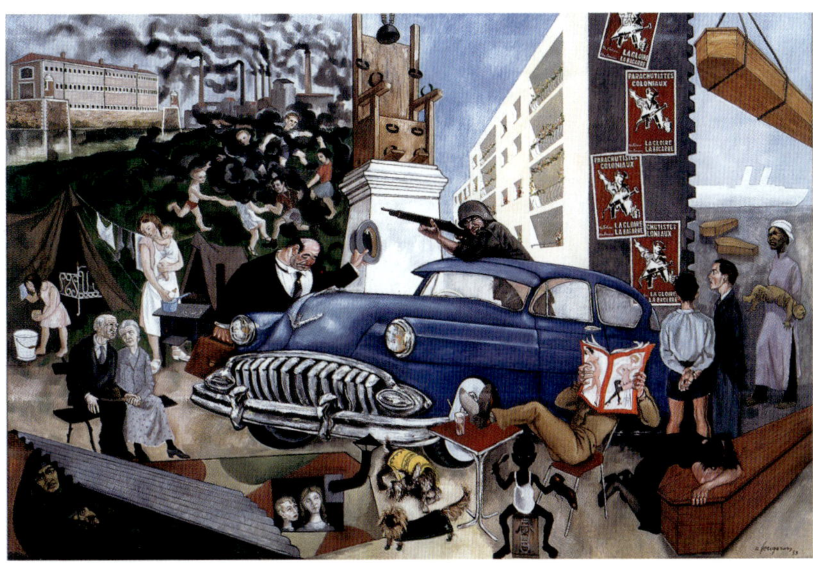

55 André Fougeron
Atlantic Civilization, 1953

America is presented in critical terms by Fougeron, in the form of an iconic automobile, an electric chair (an allusion to the execution of Joshua and Ethel Rosenberg that year), and a GI enjoying a soft-porn magazine while famine, death, and pollution unfold around him. France too comes under assault, notably for its colonial war in Indo-China (signified by recruitment posters for parachutists) and its colonial exploitation of Algeria (signified by the women huddled under the corrugated iron).

Curtain' being drawn across Europe. The mutual antagonism between the United States and the Soviet Union, then led by President Harry S. Truman and Joseph Stalin respectively, would intensify in the following years, especially in the 1950s. The culture of the 'Cold War' was born, a culture that fuelled fear and paranoia. This was an increasingly repressive climate for many European artists, many of whom saw themselves as trapped between Stalin's totalitarian regime and aggressive American capitalism. Nowhere were the ramifications of the clash between communism and capitalism clearer than in the widespread fear of the atomic and then hydrogen bomb, which penetrated both popular culture and the work of artists of various styles and political persuasions. While New York was deemed to have stolen modern art from Paris with the exile of so many painters, America was still seen in French eyes—especially in communist eyes—as a land of sexual consumption rather than ideas and cultural advance. Thus in André Fougeron's (1913–98) large-scale painting *Atlantic Civilization* (1953) **[55]**, exhibited at the Salon d'Automne in Paris that year, we see how an official French communist artist represents America in xenophobic terms: a businessman wows over an American car, an electric chair above him alludes to the execution of the Rosenbergs in America in June 1953, imperialism in general (French too—notably in Indo-China and Algeria) is attacked, as is nuclear war, and an American GI devours a porn magazine, since erotic and pornographic material was much more readily available in post-war Paris than in the United States. The painting mocks America as the supposed land of freedom even though political purging was rife at this time, as well as suggesting that the decline of France was due to the impact of American, Hollywoodian culture.

In this post-war climate, eroticism inevitably continued to be adopted by artists as a political metaphor. Formless figures and deliberately crude painting styles suggested a spiritual malaise and a desperate search for a formal language that could portray the horror of the war, the Holocaust, and the bombings of Hiroshima and Nagasaki. Post-war nudes tended to be emaciated and fragmented, their decrepit forms mirroring the ravaged state of Europe as it attempted to rebuild itself. The representation of the female body was particularly revealing. In France, the metaphoric use of the female form in art—traditionally associated with the heroic, fertile, and beautiful Marianne—shifted to images of fallibility and vulnerability, often in recognition of Vichy France's capitulation to the Nazis and the need to 'purge' France of such collaborators. After the war, the majority of artists felt that France could no longer portray herself simply as the ideal image of 'La Belle République', a bastion of liberty, equality, and fraternity. That image had been shattered. Whereas before the war, the soil was synonymous with rural nostalgia and the feminine with rejuvenation, after the war the soil became synonymous with corruption and the feminine with victimhood.

Some artists, such as Jean Dubuffet (1901–85), sought to render the canvas as a physical, tactile, and erotic object in itself by literally smearing it with earth and grit in a manner that echoed the trauma of their nation as well as the formal innovations of Jackson Pollock and Willem de Kooning across the Atlantic. This may be seen in Dubuffet's Art Brut canvases such as *Miss Cholera* (1946) and *Le Mafisyx* (1950), where a crude, muddy surface reinforces the baseness of the flesh. Other artists such as Jean Fautrier (1898–1964) and Wols (Alfred Otto Wolfgang Schulze, 1913–51) shared Dubuffet's interest in primitive, bodily images. Their muddy styles and bleak representations of the body may be theorized in terms of Michel Tapié's *Art Informel*, a term he coined in 1950 to depict an artistic turn to the shapeless, a refusal of traditional figuration in favour of a gestural spontaneity with paint. In *Head of a Hostage, No. 1* (1944) **[56]**, Fautrier's combination of gestural strokes and surface play reminds one both of prehistoric art and blood stains. As such, it reflects a turn away from modern European culture and towards a primal or pre-cultural state, just as it responds to the sheer brutality of the war. Fautrier painted a series of hostage paintings that the writer Francis Ponge described in 'crucified' terms in 1946: 'The shot victim replaces the crucified One, the anonymous man replaces the painted Christ' with an anonymous, amorphous female form.[29] Fautrier portrays woman,

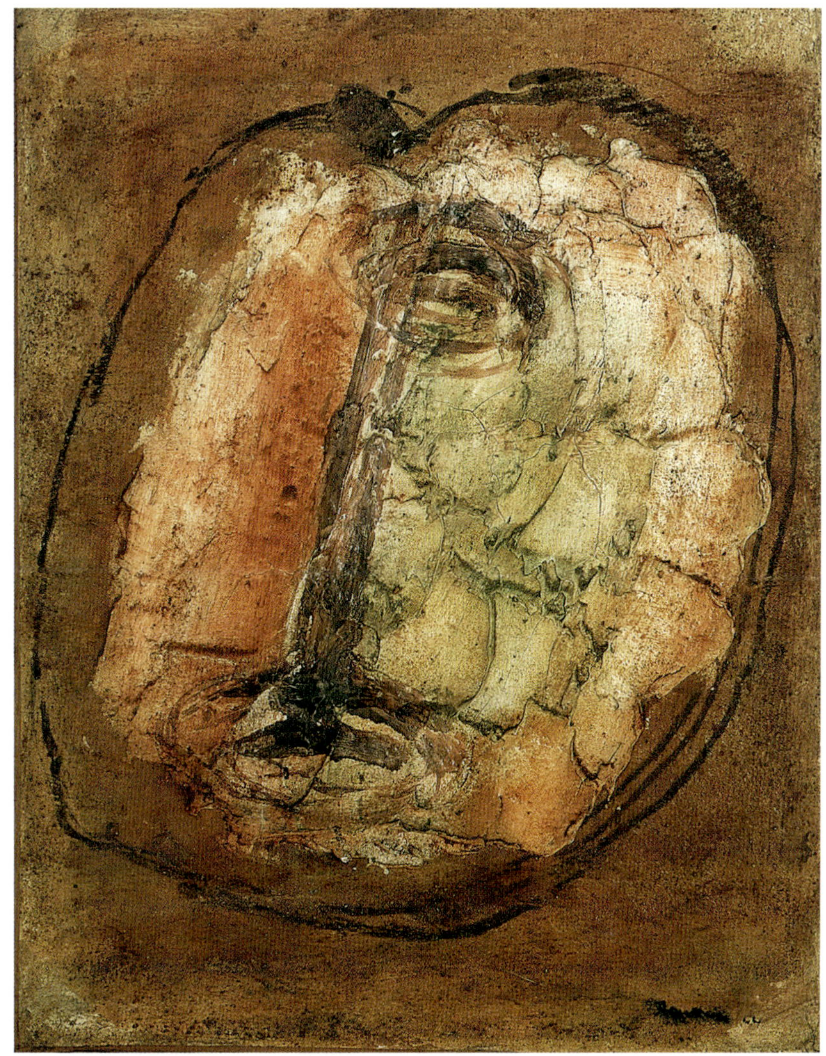

56 Jean Fautrier
Head of a Hostage, No. 1, 1944

The writer Francis Ponge's 1946 description of Fautrier's macabre, wartime series of paintings of hostages captures their moving combination of a visceral brutality and transcendent spirituality: 'The shot victim replaces the crucified One, the anonymous man replaces the painted Christ.'

no longer as curvaceous, erotic, or idyllic, but as a gash, as crushed, as mutilated.

This was also the epoch of existentialism, which defied the idea that culture was part of a historical process and insisted instead that the making of a work of art is a deliberate choice on the part of the artist. As with Pollock, de Kooning, and Dubuffet, the sculptural work of Alberto Giacometti (1901–66) and Germaine Richier (1904–59) echoes existentialism's doctrine of action, engagement, and authenticity, suggesting we have a post-war international 'existential eroticism'. For Jean-Paul Sartre, Giacometti was an existentialist artist because his art portrayed these qualities and because the artist himself had witnessed the ultimate

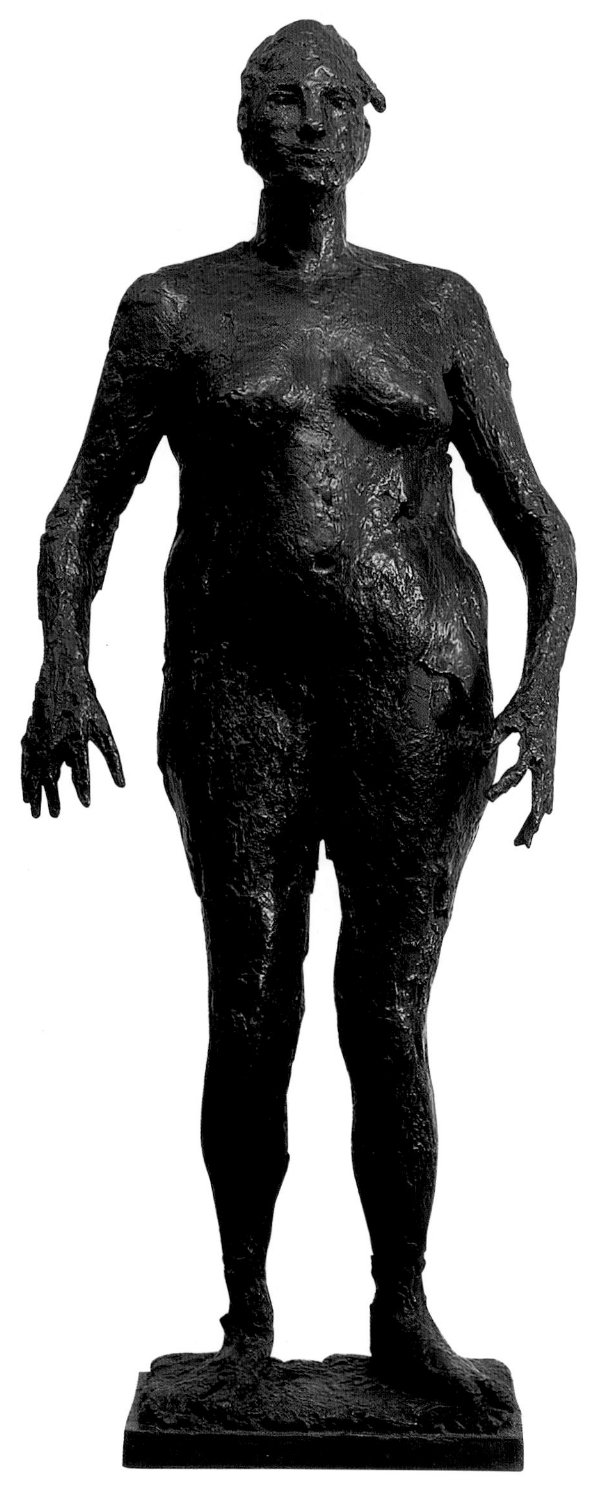

57 Germaine Richier
Hurricane Woman, 1948–9

Richier's pantheist vision comes to the fore in this sculpture, one of many 'Personages' she produced in the aftermath of World War II. Man and nature are presented as one, the upright woman seeming to resist and embody the force of a hurricane in her bronze form.

existential act—the killing of a human—in 1921. Experience was central to Sartre's vision of art, and Giacometti fulfilled that prerequisite in producing art that was not just about life but about agency. Giacometti had been briefly involved with the Surrealist group in Paris in 1935, but he turned away from his Surreal, fetish-like objects—such as his *Disagreeable Objects* (1931)—to focus on drawing and new sculptural styles from 1935–45. While in Switzerland during the war he began to have visions of heads in the void. These visions frightened him but inspired him to create totemic, elongated figures in paintings and sculpture. They still harked back to his art of the 1930s and focused on the female form, drawing inspiration from the brothels—notably the Sphinx brothel in Paris—that Giacometti liked to frequent until their closure by the French state in 1946. It was these works—interpreted at the time as existentialist—that Sartre would praise in the catalogue for Giacometti's first show in the Pierre Matisse Gallery in Paris in 1948. In the preface, entitled 'The Quest for the Absolute', Sartre compared Giacometti's figures to the palaeolithic hunters of southern France, free of notions of beauty and ugliness in their crude, roughly formed surfaces modelled on primitive man.[30] Sartre also admired the artist for retaining a distance from his models despite wanting 'to touch their lush flesh', interpreting this as a rejection of 'promiscuity, the fruit of close proximity' in favour of higher things—'friendship, love'.[31] Sartre did not refer to Giacometti's 1946 essay in homage to the Sphinx brothel and his nostalgia for the 'strange legs, long, thin and slender' of prostitutes.[32]

Interestingly, while Germaine Richier's sculptures were equally challenging in their rough surfaces and totemic forms, they did not gain such intellectual recognition at the time. Yet her bronze *Hurricane Woman* (1948–9) **[57]** is a forceful rendition, embodied in a healthy, ungainly but curvaceous woman, of the power of nature to recover after a political storm. *The Exhumed* (1955) **[58]**, by the Polish sculptress Alina Szapocznikow (1926–73) and made of cement and iron splinters, seems to lie somewhere between the styles of Giacometti and Richier as it has both a concern with space as form and with the sculptor's craft. A survivor of the Nazi camps at Auschwitz, Bergen-Belsen, and Terezin, Szapocznikow here denies the figure its fleshy sexuality while reinforcing its indestructible life force. She celebrates the imperfections of the hand as revealed in the sculptural process (in contrast to the impersonal efficiency of the machine) and portrays the vulnerability of the body.

We find a very different approach to the erotic potential of the sacred in the drawings of the philosopher and writer Pierre Klossowski (1905–2001), the brother of the artist Balthus, whose art has been described by

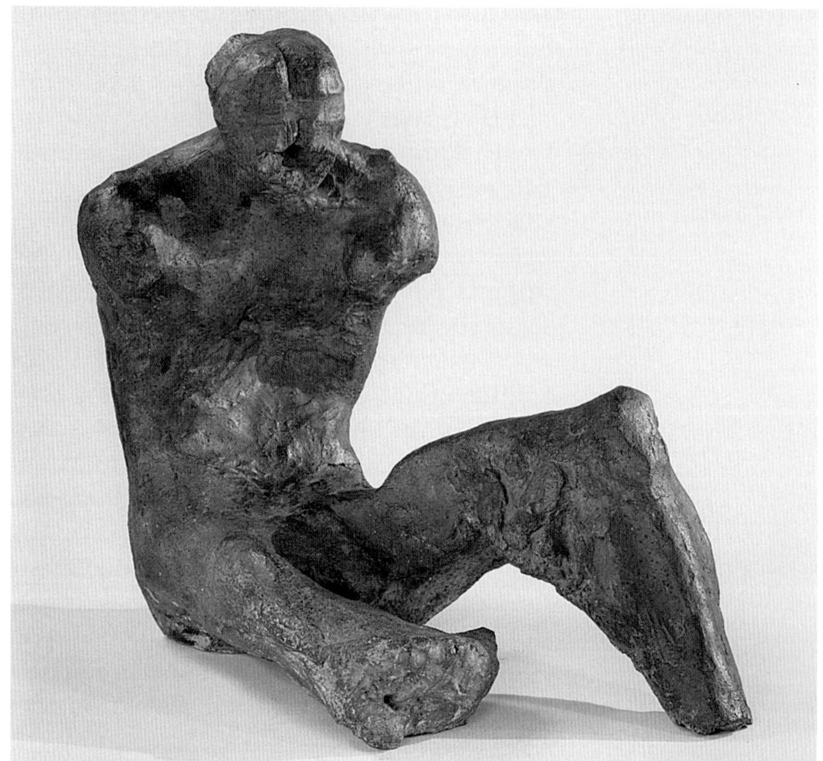

58 Alina Szapocznikow
The Exhumed, 1955
This Polish sculptor, who described the body as 'a total erotogenic zone', captured both the extremes of love and pain, sensuality and anguish, in her art. Her experience of the war (as a Jewish prisoner in Auschwitz, Bergen-Belsen, and Terezin) and her later experience of breast cancer (which eventually killed her) informed her humane approach to mankind in her sculptures, which represented the human body as an exhumed archaeological find.

philosopher Gilles Deleuze as 'theo-pornology' since he unites theological debate and 'superior pornography'.[33] In his treatise *Sade mon prochain* (1947), Klossowski (who spent two years in the Dominican order during the war) argued that Sade's evocation of absolute Evil in his fiction was the necessary proof of the great need for God in society and that Sade should be understood as a moralist. Just as taboo is necessary for transgression so we need to be able to contemplate evil to be inspired to lead better lives. In his fictional trilogy *The Laws of Hospitality* (1954–60)—dedicated to the heroine Roberte, who is as sexually carnivorous as any Sadean heroine as she goes about her daily business in contemporary Paris—Klossowski continues this line of argument. The trilogy's so-called 'laws of hospitality' are essentially one law: the giving of one's wife to the guests of the house. This law allows Roberte to pursue a number of sexual liaisons, and her husband, Octave, to experience voyeuristic pleasure. Their lifestyle is both 'the subject of conjugal myth' and the 'projection of the virile imagination' but it also allows them to lead lives that are open and honest.[34]

In his pencil drawing *The Parallel Bars* of 1967, or a later version of 1980 **[59]**, Klossowski gives form to a scene in the trilogy in which

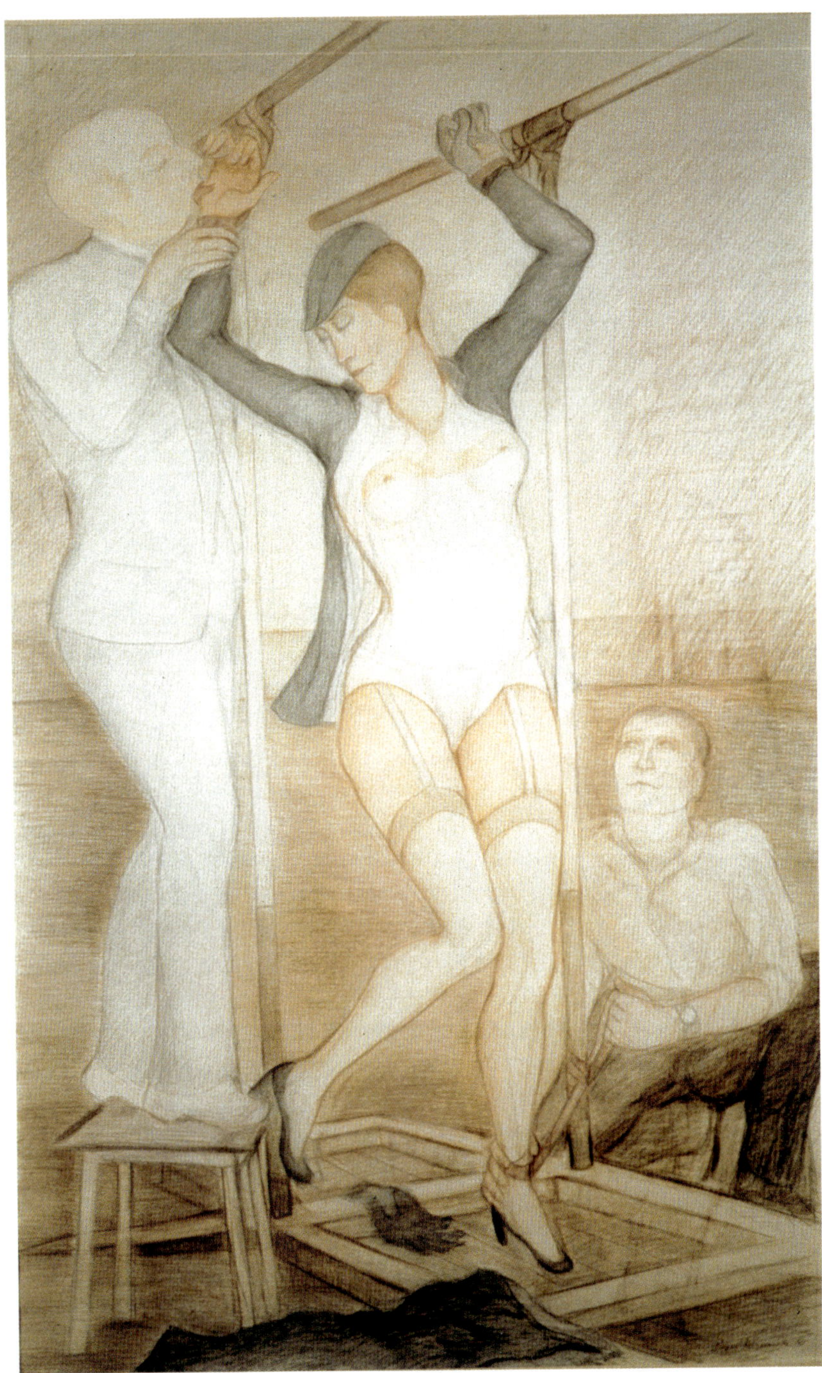

59 Pierre Klossowski
Roberte and the Parallel Bars, 1980

This drawing exemplifies the Sadean flavour of Klossowski's fiction and art. It is a scene depicted in Klossowski's novel *The Revocation of the Edict of Nantes* (1959) and in many subsequent drawings: an encounter in a dark cellar near the Louvre between the beautiful Roberte, a 'giant', and a 'short fellow'. The men strap Roberte's wrists and ankles to parallel bars and an erotic game begins: the giant licks her palm, her knees rise, and her body arches as she reaches the heights of sexual pleasure.

Roberte has a sexual encounter with two strangers, a giant and a dwarf, in a dark basement equipped with gymnast bars, near the Louvre museum. With her naked legs spread open, Roberte is in the process of being hoisted on to the bars as the giant ties and licks her hands and the dwarf ties her feet. Here we find Klossowski fusing the fear of sexual violence and an excitement for spiritual epiphany in a provocative modern-day version of the famed spiritual ecstasy of St Teresa as Roberte appears to undergo a spiritual catharsis greater than her physical pleasure or pain.

In 1947 the Surrealists also announced their return to Paris in their first post-war exhibition at the Galerie Maeght in Paris. The catalogue for the show indicated that exile in America had not quashed their erotic spirit. Designed by Marcel Duchamp and Enrico Donati (b. 1909), a young artist based in New York, the catalogue cover had a false breast on it, set against swatch of black velvet and ironically titled *Please Touch* **[60]**. Where art exhibitions and galleries usually insist on a safe distance from the art object, the Surrealists did the opposite. Before reading the Surrealist word, the viewer literally fondled a bare breast—an American 'falsie', hand-painted to look more fleshlike. While Donati saw this luxury catalogue as suggestive of a naked breast, escaped from a luxurious evening dress, it also had rather macabre connotations—one breast might also suggest sexual violence, a perverse trophy, or cannibalism, even. Certainly, this more Sadean vision of eroticism was taken to a fantastically titillating and subversive extreme in the Surrealists' 1959 exhibition held at the Galerie Daniel Cordier in Paris and dedicated in title and theme to 'EROS'.[35] The exhibition was launched with a performance on 2 December in the apartment of the Surrealist poet Joyce Mansour by Jean Benoît (b. 1922), entitled *The Execution of the*

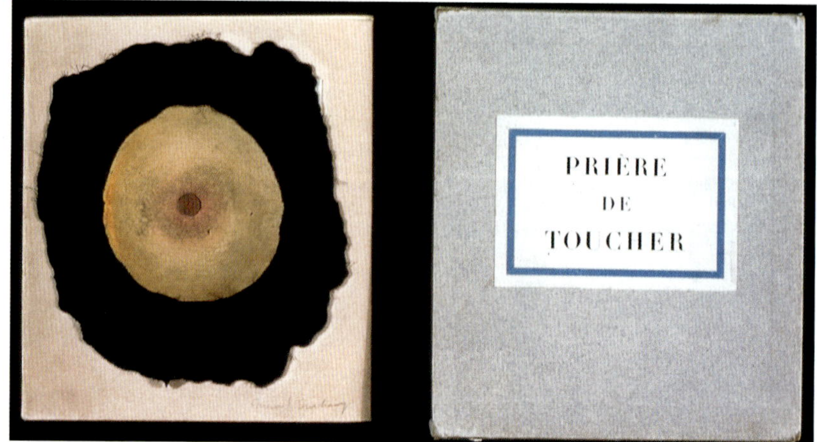

60 Marcel Duchamp and Enrico Donati
Prière de Toucher (Please Touch), 1947
This luxury catalogue, produced for the 1947 international Surrealist exhibition at the Galerie Maeght in Paris, was the combined work of Duchamp and the younger Italian artist Donati, both of whom were living in New York. They purchased 999 'falsies' (foam rubber breasts) from a warehouse in Brooklyn, and painted them so that they were more natural in appearance before gluing them to swatches of black velvet. Presenting the viewing public with erotically charged catalogue-objects, Duchamp came up with the idea of adding the ironic warning 'Please Touch'.

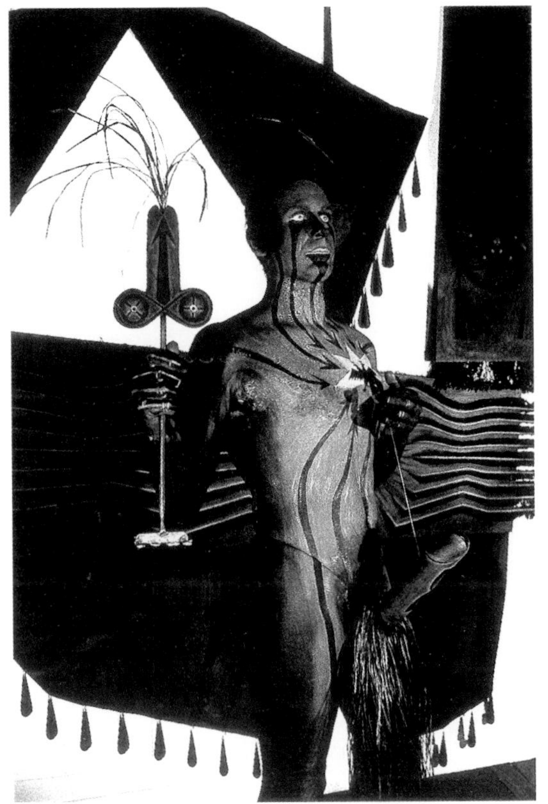

61 Jean Benoît
Testament to the Marquis de Sade, 1959
Benoît's proto-Happening was performed in the apartment of Surrealist poet Joyce Mansour on 2 December 1959, the 145th anniversary of Sade's death. He paid homage to the great libertine by enacting a dramatic striptease to the recorded sounds of city noise, 'unshackling' himself from an elaborate costume that symbolized both the repressive morality of modern society and the need to celebrate Eros. At the end of the performance he stood in his naked, painted flesh, wearing only a gargantuan phallus and wielding a phallic branding iron before burning the letters S-A-D-E onto his chest.

Testament to the Marquis de Sade **[61]**. Benoît had come to Paris from Montreal in 1947 and been invited to join the Surrealist group in 1959. In his performance he enacted a symbolic reburial of Sade, who had been buried in a cemetery at Charenton in 1808 despite his will that he be buried in an unmarked grave in his estate at Malmaison. In an elaborate striptease—where piece by piece Benoît cast off a mask, wooden crutches, wooden panels, and a huge medallion with an image of a man behind bars painted and the words 'Tout ce qui signe Sade est amour' (all that is under Sade's name is love) on it—the revolutionary eroticism of Sade was celebrated until the artist stood naked except for a gargantuan wooden phallus, his body dramatically painted with arrows. Every item of costume from which he had been 'liberated' denoted the shackling of man's desires in so-called 'enlightened' society. The finale came when, in homage to the great libertine, Benoît branded his bare chest with the letters 'S-A-D-E'. Such Sadean drama did not end with the performance but continued in the EROS exhibition itself in a gallery with velvet-covered walls, sand on the floors, and heaving walls that sighed orgasmically (thanks to hidden air pumps and a recording

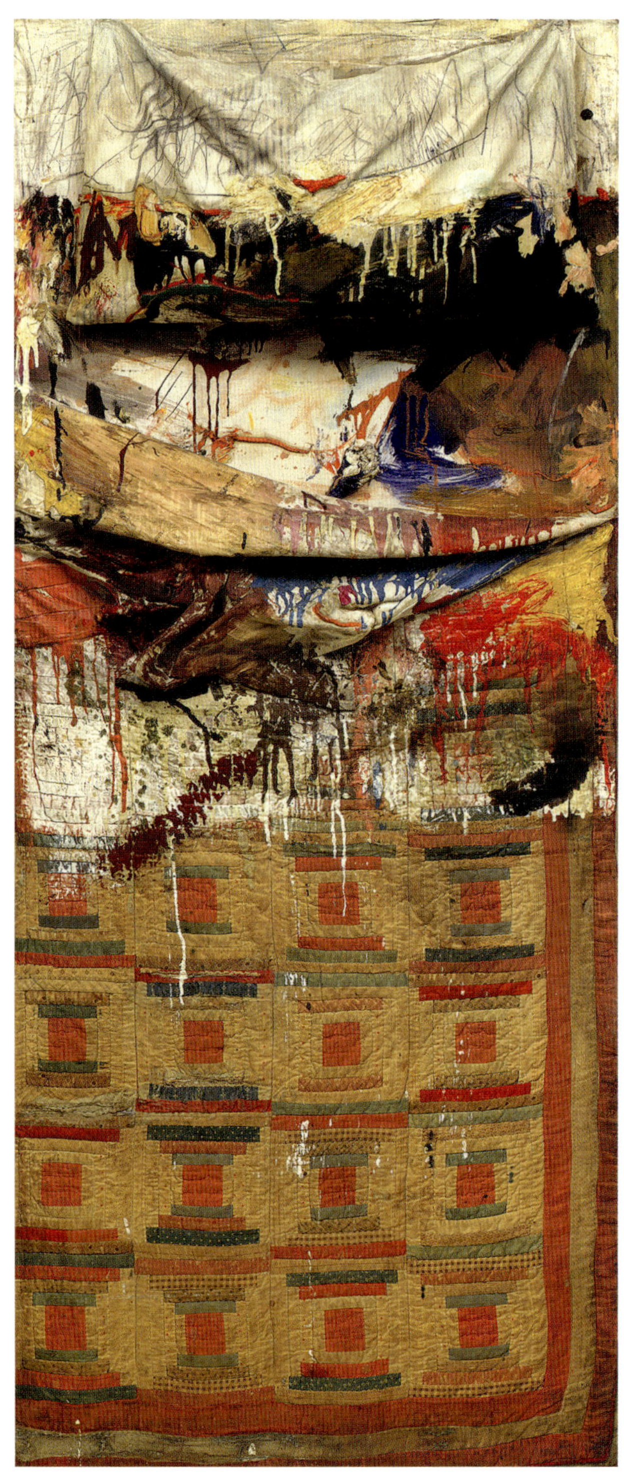

62 Robert Rauschenberg
Bed, 1955

Part sculpture, part painting, Rauschenberg's upright *Bed* pays homage to Marcel Duchamp's ready-mades while also posing a challenge to Jackson Pollock's drip paintings. Given it is the artist's own bedding and the quilt and sheet are turned down, it suggests an invitation to the spectator to enter the artist's intimate world; perhaps it is not surprising that it has been interpreted as an allusion to his romantic relationship with the young artist Jasper Johns.

created by the poet Radovan Ivsic). Mimi Parent (b. 1924), also from Montreal and the wife of Benoît, designed a velvet-lined fetish room for a wall of fetish objects and for Benoît's costume. She contributed her *Masculine-Feminine* (1959) object: a tie made of flowing female hair, Parent's own, against a white shirt and jacket lapels: a quintessentially male object turned female and monstrous, and so all the more fetishistically charged. Meret Oppenheim took the eroticism of her *Object (Breakfast in Fur)* theme to new heights too in staging a *Cannibal Feast* of luxury food (lobster, fruits, champagne) on the body of a naked, gold-painted model. Again the macabre and cannibalistic was evoked in this dramatic installation by a female artist in an exhibition space that radically did away with the neutral 'white cube' exhibition experience. Guest artists in the exhibition included the American Robert Rauschenberg (b. 1925), whose *Bed* (1955) **[62]** was selected for the show: an upright assemblage made of oil paint, a pillow, quilt, and sheet, all on wooden supports and hanging from the wall like a relief. A 'combine painting' (in the artist's own terms), it fused Abstract Expressionist brushstrokes with a Duchampian use of the 'found object' (the bed and bedding). Rauschenberg's bed is an exciting example of the marriage of American and European traditions leading to erotic intrigue.

Surrealist exhibitions and their opening-night performances would later inspire younger generations of performance, Happening, and installation artists, but they also led younger artists to reject overt eroticism and to pursue new, different means of corporeal expression. Yves Klein (1928–62) was introducing a different form of erotic performance to his canvases in the 1950s. Where Pollock dripped paint, Klein orchestrated nude models covered in his custom-made International Klein Blue (coined in 1955) paint, literally using the female body as a living brush. His *Anthropometry* (1960) **[63]** shows how he turned action painting and erotic painting in a new direction, reveling in erotic flesh and yet remaining distant throughout. It was performed at the International Gallery of Contemporary Art (Galerie Internationale d'Art Contemporain) in Paris on 9 March 1960: a chamber orchestra played his *Monotone* symphony created in 1947 (40 minutes of one continuous sound, with no beginning or end, to give 'a sense of aspiration, or a sensibility outside and beyond time'), while the artist, dressed in a tuxedo and wearing white gloves, directed naked, nubile young women to pour paint on themselves and roll on paper that covered the floor like a theatre stage. The twists and turns of their bodies left breast, belly, and buttock prints on the paper—the traces or 'stains' of the whole erotic performance. Klein was keen to distinguish himself from Pollock's Abstract Expressionism (the *Life* magazine feature on Pollock would not

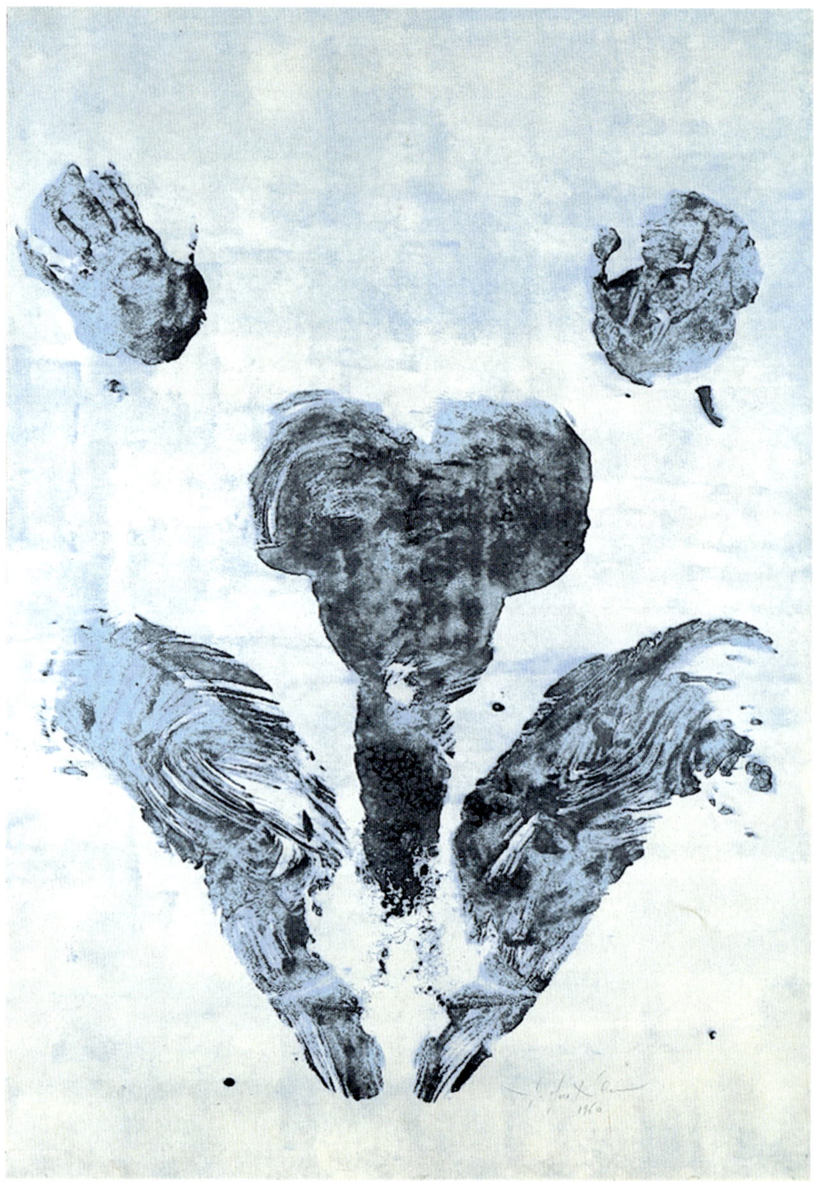

63 Yves Klein
Anthropometry, 1960
Klein's anthropometry was created with a live model who was covered in his trademark ultramarine blue paint (created in 1956 and named IKB, International Klein Blue) and used as a living paintbrush.

have gone unnoticed by French artists) as well as the Paris action art of Georges Mathieu, stating that his art was 'opposed to "action painting" in that I am actually completely detached from the physical work during its creation'.[36] He brought the notion of auteurship to a whole new dramatic significance, while also combining a number of influences—his experience as a Judo black belt, his exposure to Zen Buddhism and the writings of Gaston Bachelard, his love of Giotto's blue in the Basilica of St Francis at Assisi, and his Catholic childhood. He believed his anthropometries were spiritual as well as physical, comparable to religious relics (such as St Veronica's veil, used to wipe the face of Christ on the road to Calvary and miraculously displaying his visage afterwards), and were imbued with an 'anthropophagous' spirit, fusing Eros and Thanatos, in European man. As Klein wrote in his 1957 diary: 'What an immense, great human body it [Europe] represents. Europe is truly made of pure "flesh", gorged with the blood of past civilizations and speechless from inner joy.'[37] While Klein may have kept a safe distance from his naked models and their painted bodies, his performance art brought the female model and her eroticism into the real presence of the viewer, shifting the erotic space out of the private studio and into the public arena. With this act, erotic art was now on the cusp between the modern and the postmodern; the decade of the 1960s would see both movements battling it out.

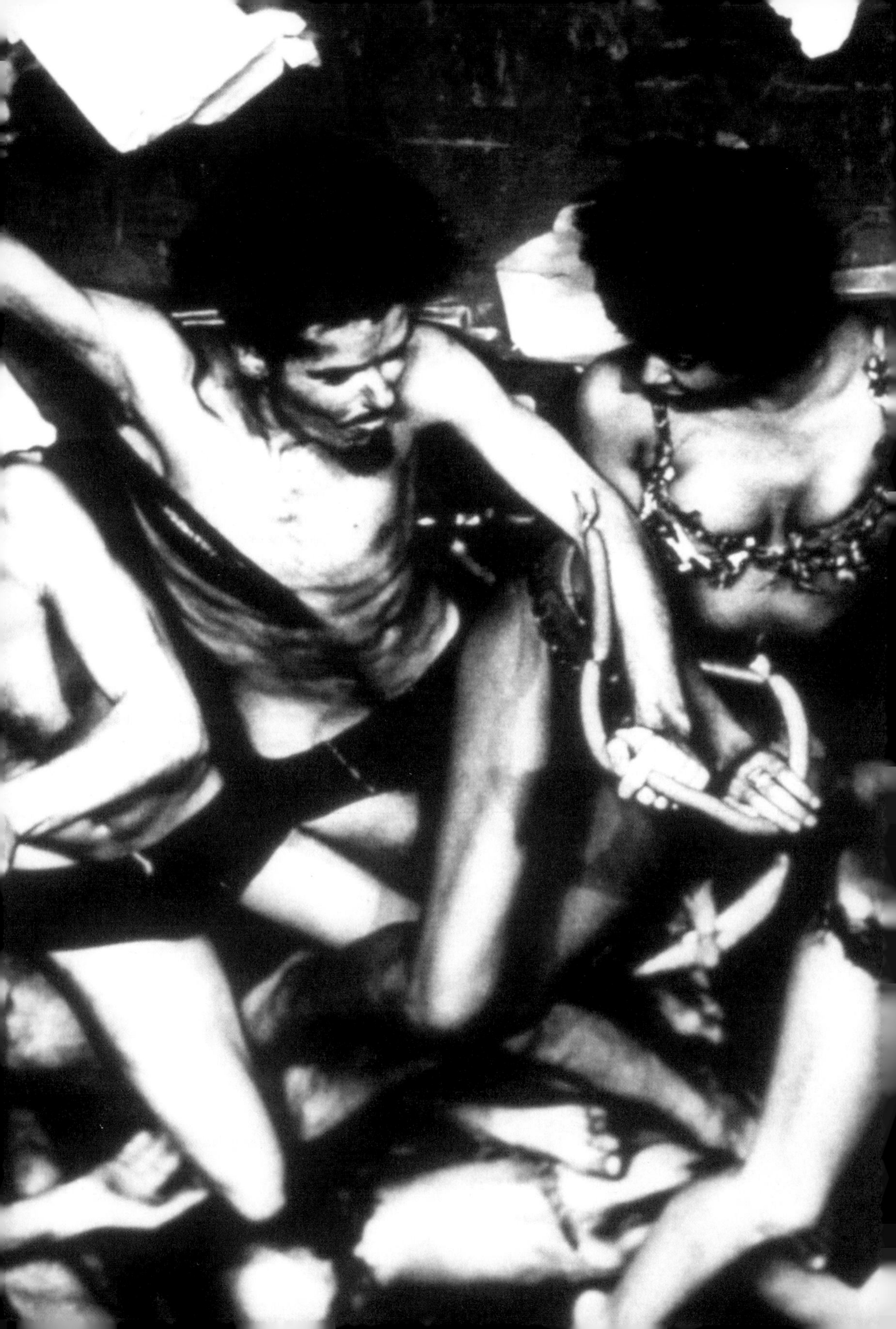

7

Eros and the 1960s

Post-war angst gave way to kitsch, absurdity, and counterculturalism in the 1960s. The Abstract Expressionism of Jackson Pollock in the United States and the *Anthropometries* of Yves Klein in France gave way to Pop art and performance art which brought the street into art and art into the streets. These new movements shared an energy and irreverence for high art traditions, and a sense of *irony* when it came to eroticism. Perhaps one of the defining feature of the 1960s was the conspicuous role played by the United States in the art world and market. The tensions between American 'high' art and 'low' mass culture, between the glamour of popular culture and the banalities of life in Middle America, became the subject of art for a new generation. And yet the culture of mass consumerism, America's Cold War faith in technology and weapons of mass destruction, and intervention in the civil war between the Communist North Vietnam and pro-Western South Vietnam (1964–73) was also the *object* of vehement attack in the increasingly politicized art of this generation. If erotic art enjoyed a new non-conformist sexualization (and often masculinization) in Pop art in the first half of the decade, it soon gave way to countercultural radicalism in the latter half.

64 Carolee Schneemann
Meat Joy, 1964

Meat Joy developed from a series of 'dream sensation images' that the artist had been recording since 1960. Its title was inspired by the Beat writer Michael McClure's *Meat Science Essays* (1963). For Schneemann the performance was an 'erotic rite: excessive, indulgent; a celebration of flesh as material'.

In *Understanding Media: The Extensions of Man* (1964) Marshall McLuhan presented a radical view of the world, claiming that the new technologies of the modern age (television, radio, telephones, cinema, computers) were creating a 'global village' that would radically alter the way people lived and their visual experience of the world (television adverts, billboards, comics, Hollywood films). Mass media increasingly mediated the individual's knowledge of the world: the generation of artists reaching adulthood in the 1960s inevitably incorporated in their art the global and visual influence of television (from documentaries about non-Western cultures and news reports from war zones, to commercials, political broadcasts, and cartoons). Artists turned to popular iconography as a means of expressing the sensibility of the 1960s, reflecting this new and distinctly immediate visual culture and its values, but from a new critical perspective.

Artists turned more and more to popular depictions of sex as source material: teen romance, soft-porn magazines, television and film sex symbols, street fashion, and advertising campaigns based on the sex appeal of consumer goods. The Sexual Revolution of the 1960s brought to a peak the general trend of increasingly liberal attitudes to sex in many Western countries after World War II. The term 'Sexual Revolution' was in general popular use in American society by 1963. It was manifest in the heightened sexualization of everyday popular culture (notably in advertising and men's and women's magazines), the increased prevalence of extra-marital sex and of cohabitation instead of marriage, and (in visual culture) in the deliberate use of sexually explicit imagery and performance as a revolutionary shock weapon against bourgeois morality. *Cosmopolitan* magazine was relaunched by Helen Gurley Brown in 1965 to cater to the needs of sexually active single woman. Famous for her book *Sex and the Single Girl*, published in 1962, Gurley Brown advised young womenfolk: 'You do not need men every step of the way, and they are often cheaper emotionally and more fun by the dozen.'[1] Women's performance art, meanwhile, saw women not just claiming their sexual identities but celebrating them. Too long relegated to the status of erotic object, women now claimed their status as erotic subjects. At the same time new models of masculinity, notably the 'Playboy' who enjoyed luring the sexually active single woman back to his Hugh Hefner-styled leopard-printed boudoir, came to the fore of Pop art.

Pop Art and the All-American Nude

As the term itself indicates, Pop art took its inspiration from popular culture—billboards, television commercials, magazines, movie posters. Pop art maintained the epic scale typical of the Abstract Expressionist canvases of Jackson Pollock while rejecting their gesturalism, mental intensity and angst, and emphasis on painting as performance. Avoiding connotations of creativity, Pop artists set out to *produce* works of art that used familiar, popular cultural imagery and bold flat colour, working with mechanical and impersonal techniques of commercial art such as silkscreen, Ben Day dots, and the airbrush. Pop art seemed to promote the American dream while also questioning it, bringing consumer culture into high art and yet undermining the very concept of high art in the process. Claes Oldenburg's (b. 1929) 1961 text voices this tension:

> I am for an art that is political-erotical-mystical, that does something other than sit on its ass in a museum.
>
> I am for an art that grows up not knowing it is art at all, an art given the chance of having a starting point of zero.
>
> I am for an art that embroils itself with the everyday crap and still comes out on top.
>
> I am for an art that imitates the human, that is comic, if necessary, or violent, or whatever is necessary.
>
> I am for an art that takes its form from the lines of life itself, that twists and extends and accumulates and spits and drips, and is heavy and coarse and blunt and sweet and stupid as life itself . . .[2]

Oldenburg wrote during the Kennedy era, a period of great economic growth and national optimism, but within that optimism Pop art detected a weakness: the tendency of youth and television culture towards convenience and the throw-away. The 1961 reprinting of Clement Greenberg's 1939 essay 'Avant-Garde and Kitsch' fuelled the critical perception of Pop art as a new expression of kitsch—an art that was high-gloss, impersonal, and garish. Certainly Pop art's pirating of consumer culture seemed to confirm that suspicion, but kitsch has a subversive edge to it too. Even when we are faced with the most blatantly materialist and sexist imagery we find the boundaries of high and low culture, masculine and feminine space, public and private sexuality, being blurred.

Roy Lichtenstein (1923–97) focused on a very particular aspect of 1960s consumer culture, the teen idol comic, paying homage to the comic strip in his use both of mechanical printing methods (especially the magnified Ben Day dots prominent in his blown-up graphics) and in quotes from actual comic storyboards. The impersonal style of his compositions, coupled with his parodic idealization of swooning girls and comic strip heroes was intended to create an emotional directness. Lichtenstein took his subject-matter from popular, uncontroversial comics endorsed by the Comics Code Authority (set up in 1954). These comics offered the perfect vehicle for the exploration of teenage dramas—broken hearts, crushes on boys, and fantasies of being a heroic wartime fighter pilot. Lichtenstein did not reproduce images from the original comics directly but *recomposed* their elements, enlarging a particular frame from a story to the size of a history painting while still retaining its balloon dialogue in order to undercut ironically the themes of life and death, love and despair. In *Drowning Girl* of 1963 **[65]** we see a tearful, pretty girl with a perfect pout drowning in the sea but thinking 'I don't care! I'd rather sink than call Brad for help!' The image was borrowed from a 1962 panel from the story 'Run for Love!' in the

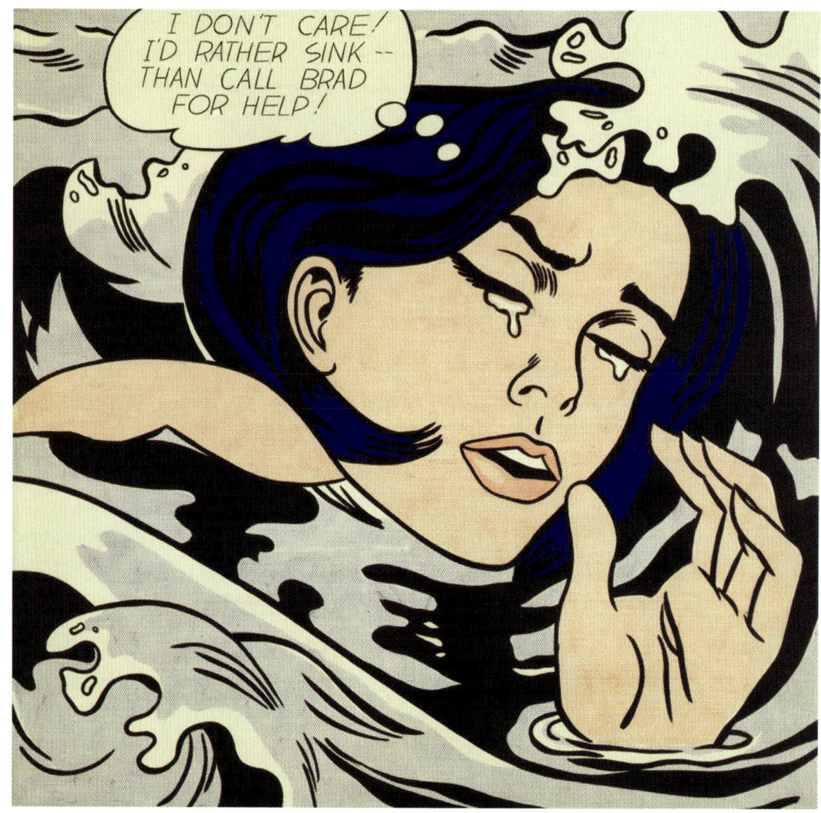

65 Roy Lichtenstein
Drowning Girl, 1963
Lichtenstein's comic strip painting borrows its composition from 'Run for Love!', a picture story in a 1962 edition of the *Secret Hearts* comic. The artist mimics low culture, invoking the teen romance and sexuality of Middle America while ironically elevating comic book imagery to the status of high art.

Secret Hearts comic but Lichtenstein changed the boy's name to make the scene all the more 'American'—replacing the comic's 'Mal' with the all-American name 'Brad'.[3] Lichtenstein perpetuated a particular idea of sexual desire that was already rapidly disappearing from view: his images—of crying girls whose sole mission in life is to get married and of muscular boys who want to protect their women—stand in stark contrast to the sexual politics of the counterculture that would emerge with full force in the second half of the decade. Lichtenstein's teen romance would give way to the sexual experimentation and revolutionary ideals increasingly characteristic of American youth after the assassination of President Kennedy in November 1963. As political tensions grew more acute, questions were asked about just how ironic or critical Pop art really was. Indeed, as early as the summer of 1963, Peter Selz, a curator at the Museum of Modern Art in New York, suggested in *Partisan Review* that Pop art was just slick national and sexual chauvinism.[4]

Tom Wesselmann (1931–2004) exposed himself to such criticism in his billboard-scale stylized nudes. Born in Cincinnati, he studied at the Cooper Union School of Art and Architecture in New York from 1956 to

1959; his early style was heavily influenced by Abstract Expressionism and the figurative art of de Kooning. However, in the 1960s his art took a dramatic turn towards kitsch with his *Great American* nude series. His mixed-media *Great American Nude #6* (1961) exemplifies his fusion of high art and American iconography: the flattened, naive perspective refers to Matisse's odalisques of the 1920s, while a portrait by Amedeo Modigliani (1884–1920) hangs on the wall behind her. A little kitten has a central position in the work, no doubt alluding to the first great 'real' nude, Manet's *Olympia*. Here Wesselmann makes high art decorative and domestic, acknowledging that mass reproduction has allowed European art to lose its elitist aura and to infiltrate an all-American suburban interior. In another mixed-media work of the same year, *Little Great American Nude #6*, a Matisse-like pink nude poses against American high art: the American flag and a portrait of George Washington. Even the colour scheme of the interior is nationalistic—red and white bedding and a blue wall. The large scale of Wesselmann's work, coupled with the title 'Great', made an ironic statement on the high art tradition of the nude. Five years later, his *Great American Nude #77* presents an even more stylized recumbent American odalisque as the ultimate commodity. Her faceless body has been reduced to sexual shapes: a bright red nipple on a white breast exposed to the summer sun. Similarly, in *American Nude* (1967) the nude's bikini tan-lines strategically lead the eye to her breasts and pubis, and vibrant red tones to her open lips; while stockings, splayed legs, and leopard-print bedding leave little to the imagination. In these works Wesselman's nudes are depersonalized, echoing the style of contemporary advertising. As Sidra Stich has pointed out, though, they also echo the new 'genre' of the nude that now populated American life: the slick soft-porn centrefold made famous by *Playboy* magazine. The nudes in Wesselmann's art were part of the new sexual culture *Playboy* was promoting with its combination of fiction, advertisements, and nude photograph spreads; they were to be viewed as 'a status symbol, associated with the good life in America'.[5] Certainly, many of Wesselmann's nudes re-stage the clichéd erotic scenes of soft porn. In *Smoker, 1 (Mouth 12)*, also of 1967, Wesselmann reduces the female body to its ultimate erotic sign: a red-painted mouth, lips parted, from which a cigarette hangs as smoke seems to filter out of the canvas. Wesselmann alludes to pin-ups of Hollywood starlets and billboard campaigns advertising cigarette brands. He is not just painting the allure of the all-American blonde, he is teasing the all-American male fantasist.

As Cécile Whiting has argued, in his art Wesselmann conflated highbrow male taste for the nude with middlebrow female taste for consumer objects and chic domestic interiors. His eroticism was 'bawdy', it conformed to pornographic codes and 'violated the consumer's standard of restraint and modesty seen in women's magazines', as well as the restraints promoted by Greenbergian modernism.[6] Whiting also concludes that Wesselmann's art privileges the male gaze and the *Playboy* view of the world. However, we might also view his nudes as configuring a 'new woman' who is conscious that she is both subject and object of the male gaze and happy in her role as both the sexual commodity and the sexual consumer—Wesselmann may be promoting a 'Playgirl' who rejects bourgeois values.[7] While Wesselmann admitted in an interview in 1964 that he did not see Pop as revolutionary, he did admit that Dada had 'something to do with my work'.[8] When looking at Wesselmann we should perhaps recall Duchamp's parody of Leonardo da Vinci's *Mona Lisa* in 1919 when, on a cheap postcard reproduction of the famous painting, he added a moustache to her enigmatic face and the letters 'L.H.O.O.Q.' below her hands—letters that read as 'Elle a chaud au cul!' (She's got a hot ass!) when pronounced in French.

The Californian artist Mel Ramos (b. 1935) also takes on the public advertising machine and the private reader of soft-porn magazines in his art, though in a style that has led critics to emphasize the sensuality of his thickly pigmented surfaces and to read this surface 'play' as a commentary on mass versus fine art and a peculiarly San Francisco Bay Area approach to Pop.[9] Ramos has produced a number of images of female sex symbols, from Jane Russell to Wonder Woman, in a style reminiscent of comic books but with the sexual humour and 'peek-a-boo' compositions typical of *Playboy* magazine. Like *Playboy* pin-ups, his nudes are streamlined, highly staged, physically flawless, and with the veiled eroticism of the girl next door. Yet Ramos also professed to have been influenced by Dalí and de Kooning. The former's illusionistic approach to eroticism and the latter's obsession with the female nude have certain traces in Ramos's distinctly individual art. One critic's 1966 account of Ramos's talents still rings true, however, and captures the artist's emphatically male and uncomplicated view of woman as sexual object: 'He presents us with a bevy of luscious broads, starkers all, whose denture-like artificiality becomes apparent even as we begin to salivate.'[10] An example of such 'broads' include *Chiquita* (1964), a blonde nude cupping her breasts and smiling out at the viewer as she steps out of a mammoth, half-peeled Chiquita banana, and *Gorilla* (1967), a sultry buxom brunette lying on a gorilla.

Ramos advanced his subject-matter beyond the world of advertising and into the world of high art too, parodying famous art-historical nudes such as Ingres's *Turkish Bath* and Manet's *Olympia*. Yet we find no

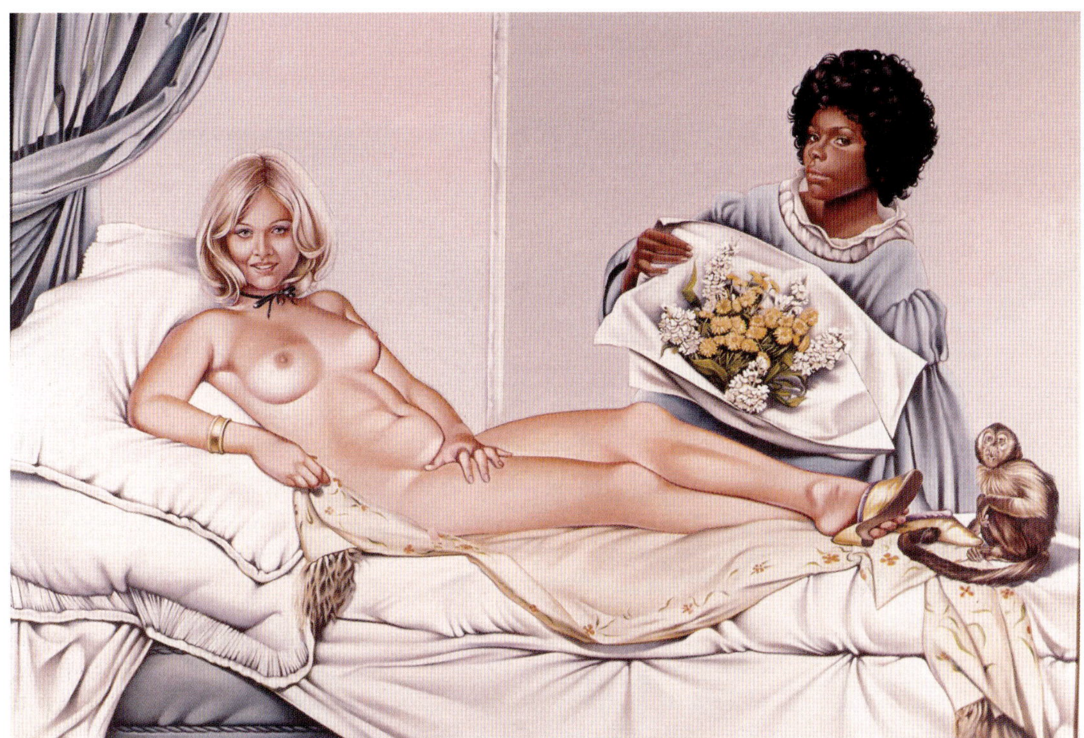

66 Mel Ramos
Manet's Olympia, 1973
Ramos claimed he just 'removed the art historical patina' of Manet's celebrated *Olympia*, as he updated it with the modern aesthetics of the pin-up and a light-hearted *Playboy* eroticism.

Dadaist spirit in these works either: as Ramos himself said, his 'odes' to these earlier erotic paintings were simply part of a process of 'cleaning up those old paintings—the images are the same, I just removed the art historical patina.'[11] He simply 'updated' masterpieces, almost out of a nostalgia for a fine art eroticism. His *Manet's Olympia* (1973) **[66]** presents a Californian blonde, bikini tan-lines showing, stretched out on a bed and grinning at the viewer as her black maidservant, complete with 1970s eye-shadow, brings her flowers. Manet's subversive use of the real body and his assault on the art academy and bourgeois morality seem to have been lost on Ramos, despite his decision to re-work this particular nineteenth-century painting. In an interview in 1979, he explained that Manet's *Olympia* 'permeates every art book published since 1945. It's become the same as the *Coca Cola* image on the billboard right there in front of you.'[12] For Ramos the nude is like a hamburger: a tasty, quick, and ephemeral treat.

Ramos stands as a useful foil to the Swedish-born but New York- and Chicago-reared Claes Oldenburg, whose Pop sculptures included *Two Cheeseburgers with Everything on Them* (1962), made of burlap soaked in plaster, and *Giant Hamburger* (1962) made of sailcloth stuffed with foam. In 1961 Oldenburg opened *The Store*, where he sold large sculptures of

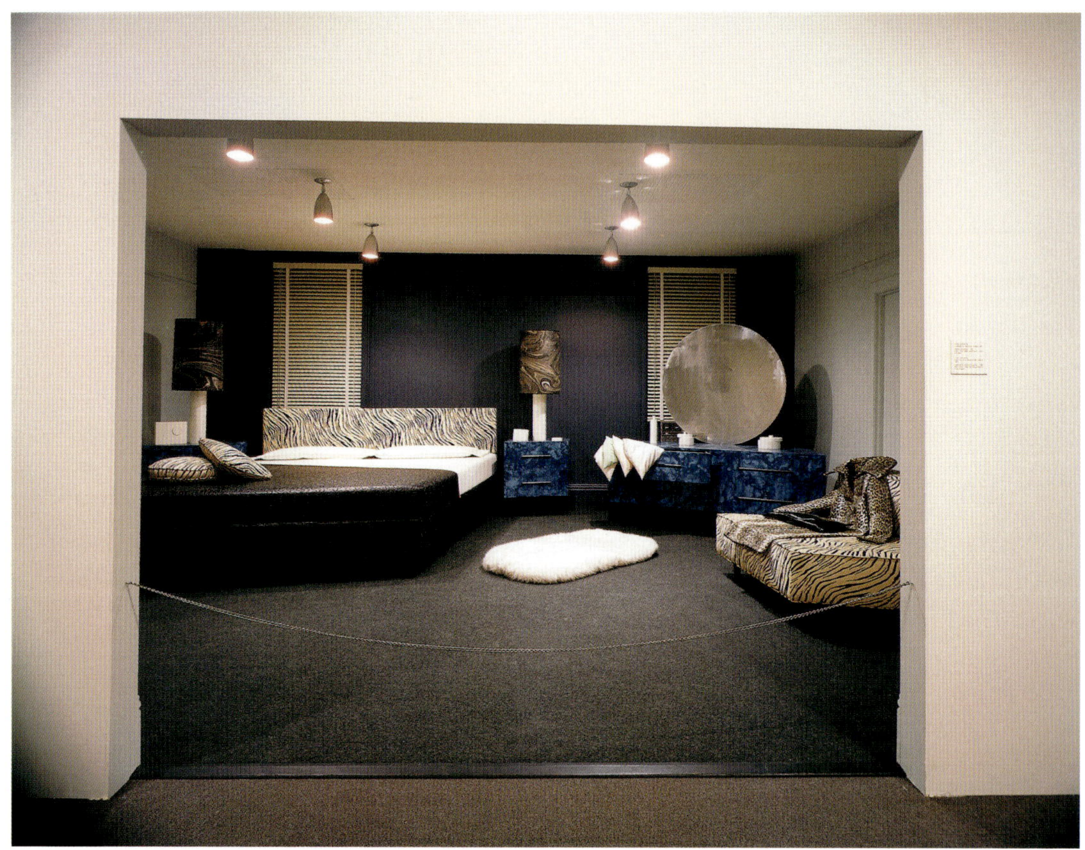

67 Claes Oldenburg
Bedroom Ensemble (1/3), 1963
This replica installation was inspired by the tacky, animal-skin themes of rooms in a Malibu motel Oldenburg had seen in his youth.

food (French fries, string beans) and basic consumer goods (a toaster, a telephone) made of plaster-soaked muslin over wire frames. They were like Abstract Expressionist renditions of consumer goods with their lumpy, crumpled surfaces and dripping colour schemes. However, in making his art available to the public in his own store—rather than in a gallery—Oldenburg made a Duchampian gesture against the art market. His *Bedroom Ensemble* (1963) **[67]**, part of his *Home* series, continued this theme in its simulacral play. Here Oldenburg re-created a bedroom interior complete with paired Formica night tables, tacky fun fur and leather bed, cushions, and sofa. The installation was based on an actual, well-known motel on the Pacific Coast Highway in Malibu in which each bedroom suite was decorated in the skin pattern of an animal—a leopard, zebra, etc. His chosen room had a zebra-patterned headboard on the bed, cushions, lampshades, and even a fake-fur rug on the floor. It was not just the re-creation of a kitsch 'erotic' setting that made this work provocative: every detail had its own sensual, phenomenological appeal. His sculptures were meant to relate to the viewer's body, to suggest body parts in their softness. As Donald Judd explained in a 1964 review, the furniture in Oldenburg's series of bedroom suites had an emotive power, ordinary things became psychosexualized, soft things seemed hard and hard things soft—such as light switches suggesting nipples.[13]

By the late 1960s, by which time American artists were increasingly concerned with political iconography and propaganda at the height of the Vietnam War, Oldenburg turned from domestic themes to emphatically public ones while still remaining true to his concern with sculptural intimacy and irony. In 1969 he constructed the large-scale *Lipstick (Ascending) on Caterpillar Tracks* on the campus of Yale University in Connecticut. This was a sculpture of steel, plastic, and wood painted in bright enamel, both monumental and anti-monumental: a banal, unimportant object made magnificent. And it was both male and female in subject, given it was a woman's personal cosmetic item made phallic. Most importantly, however, it was commissioned by dissident students in response to a remark by Herbert Marcuse on the subversive potential of satirical art; built in front of a classical war memorial, it irreverently presented itself as an anti-war monument.[14] As one critic observed in 1971, it was a 'lipstick-rocket-tank, it mocks the military erection and puts its pink finger on a culture that measures its virility in missiles'.[15] It offered a new American dream fuelled on the 1960s rally cry, 'Make Love Not War'.

Andy Warhol

The art of Andy Warhol (1928–87) is a more provocative combination of sexual liberation with commercial exploitation. In his silkscreen images of popular sex icons such as Marlon Brando, Elvis Presley, and Marilyn Monroe, and in his homoerotic art and films, he addressed both mass culture and subculture. After Monroe's death from an overdose of sleeping pills in August 1962, Warhol made more than twenty silkscreen prints based on a publicity still of her from the 1953 film *Niagara*, presenting multiple versions of the star in Technicolor and black and white. He thus created a monument to Monroe as well as a parody of Hollywood's star factory. In *Marilyn Diptych* (1962) she is memorialized in gold and yet her iconic status reminds us that she will be remembered for her image rather than her real self.[16]

Warhol's silkscreen images of Elvis—from *Triple Elvis* (1962) to *Elvis I and II* (1964) **[68]**—also present multiples of the star, drawn from a publicity still of Elvis's 1960 film *Flaming Star*. In both prints, Elvis stands in cowboy gear, legs apart, gun drawn. The repetition in the composition

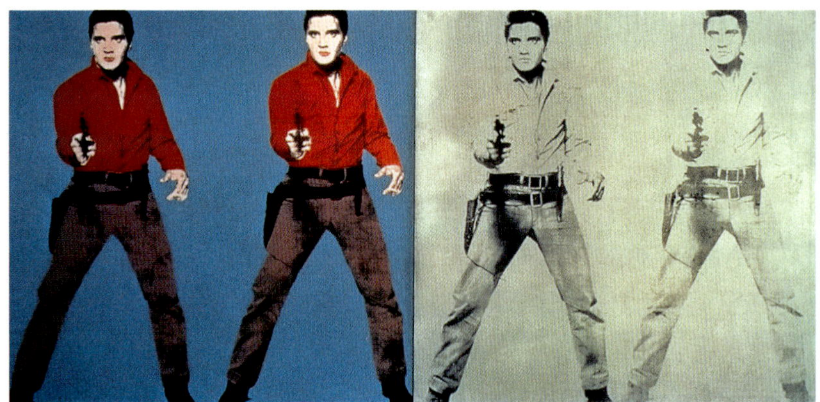

68 Andy Warhol
Elvis I and II, 1964

Having studied art at the Carnegie Institute, Pittsburgh, for four years, Warhol moved to New York in 1949, where he worked as a commercial artist. This experience would inform his Pop style and subject-matter, notably his use of silkscreen printing (where the image is transferred to the screen by photomechanical means) and his obsession with famous brands (Coca-Cola, Campbell's Soup, Brillo) and people, including Elvis Presley.

alludes to the multiple images of motion pictures, while a shift in colour from left to right in *Elvis I and II* suggests the superficiality of stardom as the sex symbol 'deteriorates' from shining movie star to faded memory in the palette shift, from vibrant red and purple on the left to newspaper grey on the right. As with Monroe, Elvis's sexual charisma is immediate and yet fleeting, while his cocked gun suggests that Warhol recognizes him as the all-American sex fantasy, for girls *and* boys.

Warhol's icons, coupled with his images of disaster—*White Burning Car III* (1963) and *Race Riot* (1964)—have been interpreted by Hal Foster as examples of 'traumatic realism'.[17] For Thomas Crow they are proof of Warhol's social engagement. Crow describes Warhol's work as a '*peinture noire* in the sense that the adjective is applied to the *film noir* genre of the forties and the fifties—a stark, disabused, pessimistic vision of American life' built on a knowing use of pulp media rather than 'the easier path of irony or condescension' seen in other Pop artists.[18] Certainly this can be seen in his 'piss paintings' entitled *Oxidations*. Begun in 1977, they paid homage to the avant-garde, notably to Duchamp's innovative use of seminal fluid in his *Wayward Landscape* of 1946. Their monochrome surfaces were coated with metallic paint striated and spotted with the oxidizing marks of urination on the canvas. Duchamp, whom he met in 1963, was a hero figure for Warhol. He paid homage to the older artist in these paintings and in his photographic self-portraits in drag, as well as in his general subversive use of camp to promote sexual liberty. It was with Warhol that the critical label 'camp' took on its emphatic homosexual connotations. Sontag had identified the origins of camp in homosexual culture, and now Warhol's art, life, and persona seemed to confirm campness as a key part of his Pop aesthetic. In *The Philosophy of Andy Warhol* (1975), the artist said he loved the sexual liberation movement of the 1960s because 'after the "lib" the things that were always a mystique became understandable and boring'.[19] Warhol's attempt to make the erotic 'boring' was perhaps his most subversive contribution to modern art.

Warhol's 'underground' film collaborations with Paul Morrissey, such as *My Hustler* (1965) and *Flesh* (1968), also brought bohemian sexuality and homosexual desire into an erotic world impossible to achieve on the canvas. Both of these films were about male prostitution, while the latter was clearly influential on the celebrated Hollywood version of male prostitution seen in John Schlesinger's *Midnight Cowboy* (1969), starring Jon Voight as Joe Buck and Dustin Hoffman as Ratso Rizzo. *Flesh*, starring Joe Dallesandro, portrays a day in the life of a male hustler, showing his homosexual and heterosexual encounters as he sells his body to make cash for his wife's girlfriend's abortion. When the film opened in September 1968 it was a great success, playing continuously in downtown and uptown New York cinemas for a year. Between his art, films, and his legendary art space known as the 'Factory'—where wannabe artists and actors, art world figures and the rock band the Velvet Underground congregated—Warhol was a key player in what cultural historian Peter Wollen has described as the 'one performance eco-system' of the 1960s.[20]

Performing the Erotic Body

Just as the Dadaists had organized cabaret evenings with nonsensical performances, it is not surprising that the emergence of a neo-Dadaism in the 1950s and 1960s also led to a return to performance art. Young artists in the United States and Europe seized upon Dada irony, use of found objects, and general subversive intent to critique art, aesthetic value, society, and politics. Marcel Duchamp remained a significant mentor figure for this generation, who could turn to Motherwell's anthology *Dada Painters and Poets* (1951), Robert Lebel's *Sur Marcel Duchamp* (1959) and Michel Sanouillet's anthology of Duchamp's writings, *Marchand du Sel: Écrits de Marcel Duchamp* (1959), to learn more of Dada and Duchamp's life, art, and artistic intent. Duchamp's *Large Glass* was also on show at the Museum of Modern Art, New York, from 1943 to 1946 and influenced young Americans who rejected Greenberg's advocacy of 'art for art's sake' and his celebration of Abstract Expressionism. Among them was Robert Rauschenberg, who, as we have seen, parodied Abstract Expressionism in his painterly *Bed* (1955) and aligned himself to the Surrealists, whom Greenberg loathed, by participating in their 1959 *EROS* exhibition.

Duchamp's own art of this period was increasingly explicit in its eroticism, though his most erotic work, an installation entitled *Étant*

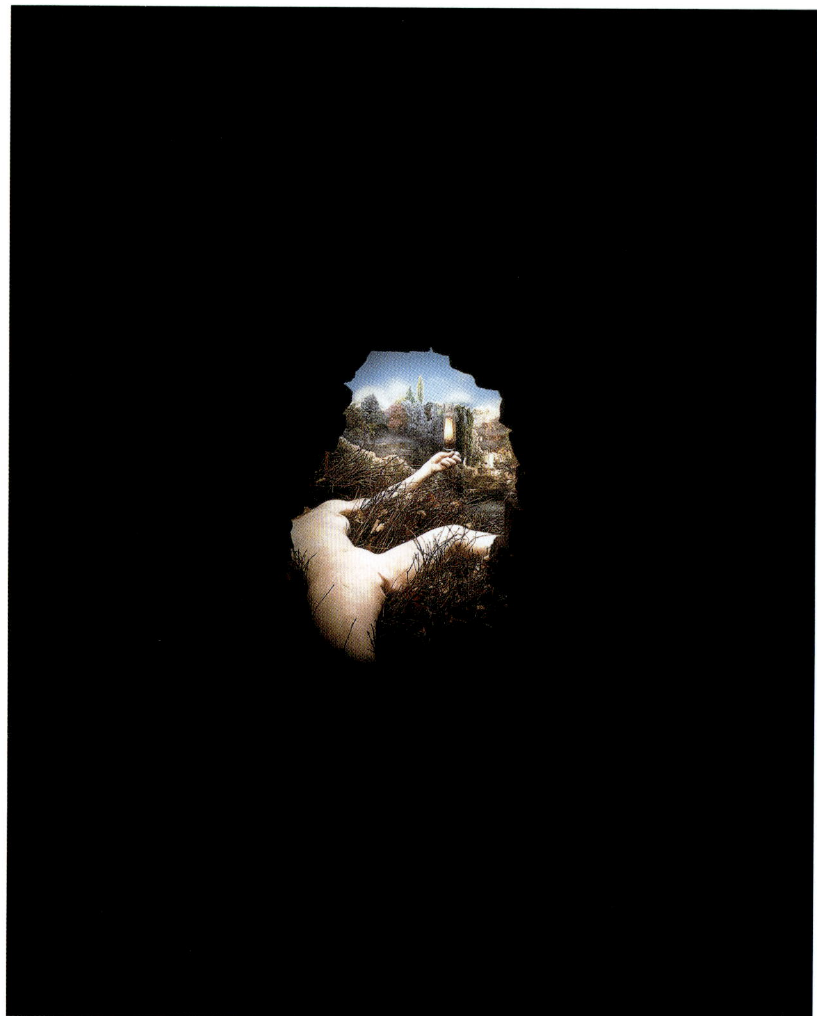

69 Marcel Duchamp
Étant donnés: 1. La Chute d'eau; 2. Le Gaz d'éclairage (Given: 1. The Waterfall; 2. The Illuminating Gas), 1946–66

This installation was kept secret by Duchamp until after his death. Its title refers to his earlier *Bride Stripped Bare by her Bachelors, Even.* Where the earlier work was intriguing for its erotic theatrics staged on transparent, glass panels, the erotic lure of *Étant donnés* lies in its impenetrable old door and the erotic landscape centred on a 'bride' holding an illuminated glass lamp, revealed only by looking through two little peep-holes.

donnés: 1. La Chute d'eau 2. Le Gaz d'éclairage (*Given: 1. The Waterfall 2. The Illuminating Gas*) (1946–66) **[69]**, was not revealed until after his death in 1968. He worked on the installation in secret for 20 years; it is now installed, following his precise instructions, in the Philadelphia Museum of Art. As with all of Duchamp's works, it needs the spectator, the final performer, for completion. In addition it is only visible to one spectator at a time. The installation consists of an old wooden door set in a brick arch, its surface cracked and splintered. There is no handle or lock on the door, but at the average eye level there are two distinct eye holes, which allow one to peep into the other side of the door. One might expect to look in and see an interior, a Sadean cell perhaps, but instead we look on to a landscape framed by the crude black outline of brick. Thus suspense is augmented as we effectively look through two 'obstacles', a door and a wall, to see into Duchamp's landscape. Unsurprisingly it is a landscape loaded with erotic thrill and unease: to the left of the jaggedly framed landscape we see a naked female, her left and part of her right breast exposed, her visible torso topped by a curl of blonde hair and ending with her spread legs. This select view allows the spectator to view her hairless pudenda and the lips of her sex, though these lips are far from anatomically accurate, as if the artist deliberately wants the female sex to look like a wound, a gash. She lies on a bed of grass and dry leaves in front of a rather romantic landscape that fills the background with purple and green trees, a running waterfall, and bright-blue sky.[21] All this is perfectly lit for the spectator's delectation, not by sunlight but by the female herself as she holds a gas burner in her left hand, its golden hue highlighting her fair flesh and smooth sex. Given her active role, what at first seems like an image of post-coital sleep—or worse, an image of the dead body of a rape victim—now takes on an even more uncanny edge. She sheds light on her own sex, thus directing the spectator's eyes back from the idyllic landscape to the very spot one's eye finds most disturbing. Duchamp seems to have brought his bride of the *Large Glass* into the third dimension, her gas burner reminding us of his peculiar erotic language in his notes for that earlier installation. We recall that when explaining the actions and sexual emissions of the nine moulds in the *Large Glass*, Duchamp refers to an 'illuminating gas' that fills the moulds, who then try to shoot up at the bride so she might experience a 'cinematic blossoming'. Thus the waterfall and gas of *Given* suggests not only uncontrollable sexual fluids but also the illuminating pleasure achieved when erotic desire is given free rein. Nonetheless, the element of unease and the suggestion of violence or violation created by the very contents of the installation also serves to remind us of the Madonna/Whore paradigm, the association between goodness and virginity that Duchamp pointed towards in his fascination with the bride. The pink texture of the naked female in *Given* might also remind us of Duchamp and Donati's painted falsie for the 1947 Surrealist catalogue, entitled *Please Touch* **[60]**. A similar sense of wanting to see and desire more—to reach out and touch the whole body—surrounds both works. Indeed, black velvet as used by Duchamp and Donati in 1947 to stage their solitary breast is used again here around the brick opening to lend a greater theatricality to the 'peeping' experience, as well as to magnify the element of shock. If this installation reminds us of one of the first works discussed in the book, Gustave Courbet's *Origin of the World* (1866) **[3]** and its dramatic staging of the female sex, then we should not be surprised either. Courbet's painting, we recall, was in the collection of Sylvie Bataille Lacan in the 1930s, concealed in a wooden hiding device constructed by the Surrealist painter André Masson. Since the Surrealists were concerned to reveal the hidden dimension of the human psyche, to bring reality and dream together and to adopt a tactic of 'profane illumination', hiding and revealing was a key part of their subversive strategy, whether in individual artists' work or collective exhibitions. Duchamp, always hailed as a father figure for Surrealism, might here be seen to owe a debt to Surrealism in turn, his erotic installation drawing on the art of Masson and Bellmer as well as the dramatic fetishistic installations and art of younger artists, notably Mimi Parent.

For installations and performances adopting a very different and wonderfully sensual stance on the *male* erotic object at this time we must turn to the Japanese artist Yayoi Kusama (b. 1929). She came to New York after the war, and from 1962 began to create collages, reliefs, and soft phallic sculptures that explored the themes of repetition, aggregation, and accumulation. Her *Sex-Obsession* (1962) and *Compulsion Furniture* (1964) brought an emphatically feminine eroticism to the forefront of American art. In these works Kusama covered everyday objects and furniture with phallic protuberances, creating installations of desire as the spectator was literally surrounded by multiple penises whose erect but bodiless form both suggested sexual excitement and castration. Her art stood between Surrealist sculpture (notably the fetishistic sculpture of Meret Oppenheim and Salvador Dalí) and the irony and kitsch of Pop art. For the feminist cultural critic Lucy Lippard, Kusama's art opened a new direction towards 'Eccentric Abstraction' in her creation of the 'sensuous object'.[22]

However, Kusama went further again with her new erotic sculptures that teased the viewer's senses: by the mid-1960s, Kusama was creating neo-Surrealist erotic environments using brightly coloured (often baby pink) sensuous sculptures, mirrors, electric lights, kinetics, and such props as kitchen tables, high heels, and mannequins. Her *Love Happenings* were often characterized as orgies, involving naked performers, nudist fashion (called 'orgy gowns' by the artist), and acts of 'free love' staged in various studios in lower Manhattan; there was also lighting, rock music, and parodic images of the establishment, from the American flag to posters of President Lyndon B. Johnson. Dressed in her orgy gown, Kusama would paint dots on other performers; they in turn kissed and fondled each other in front of the press, who had been invited to witness their 'liberation'. Kusama also organized more explicit Happenings, such as *Self Obliteration* and *Body Festivals*, in which she and four or five dancers would take to the streets (usually beginning

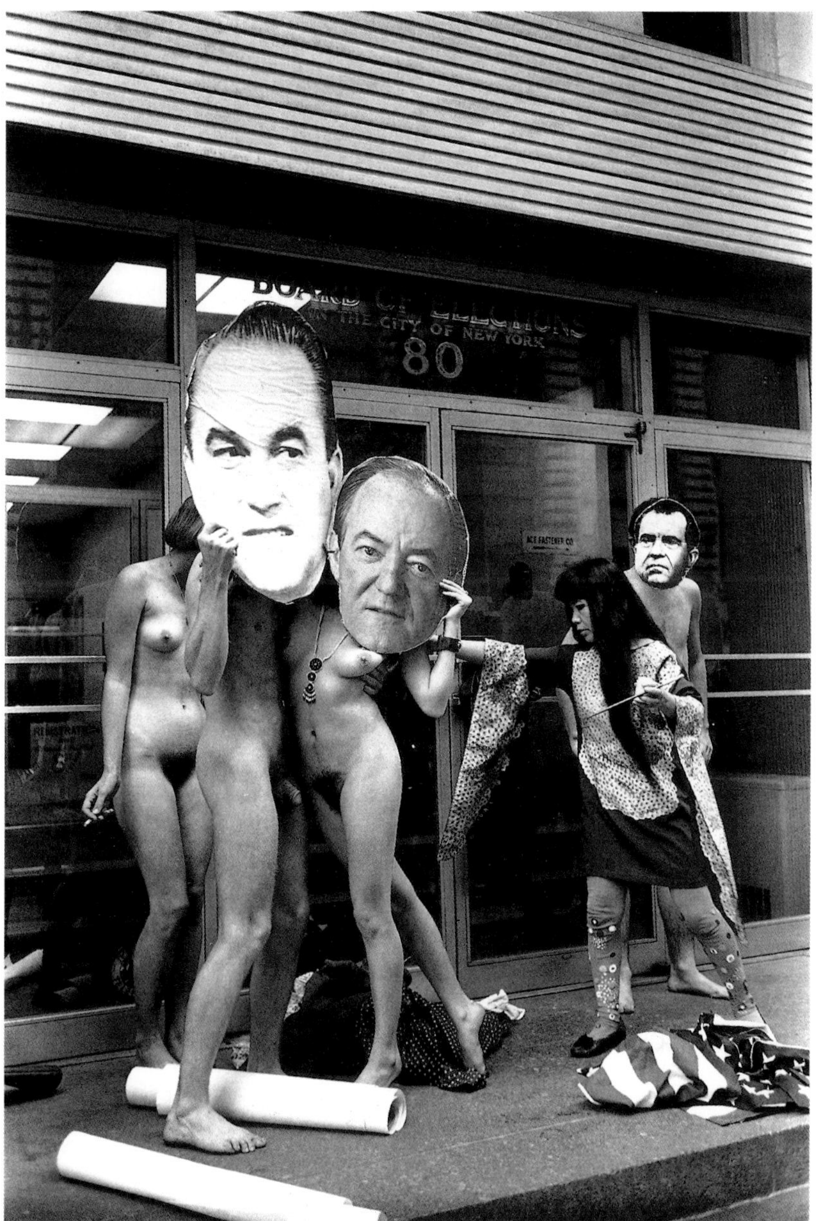

70 Yayoi Kusama
Performance at the Board of Elections, 80 Varick Street, New York, 3 November 1968

Kusama moved to New York in 1957, where her art took a distinctly fetishistic turn as she moved away from drawings and watercolours towards sculpture. In 1964–5 her art evolved from sculpture to environmental art, often including fields of phalluses, polka-dot textiles, and mirrored walls. From 1967 until her return to Japan in 1975, she was involved in Happenings, organized as political protests and sexual celebrations. This performance pilloried the three candidates in the 1968 presidential election: the Independent and Southern segregationist George Wallace (left), the then Vice-President and Democratic candidate Hubert Humphrey (centre), and Republican Richard Nixon (right), who would win later that month. It was part of an *Anatomic Explosions* series of Happenings organized by Kusama from July to November 1968.

in front of an iconic monument in New York such as the Statue of Liberty, St Patrick's Cathedral, or the Museum of Modern Art); Kusama, as 'priestess', would order her fellow performers to strip and dance before the public and invited media **[70]**. These actions were usually stopped after fifteen or twenty minutes by the police. Kusama's originality and force lay in her combination of the body, female sexuality, and the political in all of her art, while the themes of vulnerability and fragmentation perhaps presage the later art of Robert Gober and Kiki Smith.[23]

Kusama's performances were part of the startling phenomenon of the 'Happening', a new form of improvisational and provocative performance art which explored issues of sexuality and gender, the erotic body, and politics. The term 'Happening', common in African-American jazz circles in the 1950s, was first used to categorize a type of art performance by Allan Kaprow (b. 1927). In 1959 he entitled a performance staged in the experimental Reuben Gallery in New York *18 Happenings in 16 Parts*.[24] For the Happening, Kaprow divided the gallery space into three rooms with clear plastic walls; the public, whose tickets directed them to specified seats in each room at particular times, then experienced several performed events including a girl squeezing oranges and an artist lighting matches. The performers included Rauschenberg and Jasper Johns. The Happening was a kind of amateurish type of performance; it had no defined or ideological plan and evolved in the particular environment in which it was staged. Kaprow viewed the environment (a chosen space selected for a given time and a limited audience) and the Happening as interdependent: the former was man-made, the latter ready-mades. Together they created an exciting Neo-Dada space.[25]

A more erotically charged form of Happening was developing in Europe. As avant-garde film-maker Jonas Mekas excitedly reported in 1966 after a five-week trip in Europe: 'It seems that the European undergrounds are breaking open. The American Happening artists are becoming classicists in a way, concerned more with creation than destruction . . . the Happenings staged in Europe are so much wilder, messier, and so much less "art".'[26] The Happenings of the French artist Jean-Jacques Lebel particularly impressed Mekas:

> I saw one staged by Jean-Jacques Lebel in the small town of Cassis, where 5000 people came to watch a huge 800-foot rubber Priapus come into the harbour from the sea, as the loud-speakers sold free love, and it was a wild scene that broke into a near riot, with three boats sunk and tourist cars lifted into the air and plastic bombs thrown at the Living Theatre, and which ended up with Jean-Jacques Lebel being run out of town by the mayor.[27]

Jean-Jacques Lebel (b. 1936) was breaking all erotic barriers, destroying any sense of sexual inhibition, and outraging officials in promoting free love to make a political and social statement, and winning considerable international attention in the process. Influenced by Dada as well as Antonin Artaud, jazz, and Beat poetry, Lebel's aesthetic agenda was

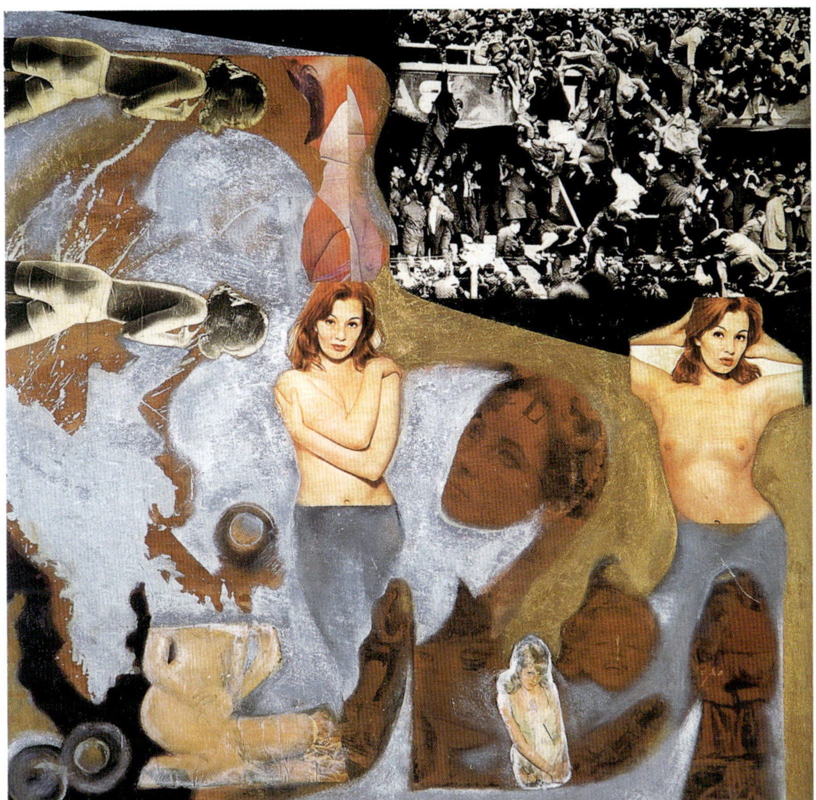

71 Jean-Jacques Lebel
Christine Keeler Icon, 1963
This is one of a series of works by Lebel devoted to Christine Keeler, the model and showgirl whose affair with Conservative Cabinet minister John Profumo caused a political scandal in Britain in 1963. Lebel uses found images, from cutouts of a centrefold of Keeler and Elizabeth Taylor to the photograph of an accident in a football stadium, to explore the power of the media machine and human 'disaster', whether political, romantic, or chance.

characterized by sexual libertarianism, anti-colonialism, and a retaliation against the commodity fetishism of capitalist society. From his collage *Christine Keeler Icon* (1963) **[71]** to his collective, improvised Happenings, Lebel countered political obscenity with sexual obscenity. In *Christine Keeler Icon* Lebel pays homage to the English call-girl Keeler who brought down the Conservative government of British Prime Minister Harold Macmillan in 1963 through her affair with John Profumo, the Secretary of State for War. His Happening strategy is evident in this collage: cutouts of Keeler, Hollywood icons (Marilyn Monroe, Elizabeth Taylor), adverts for girdle panties, and a contemporary magazine photograph of an accident at a football stadium (highlighting the 'disastrous' nature of Profumo's disgrace) are brought together in an improvised but politically pointed manner. Lebel draws these many facets of contemporary life together in swirls of paint so that the eye cannot rest easily and so that every aspect of society (social, sexual, political) is scrutinized through a dark erotic humour.

Compared to the Happenings of Kaprow, whom Lebel met in New York in 1961, Lebel's Happenings might be viewed as deploying a sexual

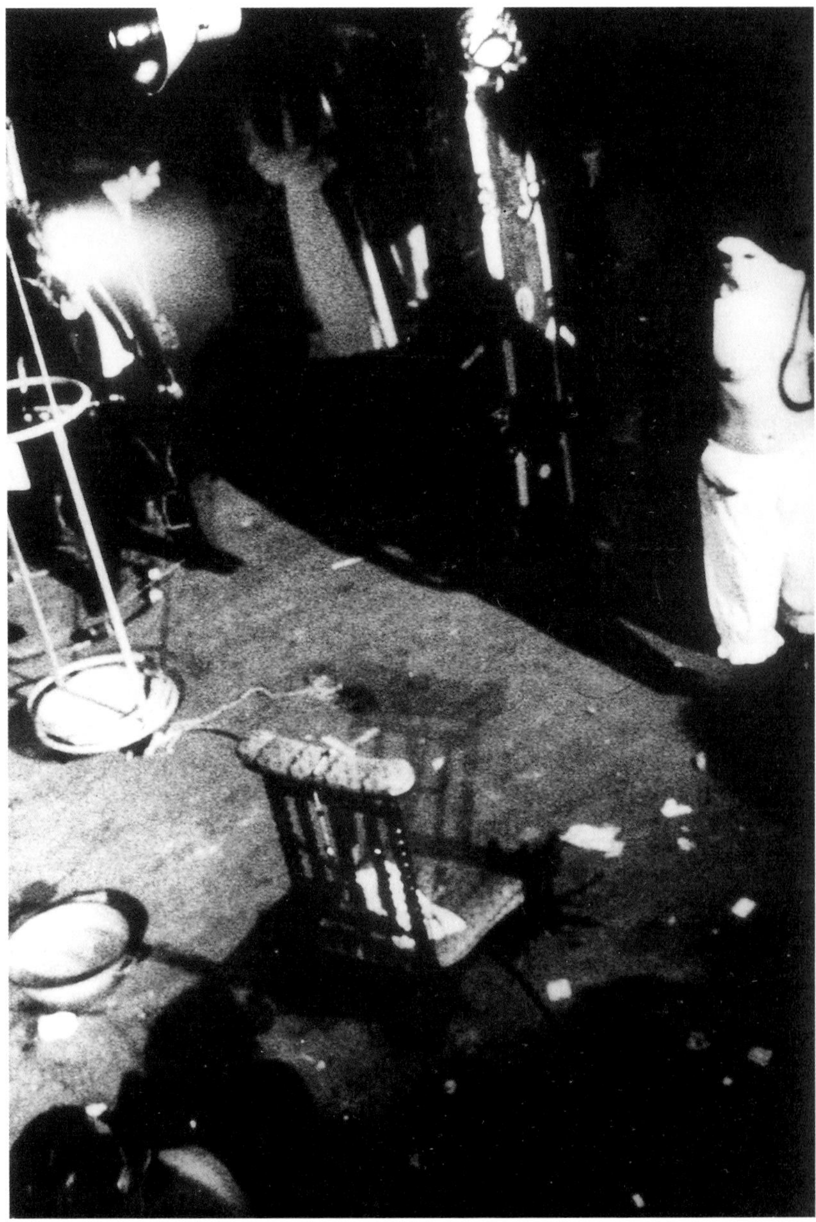

72 Jean-Jacques Lebel
120 Minutes Dedicated to the Divine Marquis, 1966
Performed at the Théâtre de la Chimère, 42 rue Fontaine, Paris, Lebel's Happening invited the public into a Sadean world in which the traditional theatre/gallery space was made strange through strobe-lighting, projected film, music, and the handing out of sugar cubes laced with LSD. The improvised performances lasted 120 minutes. Participants included Frédéric Pardo, Bob and Barbara Benamou, Philippe Hiquily, B. Copley, Shirley Goldfarb, Gérard Rutten, and Cynthia, a trans-sexual who worked in Pigalle.

'terrorism', taking the improvisation of Kaprow and radically accentuating its sexual and political dimensions. The result not only disorientated but shocked and repulsed the viewer. In his 1966 Happening, *120 Minutes Dedicated to the Divine Marquis* **[72]**, performed at the third Workshop of Free Expression in the Théâtre de la Chimère in 42 rue Fontaine in Paris (the same building in which André Breton lived), Lebel created an 'open work' in a performance dedicated to the radical ideas of the Marquis de Sade. Taking Sade's *120 Days of Sodom* as a guiding principle, and celebrating the disruptive power of taboo, the performance ran for 120 minutes as Lebel and fellow performers unleashed a series of shocking actions on an unsuspecting audience. The participants included Cynthia, a trans-sexual prostitute who worked in the red-light district of Pigalle, and Denise de Casabianca, the editor of Jacques Rivette's sexually explicit and controversial film *La Religieuse* (1966), which had just been banned.[28] The audience entered the theatre by passing between two bloody meat carcasses, to find themselves surrounded by strobe lights, film clips projected on the walls, and people handing out sugar cubes laced with LSD. They then witnessed a series of erotic *détournements*. A performer (Cynthia) dressed as a nun, began to strip, before washing herself and then sodomizing herself with various vegetables; a naked, unnamed soprano singer sang a made-up song based on *120 Days of Sodom*, while another naked female, her Sadean 'twin', urinated from the theatre stands down on to the audience. The singer then lay down on a table where she was covered in Chantilly cream that members of the audience were invited to lick off. All this was provocative, to say the least, but in keeping with the avant-garde tradition of Lebel's mentors (Duchamp, Picabia, Antonin Artaud, and the Surrealists), the erotic body was not performed for its own sake; rather, it was intended to disrupt the political status quo too. This was evident in details: the nun shocked everyone when in the process of stripping she revealed a g-string with the Star of David on it; when she stripped totally she turned out to have both breasts and a penis (she was a transsexual); while the Chantilly-covered singer mocked French *patrimoine* by wearing a mask of General de Gaulle and posing bare-breasted with arms outstretched so that she seemed to embody 'the French Republic in danger', as Lebel put it.[29] Lebel's performance ended with his arrest. It was deemed an 'outrage to good morality', and he was only released following a public petition signed by leading figures in the French art and intellectual world, including Breton, Jean-Paul Sartre, Simone de Beauvoir, Jacques Rivette, and Eric Rohmer.[30] Lebel's Happening was an angry assault on society and culture, using erotic excess for all its disturbing power. As he stated in a 1996 interview: 'I'd read *Les Cent-vingt journées de Sodome* and I knew that the "revolutionization of desire" wasn't going to happen because of anything like mini-skirts, going topless or Timothy Leary's psychedelic bacchanalia.'[31]

Lebel's Workshop of Free Expression, which ran from 1964 to 1967, involved many key figures in performance art and brought avant-garde art, film, music, and poetry together. Carolee Schneemann performed

Meat Joy **[64]** with Daniel Pommereulle (1937–2003), at the first Free Expression festival in Paris in 1964. An example of her 'kinetic theatre', *Meat Joy* brought various influences together (the writings of Antonin Artaud, Wilhelm Reich, and Simone de Beauvoir), while the title of the performance was inspired by the Beat writer Michael McClure's *Meat Science Essays* (1963). *Meat Joy* developed from a series of 'dream sensation images' the artist had been recording since 1960 and has been described by Schneemann as an 'erotic rite: excessive, indulgent; a celebration of flesh as material'.[32] This excess was made manifest in the use of dead plucked chickens, dead fish, sausages, buckets of paint, brushes, rope, plastic, and scrap bits of paper in a performance of orgiastic fervour by untrained performers who were chosen by the artist, and who erotically played in their underwear only a few feet away from the audience. Schneemann envisaged a performance that would evolve from the tactile to a fleshy, meaty mess; she succeeded in creating erotic chaos as she and her fellow performers painted each other, rolled around on newspaper and debris, threw chickens at each other, and slipped and slid on stage.

In her film *Fuses* (1964–7) **[73]**, Schneemann went further. She allowed the sexual act to be seen and, most importantly, represented the female orgasm in a radically explicit way. Through the moving image she subverted the stubborn insistence on mind–body dualism in Western art by combining carnal imagery, sophisticated editing, and music, all the time ensuring that woman (Schneemann herself) was not fetishized.[33] The film presented Schneemann and her partner Jim Tenney having sex from the point of view of their pet cat. The images were transgressive in their sexual explicitness, showing the penis and vagina, ejaculate, and menstrual blood. The film celebrated what Schneemann referred to as 'the fuck', and was therefore an important step for feminist art and the idea of erotic equity: 'Fuses wasn't programmatic. The fuck was inseparable from an intimacy, an erotic generosity that was evident. Jim Tenney and I were together for thirteen years—an extraordinary and rapturous loving life together.'[34]

Schneemann's art liberated female sexuality, making her own erotic body integral to her art work. She celebrated the power of the erotic to affect the spectator and to challenge society radically, especially patriarchal society.

Yoko Ono (b. 1933) was also pushing at the boundaries of performance art and using the erotic body to confront the political. She was an early participant in the Fluxus movement founded by George Maciunas in New York in the 1960s and which fused Zen philosophy with Dada antics. Born in Tokyo, her family moved to Scarsdale, New York, in 1951.

Ono began her studies at the Sarah Lawrence College but abandoned their classical art training programme to begin her own unorthodox approach to art with her 'instruction pieces'. These were instructions, typed up in Japanese and later in English, and exhibited on a wall as works in themselves. One, made in 1962, entitled *Painting to be Worn*, carried the following instructions: 'Cut out jackets or dress from acquired paintings, such as Da Vinci, Raphael, De Kooning. You may wear the painted side in or out. You may make underwears [*sic*] with them as well.' The work made a mockery of the canonical 'Masters' of art and turned to craft and the domestic (the making of clothes) as a means of subverting conventional notions of power and gender difference. Ono's *Cut Piece* (1964) continued this theme but expanded the corporeal element and was part of what she termed 'strip-tease shows' that were to lead to the 'stripping of the mind'.[35] It was performed in Kyoto and Tokyo in 1964, in Carnegie Hall in New York the following year, and in the Africa Centre, London, in 1966. Ono sat on stage on her shins, adopting the Japanese *seiza* position assumed in formal settings, with a large pair of scissors in front of her, and invited members of the audience to cut the clothes off her body. The stoic passivity of the artist and the assault she invited on her person made a subtle stance against sexual aggression. Ono's earliest memories were set against the backdrop of war—she was 12 at the time of the bombings of Hiroshima and

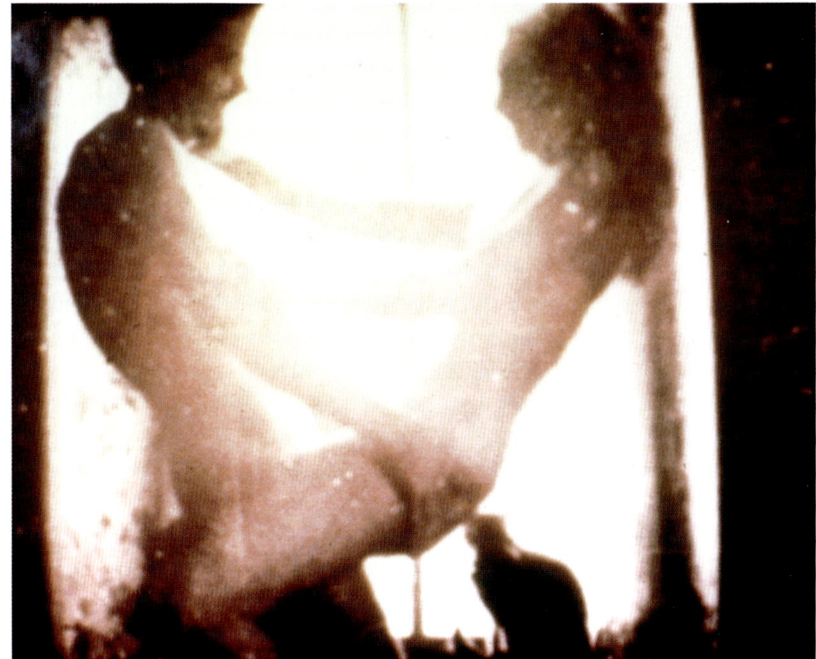

73 Carolee Schneemann
Fuses, 1964–7

This silent film was made up of sequences of lovemaking between the artist and her then partner, the composer James Tenney, shot from the perspective of her cat, Kitch, and with the addition of various visual effects. It was intended to capture both the intimacy and the materiality of lovemaking without fetishizing woman. According to the artist, when it was screened at Cannes in 1968 'French men were ripping up the seats with razor blades and screaming because it was not truly pornographic. It was not satisfying the predictable erotic, phallocentric sequence they wanted.'

Nagasaki, and her family were so poor she would imagine delicious menus of food to distract herself from hunger pains. *Cut Piece* was performed at a time when artists were protesting against the Vietnam War, and her art spoke to this very real horror. The artist's account of the inspiration behind the performance further explains her pacifist stance before the war: the story of Buddha who allows a tiger to attack him and rip his body to shreds so that his soul can achieve supreme enlightenment. Through allowing members of the public to (sexually) threaten her body, Ono hoped they would achieve enlightenment. Presaging Ono and John Lennon's later *Bed-In* performance (1969) and their installation of a billboard stating 'War Is Over' in Times Square, New York, in 1969, Ono's art practice involved methods that were so far removed from high art that the establishment did not know how to silence her.[36]

In September 2003 Ono performed *Cut Piece* again in the Théâtre Ranelagh in Paris at the age of 70 **[74]**. Some 200 members of the public were invited to cut a postcard size piece of her clothing (a black skirt and long sleeved top) off and to send the fragment to a loved one. After about an hour the artist was left facing her audience in her underwear. In her statement about it, Ono emphasized that the performance was not about violence but about trust—trusting someone with scissors, an object that could be a lethal weapon. As always, her art was a direct response to sociopolitical circumstance. In 2003 her pacifist stance was inspired by the terrorist attacks on the World Trade Center in New York on 9 September 2001. As she stated in her press release: 'Following the political changes through the year after 9/11, I felt terribly vulnerable—like the most delicate wind could bring me to tears. *Cut Piece* is my hope for world peace.'[37]

Yoko Ono reminds us that the 1960s were not just a moment in history but an attitude and aesthetic that continued into the 1970s and is equally relevant today. However, the use of free love by a small but influential minority as a revolutionary weapon against the status quo would inevitably be short-lived—the explicit erotic body would take on very different forms for the next generation of artists, largely due to the threat of AIDS, as we shall see. However, the words of John Sinclair, the poet, manager of MC5, and founder of the radical White Panther Party, in the March 1968 edition of the Detroit underground newspaper, the *Sun*, powerfully evoke the sexual dynamics of the decade and its radical vision of Eros:

> Our position is that all people must be free to fuck freely, whenever and wherever they want to, or not to fuck if they don't want to—in bed, on the floor, in the chair, in the parks and fields, 'back street boogie for the high

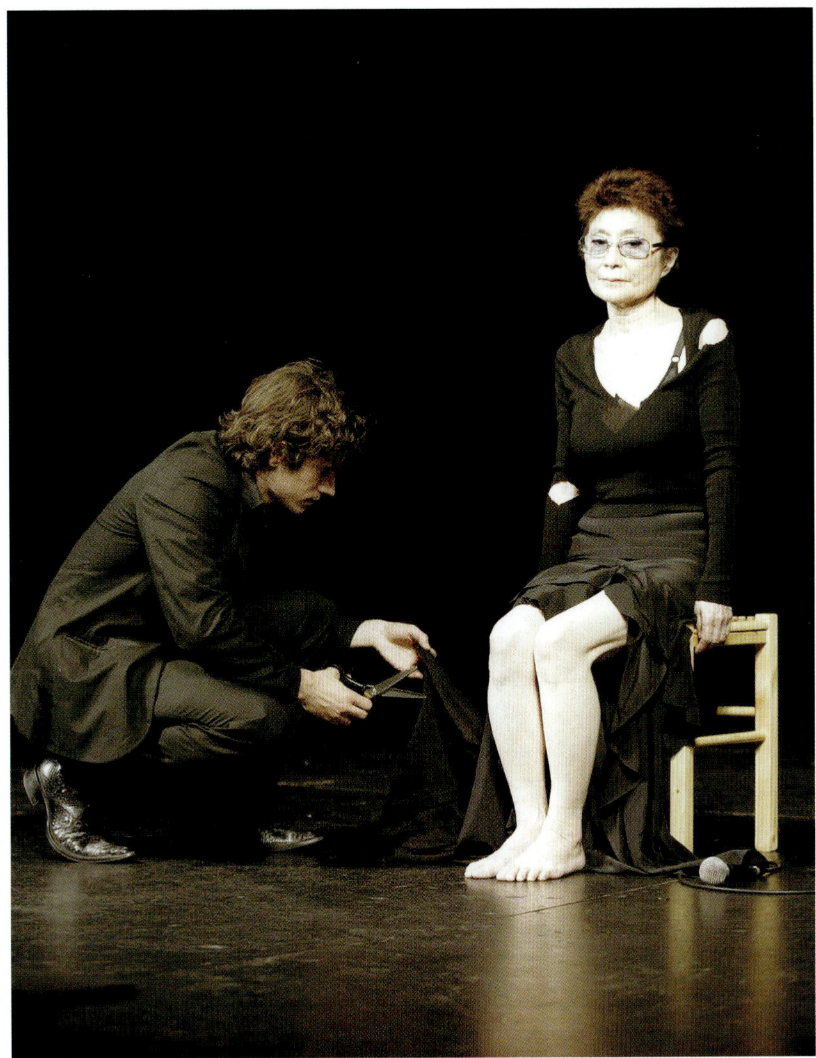

74 Yoko Ono
Cut Piece, as recreated at the Théâtre Ranelagh, Paris, 2003

First performed in 1964, *Cut Piece* was a sadistic-masochistic performance involving the disrobing of the artist as members of the public cut away her clothing while she sat motionless on stage in the traditional Japanese seating position for a woman, with legs folded underneath her. The performance probed the relationship between artist/spectator, man/woman, oppressor/oppressed. In 1966 the artist wrote: 'People went on cutting the parts they do not like of me finally there was only the stone remained of me that was in me but they were still not satisfied and wanted to know what it's like in the stone.'

> school kids' sing the Fugs who brought it all out in the open on stage and in their records, fuck whoever wants to fuck you and everybody else do the same. America's silly sexual 'mores' are the end product of thousands of years of deprivation and sickness, of marriage and companionship based on the ridiculous misconception that one person can 'belong' to another person, that 'love' is something that has to do with being 'hurt', sacrificing, holding out, 'teardrops on your pillow' and all that shit.[38]

In the 1960s, sex and eroticism were celebrated as manifestations of life, in opposition to war; and of pleasure, in opposition to a corrupt and puritanical value system.

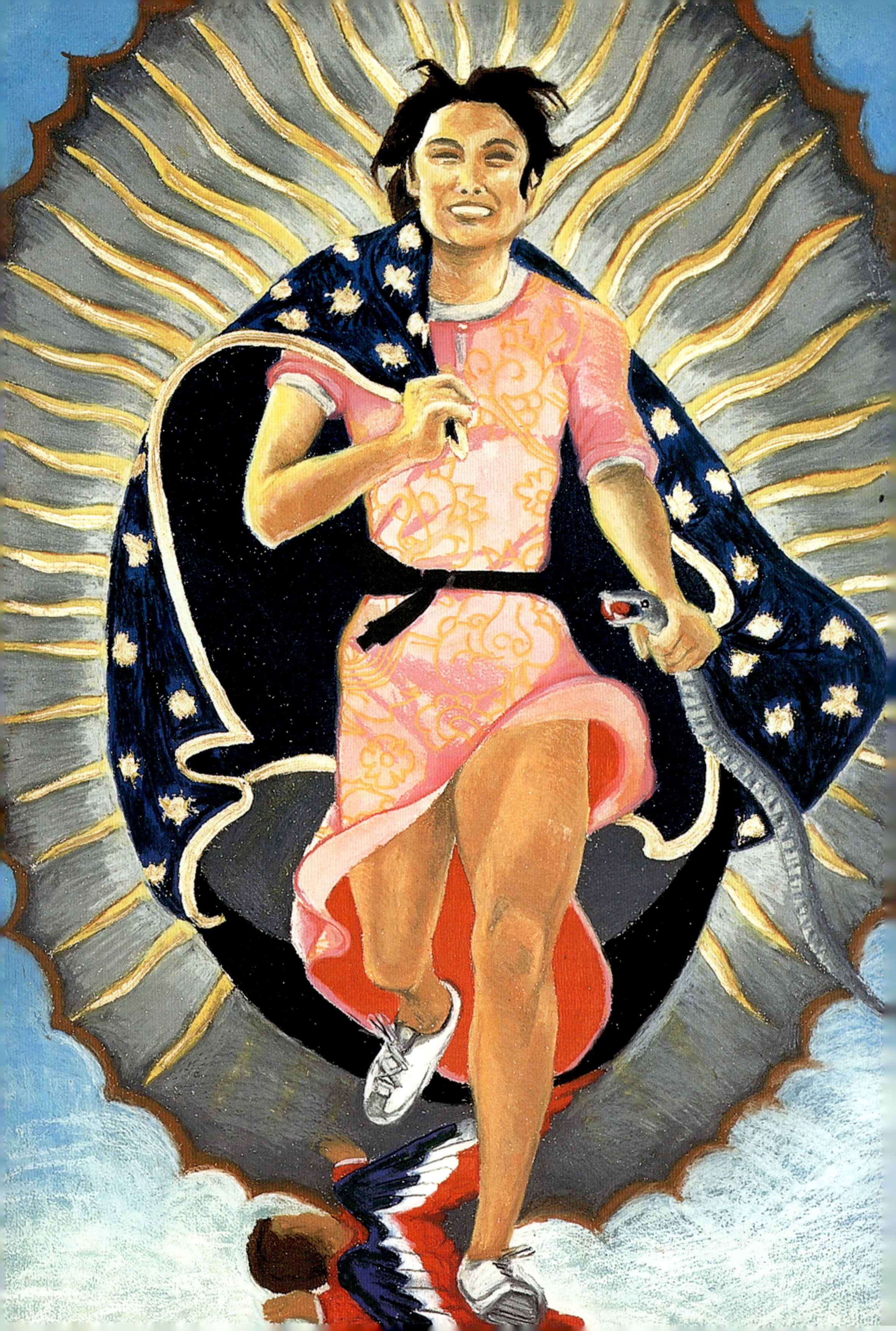

8

Visual Pleasure and Identity Politics

If Pop art in the 1960s signalled the 'end' of modern art and its formalist agendas, the 1970s signalled the birth of the postmodern era. Of course this was not a seamless transition: as the French philosopher Jean-François Lyotard observed, postmodernism was not just the birth of a new historical period or shift, but a state of mind characterized by the computerization of society, a plurality of 'language games', and the liberation of culture from 'grand narratives'.[1] Postmodern art demonstrates this ludic plurality in a type of *bricolage* in which artists quote elements from previous art styles and historical periods, looking back to those periods with a sense of irony or pastiche.

Yet given the breakdown of master narratives, postmodernism can also be seen as the end of an era: the end of modernism, the end of avant-gardism, the end of ideology. It signals the end of those subversive movements in art we have so far assessed, including Dada and Surrealism, and their use of the erotic for shocking, political, effect. Accordingly, for some theorists postmodern culture cannot be viewed in academic and intellectual terms alone; it should be seen as a departure from the radical goals of modernism and, by extension, as an indicator of the continued success of capitalism. Frederic Jameson sees postmodernism as the cultural logic of the third great phase of capitalism, late capitalism, which was born out of the ashes of World War II; it signals both the end of modernism's critical, scandalous voice of dissent and the erosion of the modern distinction between high and low culture which often fuelled the expressive means of that dissent.[2] The end of modernism signalled the end of stylistic innovation, the recourse to never-ending recycling of historical styles, and the imprisonment of art within its own history rather than the radical advancement of art in the name of resistance. Within this rather pessimistic frame, artists who battled to bring the lowly subject of sexual desire into high culture—Picasso, Duchamp, Warhol—were successes for the art world and market but failures to their radical intent. While they had

Detail of 86

pushed back the boundaries of art they had still been co-opted into high art, into the canon, and were being taught in the academy alongside the very artists they mocked. By the 1970s, their established status meant that all erotic art to follow, however sexually explicit it might be, could never have the same shocking impact on art and society. As Jameson puts it, even the 'most offensive forms of [contemporary] art—punk rock, say, or what is called sexually explicit material—are all taken in stride by society, and they are commercially successful, unlike the productions of the older high modernism'.[3]

Opposition did not die with modernism, however. Even if avant-garde artists were drawn into the academic canon, that canon was undergoing a dramatic overhaul. And while resistance certainly splintered into various identity politics groups from the 1970s on, eroticism continued to be used as a means of common resistance. Society did not turn a blind eye to 'sexually explicit material'; if anything, it grew increasingly sensitive to it as radical feminist, gay, lesbian, and race politics attacked the status quo. Artists not only forced the disciplines of art history and cultural theory to undergo dramatic self-questioning but also began to enact a critique of the critical language of art history and aesthetics. During the 1970s there was increased concern over the production and reception of art—from the artist to the museum, to the art critic and art historian—while increased internationalism and globalization meant that the geographical frames used to view most modern art would no longer suffice. Indeed, the 1970s might be seen as a decade in which identity politics (the Self) and the politics of identity (race, gender, sexuality, community) moved from the periphery to the centre.

To address the political dimension of identity, artists and theorists often refer to the 'gaze'. The gaze is a term loaded with psychoanalytic significance. It is to Freud that theorists turn to explain the power structure behind the act of looking, specifically behind *scopophilia* (the pleasure of looking at others). In *Three Essays on the Theory of Sexuality* (1905), Freud wrote that 'visual impressions remain the most frequent pathway along which libidinal excitation is aroused', reasoning that it encouraged 'the development of beauty in the sexual object' and the 'concealment of the body' which keeps 'sexual curiosity awake'.[4] Art, he also argued, allowed for the sublimation of this instinct, allowing natural sexual curiosity expressed in the act of seeing, to be diverted from the genitals to the body. However, this pleasure in looking was open to perversion: when looking was restricted exclusively to the genitals; when it was connected to disgust (he gives the example of getting a voyeuristic thrill from watching excretory functions); or when normal sexual looking results in exhibitionism—exhibiting one's genitals in order to enjoy a reciprocal view of another person's genitals.[5] Typical forms of perversions for Freud, whether expressed in one or all of these three directions, included sadism and masochism.

For artists and theorists in the 1970s, especially feminists, scopophilia as described by Freud offered a new means of reassessing the latent and subliminal messages behind representations of the female body in art and Western culture in general. In a seminal essay of 1975 entitled 'Visual Pleasure and Narrative Cinema', the film-maker, art historian, and theorist Laura Mulvey made feminist, 'political use' of Freud's theorization of the pleasure of looking.[6] She focused on Hollywood film and argued that the scopophilic gaze was the dominant power relation exercised in the moving image: it privileged the viewer who could sit back and look at the screen as if in a self-contained world. However, the nature and pleasure of the scopophilic gaze did not privilege all viewers, she argued: it privileged the *male* viewer and presented the female body as an object of scopophilic or fetishistic pleasure, she embodied 'to-be-looked-at-ness'. Freud's scenario and Western culture in general presented the male as the privileged spectator and woman as the spectacle. Mulvey's theory had—and continues to have—a tremendous impact on art and film theory. By equating spectatorship with maleness, Mulvey offered a theory with which artists, art historians, and critics could now address the politics of looking and the power struggles within representation.

Of course women artists had already been engaging with the power of the gaze, especially Dada and Surrealist artists such as Hannah Höch and Claude Cahun, as we have seen. But it was not until the 1970s that many women artists' pioneering role gained its full recognition. For example, since the 1930s the American artist Alice Neel (1900–84) had been exploring in her art this power struggle between woman as object and woman as subject. In Neel's 1933 painting of the Beat writer *Joe Gould* **[75]** we find an exciting, early example of a woman artist questioning sexual and gender roles by framing a nude male in a manner that hitherto had been the privelege of the female nude. Gould sits passively before the female artist, who stages him for the female viewer. However, while we have seen male nudes before (from Michelangelo's *David* to Eakins's *Swimming*), here we are not presented with the heroic, symbolic male nude as an icon of the virtues of masculinity (humanism, rationalism, nationalism), but as a vulnerable, naked, and so very real person, minus all the trappings of high art. Indeed, while allusions could be made to the raw portraiture of Egon Schiele, it seems that Neel chose, in her own words, 'to be the painting and the painter', as a means of defusing the traditional power relation between the painter-as-subject,

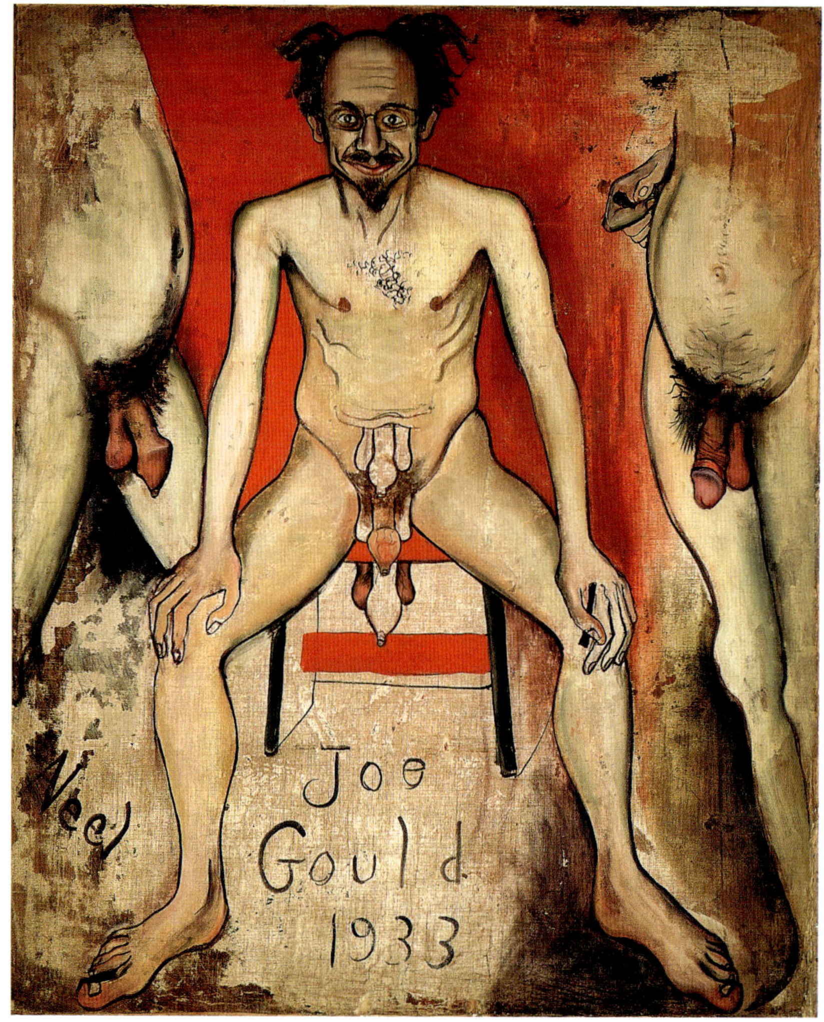

75 Alice Neel
Joe Gould, 1933

Neel's portrait of the New York bohemian Gould reverses the traditional gender roles of artist and model while offering a frank image of the naked male body. Gould's virility is sarcastically magnified through multiple penises, several decades before feminist artists would begin to question art history and its hierarchies.

wielding the brush, and the sitter-as-object, at the mercy of the brush.[7] She acknowledges this self-conscious approach to the act and power of painting by adding a humorously subversive detail to her portrait of the jovial, grinning Gould: there are three sets of genitalia, as well as three views of the man—sitting in full frontal nudity in the centre, and with two portraits either side, one with uncircumcised penis to the left and circumcised to the right. Gould's splendid phallic 'power' is here made comical, his ungainly pose and quirky expression deflating his cheeky nudity, and his portly stomach and willowy legs distracting the eye from his exposed sex. Gould's exaggerated masculinity is deflated; Neel both exposes the age-old association between the pen, brush, sword, and the phallus, as well as claiming phallic power for herself.

But it was only in 1963 that *ArtNews* proclaimed that Neel's 'portraits are not only people, they are art', and not until 1974, at the age of 74, that she was honoured with a retrospective show at the Whitney Museum of American Art in New York.[8] Then her hitherto unfashionable, personal, brutally realist portraits were critically celebrated and commercially valued. This was largely due to the influence of feminist art historians and their fierce campaign to reclaim women artists for art history. Notably, Linda Nochlin revolutionized the discipline of art history by posing the question 'Why Have There Been No Great Women Artists?' in 1971. She argued that 'greatness' had always been categorized in art in male terms, and that genius remained tied to phallic power as it was gendered (that is, it was deemed to be the privilege of male self-expression); and given both their historical exclusion from art academies and this particular association between maleness and greatness, women artists had been excluded from consideration. She called for a feminist critique of the discipline of art history, a paradigm shift.[9] In keeping with this challenge to the art canon and the demand to expand its boundaries not merely to include women and 'female' subjects, but also to realize that the 'so-called woman question' could now act as a catalyst for radical change in art and its history, many women artists' work was reassessed and younger generations inspired. Neel's portraits of society figures, friends, the men in her life, her children and grandchildren, were finally recognized as explorations of the Self, of domestic space, of a woman's struggle as artist, mother, and lover. The personal nature of her art was appreciated as political, and her choice of palette, attention to clothing and background detail were re-interpreted as not just honest depiction of life but subtle commentaries on the social and gender politics that run through everyday life. For example, Neel's 1962 portrait of eminent art dealer Ellie Poindexter, in which the sitter's large breasts under a startling yellow dress are emphasized through crude daubs of paint, could be read as a symbolic celebration of female power.

Sylvia Sleigh's (b. 1925) reworking of the canonical Ingres female nude in her *The Turkish Bath* (1973) **[76]** turns Freudian theory on its head as a feminist artist's reappropriation of male scopophilic pleasure. Here Sleigh not only presents us with lounging male nudes rather than traditional female ones, she also pokes fun at the male-dominated art establishment too in choosing models from the art world—Scott Burton, John Perreault, Carter Ratcliff, and Lawrence Alloway, her husband—and in framing them between two views of her favourite male model, the beautiful black-haired Paul Rosano. Sleigh enters into a *dialogue* with dominant erotic fantasy, reinterpreting the past by playing

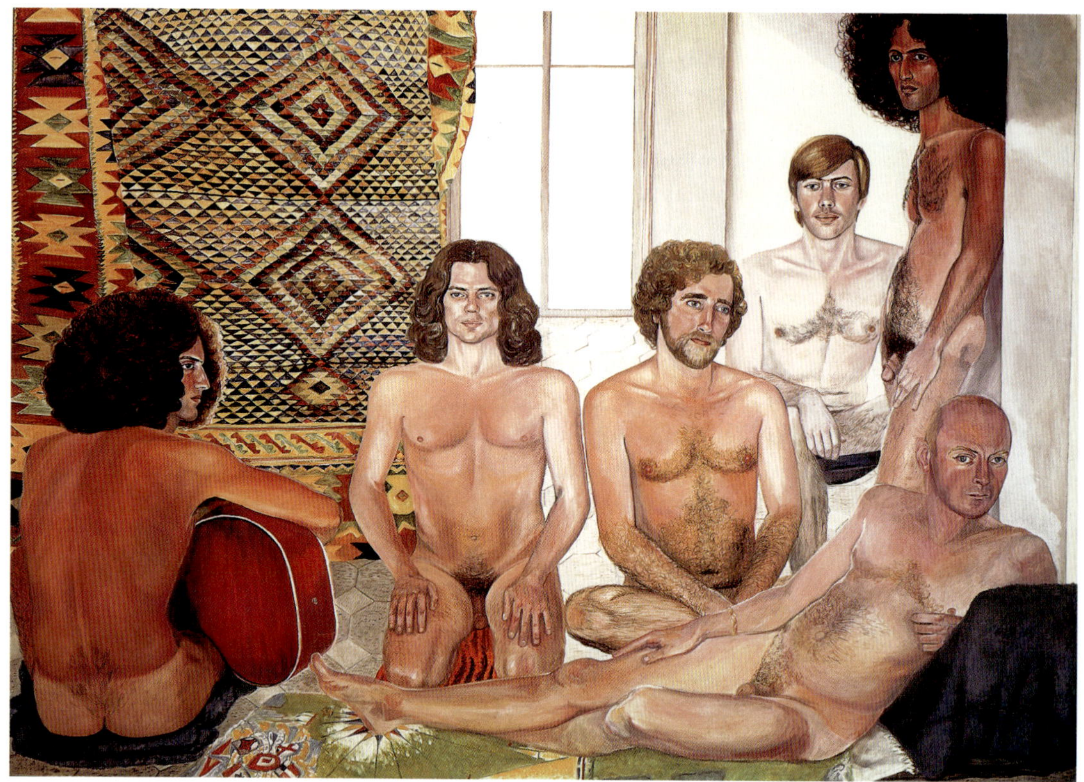

76 Sylvia Sleigh
The Turkish Bath, 1973
Born in Wales and trained at the Brighton School of Art in Sussex, Sleigh moved to New York in the 1960s after marrying the art critic Lawrence Alloway. She became known for her feminist art, including this parody of Ingres's *Turkish Bath*. In it Sleigh replaces Ingres's female beauties with her own selection: the sculptor, Scott Burton, the poet John Perreault, the art critic Carter Ratcliff, and her husband, Alloway, as well as her favourite model Paul Rosano.

with what Linda Nochlin calls 'the cultural patrimony'—patrimony to be taken in the literal sense of 'that which is inherited from the father.'[10] She uses her power as an artist—as the controller of the image—to turn the tables and present the male body as the object of desire, there to please the female spectator.

Sexual Politics

In 1970 Neel's portrait of feminist activist Kate Millett was used as the cover of an edition of *Time* magazine dedicated to 'The Politics of Sex'. Millett, in her highly influential book *Sexual Politics* (1970), argued that sex is a site of oppression by presenting a critical reading of patriarchal society through an exposé of how male writers—including D. H. Lawrence, Henry Miller, and Norman Mailer—use sex to degrade women. At the same time vocal and influential feminists—such as Germaine Greer, in her *The Female Eunuch* (1970)—attacked society's gender conditioning of women; feminist women artists, women art critics, and historians began collectively and systematically to protest for women's rights in the visual, institutional, and political realm. Feminist artists also began a very conscious and strategic battle to reclaim eroticism and sexuality for women. The artist Lynda Benglis (b. 1941) made one of the most dramatic feminist statements in the November 1974 issue of *Artforum* when she posed with her hands on her hips stark naked except for her sunglasses and a proudly displayed gargantuan dildo **[77]**. Initially intended as an artist's statement, she had to buy advertising space in

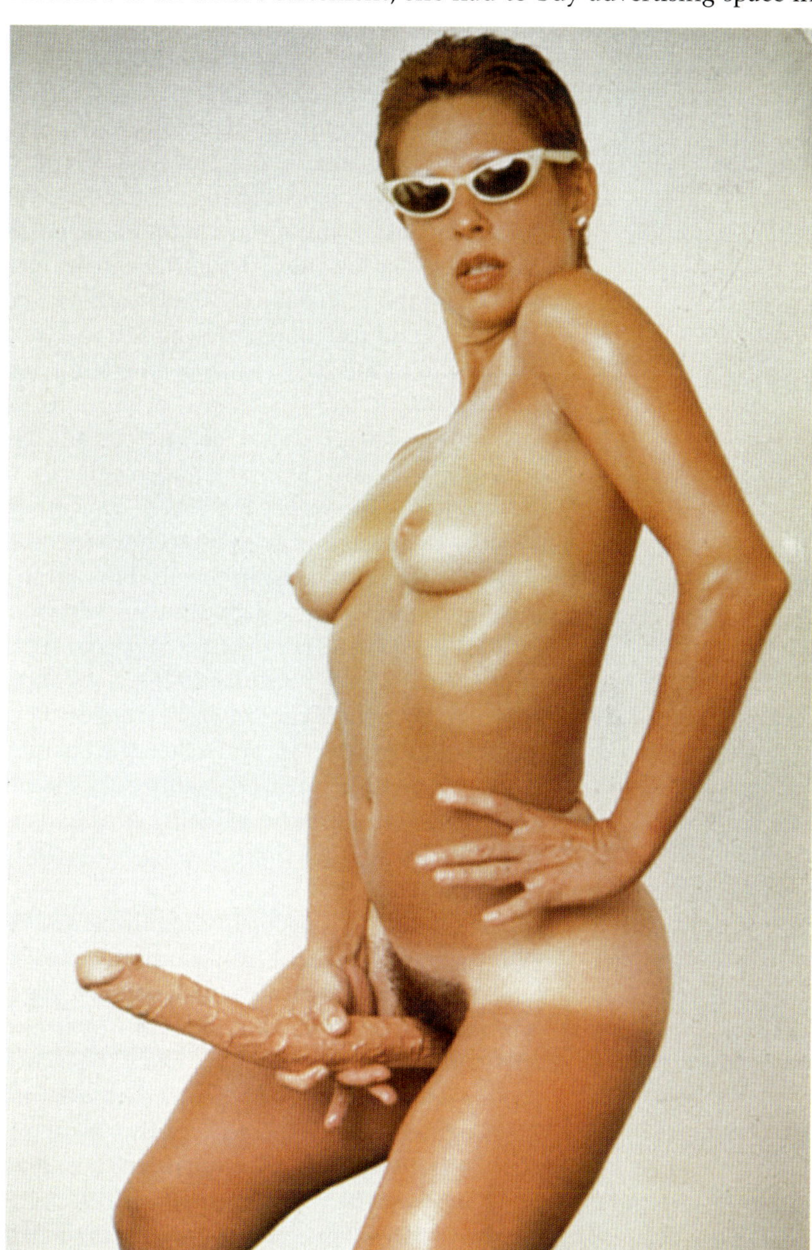

77 Lynda Benglis
Untitled, Artforum,
November 1974

Benglis's controversial advert in the art journal *Artforum* has become a classic feminist art statement. It was a protest against the art establishment and its privileging of male artists, and mocked the sexism of popular culture and the pin-up. But Benglis also tested feminism, insisting on the need for women and women artists to be allowed to enjoy and play with their sexuality.

the journal, using her gallery's name so that she could evade censorship and have the image reproduced. She later decided though that this added a further subversive edge: 'placing the gallery's name on the work strengthened the statement, thereby mocking the commercial aspect of the ad, the art-star system and the way artists use themselves, their persona, to sell their work. It was mocking sexuality, masochism, and feminism.'[11]

The 1970s saw the formation of a feminist movement to campaign against the patriarchal system of values and the Western art canon, arguing that women had been effectively outlawed from mainstream cultural recognition. Artists such as Kusama, Schneemann, and Yoko Ono did not just re-examine eroticism in Western art and the traditional objectification of woman for erotic purposes, they offered a new erotic methodology for art. Feminist artists reclaimed the female body, insisted on the inter-subjective relations between eroticism and sexual, social, and political hierarchies, and then used their own body or dominant erotic motifs as a means of liberating and performing their own erotic selves.

'The Personal Is Political' became the rally cry of early feminism, and some women artists chose to turn to their own bodies—which had been traditionally objectified, fetishized, and tabooed in Western art and society—as a means of both reclaiming the female body and empowering it, and for celebrating its unruly, biological, and desiring qualities so threatening to Western masculinity and civilization. The political also became personal as groups like Women Artists in Revolution (WAR) were set up. Nancy Spero (b. 1926), a vocal participant of this group, began in 1974 her *Torture of Women* series: 14 panels documenting the torture of women in war. Since then she has only used images of women in her art, and explores, predominantly, the relationship between the war of the sexes and the sexuality of war, as well as the easy slippage between the human drive to procreate (Eros) and the drive to kill (Thanatos).

The pursuit of a peculiarly feminine and feminist eroticism began with what feminist art historians have called 'vulvic art' or 'cunt art'—that is, art that provocatively challenged the traditional, passive, and submissive role ascribed to woman in patriarchal society, and which celebrates the fact that to be woman is to be 'formed round a central core and have a secret place which can be entered and which is also a passageway from which life emerges'.[12] Judy Chicago's (b. 1939) *Cock and Cunt Play* **[78]**, written in 1970 and performed in 1972, is a provocative example of the ways 'cunt art' brought feminist politics dramatically into the foreground of art practice.[13] The play was a parodic comedy performed

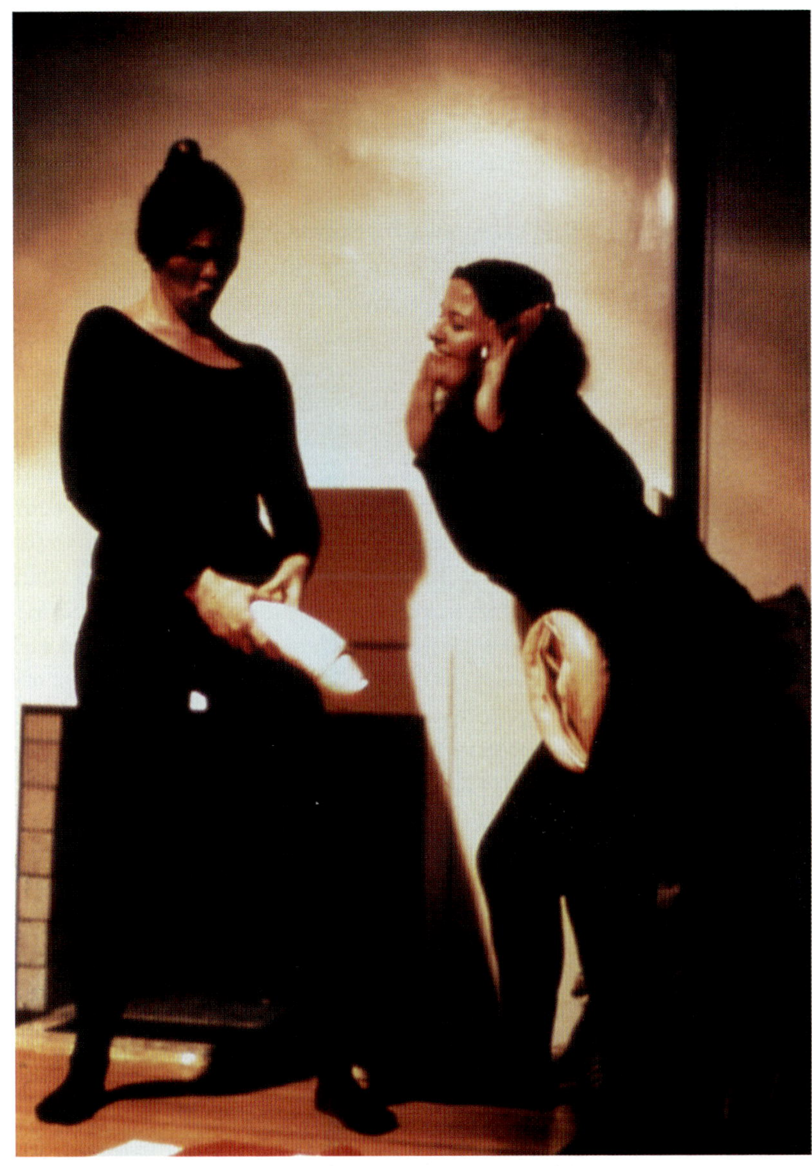

78 Judy Chicago
Cock and Cunt Play, from *Womanhouse*, 1972

Chicago's play, performed at Womanhouse in 1972, parodied the association between men and genius and attacked society's oppression of woman. The play's two characters, 'He' and 'She' (played by Faith Wilding and Janice Lester), argued over such stereotypical assertions as 'A cock means you don't wash dishes. A cunt means you wash dishes.'

by two women in black, one wearing a plastic vulva, the other a large plastic penis. The 'battle' of the sexes was performed in a sing-song way with such stereotypical assertions made as 'A cock means you don't wash dishes. A cunt means you wash dishes.' It ends with the Cock tearing off his penis (so enacting self-castration) and demanding sexual gratification while beating Cunt to death with his penis. This 'Punch and Judy'-like play was a very literal exposé of the subordination of woman in society for her phallic 'lack', which for Freud was a sign of her inferiority. Chicago's choice of title for the play also alerts us to the deliberate use of 'obscene' sexual language to expose political and social obscenity.

In keeping with the feminist movement's interrogation of the Western art canon's privileging of male artists, male subject-matter (myth, historical battles, political portraiture) and exclusion of women, Chicago was instrumental in creating new cultural spaces for women artists and in documenting and celebrating woman power. She founded the first feminist art programme at Fresno State University in 1970 and, with artist Miriam Schapiro (b. 1923), Womanhouse at California Institute of the Arts in Valencia in 1972, both of which were intended to develop visual art education based on feminism. Womanhouse was a building with feminine spaces devoted to women's art. It included a menstruation bathroom that one viewed through a veil of gauze, to see sanitary products and a bin full of bloody tampons, and a kitchen in which fried eggs metamorphosed into breasts. Together the students and teachers organized activities that challenged gender stereotypes and patriarchal institutions, and promoted instead feminist principles and art. Chicago's *Dinner Party* (1974–9) is a celebrated visual enactment of such principles and the feminist project of reclamation. Here Chicago encouraged consciousness-raising and solidarity among women in constructing a large triangular table for 39 'guests' made up of women who played key roles in history. As a collective group seated round a triangular-shaped table, Chicago here gave visual form to her belief that 'Power begins with claiming your own sexuality, your own womanhood.'[14] The triangle was made of three tables, each devoted to mythological and historical women, including the Fertile Goddess, Eleanor of Aquitaine, and Virginia Woolf. One living artist, Georgia O'Keeffe, was there too, as Chicago felt she shared something with the older artist: 'I felt that O'Keeffe made a similar connection between herself and her work. In her paintings, the flower suggests her own femininity, through which the mysteries of life could be revealed.'[15] One table was devoted to women from pre-history, the second to women from Christianity to the Reformation, and the third to women from the seventeenth to the twentieth centuries. Each had a carefully designed place setting: on top of elaborate runners sat exotic plates, each with a vulvic design, cutlery, and a goblet. This was a feast for females, subverting the most iconic male feast of Western art history, the Last Supper. For Chicago the arrangement suggested the 'gradual destruction of these female-orientated societies and the eventual domination of women by men, tracing the institutionalizing of that repression and women's response to it'.[16] She was assisted by a team of women who used their artisan skills to make beautiful banners, runners, china plates and floor tiles for the installation. The agenda was for women 'to transform our circumstances into our subject matter . . . to use them to reveal the whole nature of the human condition.'[17] Chicago believed in the need to reclaim the ancient 'Great Goddess' in art and performance as a means of uniting women through their common biological and spiritual heritage. This universal stance, and collective feminine spirit, was at great odds with the aims and agendas of modernist artists in previous decades of the twentieth century, where, in the words of Lippard, art had been dominated by an 'egotistical monologue' and where the speaker, was of course, male.[18]

It was at this time that Carolee Schneemann turned to vulvic power too. In 1975 she performed *Interior Scroll* **[79]**, a celebration of her creative Self and (in her own words) her 'vulvic space' as the source of 'interior knowledge'.[19] She performed naked (except for a sheet half-wrapped around her) before an audience of women in a town hall in East Hampton, New York. Standing on a table, Schneemann read from her own feminist text *Cézanne, She Was a Great Painter* (1975) (in which she recounts how as a little girl hearing about 'great artists' she presumed

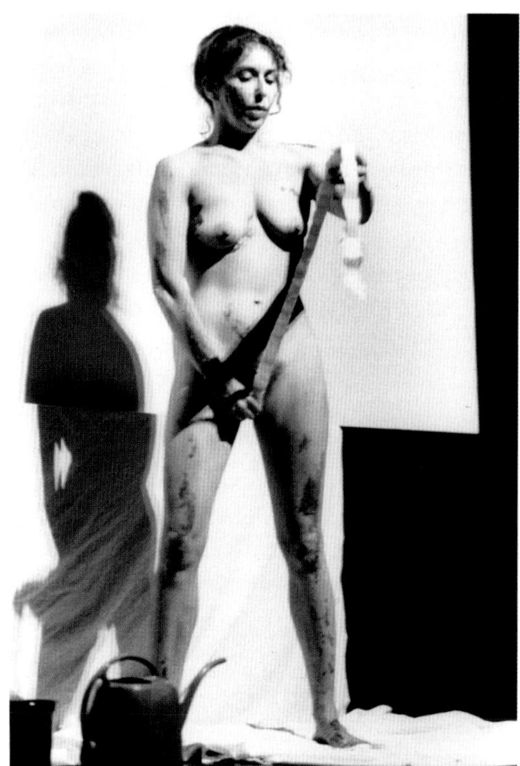

79 Carolee Schneemann
Interior Scroll, 1975

In this performance at Women Here and Now, East Hampton, Long Island, Schneemann slowly extracted a scroll from her vagina, from which she read a text, *Kitch's Last Meal* (1973–8). The performance was an investigation and celebration of vulvic space and its symbolism, inspired by the artist's study of ancient cultures. As she has stated: 'I thought of the vagina in many ways—physically, conceptually: as a sculptural form, an architectural referent, the sources of sacred knowledge, ecstasy, birth passage, transformation.'

Céz-anne was female—given the 'Anne' in the name) and adopted the 'action poses' of a life model. At the conclusion of her reading, she dropped the book and the sheet, painted her naked body with daubs of paint, as if drawing the contours of her own face and body, and then stood up on the table, pulled a long thin tampon-like scroll of paper from her vagina, inch by inch unrolling it and reading it to her audience. The scroll contained further excerpts from her own feminist writing: 'he said we can be friends | equally though we are not artists | equally I said we cannot | be friends equally and we | cannot be artists equally'.[20] It was an enactment of 'the movement from interior thought to external signification' and the scroll was a reference to 'an uncoiling serpent, to actual information (like ticker tape, rainbow, Torah in the Ark, chalice, choir loft, plumb line, bell tower, the umbilicus, and tongue)'.[21] Schneemann's eroticism was primitive, obscene, devouring—the antithesis of the traditional erotic female.

The exploration of vulvic power and 'cunt art' attracted criticism from other women artists. They feared it promoted an essentialist, reductionist view of woman in its emphasis on woman's body, and thought it too separatist in its emphasis on women's spaces and communities. Hannah Wilke (1940–93) disliked Chicago's *Dinner Party*, arguing that 'By labelling woman as a vagina . . . the piece [is] denigrating to women.'[22] Yet Wilke also used vaginal imagery. In the early 1960s, Wilke began to make what Lowery Sims has called her 'signature cunt/scar forms'.[23] These terracotta sculptures began a particular soft sculptural form that became a regular feature of her art: made of lint, clay, erasers, and chewing gum, they were moulded to take on curling, petal-like forms, like the folds of a vulva. Wilke was concerned to develop a specifically female iconography, and saw this as a direct assault on American society which, in her own words, 'prohibited its citizens from and sometimes arrested them for using the words fuck, cock and prick'.[24] She wanted to celebrate the cunt, to destroy its taboo connotations, and to defy phallocentric society and its language. Her soft forms in fleshy pink colours challenged the hard-edge minimalism of such celebrated contemporary male artists as Frank Stella or Donald Judd, while still retaining the Minimalists' fascination with touch and space. In this way Wilke did not advocate separatism but difference. Her *Single-Fold Gestural Sculptures* (1973–4) bring two forms together to create a feminine third: circles of ceramics, rectangle gum, both twisted to become a three-dimensional shape, which is soft and layered and vulvic. Wilke 'dirtied' Minimalist purity with the erotic.[25]

Wilke also exposed her vulnerable private self through a process of dramatic exhibitionism in naked performances begun in 1970. These

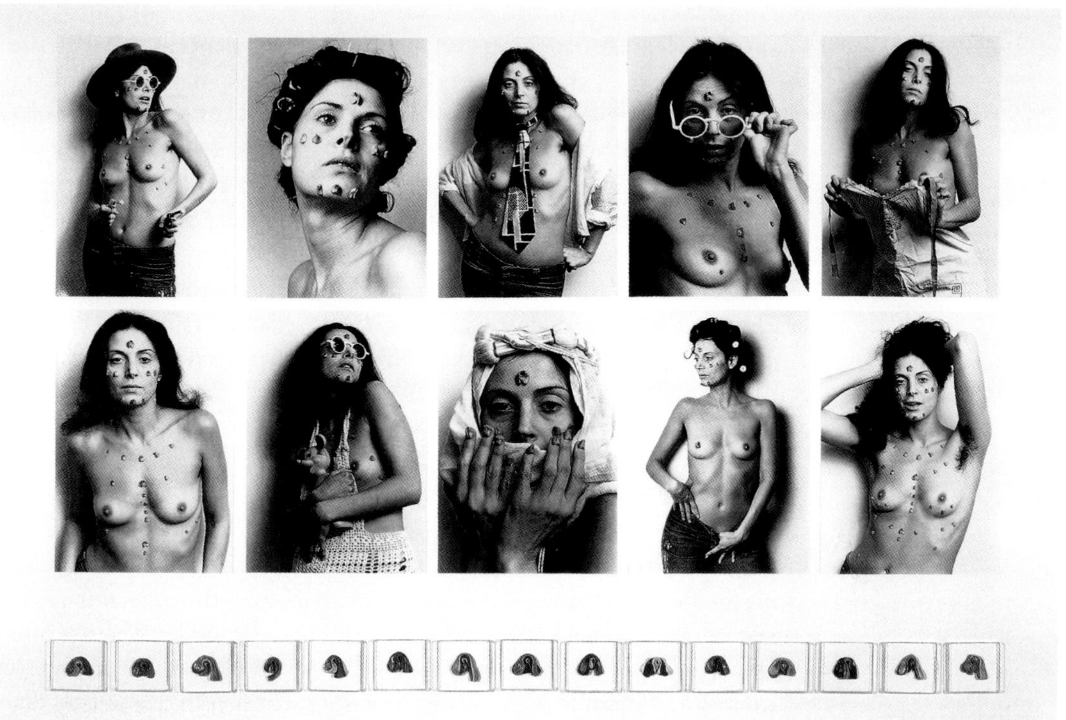

80 Hannah Wilke
S.O.S. Starification Object Series, 1974–82
'Tattooing' her half-naked body with lumps of masticated chewing gum which she sculpted so that they took on a vulvic form, Wilke poses in this series of 'performalist self-portraits' that mock fashion models, movie stars, and the sexy suburban housewife, undermining notions of fixed femininity and the taboo that surrounds vaginal forms.

included *S.O.S. Starification Object Series* (1974–1982), *Intercourse with . . .* (1977), *So Help Me Hannah* (1979, 1982, 1985), and her Duchamp tribute, *I Object* (1977–8). In *S.O.S. Starification Object Series* **[80]**, she presented herself in a series of topless black-and-white photographs, her body in each frame variously 'tattooed' with lumps of masticated chewing gum sculpted to take on a vulvic form. With her model-like good looks, Wilke's brash exhibitionism, bare-breasted and provocatively posed before the world, was undercut by this comic and parodic vulvic 'detailing'. These bizarre scars exposed 'internal wounds, made from external situations', including the trauma of her own mother's mastectomy in 1970. In *So Help Me Hannah*, the artist posed again in a manner that parodied the tradition of the nude and the glossy magazine pin-up. In one photograph from the piece we see Wilke naked, over a toilet bowl, urinating into it and holding a pistol. The photograph is titled 'HIS FARCED EPISTOL', quoting James Joyce, and makes direct reference to Duchamp and his urinal *Fountain* **[32]** (1917). Wilke plays with Duchampian puns—she is literally a fountain, 'pissing' in the bowl, wielding a *pistolet* (the French for gun), and confronting the viewer as she boldly stares out of the image. Indeed, Wilke takes Duchamp's erotic humour a step further in *I Object* (1977–8): we find Wilke naked again, now reproduced on the front and back of a fake book jacket, with her legs askew like the nude in Duchamp's *Étant données* **[69]**. The photograph was taken by Richard Hamilton on rocks in Cadaques, where Marcel and Tiny Duchamp had a summer retreat. It was a provocative response to Duchamp's installation. Wilke found Duchamp's macabre nude too disturbing not to engage with in her own art, explaining: 'I find *Étant Donnés* . . . repulsive, which is perhaps its message. She has a distorted vagina. Its voyeuristic vulgarity justifies impotence.'[26] Wilke used her own body to confront the safe distance of the erotic gaze, and did not resort to the mannequin for shock effect: her body *is* the found erotic object. She replaced Duchamp's surreal eroticism with something much more confrontational—the real.

The legacy of Duchamp was also apparent in the sculptures of Louise Bourgeois (b. 1911). In 1968, she produced two sculptures that were humorous and shocking at the same time: *Fillette* **[81]** and *Janus Fleuri*. The former, a latex sculpture, undermines the iconic status of the male phallus in its choice of title, 'Little girl'. It fuses male and female genitalia so that the base of the sculpture may be read as breast and/or testicles, or hip ball-joints framing a pudenda. However, it revels in the castrative power of the desired female too, as it may also be interpreted as an excited phallus rising up only to be hooked from the ceiling like a raw bloody carcass about to be sliced. On the one hand it captures the moment of heterosexual copulation or fusion of opposites with the orgasm (*la petite mort*) and its intense tenderness, on the other hand it plays with the Freudian idea that every woman wants to give birth to her own penis (a son) to compensate for her own phallic lack. The bronze sculpture *Janus Fleuri* continues this titillating play, but in bronze: it is a hanging 'Flowering Janus' that brings Courbet's *Origin of the World* into the third dimension. Here too we find a genital slit that is more of a smile than a Freudian wound; bronze, the archetypal medium of classical sculpture, lends a heroism to a disembodied vagina, which emerges from two mounds that simultaneously evoke breast, hips, and buttocks, as if reclaiming the metamorphic power of the female form from Western art and the dolls of Hans Bellmer. *Janus*, the Latin for archway, also reminds us of classical myth: for the Romans, Janus was the god of gateways and new beginnings, and was often represented as split, with two heads looking in opposite directions. Bourgeois seeks to bring both faces, sides, directions together in a new hybrid form. Her description of her art as 'I Do, I Undo, I Redo' is perhaps the best synopsis of the objective of the first wave of feminist art.[27]

81 Louise Bourgeois
Fillette, 1968

This two-foot phallus is half cadaver, half infant, its latex form lending it a monstrous viscerality, its scale suggesting something one could cradle—as indicated by the artist's titling of the work, 'little girl'. Bourgeois also conflates the male and female sex in this sculpture: its erect head ends in a swollen vaginal form, undermining phallic power and suggesting male vulnerability.

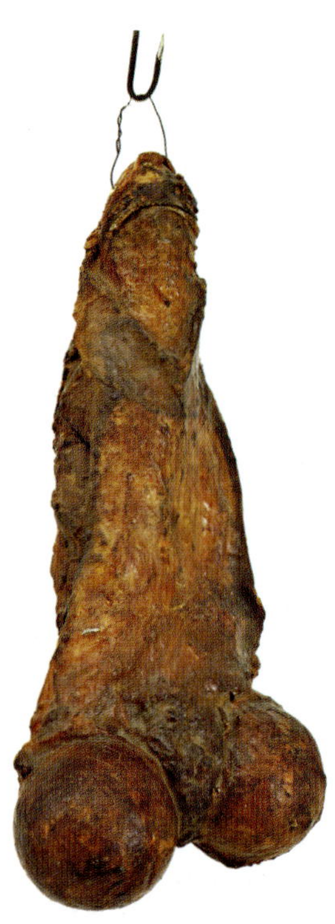

Same-sex Politics

Same-sex eroticism became a particular issue in art between the Stonewall rebellion in New York in 1969 and the first gay rights march in Washington in 1979. In 1969, patrons of the Stonewall Inn, the gay bar in Greenwich Village, New York, fought back in a police raid, sparking three days of violence. This is usually taken as the start of the gay liberation movement and the questioning of the heterosexual conceptualization of sexual 'normality'. The 1979 event involved some 100,000 participants and marked the end of a number of important battles for gay rights in America, including the decriminalization of homosexuality between consenting adults in private (only one state, Illinois, had decriminalized it at time of Stonewall) and the removal in 1973 of homosexuality from the American Psychiatric Association's list of mental disorders.

The male nude was always present in the Western art canon but it gained a new meaning with the increased visibility and political activism of gay culture. As we have seen, in his series based on Elvis, Andy Warhol seized the iconography of the Hollywood star and re-presented it through a gay erotic eye, exposing the homoerotic potential of icons for marginal audiences. Warhol fabricated his own erotic image too in his highly contrived photographic self-portraits: with his almost vacant expression, spiked white hair, and pale skin he presented himself as a persona than a person. The attempt on his life in 1968—when Valerie Solanis, founder and sole member of SCUM (Society for Cutting Up Men) walked into his studio, the 'Factory', and shot him three times in the chest—further testified and contributed to his fame. His *Self-Portrait in Drag (Long Reddish Blonde Wig and Plaid Tie)* of 1981–2, while taken towards the end of his career, reminds us of how Warhol played with sexual and gender politics in all his art despite his cult status. He turns to drag, which imitates gender stereotypes, to expose the imitative structure of gender itself. He not only performed gender, he used 'camp' as a subversive strategy for destabilizing gender norms.

In the Victorian era 'camp' was a slang word used to denote exaggerated actions and gestures and was linked to homosexuals (Oscar Wilde, who was sentenced to two years in prison in 1895 for 'unnatural acts', was accused of being 'camp'). But in the 1960s camp was turned from a word of disdain to a word of pride, becoming a popular 'style' and a characteristic associated with a growing homosexual culture. As noted in the previous chapter, Susan Sontag's highly influential 1964 essay 'Notes on "Camp"' contributed to this shift. For Sontag camp was a 'cult name' for a particular sensibility, one that was emphatically theatrical and ironic: 'Camp sees everything in quotation marks . . . To perceive Camp in objects and personas is to understand Being-as-Playing-a-Role. It is the farthest extension, in sensibility, of the metaphor of life as theatre'.[28] Sontag presented camp as an aesthetic strategy, and gay artists seized upon its subversive potential.

Photography took on a particular importance in both expressing same-sex desire and its camp theatrical potential. Certain gay artists were particularly influential in paving the way for the 1970s generation of gay artists, and especially for the gay photographer who would soon take the art world by storm, Robert Mapplethorpe. As mentioned in Chapter 6, the American photographer Georges Platt Lynes was very influential on Mapplethorpe's subject-matter and photographic style. Lynes conflated low art types (the muscle man, the sailor, etc.) with high art compositions (the seated or standing muscular male nude), and staged the male figure so that light and shade emphasized body contour and muscle to an almost marmoreal degree. As a result his photographs are sensually erotic while remaining within the classical tradition.

Mapplethorpe began his career with collage works, using pornography magazine cutouts and exploring notions of taboo and transgression in his careful framing of homoerotic images. For example, in *Leatherman I* (1970) he used black mesh to conceal an image of a semi-naked man in leather cap, gloves, and jacket, holding a bull-whip and sitting on a stool so that his genitals are visible to all. Mapplethorpe blocks out the *Leatherman*'s eyes with silver tape and sets the whole meshed image against vivid red paper and old-fashioned sky-blue wallpaper with a white velvet foliage pattern. The sexually explicit and the domestic are juxtaposed and the tension between desire and repression made visible through the layering of the image. Mapplethorpe's photographs from 1977 to 1980 which explore sado-masochism are usually referred to as 'the sex pictures'. They depicted people Mapplethorpe met on the S/M scene in New York and San Francisco whom he invited to his studio, where they could pose in their own preferred sado-masochistic 'costuming'. *Helmut* (1978) **[82]** is from his *X Portfolio* of 13 sado-masochistic photographs. In 1979 at the Richard Miller Gallery in New York, Mapplethorpe exhibited the *X Portfolio* alongside a *Y Portfolio* made up of delicate flower studies, Mapplethorpe delighting in his *Portfolios*' juxtaposition of the distasteful (the homoerotic) with the tasteful (the still life). However, even his flowers had an erotic tension to them as Mapplethorpe's lens caught the arch of a phallic tulip or the vulnerability of a lily, reminding us of the sexual interpretation of Georgia O'Keeffe's flower studies. The *X Portfolio* had a similar tension

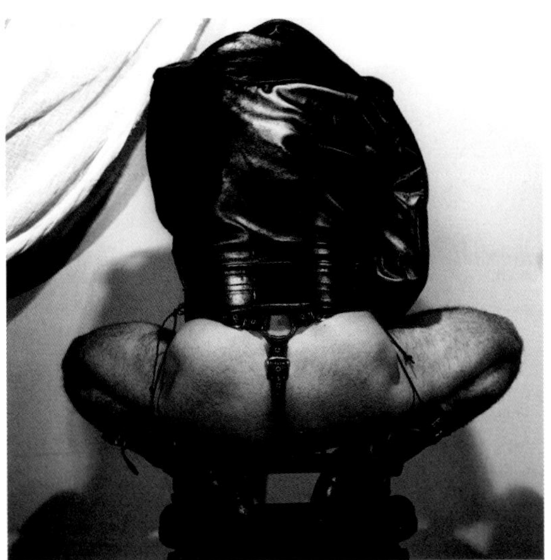

82 Robert Mapplethorpe
Helmut, 1978

This photograph's eroticism lies in what we do *not* see, as much as in what we do; its originality comes from its staging of leather sex as if a conventional still-life photograph, so that the viewer is not only startled by the subject-matter but seduced by the formal rendition of the black leather, the white drape, and the harness that divides the model's buttocks. In the process, S/M subculture is made beautiful.

despite the startlingly different subject-matter: even in portraying auto-eroticism or sado-masochism Mapplethorpe did so as if he was framing a vase of flowers in his attention to light and shade, balanced composition, and pictorial beauty. His assertion of 1979, 'I don't think there's that much difference between a photograph of a fist up someone's ass and a photograph of carnations in a bowl', needs to be kept in mind in looking at all his work.[29]

Helmut shows the back of a semi-naked man in leather bondage gear squatting on top of a pedestal. He wears only leather jacket, boots, and harness but his bare buttocks and leather torso have become almost abstract shapes as we see no head or hands; a white drape to his left recalls the use of drapes as backdrops in traditional portraiture paintings. Mapplethorpe also designed a *mirrored* frame for the photograph, distancing the viewer even further from the individual whose buttocks appear so boldly before us. The black leather, the white drape, the harness that divides his buttocks, all these details seem to depersonalize but also beautify the male model despite his unusual pose. The photograph must still be appreciated in terms of an S/M subculture though, in denying us the frontal image. Richard Meyer reads the model's drooped head, raised left arm, and lower right arm as indicators that he is masturbating and inhaling amyl nitrate (poppers), a popular inhalant used by gays at the time. He reminds us that behind Mapplethorpe's formal beauty lies an image of 'autoerotic practice and kinky pleasure'.[30] Thus the subversive power of Mapplethorpe's eroticism lies in his conflation of the formally acceptable and tasteful with the sexually unacceptable and 'distasteful'.

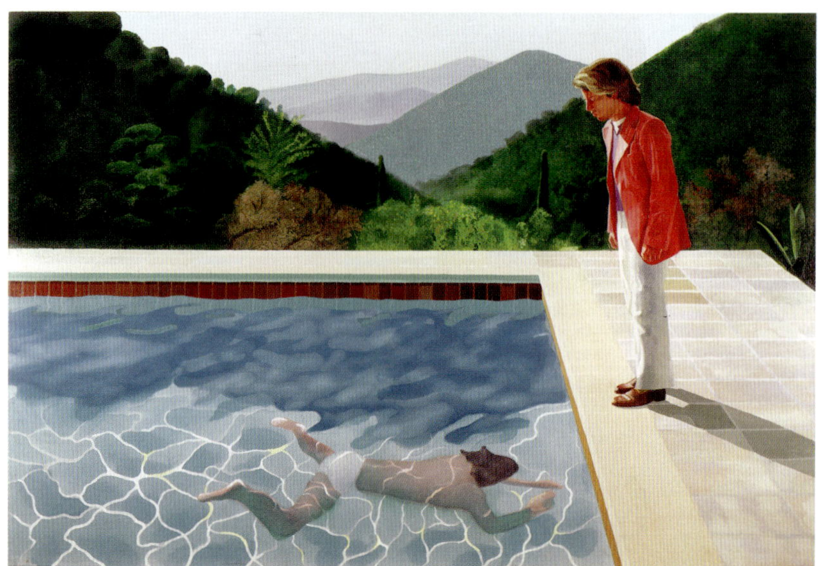

83 David Hockney
Portrait of an Artist, (Pool with Two Figures), 1972

When Hockney left Britain for California in the 1960s he was quickly inspired by its Hollywoodian glamour, sunshine, and body-beautiful culture. Swimming pools emerged as a dominant motif, most famously in *Peter Getting Out of Nick's Pool* (1966), *A Bigger Splash* (1967), and this portrait of his lover Peter Schlesinger looking down into a sun-lit outdoor pool.

While Warhol and Mapplethorpe pushed back the boundaries of the homoerotic in New York, the British artist David Hockney (b. 1937) had begun to do the same in Los Angeles in his paintings of sun-kissed males stretched out beside swimming pools or taking showers together. Los Angeles attracted the Yorkshire-born artist for its Hollywoodian glamour and camp potential. It was a city he fantasized about ever since reading John Rechy's homoerotic novel *City of Night* (1963), which documents the experiences of a young hustler in Times Square, New York, Pershing Square, Los Angeles, and the French Quarter, New Orleans. Hockney's *Portrait of an Artist (Pool with Two Figures)* of 1972 **[83]** exemplifies the erotic tension in his art. Though appearing simple in composition, the painting is based on hundreds of preparatory photographs and shows a man gazing at another man swimming underwater in a pool against a backdrop of sunlit Hollywood hills. Yet we sense a psychological tension between the male figures, a strained sense of space despite the beautiful outdoor setting. If we compare the painting to an earlier one, *Peter Getting out of Nick's Pool* (1966), we sense the tension all the more. The 1966 painting portrays the perfect sexual Los Angeles scenario: a body-beautiful male nude lifting himself out of the pool, framed by the glistening, abstract water surface and modernist architecture so that his muscular back and buttocks are caught in the sun. The 'Peter' of the painting's title was Hockney's new lover Peter Schlesinger, an art student he met while teaching at the University of California, Los Angeles, and the Nick of the title was Hockney's dealer, Nick Wilder, with whom he had lived earlier on in the year.[31] The painting rejoices in this new love. The 1972 painting speaks of the end of the affair and his loss: Hockney's relationship with Peter ended in 1971. In both paintings Hockney normalizes gay desire and love. He presents beautiful, healthy male nudes without any of the drug or sado-masochistic associations we find in Mapplethorpe's homoerotica. Yet Hockney, like Mapplethorpe, is as concerned with form as he is with subject-matter. His often lifeless, flat style in which people and buildings are built up in blocks of colour with little gestural expression might be seen as key to his normalization, and commercially successful depiction, of gay life too. While he would use the camera to advance the perspectival realism of his art from 1970 on—as indicated by his extensive use of photographs taken in April 1972 to improve *Portrait of an Artist*—his methodical approach to art as a formal exercise was and remains a consistent concern throughout his career. This was evident in the art he produced as a young student at the Royal College of Art in London. In *Figure in a Flat Style* (1961) he painted in an Abstract Expressionist style a highly stylized portrait (possibly a self-portrait) of a man masturbating. A small square canvas with a large eye painted on it stands on a larger rectangular canvas showing hands covering a phallus and the words 'the fires of furious desire'; together they stand on the supports of an easel. The words are taken from a poem by William Blake, while the masturbating hands—which 'fire' spurts of white paint up through the centre of the canvas—parody Jackson Pollock's drip technique.[32]

Race Politics

Just as with sexual and gender politics, the power of the gaze had to be considered in terms of race. Here feminist and gay activism could join forces again, as artists of colour began to question the historical narratives that define and construct race, thus pushing the boundaries of art further back in their resistance to traditional binary oppositions (male–female, heterosexual–homosexual, white–black). *I Like Olympia in Black Face* (1970)—by Larry Rivers (1923–2002), exhibited in his 1971 exhibition 'Some American History' on 'the black experience'—used *trompe l'œil* accuracy to parody the inherent racism of the Western art canon. Rivers, a white American artist, here staged two Olympias to make a point about racial stereotypes: Manet's *Olympia* as exhibited at the Paris Salon in 1865, and a 'sister' version in which Olympia is black, her maidservant and cat white.

African-American artists also turned to the female body, or their own self-portrait, as a means of redressing art history's negative images of race. They recognized that the erotic black body often carried negative social and cultural associations in Western art. The black female nude was predominantly equated with illicit sexuality and the enslaved body, and the black male with sexual, animalistic prowess. Given this stereotyping, it is not surprising that representations of the explicitly erotic racial body were rare until the 1970s. As Richard J. Powell has observed, black erotica was effectively forbidden territory for American artists in 1970—African-Americans censored themselves because of all the cultural and imperialist baggage connected with this subject, while white artists avoided it for fear of being accused of racism.[33] It took the political and sexual revolution of the 1960s to liberate the black nude in art.

African-American women artists came together in the early 1970s in the United States under the leadership of such artists as Faith Ringgold (b. 1930) and the 'Where We At' group of women artists founded in 1971. The group arrived at feminist politics out of their involvement in civil rights protests in the 1960s and their dissatisfaction with the black art movement, which was made up of male artists only. They organized the first ever African-American women's art show at the Martin Luther King Gallery in New York and were involved in the 1968–70 demonstrations against the exclusion of black and women artists from the Whitney Museum and Museum of Modern Art in New York. Ringgold produced militant paintings such as *Die* (1967), an oil painting depicting black and white men, women, and children, in a frieze-like image of violence and torture. Her *Slave Rape* series (1972) is more jubilant despite its title: it portrays the black female nude as a fertile figure of resistant fighter battling feminist and colonial politics simultaneously.

Boston-based Dana Chandler (b. 1941) and Los Angeles-based Betye Saar (b. 1926) were equally forthright in addressing racism and parodying erotic stereotyping in their art. Chandler's *American Penal System . . . Pan-African Concentration Camps and Death Houses* (1971, from the *Genocide Series*) **[84]** shows a caged black male, identifiable only by his chained erect black penis, as an American flag and a prison cage door encloses him. It offers a male sexualized image of black power to Ringgold's female one. Chandler's image should be compared to the 1970s nudes by Barkley L. Hendricks (b. 1945) where he portrays African-Americans as 'black, beautiful and suave', confidently striding towards the viewer, as in his nude *Brilliantly Endowed Self Portrait* of 1977; or Adger Cowans's (b. 1936) photograph *P.B.* (1974), where the camera frames top-lit black buttocks, emphasizing their abstract shapes while still alluding to the erotic folklore around black steatopygia.[34]

Betye Saar's *The Liberation of Aunt Jemima* (1972) turns to racist erotic stereotyping too: the black buxom 'Mammy' slave servant, with wide

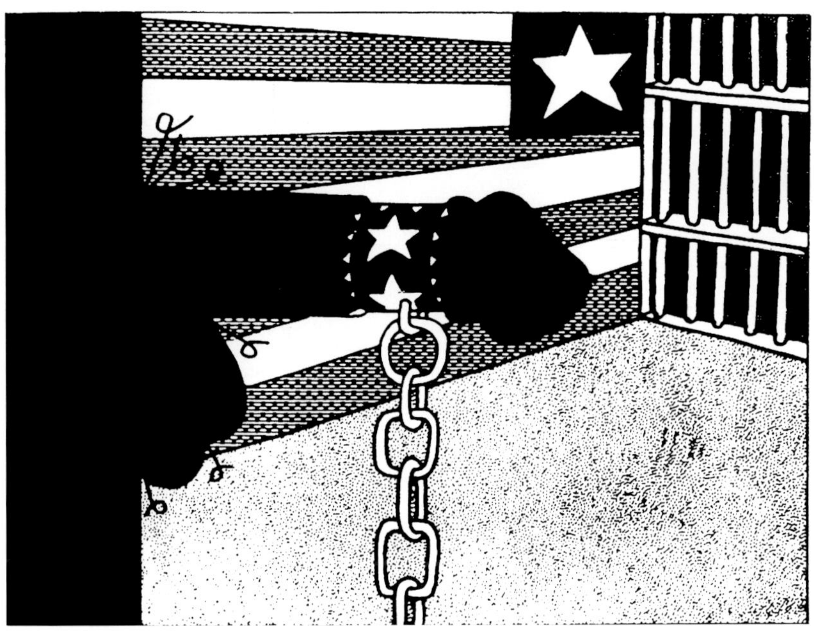

84 Dana Chandler
American Penal System . . . Pan-African Concentration Camps and Death Houses, 1971, from the *Genocide Series*

If the American flag is typically a symbol of liberty, in Chandler's lithograph it is a symbol of oppression, a signifier of the penal system for African-Americans living in the United States. Born in Lynn, Massachusetts, in 1941, Chandler studied at the Massachusetts College of Arts and at Northwestern University, where he set up the African-American Master Artists in Residency Program to encourage fellow African-American artists. In 1971, the year of the *Genocide Series*, he became a professor of art and art history at Simmons College in Boston.

smile and hair tied up in a kerchief. This Mammy icon was made famous by American merchandise as her iconic face was used to advertise pancake mix, syrup and cookie jars, and other collectible objects. Saar turns such racist packaging on its head: her boxed object is lined with Aunt Jemima product labels and shows a Mammy notebook holder that is empty but for a further Mammy image of a black servant holding a crying white baby. Mammy memorabilia is shown to be offensive and to camouflage a history of slavery. Saar makes her position clear: where this Mammy usually only held a broom and a smile, Saar puts a rifle and a Black Power fist by her side: no longer slave, she is now master of her own destiny. Black power and woman power are one in their fight against oppression.

It is interesting to note here how the next generation dealt with this legacy. Saar's daughter, Alison Saar (b. 1956), having studied African, Haitian, and Afro-Cuban art with art historian Samella Lewis at Scripps College, fuses art-historical critique with identity politics in her sculpture. In her 1981 mixed-media sculpture *Si j'étais blanc* (*If I was white*) she makes reference to a song of Josephine Baker's and so to the exotic eroticism Baker refers to in her title, only to undercut it by presenting a sculpture of a black boy, seated on a chair with his chest open. Inside his chest (which has cupboard-like doors) we see shafts of glass, while his legs are made of cement and bits of blue and white tiles. His body is the antithesis of Western society's exoticization of blackness; instead it

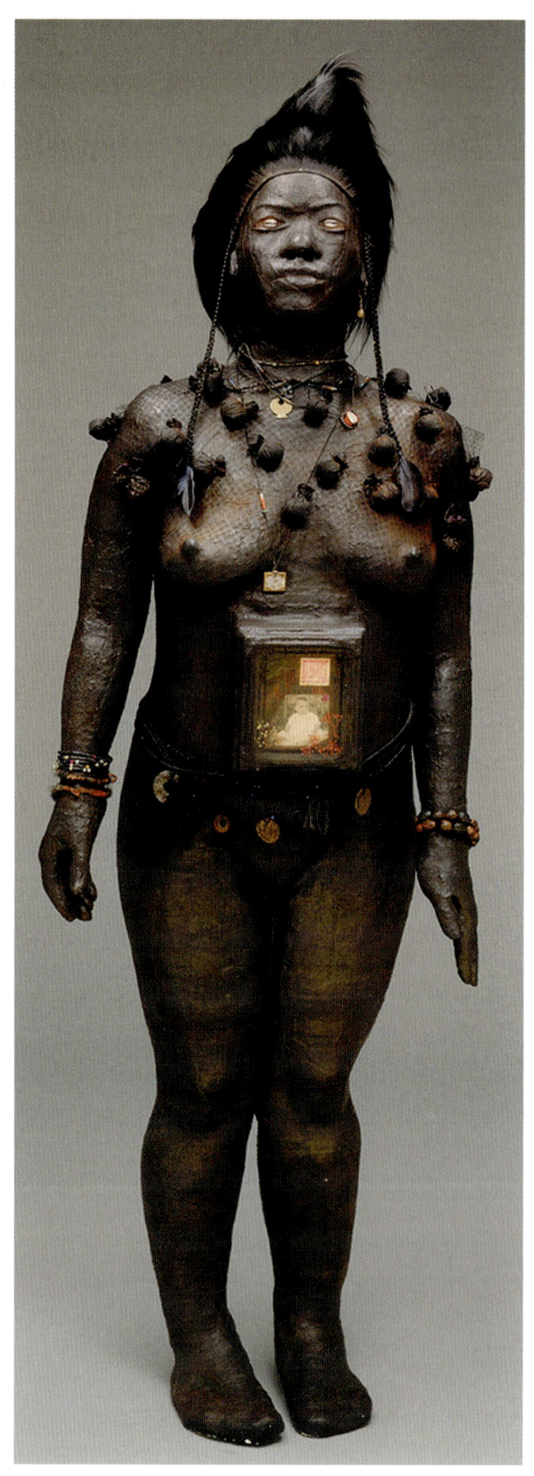

85 Renee Stout
Fetish #2, 1988

This sculpture, cast from the artist's own body, recalls *minkisi* made by the Kongo people of the present-day Democratic Republic of Congo. *Minkisi* are traditional figurines formed of man-made and natural material and are used to hold powerful medicines. They are an important part of rituals whereby chiefs communicate with ancestors.

refers to a different set of cultural symbols. In form and with its cavity, the work recalls figurative Kongo *minkisi*—figurines made of man-made and natural material used to hold powerful medicines and used by chiefs to communicate with their ancestors. Saar speaks of and to an African diasporic culture in her rejection of erotic tourism and in her insistence on a non-Western perspective in her art.[35] Renée Stout (b. 1958) also turns to the sacred power that *minkisi* hold in *Fetish #2* (1988) **[85]**. A 163 cm-tall sculpture of a black female body, naked except for bracelets and necklaces, it too holds a container in the stomach housing glass, a turn-of-the century photograph of a baby, a stamp from Niger, and dried flowers. The artist not only cast her own body for this work—thus removing the traditional power struggle between artist and sitter—she has also claimed her ancestry at the very site of her own procreative powers, her womb. The black female body here resists being objectified as an erotic object and instead is empowered and protected by its ancestors.

Ethnic Identity

Ethnicity also came under scrutiny in the 1970s. The women artists group, Las Mujeres Muralistas (Women Muralists)—whose founding members were three Chicanas, Patricia Rodríguez, Graciela Carrillo, and Irene Pérez, and a Venezuelan, Consuelo Méndez—brought gender, race, and class politics into the streets. As their collective name indicates, they turned to the theme of womanhood to express their sexual identity in their art. Motherhood in particular offered further thematic possibilities: the organic form (e.g. pregnant body), ancestry (e.g. pre-Columbian mythology), and the Madonna/whore dichotomy. Los Angeles-based muralist Judith Baca's (b. 1946) mixed-media triptych *La Tres Marías* (1976) demonstrates Chicano politics in addressing sex, colour, and class. The work was originally used for a performance and consists of three panels: a central mirror is flanked by two painted panels made of masonite over wood. On the right Baca depicts a Pachuca from the 1940s: she wears a tight skirt and white blouse, a scarf knotted at her neck, and has a back-combed 'homegirl' hairstyle with razor blades tucked into her curls. She suggestively draws on a cigarette she holds in her hand with bright-red painted fingernails. Her allegiances are clear from her dress code but are also reinforced by her LOCA tattoo—a barrio designation for Pachucas and Cholas. The opposite panel shows an updated homegirl, a Chola from the 1970s with long hair and trousers. She too has attitude, from her kohl-lined eyes to her boyish dress to her LOCA tattoo on her right arm. Her masculinity stands in stark contrast to the feminine Pachuca and yet both women display an aggressive femininity that is central to their battle for identity politics. Both women are separated by a mirror: the spectator 'completes' the triptych. As the piece is also accompanied by a text stating that the work intends to address the Virgin-Mother-Whore paradigm, the mirror compels the spectator to examine, literally and figuratively, where he/she stands.

Yolanda López (b. 1942), a San Francisco-born Chicana artist, has also prioritized the politics of looking in her art since the 1970s, a decade in which she says 'I found my voice as an artist.'[36] López addresses how Chicanos are represented stereotypically but also how they are not always sufficiently critical of those stereotypes. She insists: 'We have to be visually literate. It's a survival skill', and much of her art is concerned with her community's elevation of one particular icon—the Virgin of Guadalupe. She deconstructs the iconography of the Virgin, all the time asking 'Why doesn't she look like an Indian instead of a Mediterranean, a nice Jewish girl from the sixteenth century?'[37] In her 1978 painting *The Guadalupe Triptych*, López rooted herself in this problematic idolization of an ideal Mother in addressing the role of the Virgin for three generations: herself, her mother, and her grandmother. She portrays herself as a modern woman wearing a pink dress and sneakers, smiling and running **[86]**. In one hand she holds the blue and gold cloak of the Virgin like an Olympic athlete would hold their nation's flag; in the other she holds a serpent by the neck: symbols that suggest she has seized matriarchal power. For while in Freudian terms the serpent may symbolize phallic power, here she has literally grabbed it by the throat. It also evokes the Plumed Serpent, Quetzalcoatl, the ancient Mexican deity who created the calendar and civilization itself and who is, by

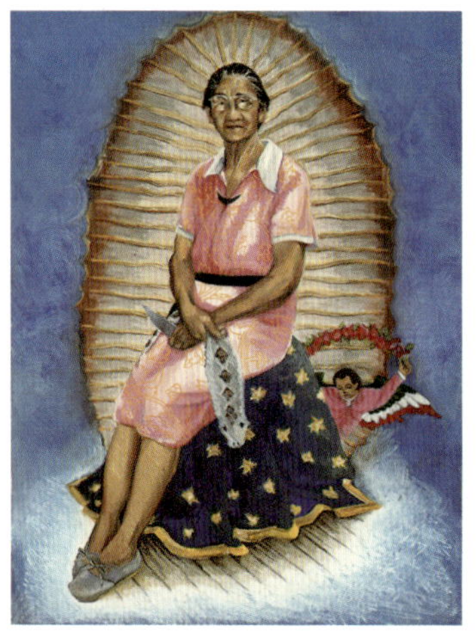

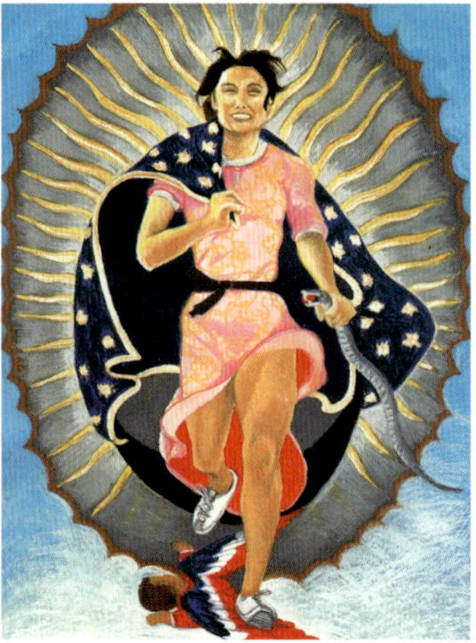

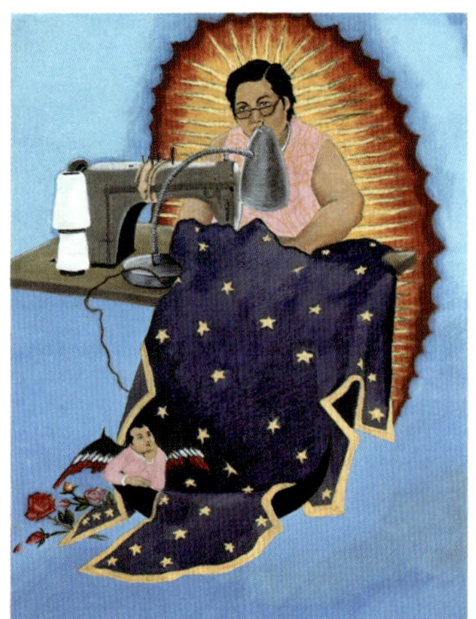

86 Yolanda López
Portrait of the Artist as the Virgin of Guadalupe, 1978

López's triptych celebrates matriarchal power while also questioning the iconic status of the Virgin of Guadalupe, the 'Queen of Mexico' for generations of Chicana women. The artist draws on Mexican folk art that typically portrays the Virgin in her blue and gold cloak, supported by an angel and with rays of light behind her.

extension, associated with feminine power as a symbol not just of the life cycle but also of the monthly cycle. The reclamation of the past for the vigorous renewal of the present and the leading of future generations into a blazing new light is reinforced in the triptych by López's triumphant smile in her self-portrait, her depiction of her grandmother skinning the snake (controlling rather than 'falling' in the Garden of Eden), and her mother using the snake as a pincushion (liberation through work).

While the Virgin reinforces the age-old Madonna/whore categorization of womankind, controlling and repressing women and their sexuality, it also speaks very specifically to a particular association between Mexico, maternalism, and mysticism. López chooses to subvert repressed notions of femininity and seize powerful, collective mythological ones instead. When a country's fertility and liberty is visualized as a feminine type, specifically a virgin mother, it again reminds us that the erotic body and body politic can never be divorced. Identity politics are thus asserted through the cultural reappropriation of the erotic body, and the boundaries of art and society begin to shift.

The vital advances of women artists and those artists concerned with sexuality and sexual politics caused a paradigm shift for art. Totally undermining traditional canonical art, they greatly expanded conceptions of artistic subject-matter of art and launched radical new means of self-expression. As the art historian Andreas Huyssen has acknowledged:

> It was especially the art, writing, film-making and criticism of women and minority artists with their recuperation of buried and mutilated traditions, their emphasis on exploring forms of gender-and-race-based subjectivity in aesthetic production and experiences, and their refusal to be limited to standard canonizations, which added a whole new critique of high modernism and the emergence of alternative forms of culture.[38]

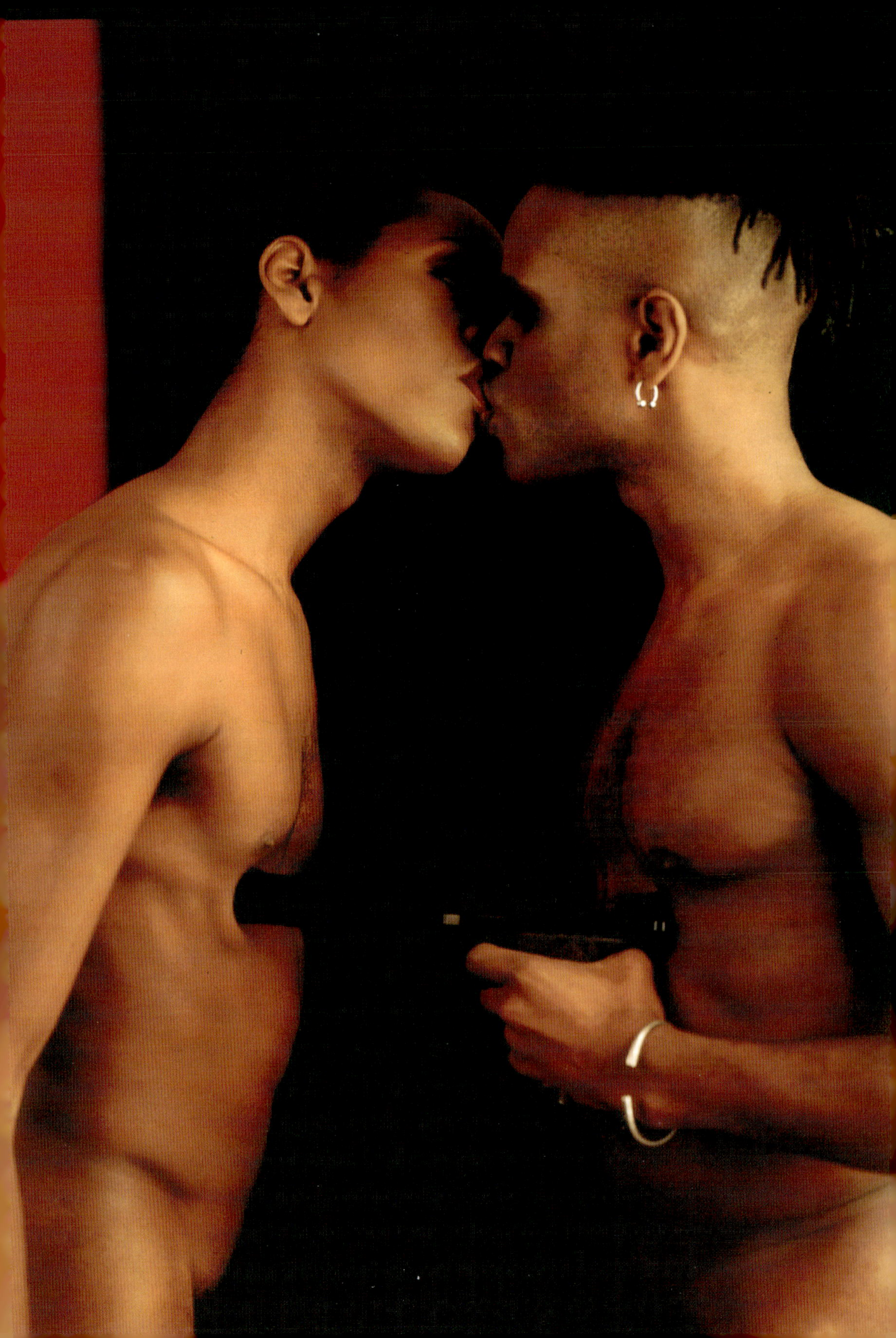

9

Eroticism and the Culture Wars of the 1980s and 1990s

While postmodern culture witnessed the rise of identity politics in the 1970s, there was an effective backlash against it in the 1980s and early 1990s, a period of the so-called 'Culture Wars'. This term signified the battle between liberalism and progressivism on the one hand, and religious orthodoxy and tradition on the other. In the United States, a shift from the liberalism of the 1970s to conservatism was signalled with the election of Republican Ronald Reagan in 1980. His government opposed abortion, promoted school prayer, and facilitated the political power of new Right-wing religious groups, notably the Moral Majority and the Christian Coalition. With similar conservative conviction, Margaret Thatcher, the 'Iron Lady', declared her wish to return to 'Victorian values' during her reign as Prime Minister in Britain from 1979 to 1990. This era also witnessed the slow thawing of the Cold War between Western capitalist democracies and the socialist countries in Eastern Europe and Asia. Mikhail Gorbachev came to power in 1985, the Berlin Wall came down in November 1989, and Reagan's successor President George H. W. Bush confidently announced 'The Cold War is over' on 17 November 1990, some 44 years after it had begun.

Major battles fought included the controversy over funding of the US National Endowment for the Arts (NEA), set up in 1965, which Reagan and Bush (elected in 1988) tried to dismantle in the 1980s. Provocative exhibitions involving Robert Mapplethorpe, David Wojnarowicz (1954–92), and Andres Serrano (b. 1950) in the late 1980s—as well as the 1999 showing of the English Royal Academy's *Sensation: Young British Art in the Saatchi Collection* exhibition in New York, featuring Chris Ofili's (b. 1968) elephant-dung-decorated *The Holy Virgin Mary* (1996) **[101]**—also led to vehement calls for NEA cutbacks. Serrano's *Piss Christ* (1987), a large colour photograph of a plastic crucifix submerged in a container of his own urine and lit in such a way as to make it radiate like a Sacred Heart statue, alerts us to some of the key tensions between art of the era and this censorship campaign. Serrano

Detail of 100

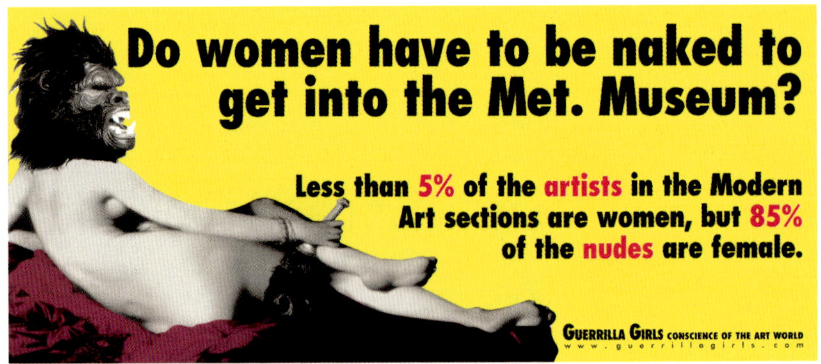

87 Guerilla Girls
Do Women Have to Get Naked to Get into the Met. Museum? 1989

An anonymous group of feminists founded in 1985, the Guerrilla Girls protest against art history's and art institutions' continued neglect of women artists, as well as sexism and racism in culture, society and politics, both through demonstrations (wearing gorilla masks), publications, posters, stickers, and their website.

conflated the sacred (Jesus) with the profane (bodily fluids), using erotic religious iconography as a means of both addressing the taboo of sexual desire and AIDS and discussing political impotence and religious intolerance before the epidemic. Jesse Helms, the Republican Senator from North Carolina, publicly decried Serrano's work, stating in the Senate: 'I do not know Mr. Andres Serrano and I hope I never meet him. Because he is not an artist, he is a jerk.'[1] The work's apparent blasphemous contents outraged the Senator but also the fact that Serrano had received a $15,000 grant from the NEA. Serrano's art was viewed as a serious threat to the morality of the nation.

Some artists, notably a group of anonymous feminists calling themselves the Guerrilla Girls, revived the militant feminism of the 1970s. Formed in 1985, the group strategically protested against the under-representation of women artists in museum collections and galleries by wearing gorilla masks and demonstrating outside. They produced posters, fliers, badges, books, and advertisements that denounced the sexism of art institutions, and gave lectures across the country.[2] One 1989 advert **[87]** asked: 'Do women have to be naked to get into the Met. Museum?' and stated that 'Less than 5% of the artists in the Modern Art Sections are women, but 85% of the nudes are female', alongside a reproduction of an Ingres nude wearing a gorilla mask.

Similar guerrilla or postmodern 'punk' tactics were employed by artists whose work engaged with eroticism: they began to wreak havoc on the limits of the erotic itself. Graphic, explicit images of sex entered the mainstream, and the pornographic imagination was let run wild. The trial of a museum director, Dennis Barrie, for exhibiting the erotic art of Robert Mapplethorpe was a major battle in the Culture Wars, while the accusation held against Barrie—obscenity and misuse of a minor in pornography—indicates the heated reception of much controversial erotic art in the last two decades of the twentieth century.

Sexual Outlaws

When Robert Mapplethorpe's retrospective show, *The Perfect Moment*—which included his images of men engaged in sado-masochism (the *X Portfolio*)—initially opened at the Institute of Contemporary Art in Philadelphia in December 1988 there was no public outcry. $10,000 had been awarded to the show by the NEA and it was to travel to five major cities. It duly travelled to Chicago, where again it attracted huge crowds and no protest. However, when it moved to Washington, to be shown in the Corcoran Gallery of Art in June 1989, it was cancelled by the director, Christina Orr-Cahall. She feared some of the photographs might cause public upset and lead to cutbacks in the gallery's public funding, a fear augmented by a recent letter signed by 36 US Senators demanding changes in NEA grant-making procedures to ensure 'shocking, abhorrent and completely undeserving art would not get money'.[3] In July, the Senate voted to limit funds to the Institute of Contemporary Art in Philadelphia for having exhibited Mapplethorpe's show, though it did not vote in favour of Jesse Helms's amendment to restrict grants supporting 'obscene or indecent art' a few months later. Yet when the show opened at the Contemporary Arts Center (CAC) in Cincinnati in April 1990 after its Washington cancellation, the director, Dennis Barrie, was charged with obscenity and misuse of a minor in pornography. The CAC was the first gallery to face prosecution for the art it exhibited; erotic art went on trial.

Mapplethorpe's art caused a crisis, firstly, over state sponsorship of art; secondly the definition of art itself was brought into question as defendants worked out a strategy to defend art that challenged the boundaries between the erotic and the pornographic. The photographs that particularly offended were sado-masochistic photographs from the *X Portfolio* and two photographs of children: *Rosie* (1976), in which a 4-year-old girl sits on a stone garden bench in a check dress, her genitals showing as she touches her foot and looks straight at the camera; and *Jesse McBride* (1976), in which a young naked boy perches on an armchair. The photographs led Helms to decry Mapplethorpe's art as 'homosexual pornography' and the artist as someone 'who died of AIDS while spending the last years of his life promoting homosexuality'. The images of children led to accusation of paedophilia: Judith Reisman, the 'associate director in charge of research' at the American Family Association, claimed that in *Rosie* 'Mr. Mapplethorpe's eye, and camera, peep under the child's skirt to expose her hairless genitalia provocatively to the world—just as thousands of other child molesters/pornographers before and after him.'[4]

It should be noted that *Rosie* was also one of the images that led to a furore over a Mapplethorpe retrospective at the Hayward Gallery in London in 1992 too. The Hayward also censored themselves for this show, taking advice from the Metropolitan Vice Squad, and chose to censor two of the works: *Rosie* and *Marty and Hank*, an image of two men having oral sex. However, it was the explicit image of a child's genitalia that caused consternation despite the fact that the model, Rosie, a grown woman aged 23 at the time of the show, had no problem with her portrait and happily displayed it in Notting Hill, London, at the restaurant she managed.

In both the United States and Britain, Mapplethorpe was accused of exploiting a child or indulging in paedophiliac desire in his photographs of children. Rosie's evident lack of trauma as an adult over her photograph—and Jessie McBride's mother's explanation that her son had simply been running around the apartment without any clothes on when Mapplethorpe took the photograph, and that 'It was all done in a spirit of fun and innocence'—were not listened to.[5] Instead Mapplethorpe was suspected of abusing his adult power and of couching children's erotic potential in formal brilliance. His homosexuality increased suspicion. That said, American photographer Sally Mann (b. 1951), who photographed her three children from about 1984 to 1996, was treated with suspicion too at the time; indeed, her photographs still make people uneasy. Mann's *Jessie at Five* (1987), in which her daughter has no top and wears lipstick and pearls as she stands coquettishly with one hip cocked, looking at the camera—is still discussed as 'not easy to look at' because 'her images upset cherished conventions of idyllic childhood'.[6]

In Mapplethorpe's case, after a week-long trial (28 September to 5 October 1990), Dennis Barrie and the CAC were acquitted: Mapplethorpe's photography was successfully defended on the grounds of artistic merit, its erotic artistry effectively saving it from the category of the obscene. His art was discussed in terms of light and shade as 'classical compositions' and the sexually explicit and/or pornographic nature of its content evaded. Mapplethorpe's classicizing tendencies saved the day as, ironically, the classical art tradition was used to remove his art from its specific social, political, and historical context and place it back within the timeless and universal frame of 'form'. His art may have been offensive in its erotic explicitness but it was still judged to be *art*. The trial did not address Mapplethorpe's wish to stage the supposedly obscene as beautiful through his formal skills. Indeed, the artist's assertion that 'it could be pornography and still have redeeming social value. It can be both, which is my whole point in doing it—to have all the elements of pornography and yet have a structure of lighting that makes it go beyond what it is' is still neglected by art historians and critics.[7] In his 1996 book on Mapplethorpe, Arthur C. Danto uses this statement to consider Mapplethorpe's art as 'transcendental'.[8] For Danto, Mapplethorpe's S/M images are ritualistic and spiritual in evoking Catholic imagery (for example, the often grotesque nature of Baroque altarpieces) and in transgressing taboo. Mapplethorpe's own reference to pornography indicates he was consciously using the risk factor of pornographic subject-matter but to make a social and sexual point, to go beyond the mass-produced genre of pornography through his artistic skill and thus to bring it safely back into the realm of the erotic imagination and form. As the French theorist Roland Barthes argued, even in his explicit close-ups of genitalia, Mapplethorpe moves from the pornographic detail to texture; his art has none of the banality of pornography. Mapplethorpe takes the spectator 'outside [the picture's] frame', leading to an animated exchange between the viewer and the viewed.[9] Again we find the active and empowering role of eroticism being asserted here: Mapplethorpe's art is far from pornographic solipsism since it forces the viewer into the erotic scenario.

The AIDS Crisis

The AIDS crisis in the 1980s and 1990s heightened public sensitivity to erotic subject-matter, notably over homosexual, abject, or sadomasochistic depictions of erotic pleasure. In the United States, political activism increased awareness about the AIDS crisis and discrimination against those suffering from AIDS-related illnesses but, as Simon Watney has argued, also led to the association between homosexuality and disease—an association often exploited by the Right.[10] When AIDS was first reported in 1981, President Reagan had been in office a year; for the next six years he neglected the AIDS crisis and evaded discussing the epidemic or funding necessary research and education on the problem until 1987. This was the year that ACT UP (AIDS Coalition to Unleash Power) was launched in the US. In 1987, one of ACT UP's members, the art historian Douglas Crimp, edited a special edition of the American art history journal *October* entitled *AIDS: Cultural Analysis/ Cultural Activism*. In this issue the renowned cultural theorist Leo Bersani addressed queer politics and the epidemic in his essay 'Is the Rectum a Grave?'[11] ACT UP was emphatically visual in its means and methods of protest—it involved people from the arts, advertising, and public relations worlds, and used posters, badges, videos, and logos in a very striking way. It also raised a lot of money through art auctions and was a vital voice of dissent at a time when the Reagan—and later Bush—administrations failed to deal with the crisis.[12]

Several artists were involved in this activist politics, including David Wojnarowicz, who tested HIV positive in 1987. He addressed his own struggle with prejudice against gays and the disease in his art and writing before dying from AIDS-related illness in 1992. His artistic career had begun in 1978–9 with an art work that paid homage to Arthur Rimbaud, when he produced 24 black and white gelatin silver prints of a friend wearing a mask of Rimbaud in a number of seedy New York locations. The artist explained: 'I didn't see myself as Rimbaud but rather used him as a device to confront my own desires, experiences, biography and to try and touch on those elusive "sites of attraction".'[13] Wojnarowicz's life was not unlike Rimbaud's a century earlier: they had hard lives, were abused by their parents, were gay and depended on strong mentors for supports—Paul Verlaine for Rimbaud, and the photographer Peter Hujar for Wojnarowicz. Both explored not just the homoerotic but also violence and rage in their art. Wojnarowicz's art might be described in Rimbaud's terms as 'a season in hell', a dark exploration of man's baser nature.[14] Certainly, Wojnarowicz presents us with his own bleak reality, depicting his horrendous experiences as a child prostitute in Times Square, New York, in such writings as *Memories that Smell like Gasoline* (1992), or in an image of his own face with his lips sewn together in the film *Silence = Death* (1990) by Phil Zwickler and Rosa Von Prauheim. This powerful image, with the title printed above a pink triangle—the Nazi symbol for homosexuality which became a global symbol of gay solidarity—was reproduced on the cover of *High Performance: A Quarterly Magazine for the New Arts* in the autumn of 1990.[15] The title spoke of resistance, but with sewn lips Wojnarowicz literally could not speak. Thus the visual impact of the image was louder than any words. The photograph was disturbingly intimate and terrorizing at the same time.

Fusing photography, paint, collage, and texts in his art works, Wojnarowicz polemically addresses the violence and hatred of the world. In *Fuck You Faggot Fucker* (1984) we find black and white photographs of naked men juxtaposed with an acrylic painted image of two men kissing. In *The Death of American Spirituality* (1987) **[88]** we find the all-American symbol, the cowboy, riding a bull that is 'coloured in' with newspaper clippings including one on Stonewall, another on a 'mob' killing, and another on AIDS. A painted bolt of electricity runs through the painting and even lassoes the arm of the cowboy, who not only refers to the ideal male Marlboro man of cigarette advertising campaigns, but also to Reagan, who was then in power. Reagan had played

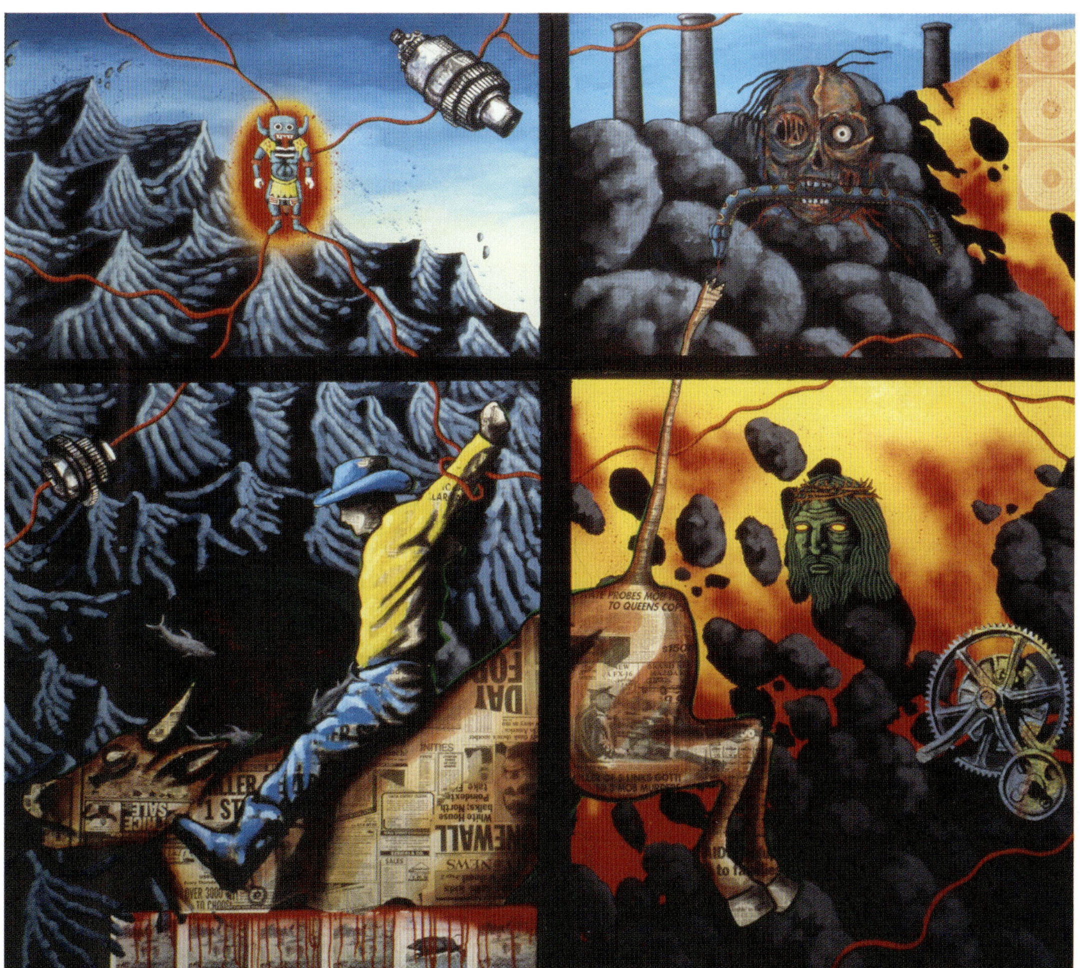

88 David Wojnarowicz
The Death of American Spirituality, 1987
Taking inspiration from Warhol and Lichtenstein in his use of popular iconography, Wojnarowicz undermines the 'American dream' in this multi-panelled painting. Collaged details include newspaper clippings on the Stonewall rebellion of 1969 and on the AIDS crisis; motifs include the cowboy, Jesus, a kachina doll, and a snake charmer.

cowboys in Hollywood Westerns (*The Bad Man* (1941) and *Law and Order* (1953)), and his political campaign imagery celebrated him as the all-American cowboy with photographs of him in a cowboy hat. Wojnarowicz exploited this association and described Reagan as a nuclear 'buckaroo' in an interview in 1987.[16] Amidst the pasted paper clippings we also see a china doll, a snake charmer, and Jesus: icons of lost faith and lost times. Wojnarowicz expresses his own experience of America through collage. As the French theorist Félix Guattari has observed, in Wojnarowicz's art we come face to face with a 'cartography' that enables the artist to reconstruct his own experience.[17]

Given his style and subject-matter it is not surprising that Wojnarowicz found outrage wherever he exhibited. In 1989, NEA funding for an exhibition dealing with AIDS entitled *Witnesses: Against Our Vanishing*,

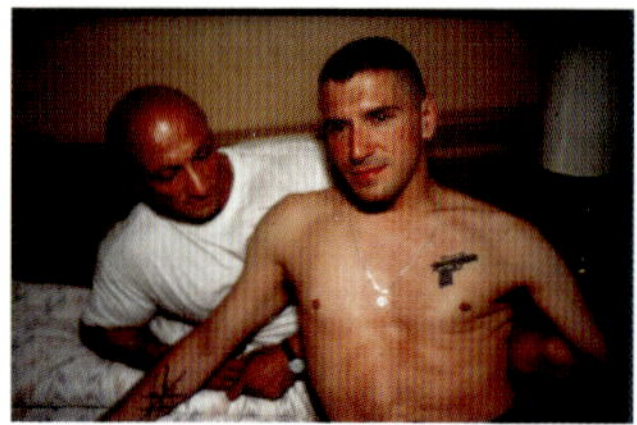
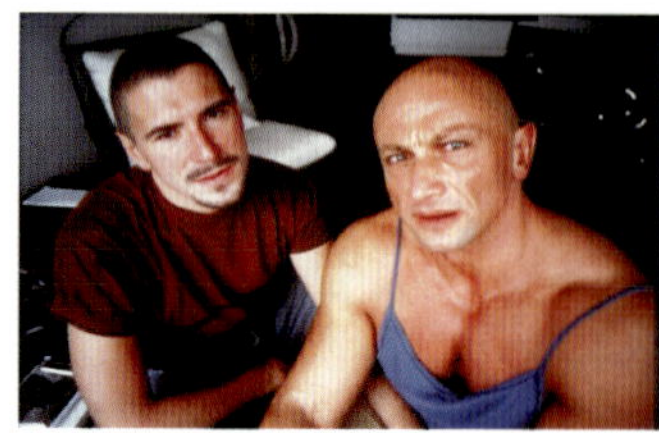
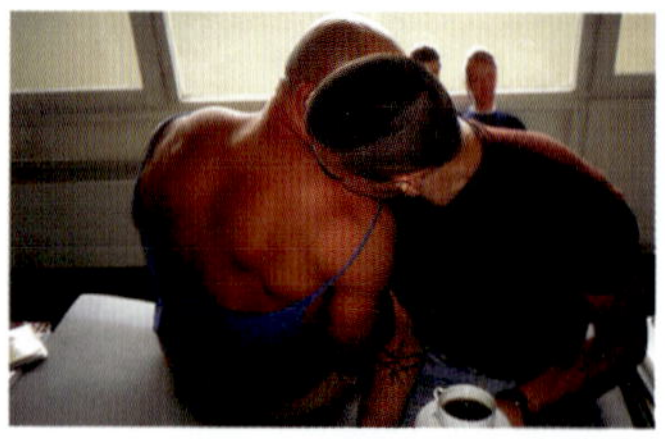

89 Nan Goldin
Gilles and Gotscho, 1992–3

These photographs document the lives of Goldin's friends, her French art dealer Gilles and his lover Gotscho, leading up to Gilles's death from AIDS in 1993. The photographs formed part of the catalogue *I'll Be Your Mirror* for her 1996 retrospective at the Whitney Museum, New York.

curated by the American photographer Nan Goldin (b. 1953) at the New York Artists Space, was withdrawn. It was not just the art that offended the then Chairman of the NEA, John Frohnmayer, but also the catalogue and an essay in it by Wojnarowicz. Entitled 'Post Cards from America: X-Rays from Hell' the obscene, deliberately provocative, language of Wojnarowicz's essay attacked the government, the Church, and American society in general for its 'diseased' stance on AIDS. The following year Wojnarowicz's solo exhibition, entitled *Tongues of Flame*, held at the Illinois State University, came under attack too. The Reverend Donald Wildmon and the American Family Association denounced the show and printed fliers headlined 'Your Tax Dollars Helped Pay for these "Works of Art"'. The fliers included some 14 details of Wojnarowicz's art—the most pornographic details—and were sent off to the US Congress. Wojnarowicz responded bravely by suing Wildmon and the American Family Association for libel and copyright infringement, insisting his art had been 'mutilated'. The US District Attorney ruled in favour of the artist on 8 August 1990, though he was only awarded $1 in damages. It was a major victory. In his short artistic career, Wojnarowicz exposed the public to the harsh reality of homosexual existence in Reagan's and Bush's America. His key strategy was not just to expose homosexuality and the AIDS crisis but to turn those aspects of society back on the institutions of power, insisting it was their reality too.

Nan Goldin was also influential in speaking out for AIDS victims. As mentioned above, she curated the major New York show *Witnesses: Against Our Vanishing* in 1989, and her photographs dealing with the epidemic act as poignant reminders of the emotional vulnerability of people when faced with a deadly disease. Goldin invites the public into her reality too. She has described her art practice as an extension of her daily life: 'It's as if my hand were a camera . . . The camera is as much a part of my everyday life as talking or eating or sex.'[18] Her large-scale photographs of friends, family, and lovers in bed, on the toilet, dressed in drag, or kissing their dying lover are poised between the documentary and the portrait. When it comes to AIDS her brutally honest approach does not change. In *Gilles and Gotscho* (1992–3) **[89]** we see a series of photographs of two lovers, beginning with them looking

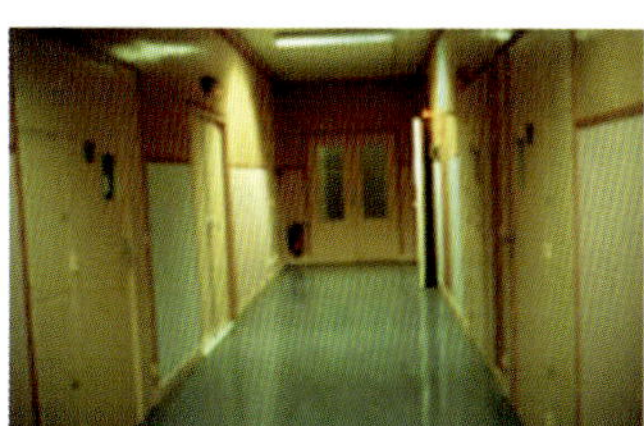

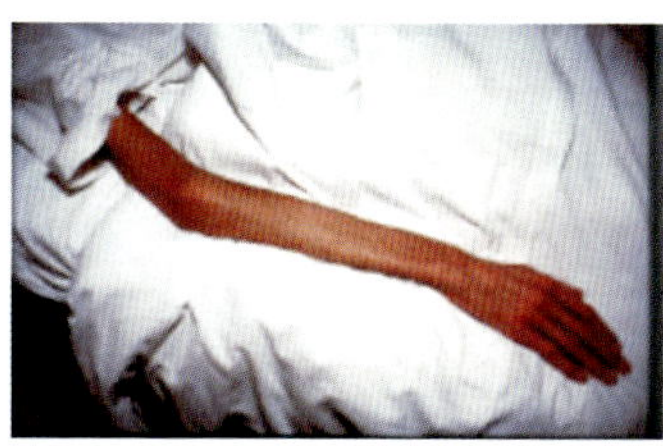

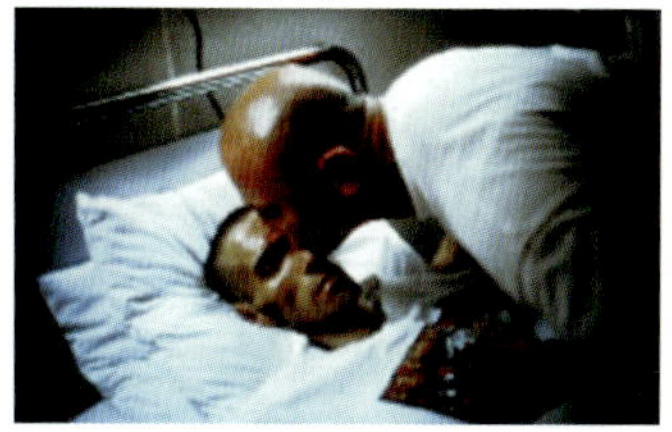

healthy and happy sitting on a bed, and ending with one tenderly kissing the other who now lies dead in a hospital bed, his skeletal body a shadow of his former handsome self. Here Goldin portrays the reality, the intimacy, and even the banality of AIDS. Her art has none of the rage of Wojanowicz and perhaps offers the kind of imagery of gay love and AIDS that the public is more comfortable viewing: a world where people love and people die but which is still a safe distance from the 'norm'.

Robert Gober's installation art seems to invite us into its own harmless world, but on closer inspection it is actually alienating and disturbing. His repeated use of truncated legs in his installations may have something to do with this. They poignantly remind the viewer not only of society's desire for the perfect, whole, ideal body but also its homophobia. In *Untitled* (1990) **[90]** male buttocks and legs emerge out of the gallery wall, the buttocks engraved with a musical score. The male body itself is banal, that of a white middle-American perhaps, but as a truncated body, exposed, and already tampered with it becomes nightmarish. The vulnerable bare and tattooed buttocks make reference to society's phobia over AIDS and the desire to make its victims visible—the work alludes specifically to the conservative writer William F. Buckley Jr's suggestion in a 1986 article in the *New York Times* that HIV-infected men should all be tattooed on their upper forearms to protect needle users and on their buttocks to 'prevent the victimization of other homosexuals'.[19] Dave Hickey has read the 'disaffection' of Gober's art as revealing aspects of the artist's personal life too: 'the homosexual son of Catholic working people, the infant blessed and damned in the earliest memory with an awareness that his "nature" is at odds with the "nature" of the culture in which he lives'.[20] For Hal Foster, Gober's art involves the child's primal fantasies as formulated by Freud—witnessing one's parents having sex, the fear of castration, the fantasy of seduction—and brings our personal desires and fears into the collective space of the museum.[21] Certainly the truncated form and emphasis on bodiless limbs suggests violence and castration, and so death. The banal staging of the objects also lends a macabre, almost clinical, air to many of Gober's sculptural objects and their installation scenes, refuting the

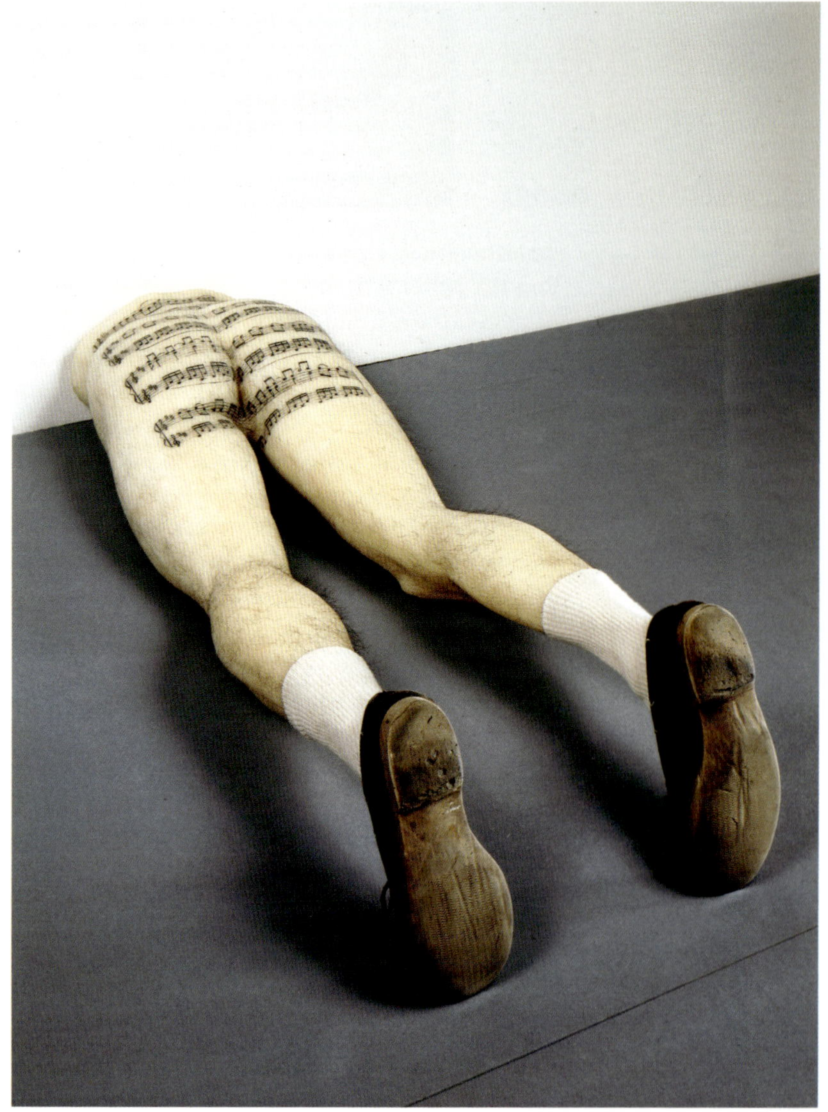

90 Robert Gober
Untitled, 1990

In his sculptures, Gober makes the familiar strange. Here the fragmented form of the truncated body-parts creates not only an uncanny mood but also a sensation of vulnerability. This work might be viewed as an example of abject masculinity as Gober defies homogeneous notions of identity and confronts social inhibitions and taboos. As Gober has explained, the tattooed score is an excerpt from a piece of found music, carefully transcribed but nonsensical when played.

usual fetishistic potential of the body part. The fragmentary peek-a-boo nature of Gober's art denies the public any perfect body or grand narrative. Gober exposes his own baggage, his own fears, but subversively exploits humankind's shared fascination with all things hidden.

Gay artists in Europe were also battling to push back both the boundaries of art and society and attitudes to AIDS. The Italian and British duo Gilbert and George (Gilbert Proesch, b. 1943, and George Passmore, b. 1942) have addressed the taboo homosexual body and the subject of AIDS in Britain. Their imagery stands in stark contrast to Wojnarowicz's, however, as they address the homoerotic and AIDS through glossy, slick images. Yet they too strive to bring the reality of AIDS into the safe haven of the art gallery and the middle-class home. In 1989, they held a *For AIDS Exhibition* at the Anthony d'Offay Gallery in London for the British AIDS charity organization CRUSAID, in which they exhibited magnified photographs of blood—the very carrier of HIV—like the post-modern offspring of Abstract Expressionism. *The Cosmological Pictures*, which toured museums in Europe from 1991 to 1993, advanced the homoerotic in more confrontational terms. These works included images of young men, as in *EDGER* (1989), a large-scale image (226 × 254 cm) of a man in tight jeans and sleeveless T-shirt, shown in profile and from a frontal view, against the urban backdrop of London. His expression and stance are sexually confident and defiant, and his physique takes on a totemic quality through the artists' use of block colours: his skin is painted red, the street behind him yellow, and his jeans a startling blue. In *DOWN to EARTH* (1989) we find the same vibrant palette of colours; we see the artists themselves, their magnified faces staring out at us as their mouths 'receive' each other's smaller phallic bodies amidst a graveyard of headstones. Gilbert and George here glorify the taboo and elevate the scatological to a saintly height. They turn abject corporeal waste —urine, faeces, semen—into abstract, glossy, images photographed under a microscope and raised to a monumental status. In many ways Gilbert and George also pay homage to Marcel Duchamp's *Fountain* of 1917 **[32]** in *Urinal* (1991), which conflates the sacred and the profane, taboo and transgression, homoeroticism and homophobia in its layering of images, including a row of urinals, a Gothic church interior and images of the two artists naked. The work addresses the taboo of homosexuality for the Church and the stereotypical association of gay sex with the public toilet. They accept responsibility for the shocking subject-matter but also deflect that shock in magnifying and glorifying its baseness. Indeed, they make the base beautiful, the glossy surface of their epic-scale works even evoking stained glass and the sublime aura of Gothic cathedrals. In using their own naked bodies, the artists also remind us that the male nude, whether heterosexual or homosexual, is often a taboo subject-matter in art.

Gilbert and George have always spoken through their own performative bodies, both in their public lives as immediately recognizable, tweed-suited dandies and in their self-portraits. The 'Englishness' of their public profile makes their art all the more subversive in its engagement with the aspects of British society that do not win public or political attention. Indeed, when they exhibited in Russia in 1990 it was not the Russians who were appalled by their homoerotic and scatological imagery but the British Council, who did not appreciate such cultural 'tourism' for Britain, one top official demanding to know why 'two homosexual fascists' were getting such attention.[22] Despite their often shocking subject-matter they explain their art as 'gentle'. George stated in 1997: 'We think we are very gentle in our approach to the viewer, really. We know how fragile we are, so we can imagine that the viewer is equally fragile . . . One of the main subjects under discussion is the human reality that there is no nakedness without a viewer: we are not naked when we are alone . . .'[23] In their recourse to the erotic Gilbert and George portray in accessible imagery the homoeroticism of London, as well as society's homophobia and its too-quick association between homosexuality and sexually transmitted disease. In this way they also present us with a very human face behind gay politics, trying to appeal to the common humanity of all.

If Gilbert and George present a 'neighbourly' homoeroticism in their art then the Milan-born, London-based artist Franko B (b. Milan, 1960) does the exact opposite. Franko B also uses his own body in his art but to enact rituals of masochistic self-mutilation before the public. Beginning in 1990, in response to the creation of 'Operation Spanner'—an anti-obscenity squad founded in 1987 and directed at homosexuals practising sado-masochism—his performances assert the rights of the sado-masochist, and involve the use of everyday objects (cages, wheelchairs, medical tools) to explore sexual control. However, Franko's pain (notably from blood letting) is always self-inflicted. In his performances in London in the 1990s, like *I'm Not Your Babe Parts 1* and *2*, or *Mama I Can't Sing Parts 1, 2 and 3* **[91]**, Franko B stands naked before his audience, his head shaved, his mouth more metal than teeth with metal caps and a tongue stud, his hairless body covered in white paint, as if already dead. He evokes Catholic martyrdom (he was raised a Catholic) as he ritualistically cuts his flesh until potentially lethal amounts of his own blood pour out of his veins. His use of medical implements is also emphatically symbolic—for example his use of a wheelchair in performances might be read as a reference to both physical *and* social paralysis, perhaps as 'symbols of blockage' and psychological impotence.[24] Between his terrorizing celebration of self-destruction and his emotive use of ritual (with lighting, sound, and catwalk-like stages), Franko B exposes psychological, sexual, and social imperialism in general and the policing of sexuality specifically. His choice of artistic medium is not paint but blood. Blood is the symbol of man (war), woman (procreation), science (disease), and taboo (S/M); as such it is the most potent medium to address the regulation of the individual. In eroticizing pain and the threat of death itself, Franko B forces the view-

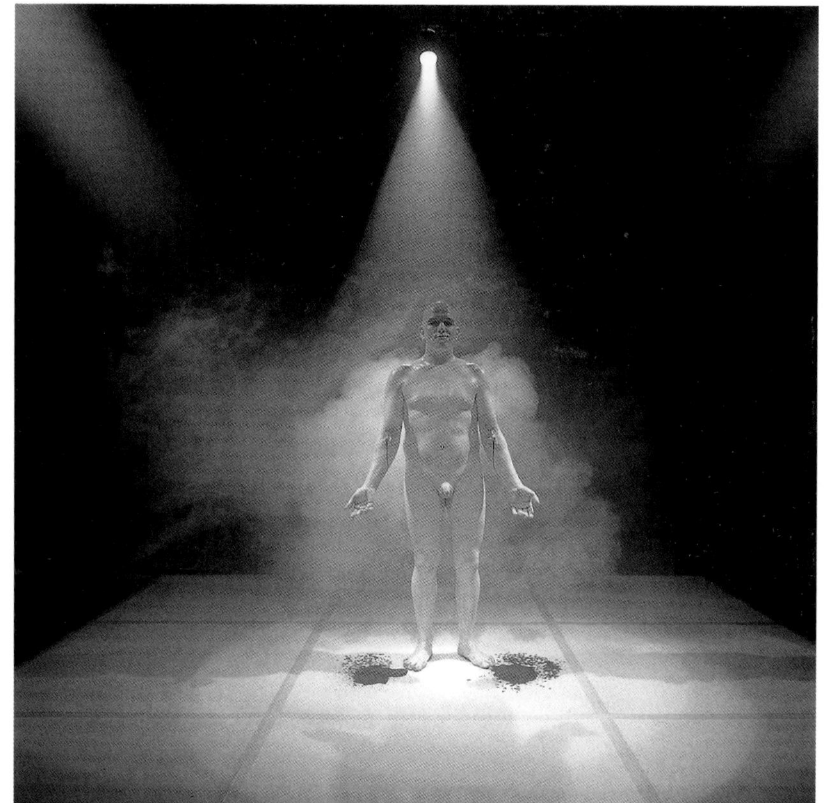

91 Franko B
Performance at the ICA, London, 1996

The Italian performance artist Franko B began his self-mutilation in 1990 in response to 'Operation Spanner', an anti-obscenity squad founded in 1987 and directed at homosexuals practising sado-masochism. In ritualized acts of self-mutilation, performed on catwalk-like stages, he pays tribute to Viennese Action Art of the 1960s while also commenting on the increased fear of the abject body and its visceral waste in a world traumatized by HIV/AIDS.

Photograph by Nicholas Sinclair

ing public to accept his sexual preferences while still retaining his sexual difference. He performs and preserves his sexual Otherness in the full knowledge that his public art would be deemed deviant in the eyes of the law were it to be staged in private.

The subject of visibility is also pertinent to the art of Irish artist Billy Quinn (b. 1954), whose life-sized photographic portraits of naked men and women express 'sex in a positive way' and 'the pain and rage around AIDS and the people we have lost'.[25] Unlike Nan Goldin, Quinn's photographs are not intimate moments snapped from real life. Rather, they are posed—sometimes kitsch—portraits of full frontal nudity. The artist often uses gold and silver leaf so that the image is endowed with an iconic status, parodying the iconography of martyrdom common to the Catholic tradition while also denying any visual referent to pain or disease. Of course such sexual explicitness, not to mention the topic of AIDS, is at odds with Ireland's image of herself—even in the 1990s. His self-portrait, *Billy* (1991) **[92]**, caused an outcry when it was shown in the 'Irish Art Now: From the Poetic to the Political' exhibition at the McMullen Museum of Art at Boston College, Massachusetts, a Jesuit

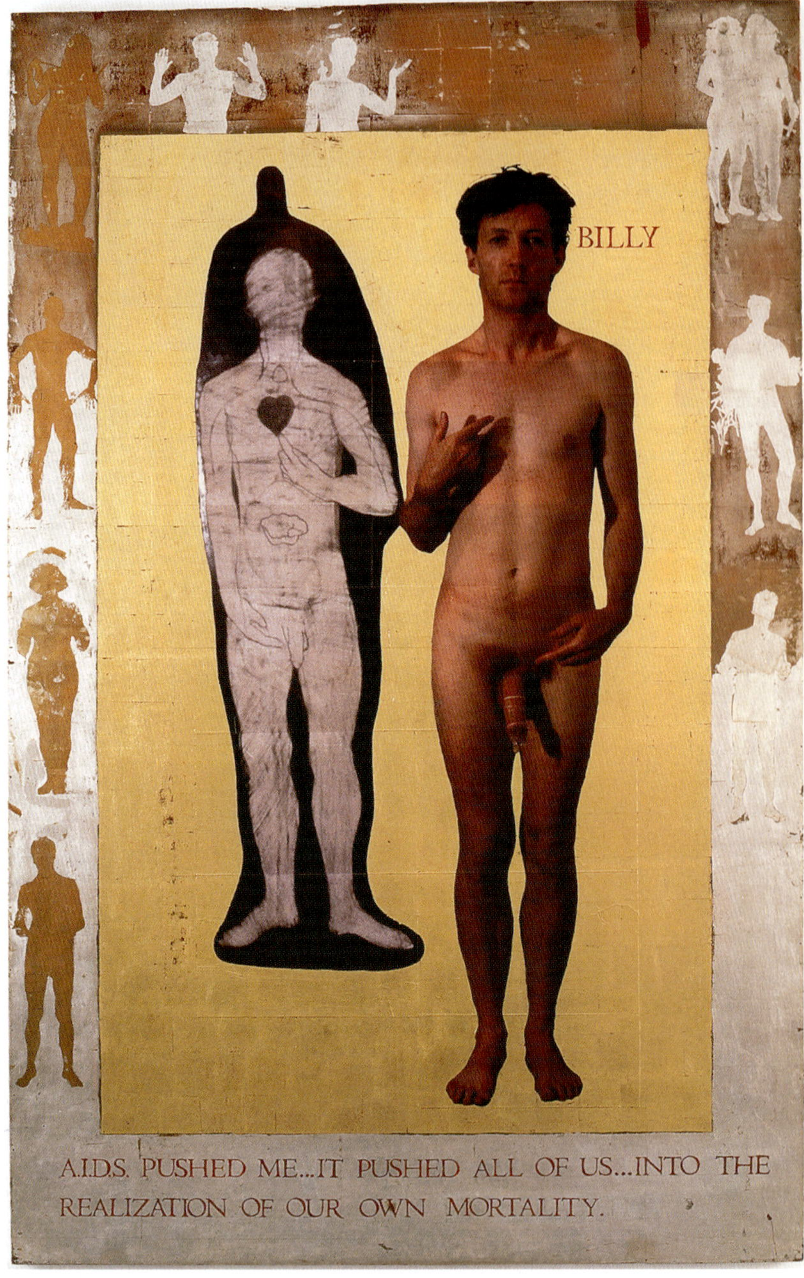

92 Billy Quinn
Billy, 1991

Quinn's self-portrait echoes the pose of the body of Christ in medieval frescoes and Renaissance painting, while his inclusion of text and use of gold leaf is reminiscent of early Christian illuminated manuscripts. The realism of the photograph is undercut by the rough, hand-drawn quality of his mirror image, which highlights the vulnerability of the major organs to which he points.

institution, from October to December 1999. The self-portrait of Billy, wearing only a condom, and posed against a gold-leaf background and the words 'AIDS pushed me . . . It pushes all of us . . . into the realization of our own mortality' was deemed anti-Catholic and, by extension, anti-Catholic Ireland. But this is the very guilt-ridden image of sexu-

aura that surrounds sexual terror. While S/M involves power dynamics, it is a sex act based on the eroticization of those dynamics, played out in fantasies of dominance and submission, and for mutual pleasure. S/M culture gained a veritable cult status in art in the 1980s and 1990s among gay and lesbians, although it was often harshly attacked by feminists taking active stances against pornography. These feminists perceived S/M, notably lesbian S/M, as dehumanizing and as perpetuating dominant gender roles and male dominance in mirroring active/passive roles.[35] Yet S/M reminds us of the Eros–Thanatos tension in erotic art. With sado-masochism, the death instinct is made visible: the outward death instinct (sadism) and the inward death instinct (masochism), the sadist deriving pleasure from inflicting pain, the masochist from suffering pain. Pain itself only gains its pleasurable significance from the actual ritual, the conditions, involved in its use, when it signifies something more than pain, when it gives physical and psychic pleasure.[36]

The photography of Grace Lau (b. 1939) from the 1980s onwards has explored the themes of bondage, S/M, and cross-dressing. In response to erotic images of male nudes in gay men's porn magazines, which tended to be sold in cellophane wrappers, Lau tightly wrapped a nude male model's buttocks in cellophane before photographing his glistening torso. In this way she 'packaged' the male body as a sexual object, enacting a role-reversal and creating an erotic *mise-en-scène* that *she* controlled. Her photographs include images of men and women in fetish gear, male and female strippers, androgynous figures, transvestites, and S/M rituals (she meets her models in clubs in London); as such they are quite documentary-like in mood. Underground sex clubs provide her with a 'visual theatre', an 'adult Disneyland', where the mood of 'intimate friendliness and warm humour' impressed her.[37] There is none of the formal classicizing seduction that we find in Mapplethorpe or the sense that Lau is a participant: her role as photographer is always that of voyeur exploring taboo territory from *outside* the erotic frame; photography, in her own words, allows her to 'sample perversion'.[38] Ultimately her work is feminist in intent and defies those feminists who believe S/M ritual only reinforces male values. The camera becomes her phallic weapon, allowing her to 'capture' people and to 'shoot' film, to dominate the erotic scenario but also to show that dominance is not gendered and that S/M is a sexual preference that involves consent and trust.

Nayland Blake (b. 1960) is much less a sexual tourist in his photographic explorations of S/M, and seeks to expose the 'unspoken power relationships in everyday life' through his theatrical approach to S/M.[39] *Restraint (Neck Prod)* (1990) is a suspended neck restraint; *Workstation #2*

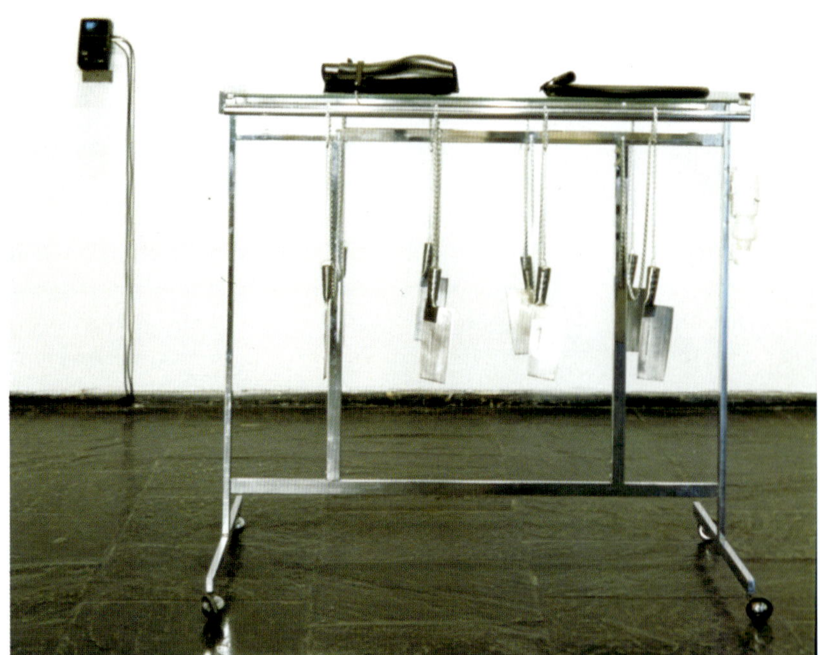

96 Nayland Blake
Work Station #5, 1989

New York-born artist Blake explores gender and sexuality, as well as his own biracial mix of African and European heritage, in his sculptures, installations, and performances. His art often presents a dialogue between gay culture and the dominant culture, as in this installation's subtle exploration of S/M, through the fetishistic power of chrome and rubber and the suggestion of bondage and pain. It also speaks, however, in more general terms to the theme of desire as a contested terrain in a postmodern capitalist society.

(Restraint) (1988) is a shiny, stainless steel bondage table, with handles and hoops, a leather-studded collar, and a sword. Sexual arousal and torture seem to be one in these works. *Work Station #5* (1989) **[96]** is an installation made of a steel clothes rack on which we see a piece of black rubber hose and rubber leggings, and several meat cleavers hanging from chains, their shiny surfaces catching the light. Blake wants to make bondage clinically clear in his art: it is about physical restraint and the satisfaction one gets from being restrained as well as the satisfaction of seeing someone in such a position. His installation entitled *The Schreber Suite* (1989)—devoted to Sigmund Freud's analysis of Daniel Paul Schreber's *Memoirs of My Nervous Illness* (1911), in which Freud effectively conflates paranoia and homosexuality—is equally calculated. This work takes issue with Freud's analysis, his neglect of the significance of Schreber's father (who had theories on child-rearing and designed armature to correct children's posture), and Schreber's very real fear of castration at the hands of his doctors as a 'cure' for his delusions. Blake hopes to reposition Schreber's book and give Schreber a voice. Indeed, Blake has stated that he sees Schreber's book as an example of 'a type of gay sensibility that exists at the base of modernism', a sensibility he also sees in Marcel Duchamp.[40] The *Suite* presents the viewer with a bizarre conflation of the scientific and the sexual, as the implements evoke cutting and castration but also the fetishistic

power of steel and leather. Blake hopes to present a different definition of a gay sensibility in his art and to confront canonical texts, like Freud's, which have influenced cultural discourse and social contracts concerning homosexuals. This intent lies behind his engagement with characters who have been at the forefront of popular culture or the mass media. In *Punch Agonistes* (1990) the puppet Punch is presented as a sadistic anti-hero of popular culture, while *Bleep* (1992) explores the 'cult' status of two homosexual mass murderers—the British mass murderer and necrophiliac Dennis Nilsen and the American mass murderer and cannibal Jeffrey Dahmer. Nilsen's and Dahmer's victims are represented by 14 chocolate heads, each cast from a bust of Wagner to evoke the fact that Dahmer's victims were mostly Asian or black and to turn symbolically Richard Wagner 'into shit', as Blake puts it, for his racism and anti-Semitism. Here Blake not only addresses the taboo of sexual violence and the theme of homosexuality as a supposed psychological perversion but also the subject of race and his own identity as a white-skinned man who is officially black (his father is African-American). For Blake, the reduction of gay male sensibility to the male gaze is too neat, too limiting, too regressive—he chooses instead to blur gender, to work against dominant readings of gay pleasure where the male gaze is simply directed to the male (as opposed to female) object, and to assert more provocatively his vision of 'the pleasure of the anus'.[41] His art is to be understood as a dialogue, notably between gay culture and dominant culture; but it also speaks in more general terms to our understanding of desire and pleasure in a capitalist society. As he explained in an interview, 'Our society trains us to all have the same desires that is what capitalism needs. Where someone takes their pleasure is highly individual . . .'[42]

Bob Flanagan, a Los Angeles-based artist who died of cystic fibrosis, also chose to explore his and society's bodily limits through ritualized pain and the fetishistic potential of science, medical equipment, and clinicality itself. Like Blake, he exploited the 'normality' of science in his sado-masochistic performances, often using hospital and medical paraphernalia as props. In this way erotic desire and a sexual regime could overpower his disease and medical regime. Assisted by his wife and collaborator Sheree Levin, aka Sheree Rose, he also documented his S/M acts (alongside his wretched daily suffering from cystic fibrosis) in his *Pain Journal*, begun in November 1994 and continued until his death. An entry dated 23 April 1995 begins 'Here again. Drugs. Computer. TV. Couch. Naked. Alligator clip on my dick. Fantasize about putting dozens and dozens of clips on my dick, but I can barely stand one.'[43] His performances coincided with a general interest in S/M and

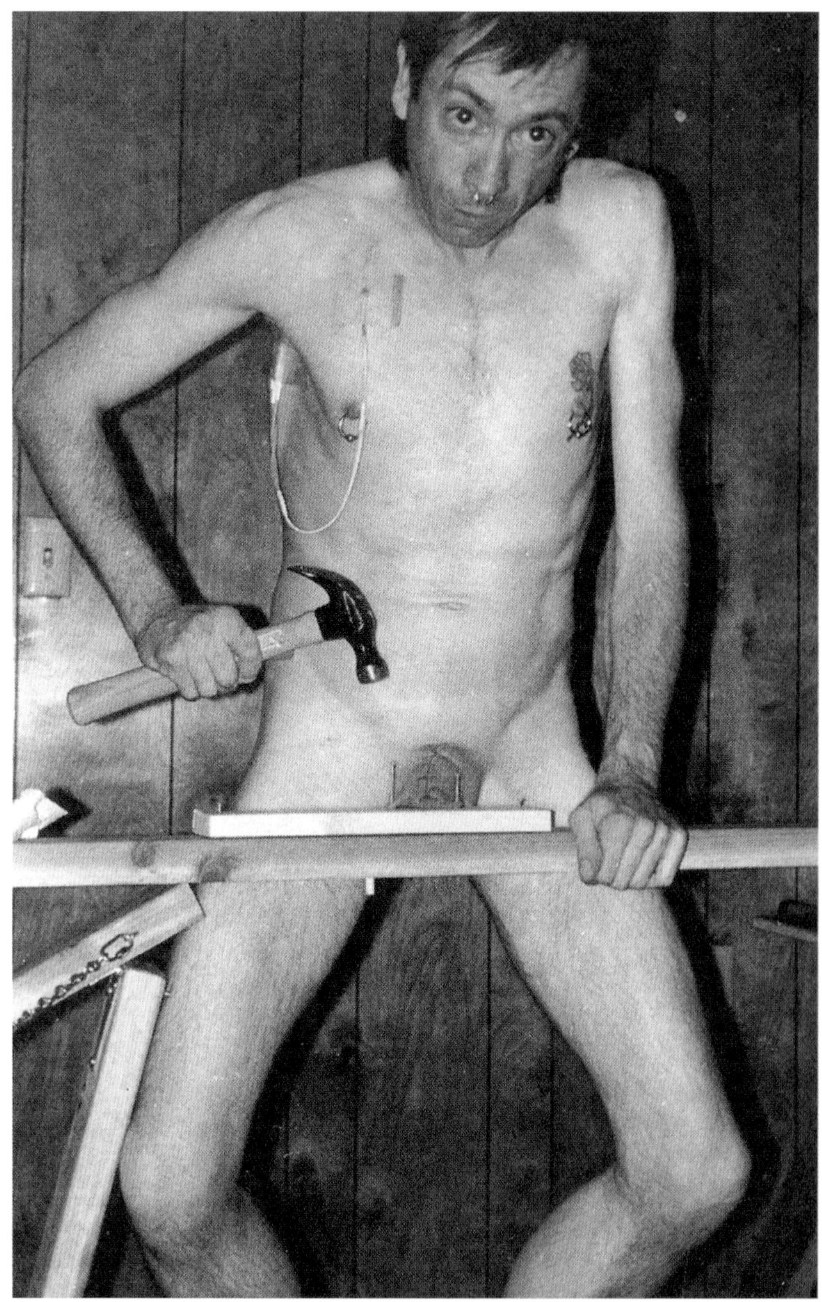

97 Bob Flanagan
If I Had a Hammer, part of the performance *Nailed* at the Olio Club, Los Angeles, 1989

Flanagan's self-mutilation contests the tradition of the heroic male nude and celebrates the pleasure of pain. He developed his art, in part, as a response to his life-long battle with cystic fibrosis. The performance may also be seen to allude to Christian martyrdom, the artist having stated that he derived pleasure from the idea that suffering 'was kind of holy'.

body modification in art and in youth culture in the United States in the 1980s and 1990s. Indeed, Flanagan became a subculture icon, being invited to perform in rock videos by Nine Inch Nails, Danzig, and Godflesh. Flanagan's sado-masochistic focus was his penis, a sign and symbol of life. His acts of self-cruelty included nailing his penis to a wooden board in a performance aptly called *Nailed* (1989), one he repeated at Q.S.M. ('Quality' Sado-Masochism location) in the San Francisco Bay Area in 1991 **[97]**. As he explained in a poem 'Why?', he chose to do this 'Because it feels good; because it gives me an erection . . . because I'm sick . . . because I say FUCK THE SICKNESS.'[44] With Rose as dominatrix, or on his own, he enacted symbolic castration, eroticizing and aestheticizing his pain. The sexual thrill lay not just in the element of control and trust so key to S/M, but in the ritualistic, religious thrill Flanagan felt from his self-sacrifice: he enjoyed 'the idea that suffering in some way was kind of holy'.[45] His art offers a radical break from the machismo performance art of the 1960s when artists like the Viennese Actionists (Otto Muehl, Hermann Nitsch, and Rudolf Schwarzkogler) reasserted the male, phallic body as a weapon of social revolt in their bloody performance art. As Amelia Jones argues, Flanagan's art pushes 'the eroticized body/self to its outer limits' through the *vulnerable*, flaccid male body.[46]

The Black Male

As AIDS forced art historians and critics to embrace the once-marginalized homosexual artist, so too did globalization and increased multicultural awareness force the subject of racialized and postcolonial identities into mainstream cultural and critical arenas. Yet this new post-modern situation threatened to deny difference and to undermine political struggle too. Just as Nayland Blake and Franco B insisted on the preservation of gay, sado-masochistic identity in their art, so too did many black artists insist on the need to preserve their racialized sexual identity in their art practice. In his 1992 essay 'What Is This "Black" in Black Popular Culture?', the sociologist Stuart Hall wrote that 'black' was the 'mark of difference *inside* forms of popular culture' and spoke to the survival of the black experience, the black aesthetic, and the black counternarratives that the black community had struggled to give a voice to.[47] This approach to cultural difference was reflected in black artists' approach to eroticism which became even more politically pro-active in an era when AIDS was attacking all members of society, black or white, indiscriminately. The stereotypical image of the black male as an exotic sexual Other became a predominant theme in black male artists' work, a trend made all the more apparent with the organization of *The Black Male* exhibition at the Whitney Museum in 1994. The foreword to the exhibition catalogue acknowledged the importance of academic programmes (postcolonial, ethnic, and gender studies) in the 1980s in

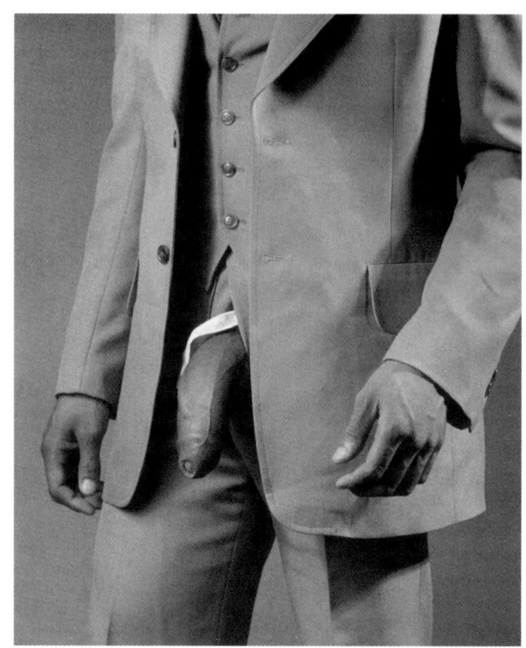

98 Robert Mapplethorpe
Man in Polyester Suit, 1980
The subject of numerous debates and articles, this 'portrait' of Mapplethorpe's lover Milton Moore may be viewed as enacting a colonial fantasy as the black male is reduced to his penis. Its fetishistic power is enhanced by the shine from the lighting and choice of monochrome film. The image is doubly subversive, transgressing both the taboo of homosexual desire and race.

bringing black masculinity to the forefront of cultural and social debate, while the primary curator for the exhibition, Thelma Golden, recognized how Robert Mapplethorpe's images of the black male expose white fears of the black male as sexual Other. She credited Mapplethorpe with making explicit 'the fear of black masculinity and more specifically of the lust and loathing of the big, black dick'.[48] Mapplethorpe had not just eroticized the black male, he brought black homoeroticism into the equation, confusing the traditional equation of blackness with heterosexual maleness.

Mapplethorpe's photograph, *Man in a Polyester Suit* (1980) **[98]**, literally depicts the black male as his penis, framing a man's torso, in a cheap polyester suit, with his fly open and his half-erect penis. It eroticizes the black male through racial stereotype, fulfilling a 'colonial fantasy'. The Martiniquan psychiatrist and cultural theorist Frantz Fanon explained this fantasy in *Black Skin, White Masks* (1952): 'one is no longer aware of the Negro, but only of a penis; the Negro is eclipsed. He is turned into a penis. He *is* a penis.'[49] Mapplethorpe's fantasy world is one of male power and potency; it is also one where the black male is portrayed as the most phallic. For cultural critic Kobena Mercer, writing in 1986, Mapplethorpe's black male nudes, especially his *The Black Book*, presents 'Black + Male = Erotic/Aesthetic Object. Regardless of the sexual preferences of the spectator, the connotation is that the "essence" of black male identity lies in the domain of sexuality.'[50] He argued that the anonymous black male body was essentialized, beautified, and fetishized by Mapplethorpe in a manner comparable to the tradition of the female nude, the dichotomy of black–white difference taking the place of the traditional male–female polarity. Where the traditional voyeuristic gaze in art is enacted by a white male on an objectified woman, with Mapplethorpe it is enacted by a white male on an objectified black man. The fetish of skin colour, which functions for Homi Bhabha as 'the most visible of fetishes', is enhanced through the manipulation of shadow and light, lending a fetishistic 'shine' to the skin.[51] Of course this emphasis on the 'shine' reinforces Freud's association between the luminous shine and the fetish and his case study example of the young man who 'had exalted a certain sort of "shine on the nose" into a fetishistic precondition'.[52] In the case of *Man in a Polyester Suit*, the skin of the exposed penis shines, magnifying a primal fantasy, allowing not only for the traditional sexual fantasy of 'difference', but also a fantasy of 'mastery', to go uncontested.[53] When discussing the image in her biography of Mapplethorpe, Patricia Morrisroe seems to support the suspicion of racism behind his erotic framing of the black male. She cites Mapplethorpe's comment to a friend (John Abbott): 'Wouldn't a nigger wear a suit like that?'[54] Yet Edmund White has argued against such a racist interpretation of the image, reading it as a homage to sexual love: Mapplethorpe's black lover Milton Moore did not want to be identified by his face in photographs, hence his nameless, faceless 'portrait'.[55] Mapplethorpe's imaging of the black male must also be considered in the light of artistic precedent. As well as the homoerotic photography of Platt Lynes, Mapplethorpe was also strongly influenced by George Dureau (b. 1930), a Louisiana-born photographer and a homosexual, known for his images of fellow African-American men. Mapplethorpe befriended Dureau in the 1970s, and after meeting him began photographing black men. *Man in a Polyester Suit* was produced in the same year that he organized Dureau's first exhibition in New York. Dureau's style of rendering the male nude heroic (whether photographing athletes or amputees) allows us to appreciate Mapplethorpe's very direct style and fascination with the black body in a new light; we can then reconsider what it is about *Man in a Polyester Suit* that we find so disturbing.

Given the personal and artistic context for its production, we might view the photograph as a portrait of black homosexuality, in defiance of traditional male–female and black–white erotic polarities; it is also a challenge to popular taste and censorship laws, given its teasing portrayal of an almost fully (and therefore censorable) erect penis. Kobena Mercer would reconsider his initial criticism of Mapplethorpe's objectification of the black male. In a 1989 article, he explained that he did not doubt his initial argument but had come to recognize that as a black gay reader of Mapplethorpe's photography, he had initially identified with the black man in Mapplethorpe's works, feeling both intrigued and threatened by their homoeroticism, and that circumstances—notably the death of Mapplethorpe in 1989 and controversy over his Corcoran Gallery exhibition, as well as 'the emergence of new aesthetic practices among black lesbian and gay artists in Britain and the United States'—had led him to temper his earlier, angry assessment of the photographer.[56] He conceded that sexual difference and differences of race were not equivalent, and that Mapplethorpe's elevation of the black male to the status of aesthetic ideal, within a white Western canon, endowed the disadvantaged and disempowered with a bold, subversive new status. It made the hitherto invisible visible. With this in mind, Mapplethorpe's erotic art might be seen to enact a double transgression across homosexuality and race, using the former as 'artistic perversion' to subvert the traditional nude, to destabilize fixed reading, and to reveal 'the political unconscious of white ethnicity'.[57] This revised reading again reminds us of how black masculinity itself was used by black artists, male and female, in the 1970s, when Mapplethorpe was looking to black artists like Dureau, and how important it is to contextualize erotic art historically. We recall Barkley L. Hendricks's *Brilliantly Endowed Self Portrait* of 1977 and Adger Cowans's photograph *P.B.* (1974), both of which 'exploited' black sexuality to address race. We might also think of *I Embody* (1975) by African-American artist Adrian Piper (b. 1948). In this painting she speaks against racism by means of racial stereotype and her own self-portrait (a recurring theme in her art, given her light-coloured skin) through a clever juxtaposition of the text 'I embody everything you most hate and fear' to one side of the image, and her self-portrait complete with Afro hairstyle, sunglasses, and cigarette to the other. On a popular level, let us not forget either Gordon Parks's blaxploitation film *Shaft* (1971), which depicted John Shaft (Richard Roundtree) as the blackest, coolest private 'dick'.

Mapplethorpe's 'contamination' of the homoerotic through racial stereotyping had an immense impact on subsequent generations of black artists. The African-American gay artist Glenn Ligon (b. 1960) has explored his own reaction to Mapplethorpe's eroticization of the black male in *The Black Book* by choosing to re-frame the work and focus on his own sexual and racial identity in the process. Ligon's *Notes on the Margin of the 'Black Book'* (1991–3), an installation piece consisting of Mapplethorpe's images and critical texts, exhibited at the 1993 Biennial at the Whitney Museum, was the first work by Ligon openly to address homosexuality as well as race. Ligon's documented his own reaction to *The Black Book* in his preparatory notes for the installation piece which he jotted on his own copy of the book. His notes demonstrate the probing nature of his work, his concern not just with how his race is represented by Mapplethorpe but the specific fetishization of blackness, asking 'Why are we always greasy? Why are we always shining?' In the installation he appropriated Mapplethorpe's images, lined them up in two rows, and divided them by printed texts taken from supportive and derogatory critical readings of Mapplethorpe's art. In this way Ligon reconceptualized Mapplethorpe's original project such that the viewer had to reconsider Mapplethorpe's problematic objectification of the black male as erotic object. In his postmodernist approach, notably citing multiple readings of Mapplethorpe and insisting on an intertextual reading of the work as a result, Ligon also refused to take his own stand on the original work. Instead he created a space for plurality, defying political correctness and insisting instead on freedom in all areas—racial, political, sexual, and artistic.

Race and erotic desire, and the concept of 'blackness' itself, are the subject of many of Ligon's works, both in terms of his own identity and the more general formation of modern black experience. In *Cocaine (Pimps)* (1993), we come face to face with a racist joke made famous by the black comic and film actor Richard Pryor, in bold orange text on a red background (painted on linen with oil stick and acrylic): 'Niggers be holding them dicks too. White people go: "Why you guys hold your things?" Say "you done took everything else motherfucker."' In this reappropriation we find Ligon again using the device of reframing to make a political point: the joke reinforces the racial stereotyping of the well-endowed black male, but in making the viewer read rather than hear it he/she becomes more conscious of the continued problem of polarized race relations in the United States. The rage of the black person may be 'contained' in a written text but it is also lent force by the angry red/orange colours.

Ligon's installation *A Feast of Scraps* (1994–8) **[99]** might be viewed as taking his questioning of Mapplethorpe and American racism further and deeper in introducing his own homoerotic desire to the debate. In this installation he juxtaposes images from his personal family album with pornographic images of black men and typed labels, many of which allude to his own homosexuality—for example, 'Mother knew', or 'Necessity is a *mother*'—by placing it under a photograph of a muscular black nude, oiled up for the viewer's gaze. The work places the public with the personal, the family with the forbidden. 'Brother' is the label given to an image of a young naked black man smiling out at the viewer,

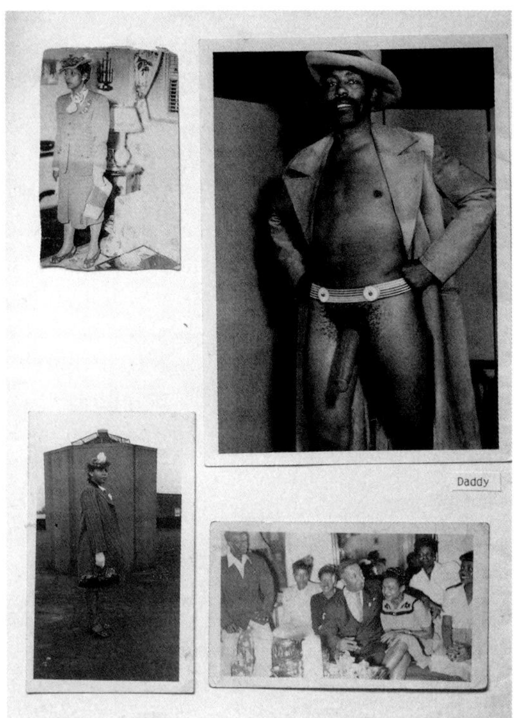

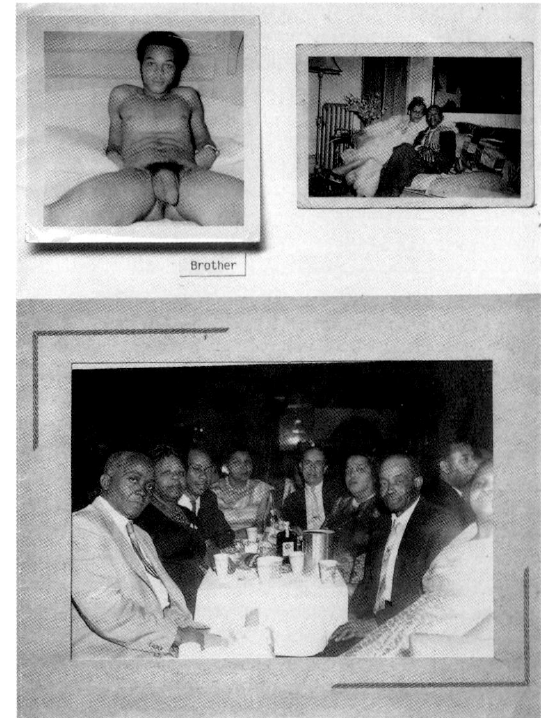

99 Glenn Ligon
Feast of Scraps, 1994–8

The painter and mixed-media artist Glenn Ligon explores his own experience as an African-American and a homosexual in his art, testing the tradition of representations of the black male, including the controversial staging of the black male by Mapplethorpe. Through the format of the family album, he juxtaposes family snapshots and vintage gay porn alongside such headings as 'Daddy', 'Brother', and 'Mother Knew' to explore the memories and stories families share, as well as those they keep secret.

and is placed beside a photograph of a black couple on a couch, dressed up for the evening, and above a photograph of four couples in a club. Ligon's art speaks to a specific African-American experience: as he said in an interview, 'blackness as a subject matter tells you about what it means to be anything else'.[58] His art does not just look at the polarities and stereotypes of black and white through the erotic, it insists on the need to explore and renegotiate the space between those poles.

Los Angeles-based artist Lyle Ashton Harris (b. 1965) also engages with this in-between space. He explores his own black gay identity through camp. David Bergman has explained camp homosexual culture as embodying 'a self-conscious eroticism that throws into question the naturalization of desire'.[59] It questions normative views of the erotic. Adopting camp as a strategy, Harris might be seen to subvert 'natural' desire through a subversive exploration of artifice. He plays male/female, straight/queer, butch/femme roles in his photographs, proposing identity itself to be highly constructed. In the process he explores, in his own words, 'the Black subject at the center of the matrix of desire, not as a fixed ideal, but in flux, liberating, complex, and self-reflecting'.[60] *Brotherhood, Crossroads and Etcetera, #2* (1994) **[100]** is the central panel of a triptych made up of colour photographs of two naked black men. One of the men is Harris, the other his brother, Thomas Allen Harris, a film-maker and performance artist. The image is meant to evoke the primal scene of Cain's treachery towards his brother Abel, symbolized by the kiss and gun. The other two photographs in the triptych show Lyle holding his fallen brother, and the brothers embracing and pointing a gun at the viewer, respectively. According to the brothers, these images draw on their individual and collaborative works, thus 'interrogating as well as re-imagining' themselves; the images also allude to 'the black literary tradition of autobiography as self-creation and self-fashioning' as a radical act of empowerment.[61] They are both concerned to stage multiple selves by drawing on African-American visual culture and disregarding bourgeois notions of taste and morality. At the same time, they express a strong sense of fraternity and spiritual communion: both men were brought to the Bethel African Methodist Episcopal Church in Harlem during the 1960s and 1970s by their grandparents. They also consciously draw on another aspect of their African-American heritage in the colour scheme of the triptych: the tricolour flag of Marcus Garvey's UNIA (Universal Negro Improvement Association), where red stands for blood, green for the land, and black for the African race. Finally, the triptych also speaks to Lyle's gay identity within his black brotherhood. He has said that at the heart of his *Brotherhood, Crossroads and Etcetera, #2* triptych is an attempt to address the promotion of 'purity around blackness' within black nationalism, an exclusionary vision of masculinity which fears male intimacy or homosexuality. Thus *Brotherhood* 'speaks to the twinning of black homophilia', to quote Paul Gilroy, 'and black-on-black violence'.[62] The brothers' naked bodies, the kiss, and the gun symbolize this tension.

The black British artist Chris Ofili also draws on Marcus Garvey and the Black Panther movement in his use of the red, green, and black colours of black nationalism in his art, as well as exploiting the erotic stereotyping of blacks in Western culture. His series of images of *Captain Shit*, a black hero with Afro hairstyle and big lips, is a case in point. The artist confronts stereotypes, asserting: 'It's what people really want from black artists. We're the voodoo king, the voodoo queen, the witch doctor, the drug dealer, the *magicien de la terre*. The exotic, the decorative. I'm giving them all of that, but it's packaged slightly differently.'[63] Ofili not only subverts street stereotypes, such as the image of the black as drug dealer (selling 'shit'), but also the exoticization of non-white culture and art. His quote refers to the ground-breaking *Magiciens de la terre* exhibition at the Centre Georges Pompidou in Paris in 1989—an exhibition that brought many non-white artists to a major museum in Europe but still came under attack as 'exoticizing' and decontextualizing

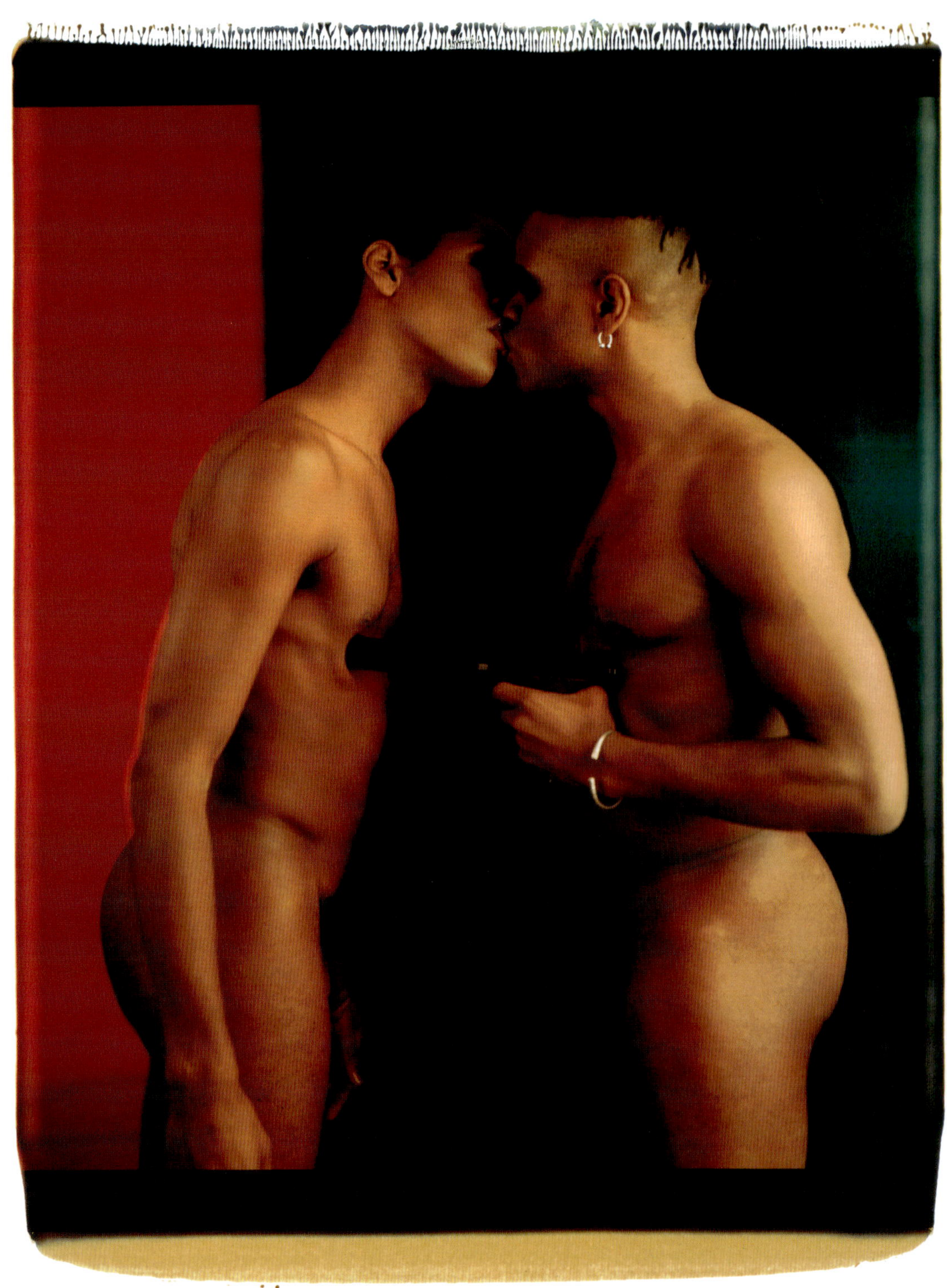

100 Lyle Ashton Harris in collaboration with Thomas Allen Harris
Brotherhood, Crossroads and Etcetera, #2, 1994
Lyle Harris questions black masculinity in his art through the themes of family, race, sexuality, gender, and masquerade, all the time disrupting the viewer's traditional expectations, as well as insisting that identity is not fixed. He explained this collaboration with his brother, the film-maker Thomas Allen Harris: '[we use] masquerade as our mode of transgression . . . challenging a construction of African nationalism that positions queers and feminists outside the black family' (*Flash Art*, 29, 1996).

race. Ofili's subversion lies in his irreverent fusion of high and low cultural sources, from the Bible to porn magazines. His use of mixed media is equally hybrid: on the one hand he paints in an age when many artists have turned to photography and video; on the other hand he is notorious for his use of elephant dung on his canvases. However, this differs from the Dadaists' agenda to 'shit on art', as Ofili is concerned with surface texture and making the supposedly ugly (shit) beautiful. In *The Adoration of Captain Shit and the Legend of the Black Stars (Part 2)* (1998), we see fans' adoring hands trying to rip the clothes off Captain Shit, an Afro-haired black 'Superman' dressed in a gold and red figure-hugging suit, a kind of fusion of Elvis and Shaft. A kitsch black star around him is decorated with cutout images of women's dark, kohl-lined eyes in a deliberate parody of the exoticizing of race in Western art. Through visual and cultural layering Ofili again camps up black eroticism for political effect. As he has explained, 'My project is not a p.c. project . . . It allows you to laugh about issues that are potentially serious.'[64]

In 1999, the year after he became the first black artist to win Britain's Turner Prize, Ofili also fell victim to the type of censorship Robert Mapplethorpe had faced ten years earlier.[65] Ofili's *The Holy Virgin Mary* (1996) **[101]** caused a huge outcry when it went on show in New York in the exhibition *Sensation: Young British Art in the Saatchi Collection*.[66] Ofili's painting was of a black Virgin Mary, surrounded by a golden halo patterned with cutouts of vaginas and buttocks from porn magazines, and a ball of elephant dung formed her right breast. Her title was even spelt out on two balls of elephant dung which act as supports for the canvas—'Virgin' on one, 'Mary' on the other, each written with little pins stuck into the shiny, resin-coated balls. The Mayor of New York, Rudolph W. Giuliani, supported by the Catholic League for Religious and Civil Rights, called for the censorship of the work, seeing Ofili's painting as an affront to Catholicism and calling the exhibition 'sick stuff'. He threatened to withdraw $7 million of public funding to the Brooklyn Museum where the exhibition was on show. The fact that Ofili was reared a Roman Catholic and was once an altar boy did not enter Giuliani's debate, nor that Ofili views the elephant dung as having multiple possible interpretations, including a reminder of the earth and the cycle of life. Instead, Ofili's fusion of the sacred and the profane, the spiritual and the excremental was deemed too great a threat for public consumption. Cries for censorship ultimately served to expose not just New York but a global audience to Ofili's art and to reinforce his personal faith in the power of art to change society. As he said in interview: 'it kind of recharged the belief that art could have

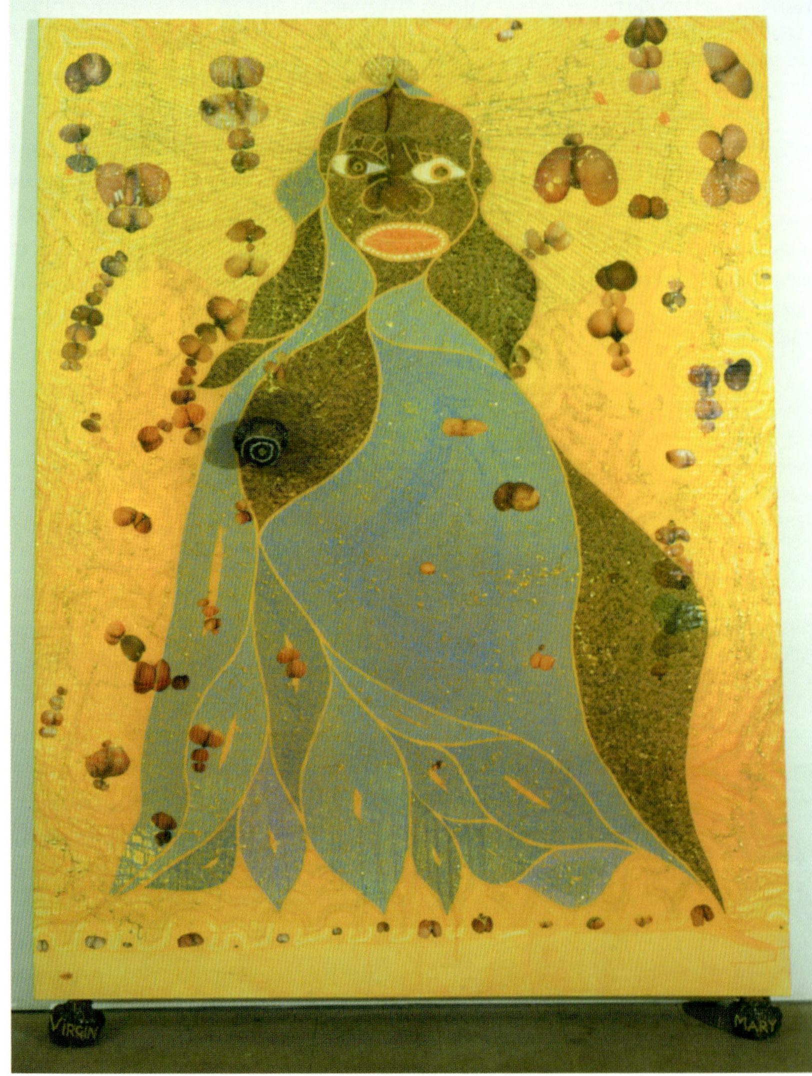

101 Chris Ofili
The Holy Virgin Mary, 1996
The 1998 winner of the Turner Prize, Ofili's representation of a black Virgin Mary exemplifies his controversial style and technique in its use of varnished balls of elephant dung, exotic decoration, and cutouts from porn magazines. It caused a scandal when it was exhibited at the Royal Academy *Sensation* show in London and New York. The Mayor of New York, Rudolph W. Giuliani, saw it as an affront to Catholicism and called for it to be censored.

power and could still make people respond. People could still feel that they had the time to go and look at something that was made by quite primitive means, really.'[67]

Ofili's art was praised in the *Sensation* catalogue for its 'homemade look that allows a gentle romantic spirit to animate the cultural mix of their making', but others have been critical of this very element.[68] Ofili's approach to ethnicity—his use of elephant dung, his appropriation of the dots used by cave painters in the Metapos Hills in Zimbabwe (both inspired after a visit to Zimbabwe, funded by the British Council), and his mapping out of a particular black British scene in London in his reference to hip hop, the Wu-Tang Clan, and the Notting Hill Carnival—has led Niru Ratnam to argue that Ofili falls victim to the hybrid nature of his art, indulging in ambiguity and allusion, a playful approach to identity, and a quintessentially 'pc' quality that means racism is not addressed head on.[69] Julian Stallabrass, in his analysis of young British art as 'high art lite', also finds Ofili's art too ambivalent in its recourse to the decorative and primitive, too gentle in its handling of serious, racial, issues and thus as lacking 'critical bite'.[70] Yet Ofili's collage-like approach to contemporary black life and culture should not just be viewed as a postmodern evasiveness: as Richard Powell points out, it is in keeping with the nature of 1990s hip hop music and Ofili's ironic and 'decidedly critical stance towards contemporary black culture, disparaging the necessity of efficacy of identity markers, sartorial or individual'.[71]

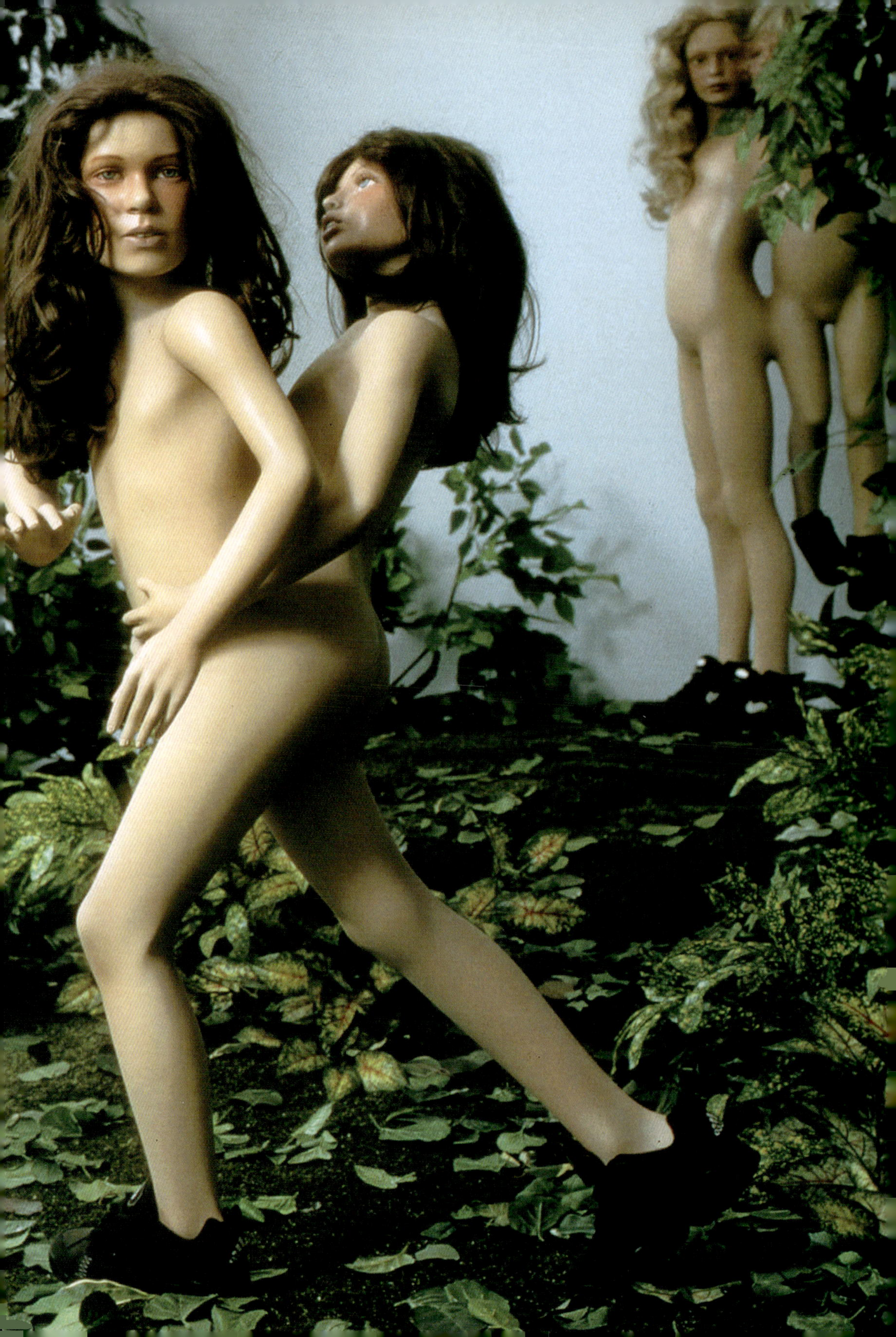

10

Erotic Fragmentation and Abjection

If the 1960s were the era of McLuhan's 'global village', the late 1980s and 1990s saw rapid global expansion and a deepening of consumer culture not only in the United States and Britain but also in the so-called 'tiger' economies of Asia, and, in the 1990s, in the former Soviet Union and China. This expansion was facilitated by the proliferation of television and an emerging digital world which made the transfer of information almost instantaneous. Society's experience of conflict (the Tiananmen Square massacre, the Gulf War, 'ethnic cleansing' in Bosnia, race riots in Los Angeles), of scientific advances (the Space Shuttle, the Hubble telescope, the cloning of Dolly the sheep), and of social and political crises (HIV-AIDS, the Clinton–Lewinsky affair) was now emphatically global and increasingly 'live'. Francis Fukuyama and other champions of Western capitalism proclaimed that the triumph of liberal democracy and Western capitalism had brought about the 'end of history'.[1] Artists responded ambivalently to these developments. Some sought to challenge what they saw not only as the increasing commodification of culture but also the sense of the body itself as a commodity and of erotic desire as a commercial transaction. Some became preoccupied by the increasing and everyday interdependence of the body and high technology, especially computers and machines, and sought to explore the body and erotic desire as mechanical or digital phenomena. Some contested what they saw as the desensitization of the public by television and new media by creating more and more explicit imagery designed to capture the attention of even the most cynical viewer. Most continued to investigate these questions in relation to their own subjective identity and physical being, though others sought to depersonalize the representation of the body and the erotic through the use of anonymous robotic or plastic forms.

Detail of 113

Gender Trouble

A number of artists focused on what they saw as the highly contrived nature of gender identity highlighted by the prevailing artificiality of consumer and media culture. In her highly influential book *Gender Trouble* (1990), Judith Butler called for a new appraisal of the gendered body, demanding that we un-fix it. She argued that gender (masculine/feminine) was all too often viewed as an extension of one's sexual biology (male/female), as a 'natural' characteristic, but it was neither natural nor fixed, it was 'unnatural', a social construct that individuals *acquire* and which then dictates desire (for the other gender). Building on the advances of Michel Foucault, she argued that gender needed to be considered in terms of performing, bending, or unlearning gender roles, and called for a gender 'troubling'. Butler's 'theatrical' perspective on gender was that of a postmodern feminist but her radical revision of gender did not just empower women, it also freed men and created a new space for those who were attracted to the same sex. Indeed, for Butler, feminists had made a mistake in choosing to focus on gender from the 1960s on, and had only served to reinforce binary gender difference. Her conceptualization of gender exposed society's attempt to regulate gender and liberated the individual to perform their gender, with all its codes and costumes, as he/she sees fit. Butler contributed to a growing body of 'Queer' theory that also questioned the psyche of the heterosexual in society, the notion of 'straight' principles, and the dominant social and epistemological binarisms that tend to reify identity (masculine/feminine, identity/difference, private/public, etc.). Erotic art offered the perfect stage for queering identity and exploring the disorientating power of masquerade.

Yasumasa Morimura (b. 1951) destabilizes gender by restaging masterpieces from the Western art canon. He takes on the role of both Manet's Olympia and her black maidservant in *Portrait (Futago)* of 1988 **[102]**, appearing not only as female but as both black and white females, despite being gay and Japanese. He adds his own costuming too: his Olympia has Marilyn Monroe-like peroxide hair and lies on a richly coloured kimono. In adopting the guises of both of Manet's female characters in this large (almost lifesize) photographic print, Morimura also make a direct connection between the women's sexual status in modern society—Olympia as a 'Hottentot Venus', her black maidservant as a Hottentot—as well as his 'queer' sexual status in postmodern society. Indeed, Morimura may be queering the original too, exploiting the lesbian fantasy encouraged by juxtaposing two women in close proximity—as Paul Franklin sees it, Morimura claims Olympia as a

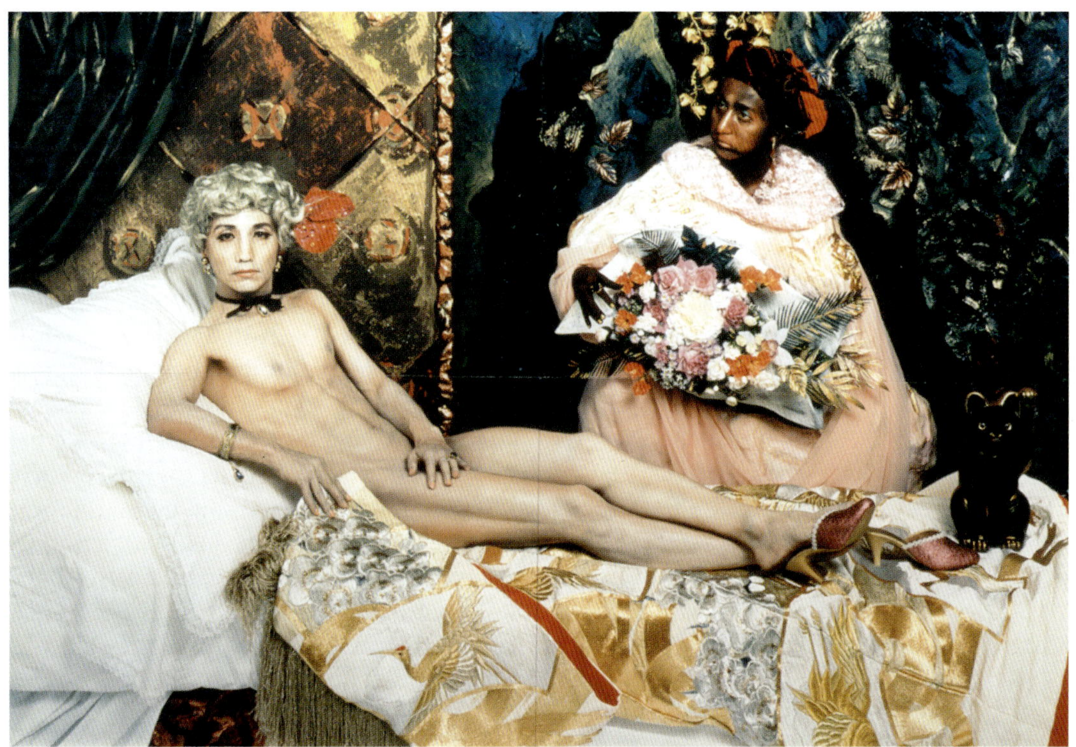

102 Yasumasa Morimura
Portrait (Futago), 1988
Morimura's queering of Manet's *Olympia* exploits the lesbianism of Victorine Meurent and the hierarchy of the white model over the black. Yet, as a gay Japanese artist, he identifies with both the lesbian and the black woman, as indicated by his performance of both roles and the luxurious kimono underneath him.

fellow queer given that the model, Victorine Meurent, was reported to be a lesbian.[2] Morimura and Olympia are exotic sexual outsiders. In resorting to the fantasy of *metalepsis*, continuing tropes from past art works in his own, Morimura not only camps up the past, he also presents sex, gender, and race as theatrical performances that are enhanced by make-up and costume. He adds a particular Japanese element to his gender-troubling too. For he may be seen to update the Japanese seventeenth-century theatrical tradition of Kabuki in which fantastic costume and make-up was employed, the actors were all young males, many of whom also worked as prostitutes. Some were so beautiful and popular that performances would lead to violent brawls among the male spectators; Kabuki performances were clamped down on at the same time as male prostitution was outlawed, in 1652.[3] Morimura thus speaks to particular historical traditions both in his own country and in France, as well as to the continued fear of, and racial slurring against, those who do not conform to sexual and gender 'norms'.

To be able to draw similarities between a Japanese gay artist and a California-born person previously known as a lesbian and now living in London, is surely a testimony to the global nature of postmodern culture and the vision of queer as a category that escapes the restriction of class, race and gender. Della Grace (b. 1957), also known as Della Disgrace and for the past ten years as Del LaGrace Volcano, also insists on a queer view of eroticism, but through very different tactics. Volcano is a gender variant visual artist and cultural producer working with the body and gender/sexual identity notions for social, political, artistic and personal purposes. Volcano professes to be a 'gender terrorist and intentional mutation', contesting rigid notions and labels of gender as the last bastion of male Western civilization. In *The Ceremony* (1988), a butch and a femme lesbian couple are photographed in black and white wearing leather biker gear and a wedding veil respectively, all the time contesting what it is to be she/he. In the black and white photograph *Tongue in Cheek* (1992) **[103]**, Grace assaults audiences' preconceived notions of the boundaries between art and pornography. Contesting the fact that these boundaries are usually played out on the heterosexual terrain, Grace also explores masculinity in lesbianism and thus addresses some feminists' critique of lesbian S/M as gender mimicry. In photographing and 'exposing' herself and her models, Della Grace performs gender, however, and claims it as fluid—just as Butler does—thus revealing cultural prejudices. The artist asks the viewer of *Tongue in Cheek*:

> What do you see when you look at the women in these photographs? Skinhead racists? Lesbian perverts? Concentration camp survivors? Mannequins? Alien Dykes from Hell?! Strong beautiful women? If we look different it's because we are and we like it this way. We don't look or act the way women or even lesbians are supposed to. We are entirely ourselves, creating and changing our gender as we go along.[4]

After some twenty years as artist Della Grace, as Volcano this artist continues to challenge gender 'norms', taking testosterone to amplify the hermaphroditic qualities of his body. Volcano's gender identity has thus gone through several 'mutations' by design—from lesbian to hermaphrodyke to transman to intersexed. On this process, the artist has stated:

> I have accessed technologies of gender in order to amplify the hermaphroditic traces genetically inscribed upon my body by my intersex ancestors that I formerly attempted to disguise. I aim to be part of remapping the social terrain and creating new gendered geographies that have the potential and the ambition to see difference as a valuable social asset and resource.[5]

Volcano's art projects in the 1990s—such as *Hermaphrodyké: Self Portraits of Desire, TransGenital Landscapes*, and *The FTM Visibility Project*—increasingly explore intersex hybridity, continuing to probe at society's

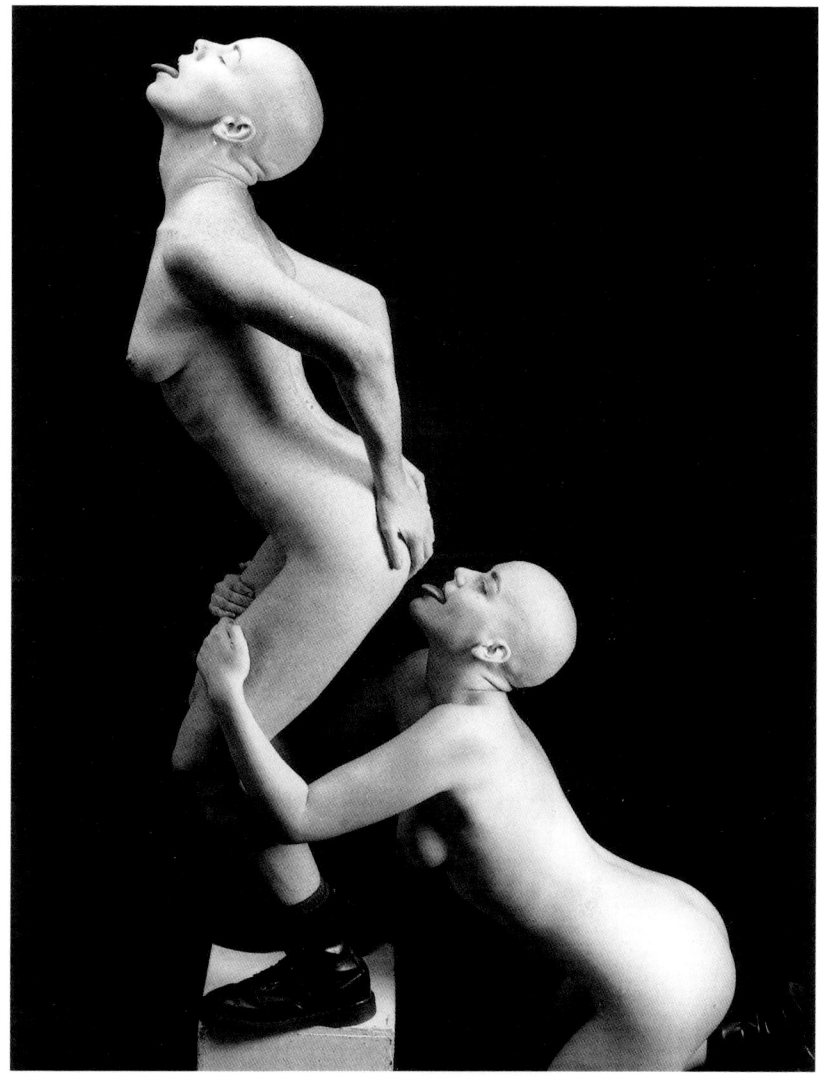

103 Del LaGrace Volcano
Tongue in Cheek, 1992
Volcano's art challenges gender polarities and 'norms', offering 'new gendered geographies' that celebrate difference, as in this photograph's provocative challenge to society's preconceived notions of how a lesbian looks and acts.

fear of sexual 'deviancy', of sexual 'mutancy', all the while speaking for the space and desires of someone living an intersexed life.

Chicana lesbian photographer Catherine Opie (b. 1961) also became prominent in art circles in the 1990s for her photographs of S/M, transvestite, and female-to-male trans-sexual communities in Los Angeles in the 1990s. Her art addresses sexual experimentation but also refutes sexual labels, thus adopting Butler's insistence that gender is not 'natural' but performed. Opie's colour photography is much more seductive technically than Grace's, however: the glossy finish lends a sense of gravitas to her framed sitters, while the close range of many portrait shots is both intimate and disarming for the viewer. In her series *Being and Having* (1991), photographic portraits are uniformly presented against a vivid yellow backdrop and sitters' heads are cropped so that we see only their faces, from the chin to the forehead, without the gender distraction of hair and necks. These are images of women (with such names as 'J' or 'Wolfe') who have beards or moustaches, their deadpan expressions deflecting any fear the viewer might have. In *Self Portrait* (1993) Opie continues her transgendering. She defies traditional portraiture in photographing her back, confusing the mind's eye so that we are unsure if we are looking at the back of a man or a woman. The answer lies in the graffiti that has been cut into the artist's naked flesh,

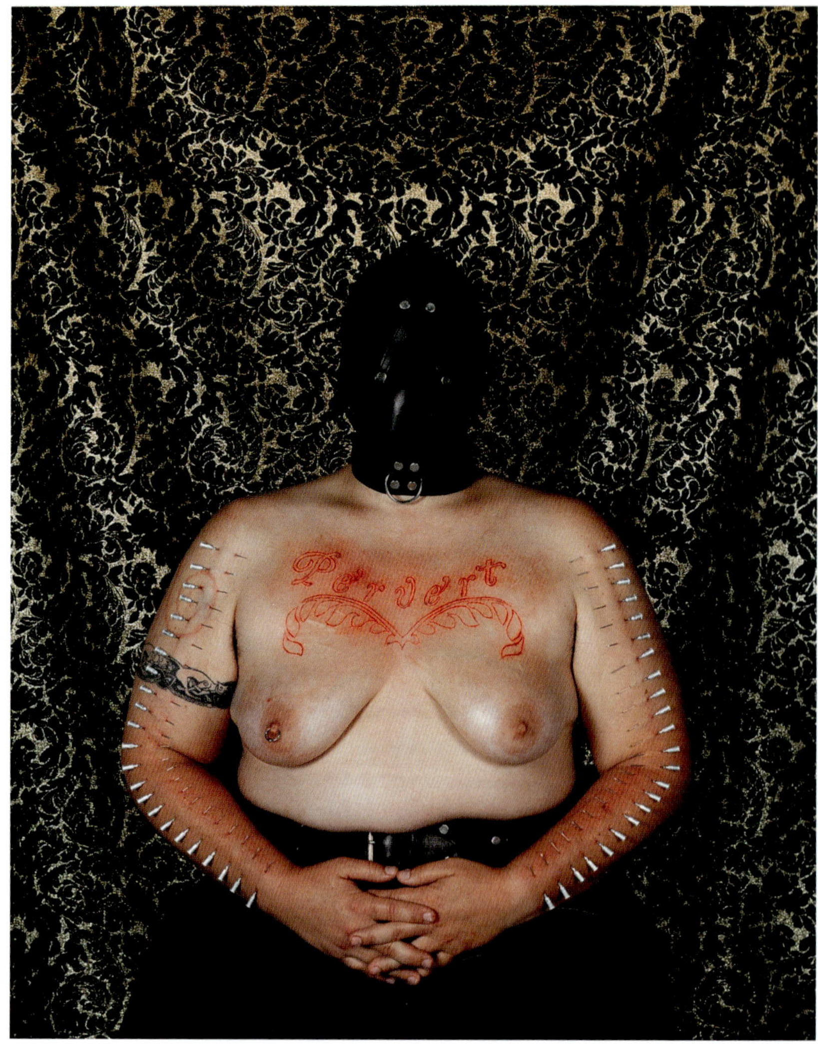

104 Catherine Opie
Self-Portrait/Pervert, 1994

In her self-portrait, lesbian artist Opie challenges notions of public decency and engages with feminist debates over lesbian S/M. She cuts her own chest with the word 'pervert' but undermines the 'threat' posed by her leather trousers, hood, nipple ring, and pierced arms with her matter-of-fact posture and choice of floral drape behind.

however: a child-like, stick image of a house, sun, cloud, and birds, and a happy couple holding hands—two *female* stick figures. *Self Portrait/ Pervert* (1994) **[104]** is a frontal self-portrait, where her self-mutilation is more disturbing: she is hooded in a black leather bondage mask, 'pervert' is cut into the skin above her breasts in cursive script, one nipple is pierced, and the length of both of her arms is threaded with a series of needles. And yet again Opie deflects society's fear of sexual nonconformity: she sits before a floral-patterned backdrop, with her hands on her lap as if for a banal, commercial studio portrait. In another self-portrait, *Bo* (1994), we come face to face with a full-length photograph of Opie, in jeans and cut-off check shirt with a moustache and her prominent arm tattoo—this is Opie as arch-male, as truck-driver, womanizer. The image speaks to two sets of stereotypes, that of the lesbian butch and the check-shirted American worker, but Opie defies both. This defiance continues in her more recent work in which she has photographed lesbian couples from one state to another across America. Opie presents a portrait of an unseen America, one whose subversion lies in its banality, its sameness, rather than its difference to the heterosexual family.

Like Opie, the Californian artist Laura Aguilar (b. 1959) also uses strategies of traditional documentary photography to portray difference, but Aguilar insists on the need for inclusion. She is third-generation Mexican-American on her father's side and Irish-American on her mother's, but has described herself as a 'Latina lesbian'—the name of one of her photography series begun in 1986 and still ongoing. In *Three Eagles Flying* (1990) **[105]**, Aguilar expresses in terms of race and gender both her bicultural identity as a Mexican-American and her own sexual identity. In this self-portrait, a black and white photograph, she stands semi-naked between the American and Mexican flags. Her lower body is clothed in the Stars and Stripes, while her head is hooded in a Mexican flag, its eagle insignia covering her face. A rope binds her neck, hand, and thighs, making this 'self-fashioning' all the more macabre.

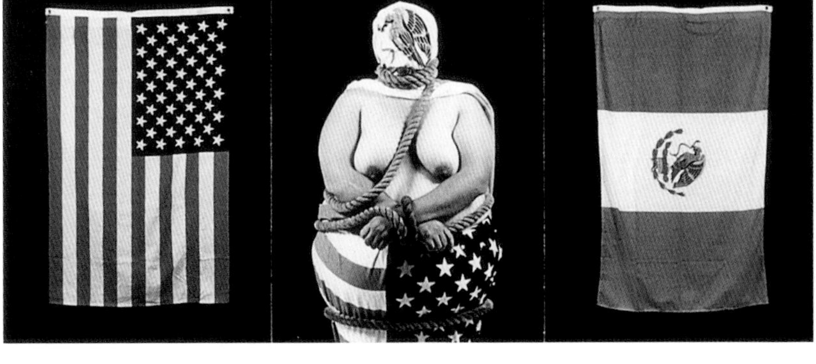

105 Laura Aguilar
Three Eagles Flying, 1990
'Latina lesbian' photographer Aguilar here explores ethnic identity in a macabre self-portrait in which she stands between the Mexican and American flags, her large, bare-breasted body seeming to parody Delacroix's *Liberty Leading the People* (1830), its bindings insisting on political oppression rather than emancipation.

Her large body is sexualized in a particular racial way. Where Delacroix's bare-breasted Liberty in *Liberty Leading the People* (1830) wielded the tricoleur as a symbol of freedom, Aguilar portrays both flags as restrictive, as binding, and the Mexican flag as a literal and symbolic suffocation threat (the central eagle on the flag also puns on her name, *aguila*, the Spanish for eagle). Amelia Jones reads this work in geopolitical terms: 'the flags mark Aguilar's body not as "authentic" but, rather, as annihilated by the very signs that are meant to secure its ethnic identity and so its socioeconomic position in relation to the geopolitical mapping of power'.[6] Yet the artist herself chooses to downplay the politically particular and instead to emphasize 'the universal elements' in her art, refuting the reification of identity that Jones and others would impose.[7]

In her photographs of individuals from gay, lesbian, and/or persons of colour communities, Aguilar again uses sexual metaphor to expose political, racial, and social limitations and to address the theme of the universal through the particular. Whether her sitters are clothed or unclothed (as in her series *Clothed and Unclothed*, 1990 ongoing), whether they sit with friends, family or lovers, she aims to expand our concept of 'normal' through a parody of both the documentary portrait and the tradition of the nude. For example, *Cheri and Sue* (1994) is a portrait of two women, made up of two black-and-white photographs. In one photograph, both women are clothed, one woman touching the other's pregnant body; in the other, both are naked, and touching but now in what is clearly a lovers' embrace. The former might be read as an image of loving family members, the latter is clearly a portrait of a lesbian couple. The politics of dress, social codes of behaviour, and definitions of what a 'family' is are here subtly addressed. Aguilar and Opie might be linked as Chicana women, as 'lesbian artists' (a category that only came into open existence after 1970), but of course their art insists that there is no such thing as a fixed Chicana or lesbian identity. Rather, they both engage with the mutability of identity.

'Bad Girls of Contemporary British Art'[8]

A very different approach to gender performance is found in one of the leading players of contemporary British art—Sarah Lucas (b. 1962). Like Ofili, Lucas is one of the 'yBa's (young British artists), the generation of artists championed by private collector Charles Saatchi, who grew up in Thatcherite Britain and adopted Thatcher's aggressive spirit of private entrepreneurship.[9] Lucas's art explores gender through often graphically—if not pathetically—crude visual puns that nevertheless also speak to universal prejudice. For example, in *Two Fried Eggs and a*

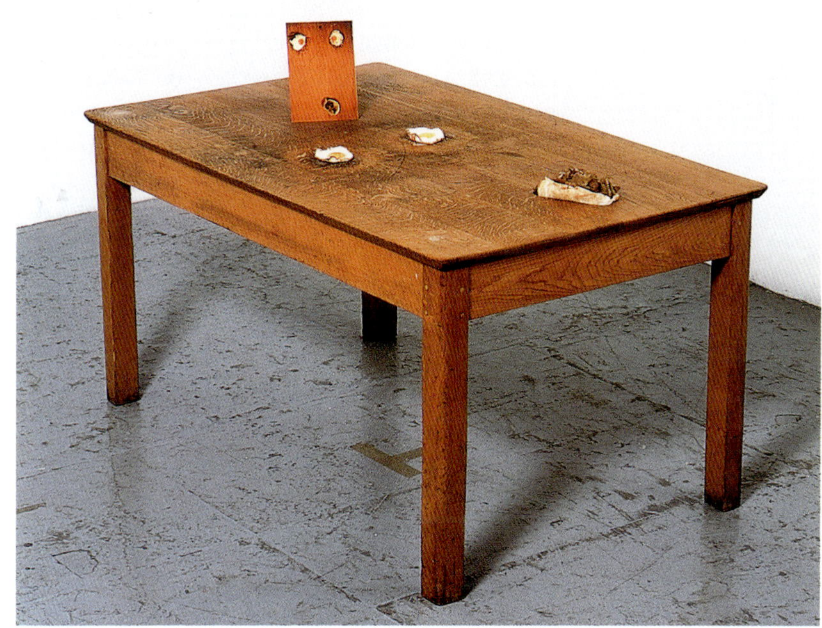

106 Sarah Lucas
Two Fried Eggs and a Kebab, 1992

A 1987 graduate from Goldsmiths College, London, and one of Charles Saatchi's chosen 'young British artists', Lucas's sculpture subverts high and low culture as a postmodern pastiche of Magritte's *Rape* and provides a commentary on tabloid journalism's sexist puns and humour.

Kebab (1992) **[106]** Lucas arranged two fried eggs, a doner kebab, and an upright framed photograph of the same arrangement on a wooden kitchen table so that the food suggested a woman's breasts and genitalia (the photograph, at the top of the table, showed the 'still life' in an upright position, to reinforce the face idea). The installation might be seen as a postmodern pastiche of René Magritte's *Rape* (1934) **[45]** where he conflated a woman's face with her naked body, but here Lucas has reduced Magritte's original to its most basic joke. Yet Lucas speaks to the local as well as the timeless nature of male desire, and one perhaps recalls the women-furniture of British Pop artist Allen Jones (b. 1937) in which he conflated naked mannequins in black stiletto boots with mass-produced domestic furniture.[10] Lucas's art certainly cannot be fully appreciated without a glance to British, 'laddish', sexual culture and its smutty allusions to food and objects when 'discussing' women. As the artist explained in an interview in 1994, the comparison between a woman's body and a take-away is deliberate: '"If I make *Two Fried Eggs and a Kebab* it's because I live with remarks like that all my life. And I think, well yeah, I can make that same kind of remark just like you can, and I make it look fucking good into the bargain.'[11]

Bitch (1994) continues this aggressive tone against Pop art's recourse to soft porn, illustrating Lucas's reappropriation of tabloid humour and defiance of the all-too-quick dismissal of the postmodern as superficial pastiche. The installation shows a wooden table, again acting as a woman's body but now 'wearing' a tight white T-shirt from which melons hang, like full breasts, and sporting a dead fish at its 'penetrable' rear end. The installation evokes wet T-shirt competitions, page 3 tabloid pin-up girls, and also the sheer banality of sexism in the mass media. It is a three-dimensional exploration of her earlier engagement with tabloid imagery, *'Sod you gits . . . men go wild for my body'* (1990), when she magnified images from the *Sun* newspaper, presenting their sexist spreads complete with their topless girls and crude headlines. In this work Lucas magnifies the tabloid story of a sex-symbol midget, Sharon Lewis, shown topless and proud of her erotic niche as an exotic topless kissogram. Lucas hijacks mass-produced images and the tactics of tabloid journalism to question the supposed gap between 'low' and 'high' art sexism in the process. Lucas has said that feminist texts encouraged her to look at pornography—'Certain feminist literature, like Andrea Dworkin, opened up the idea for me of having more subject matter'—though where Dworkin insists women should call for the censoring of pornography, Lucas adopts a reverse psychology: rather than condemning the soft porn of tabloids she magnifies and frames it.[12] Her strategy might be viewed as that of a postmodern feminist, one who builds on but also critiques feminism's emphasis on gender politics. Certainly her photographic self-portraits suggest so. In *Self-Portrait with Fried Eggs* (1996), she sits in a macho pose in jeans and T-shirt with fried eggs covering her own breasts. We think of Chicago and Shapiro's *Womanhouse* (1972), where eggs morphed into breasts in the kitchen, and suspect that Lucas is challenging male sexism and female essentialism in her art.

Tracey Emin also turns to the theme of sexuality and sexual power in her art through recourse to the banal, the everyday. Emin's *My Bed* (1998/9) **[107]** was exhibited in Tokyo, London, and New York in 1998 and 1999, and was short-listed for the Turner Prize in 1999. It was also purchased at auction by Charles Saatchi for £150,000. Emin's art style is provocative but in a quite different way from her fellow yBa, Sarah Lucas. The installation, when exhibited at the Tate Gallery in London for the Turner Prize, was made up of a bed with crumpled, used sheets, and debris to one side—bloodstained knickers, contraceptive pills, condoms, an empty bottle of Vodka, cigarettes. On the other side of the bed were two bound suitcases and, on the wall, a blanket work entitled *No Chance* (1999), a neon work *Every Part of Me's Bleeding* (1999), and, in a separate room, a number of video pieces including *Tracey Emin's CV. Cunt Vernacular* (1999). These other works amplified details of the artist's personal profile not otherwise deducible from the installation presented to the public. From details about the bed (the artist's own)

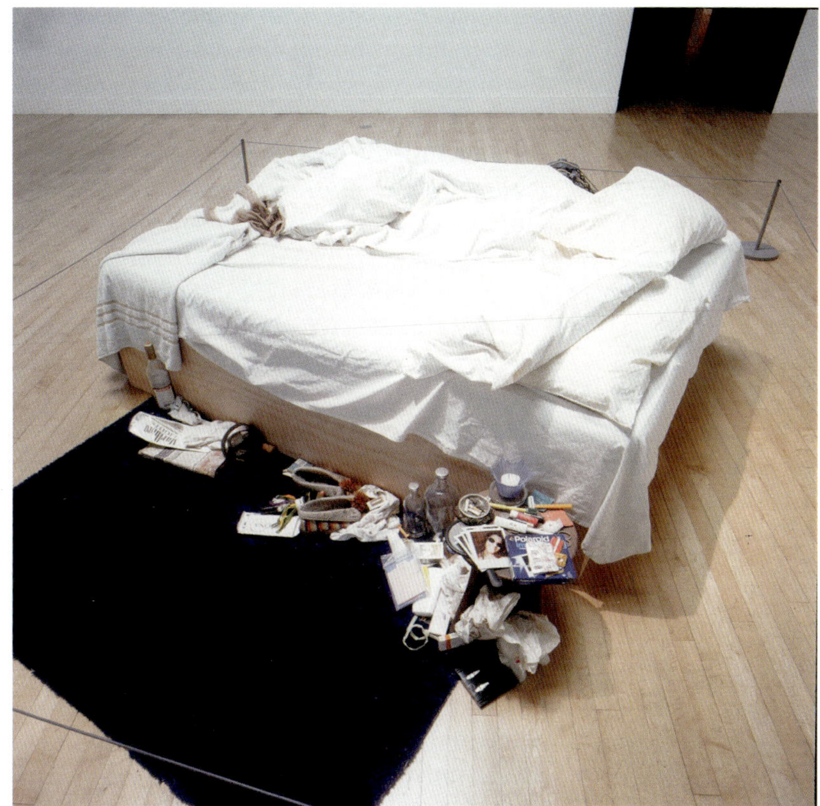

107 Tracey Emin
My Bed, 1998/9

Emin's art and life are inextricably linked. Her provocative use of her own bed and all her personal bedside paraphernalia—from soiled knickers and cigarette butts to vodka bottles—caused quite a media storm when it was short-listed for the Turner Prize in 1999. However, the majority of critics failed to appreciate it as anything other than a schoolgirl prank, despite its obvious layers of personal and feminist meaning.

and the video works on show, Emin allowed the public to 'investigate' the work beyond its initial messy confusion. They learnt that she tried to commit suicide in 1982, and that she had had two abortions. Yet critics were quick to denounce Emin and to view the work as lacking in any significant meaning. One newspaper, *The Independent on Sunday*, ran a debate asking readers 'would you show your bed to the public?' (24 October 1999). *The News of the World*, a paper whose news is dominated by sex scandals and celebrity gossip, claimed a furious housewife had to be stopped from cleaning it all up (31 October 1999). A critic in the *Sunday Times* claimed it only appealed to 'naughty schoolgirls'.[13] Most art critics saw it as adolescent, as naughty. But Emin's *My Bed* was not a cynical, schoolgirl prank. The very fact it succeeded in outraging British journalists indicated that it went beyond that. In many ways it continued a subversive use of bedding and soiled matter in modern art, reminding us of Rauschenberg's *Bed* (1955) **[62]** and Chicago's *Menstruation Bathroom* installation at Womanhouse (1972). Chicago's installation also presents us with a domestic, feminine space and the taboos of bodily waste—especially female menstrual blood—and woman's body in general. Chicago's work speaks specifically of puberty as a time when a female must confront her taboo body in its abjection; hence when the British press refers to bold and naughty teenage girls in their analyses of Emin's *My Bed* it inadvertently evokes the same theme. But Emin's *My Bed* goes further again than Chicago. It suggests not just the private made public, nor the need to confront the still taboo subject of woman's body, it also seems to stage a scene of sexual violence, or of suicide perhaps (in Tokyo and New York, the installation included a rope noose suspended from the ceiling). In the artist's own words, *My Bed* 'looks like the scene of a crime as if someone has just died or been fucked to death'.[14] Emin's installation in fact provokes members of the public to reveal their own unconscious fears about woman, sexuality, and death—the desire to mock this art work or to laugh at it is best understood as nervousness in the face of the abject.

Abject Suffering and Desire

From the Latin for 'to cast away from' (*ab-jacere*), the abject is the space of the outcast. Abjection, as conceptualized by the French theorist Julia Kristeva, 'disturbs identity, system, order. What does not respect borders, positions, rules. The in-between, the ambiguous, the composite.'[15] While often denoting the marginal and the impure, the abject is also wonderfully intimate, it is where intimate suffering and loss can also join intimate sexual desire and excess as the body and mind, physical and psychic, come together. Abject art reveals this peculiar mixture of disgust and intimacy as artists seize the materiality of the erotic, sexually active body in all its corporeal matter—blood, milk, urine, cum, excrement, skin, hair—as a medium and theme in itself.

Abjection also returns us to one of the pressing tensions behind erotic art, as discussed in the Introduction, notably the tension between the sacred and profane body, pure and impure desires, and the tension between Eros and Thanatos. Bodily waste, cut flesh, open wounds, and fragility all suggest the corpse and decay and thus hark back to the fear and reality of death. Inevitably, contemporary artists also invoke religious symbolism in their exploration of abjection, choosing either to challenge or endorse the tendency of religion to purify the abject.

Not only has abjection permeated much of the history of Western art, it has provided a subtext to much of the art we have already seen, from Dalí's *The Lugubrious Game* **[43]** to Schneemann's *Interior Scroll* **[79]**. The abject art of the 1990s was indebted to the abject art before it, especially during the 1960s and 1970s where it had radically altered the very processes of the making of art. *Trademarks* (1970) by Vito Acconci

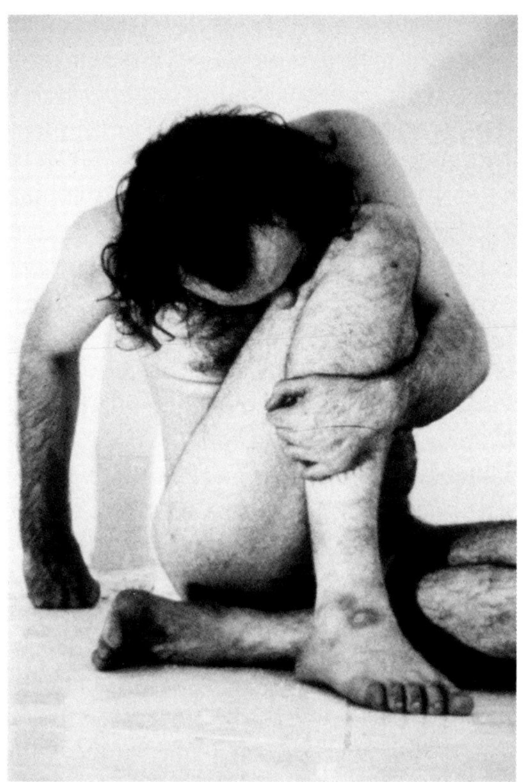

108 Vito Hannibal Acconci
Trademarks, photo-performance, 10 September 1970. 'Biting myself: biting as much of my body as my mouth can reach. Stamping my bite-print on the world around me: making the world around me mine'

In this performance, Acconci used his own body as target, presenting himself as object rather than artist. He sat naked on the floor and bit as many parts of his body as his mouth could reach, applied printer's ink to the bites, and stamped bite-prints onto various surfaces.

(b. 1940) **[108]** was particularly influential. Photographs of this performance document Acconci biting his naked body. He then inked those parts of his bitten flesh and made prints of the traces of his action. These were the (orthodox) marks of his (unorthodox) actions, his self-inflicted wounds transmuted into concrete prints. Acconci's performance enacted a kind of auto-eroticism based on an almost narcissistic desire to consume his own flesh. His religious upbringing, specifically in terms of the Catholic fascination with flesh and blood, is highly relevant. Acconci grew up in an Italian Catholic neighbourhood in the 1940s and as child chose to attend an Irish Catholic school rather than an Italian one. As he explained in a recent interview, 'I wanted to belong to that neat, clean, whitewashed Catholic church; not the messy church of Italian Catholicism, as it seemed to me. Through the Irish church came sin: I found out about it, I learned it, I introduced it at home.'[16] The abject art of the 1990s drew on the advances in 'Body Art' (where the artist's body is the canvas) from the 1960s on, but with different intentions.[17] It increasingly focused on abject fluids to celebrate the abject power of the base and/or feminine body and to acknowledge how AIDS radically altered the public's conceptualization of bodily waste. It also contested the 'finish fetish' of both 1970s Minimalist art and the slick advertising style of contemporaries, like Jeff Koons.[18]

The sculptures of Kiki Smith (b. 1954) from the 1990s exemplify this shift from high finish to the abject. Smith was born in Nuremberg, Germany, but she grew up in New Jersey and has been living in New York City since 1976. In her art she explores, in her own words, 'the abject loss of selfhood-recognition-necessity, loss of flesh, sex, fluid'.[19] She politicizes the body's corporeal reality through the abject, all the time recognizing the effect AIDS has had in making the public more aware of the body as a social, sexual, and political threat. The putrefaction of Dalí's art enters into the third dimension with Smith and has new, more frightening, potential. The installation *Untitled* (1990) is of lifesize nude male and female wax mannequins, suspended on metal stands, and lifeless apart from their bodily fluids: milk weeps from the female's breasts, ejaculate from the male's penis. Here abject fluids are not horrific, rather they act as the one sign of life in a macabre installation. The inside and outside of the body, the skin that contains and the fluids that leak out, purity and its dangerous opposite filth, are brought together.

A similar use of dead flesh to express living desire also informs the art of Irish artist Alice Maher (b. 1956). The title of her show *The History of Tears* (2001) drew on a work by feminist Conceptualist artist Barbara Kruger (b. 1945) entitled 'Who will write the history of tears?', thus aligning her use of the abject to feminist art practice. Maher exhibited self-portraits in which she wears a necklace of lambs' tongues **[109]** and a choker made of the hearts of lambs. She dons another animal's raw flesh not just to question our popular notions of beauty and desire (the beauty

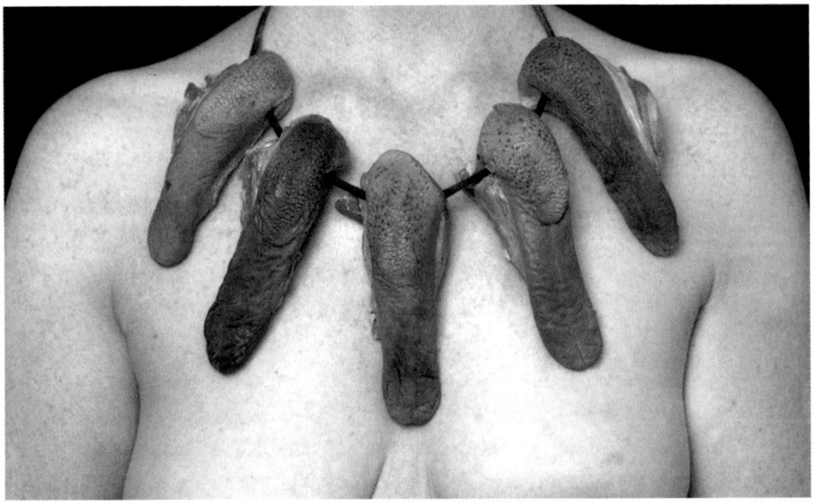

109 Alice Maher
Necklace of Tongues, 2000

Maher explores female identity in her art, this self-portrait using the abject power of raw meat to contest traditional notions of beauty. The tongue is both a part of the body where the inside and outside of the body meet and the organ with which we communicate. In threading lambs' tongues into a necklace Maher also reinvests these dead animal parts with new symbolic significance by alluding to the power of speech and language, including the decline of the Irish language in contemporary Ireland.

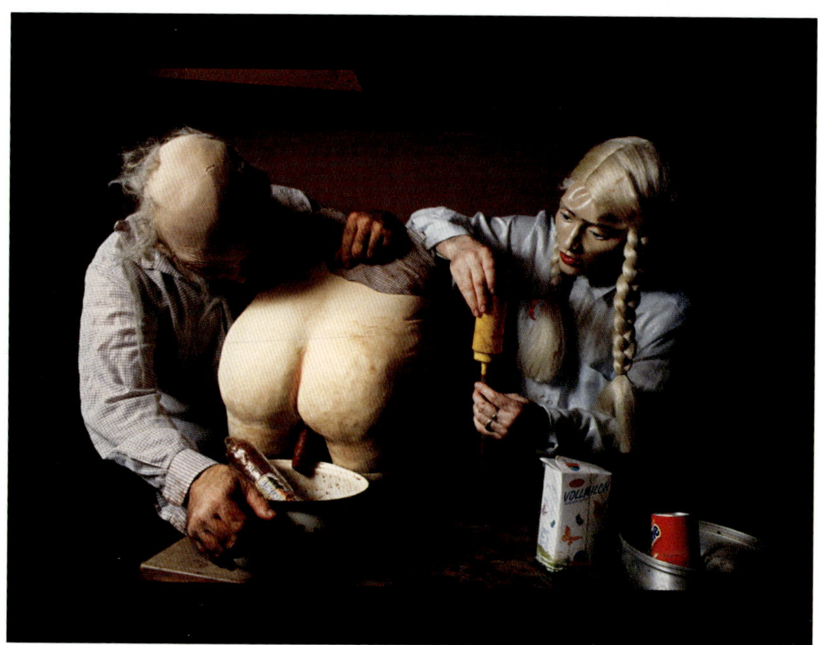

110 Paul McCarthy and Mike Kelley
Heidi: Midlife Crisis Trauma Center and Negative Media-Engram Abreaction Release Zone, 1992

In this video performance, McCarthy and Kelley turn the quaint story of Swiss girl Heidi into a theatre of cruelty, drawing on Adolf Loos's 1908 treatise on 'Ornament and Crime' in their plot and scatological details. As in many of their works, the artists explore oral and anal eroticism through a visceral use of food and faeces, all the time ensuring the spectator is confronted with a disturbing sense of the uncanny.

of the nape of a woman's neck, or jewellery as a sign and symbol of love, notably as a gift from a man) but also—in the words of Maher—to make 'visceral something that is usually only imagined or miniaturized, kept locked up. You are turning the body inside out, opening the forbidden chamber.'[20] Like Smith, she seizes the feminine power of the abject to create new uncanny erotic spaces.

Abjection is not a theme we only find in women's art, however. In their collaborative work Mike Kelley and Paul McCarthy have boldly revelled in abject taboo to subvert American society and its regulation of the individual. In their 1992 collaboration *Heidi: Midlife Crisis Trauma Center and Negative Media-Engram Abreaction Release Zone* **[110]**, we find Joanna Spyri's 1881 tale of *Heidi* perverted into a hideous theatre of erotic, abject cruelty where Heidi (played by Kelley) and the city 'Sick Girl' of the story (a mannequin with a Madonna mask) are the victims of sexual and physical abuse at the hands of Heidi's supposedly doting grandfather (played by McCarthy). Kelley and McCarthy stage this abuse in an installation that includes Heidi's chalet home, the façade of Adolf Loos's American bar in Vienna, and a 60-minute fragmented videotape recorded, and played, in the space. Their installation design specifically mocks Loos's 1908 treatise on 'Ornament and Crime' in which he vilified ornament as the perverse enemy of civilization. This text is quoted in a critical moment in the video when Heidi's grandfather reprimands her for tattooing her buttock with an image of a rose and a cube, perversely referencing Loos's view of ornament as 'tattooing' nature. The installation is a battleground between abject forces and society's desire to regulate the unruly, and culminates with the grandfather enacting a *Texas Chainsaw*-like massacre of both females. While choosing an alpine story and setting for the work, the artists' amoral world is a direct attack on their home country, the United States. This is political satire voiced through abject eroticism, McCarthy describing *Heidi* as 'Americanized in a sort of dysfunctional horror film'.[21]

In their 45-minute video piece *Fresh Acconci* (1995), Kelley and McCarthy repeat this brutally abject approach to eroticism to expose the supposedly safe confines of the family and the nation state. The work mocks the vogue for new media in contemporary art and pays homage to the aims of 1970s' abject performance art. It specifically incorporates Vito Acconci's early video performances—*Contacts* (1971), *Theme Song* (1973), *Claim Excerpts* (1971), and *Focal Points* (1971)—but replaces the often spotty-bottomed Acconci with naked statuesque models who are closer to soft-porn movie stars than 1970s performance Actionists. In this manner the avant-gardism of Acconci and his abject resistance to the status quo becomes 'fresh'—new but lewd. As Timothy Martin has written, *Fresh Acconci* is 'more like an inflatable sex surrogate than a remake [of the original Acconci works]. It directly supplements Acconci's works while stimulating the desire to return to it.'[22] It also speaks to the postmodern condition and the loss of the impact and intimacy video art once had. While Kelley and McCarthy use video, as Acconci did, their art recognizes the end of medium-specificity in an age when the art public have multiple international television stations at their fingertips and can surf the World Wide Web with ease. It speaks to what Rosalind Krauss has called our 'post-medium condition' where we must appreciate art not in terms of the medium but the idea behind the medium.[23] Finally, Kelley and McCarthy do not merely pay homage to an earlier era of performance and video art, they also mock the cult of beauty that emerged in the 1990s, exposing its conservative tendencies. Parodying artists like Jeff Koons and his airbrushed pornographic self-portraits with La Cicciolina, they call for abject resistance through its absence.

Within artists' turn to abjection came a renewed libidinous appreciation of the *wound*. As a cut, a leaking tear in the skin, the breaking of tissue, the wound again evoked death but also, more importantly, the ecstasy before death that was so key to Christian martyrdom. It spoke not only to physical and mental trauma but also to a powerful fusion of the body and soul, as the former suffered and the latter rose above that suffering. Artists who ritualistically wounded themselves before the viewing public used the wound as a strategy to traumatize the 'me' mentality of postmodern society where instant gratification is expected and emphasized, and to insist on *authenticity* and the *real* in an era of postmodern simulacra and the hyperreal.

The French artist Orlan (b. 1947), a performance artist since the 1970s, interrogated corporeal, medical, and technological boundaries in her performances in the 1990s in which she combined personal theatrics (costume, readings from a selection of texts, the use of assistants) and plastic surgery. Orlan calls these performances 'carnal art', so emphasizing the relationship between the flesh (and the wounding of the flesh) and the sexual appetite. Orlan's approach to pain and the wound is emphatically unhysterical, defying traditional associations between femininity and hysteria—a word whose origins lie in the Greek for womb (*hystera*), the ancients believing that the 'rising of the womb' lay behind fits.[24] Through new technological advances, notably live broadcasts of her performances, Orlan made use of the global nature of our existence and exposure to trauma and terror worldwide. She thus exploited the immediate, shocking impact, and the voyeuristic thrill, of the experience for those who witnessed her art.

Carried out in operating theatres, the performances were stages in a bigger project: to refashion the artist's face into a monstrous amalgamation of the facial features of Western art's great erotic beauties to subvert the canon of beauty. Her selection was made up of the chin of Botticelli's Venus, the Fontainebleau school's Diana, the lips of Gustave Moreau's Europa, the nose of Gérôme's Psyche, and the brow of Leonardo's Mona Lisa. In Orlan's performances her body becomes a canvas, fashioned by the surgeon according to the artist's design, but Orlan dominates by explaining the metaphysical theory behind the procedure to her unseen audience who watch, live, from a selection of international galleries. In *Seventh Surgery-Performance*, entitled *Omniprésence* (1993) **[111]**, Orlan wore an Issey Miyake dress and talked to her audience about Graeco-Roman iconography as her feminist surgeon Dr Marjorie Cramer cut into her face, lifting the skin and inserting implants. A male assistant dressed in a black mask translated Orlan's words into English, another assistant dressed in green signed for the deaf. Transmitted live to the Sandra Gering Gallery, New York, The Multimedia Centre in Banff, Canada, and the Pompidou Centre, Paris, the performance exploited the public's ease with gory documentary film while refusing to allow the safe distance between viewer and documentary object. For Orlan spoke directly to audience, augmenting their traumatic experience. As the surgeon inserted the last implant over Orlan's left brow (which

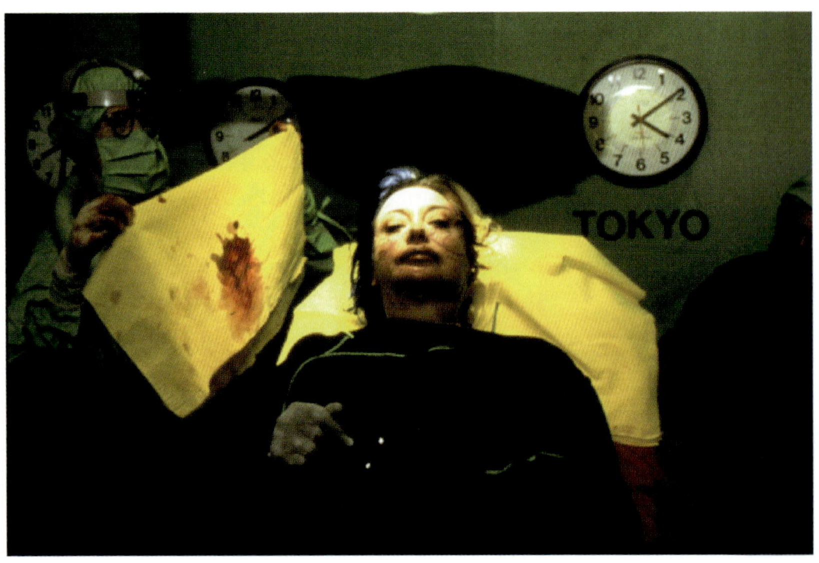

111 Orlan
Seventh Surgery-Performance, titled *Omniprésence*, New York: 21 November 1993

Since 1990, Orlan's use of cosmetic and reconstructive surgery in her performance art has challenged the traditional Western canon of beauty and society's demands on women. As part of her 'Carnal Art' aesthetic, Orlan uses modern technology in her self-portraiture, literally inviting surgeons to cut and refashion her face. In using her own flesh and body as a 'modified ready-made' she explains that her art 'does not long for pain' but aims to make the body 'the subject of public debate'.

would give Orlan two little 'horns') the artist asked her audience: 'Am I very pretty?'

Orlan exposes plastic surgery as a sign not of society's technological advance but of its technological subordination; yet she also speaks to the liberation of the Self—of identify—from the flesh and the body and the sex one is born with. These performances are problematic: on the one hand Orlan subverts Western, patriarchal ideals of beauty in cutting up great icons of female beauty; on the other she literally objectifies her own body, seeming to continue the objectification of woman in Western society. Sarah Wilson makes the important point that the genesis of Orlan's art work lies in an experience of local anaesthetic for an operation on an ectopic pregnancy in 1979, which led to 'an extraordinary ambivalence concerning the relationship between anaesthesia, aesthetics, psychic pain and its mastery'.[25] For Parveen Adams, Orlan's art is about Orlan's *female* relationship to the wound too: we should understand Orlan's acts as turning herself into 'an art-historical morph', as 'an image trapped in the body of a woman'.[26] Building on Orlan's explanation of her art as 'woman-to-woman trans-sexualism', Adams interprets her art as a feminist reappropriation of the flesh to expose the emptiness of the image, the emptiness of idealized beauty and its desirability. Not unlike Claude Cahun, Orlan's performances revel in masquerade, as one mask is peeled off only to reveal yet another; yet we are witness not to photography or collage but to Orlan's real pain, the peeling away of her real face, a self-sacrifice that allows her to interrogate, in her own words, 'the status of the feminine body, via social pressures, those of the present or in the past'.[27] In Bataillean spirit, the sacred is never far from her seemingly profane acts, as the artist refers to her art's reversion to 'the Christian principle of the word made flesh and the flesh made word, because it is in the flesh that my word inscribes itself as an artist's word'.[28] This is at the heart of Orlan's conception of the erotic in her ritualized and witnessed self-wounding.

The San Francisco-born artist Matthew Barney (b. 1967) has also contributed to the emergent cultural formation of a techno-body and has investigated its gender (or lack of) in his *Cremaster* film series (1994–2002). The title of the series indicates the erotic dimension from the outset as the cremaster muscle is present in both sexes but only develops to its full extent in males: it is the muscle surrounding the testicles and assists in the production of sperm cells as well as raising or lowering the testicles depending on temperature, stimulation, excitement, or fear. In keeping with this motif, *Cremaster 1* represents the most 'erect' state, *Cremaster 5* the 'lowest' state. Yet despite its biological meaning, the cremaster world is emphatically feminine and intra-uterine. In *Cremaster 1*, bulbous Goodyear blimps housing glamorous flight attendants in 1930s uniforms designed by Isaac Mizrahi float in the sky only to be roped in by Miss Goodyear in all her platinum-haired glory as she leads a troupe of Busby Berkeley-like hoop-skirted chorus girls around a football stadium in Boise, Idaho; in *Cremaster 5*, Ursula Andress—described by Barney as 'a proto-athletic sex symbol, whose shoulders are bigger than her hips'—makes a star appearance; in *Cremaster 2*, the convicted killer Gary Gilmore—said to be the grandson of Houdini, and the subject of Norman Mailer's *The Executioner's Song* (1979)—finds himself sandwiched in the interior of two 1966 Mustangs linked by a kind of umbilical tunnel coated in slimy Vaseline (his character is played by Barney, and Houdini by Mailer).[29] Mechanisms frequently present themselves as 'desiring machines', in Gilles Deleuze and Félix Guattari's terms: they are 'machines being driven by other machines, with all the necessary couplings and connections'; they are driven by and produce desire.[30] Like Deleuze and Guattari, Barney fantasizes about the internal mechanisms of the body and visualizes the body as machine and the machine as body and all as producing desire in constant flow: 'Amniotic fluid spilling out of the sac and kidney stones; flowing hair; a flow of spittle, a flow of sperm, shit or urine that are produced by partial objects and constantly cut off by other partial objects, which in turn produce other flows, interrupted by other partial objects.'[31] Barney insists on fluidity and defies order from the outset, by shooting these works on video before transferring them to film and

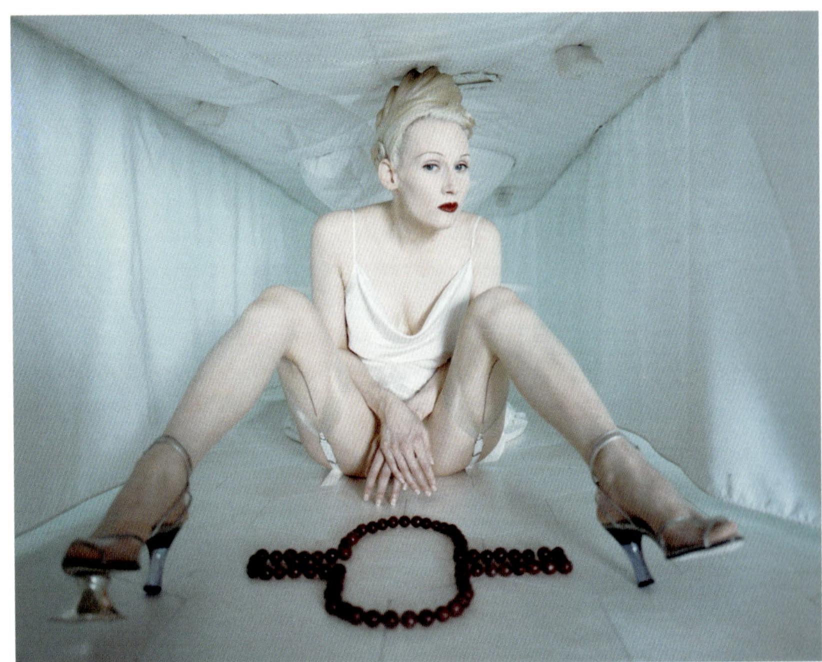

112 Matthew Barney
Cremaster 1, 1995

Barney's *Cremaster* cycle wallows in visual pleasure while offering a sophisticated tale of sex, gender, performance, and spectacle. In *Cremaster 1* we find glamorous, 1930s-styled air hostesses in Goodyear Blimps that float over Boise's Bronco Stadium at night-time. Goodyear, a platinum blonde, resides in both blimps, trapped under a grape-strewn table in a womb-like space. From an opening she steals grapes, mapping out patterns that miraculously create the choreographed dances of a troop of chorus girls in the stadium below.

then beginning his series with *Cremaster 4* (1994); *Cremasters 1* (1995) **[112]**, *5* (1997), *2* (1999), and *3* (2002) follow. *Cremaster 4* introduces the key narratival themes (mythology, ecology, biology, and biography) and erotic themes in the series (masculinity, trans-sexualism, fetishism; genital, oral, and anal pleasure), with Barney appearing as a handsome satyr, half-man, half-beast, who aspires to be a Loughton Ram, a four-horned breed of ram from the Isle of Man. Drawing on film history from Hollywood musicals to David Lynch's neo-Surrealism in his exploitation of dance, epic architectural settings, and costume, Barney's fantasia is one of hybrid creatures and abject fluids where natural and manmade forms all take on a nightmarish, all-engulfing, erotic potential. While using new media technology to unfix biological sex and to insist on the polymorphous nature of sexual desire, his art still smacks of Surrealism in its bizarre juxtapositions, slippage between dream and real states, and fetishistic use of costume, objects, and space itself. It also recalls Duchamp's erotic play in Barney defiance of fixed gender and his exploration of the easy slippage or blurring between the masculine and the feminine.[32] Barney might be viewed as updating Surrealism's uncanny play by toying with our fear of genetic modification and monstrous mutancy. We are repeatedly presented with emasculated males in the film series; Barney himself repeatedly appears as a dandy or sexless male. This effeminate role is emphasized all the more by the inclusion of 'Alpha' males in the series—Mailer as Houdini in *Cremaster 2* and the sculptor Richard Serra as the architect Hiram Abiff, the chief architect of Solomon's Temple, in *Cremaster 3*.[33] Furthermore, while the title of the series refers to the excited or fearful status of the cremaster muscle, this muscle is also associated with sexual differentiation in the womb. Barney began his university career in medicine before switching to art: he combines both interests in his series, presenting us with a story that is an ultimately utopian fantasy world 'developed about a sexual system that could move at will, and within this fantasy the cremaster muscle would control that, although in fact it does not'.[34]

A fascination with desiring-machines also informs the art of two British artist brothers, Jake Chapman (1966) and Dinos Chapman (1962). The Chapmans began to collaborate in 1992, and since then have explored the themes of corporeal excess in sculptures and installations that owe their greatest debt to the writings of Georges Bataille; Deleuze and Guattari have acknowledged his influence too. All share a deep concern with transgression and its transformative powers.[35] In *The Tears of Eros* (*Les Larmes d'Éros*, 1961)—cited by Jake Chapman as of seminal importance for the brothers' ideas and art—Bataille recounts the history of the representation of Eros from prehistoric cave painting at Lascaux, to the role and depiction of eroticism from antiquity, through mannerism, to Sade and Surrealism. While he relates the relationship between the erotic and death drive to the sexual act and orgasm, his key concern is with the ecstasy of the torturer and the tortured.[36] The book concludes with a chapter on a particularly horrific form of torture, the Chinese torture of 'Cent Morceaux' (one hundred pieces), with photographs of a man 'ecstatically' suffering this harrowing ritual wherein he is hung up on a cross and given opium to extend his capacity for torture while up to one hundred parts of his body are hacked off.[37] A similar intrigue with erotic excess and violence is apparent in the Chapman's art. The two figures of the 1994 sculptural pair *Mummy and Daddy Chapman* have multiple genitalia and skin punctuated with red sores. Mummy has a penis emerging out of her forehead, two more from the front of her neck, a vaginal slit between her breasts, and another on her left nipple. The viewer inevitably asks, as Norman Rosenthal of the Royal Academy in London once did, 'is *Mummy Chapman* a menacing fertility goddess, or one of the walking wounded, crippled by some uncontrollable sex drive?'[38]

In their *Tragic Anatomies* (1996) **[113]**, the Chapmans staged a perverse theatre of cruelty, a Garden of Eden gone wrong, with lifesize mutant mannequin children running around in designer trainers with sexless pudenda but multiple sexual orifices and protrusions. If *Mummy*

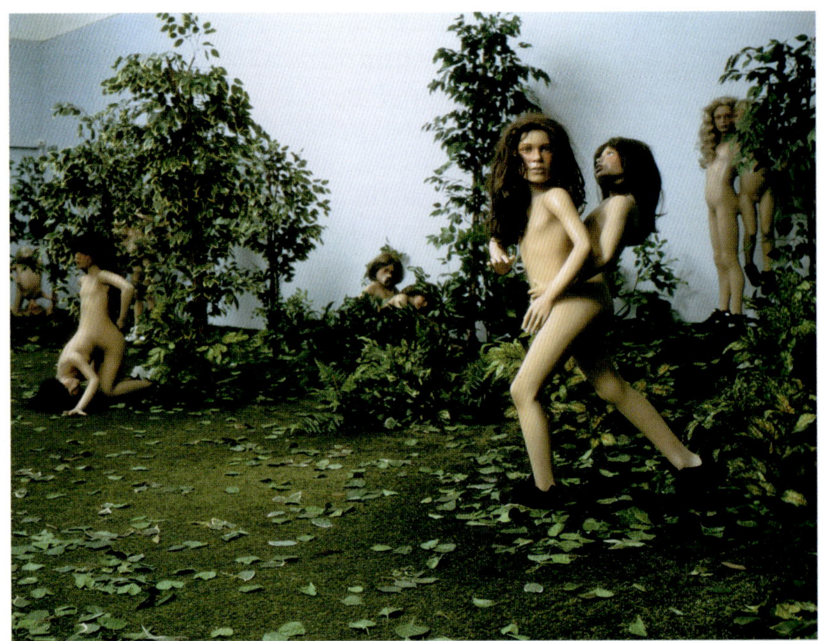

113 Jake and Dinos Chapman
Tragic Anatomies, 1996
The Chapmans' installation controversially presented naked, sexually mutated children in an Edenic garden. Influenced by the dolls of Hans Bellmer and Bataillean ideas of base desire and erotic excess, these creatures test the boundaries of art, largely through their allusion to paedophilia.

and Daddy Chapman embody sexual desire and sexual disease simultaneously, their tragic offspring seem to embody transgression itself, as they take on hybrid, trans-sexed forms and run riotously free in an arcadia that only the Marquis de Sade would have loved. The installation updates Bataille's fascination with the violent, ritualistic side of eroticism, however, and Deleuze and Guattari's vision of desiring-machines, by introducing a 'cyborg' (cybernetics/organism) element, made visual here in hybrids that are half human, half sex machines. The cyborg is the erotic subject par excellence as, in Donna Haraway's words, it 'is resolutely committed to partiality, irony, intimacy, and perversity. It is oppositional, utopian, and completely without innocence.'[39] Indeed, *Tragic Anatomies* seems to bring Haraway's observation that 'A cyborg body is not innocent; it was not born in a garden . . . it takes irony for granted' into the third dimension.[40] At the same time it picks at a very real sore in society, paedophilia, given its blatant conflation of childhood innocence and sexual perversion. But is also alludes to the fears and desires of art throughout the ages as it explores the easy slippage between the fairy tale and the horror story: the mutant children run riot in nature, free from civilization and all notions of bodily and sexual taboo, but the viewer is voyeur to their freedom and finds their antics more in keeping with the Marquis de Sade's anti-Enlightenment story of the cruel Juliette than Jean-Jacques Rousseau's Enlightenment hero Émile. In this way it is true to the Chapmans' vision of contemporary art in general—it is 'anthropological, and it's social'—as well as their desire to present art that refuses recuperation.[41] Like Bataille's photographs of Chinese torture, these works' sexual violence and erotic excesses cannot be appropriated.

In creating these hybrid trans-sexual creatures, the Chapmans play God—for, as Freud recognized, technology allows man to become 'a kind of Prosthetic God'.[42] But they do so with a neo-Surrealist (or dissident, Bataillean Surrealist) black humour, not merely dismembering the unified body but cruelly perverting its every erotic, libidinal potential. In their first joint anti-art statement, printed in adhesive letters on a mud-smeared wall at their *We Are Artists* exhibition of 1992, the Chapmans made this 'legacy' clear. While their statement opened with the admission 'We are sore-eyed scopophiliac oxymorons. Or, at least, we are desensitised aristocrats, under siege from our feudal heritage', it ended 'we phantasise emancipation from this liberal polity, into a superheavyweight no-holds-barred all-in mud wrestling league, a scatological aesthetics for the tired of seeing.'

Once again the erotic is employed by the artist as a deviant strategy to unsettle the viewer's social, psychological, and cultural assumptions, to incite a crisis in aesthetic taste and moral values. And behind that resistance lies a dream of a better world, a fantasy of new erotic bliss, an erotic dystopia that reminds us of eroticism's continued vital power to unsettle us, probe us, and even make us act differently.

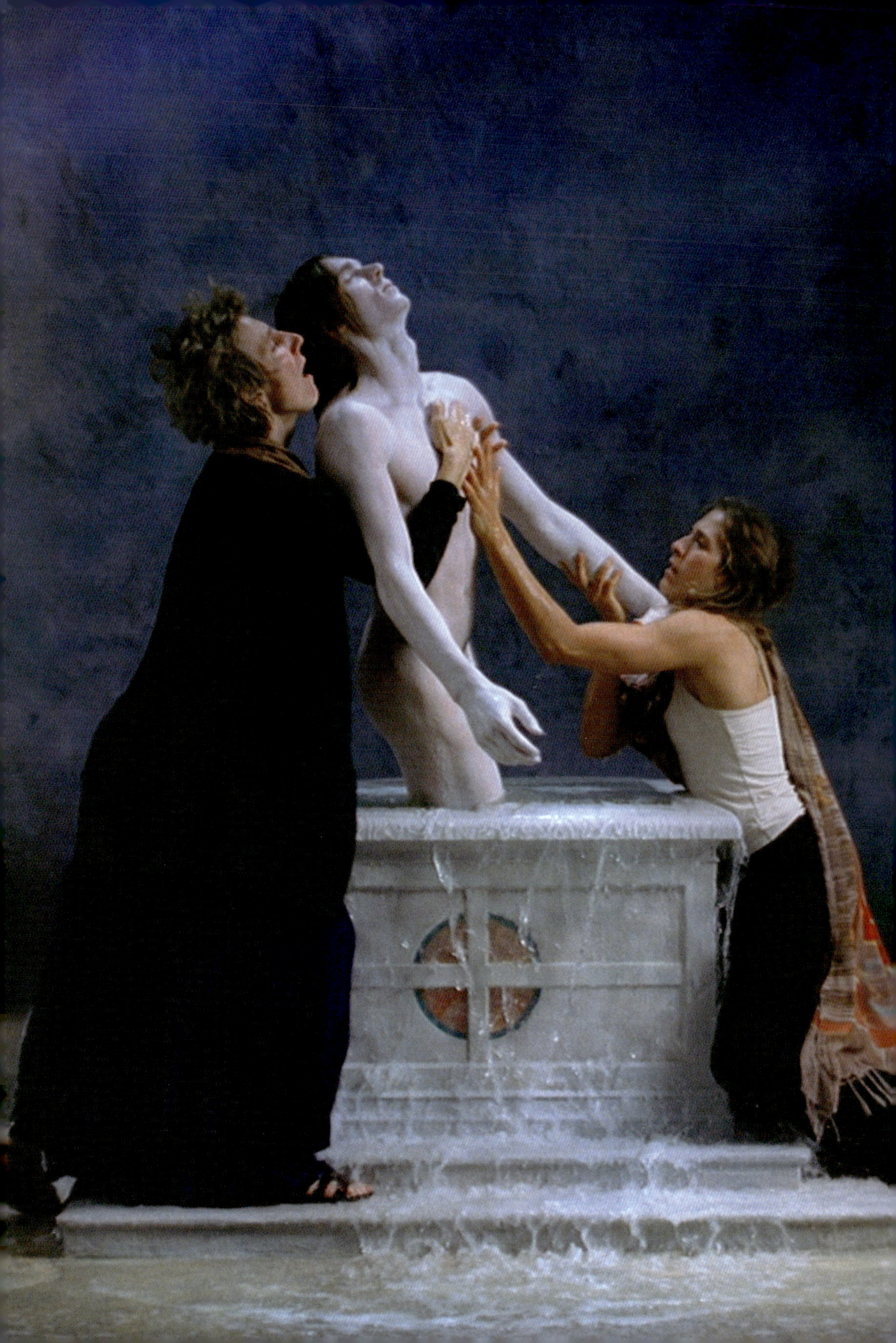

Conclusion

The fact that so much erotic art of the last decades of the twentieth century tended to explore the dark and deathly face of man's erotic urges might lead one to assume that such tendencies would continue in the twenty-first century. Postmodern art since the 1970s has insisted on the inseparability of Eros and Thanatos, desire and violence, with artists recognizing Thanatos in particular as a powerful and polemical vehicle through which to capture the attention of the public and to attempt to make them see the world differently. They have looked back through the history of art and its erotic iconography, but in drawing from the past have tended to emphasize not the erotic as pleasure so much as the pleasure men and women take in inflicting pain on each other. This might strike us as a postmodern pursuit of martyrdom and the ecstatic, of the spiritual potential of physical suffering, especially in a world home to such a disconnection between our desperate need to believe in goodness, innocence, and civilized order, on the one hand, and the warring, brutal, realities of the world in which we actually live. And yet we must not be too quick to try to beautify or redeem the erotic spirit and riotous pursuit of excess and transgression we have seen artists celebrate. *Jouissance*, that orgasmic experience of pleasure without fear of the ends or consequences, fuels both the pursuit of sado-masochistic pleasure in Bob Flanagan's performances as much as the sticky Vaseline-coated, gender-liberated world of Matthew Barney.

114 Bill Viola
Emergence (detail), 2002
Inspired by medieval and early Renaissance devotional imagery, Viola's art brings the tradition of the sacred into the postmodern world, presenting an image of mourning, as two women administer to a Christ-figure who emerges out of a marble cistern in a small courtyard. He rises out of the water, bringing hope and rebirth at a time of loss and despair.

If yBa artists like the Chapman brothers offer glimmers of hope in their work despite their generally dystopian image of the world, the recent work of the American video artist Bill Viola (b. 1951)—one of the most provocative of contemporary artists in his deployment of the body as erotic sacred object—may suggest that far from pursuing the obscene in a downward spiral of transgressive fury, erotic art in the future will continue cyclically to return to age-old themes while expanding them in new directions. Viola's video series *The Passions* (2000–3) refigures many of the themes articulated across the generations and aesthetic diversity of the art works discussed throughout the course of this book. *The Passions* explores not only human emotions but also the texture, volume, and tactility of the human body. Taking inspiration from medieval and Renaissance devotional images but 'translating' them into a postmodern context, Viola uses very large flat-panel digital video screens installed in the gallery space to display slow-motion moving image reproductions of scenes from the life of Christ. The seductive images of *The Passions* address the controlled eroticism of devotional imagery, the taboo of violence, blood, and nakedness, the pursuit of spiritual ecstasy and enlightenment through corporeal pain, the trauma of witnessing the real body rather than the painted or sculpted form, and the containment and purification of abjection which has always been central to Christian iconography and which remains central to the pleasure principle of mainstream aesthetics today.

Indeed, Viola sees art as having a 'healing function' as 'part of the life process'; *The Passions* was produced and exhibited in the aftermath of the attacks of 11 September 2001, events Viola has acknowledged to have resonances in his work.[1] A member of the post-World War II baby-boom generation, the first to grow up with a close relationship to television, Viola graduated from Syracuse University in 1973 and took inspiration from the first wave of artists such as Vito Acconci who used video as an experimental art form. As such, Viola's work emanates from a radically new cultural and technological moment, but it also harks back to the past, drawing, for example, upon both the religiously reverent Renaissance painting of Mantegna and the satirical Enlightenment-era prints of Goya. In *The Passions*, Viola deliberately and insistently slows down the usually rapid pace of motion picture imagery in order to use the medium of digital video to reclaim a classical vision of sublime beauty and form in which the image of the body somehow stands outside of modernity; in doing so it gains an erotic charge. The spectator of Viola's work, watching his actors enact ancient scenes from the life of Christ, is forced to slow down to the speed of the images themselves and to contemplate the video image as if it was a sixteenth-century altarpiece. The technology is today's but the experience is timeless.

Through *The Passions* Viola revisits universal themes such as love, hate, birth, and death, but celebrates them as 'life-giving' mysteries.[2] In doing so, he echoes Bataille's notion of the sacred element of eroticism, for Christ's story is one of brutal violence, agony, and final ecstasy, in which taboos (notably murder) are broken and sacred redemption is achieved through the profane acts of others. What Bataille recognizes as the 'excessive pleasure of the licentious' in the abuse of the figure of Christ is essential to the imagery and meaning of *The Passions*.[3] The emotions expressed by the actors in the series range from total anguish and wailing despair to rage and pious happiness, recalling Bataille's insight that man goes constantly in fear of his erotic drives; the death of

Christ itself is the perfect illustration of the battle between Eros and Thanatos.

The Passions appears to the gallery spectator as a temple dedicated to this battle, the imagery on its large and spectacular plasma screens reinforced by a sophisticated and layered use of digital sound, filling the gallery space with reminders of man's inhumanity to man (Christ's suffering, death, and resurrection) but also of the power of humanity to forgive, to heal, and to go on. In *Surrender* (2001), the screens are mounted vertically end-to-end, presenting the bodies of a male and female actor reflected in water as mirror opposites. They bend as if to kiss, breaking the water's surface, and emerging with faces of anguish, before the image itself dissolves and begins again. *Emergence* (2002) **[114]**, based on a fresco by Masolini depicting Mary and John the Evangelist beside the corpse of Jesus in the tomb, imbues Masolini's motionless painted iconography with activity and time: two women (played by Weba Garretson and Sarah Steben) sit by a tomb, waiting, mourning, their grief gradually turning to disbelief as the head of a young man begins to emerge from the tomb, their tears of sorrow turning to tears of joy as the once-dead man (played by John Hay) rises up triumphantly. The naked, sculpturesque body of Christ breathes the essence of taboo: the sacred and yet the forbidden. Viola's rendition harks back to Giotto, recapitulating the pulsating power of his human forms and yet extending them in a controlled but elongated narrative that demands of the spectator—in reaction to the seductively high production values and almost fetishistic gloss of the screen image itself—passionate and emotional but also bodily responses. In *The Passions*, the erotic lies in the emotion, the passion of the characters, the involvement of the viewer, the overwhelming technological seduction of the viewing experience, and the theme of corporeal intensity and suffering in the name of spiritual ecstasy.

Produced during a time of war and insecurity, the eroticized sacred art of Viola's *The Passions* offered a moment of quiet contemplation in the gallery space. It did not present itself as already complete but as evolving before the viewer's eyes, unsettling the senses, giving visceral and virtual form to desire, but calling on the viewer to complete the work of art, and in completing it contemplating its eroticism as a response to a global environment and historical moment dominated by Thanatos. The sublimity of the work may have left it open to recuperation; yet its denial of closure, and its resurrection of the erotic just at the moment when a new millennium was born, demonstrated that erotic art would continue to urge man to overcome his erotic fears, to recognize that the body and soul, the passions and reason, are indeed one.

Notes

Introduction

1 *Oxford English Dictionary*, 2nd edn, vol. V, Oxford: Clarendon Press, 1989, p. 374, and *Collins English Dictionary and Thesaurus*, Glasgow: HarperCollins, 1998, p. 380.

2 Plato, *The Symposium*, trans. with introduction by Christopher Gill, London: Penguin Books, 1999, 2003 reprint, 205d, p. 42. This ideal of love is expressed by Socrates, recounting the speech of his teacher, the priestess Diotima, on love.

3 David Hume, *A Treatise of Human Nature*, Book 2. Of the Passions, part III, sec. III, eds. David Fate Norman and Mary J. Norton, Oxford: Oxford University Press, 2004, p. 265

4 Simon Blackburn, *Lust, The Seven Deadly Sins*, New York and London: Oxford University Press, 2004. Blackburn's study is indebted to Hume's position on lust and offers an insightful and lively philosophical defence to drag it 'from the category of sin to that of virtue'.

5 David Hume, *Enquiry Concerning the Principles of Morals*, ed. David Berman, 3rd edn rev. P. H. Nidditch, Oxford: Oxford University Press, 1975, sec. IX, p. 268, cited in Blackburn, *Lust*, p. 3. See also Simon Blackburn, 'Why Do We Need to Feel? Hearts and Minds: The Place of Emotion in Rational Thought', *Times Literary Supplement*, 29 October 1999, pp. 3–4, p. 3.

6 Immanuel Kant, *Lectures on Ethics*, trans. Louis Infield, New York: Harper and Row, 1963, p. 1634.

7 Georges Bataille, *Eroticism* (1957), trans. Mary Dalwood, London: Marion Boyars, 1987, p. 11.

8 Ibid., p. 256. The term taboo originated in the islands of the Pacific and was brought back to European shores by travellers in the eighteenth century, including Captain Cook. As originally used, taboo designates something consecrated, forbidden to all except a king, god, priest, or chief. Today its sacred origins are all too often overlooked, and the term is loosely employed to describe 'an expression or topic considered offensive and so avoided or prohibited by social custom'. See *Oxford English Dictionary*, p. 521.

9 In *Discipline and Punish* (1975), and the first two volumes of *The History of Sexuality* (1976; 1984), Michel Foucault (1926–84) argued that power is inscribed on the body by the individual him/herself and by social regulation and discipline. In her writings, notably in *Revolution in Poetic Language* (1974), *Desire in Language* (1980), and *Powers of Horror: An Essay in Abjection* (1980) Julia Kristeva (b. 1941) explored the maternal, pre-Oedipal body and its abject 'threat' to the social order which leads to the reduction and oppression both of woman and the feminine to the abject maternal function. She also presented the maternal as operating *between* nature and culture, in contrast to the traditional view of woman, especially of the maternal woman as solely natural.

10 See Ann Rosalind Jones, 'Writing the Body: Toward an Understanding of l'Écriture féminine' in *The New Feminist Criticism, Essays on Women, Literature and Theory*, ed. Elaine Showalter, London: Virago Press, 1986, pp. 361–77, p. 375, footnote 2.

11 *Oxford English Dictionary*, p. 136 (from Dunglison Medical Dictionary 1857), and *Collins English Dictionary and Thesaurus*, p. 885.

12 This definition of 'hardcore pornography' is from *The Lancet*, 11 June 1977, cited under 'pornography' in the *Oxford English Dictionary*, p. 136.

13 Gloria Steinem, 'Erotica vs. Pornography' (1977 and 1978) in *Acts and Everyday Rebellions*, London: Fontana, 1984, pp. 219–30, p. 222. Catharine A. MacKinnon offers a feminist definition of pornography too as 'a form of forced sex, a practice of sexual politics, an institution of gender inequality'. See Catharine A. MacKinnon, 'Pornography: Not a Moral Issue', *Women's Studies International Forum*, vol. 9, no. 1, 1986, pp. 63–8, p. 65.

14 Steinem, 'Erotica vs. Pornography', p. 222.
15 Catharine A. MacKinnon, *Only Words*, Cambridge MA: Harvard University Press, 1993, p. 22, and Andrea Dworkin and Catharine A. MacKinnon, *Pornography and Civil Rights: A New Day*, Minneapolis MN: Organizing Against Pornography, 1988.
16 Roger Scruton, *Sexual Desire, A Philosophical Investigation*, London: Weidenfeld and Nicolson, 1986, p. 154. This painting falls under Scruton's understanding of the 'obscene' as it focuses on the female genitals, unlike 'true erotic art' in which 'it is usually the face and not the sexual organ that provides the focus of attention' (ibid.). Scruton's study (in contrast to this book) claims the erotic must retain an element of beauty, thus removing the sexually explicit—let alone abject or sado-masochistic desire—from our understanding of eroticism.
17 On Bouguereau's life and vision of art see *William Bouguereau 1825–1905*, exh. cat., Montreal: Montreal Museum of Fine Arts, 1984.
18 See Walter F. Otto, *Dionysus: Myth and Cult*, Bloomington IN and London: Indiana University Press, 1965. For an excellent introduction to classical art see Mary Beard, *Classical Art: From Greece to Rome*, Oxford: Oxford University Press (History of Art Series), 2001.
19 It is the portrayal of the erect penis and of penetration by objects that distinguishes 'hardcore' pornographic, violent, obscene sex from acceptable, 'softcore' pornography (as in 'girlie' magazines).
20 Saint Augustine, *The Confessions of St. Augustine*, trans. Rex Warner, introduction Vernon J. Bourke, New York: Mentor-Omega Books, 1963, Book X, Chapter 30, p. 237.
21 Giorgio Vasari, *Lives of the Artists*, vol. 1 (1568), trans. George Bull, Harmondsworth: Penguin Books, 1965, 2003 reprint, p. 58
22 *The Life of St Teresa of Avila by Herself*, trans. and introduction by J. M. Cohen, Harmondsworth: Penguin Books, 1957, p. 210.
23 W. B. Yeats, 'The Censorship and St. Thomas Acquinas', *Irish Statesman*, 11, 1928, pp. 47–8, reprinted in *Banned in Ireland: Censorship and the Irish Writer*, ed. Julia Carson, London: Routledge, 1990, pp. 130–2, p. 131. Yeats's essay was a protest against censorship in Ireland, the year before the Censorship of Publications Act (1929) was made law, pointing out that the equation of the 'indecent' with that which incites 'sexual passion' would deny the Irish people a whole history of religious and secular art.
24 Vasari, *Lives of the Artists*, vol. 1, p. 339.
25 Kenneth Clark, *The Nude, A Study of Ideal Art*, Harmondsworth: Penguin Books, 1956, p. 54.
26 Dominique Fernandez, *A Hidden Love: Art and Homosexuality*, New York: Prestel, 2002, pp. 77 and 49 respectively. See also James Saslow, *Ganymede in the Renaissance: Homosexuality in Art and Society*, New Haven CT: Yale University Press, 1986.
27 D. A. F. de Sade, *Philosophy in the Boudoir* (1795) in Sade, *Justine, Philosophy in the Boudoir, Eugénie de Franval and Other Writings*, eds. Richard Seaver and Austryn Wainhouse, London: Arrow Books, 1965, p. 185.
28 Maurice Blanchot, 'Sade' in Sade, *Justine, etc.*, eds. Seaver and Wainhouse, pp. 37–72, p. 57.
29 Clark, *The Nude*, p. 140.
30 Micheal Farrell and Gerry Walker, 'The Journal of a Meathman as an Intellectual' in *Micheal Farrell*, Cork: Gandon Editions, 1998, p. 43.
31 Ibid., p. 15.
32 Michel Foucault, *The History of Sexuality, Volume One: An Introduction* (1976), Harmondsworth: Pelican Books, 1981, pp. 25–6.
33 Ibid., p. 148.
34 See G. Boas, 'Il faut être de son temps', *Journal of Aesthetics*, vol. 1, 1941, pp. 52–65.
35 A thematic approach to eroticism and aesthetics (with chapter headings including Cruel Fantasies, Love for Sale, Pleasurable Pains, and Here Comes a Whopper), which tends to neglect the sociopolitical context, is adopted by Edward Lucie-Smith in his *Eroticism in Western Art*, London: Thames and Hudson, 1972, reprinted as *Sexuality in Western Art* in 1991; Gilles Néret's *Twentieth-century Erotic Art*, Cologne: Benedikt Taschen, 1993, is comparable in approach (with such headings as Nudity Veiled, The Anatomy of Love, and The Perverse Art of Playing with Dolls).

Chapter 1: The Rhetoric of the Nude

1 Plato, *The Republic*, ed. G. R. F. Ferrari, trans. Tom Griffith, Cambridge: Cambridge University Press, 2004, Book 10, 597e, p. 316.
2 Ibid., Book 10, 602c, p. 322.
3 Aristotle, *Poetics*, trans., introduction, and notes by Malcolm Heath, London: Penguin Books, 1996, 11.3, (i), p. 45.
4 See Rosika Parker and Griselda Pollock, *Old*

Mistresses: Women Art and Ideology, London: Routledge and Kegan Paul, 1981, p. 119.

5 See Lynda Nead, *The Female Nude: Art, Obscenity and Sexuality*, London and New York: Routledge, p. 192, especially her synopsis of the discourse on the naked and the nude, pp. 5–33.

6 Or as John Berger put it in his highly influential television series and book, *Ways of Seeing*, '*men act* and *women appear*. Men look at women. Women watch themselves being looked at.' See John Berger, *Ways of Seeing*, London: British Broadcasting Corporation and Penguin Books, 1972, p. 47.

7 Griselda Pollock, *Vision and Difference: Femininity, Feminism, and the Histories of Art*, London and New York: Routledge, 1988, p. 147.

8 J. F. de Bourgoing, cited in *Nineteenth Century Art: A Critical History*, ed. Stephen F. Eisenman, London: Thames and Hudson, 1994, p. 84.

9 Ibid., pp. 85–6. See also Francis D. Klingender, *Goya in the Democratic Tradition*, London: Sidgwick and Jackson, 1948.

10 Anthony Hull, *Goya: Man among Kings*, London and New York: Hamilton Press, 1987, p. 98.

11 See Roger Benjamin, 'The Oriental Mirage' in *Orientalism: Delacroix to Klee*, ed. Benjamin, exh. cat., London: Thames and Hudson and The Art Gallery of New South Wales, 1997, pp. 7–31.

12 Roger Benjamin (ed.), *Orientalism: Delacroix to Klee*, exh. cat., London: Thames and Hudson and The Art Gallery of New South Wales, 1997, p. 67; see also Carol Ockman, *Ingres' Eroticized Bodies: Retracing the Serpentine Line*, New Haven CT: Yale University Press, 1995, p. 36.

13 Berger, *Ways of Seeing*, p. 55.

14 See Norman Bryson's reading of Ingres as the postponement of satisfaction in *Tradition and Desire: From David to Delacroix*, Cambridge: Cambridge University Press, 1984.

15 Nicolas de Nicolay, Lord of Arfeuile, was the chamberlain and geographer to Henry II and accompanied the second embassy of Gabriel d'Aramon to Suleiman in 1551. His *Les Quatre Premiers Livres des navigations, pérégrinations et voyages* (1567) was translated into English as *The Navigations, Peregrinations, and Voyages, Made into Turkee*, in 1585. See Leslie Luebbers, 'Documenting the Invisible: European Images of Ottoman Women, 1567–1867', *The Print Collector's Newsletter*, vol. 24, no. 1, March–April 1993, pp. 1–7.

16 Théophile Gautier, 'Beaux-Arts: Collection Khalil Bey', *Le Moniteur universel*, 14 December 1867, cited in Benjamin, *Orientalism*, p. 70.

17 Edward Said, *Orientalism: Western Conceptions of the Orient* (1978), Harmondsworth: Penguin Books, 1995, p. 3.

18 Seminal postcolonial texts to address the binary logic of identity and difference, Self and Other, include Homi Bhabha, *The Location of Culture*, New York and London: Routledge, 1994, and Gayatri C. Spivak, 'Can the Subaltern Speak?' in *The Postcolonial Studies Reader*, eds. Bill Ashcroft, Garther Griffiths, and Helen Tiffin, New York: Routledge, 1995, pp. 24–8.

19 See Reina Lewis, *Gendering Orientalism: Race, Femininity and Representation*, London and New York: Routledge, 1996, pp. 111–12.

20 For more on the reception of the painting, see Jack J. Spector, *Delacroix: The Death of Sardanapalus*, New York: Viking Press, 1974.

21 Linda Nochlin, *The Politics of Vision, Essays on Nineteenth-century Art and Society* (1989), London: Thames and Hudson, 1991, p. 44.

22 See chapters 3 and 4 of Lewis, *Gendering Orientalism*. On Browne's life see also Charlotte Yeldham, 'Henriette Browne' in *Women Artists in Nineteenth-century France and England*, 2 vols., New York and London: Garland Publishing, 1984, vol. 1, pp. 345–50.

23 See Mary Roberts, 'Contested Terrains: Women Orientalists and the Colonial Harem' in *Orientalism's Interlocutors. Painting, Architecture, Photography*, eds. Jill Beaulieu and Mary Roberts, Durham NC and London: Duke University Press, 2002, pp. 179–203.

24 Olivier Merson, *Exposition de 1861: La Peinture en France*, Paris: Libraire de la Société des gens de lettres, 1861, p. 276, cited in Roberts, 'Contested Terrain', p. 181.

25 Abigail Solomon-Godeau, *Male Trouble: A Crisis in Representation*, London: Thames and Hudson, 1997, p. 178.

26 Walter Pater, *Greek Studies* (1895), Oxford: Blackwell, and New York: Johnson Reprint Corp., 1967, p. 221.

27 Leonée and Richard Ormond, *Lord Leighton*, New Haven CT: Yale University Press, 1975, p. 48; and Peter Webb, *The Erotic Arts*, London: Secker and Warburg, 1983, p. 189.

28 Henry James, 'The Picture Season in London' (1877) in Henry James, *The Painter's Eye: Notes and Essays on the Pictorial Arts*, ed. J. L. Sweeney, London: Hart-Davis, 1956, pp. 130–51, p. 149.

29 Elizabeth Prettejohn, 'The Modernism of Frederic Leighton' in *English Art 1860–1914:*

Modern Artists and Identity, eds. David Peters Corbett and Lara Perry, Manchester: Manchester University Press, 2000, pp. 31–48, p. 45. See also Tim Barringer and Elizabeth Prettejohn, *Frederic Leighton, Antiquity, Renaissance, Modernity*, New Haven CT: Yale University Press, pp. xiv–xv.

30 Joseph A. Kestner, *Mythology and Misogyny: The Social Discourse of Nineteenth-century British Classical-Subject Painting*, Madison WI and London: The University of Wisconsin Press, 1989, p. 145.

31 Ibid., pp. 145–6.

32 Colin Cruise '"Lovely devils": Simeon Solomon and Pre-Raphaelite Masculinity' in *Re-framing the Pre-Raphaelites: Historical and Theoretical Essays*, ed. Ellen Harding, Aldershot: Scolar Press, 1996, pp. 195–210, p. 202.

33 Ibid., p. 206.

34 Walter Hamilton, *The Aesthetic Movement in England*, London: Reeves and Turner, 1882, p. 82, cited in Cruise, '"Lovely devils"', p. 196.

35 It must be said that this was not a male-only movement—as recent scholarship has rightly shown, we must acknowledge a Pre-Raphaelite 'sisterhood' too. See Jan Marsh, *The Pre-Raphaelite Sisterhood*, London and New York: Quartet Books, 1985, and Jan Marsh and Pamela Gerrish Nunn, *Pre-Raphaelite Women Artists*, exh. cat., Manchester: Manchester City Art Galleries, 1998.

36 Pollock, *Vision and Difference*, p. 128.

37 J. B. Bullen, *The Pre-Raphaelite Body: Fear and Desire in Painting, Poetry and Criticism*, Oxford: Clarendon Press, 1998, p. 92.

38 See Elaine Showalter, *The Female Malady: Women, Madness and English Culture, 1830–1980*, London: Virago Press, 1987, p. 11. Showalter takes this flower convention further and sees Ophelia, in giving away her flowers, as symbolically 'deflowering' herself.

39 Algernon Swinburne, recorded in *The Diaries of George Price Boyce*, ed. V. Surtees, Norwich, 1980, p. 89, cited in Pollock, *Vision and Difference*, p. 215 footnote 17.

40 Kestner, *Mythology and Misogyny*, p. 77.

41 See ibid., pp. 92–4.

42 Charles Darwin, *The Descent of Man* (1871), reprint Princeton NJ: Princeton University Press, 1981, pp. 326–7.

43 See Sir Joshua Reynolds, *Discourses on Art*, New Haven CT: Yale University Press, 1981, no. 9, p. 171.

44 Barbara Groseclose, *Nineteenth-century American Art*, Oxford: Oxford University Press, 2000, pp. 23–5. See also Joy Kasson, *Marble Queens and Captives*, New Haven CT and London: Yale University Press, 1990, pp. 49–51.

45 J. B. Atkinson, *Saturday Review*, 14 May 1870, p. 642, cited in Alison Smith, *The Victorian Nude: Sexuality, Morality and Art*, Manchester: Manchester University Press, 1996, p. 151.

46 Smith, *The Victorian Nude*, pp. 154–5.

47 Lynda Nead has read the painting in the light of these social changes. See Nead, 'Representation, Sexuality and the Female Nude', *Art History*, vol. 6, no. 2, June 1983, pp. 227–336. See also Nead's *Myths of Sexuality: Representations of Women in Victorian Britain*, Oxford: Basil Blackwell, 1988.

48 On the Académie Julian see *Overcoming All Obstacles: The Women of the Académie Julian*, eds. Gabriel P. Weisberg and Jane R. Becker, exh. cat., New York: The Dahesh Museum, and New Brunswick NJ and London: Rutgers University Press, 1999. See also Tamar Garb, *Sisters of the Brush: Women's Artistic Culture in Late Nineteenth-Century Paris*, New Haven CT: Yale University Press, 1994; and for a history of women artists and the obstacles that impeded their artistic careers, see Germaine Greer, *The Obstacle Race: The Fortunes of Women Painters and Their Work*, London: Secker and Warburg, 1979.

49 Charles Baudelaire, 'The Modern Public and Photography' (1862), cited in *Classic Essays on Photography*, ed. Alan Trachtenberg, New Haven CT: Leete's Island Books, 1980, p. 87.

50 Carol Mavor, *Pleasure Taken: Performances of Sexuality and Loss in Victorian Photographs*, Durham NC and London: Duke University Press, 1995, p. 3.

51 Morton Cohen, *Lewis Carroll, Photographer of Children: Four Nude Studies*, New York: Potter, 1978, p. 4.

52 See Nina Auerbach's reading of the photograph in *Romantic Imprisonment: Women and Other Glorified Outcasts*, New York: Columbia University Press, 1986, p. 168.

53 Joris-Karl Huysmans, cited in Griselda Pollock, *Mary Cassatt: Painter of Modern Woman*, London: Thames and Hudson, 1998, p. 185. Pollock identifies the painting Huysmans refers to as *A Goodnight Hug* (1880).

Chapter 2: The Naked Truth

1 Clement Greenberg, 'Avant-Garde and Kitsch', published in *Partisan Review*, vol. 6, no. 5, New

York, Fall 1939, pp. 34–48, reproduced in *Art in Theory 1900–1990: An Anthology of Changing Ideas*, eds. Charles Harrison and Paul Wood, Oxford: Blackwell, 1992, pp. 529–41.

2 See the catalogue entry on *The Sleepers* in Sarah Faunce and Linda Nochlin, *Courbet Reconsidered*, exh. cat., New York: The Brooklyn Museum, 1988, pp. 175–6. *The Sleepers* was apparently also commissioned by Khalil Bey and would be one of the items included in a police dossier begun on the artist in 1868. It was deemed to be indicative of his communard stance and 'reprobate status'.

3 The whereabouts of the painting is now unknown though the history of the painting's ownership is fascinating. After Khalil Bey (who had to sell his collection in 1868 due to gambling debts) and Sylvie Bataille Lacan, it was subsequently in the collection of the Museum of Fine Arts, Budapest, before disappearing during the war and being sold to an unspecified buyer in Paris in the 1950s. See Linda Nochlin, 'The Origin without an Original', *October*, no. 37, Summer 1986, pp. 77–86.

4 Francis Haskell suggests that Khalil Bey may have shown Ingres's *The Turkish Bath* to Courbet. See Francis Haskell, 'A Turk and His Pictures in Nineteenth-century Paris', *Oxford Art Journal*, vol. 5, no. 1, 1982, pp. 40–7, p. 45.

5 Charles Baudelaire, 'The Painter of Modern Life' (1863) in *The Painter of Modern Life and Other Essays*, trans. and ed. Jonathan Mayne, London: Phaidon, 1995, p. 12.

6 Ibid., p. 36.

7 See Eunice Lipton's engaging history of Meurent's life, artistic career, and lesbianism in *Alias Olympia: A Woman's Search for Manet's Notorious Model and Her Own Desire*, New York: Charles Scribner's Sons, 1992. Meurent was also the unclothed model in the foreground of Manet's *Déjeuner sur l'herbe* (1863).

8 For the numerous criticisms of the painting, see George Heard Hamilton, *Manet and His Critics*, New York: W. W. Norton, 1969.

9 Amédée Cantaloube, *Le Grand Journal*, 21 May 1865, cited in T. J. Clark, 'Preliminaries to a Possible Treatment of Olympia in 1865' (1980) in *Modern Art and Modernism*, eds. Francis Frascina and Charles Harrison, London: Harper and Row, 1982, pp. 259–73, p. 263.

10 Émile Zola, 'Édouard Manet' (1867) in *Modern Art and Modernism: A Critical Anthology*, eds. Francis Frascina and Charles Harrison, London: Harper and Row, 1982, pp. 29–39, p. 30.

11 For an excellent history of the lives of prostitutes and the regulation of prostitution at this time see Alain Corbin, *Women for Hire: Prostitution and Sexuality in France after 1850*, trans. Alan Sheridan, Cambridge MA and London: Harvard University Press, 1990.

12 See Loraine O'Grady, 'Olympia's Maid: Reclaiming Black Female Sexuality', *Afterimage*, vol. 20, no. 1, Summer 1992,pp. 14–15, p. 14.

13 Émile Zola, *Nana* (1880), trans. and introduction by George Holden, Harmondsworth: Penguin Classics, 1972, p. 44.

14 Georges Holden, 'Introduction', *Nadja*, pp. 5–16, p. 14.

15 Zola, *Nana*, pp. 44–5.

16 Tamar Garb, *Bodies of Modernity: Figure and Flesh in Fin-de-siècle France*, London: Thames and Hudson, 1998, p. 146.

17 Albert Wolf and Zola, cited in Sophie Monneret, *Renoir*, Paris: Éditions du Chêne, 1989, p. 62.

18 As Romy Golan notes, the 1920s witnessed 'the sudden vogue for Renoir's corporeal late nudes'; and in his 1924 publication *Le Nu dans la peinture moderne (1863–1920)*, Francis Carco confidently asserted that after the decline of the nude with the Impressionists, Fauves, and Cubism, the nude was back. See Romy Golan, *Modernity and Nostalgia: Art and Politics in France between the Wars*, New Haven CT and London: Yale University Press, 1995, pp. 19–20.

19 J.-K. Huysmans, *Certains*, Paris (1889), 1908, pp. 22–7, trans. M. L. Landa in P. Cabanne, *Edgar Degas*, Paris and New York, p. 120, cited in Norma Broude, 'Degas's "Misogyny"' (1977) in *Feminism and Art History: Questioning the Litany*, eds. Norma Broude and Mary D. Garrard, New York: Harper and Row, 1982, pp. 247–69, p. 247. See also Carol Armstrong on Huysmans and the 1886 series of nudes in *Odd Man Out: Readings of the Work and Reputation of Edgar Degas*, Chicago: Chicago University Press, 1991, pp. 157–209.

20 J. M. Michel, *La Petite Gazette*, 18 May 1886, np, cited in Heather Dawkins, *The Nude in French Art and Culture, 1870–1910*, Cambridge and New York: Cambridge University Press, 2002, p. 68.

21 Georges Rivière, *Mr. Degas, Bourgeois de Paris*, Paris, 1935, p. 18, cited in Broude, 'Degas's "Misogyny"', p. 250.

22 Alice Michel, 'Degas et son modèle', *Mercure de France*, 16 February 1919, pp. 457–8. Dawkins

reproduces many excerpts from this text in her analysis of it in *The Nude*, pp. 86–114.

23 Dawkins, *The Nude*, p. 123.

24 Broude, 'Degas's "Misogyny"', p. 264. Broude also compares Degas's dancers to a relief from the Temple of Athena Nike and his *The Laundresses* (*c.* 1884) to Michelangelo's *Slave*, which Degas had sketched.

25 Anthea Callen, *The Spectacular Body: Science, Method and Meaning in the Work of Degas*, New Haven CT: Yale University Press, 1995, p. 147.

26 Garb, *Bodies of Modernity*, pp. 49–51.

27 Maurice Merleau-Ponty, 'Cézanne's Doubt' in *Sense and Non-sense*, trans. Herbert L. Dreyfus and Patricia Allen Dreyfus, Evanston IL: Northwestern University Press, 1964, pp. 9–25, pp. 11 and 19 respectively.

28 Émile Zola, 'To My Friend Paul Cézanne', Paris, 20 May 1866, in *Paul Cézanne, Letters*, ed. John Rewald, trans. Marguerite Kay, Oxford: B. Cassirer, 1976, pp. 105–8.

29 Zola recounts such sunny carefree days in his semi-autobiographical novel *L'Œuvre* (1886), trans. Thomas Walton as *The Masterpiece*, London: Elek Books, 1950.

30 Joachim Gasquet, *Cézanne*, 2nd edn, Paris: Bernheim-Jeune, 1926, p. 55.

31 Shearer West, *The Visual Arts in Germany 1890–1937: Utopia and Despair*, Manchester: Manchester University Press, 2000, p. 19.

32 See Timothy d'Arch Smith, *Love in Earnest: Some Notes on the Lives and Writings of English 'Uranian' Poets from 1889 to 1930*, London: Routledge and Kegan Paul, 1970.

33 Henry Scott Tuke, Sonnet, no. 1076, published anonymously in *The Artist*, and reproduced as Appendix III in David Wainwright and Catherine Dinn, *Henry Scott Tuke, 1858–1929, Under Canvas*, London: Sarema, 1989, p. 157.

34 Emmanuel Cooper, *The Life and Work of Henry Scott Tuke (1858–1929): A Monograph*, London: GMP, 1987, p. 33. Note that Cooper identifies the second boy in *Noonday Heat* as Fouracre, whereas Wainwright and Dinn, in *Henry Scott Tuke*, name him as Harry Cleave.

35 See Gordon Hendricks, *The Photographs of Thomas Eakins*, New York: Grossman Publishers, 1972. While often titled *The Swimmong Hole*, the original title for the painting was *Swimming*. See Marc Simpson, '*Swimming* through Time: An Introduction' in *Thomas Eakins and the Swimming Picture*, eds. Doreen Bolger and Sarah Cash, Fort Worth TX: Amon Carter Museum, 1996, pp. 1–12.

36 Marc Simpson, 'Thomas Eakins and His Arcadian Works', *Smithsonian Studies in American Art*, vol. 1, no. 2, Fall 1987, pp. 71–95, p. 74.

37 See Michael Hatt's analysis of the painting as a homoerotic, as opposed to homosexual, image in 'The Male Body in Another Frame: Thomas Eakins' *The Swimming Hole* as a Homoerotic Image' in *The Body, Journal of Philosophy and the Visual Arts*, ed. Andrew Benjamin, 1993, pp. 9–21.

38 Randall C. Griffin, 'Thomas Eakins' Construction of the Male Body, or "Men Get to Know Each Other Across the Space of Time"', *The Oxford Art Journal*, vol. 18, no. 2, 1995, pp. 70–80, p. 78.

Chapter 3: Primitive Drives

1 Clement Greenberg, 'Modernist Painting' (1965) in *Modern Art and Modernism: A Critical Anthology*, eds. Francis Frascina and Charles Harrison, London: Harper and Row, 1982, pp. 5–10, p. 5.

2 William Rubin (ed.), 'Modernist Primitivism: An Introduction' in *'Primitivism' in 20th-Century Art: Affinity of the Tribal and Modern*, exh. cat., 2 vols, New York: MoMA, 1984, vol. I, pp. 1–81, p. 1. As Rubin notes (footnote 1, p. 74), 'the terms primitive and tribal are both problematic. The former is sometimes avoided lest it have pejorative, Darwinian connotations. The latter is a term which was used by anthropologists up until the 1960s as a means of addressing art across continents and culture, but it has also been criticized, African scholars in particular seeing it as too Eurocentric.'

3 This association between the tribal arts and twentieth-century painting was largely spearheaded by the art historian Robert Goldwater and his seminal text *Primitivism and Modern Painting*, New York 1938 (enlarged edn, Cambridge MA: Belknap Press, 1986). More recent studies that provide excellent introductions to the influence of primitive art on modern art include Colin Rhodes, *Primitivism and Modern Art*, London: Thames and Hudson, 1994, and Gill Perry, 'Primitivism and the "Modern"' in *Primitivism, Cubism, Abstraction: The Early Twentieth Century*, eds. Charles Harrison, Francis Frascina, and Gill Perry, New Haven CT and London: Yale University Press in association with the Open University, 1993, pp. 3–85.

4 Paul Gauguin, 'Diverse chose, 1896–97' in *Theories of Modern Art: A Source Book by Artists and Critics*, ed. Herschel B. Chipp, Berkeley CA: University of California Press, 1975, p. 65.
5 Louis-Antoine de Bougainville, *Voyage round the World* (1771), cited in Kirk Varnedoe, 'Gauguin' in *'Primitivism' in 20th-Century Art*, ed. Rubin, vol. I, p. 188.
6 Paul Gauguin, 'Une Lettre inédite de Gauguin', *Les Marges*, vol. 14, May 1918, pp. 168–9, cited in Stephen F. Eisenman, *Gauguin's Skirt*, London: Thames and Hudson, 1997, p. 56.
7 Gauguin, cited in Varnadoe, 'Gauguin', pp. 199–200. See also Bengt Danielsson, 'Gauguin's Tahitian Titles', *Burlington Magazine*, vol. 109, no. 769, April 1967, pp. 228–33.
8 Belinda Thomson, *Gauguin*, London: Thames and Hudson, 1987, p. 156.
9 See Abigail Solomon-Godeau, 'Going Native', *Art in America*, vol. 77, July 1989, pp. 119–28, and Griselda Pollock, *Avant Garde Gambits 1888–1893: Gender and the Colour of Art History*, London: Thames and Hudson, 1992, for their readings of Gauguin's racist and sexist objectification of Tahitian woman.
10 Bengt Danielsson, *Gauguin in the South Seas*, trans. Reginald Spink, London: George Allen and Unwin, 1965, p. 282.
11 Eisenman, *Gauguin's Skirt*, p. 66.
12 See Jack Flam, 'Matisse and the Fauves' in *'Primitivism' in 20th-Century Art*, ed. Rubin, vol. I, pp. 224–6.
13 James D. Herbert, *Fauve Painting: The Making of Cultural Politics*, New Haven CT and London: Yale University Press, 1992, p. 157.
14 Freud defines the fetish as both 'a token of triumph over the threat of castration and a protection against it'. See Sigmund Freud, 'Fetishism' (1927) in *On Sexuality: Three Essays on the History of Sexuality and Other Works*, The Pelican Freud Library, vol. VII, Harmondsworth: Penguin, 1977, p. 353. As anthropologist William Pietz has shown, the origin of the term 'fetish' lies in the Afro-Portuguese word *fetisso*—based on the Portuguese *feitiço* (magical practice), which derives from the Latin *facticius* (manufactured), and was used by those Portuguese who traded along the west coast of Africa in the sixteenth and seventeenth centuries. The term had religious, exotic, and economic significance, but the symbolic and ritualistic importance of the fetish object itself was not appreciated or understood by traders. See Pietz, 'The Problem of the Fetish I', *Res*, 9, Spring 1985, pp. 5–17, and 'The Problem of the Fetish II', *Res*, 13, 1987, pp. 23–45.
15 See Robert Rosenblum, '*Les Demoiselles d'Avignon* et le théâtre érotique de Picasso' in Jean Clair et al., *Picasso érotique*, exh. cat., Paris: Galerie Nationale du Jeu de Paume/Réunion des Musées Nationaux, 2001, pp. 94–9, pp. 94–5.
16 William Rubin offers the most thorough reading of the tribal influences on Picasso's art in his essay 'Picasso' in *'Primitivism' in 20th-Century Art*, ed. Rubin, vol. I, pp. 241–343.
17 Other influences on Picasso's *Les Demoiselles d'Avignon* (1907) may include the nude on the far left of Henri Matisse's *The Joy of Life* (1905–6) as well as Michelangelo's marble sculpture of a *Dying Slave* (1513–16) in the collection of the Louvre, Paris. On these possible inspirations see 'Choses vues' in *Les Demoiselles d'Avignon*, ed. Hélène Seckel, exh. cat., Paris: Musée Picasso, 1988, pp. 4–13 and Chapter One of William Rubin, *Les Demoiselles d'Avignon, Studies in Modern Art 3*, New York: Museum of Modern Art, 1994.
18 See Patricia Leighten, 'Colonialism, l'art nègre, and *Les Demoiselles d'Avignon*' in *Les Demoiselles d'Avignon*, ed. Christopher Green, Cambridge: Cambridge University Press, 2001, pp. 77–103.
19 See for example Carol Duncan, 'The MoMA's Hot Mamas', *Art Journal*, vol. 48, no. 2, Summer 1989, pp. 171–8, and Anna Chave, 'New Encounters with *Les Demoiselles d'Avignon*: Gender, Race and the Origins of Cubism', *The Art Bulletin*, vol. 76, no. 4, December 1994, pp. 596–611.
20 On Picasso's pursuit of eroticism in terms of Eros and Thanatos see Jean Clair, *Picasso et l'abîme: Éros, Nomos et Thanatos*, Paris: L'Échoppe, 2000, and his essay 'Leçon d'abîme' in *Picasso Érotique*, pp. 14–26.
21 Leo Steinberg's influential 1972 analysis of the painting also refers to it in philosophical terms, as a traumatic exposé of the artist's fears. See Leo Steinberg, 'The Philosophical Brothel', *ArtNews*, vol. 71, no. 5, September 1972, pp. 22–9 (part I) and no. 6, October 1972, pp. 38–47 (part II).
22 Müller joined in 1910 following Nolde and Pechstein's foundation of the 'New Secession' that year in response to their rejection by the Berlin Secession group, with whom they had exhibited in 1909.
23 Emil Nolde, *Artistic Expression of Primitive*

Peoples (1912), trans. in *Theories of Modern Art*, ed. Chipp, pp. 150–1.

24 Emil Nolde, letter to Hans Fehr, March 1914, in Nolde, *Welt und Heimat. Die Südseereise, 1913–1918* (1936), Cologne: DuMont Schauberg, 1965, 1971 edn, p. 88, cited in trans. in William S. Bradley, *Emil Nolde and German Expressionism: A Prophet in His Own Land*, Ann Arbor MI: University of Michigan Press, 1986, p. 86.

25 Friedrich Nietzsche, *The Will to Power*, trans. Walter Kaufmann and R. J. Hollingdale, New York: Vintage, 1968, p. 424, cited in Donald E. Gordon, 'German Expressionism' in *'Primitivism' in 20th-Century Art*, ed. Rubin, vol. II, pp. 369–403, p. 371.

26 Gordon, 'German Expressionism', p. 370.

27 Gill Perry, 'Primitivism and the "Modern"' in *Primitivism, Cubism, Abstraction*, eds. Harrison, Frascina, and Perry, p. 73. See also J. Lloyd, *German Expressionism: Primitivism and Modernity*, New Haven CT and London: Yale University Press, 1991.

28 Gordon, 'German Expressionism', pp. 372–3.

29 Shearer West, *The Visual Arts in Germany 1890–1937: Utopia and Despair*, Manchester: Manchester University Press, 2000, pp. 52–3.

30 See Sherwin Simmons, 'Ernst Kirchner's Streetwalkers: Art, Luxury, and Immorality in Berlin, 1913–16', *The Art Bulletin*, vol. 82, no. 1, March 2000, pp. 117–48.

31 Sigmund Freud, 'Lecture XXIII: The Paths of the Formation of Symptoms', *Introductory Lectures on Psycho-Analysis (Part III)*, ed. and trans. James Strachey, The Standard Edition of the Complete Psychological Works of Sigmund Freud, vol. XVI, London: Hogarth Press, 1963, p. 376.

32 Sigmund Freud, 'Femininity' in *New Introductory Lectures on Psychoanalysis*, ed. and trans. James Strachey, Pelican Freud Library, vol. II, Harmondsworth: Penguin Books, 1973, p. 169.

33 See Werner Hofmann, 'Gustav Klimt' in *Vienne 1880–1938: L'Apocalypse joyeuse*, ed. Jean Clair, exh. cat., Paris: Éditions du Centre Pompidou, 1986, pp. 192–202; and Jean-Paul Bouillon, *Klimt: Beethoven, The Frieze for the Ninth Symphony*, Lausanne: Skira, 1987. Note that Schiele and Klimt did not survive the end of the war; only Kokoschka lived to see the Austrian government overthrown once more, by Hitler in 1938. Kokoschka spent the remainder of his very long life in exile, first in Czechoslovakia, then in England, and finally in Switzerland.

34 Oskar Kokoschka and Egon Schiele were supported by Klimt. Indeed, Klimt introduced Schiele to the Vienna Workshop and to the Lederer family, who would become important patrons for the young artist.

35 See Arthur Roessler, *Egon Schiele en prison* (1922), Lyon: La Fosse aux Ours, 2000.

36 Kirk Varnedoe in *Vienna 1900*, exh. cat., New York: Museum of Modern Art, 1986, quoted in Jill Lloyd, 'L'Expressionisme Autrichien' in *La Verité nue: Gerstl, Kokoschka, Schiele, Boeckl*, exh. cat., Paris: Fondation Dina Vierny-Musée Maillol, 2001, pp. 21–37, and in trans. pp. v–xv, p. xii.

Chapter 4: The Erotic Body between the Wars

1 Henri de Saint-Simon, *Literary, Philosophical and Industrial Opinion* (1825), excerpt in *Art in Theory 1815–1900: An Anthology of Changing Ideas*, eds. Charles Harrison and Paul Woods, Oxford: Blackwell, 1998, p. 40.

2 Gabriel-Désiré Laverdant, *De la Mission de l'art et du rôle des artistes*, Paris, 1845, cited in Renato Poggioli, *The Theory of the Avant-Garde* (1962), trans. Gerald Fitzgerald, Cambridge MA: Harvard University Press, 1968, p. 9.

3 See Peter Bürger, *Theory of the Avant-Garde* (1974), trans. Michael Shaw, foreword by Jochen Schulte-Sasse, Minneapolis MN: University of Minnesota Press, 1984, p. 54.

4 Suzanne Pagé et al., *Francis Picabia: Singulier idéal*, exh. cat., Paris: Musée d'Art Moderne de la Ville de Paris, 2002, p. 214.

5 See *Picabia et la Côte d'Azur*, exh. cat., Nice: Musée d'Art Moderne et d'Art Contemporain, 1991, and Sara Cochran, 'La Peinture de Francis Picabia pendant la Seconde Guerre Mondiale', *Art Press*, no. 222, 1997, pp. 48–9.

6 Man Ray, *Self Portrait* (1986), with afterword by Juliet Man Ray and foreword by Merry A. Foresta, Boston MA: Bullfinch Press, 1998, p. 26.

7 Volume 2 of *Studies in the Psychology of Sex* by Henry Havelock Ellis (1859–1939), devoted to *Sexual Inversion*, was published in England in 1897 but the bookseller who sold it, George Bedborough, was prosecuted and the *Studies* deemed obscene by a British judge. The subsequent volumes were published in America. *Sexual Inversion* documented the cases of 80 homosexuals without presenting homosexuality as a perversion or crime.

8 See Anne McCauley, 'Alfred Stieglitz et le nu féminin', *4814 La revue du Musée d'Orsay*, no. 19,

Autumn 2004, pp. 78–92. McCauley documents how Stieglitz had procured the six volumes of Henry Havelock Ellis's *Studies in the Psychology of Sex* in 1911 and that a letter of his from October 1911 specifically refers to Ellis's *The Evolution of Modesty*, volume 1.

9 Marcel Duchamp, in Pierre Cabanne, *Dialogues with Marcel Duchamp* (1967), trans. Ron Padgett, New York: Da Capo Press, 1987, p. 88.

10 F. T. Marinetti, Futurist 'Founding Manifesto' (1909) in *Art in Theory 1900–1990: An Anthology of Changing Ideas*, eds. Charles Harrison and Paul Wood, Oxford: Blackwell, 1992, pp. 145–9, p. 147.

11 This is Calvin Tomkins's term. See Tomkins, *Duchamp: A Biography*, London: Chatto and Windus, 1997, and *The Bride and the Bachelors*, New York: Penguin Books, 1965. See also David Hopkins's analysis of Catholicism in Duchamp in his study *Marcel Duchamp and Max Ernst: The Bride Shared*, Oxford: Clarendon Press, 1998.

12 See Marcel Duchamp, *Notes and Projects for the Large Glass*, ed. Arturo Schwarz, London: Thames & Hudson, 1969.

13 André Breton, 'Phare de la Mariée' (Lighthouse of the Bride), *Minotaure*, no. 6, Winter 1935, pp. 45–9, p. 48 ('une interprétation mécaniste, cynique, du phénomène amoureux').

14 Jean Clair, *Sur Marcel Duchamp et la fin de l'art*, Paris: Gallimard, 2000. This should be contrasted with Thierry de Duve, *Kant after Duchamp*, Cambridge MA and London: MIT Press, 1999, in which de Duve argues that Duchamp's attack on art and 'retinal pleasure' may be understood as an attack on the Enlightenment equation of art with beauty.

15 In this way Rrose Sélavy is comparable to Monique Lerbier, the heroine of Victor Margueritte's bestselling novel devoted to the new flapper, *La Garçonne* (1922).

16 Hugo Bettauer, 'The Erotic Revolution' (Die erotische Revolution), *Er und Sie I* (1924), reproduced in *The Weimar Republic Sourcebook*, eds. Anton Kaes, Martin Jay, and Edward Dimendberg, Berkeley, Los Angeles, and London: University of California Press, 1994, pp. 698–700, p. 700.

17 George Grosz, autobiographical essay of 1928 cited in Beth Irwin Lewis, *George Grosz: Art and Politics in the Weimar Republic*, 2nd edn, Princeton NJ: Princeton University Press, 1991, p. 66. See also Frank Whitford, 'The Many Faces of George Grosz' in *The Berlin of George Grosz: Drawings, Watercolours and Prints, 1912–1930*, exh. cat., London: Royal Academy of Arts, 1997, pp. 1–27, p. 6.

18 Kaes et al., *The Weimar Republic Sourcebook*, p. 641.

19 Maud Lavin, *Cut with the Kitchen Knife: The Weimar Photomontages of Hannah Höch*, New Haven CT and London: Yale University Press, 1993, p. 202.

20 Ibid., p. 186.

21 The association of fascism with fantasy was most notably articulated by Klaus Theweleit in his influential study *Male Fantasies, Vol. I: Women, Floods, Bodies, History* (1977), trans. Stephen Conway, Erica Carter, and Chris Turner, Minneapolis MN: University of Minnesota Press, 1987. See also Susan Sontag on the eroticization of fascism in 'Fascinating Fascism' in *Under the Sign of Saturn*, New York: Farrar, Straus, Giroux, 1980, pp. 73–105.

22 Walter Benjamin famously alerted the public to the phenomenon of 'the aestheticization of politics and the politicization of aesthetics' in his 1936 essay 'The Work of Art in the Age of Mechanical Reproduction', reproduced in Walter Benjamin, *Illuminations*, trans. Harry Zohn, ed. and introduction by Hannah Arendt, London: Jonathan Cape, 1970, pp. 219–53.

23 In his own vision of the Superman, Mussolini was influenced by the writings of the German philosopher Friedrich Nietzsche (1844–1900) who wrote of the death of God but also the god-like potential of man, most notably in *The Gay Science* (1882).

24 Gigliola Gori, 'Model of Masculinity: Mussolini, the "New Italian" of the Fascist Era' in *Superman Supreme: Fascist Body as Political Icon—Global Fascism*, ed. J. A. Mangan, London: Frank Cass, 2000, pp. 27–61, p. 49, and footnote 87, p. 60.

25 Though this law was abandoned in 1938. See Jonathan Petropoulos, *Art as Politics in the Third Reich*, Chapel Hill NC: University of North Carolina Press, 1996, p. 72.

26 Peter Adam, *Art of the Third Reich*, New York: Harry N. Abrams, 1995, p. 116.

27 See Stephanie Barron et al., *'Degenerate Art': The Fate of the Avant-Garde in Nazi Germany*, Los Angeles: Los Angeles County Museum of Art, exh. cat., 1991.

Chapter 5: Surrealism's Erotic Politics

1 On the life of Bellmer, see Peter Webb and Robert Short, *Hans Bellmer*, New York: Quartet Books, 1985, and Pierre Dourthe, *Bellmer: Le*

Principe de perversion, Paris: Jean-Pierre Faur, 1999.

2 Bellmer, interview with Peter Webb, Paris, 15 January 1972, in Peter Webb, *The Erotic Arts*, Appendix III, London: Secker and Warburg, 1983, pp. 366–70, p. 370.

3 André Breton, interview with Charles-Henri Ford, *View*, nos. 7–8, Surrealist Number, October–November 1941; reproduced in André Breton, *What Is Surrealism? Selected Writings*, ed. Franklin Rosemont, New York: Monad Press, 1978, pp. 263–72, p. 266.

4 See *Investigating Sex: Surrealist Discussion 1928–1932*, trans. Malcolm Imrie, ed. José Pierre, and afterword by Dawn Ades, London and New York: Verso, 1992.

5 André Breton, 'First Surrealist Manifesto' in *Manifestoes of Surrealism*, trans. Richard Seaver and Helen R. Lane, Ann Arbor MI: University of Michigan Press (1969), 1972 edn, pp. 1–47, p. 26.

6 André Breton, 'Surrealism and Painting' (1928) in *Surrealism and Painting*, trans. Simon Watson-Taylor, Boston MA: MFA Publications, 2002, pp. 1–48, p. 36.

7 René Magritte, *Écrits complets*, ed. André Blavier, Paris: Flammarion, 2001, no. 194, p. 636.

8 Ian Gibson, *The Shameful Life of Salvador Dalí*, London: Faber and Faber, 1997, p. 46.

9 Georges Bataille, 'The Lugubrious Game', originally published as 'Le Jeu Lugubre' in *Documents*, no. 7, Paris, December 1929, reproduced in edited form in *Art in Theory 1900–1990: An Anthology of Changing Ideas*, eds. Charles Harrison and Paul Wood, Oxford: Blackwell, 1992, pp. 476–8, p. 478.

10 Breton, *Manifestoes of Surrealism*, p. 186.

11 Robert Desnos, *Liberty or Love!* (1927), trans. and introduction by Terry Hale, London: Atlas Press, 1993, p. 123.

12 Maurice Blanchot, *Lautréamont et Sade* (Paris: Minuit, 1949), cited in translation in Georges Bataille, 'The Meaning of Eroticism' (1957; first published in *Revue de la Bibliothèque Nationale*, no. 17, Fall 1985) in *Erotic Art from the Seventeenth Century to the Twentieth Century*, ed. Peter Weiermair, exh. cat., Frankfurt: Frankfurter Kunstverein and Edition Stemmle, 1995, pp. 10–12, p. 12.

13 For a psychoanalytic reading of the film see Linda Williams, *Figures of Desire: A Theory and Analysis of Surrealist Film*, Berkeley CA and Oxford: University of California Press, 1992. For a thorough history and analysis of the relationship between Dalí and Buñuel see Robert Short, *The Age of Gold: Surrealist Cinema*, New York: Creation Books, 2003.

14 This synopsis does not fully do justice to the film's symbolism and *mise-en-scène*. For a closer analysis of this film see Allen S. Weiss's excellent essay, 'Between the Sign of the Scorpion and the Sign of the Cross: *L'Age d'or*' in *Dada and Surrealist Film*, ed. R. Kuenzli, Cambridge MA and London: MIT Press, 1987, pp. 159–75.

15 Of course while Magritte repeatedly rejected psychoanalytic readings of his art, in *The Interpretation of Dreams* Freud wrote of the representation of the genitals by other parts of the body in the dream state. As Jack Spector points out, in 1906 Freud referred to the idea often represented by cartoonists of a violin as a woman and violin bow as a penis, and in *Totem and Taboo* refers to this French expression for onanism, *jouer au violon*. See Jack Spector, *The Aesthetics of Freud*, London: Allen Lane, 1972, p. 174.

16 André Breton et al., *Violette Nozières*, Brussels: Editions Nicolas Flamel, 1933, reprinted with preface by José Pierre, Paris: Terrain Vague, 1991.

17 Antonin Artaud, *La Nouvelle Revue Française*, May 1934, cited in Gilles Néret, *Balthus*, Taschen 2003, p. 7. Here Artaud was referring specifically to Balthus's painting *Alice* (1933). Balthus met the writer, actor, and artist Artaud in 1934 and the following year designed the set and costumes for Artaud's adaptation from Shelley and Stendhal, *Les Cenci*.

18 Ivan Goll, 'The Negroes Are Conquering Europe' (Die Neger erobern Europa), *Die literarische Welt*, no. 2, 15 January 1926, pp. 3–4, reproduced in *The Weimar Republic Sourcebook*, eds. Anton Kaes, Martin Jay, and Edward Dimendberg, Berkeley, Los Angeles, and London: University of California Press, 1994, pp. 559–60, p. 559.

19 Mary Ann Caws, *The Surrealist Look: An Erotics of Encounter*, Cambridge MA and London: MIT Press, 1997, p. 130.

20 Rosalind Krauss, 'Photography in the Service of Surrealism', in Krauss and Jane Livingston, *L'Amour Fou: Photography and Surrealism*, London: Arts Council of Great Britain, 1986, pp. 15–54.

21 Meret Oppenheim in Robert J. Belton, 'Androgyny: Interview with Meret Oppenheim' in *Surrealism and Women*, eds. Mary Ann Caws,

Rudolf E. Kuenzli, and Gwen Raaberg, Cambridge MA and London: MIT Press (1991), 1993 edn, pp. 63–75, p. 69.

22 André Breton in 7th Session (6 May 1928), in *Investigating Sex*, p. 105.

23 Xavière Gauthier, *Surréalisme et sexualité*, Paris: Gallimard, 1971, paved the way in the critical reconsideration of male Surrealists' attitude to and frequent objectification of woman; Whitney Chadwick, *Women Artists and the Surrealist Movement*, London: Thames and Hudson, 1985, began the important task of documenting the role of women Surrealists and their stance on Breton's Surrealism as well as such themes as desire.

24 Bohuslav Brouk in Vítězslav Nezval and Jindřich Štyrský, *Edition 69*, trans. Jed Slast, Prague: Twisted Spoon Press, 2004, p. 119. Brouk (1912–78) was another member of the Czech Surrealist group; his writings included *Autosexualismus a psychoerotismus*, published by Edice Surrealismus in 1935.

25 For more on the relationship between Carrington and Ernst see Susan Rubin Suleiman, 'Leonora Carrington and Max Ernst' in *Significant Others: Creativity and Intimate Partnership*, eds. Whitney Chadwick and Isabelle de Courtivron, London: Thames and Hudson, 1993, pp. 97–117.

26 Leonora Carrington, 'The Debutante', in *The House of Fear: Notes from Down Below*, trans. Katharine Talbot and Marina Warner, London: Virago, 1989, pp. 44–8.

27 Leonora Carrington, 'Oval Lady' in *The House of Fear: Notes from Down Below*, trans. Katharine Talbot and Marina Warner, London: Virago, 1989, pp. 37–43, p. 43.

28 See Rosalind Krauss, *Bachelors*, Cambridge MA and London: MIT Press, 1999, p. 42. For the most thorough introduction to Cahun's life see François Leperlier, *Claude Cahun: L'Écart et la métamorphose*, Paris: Éditions Jean Michel Place, 1992.

29 Joan Riviere, 'Womanliness as a Masquerade', *International Journal of Psycho-analysis* (1929) reprinted in *The Inner World and Joan Riviere: Collected Papers, 1920–1958*, London: Karnac Books, 1991, pp. 90–101, p. 94.

30 Claude Cahun, *Écrits*, ed. François Leperlier, Paris: Éditions Jean-Michel Place, 2002, p. 366.

31 For a reading of Cahun and her 'heroines' see Katharine Conley, 'Claude Cahun's Iconic Heads: From "The Sadistic Judith" to *Human Frontier*', *Papers of Surrealism*, Issue 2, Summer 2004, http://www.surrealismcentre.ac.uk/publications/papers/journal2/. For a reading of Cahun's self-portraits in lesbian terms, see also Abigail Solomon-Godeau's 'The Equivocal "I": Claude Cahun as Lesbian Subject' in *Inverted Odysseys*, ed. Shelley Rice, Cambridge MA: MIT Press, 1999, pp. 111–25.

Chapter 6: Erotic Art in Wartime and After

1 See Varian Fry, *Surrender on Demand*, Boulder CO: Johnson Books in conjunction with the United States Holocaust Memorial Museum, 1997.

2 See Anna C. Chave, 'O'Keeffe and the Masculine Gaze' in *Reading American Art*, eds. Marianne Doezema and Elizabeth Milroy, New Haven CT: Yale University Press, 1998, pp. 350–70.

3 Georgia O'Keeffe in Lucy R. Lippard, 'Fragments' in *From the Centre: Feminist Essays on Women's Art*, New York: Dutton, 1976, p. 71.

4 For an analysis of the dispute between Benton and Davis that followed Davis's accusation, see chapter four of Susan Platt, *Art and Politics in the 1930s: Modernism—Marxism—Americanism. A History of Cultural Activism during the Depression Years*, New York: Midmarch Arts Press, 1999.

5 Indeed, it was in 1934 that the term Regionalist was developed and promoted by the New York art dealer Maynard Walker, whose efforts then inspired Henry Luce to write a feature on it for *Time* magazine. The other two Regionalists praised were Grant Wood and John Steuart Curry. See Henry Adams, *Thomas Hart Benton: An American Original*, New York: Alfred A. Knopf, 1989, p. 216.

6 Mike Davis, 'Bunker Hill: Hollywood's Dark Shadow' in *Cinema and the City: Film and Urban Societies in a Global Context*, eds. Mark Shiel and Tony Fitzmaurice, Oxford: Blackwell Publishers, 2001, pp. 33–45, p. 38.

7 Richard Meyer, *Outlaw Representation. Censorship and Homosexuality in Twentieth-Century American Art*, Boston MA: Beacon Press, 2004, p. 40.

8 Ibid., p. 93.

9 Robb Baker, 'The Trials of Lucifer: An Interview with Kenneth Anger', *Soho Weekly News*, 28 October 1976, p. 16.

10 Clement Greenberg, 'Surrealist Painting', *Nation*, 12 and 19 August 1944, reprinted in *Clement Greenberg: The Collected Essays and*

Criticism, vol. I: Perceptions and Judgements 1939–1944, ed. John O'Brian, Chicago: University of Chicago Press, 1986, pp. 225–31, p. 229.

11 Salvador Dalí, 'Declaration of the Independence of the Imagination and the Rights of Man to His Own Madness', distributed as a leaflet and reprinted in Julien Levy, *Memoir of an Art Gallery*, New York: Putnam's, 1977, pp. 219–22.

12 *Time*, 26 June 1929, p. 10, cited in Ingrid Schaffner, with photographs by Eric Schaal, *Salvador Dalí's Dream of Venus: The Surrealist Funhouse from the 1939 World's Fair*, New York: Princeton Architectural Press, 2002, p. 136.

13 'Declaration VVV' (trans. unknown), reproduced in André Breton, *What Is Surrealism? Selected Writings*, ed. Franklin Rosemont, New York: Monad Press, 1978, pp. 337–8. This declaration appeared on the title page of each of the three issues of *VVV*.

14 André Breton, interview with Charles-Henri Ford, *View*, nos. 7–8, Surrealist Number, October–November 1941; reproduced in Breton, *What Is Surrealism?* pp. 263–72, p. 266.

15 Whitney Chadwick, *Women Artists and the Surrealist Movement*, London: Thames and Hudson, 1985, p. 93.

16 *10 Recent Paintings and a Biography*, exh. cat., New York: Gimpel-Weitzenhoffer Gallery, 1979, n.p., cited in Chadwick, *Women Artists*, p. 138.

17 On New York's appropriation of modern art from Paris see Serge Guilbaut, *How New York Stole the Idea of Modern Art: Abstract Expression, Freedom, and the Cold War*, trans. Arthur Goldhammer, Chicago: University of Chicago Press, 1985.

18 Norman Mailer, quoted in John Montgomery, *The Fifties*, London: Allen and Unwin, 1965, title page.

19 See Robert Rosenblum, 'American Painting since the Second World War' (first published as 'La Peinture américaine depuis la seconde guerre mondiale' in *Aujourd'hui: Art et architecture*, vol. 3, no. 18, July 1958, pp. 12–18), reproduced in English in *On Modern American Art, Selected Essays*, New York: Harry N. Abrams, 1999, pp. 62–71.

20 Harold Rosenberg, 'The American Action Painters' (1952), *The Tradition of the New*, Chicago and London: University of Chicago Press, 1960, pp. 26–7.

21 Clement Greenberg, 'Byzantine Parallels', reprinted in *Art and Culture: Critical Essays*, Boston MA: Beacon Press, 1961, pp. 167–70, p. 169.

22 Clement Greenberg, '"American-Type" Painting', *Partisan Review* (1955), reprinted in *Art and Culture*, pp. 208–29, p. 211.

23 Lisa Phillips, *The American Century: Art and Culture 1950–2000*, exh. cat., New York: Whitney Museum of American Art and W. W. Norton and Company, p. 36. For an analysis of the Right's and Dondero's attack on Abstract Expressionism see William Hauptman, 'The Supression of Art in the McCarthy Decade', *Artforum*, vol. 12, no. 2, October 1973, pp. 48–52.

24 Herbert Marcuse, *Eros and Civilization: A Philosophical Inquiry into Freud* (1956), London: Routledge, 1998, pp. 144 and 185 respectively.

25 When City Lights Bookshop, San Francisco, published Ginsberg's *Howl and Other Poems* (1956), an obscenity charge was issued against the publisher, fellow poet Lawrence Ferlinghetti. The highly publicized trial in 1957 resulted in his acquittal, however.

26 Alfred Kinsey, *Sexual Behavior in the Human Female*, Philadelphia PA: Saunders, 1953, pp. 287, 315, and 239, and Alfred Kinsey, Wardell B. Pomeroy, and Clyde E. Martin, *Sexual Behavior in the Human Male*, Philadelphia PA: Saunders, 1948, p. 625, cited in Beth Bailey, 'Sexual Revolution(s)' in *The Sixties: From Memory to History*, ed. David Farber, Chapel Hill NC and London: University of North Carolina Press, 1994, pp. 235–62, pp. 236–7.

27 See Vern L. Bullough, 'Alfred Kinsey and the Kinsey Report: Historical Overview and Lasting Contributions', *Journal of Sex Research*, vol. 35, no. 2, 1998, pp. 127–31.

28 'Playboy Panel', *Playboy*, June 1962, pp. 43–4, cited in Bailey, 'Sexual Revolution(s)', p. 247.

29 Francis Ponge, *Note sur Les Otages*, Paris 1946, p. 25, cited in translation in Sarah Wilson, 'Paris Post War: In Search of the Absolute' in *Paris Post War: Art and Existentialism 1945–55*, ed. Frances Morris, exh. cat., London: Tate Gallery, 1993, pp. 25–52, p. 27.

30 Jean-Paul Sartre, 'The Quest for the Absolute' in *Essays in Existentialism*, ed. and foreword by Wade Baskin, New York: Citadel Press, 1993, pp. 388–401. It should be noted that Giacometti himself did not use the word 'existentialist' when discussing his art, he simply claimed his primary concern was to capture as accurately as possible what he saw.

31 Jean-Paul Sartre, 'The Paintings of Giacometti'

in *Essays in Existentialism*, pp. 402–18, p. 404.

32 Alberto Giacometti, 'The Dream, The Sphinx and the Death of T.', *Labyrinthe*, December 1946, cited in Patrick Elliott, 'Alberto Giacometti: An Introduction' in Toni Stoos and Patrick Elliott, *Alberto Giacometti, 1901–1966*, exh. cat., Vienna: Kunsthalle and Edinburgh: National Galleries of Scotland, 1996, pp. 11–25, p. 21.

33 Gilles Deleuze, 'Pierre Klossowski ou les corps-langage', *Critique*, no. 214, March 1965, pp. 199–219, p. 200. See also Alyce Mahon, 'Pierre Klossowski, Theo-Pornologer', critical introduction to *Pierre Klossowski: Decadence of the Nude/La Décadence du nu*, ed. Sarah Wilson, London: Black Dog Publishing, Revisions Series, 2002, pp. 33–101.

34 Pierre Klossowski, 'Aux limites de l'indiscrétion', interview with Jean-Maurice Monnoyer, *La Nouvelle Revue française*, no. 325, 1 February 1980, pp. 70–86, pp. 72 and 75 respectively.

35 For a detailed analysis of the EROS exhibition see chapter four of Alyce Mahon, *Surrealism and the Politics of Eros 1938–1968*, London: Thames and Hudson, 2005.

36 Yves Klein, 'Due to the Fact That' (1961), cited in Nan Rosenthal, 'Assisted Levitation: The Art of Yves Klein' in *Yves Klein 1928–1962, A Retrospective*, Houston: Institute of the Arts, Rice University, 1982, p. 124.

37 Yves Klein, 'Quelques extraits de mon journal en 1957' in *Yves Klein*, exh. cat., Paris: Musée des Arts Décoratifs, 1969, p. 75, cited in Sidra Stich, *Yves Klein*, exh. cat., London: Hayward Gallery and Cantz, 1995, p. 180. Stich makes the analogy with St Veronica's veil on p. 179.

Chapter 7: Eros and the 1960s

1 Helen Gurley Brown, *Sex and the Single Girl*, New York: Bernard Geis Associates, 1962, p. 2, cited in Beth Bailey, 'Sexual Revolution(s)' in *The Sixties: From Memory to History*, ed. David Farber, Chapel Hill NC and London: University of North Carolina Press, 1994, pp. 235–62, p. 249.

2 Claes Oldenburg, 'I Am for an Art . . .', first published in exhibition catalogue, *Environments, Situations and Spaces*, Martha Jackson Gallery, May–June 1961. This statement was revised and republished in *Oldenburg*, exh. cat., London: Arts Council of Great Britain, 1970, published in *Art in Theory 1900–1990*, eds. Charles Harrison and Paul Wood, Oxford: Blackwell, 1992, pp. 728–30, p. 728.

3 Kirk Varnedoe and Adam Gopnik, *High and Low: Modern Art and Popular Culture*, exh. cat., New York: Museum of Modern Art, 1991, p. 199.

4 Peter Selz, 'Variety: Pop Goes the Artist', *Partisan Review*, Summer 1963, pp. 314–16.

5 Sidra Stich, *Made in USA: An Americanization in Modern Art, the '50s & '60s*, Berkeley and Los Angeles CA: University of California Press, 1987, pp. 30–1.

6 See Cécile Whiting, *A Taste for Pop: Pop Art, Gender and Consumer Culture*, Cambridge 1997, pp. 72–8, quotes from p. 78.

7 Of course *Playgirl* is the title of the soft-porn magazine for women launched in 1973.

8 Tom Wesselmann, interview cited in G. R. Swenson, 'What Is Pop Art?', *ArtNews*, February 1964, pp. 40–1, p. 41.

9 See Stich, *Made in USA*, pp. 151–2, and Thomas Albright, *Art in the San Francisco Bay Area, 1945–1980*, Berkeley: University of California Press, 1985, p. 131.

10 Jay Jacobs, 'In the Galleries: Mel Ramos', *Arts*, January 1966, p. 56, reproduced in *Pop Art: A Critical History*, ed. Steven Henry Madoff, Berkeley and Los Angeles CA: University of California Press, 1997, p. 324.

11 Mel Ramos, *The Girls of Mel Ramos*, Chicago: Playboy Press and New York: Simon and Schuster, 1975, p. 142.

12 Mel Ramos and Carl Belz, December 1979 interview, in *Mel Ramos, A Twenty-Year Survey*, exh. cat., Waltham MA: Rose Art Museum, Brandeis University, 1980, p. 24.

13 Donald Judd, 'In the Galleries: Claes Oldenburg', *Arts*, Sept 1964, p. 63, reproduced in *Pop Art*, ed. Madoff, p. 225.

14 Stich, *Made in USA*, p. 202. For more on *Lipstick (Ascending) on Caterpillar Tracks*, see Susan P. Casteras, *The "Lipstick" Comes Back*, exh. cat., New Haven CT: Yale University Art Gallery, 1974.

15 Andrew Forge, 'Forces against Object-Based Art', *Studio International*, January 1971, p. 33, cited in Irving Sandler, *American Art of the 1960s*, New York: Harper and Row, 1988, p. 187.

16 Others paid homage to Monroe too, notably James Rosenquist in *Marilyn Monroe I* (1962) and Willem de Kooning in *Marilyn Monroe* (1954).

17 Hal Foster, *The Return of the Real*, Cambridge MA: MIT Press, 1996, pp. 127–36.

18 Thomas Crow, *Modern Art in the Common*

Culture, New Haven CT: Yale University Press, 1996, p. 63.

19 Andy Warhol, *The Philosophy of Andy Warhol (From A to B and Back Again)*, New York: Harcourt Brace and Company, 1975, p. 45.

20 Peter Wollen, 'Little Stabs at Happiness', *Frieze*, issue 16, May 1994, p. 44.

21 The landscape consists of a manipulated photograph taken when Duchamp was holidaying at Chexbres on Lake Léman in Switzerland in 1946. See Dawn Ades, Neil Cox, and David Hopkins, *Marcel Duchamp*, London: Thames and Hudson, 1999, p. 193. See also Anne d'Harnoncourt and Walter Hopps, '*Étant donnés: 1. La chute d'eau 2. Le gaz d'éclairage*: Reflections on a New Work by Marcel Duchamp', *Philadelphia Museum of Art Bulletin*, vol. 64, nos. 299–300, Spring/Summer 1969.

22 Lucy Lippard, cited in Alexandra Munroe, 'Obsession, Fantasy and Outrage: The Art of Yayoi Kusama' in *Yayoi Kusama: A Retrospective*, ed. Bhupendra Karia, exh. cat., New York: Center for International Contemporary Arts, 1989, pp. 11–35, p. 25.

23 Lynn Zelevansky, 'Dricing Image: Yayoi Kusama in New York' in Zelevansky et al., *Love Forever: Yayoi Kusama, 1958–1968*, exh. cat., Los Angeles: Los Angeles County Museum of Art, 1998, pp. 11–41, p. 30.

24 Other artists who were producing Happenings in the United States too but simply did not use this generic term were Claes Oldenburg and his 'Ray Gun Theater' and Ken Dewey and his 'Action Theater'.

25 See Allan Kaprow, *Assemblages, Environments & Happenings*, New York: H. N. Abrams, 1966.

26 Jonas Mekas, 'Movie Journal' in *The Village Voice*, 1 September 1966, in *Jean-Jacques Lebel, retour d'exil: Peintures, dessins, collages 1954–1988*, exh. cat., Paris: Galerie 1900–2000, 1988, p. 73.

27 Ibid.

28 *La Religieuse* (1966) was based on Diderot's eighteenth-century classical tale of a young girl forced to join a convent against her will. It was banned primarily because of the objections of the Catholic Church.

29 Jean-Jacques Lebel and Arnaud Labelle-Rojoux, *Poésie directe, des happenings à polyphonix*, Paris: Opus International Edition, 1994, p. 76.

30 For a detailed analysis of this Happening and its reception see Alyce Mahon, 'Outrage aux bonnes mœurs: Jean-Jacques Lebel and the Marquis de Sade' in *Jean-Jacques Lebel: Paintings, Sculptures, Installations*, eds. Uli Todoroff and Sophie Haaser, exh. cat., Vienna: Museum Moderner Kunst Stiftung Ludwig Wien, 1998, pp. 93–112.

31 Catherine Millet, 'Jean-Jacques Lebel, oppositionnel', *Art Press*, May 1996, no. 213, pp. 20–7, p. 22.

32 Carolee Schneemann, 'Meat Joy', *Imaging Her Erotics: Essays, Interviews, Projects*, Cambridge MA: MIT Press, 2002, pp. 61–2, p. 61.

33 Carolee Schneemann, interview with Kate Huag (1977) in Schneemann, *Imaging Her Erotics*, pp. 21–44, p. 21. On the censorship of *Fuses* at the Moscow Film Festival in 1989, see also Aviva Rahmani, 'A Conversation on Censorship with Carolee Schneemann', *M/E/A/N/I/N/G*, no. 6, 1989, pp. 3–7, reproduced in *Feminism—Art—Theory: An Anthology 1968–2000*, ed. Hilary Robinson, Oxford: Blackwell, 2001, pp. 147–52.

34 Schneemann, interview with Kate Huag in *Imaging Her Erotics*, p. 27.

35 Yoko Ono, 'To the Wesleyan People (Who Attended the Meeting)' in *The Stone*, exh. cat., New York: Judson Gallery, 1966, reprinted in Yoko Ono, *Grapefruit*, New York: Simon and Schuster, 1970, unpaginated.

36 Yoko Ono states this fact herself in 'What Is the Relationship between the Artist and the World?', written for the Cannes Film Festival, 1971, reprinted in Barbara Haskell and John G. Hanhardt, *Yoko Ono: Arias and Objects*, Salt Lake City UT: Peregrine Smith Books, 1991, p. 109.

37 See also Julia Bryan-Wilson's insightful essay 'Remembering Yoko Ono's *Cut Piece*', *Oxford Art Journal*, vol. 26, no. 1, 2003, pp. 99–123.

38 John Sinclair in the *Sun* underground newspaper of March 1968, reproduced in Sinclair, *Guitar Army: Street Writings/Prison Writings*, New York: Douglas, 1972, p.69, quoted in Bailey, 'Sexual Revolution(s)', p. 256.

Chapter 8: Visual Pleasure and Identity Politics

1 Jean-François Lyotard, *The Postmodern Condition*, Manchester: Manchester University Press, 1984.

2 Frederic Jameson, 'Postmodernism, or the Cultural Logic of Late Capitalism', *New Left Review*, no. 146, July–August 1984, pp. 53–92.

3 Frederic Jameson, 'Postmodernism and Consumer Society' in *Postmodern Culture*, ed. Hal Foster, London: Pluto Press, 1985, pp. 111–25, p. 124.

4 Sigmund Freud, *On Sexuality: Three Essays on the History of Sexuality and Other Works*, The Pelican Freud Library, vol. VII, Harmondsworth: Penguin, 1977, p. 69.
5 Ibid., p. 70.
6 Laura Mulvey, 'Visual Pleasure and Narrative Cinema', *Screen*, vol. 16, no. 3, Autumn 1975, pp. 6–18.
7 Alice Neel, untitled and undated typescript, Neel Archives, Neel Arts, New York, cited in Ann Temkin, 'Alice Neel: Self and Others' in *Alice Neel*, ed. Temkin, exh. cat., New York: Whitney Museum of American Art, 2000, pp. 13–31, p. 13.
8 Kim Levin, 'Reviews and Previews: Alice Neel', *ArtNews*, vol. 62, no. 6, October 1963, p. 11.
9 Linda Nochlin, 'Why Have There Been No Great Women Artists?', *ArtNews*, vol. 69, no. 9, January 1971, pp. 22–39, 67–71; reprinted in Nochlin, *Women, Art and Power and Other Essays*, London: Thames and Hudson, 1989, pp. 145–78.
10 Linda Nochlin, 'Pornography as a Decorative Art', introduction to Joyce Kozloff, *Patterns of Desire*, exh. cat., New York: Hudson Hills Press, 1990, p. 11.
11 Lynda Benglis, quoted by Susan Keane, *Lynda Benglis: Dual Natures*, exh. cat., Atlanta GA: High Museum of Art, 1991.
12 Miriam Schapiro and Judy Chicago, 'Female Imagery', *Womanspace Journal*, no. 1, Summer 1973, pp. 11–14, cited in *The Power of Feminist Art: The American Movement of the 1970s, History and Impact*, eds. Norma Broude and Mary D. Garrard, New York: Harry N. Abrams, 1994, p. 23.
13 Judy Chicago was born Judy Cohen. In 1971 she changed her name to the nickname her Los Angeles dealer, Rolf Nelson, had given her due to her accent. Her name change allowed her to cast off her married name under which she had been exhibiting (Gerowitz).
14 Judy Chicago, interview with Broude and Garrard, *The Power of Feminist Art*, p. 71.
15 Judy Chicago, *Through the Flower: My Struggle as a Woman Artist*, New York: Anchor/Doubleday Books, 1975, p. 142.
16 Judy Chicago, *The Dinner Party*, New York: Anchor Books, 1979, p. 53.
17 Judy Chicago, statement in *Artforum*, September 1974, quoted in *The Power of Feminist Art*, eds. Broude and Garrard, p. 22.
18 Lucy Lippard, cited in ibid.
19 Carolee Schneemann, 'Interior Scroll' (1975) in Carolee Schneemann, *Imaging Her Erotics: Essays, Interviews, Projects*, Cambridge MA: MIT Press, 2002, pp. 153–5, p. 153.
20 Many of the quotes, including these phrases, were from Schneemann's *Kitch's Last Meal*, a super-8 mm film of 1975.
21 Schneemann, 'Interior Scroll', p. 154.
22 Hannah Wilke, cited in Susan Paul, 'The Just Desserts: "Dinner Party", Now Closed, Draws Praise and Attack', *The Phoenix*, 12 February 1981, p. 19, cited in Amelia Jones, 'Sexual Politics: Feminist Strategies, Feminist Conflicts, Feminist Histories' in *Sexual Politics: Judy Chicago's Dinner Party in Feminist Art History*, ed. Jones, Berkeley CA: UCLA and the Hammer Museum of Art in association with University of California Press, 1996,footnote 9, p. 38.
23 Lowery Sims, 'Hannah Wilke: The Body Politic of the Adventures of a Good-Looking Feminist' in Benjamin H. D. Buchloh et al., *Art and Ideology*, exh. cat., New York: The New Museum of Contemporary Art, 1984, p. 48.
24 Hannah Wilke, 'Intercourse with . . .', text used in videotape performance and lecture at the London Art Gallery, London, Ontario, Canada, 17 February 1977; reproduced in *Hannah Wilke, A Retrospective*, ed. Thomas H. Kochheiser, Columbia MO and London: University of Missouri Press, 1989, p. 140.
25 Joanna Frueh makes this suggestion in *Hannah Wilke, A Retrospective*, p. 20.
26 Hannah Wilke, conversation with Joanna Frueh, New York, June 1988, cited in ibid., p. 35.
27 Louise Bourgeois, 'I Do, I Undo, I Redo', 28 February 2000, in *Louise Bourgeois, Destruction of the Father Reconstruction of the Father: Writings and Interviews 1923–1997*, eds. Marie-Laure Bernadac and Hans-Ulrich Obrist, London: Violette Editions, 2000, p. 368.
28 Susan Sontag, 'Notes on "Camp"' (*Partisan Review*, 1964) in *Against Interpretation*, London: André Deutsch, 1987, pp. 275–92, p. 280.
29 Robert Mapplethorpe, interview with Parker Hodges, 'Robert Mapplethorpe: Photographer', *Manhattan Gaze*, 10 December 1979 to 6 January 1980, cited in Richard Meyer, *Outlaw Representation: Censorship and Homosexuality in Twentieth-Century American Art*, Boston MA: Beacon Press, 2004, p. 187.
30 Ibid.
31 Peter Schlesinger features in *A Bigger Splash* (Jack Hazan's film on Hockney, begun in the summer of 1971 and released in 1974), notably in a controversial sex scene with the artist.

32 Marco Livingstone, *David Hockney*, London: Thames and Hudson, 1996, p. 43.
33 Richard J. Powell, *Black Art, A Cultural History*, London: Thames and Hudson, World of Art series, 1997 and 2002, 2002 edition, p. 146.
34 Powell, *Black Art*, p. 149.
35 See Susan Krane, *Art on the Edge: Alison Saar/Fertile Ground*, exh. cat., Atlanta GA: High Museum of Art, 1993.
36 Yolanda M. López, interview by Moira Roth, California, 10 July 1993, cited in Yolanda M. López and Moira Roth, 'Social Protest: Racism and Sexism' in *The Power of Feminist Art* eds. Broude and Garrard, pp. 140–57, p. 146.
37 Yolanda López, interview with Lucy Lippard, October 1988, quoted in Lucy Lippard, *Mixed Blessings: New Art in Multicultural America*, New York: Pantheon Books, 1990, p. 42.
38 Andreas Huyssen, 'Mapping the Postmodern' in *After the Great Divide: Modernism, Mass Culture, Postmodernism*, Bloomington IN: Indiana University Press, 1986, p. 185.

Chapter 9: Eroticism and the Culture Wars of the 1980s and 1990s

1 Senator Helms, *Congressional Record*, 18 May 1989, S5595, cited in Richard Meyer, *Outlaw Representation: Censorship and Homosexuality in Twentieth-Century American Art*, Boston MA: Beacon Press, 2004, p. 207.
2 See for example the Guerrilla Girls' critique of Western art and female stereotypes in *The Guerrilla Girls' Bedside Companion to the History of Western Art*, London: Penguin, 1998, and *Bitches, Bimbos and Ballbreakers: The Guerrilla Girls' Illustrated Guide to Female Stereotypes*, London: Penguin, 2003.
3 Christina Orr-Cahall, cited in Patricia Morrisroe, *Mapplethorpe: A Biography*, New York: Random House, 1995, p. 372. Morrisroe gives a full chronology of the 'Perfect Moment' controversy on pp. 371–5.
4 Judith Reisman, cited in ibid., p. 166.
5 Clarissa Dalrymple, cited in ibid., p. 167.
6 Anne Higonet, *Pictures of Innocence: The History and Crisis of Ideal Childhood*, London: Thames and Hudson, 1998, p. 203.
7 Bart Everly, 'Robert Mapplethorpe', *Splash*, April 1988, cited in Arthur C. Danto, *Playing with the Edge: The Photographic Achievement of Robert Mapplethorpe*, Berkeley and Los Angeles CA: University of California Press, 1996, p. 90.
8 Ibid.
9 Roland Barthes, *Camera Lucida*, London: Jonathan Cape, 1982, p. 59.
10 Simon Watney, *Policing Desire: Aids, Pornography and the Media*, London: Comedia, 1987.
11 Leo Bersani, 'Is the Rectum a Grave?' in *AIDS: Cultural Analysis/Cultural Activism*, ed. Douglas Crimp, special issue of *October*, no. 43, Winter 1987, published as a book by MIT Press (Cambridge MA) in 1988, pp. 197–222.
12 See Tina Takemoto, 'The Melancholia of AIDS: Interview with Douglas Crimp', *Art Journal*, Winter 2003, pp. 80–90, p. 93.
13 David Wojnarowicz, unpublished artist's exhibition statement, *David Wojnarowicz: In the Garden*, exh. cat., New York: PPOW Gallery, November 1990 cited in Mysoon Rizk, 'Constructing Histories: David Wojnarowicz's *Arthur Rimbaud in New York*' in *The Passionate Camera: Photography and Bodies of Desire*, ed. Deborah Bright, London: Routledge, 1998, pp. 178–9, p. 179.
14 Donald Kuspit, 'David Wojnarowicz: The Last Rimbaud', *Art in New England*, vol. 20, no. 4, June/July 1999, p. 11 .
15 The photograph of the image from *Silence = Death* (1990), which was reproduced on the cover of *High Performance: A Quarterly Magazine for the New Arts* in the Fall of 1990, was photographed by Andreas Sterzing.
16 Wojnarowicz, in conversation with Jonathan Fineberg, in Wojnarowicz's studio, 13 November 1987, cited in Jonathan Fineberg, *Art Since 1940: Strategies of Being*, New York: Harry N. Abrams, 1995, p. 454.
17 See Félix Guattari, 'David Wojnarowicz', *Rethinking Marxism*, vol. 3, no. 1, Spring 1990, pp. 76–7.
18 Nan Goldin, introduction to *The Ballad of Sexual Dependency*, New York: Aperture, 1986, p. 6.
19 William F. Buckley, 'Crucial Steps in Combating the AIDS Epidemic: Identify All the Carriers', *New York Times*, 18 March 1986, A27.
20 Dave Hickey, 'In the Dancehall of the Dead' in *Robert Gober*, ed. Karen Marta, exh. cat., New York: DIA Center for the Arts, 1992, p. 37.
21 Hal Foster, 'The Art of the Missing Part' in Foster and Paul Schimmel, *Robert Gober*, exh. cat., Los Angeles: MOCA, 1997, pp. 57–68.
22 Daniel Farson, *With Gilbert & George in Moscow*, London: Bloomsbury, 1991, p. 29. Of course Gilbert and George were in the luxurious position of being able to fund that exhibition themselves, without the support of the British Council.

23 George, statement from 1997, cited in Robert Rosenblum, *Introducing Gilbert & George*, London: Thames and Hudson, 2004, p. 128.
24 Stuart Morgan, 'The Illustrated Man: Franko B' in Lois Keidan and Stuart Morgan, *Franko B*, London: Black Dog Publishing, 1998, n.p.
25 Billy Quinn, *A Plague of Angels*, exh. cat., Chicago: Mindy Oh Gallery, 1993, n.p.
26 Billy Quinn, cited in Anna O'Sullivan, 'Irish Art in New York', *Circa*, no. 64, Summer 1993, p. 22.
27 Angela Carter, 'Polemical Preface: Pornography in the Service of Women', *The Sadeian Woman and the Ideology of Pornography*, New York: Pantheon Books, 1979, pp. 3–19.
28 Andrea Dworkin, *Pornography: Men Possessing Women*, London: Women's Press, 1981, p. 200.
29 Linda Williams, *Hard Core: Power, Pleasure, and the 'Frenzy of the Visible'*, Berkeley and Los Angeles CA: University of California Press (1989), 1998, p. 56.
30 Annie Sprinkle, *Post Porn Modernist*, Amsterdam: Torch Books, 1991, p. 112.
31 Sprinkle first wrote, produced, and enacted *Annie Sprinkle—Post Porn Modernism* in 1989 and performed it in such venues as the Kitchen and the Joseph Papp Theater in New York, De Kleine Comedie Theater in Amsterdam, and the Schmidt Theater in Hamburg.
32 Jeff Koons, Artist Panel Discussion, 19 March 2004, at *Persistence and Memory: New Critical Perspectives on Dalí at the Centennial*, Salvador Dalí Museum, St Petersburg, Florida.
33 Jeff Koons cited in Dodie Kazanjian, 'Koons Crazy', *Vogue* (New York), August 1990, pp. 338–43, p. 338.
34 Amanda Cruz, 'Movies, Monstrosities, and Masks: Twenty Years of Cindy Sherman' in Cruz et al., *Cindy Sherman Retrospective*, exh. cat., Los Angeles: Museum of Contemporary Art, and Chicago: Museum of Contemporary Art, and London: Thames and Hudson, 1997, pp. 1–17, p. 12; Cruz notes that she obtained this information from an interview with Sherman on 6 May 1997.
35 See for example Robin Ruth Linden et al., *Against Sadomasochism*, East Palo Alto CA: From Frog in the Wall, 1982.
36 See Gilles Deleuze on Thanatos in Chapter X, 'The Death Instinct' in Gilles Deleuze and Leopold von Sacher-Masoch, *Masochism: Coldness and Cruelty & Venus in Furs*, New York: Zone Books, 1991.
37 Grace Lau, 'Perversion through the Camera', *New Formations, A Journal of Culture/Theory/Politics: Perversity*, no. 19, Spring 1993, pp. 45–6, p. 45. See also Grace Lau and Amanda Hopkinson, *Adults in Wonderland: A Retrospective*, London: Serpent's Tail, 1997.
38 Lau, 'Perversion through the Camera', p. 45.
39 Nayland Blake, 'Behaviour', interview with Stuart Morgan, *Frieze*, issue 5, June–August 1992, p. 39.
40 John Gange and Stephen Johnstone, '"Believe me, everybody has something pierced in California": An Interview with Nayland Blake', *New Formations, A Journal of Culture/Theory/Politics: Perversity*, no. 19, Spring 1993, pp. 51–68, p. 54.
41 Blake, 'Behaviour', p. 43.
42 Blake in Gange and Johnstone, '"Believe me, everybody has something pierced in California"', p. 68.
43 Bob Flanagan, *The Pain Journal*, Los Angeles CA: Semiotext(e)/Smart Art Press, 2000, p. 42.
44 Bob Flanagan, 'Why?' in *Dear World*, eds. Camille Roy and Nayland Blake, San Francisco CA: self-published, 1991, pp. 55–6.
45 Bob Flanagan, *Bob Flanagan: Super Masochist*, eds. Andrea Juno and V. Vale, San Francisco CA: Re/Search Press, 1993, p. 13.
46 Amelia Jones, *Body Art: Performing the Subject*, Minneapolis MN and London: University of Minnesota Press, 1998, p. 235.
47 Stuart Hall, 'What Is This "Black" in Black Popular Culture?' in *Black Popular Culture*, ed. Gina Dent, Seattle WA: Bay Press, 1992, pp. 21–33.
48 Thelma Golden, 'My Brother' in Golden, *Black Male: Representation of Masculinity in Contemporary American Art*, exh. cat., New York: Whitney Museum of American Art, 1994, pp. 19–43, p. 33.
49 Frantz Fanon, *Black Skin, White Masks* (1952), trans. Charles Lam Markmann, London: Pluto Press, 1986, p.170. This explanation is part of Fanon's analysis of the fear of and lust for the black penis, and follows his choice of excerpt from Michel Cournot's *Martinique* (Paris: Gallimard, 1948) in which Cournot writes that the black man's penis is like a sword and that 'Four Negroes with their penises exposed would fill a cathedral.'
50 Kobena Mercer, 'Reading Racial Fetishism: The Photographs of Robert Mapplethorpe' (combining two earlier essay by Mercer, 'Imaging the Black Man's Sex' of 1986 and 'How Do I Look?' of 1989) in *Welcome to the Jungle: New Positions in Black Cultural Studies*, London

and New York: Routledge, 1994, pp. 171–219, p. 174.

51 Homi Bhabha, 'The Other Question: The Stereotype and Colonial Discourse', *Screen*, vol. 24, no. 4 , 1983, p. 30, cited in Mercer, 'Reading Racial Fetishism', p. 183.

52 See Sigmund Freud, 'Fetishism' (1927) in *On Sexuality: Three Essays on the Theory of Sexuality*, The Pelican Freud Library, vol. VII, Harmondsworth: Penguin Books, 1977, p. 351.

53 Mercer, 'Reading Racial Fetishism', p. 177.

54 Morrisroe, *Mapplethorpe*, p. 248.

55 Edmund White, 'Altars: The Radicalism of Simplicity' in Robert Mapplethorpe, *Altars*, London: Jonathan Cape, pp. 128–34, p. 130.

56 Mercer, 'Reading Racial Fetishism', p. 190.

57 Ibid., p. 201.

58 Glenn Ligon, interview with artist Byron Kim, in *Glenn Ligon: Unbecoming*, ed. Judith Tannenbaum, exh. cat., Philadelphia PA: Institute of Contemporary Art, University of Pennsylvania, 1998, pp. 51–5, p. 55.

59 David Bergman, introduction in his edited volume, *Camp Grounds: Style and Homosexuality*, Amherst MA: University of Massachusetts Press, 1993, pp. 3–16, pp. 4–5.

60 Lyle Ashton Harris, quote to accompany series of photographs reproduced in *Ten 8*, vol. 2, no. 1, Spring 1991, pp. 50–61, p. 61.)

61 Lyle Ashton Harris and Thomas Allen Harris, 'Black Widow, a Conversation' in *The Passionate Camera: Photography and Bodies of Desire*, ed. Deborah Bright, London: Routledge, 1998, pp. 248–62, p. 249.

62 Ibid., p. 253. Paul Gilroy's influential studies of black culture and society include *Ain't No Black in the Union Jack*, London and New York: Routledge, 1987, and *The Black Atlantic: Modernity and Double Consciousness*, London: Verso, 1993.

63 Chris Ofili, interview with Marco Spinelli, *'Brilliant!': New Art from the London*, Minneapolis, MN: Walker Art Center, 1995, p. 67.

64 Chris Ofili, in Lisa G. Corrin, Stephen Snoddy, and Godfrey Worsdale, *Chris Ofili*, exh. cat., Southampton City Art Gallery/Serpentine Gallery, 1998, p. 83.

65 The Turner Prize is an annual national prize for a British artist under the age of 50 founded by the Patrons of New Art (PNA), a group administered by the Friends of the Tate Gallery, London, and launched in 1984.

66 The *Sensation: Young British Artists from the Saatchi Collection* exhibition was selected by Norman Rosenthal and Charles Saatchi and exhibited at the Royal Academy, London (18 September to 28 December 1997), Hamburger Bahnhof, Berlin (30 September 1998 to 21 February 1999) and Brooklyn Museum of Art, New York (2 October 1999 to 9 January 2000).

67 Chris Ofili, interview with Jonathan Jones in 'Paradise Reclaimed', *The Guardian (Weekend)*, 15 June 2002, pp. 18–23, p. 20.

68 Martin Maloney, 'Everyone a Winner! Selected British Art from the Saatchi Collection 1987–97' in Norman Rosenthal et al., *Sensation: Young British Artists from the Saatchi Collection*, exh. cat., London: Royal Academy of Arts, 1997, pp. 26–34, p. 29.

69 Niru Ratnam, 'Chris Ofili and the Limits of Hybridity', *New Left Review*, no. 235, May/June 1999, pp. 153–9.

70 Julian Stallabrass, *High Art Lite: British Art in the 1990s*, London and New York: Verso, 1999, p. 117.

71 Richard J. Powell, *Black Art, A Cultural History*, London: Thames and Hudson, World of Art series, 1997 and 2002, 2002 edition, p. 232.

Chapter 10: Erotic Fragmentation and Abjection

1 Francis Fukuyama, *The End of History and the Last Man*, London: Hamish Hamilton, 1992.

2 Paul B. Franklin, 'Orienting the Asian Male Body in the Photography of Yasumasa Morimura', *The Passionate Camera, Photography and Bodies of Desire*, ed. Deborah Bright, pp. 233–47, p. 237.

3 Ibid., p. 240. Franklin footnotes *Studies in Kabuki: Its Acting, Music and Historical Context*, eds. James R. Brandon, William P. Malm, and David Shively, Honolulu: University of Hawaii Press, 1978, for further reading on this topic.

4 Della Grace, 'Xenomorphisis', *New Formations, A Journal of Culture/Theory/Politics: Perversity*, no. 19, Spring 1993, pp. 123–4, p. 123. See also Parveen Adams, 'The Three (Dis)Graces' in the same issue, pp. 131–8.

5 Artist's statement, www.dellagracevolcano.com

6 Amelia Jones, *Body Art: Performing the Subject*, Minneapolis MN and London: University of Minnesota Press, 1998, p. 222.

7 Jones acknowledges this difference of reading in ibid., footnote 74, p. 222. Aguilar refers to her

universal agenda in her artist's statement in *Nueva Luz: A Photographic Journal*, vol. 4, no. 2, 1993, p. 22.

8 Virginia Button, *The Turner Prize: Twenty Years*, London: Tate Gallery, 2003, pp. 154–6. Button refers to Tracey Emin, short-listed for the 1999 Turner Prize, as 'one of the so-called Bad Girls of Contemporary British Art'.

9 'yBa' is the collective label advertising magnate Charles Saatchi created for them in the press release for *Young British Artists I*, a 1992 exhibition at his private gallery.

10 See Julian Stallabrass's reading of the work in *High Art Lite: British Art in the 1990s*, London and New York: Verso, 1999, pp. 91–3.

11 Sarah Lucas, interview with Carl Freedman, 'A Nod's as Good as a Wink', *Freize*, issue 17, June–July–August 1994, p. 31.

12 Ibid.

13 Articles cited in Mandy Merck, 'Bedtime', and Deborah Cherry, 'On the Move: *My Bed*, 1998 to 1999' in *The Art of Tracey Emin*, eds. Mandy Merck and Chris Townsend, London: Thames and Hudson, 2002, pp. 119–33, p. 121 and pp. 134–54, p. 142, respectively.

14 Tracey Emin quoted in Sarah Kent, 'Bleeding Art', *Time Out*, 8–15 October 1999, p. 24, cited in Cherry, 'On the Move', p. 149.

15 Julia Kristeva, *Powers of Horror: An Essay on Abjection*, trans. Leon S. Roudiez, New York: Columbia University Press, 1982, p. 4.

16 Vito Acconci in 'Vito Acconci, Yvonne Rainer, interviewed by Christophe Wavelet', at Acconci Studio, Brooklyn, 24 August 2003, in *Vito Hannibal Acconci Studio*, ed. Corinne Diserens, exh. cat., Barcelona: Museu d'Art Contemporani de Barcelona, 2004, pp. 12–45, p. 13. Acconci also went to college in a Catholic institution, the Holy Cross College in Massachusetts.

17 According to Acconci, the term 'Body Art' was coined by William Sharp, editor-in-chief of the art magazine *Avalanche*, published in New York. See *Vito Hannibal Acconci Studio*, p. 33.

18 On the 'finish fetish' of Minimalism, see Paul Schimmel, 'Into the Maelstrom: L.A. Art at the End of the Century', *Helter Skelter: L.A. Art in the 90s*, ed. Catherine Guidis, exh. cat., Los Angeles: MOCA, 1992, pp. 19–22, p. 19.

19 Kiki Smith, handwritten notes in *Kiki Smith: Silent Work*, exh. cat., Vienna: MAK Austrian Museum of Applied Arts, 1992, p. 27, cited in Simon Taylor, 'The Phobic Object: Abjection in Contemporary Art' in *Abject Art: Repulsion and Desire in American Art*, exh. cat., New York: Whitney Museum, 1993, pp. 59–83, p. 65.

20 Alice Maher in Fiona Barber, 'Hybrid Histories: Alice Maher', *Art History*, vol. 26, no. 3, June 2003, pp. 406–21, p. 419.

21 Paul McCarthy cited in Philip Monk, 'A Twisted Pedagogy' in *Mike Kelley and Paul McCarthy: Collaborative Works*, ed. Lisa Gabrielle Mark, exh. cat., Toronto: The Power Plant Contemporary Art Gallery, 2000, pp. 8–19, p. 14.

22 Timothy Martin, 'Fresh Acconci, Beautiful Acconci' in *Mike Kelley and Paul McCarthy*, ed. Mark, pp. 30–7, p. 36.

23 See Rosalind Krauss, *'A Voyage on the North Sea': Art in the Age of the Post-Medium Condition*, London: Thames and Hudson, 2000.

24 Showalter, *The Female Malady*, p. 130.

25 Sarah Wilson, '*L'Histoire d'O*, Sacred and Profane' in *Orlan: This Is My Body . . . This Is My Software*, ed. Duncan McCorquodale, London: Black Dog Publishing, 1996, pp. 8–17, p. 14. While Wilson writes that the operation occurred in 1978, Orlan's website (www.orlan.net) dates it 1979.

26 Parveen Adams, *The Emptiness of the Image: Psychoanalysis and Sexual Difference*, London: Routledge, 1996, pp. 143–4.

27 Orlan, 'Conférence' in *Orlan: This Is My Body . . .*, ed. McCorquodale, pp. 82–93, p. 84.

28 Orlan, 'Virtuel et réel: dialectique et complexité' in Dominique Baqué, Marek Bartelik, and Orlan, *Orlan: Refiguration Self-Hybridations, Série Précolombienne*, exh. cat., Lyon: Galerie de Bellecour, Paris: Éditions Al Dante, 2001, p. 50.

29 Matthew Barney, interview with Hans Ulrich Obrist, *Tate Magazine*, issue 2, 2002, online edition, http://www.tate.org.uk/magazine/issue2/barney.htm. It should be noted that while Vaseline abounds in Barney's *Cremaster* series it was a feature of earlier work too. His earliest video work, *Scabaction* (1988), involved Barney cutting his skin with a razor before applying Vaseline and a gel pack to it to help it heal.

30 Nancy Spector makes this observation in 'Only the Perverse Fantasy Can Still Save Us' in Nancy Spector, *Matthew Barney: The Cremaster Cycle*, exh. cat., New York: Guggenheim Museum, 2002, pp. 2–91, p. 23. See Gilles Deleuze and Félix Guattari, *Anti-Oedipus: Capitalism and Schizophrenia*, with preface by Michel Foucault, London: Athlone Press, 1994, p. 1.

31 Deleuze and Guattari, *Anti-Oedipus*, pp. 6–7.
32 In the guise of a ram, Barney's re-created self with horns recalls those horns sculpted by Marcel Duchamp with shaving soap in a series of photographs taken by Man Ray around seventy years earlier, one of which was used for Duchamp/Rrose Sélavy's *Monte Carlo Bond* (1924). In addition, given Duchamp's horns have been linked to Michelangelo's marble sculpture of *Moses* (*c.*1513–16) for the tomb of Pope Julius II in San Pietro in Vincoli, Rome, further layers of meaning can be found in Barney's ludic fusion of man and beast, new technology and classical referent. Stuart Morgan offers an interesting analysis of the links between Duchamp and Barney in 'Of Goats and Men', *Frieze*, 6, January–February 1995, pp. 34–8.
33 However, as Nancy Spector points out, Barney continued his gender-bending even with such males, as Houdini would mysteriously switch places with his wife in his theatrical performances. See Spector, 'Only the Perverse Fantasy Can Still Save Us', p. 41.
34 Barney, *Tate Magazine*, issue 2.
35 Whereas Bataille's notion of transgression remained within the human realm, Deleuze and Guattari intermixed human, animal, and plant in their conceptualization of transgression.
36 Georges Bataille, *The Tears of Eros* (1961), San Francisco: City Lights Books, 1989. As Denis Hollier suggests, it might have been titled the 'blades' (*lames*) of Eros due to Bataille's fascination with torture. See Denis Hollier, *Against Architecture: The Writings of Georges Bataille*, trans. Betsy Wing, Cambridge MA and London: MIT Press, 1992, p. 85.
37 Bataille first saw this method of torture in a photograph reproduced in Georges Dumas's *Traité de psychologie* of 1923. He acquired his own copy of the photograph in 1928 from his psychoanalyst Dr Borel, which he printed in his review *Documents*.
38 Norman Rosenthal, 'Apocalypse: Beauty and Horror in Contemporary Art' in Rosenthal et al., *Apocalypse: Beauty and Horror*, exh. cat., London: Royal College of Art, 2002, p. 213.
39 Donna Haraway, 'A Manifesto for Cyborgs: Science, Technology, and Socialist Feminism in the 1980s', *The Socialist Review*, vol. 16, no. 2, March/April 1985, pp. 65–107, p. 67.
40 Ibid., p. 99.
41 Jake Chapman in 'Jake Chapman on Georges Bataille: An Interview with Simon Baker', *Papers of Surrealism*, Issue 1, Winter 2003, http://www.surrealismcentre.ac.uk/publications/papers/ For a Bataillean analysis of the Chapmans' art, see also Douglas Fogle, 'A Scatological Aesthetics for the Tired of Seeing' in Jake and Dinos Chapman, *Chapmanworld*, exh. cat., London: Institute of Contemporary Arts, 1996, n.p.
42 Sigmund Freud, *Civilization and Its Discontents* (1930), trans. and ed. James Strachey, New York: Norton, 1961, pp. 38–9.

Conclusion

1 Bill Viola cited in John Walsh, 'Emotions in Extreme Time, Bill Viola's Passions Project', *Bill Viola, The Passions*, ed. John Walsh, exh. cat., Los Angeles: J. Paul Getty Museum, 2003, pp. 25–63, p. 25.
2 Ibid., p. 57.
3 Georges Bataille, *Eroticism* (1962), trans. Mary Dalwood, London: Marion Boyars, 1987.

Bibliography

Abject Art: Repulsion and Desire in American Art, exh. cat., New York: Whitney Museum, 1993.

Adam, Peter, *Art of the Third Reich*, New York: Harry N. Abrams, 1995.

Adams, Henry, *Thomas Hart Benton: An American Original*, New York: Alfred A. Knopf, 1989.

Adams, Parveen, 'The Three (Dis)Graces', *New Formations, A Journal of Culture/Theory/Politics: Perversity*, no. 19, Spring 1993, pp. 131–8.

Adams, Parveen, *The Emptiness of the Image: Psychoanalysis and Sexual Difference*, London: Routledge, 1996.

Ades, Dawn, Neil Cox, and David Hopkins, *Marcel Duchamp*, London: Thames and Hudson, 1999.

Aguilar, Laura, 'Artist's Statement', *Nueva Luz: A Photographic Journal*, vol. 4, no. 2, 1993, p. 22.

Akomfrah, John, 'On the Borderline' (with photographs by Lyle Ashton Harris), *Ten 8, Bodies of Excess*, vol. 2, no. 1, Spring 1991, pp. 50–61.

de Alba, Alicia Gaspar, *Inside/Outside the Master's House: Cultural Politics and the CARA Exhibition*, Austin TX: University of Texas Press, 1998.

Albright, Thomas, *Art in the San Francisco Bay Area, 1945–1980*, Berkeley CA: University of California Press, 1985.

Aristotle, *Poetics*, trans., introduction, and notes by Malcolm Heath, London: Penguin Books, 1996.

Armstrong, Carol, *Odd Man Out: Readings of the Work and Reputation of Edgar Degas*, Chicago: Chicago University Press, 1991.

Ashcroft, Bill, Garther Griffiths, and Helen Tiffin (eds.), *The Postcolonial Studies Reader*, New York and London: Routledge, 1995.

Auerbach, Nina, *Romantic Imprisonment: Women and Other Glorified Outcasts*, New York: Columbia University Press, 1986.

Saint Augustine, *The Confessions of St. Augustine*, trans. Rex Warner, introduction by Vernon J. Bourke, New York: Mentor-Omega Books, 1963.

Bailey, Beth, 'Sexual Revolution(s)' in *The Sixties: From Memory to History*, ed. David Farber, Chapel Hill NC and London: University of North Carolina Press, 1994, pp. 235–62.

Baker, Robb, 'The Trials of Lucifer: An Interview with Kenneth Anger', *Soho Weekly News*, 28 October 1976, p. 16.

Barber, Fiona, 'Hybrid Histories: Alice Maher', *Art History*, vol. 26, no. 3, June 2003, pp. 406–21.

Barringer, Tim and Elizabeth Prettejohn, *Frederic Leighton: Antiquity, Renaissance, Modernity*, New Haven CT: Yale University Press.

Barron, Stephanie and Wolf-Dieter Dube (eds.),*German Expressionism: Art and Society*, London: Thames and Hudson, 1997.

Barron, Stephanie et al., *'Degenerate Art': The Fate of the Avant-Garde in Nazi Germany*, exh. cat., Los Angeles CA: Los Angeles County Museum of Art, 1991.

Barthes, Roland, *Camera Lucida*, London: Jonathan Cape, 1982.

Bataille, Georges, 'The Lugubrious Game', originally published as 'Le Jeu lugubre' in *Documents*, no. 7, Paris, December 1929; reprinted in *Art in Theory 1900–1990: An Anthology of Changing Ideas*, eds. Charles Harrison and Paul Wood, Oxford: Blackwell, 1992, pp. 476–8.

Bataille, Georges, *Eroticism* (1957), trans. Mary Dalwood, London: Marion Boyars, 1987.

Bataille, Georges, 'The Meaning of Eroticism' (1957) in *Erotic Art from the Seventeenth Century to the Twentieth Century*, ed. Peter Weiermair, exh. cat., Frankfurt: Frankfurter Kunstverein and Edition Stemmle, 1995, pp. 10–12.

Bataille, Georges, *The Tears of Eros* (1961), trans. Peter Connor, San Francisco CA: City Lights Books, 1989.

Baudelaire, Charles, *The Painter of Modern Life and Other Essays*, trans. and ed. Jonathan Mayne, London: Phaidon, 1995.

Beard, Mary and John Henderson, *Classical Art: From Greece to Rome*, (Oxford History of Art) Oxford: Oxford University Press, 2001.

Beaulieu, Jill and Mary Roberts (eds.), *Orientalism's Interlocutors: Painting, Architecture, Photography*, Durham NC and London: Duke University Press, 2002.

Belton, Robert J., 'Androgyny: Interview with Meret Oppenheim' in *Surrealism and Women*, eds. Mary Ann Caws, Rudolf E. Kuenzli, and Gwen Raaberg, Cambridge MA and London: MIT Press, 1991, pp. 63–75.

Benjamin, Roger, 'The Oriental Mirage' in *Orientalism: Delacroix to Klee*, ed. Roger Benjamin, exh. cat., London: Thames and Hudson and The Art Gallery of New South Wales, 1997, pp. 7–31.

Benjamin, Roger (ed.), *Orientalism: Delacroix to Klee*, exh. cat., London: Thames and Hudson and The Art Gallery of New South Wales, 1997.

Benjamin, Walter, *Illuminations*, trans. Harry Zohn, ed. and introduction by Hannah Arendt, London: Jonathan Cape, 1970.

Berger, John, *Ways of Seeing*, London: British Broadcasting Corporation and Penguin Books, 1972.

Bergman, David (ed.), *Camp Grounds: Style and Homosexuality*, Amherst MA: University of Massachusetts, 1993.

Bersani, Leo, 'Is the Rectum a Grave?' in *AIDS: Cultural Analysis/Cultural Activism*, ed. Douglas Crimp, special issue of *October*, no. 43, Winter 1987, published as a book, Cambridge MA: MIT Press, 1988, pp. 197–222.

Bettauer, Hugo, 'The Erotic Revolution' (Die erotische Revolution), from *Er und Sie I* (1924), reprinted in *The Weimar Republic Sourcebook*, eds. Anton Kaes, Martin Jay, and Edward Dimendberg, Berkeley CA and London: University of California Press, 1994, pp. 698–700.

Bhabha, Homi, *The Location of Culture*, New York and London: Routledge 1994.

Blackburn, Simon, 'Why Do We Need to Feel? Hearts and Minds: The Place of Emotion in Rational Thought', *Times Literary Supplement*, 29 October 1999, pp. 3–4.

Blackburn, Simon, *Lust: The Seven Deadly Sins*, New York and London: Oxford University Press, 2004.

Blanchot, Maurice, 'Sade' in D. A. F. de Sade, *Justine, Philosophy in the Boudoir, Eugénie de Franval and Other Writings*, eds. Richard Seaver and Austryn Wainhouse, London: Arrow Books, 1965, pp. 37–72.

Boas, G., 'Il faut être de son temps', *Journal of Aesthetics*, vol. 1, 1941, pp. 52–65.

Bolger, Doreen and Sarah Cash, *Thomas Eakins and the Swimming Picture*, exh. cat., Fort Worth TX: Amon Carter Museum, 1996.

William Bouguereau 1825–1905, exh. cat., Montreal: Montreal Museum of Fine Arts, 1984.

Bouillon, Jean-Paul, *Klimt: Beethoven, The Frieze for the Ninth Symphony*, Lausanne: Skira, 1987.

Bourgeois, Louise, *Louise Bourgeois: Destruction of the Father Reconstruction of the Father, Writings and Interviews 1923–1997*, eds. Marie-Laure Bernadac and Hans-Ulrich Obrist, London: Violette Editions, 2000.

Bradley, William S., *Emil Nolde and German Expressionism: A Prophet in His Own Land*, Ann Arbor MI: UMI Research Press, 1986.

Brandon, James R., William P. Malm, and David Shively (eds.), *Studies in Kabuki: Its Acting, Music and Historical Context*, Honolulu HI: University of Hawaii Press, 1978.

Breton, André et al., *Violette Nozières* (1933), reprinted with preface by José Pierre, Paris: Terrain Vague, 1991.

Breton, André, 'Phare de la Mariée' (Lighthouse of the Bride), *Minotaure*, no. 6., Winter 1935, pp. 45–9.

Breton, André, *Manifestoes of Surrealism*, trans. Richard Seaver and Helen R. Lane, Ann Arbor MI: University of Michigan Press, 1972 (1969).

Breton, André, 'First Surrealist Manifesto' in *Manifestoes of Surrealism*, trans. Richard Seaver and Helen R. Lane, Ann Arbor MI: University of Michigan Press, 1972 (1969), pp. 1–47.

Breton, André, *What Is Surrealism? Selected Writings*, ed. Franklin Rosemont, New York: Monad Press, 1978.

Breton, André, *Surrealism and Painting*, trans. Simon Watson Taylor, Boston MA: MFA Publications, 2002.

Bright, Deborah (ed.), *The Passionate Camera: Photography and Bodies of Desire*, London: Routledge, 1998.

'Brilliant!', New Art from London, exh. cat., Minneapolis MN: Walker Art Center, 1995.

Broude, Norma and Mary D. Garrard (eds.), *Feminism and Art History: Questioning the Litany*, New York: Harper and Row, 1982.

Broude, Norma and Mary D. Garrard (eds.), *The Power of Feminist Art: The American Movement of the 1970s, History and Impact*, New York: Harry N. Abrams, 1994.

Brown, Helen Gurley, *Sex and the Single Girl*, New York: Bernard Geis Associates, 1962.

Bryson, Norman, *Tradition and Desire: From David to Delacroix*, Cambridge: Cambridge University Press, 1984.

Buchloh, Benjamin H., Lucy Lippard, and Donald B. Kuspit, *Art and Ideology*, New York: The New Museum of Contemporary Art, 1984.

Buckley, William F., 'Crucial Steps in Combating

the AIDS Epidemic: Identify All the Carriers', *New York Times*, 18 March 1986, A27.
Bullen, J. B., *The Pre-Raphaelite Body: Fear and Desire in Painting, Poetry and Criticism*, Oxford: Clarendon Press, 1998.
Bullough, Vern L., 'Alfred Kinsey and the Kinsey Report: Historical Overview and Lasting Contributions', *Journal of Sex Research*, vol. 35, no. 2, 1998, pp. 127–31.
Bürger, Peter, *Theory of the Avant-Garde* (1974), trans. Michael Shaw, foreword by Jochen Schulte-Sasse, Minneapolis MN: University of Minnesota Press, 1984.
Button, Virginia, *The Turner Prize: Twenty Years*, London: Tate Gallery, 2003.
Cabanne, Pierre, *Dialogues with Marcel Duchamp* (1967), trans. Ron Padgett, New York: Da Capo Press, 1987.
Cahun, Claude, *Écrits*, ed. François Leperlier, Paris: Éditions Jean-Michel Place, 2002.
Callen, Anthea, *The Spectacular Body: Science, Method and Meaning in the Work of Degas*, New Haven CT: Yale University Press, 1995.
Carrington, Leonora, *The House of Fear: Notes from Down Below*, trans. Katharine Talbot and Marina Warner, London: Virago, 1989.
Carson, Julia (ed.), *Banned in Ireland: Censorship and the Irish Writer*, London: Routledge, 1990.
Carter, Angela, *The Sadeian Woman and the Ideology of Pornography*, New York: Pantheon Books, 1979.
Casteras, Susan P., *The 'Lipstick' Comes Back*, exh. cat., New Haven CT: Yale University Art Gallery, 1974.
Caws, Mary Ann, *The Surrealist Look: An Erotics of Encounter*, Cambridge MA and London: MIT Press, 1997.
Caws, Mary Ann, Rudolf E. Kuenzli, and Gwen Raaberg (eds.), *Surrealism and Women*, Cambridge MA and London: MIT Press, 1993.
Chadwick, Whitney, *Women Artists and the Surrealist Movement*, London: Thames and Hudson, 1985.
Chadwick, Whitney and Isabelle de Courtivron (eds.), *Significant Others: Creativity and Intimate Partnership*, London: Thames and Hudson, 1993.
Chapman, Jake, 'Jake Chapman on Georges Bataille: An Interview with Simon Baker', *Papers of Surrealism*, no. 1, Winter 2003, http://www.surrealismcentre.ac.uk/publications/papers/journal1.
Chapman, Jake and Dinos Chapman, *Chapmanworld*, exh. cat., London: Institute of Contemporary Arts, 1996.
Chave, Anna, 'New Encounters with *Les Demoiselles d'Avignon*: Gender, Race and the Origins of Cubism', *The Art Bulletin*, vol. 76, no. 4, December 1994, pp. 596–611.
Cherry, Deborah, 'On the Move: *My Bed*, 1998 to 1999' in *The Art of Tracey Emin*, eds. Mandy Merck and Chris Townsend, London: Thames and Hudson, 2002, pp. 134–54.
Chicago, Judy, *Through the Flower: My Struggle as a Woman Artist*, New York: Anchor/Doubleday Books, 1975.
Chicago, Judy, *The Dinner Party*, New York: Anchor Books, 1979.
Chipp, Herschel B. (ed.), *Theories of Modern Art: A Source Book by Artists and Critics*, Berkeley CA: University of California Press, 1975.
Clair, Jean (ed.), *Vienne 1880–1938: L'Apocalypse joyeuse*, exh. cat., Paris: Éditions du Centre Pompidou, 1986.
Clair, Jean, *Sur Marcel Duchamp et la fin de l'art*, Paris: Gallimard, 2000.
Clair, Jean, *Picasso et l'abîme: Éros, Nomos et Thanatos*, Paris: L'Échoppe, 2000.
Clair, Jean, 'Leçon d'abîme' in *Picasso érotique*, exh. cat., Paris: Galerie Nationale du Jeu de Paume/Réunion des Musées Nationaux, 2001, pp. 14–26.
Clark, Kenneth, *The Nude: A Study of Ideal Art*, Harmondsworth: Penguin Books, 1956.
Clark, T. J., 'Preliminaries to a Possible Treatment of Olympia in 1865' (1980) in *Modern Art and Modernism*, eds. Francis Frascina and Charles Harrison, London: Harper and Row, 1982, pp. 259–73.
Clark, T. J., *The Painting of Modern Life: Paris in the Age of Manet and His Followers*, Princeton NJ: Princeton University Press, 1984.
Cochran, Sara, 'La Peinture de Francis Picabia pendant la Seconde Guerre Mondiale', *Art Press*, no. 222, 1997, pp. 48–9.
Cohen, Michael, 'Lyle Ashton Harris', *Flash Art*, May–June 1996, p. 107.
Cohen, Morton, *Lewis Carroll, Photographer of Children: Four Nude Studies*, New York: Potter, 1978.
Combalía, Victoria and Jean-Jacques Lebel, *Jardín de éros*, exh. cat., Barcelona: Institut de Cultura de Barcelona/Electa, 1999.
Conley, Katharine, 'Claude Cahun's Iconic Heads: from "The Sadistic Judith" to Human Frontier', *Papers of Surrealism*, no. 2, Summer 2004, http://www.surrealismcentre.ac.uk/publications/papers/journal2.
Corbett, David Peters and Lara Perry (eds.), *English Art 1860–1914: Modern Artists and Identity*, Manchester: Manchester University Press, 2000.

Corbin, Alain, *Women for Hire: Prostitution and Sexuality in France after 1850*, trans. Alan Sheridan, Cambridge MA and London: Harvard University Press, 1990.

Corrin, Lisa G., Stephen Snoddy, and Godfrey Worsdale, *Chris Ofili*, exh. cat., Southampton: Southampton City Art Gallery, and London: Serpentine Gallery, 1998.

Crimp, Douglas (ed.), *AIDS: Cultural Analysis/Cultural Activism*, special issue of *October*, no. 43, Winter 1987; published as a book by MIT Press (Cambridge MA) in 1988.

Crow, Thomas, *Modern Art in the Common Culture*, New Haven CT: Yale University Press, 1996.

Cruise, Colin, '"Lovely devils": Simeon Solomon and Pre-Raphaelite Masculinity' in *Re-framing the Pre-Raphaelites: Historical and Theoretical Essays*, ed. Ellen Harding, Aldershot: Scolar Press, 1996, pp. 195–210.

Cruz, Amanda, 'Movies, Monstrosities, and Masks: Twenty Years of Cindy Sherman' in *Cindy Sherman Retrospective*, Amanda Cruz, Elizabeth A. T. Smith, and Amelia Jones, exh. cat., Los Angeles CA: Museum of Contemporary Art, and London: Thames and Hudson, 1997, pp. 1–17.

Cruz, Amanda, Elizabeth A. T. Smith, and Amelia Jones, *Cindy Sherman Retrospective*, exh. cat., Los Angeles CA: Museum of Contemporary Art, and London: Thames and Hudson, 1997.

Dalí, Salvador, 'Declaration of the Independence of the Imagination and the Rights of Man to His Own Madness', published in *Memoir of an Art Gallery*, Julien Levy, New York: Putnam's, 1977, pp. 219–22.

Danielsson, Bengt, *Gauguin in the South Seas*, trans. Reginald Spink, London: George Allen and Unwin, 1965.

Danielsson, Bengt, 'Gauguin's Tahitian Titles', *Burlington Magazine*, vol. 109, no. 769, April 1967, pp. 228–33.

Danto, Arthur C., *Playing with the Edge: The Photographic Achievement of Robert Mapplethorpe*, Berkeley and Los Angeles CA: University of California Press, 1996.

Darwin, Charles, *The Descent of Man* (1871), reprint, Princeton NJ: Princeton University Press, 1981.

Davis, Mike, 'Bunker Hill: Hollywood's Dark Shadow' in *Cinema and the City: Film and Urban Societies in a Global Context*, eds. Mark Shiel and Tony Fitzmaurice, Oxford: Blackwell Publishers, 2001, pp. 33–45.

Dawkins, Heather, *The Nude in French Art and Culture, 1870–1910*, Cambridge and New York: Cambridge University Press, 2002.

Deleuze, Gilles, 'Pierre Klossowski ou les corps-langage', *Critique*, no. 214, March 1965, pp. 199–219.

Deleuze, Gilles and Félix Guattari, *Anti-Oedipus: Capitalism and Schizophrenia*, with preface by Michel Foucault, London: Athlone Press, 1994.

Deleuze, Gilles and Leopold von Sacher-Masoch, *Masochism: Coldness and Cruelty and Venus in Furs*, New York: Zone Books, 1991.

Dent, Gina (ed.), *Black Popular Culture*, Seattle WA: Bay Press, 1992.

Desnos, Robert, *Liberty or Love!* (1927), trans. and introduction by Terry Hale, London: Atlas Press, 1993.

Diserens, Corinne (ed.), *Vito Hannibal Acconci Studio*, exh. cat., Barcelona: Museu d'Art Contemporani de Barcelona, 2004.

Doezema, Marianne and Elizabeth Milroy (eds.), *Reading American Art*, New Haven CT: Yale University Press, 1998.

Dourthe, Pierre, *Bellmer: Le Principe de perversion*, Paris: Jean-Pierre Faur, 1999.

Duchamp, Marcel, *Notes and Projects for the Large Glass*, ed. Arturo Schwarz, London: Thames and Hudson, 1969.

Duncan, Carol, 'The MoMA's Hot Mamas', *Art Journal*, vol. 48, no. 2, Summer 1989, pp. 171–8.

Dutt, Robin, *Gilbert and George*, London: Philip Watson Publishers, 2004.

de Duve, Thierry, *Kant after Duchamp*, Cambridge MA and London: MIT Press, 1999.

Dworkin, Andrea, *Pornography: Men Possessing Women*, London: Women's Press, 1981.

Dworkin, Andrea and Catharine A. MacKinnon, *Pornography and Civil Rights: A New Day*, Minneapolis MN: Organizing Against Pornography, 1988.

Eisenman, Stephen F. (ed.), *Nineteenth Century Art: A Critical History*, London: Thames and Hudson, 1994.

Eisenman, Stephen F., *Gauguin's Skirt*, London: Thames and Hudson, 1997.

Elliott, Patrick, 'Alberto Giacometti: An Introduction' in *Alberto Giacometti, 1901–1966*, eds. Toni Stoos and Patrick Elliott, exh. cat.,Vienna: Kunsthalle, and Edinburgh: National Galleries of Scotland, 1996, pp. 11–25.

Ellis, Henry Havelock, *Studies in the Psychology of Sex*, 7 vols., Philadelphia PA: F. A. Davis, 1920–8.

Fanon, Frantz, *Black Skin, White Masks* (1952), trans. Charles Lam Markmann, London: Pluto Press, 1986.

Farber, David (ed.), *The Sixties: From Memory to*

History, Chapel Hill NC and London: University of North Carolina Press, 1994.
Farson, Daniel, *With Gilbert and George in Moscow*, London: Bloomsbury, 1991.
Faunce, Sarah and Linda Nochlin, *Courbet Reconsidered*, exh. cat., New York: Brooklyn Museum, 1988.
Fernandez, Dominique, *A Hidden Love: Art and Homosexuality*, New York: Prestel Publishing, 2002.
Fineberg, Jonathan, *Art since 1940: Strategies of Being*, New York: Harry N. Abrams, Publishers, 1995.
Flam, Jack, 'Matisse and the Fauves' in *'Primitivism' in 20th-Century Art: Affinity of the Tribal and Modern*, vol. I, ed. William Rubin, exh. cat., New York: Museum of Modern Art, 1984, pp. 224–6.
Flanagan, Bob, 'Why?' in *Dear World*, eds. Camille Roy and Nayland Blake, San Francisco CA: self-published, 1991, pp. 55–6.
Flanagan, Bob, *Bob Flanagan: Super Masochist*, eds. Andrea Juno and V. Vale, San Francisco CA: Re/Search Press, 1993.
Flanagan, Bob, *The Pain Journal*, Los Angeles CA: Semiotext(e)/Smart Art Press, 2000.
Foster, Hal (ed.), *Postmodern Culture*, London: Pluto Press, 1985.
Foster, Hal, *The Return of the Real*, Cambridge MA: MIT Press, 1996.
Foster, Hal, 'The Art of the Missing Part' in Hal Foster and Paul Schimmel, *Robert Gober*, exh. cat., Los Angeles CA: Museum of Contemporary Art, 1997, pp. 57–68.
Foster, Hal and Paul Schimmel, *Robert Gober*, exh. cat., Los Angeles CA: Museum of Contemporary Art, 1997.
Foucault, Michel, *Discipline and Punish: The Birth of the Prison* (1975), trans. Alan Sheridan, New York: Vintage, 1977.
Foucault, Michel, *The History of Sexuality, Volume One: The Will to Knowledge* (1976), trans. Robert Hurley, New York: Random House, 1978.
Foucault, Michel, *The History of Sexuality, Volume Two: The Use of Pleasure* (1984), trans. Robert Hurley, New York: Random House, 1985.
Franklin, Paul B., 'Orienting the Asian Male Body in the Photography of Yasumasa Morimura' in *The Passionate Camera: Photography and Bodies of Desire*, ed. Deborah Bright, London: Routledge, 1998, pp. 233–47.
Frascina, Francis and Charles Harrison (eds.), *Modern Art and Modernism: A Critical Anthology*, London: Harper and Row, 1982.
Freud, Sigmund, *Civilization and Its Discontents* (1930), trans. and ed. James Strachey, New York: Norton, 1961.
Freud, Sigmund, *Introductory Lectures on Psycho-Analysis (Part III)*, ed. and trans. James Strachey, The Standard Edition of the Complete Psychological Works of Sigmund Freud, vol. XVI, London: Hogarth Press, 1963.
Freud, Sigmund, *New Introductory Lectures on Psychoanalysis*, ed. and trans. James Strachey, Pelican Freud Library, vol. II, Harmondsworth: Penguin Books, 1973.
Freud, Sigmund, *On Sexuality: Three Essays on the Theory of Sexuality and Other Works*, ed. and trans. James Strachey, The Pelican Freud Library, vol. VII, Harmondsworth: Penguin Books, 1977.
Fry, Varian, *Surrender on Demand*, Boulder CO: Johnson Books in conjunction with the United States Holocaust Memorial Museum, 1997.
Fukuyama, Francis, *The End of History and the Last Man*, London: Hamish Hamilton, 1992.
Gange, John and Stephen Johnstone, '"Believe Me, Everybody Has Something Pierced in California": An Interview with Nayland Blake', *New Formations, A Journal of Culture/Theory/Politics: Perversity*, no. 19, Spring 1993, pp. 51–68.
Garb, Tamar, *Sisters of the Brush: Women's Artistic Culture in Late Nineteenth-Century Paris*, New Haven CT: Yale University Press, 1994.
Garb, Tamar, *Bodies of Modernity: Figure and Flesh in Fin-de-Siècle France*, London: Thames and Hudson, 1998.
Gasquet, Joachim, *Cézanne*, 2nd edn, Paris: Bernheim-Jeune, 1926.
Gauguin, Paul, 'Diverses choses, 1896–97' in *Theories of Modern Art: A Source Book by Artists and Critics*, ed. Herschel B. Chipp, Berkeley CA: University of California Press, 1975, pp. 65–6.
Gauthier, Xavière, *Surréalisme et sexualité*, Paris: Gallimard, 1971.
Gibson, Ian, *The Shameful Life of Salvador Dalí*, London: Faber and Faber, 1997.
Robert Gober, exh. cat., Minneapolis MN: Walker Art Center, 1999.
Gilman, Sander, *Difference and Pathology: Stereotypes of Sexuality, Race and Madness*, Ithaca NY: Cornell University, 1985.
Golan, Romy, *Modernity and Nostalgia: Art and Politics in France between the Wars*, New Haven CT and London, 1995.
Golden, Thelma, 'My Brother' in *Black Male: Representation of Masculinity in Contemporary American Art*, ed. Thelma Golden, exh. cat., New York: Whitney Museum of American Art, 1994, pp. 19–43.

Golden, Thelma, *Black Male: Representation of Masculinity in Contemporary American Art*, exh. cat., Whitney Museum of American Art, New York, 1994.

Goldin, Nan, *The Ballad of Sexual Dependency*, New York: Aperture, 1986.

Goldwater, Robert, *Primitivism and Modern Painting* (1938), enlarged edition Cambridge MA: Belknap Press, 1986.

Goll, Ivan, 'The Negroes Are Conquering Europe' (Die Neger erobern Europa), from *Die literarische Welt*, no. 2, 15 January 1926, pp. 3–4; reprinted in *The Weimar Republic Sourcebook*, eds. Anton Kaes, Martin Jay, and Edward Dimendberg, Berkeley CA and London: University of California Press, 1994, pp. 559–60.

Gordon, Donald E., 'German Expressionism' in *'Primitivism' in 20th-Century Art: Affinity of the Tribal and Modern*, ed. William Rubin, vol. II, exh. cat., New York: Museum of Modern Art, 1984, pp. 369–403.

Gori, Gigliola, 'Model of Masculinity: Mussolini, the "New Italian" of the Fascist Era' in *Superman Supreme: Fascist Body as Political Icon—Global Fascism*, ed. J. A. Mangan, London: Frank Cass, 2000, pp. 27–61.

Grace, Della, 'Xenomorphisis', *New Formations, A Journal of Culture/Theory/Politics: Perversity*, no. 19, Spring 1993, pp. 123–4.

Green, Christopher (ed.), *Les Demoiselles d'Avignon*, Cambridge: Cambridge University Press, 2001.

Greenberg, Clement, 'Avant-Garde and Kitsch', *Partisan Review*, vol. 6, no. 5, New York, Fall 1939, pp. 34–48; reprinted in *Art in Theory 1900–1990: An Anthology of Changing Ideas*, eds. Charles Harrison and Paul Wood, Oxford: Blackwell, 1992, pp. 529–41.

Greenberg, Clement, *Art and Culture: Critical Essays*, Boston MA: Beacon Press, 1961.

Greenberg, Clement, 'Modernist Painting' (1965) in *Modern Art and Modernism: A Critical Anthology*, eds. Francis Frascina and Charles Harrison, London: Harper and Row, 1982.

Greenberg, Clement, *The Collected Essays and Criticism, vol. I: Perceptions and Judgements, 1939–1944*, ed. John O'Brian, Chicago: University of Chicago Press, 1986.

Greer, Germaine, *The Obstacle Race: The Fortunes of Women Painters and Their Work*, London: Secker and Warburg, 1979.

Griffin, Randall C., 'Thomas Eakins' Construction of the Male Body, or "Men Get to Know Each Other across the Space of Time"', *Oxford Art Journal*, vol. 18, no. 2, 1995, pp. 70–80.

Groseclose, Barbara, *Nineteenth-century American Art*, (Oxford History of Art) Oxford: Oxford University Press, 2000.

The Berlin of George Grosz, Drawings, Watercolours and Prints, 1912–1930, exh. cat., London: Royal Academy of Arts 1997.

Guattari, Félix, 'David Wojnarowicz', *Rethinking Marxism*, vol. 3, no. 1, Spring 1990, pp. 76–7.

Gudis, Catherine (ed.), *Helter Skelter, L.A. Art in the 90s*, exh. cat., Los Angeles CA: Museum of Contemporary Art, 1992.

Guilbaut, Serge, *How New York Stole the Idea of Modern Art: Abstract Expression, Freedom, and the Cold War*, trans. Arthur Goldhammer, Chicago: University of Chicago Press, 1985.

Hall, Stuart, 'What Is this "Black" in Black Popular Culture?' in *Black Popular Culture*, ed. Gina Dent, Seattle WA: Bay Press, 1992, pp. 21–33.

Hamilton, George Heard, *Manet and His Critics*, New York: W. W. Norton, 1969.

Hamilton, Walter, *The Aesthetic Movement in England*, London: Reeves and Turner, 1882.

Hammond, Harmony, *Lesbian Art in America: A Contemporary History*, New York: Rizzoli, 2000.

Haraway, Donna, 'A Manifesto for Cyborgs: Science, Technology, and Socialist Feminism in the 1980s', *The Socialist Review*, vol. 16, no. 2, March/April 1985, pp. 65–107.

Harding, Ellen (ed.), *Re-framing the Pre-Raphaelites: Historical and Theoretical Essays*, Aldershot: Scolar Press, 1996.

d'Harnoncourt, Anne and Walter Hopps, '*Étant donnés: 1. La Chute d'eau 2. Le Gaz d'éclairage*: Reflections on a New Work by Marcel Duchamp', *Philadelphia Museum of Art Bulletin*, vol. 64, nos. 299–300, Spring/Summer 1969.

Harris, Lyle Ashton and Thomas Allen Harris, 'Black Widow, a Conversation' in *The Passionate Camera: Photography and Bodies of Desire*, ed. Deborah Bright, London: Routledge, 1998, pp. 248–62.

Harrison, Charles and Paul Wood (eds.), *Art in Theory 1815–1900: An Anthology of Changing Ideas*, Oxford: Blackwell, 1998.

Harrison, Charles, Francis Frascina, and Gill Perry, *Primitivism, Cubism, Abstraction: The Early Twentieth Century*, New Haven CT and London: Yale University Press in association with The Open University, 1993.

Haskell, Barbara and John G. Hanhardt, *Yoko Ono: Arias and Objects*, Salt Lake City UT: Peregrine Smith Books, 1991.

Haskell, Francis, 'A Turk and His Pictures in Nineteenth-Century Paris', *Oxford Art Journal*, vol. 5, no. 1, 1982, pp. 40–7.

Hatt, Michael, 'The Male Body in Another Frame: Thomas Eakins' *The Swimming Hole* as a Homoerotic Image' in *The Body, Journal of Philosophy and the Visual Arts*, ed. Andrew Benjamin, 1993, pp. 9–21.

Hauptman, William, 'The Supression of Art in the McCarthy Decade', *Artforum*, vol. 12, no. 2, October 1973, pp. 48–52.

Hendricks, Gordon, *The Photographs of Thomas Eakins*, New York: Grossman Publishers, 1972.

Herbert, James D., *Fauve Painting: The Making of Cultural Politics*, New Haven CT and London: Yale University Press, 1992.

Hickey, Dave, 'In the Dancehall of the Dead' in *Robert Gober*, ed. Karen Marta, exh. cat., New York: DIA Center for the Arts, 1992, p. 37.

Higonet, Anne, *Pictures of Innocence: The History and Crisis of Ideal Childhood*, London: Thames and Hudson, 1998.

Hindry, Ann (ed.), *Artstudio: Spécial Roy Lichtenstein*, Spring 1991, Paris: Tobeart.

Hofmann, Werner, 'Gustav Klimt' in *Vienne 1880–1938: L'Apocalypse joyeuse*, ed. Jean Clair, exh. cat., Paris: Éditions du Centre Pompidou, 1986, pp. 192–202.

Hollier, Denis, *Against Architecture: The Writings of Georges Bataille*, trans. Betsy Wing, Cambridge MA and London: MIT Press, 1992.

Hopkins, David, *Marcel Duchamp and Max Ernst: The Bride Shared*, Oxford: Clarendon Press, 1998.

Hull, Anthony, *Goya: Man among Kings*, London and New York: Hamilton Press, 1987.

Hume, David, *Enquiry Concerning the Principles of Morals*, ed. David Berman, 3rd edn rev. P. H. Nidditch, Oxford: Oxford University Press, 1975.

Hume, David, *A Treatise of Human Nature*, ed. David Fate Norman and Mary J. Norton, Oxford: Oxford University Press, 2004.

Huyssen, Andreas, *After the Great Divide: Modernism, Mass Culture, Postmodernism*, Bloomington IN: Indiana University Press, 1986.

Jacobs, Jay, 'In the Galleries: Mel Ramos', *Arts*, January 1966, p. 56; reprinted in *Pop Art: A Critical History*, ed. Steven Henry Madoff, Berkeley CA: University of California Press, 1997, p. 324.

James, Henry, *The Painter's Eye: Notes and Essays on the Pictorial Arts*, ed. J. L. Sweeney, London: Hart-Davis, 1956.

Jameson, Frederic, 'Postmodernism or the Cultural Logic of Late Capitalism', *New Left Review*, no. 146, July–August 1984, pp. 53–92.

Jones, Amelia (ed.), *Sexual Politics, Judy Chicago's Dinner Party in Feminist Art History*, Berkeley CA: University of California Press in association with the Hammer Museum of Art, UCLA, 1996.

Jones, Amelia, 'Sexual Politics: Feminist Strategies, Feminist Conflicts, Feminist Histories' in *Sexual Politics: Judy Chicago's Dinner Party in Feminist Art History*, ed. Amelia Jones, Berkeley CA: University of California Press in association with the Hammer Museum of Art, UCLA, 1996, pp. 22–38.

Jones, Amelia, *Body Art: Performing the Subject*, Minneapolis MN and London: University of Minnesota Press, 1998.

Jones, Ann Rosalind, 'Writing the Body: Toward an Understanding of l'Écriture féminine' in *The New Feminist Criticism: Essays on Women, Literature and Theory*, ed. Elaine Showalter, London: Virago Press, 1986, pp. 361–77.

Jones, Jonathan, 'Paradise Reclaimed', *The Guardian (Weekend)*, 15 June 2002, pp. 18–23.

Jones, Leslie C., 'Transgressive Femininity: Art and Gender in the Sixties and Seventies' in *Abject Art: Repulsion and Desire in American Art*, exh. cat., New York: Whitney Museum, 1993, pp. 33–57.

Judd, Donald, 'In the Galleries: Claes Oldenburg', *Arts*, September 1964, p. 63, reprinted in *Pop Art: A Critical History*, ed. Steven Henry Madoff, Berkeley CA: University of California Press, 1997, p. 225.

Kaes, Anton, Martin Jay, and Edward Dimendberg (eds.), *The Weimar Republic Sourcebook*, Berkeley CA and London: University of California Press, 1994.

Kant, Immanuel, *Lectures on Ethics*, trans. Louis Infield, New York: Harper and Row, 1963.

Kaprow, Allan, *Assemblages, Environments and Happenings*, New York: H. N. Abrams, 1966.

Karia, Bhupendra (ed.), *Yayoi Kusama: A Retrospective*, exh. cat., New York: Center for International Contemporary Arts, 1989.

Kasson, Joy, *Marble Queens and Captives*, New Haven CT and London: Yale University Press, 1990.

Kazanjian, Dodie, 'Koons Crazy', *Vogue* (New York), August 1990, pp. 338–43.

Keane, Susan, *Lynda Benglis: Dual Natures*, exh. cat., Atlanta GA: High Museum of Art, 1991.

Keidan, Lois and Stuart Morgan, *Franko B*, London: Black Dog Publishing, 1998.

Kendrick, Walter, *The Secret Museum: Pornography in Modern Culture*, Berkeley CA: University of California Press, 1987.

Kestner, Joseph A., *Mythology and Misogyny: The Social Discourse of Nineteenth-Century British Classical-Subject Painting*, Madison WI and London: University of Wisconsin Press, 1989.

Kinsey, Alfred, *Sexual Behavior in the Human Female*, Philadelphia PA: Saunders, 1953.

Kinsey, Alfred, Wardell B. Pomeroy, and Clyde E. Martin, *Sexual Behavior in the Human Male*, Philadelphia PA: Saunders, 1948.

Yves Klein, exh. cat., Paris: Musée des Arts Décoratifs, 1969.

Klingender, Francis D., *Goya in the Democratic Tradition*, London: Sidgwick and Jackson, 1948.

Klossowski, Pierre, 'Aux limites de l'indiscrétion', interview with Jean-Maurice Monnoyer, *La Nouvelle Revue française*, no. 325, 1 February 1980, pp. 70–86.

Kochheiser, Thomas H. (ed.), *Hannah Wilke, A Retrospective*, Columbia MO and London: University of Missouri Press, 1989.

Kozloff, Joyce, *Patterns of Desire*, exh. cat., New York: Hudson Hills Press, 1990.

Krane, Susan, *Art on the Edge: Alison Saar/Fertile Ground*, exh. cat., Atlanta GA: High Museum of Art, 1993.

Krauss, Rosalind, 'Photography in the Service of Surrealism' in Krauss and Jane Livingston, *L'Amour Fou: Photography and Surrealism*, London: Arts Council of Great Britain, 1986, pp. 15–54.

Krauss, Rosalind, *Bachelors*, Cambridge MA and London: MIT Press, 1999.

Krauss, Rosalind, *A Voyage on the North Sea: Art in the Age of the Post-Medium Condition*, London: Thames and Hudson, 2000.

Krauss, Rosalind and Jane Livingston, *L'Amour Fou: Photography and Surrealism*, London: Arts Council of Great Britain, 1986.

Kristeva, Julia, *Revolution in Poetic Language* (1974), trans. Margaret Waller, New York: Columbia University Press, 1984.

Kristeva, Julia, *Desire in Language: A Semiotic Approach to Literature and Art* (1980), ed. Leon S. Roudiez and trans. Thomas Gora, Alice Jardine, and Leon S. Roudiez, Oxford: Blackwell, 1982.

Kristeva, Julia, *Powers of Horror: An Essay on Abjection* (1980), trans. Leon S. Roudiez, New York: Columbia University Press, 1982.

Kuenzli, Rudolf E. (ed.), *Dada and Surrealist Film*, Cambridge MA and London: MIT Press, 1987.

Yayoi Kusama: A Retrospective, exh. cat., New York: Center for International Contemporary Arts, 1989.

Kuspit, Donald, 'David Wojnarowicz: The Last Rimbaud', *Art in New England*, vol. 20, no. 4, June/July 1999, p. 11.

Lau, Grace, 'Perversion through the Camera', *New Formations, A Journal of Culture/Theory/Politics: Perversity*, no. 19, Spring 1993, pp. 45–6.

Lau, Grace and Amanda Hopkinson, *Adults in Wonderland: A Retrospective*, London: Serpent's Tail, 1997.

Lavin, Maud, *Cut with the Kitchen Knife: The Weimar Photomontages of Hannah Höch*, New Haven CT and London: Yale University Press, 1993.

Lebel, Jean-Jacques and Arnaud Labelle-Rojoux, *Poésie Directe, des Happenings à Polyphonix*, Paris: Opus International Edition, 1994.

Jean-Jacques Lebel, retour d'exil: peintures, dessins, collages 1954–1988, exh. cat., Paris: Galerie 1900–2000, 1988.

Leighten, Patricia, 'Colonialism, l'art nègre, and *Les Demoiselles d'Avignon*' in *Les Demoiselles d'Avignon*, ed. Christopher Green, Cambridge: Cambridge University Press, 2001, pp. 77–103.

Leperlier, François, *Claude Cahun: L'Écart et la métamorphose*, Paris: Éditions Jean Michel Place, 1992.

Levin, Kim, 'Reviews and Previews: Alice Neel', *ArtNews*, vol. 62, no. 6, October 1963, p. 11.

Levy, Julien, *Memoir of an Art Gallery*, New York: Putnam's, 1977.

Lewis, Beth Irwin, *George Grosz: Art and Politics in the Weimar Republic*, 2nd edn, Princeton NJ: Princeton University Press, 1991.

Lewis, Reina, *Gendering Orientalism: Race, Femininity and Representation*, London and New York: Routledge,1996.

Ligon, Glenn, interview with artist Byron Kim, in *Glenn Ligon, Unbecoming*, Judith Tannenbaum, exh. cat., Philadelphia PA: Institute of Contemporary Art, University of Pennsylvania, 1997, pp. 51–5.

Linden, Robin Ruth et al., *Against Sadomasochism*, East Palo Alto CA: From Frog in the Wall, 1982.

Lippard, Lucy R., *From the Centre: Feminist Essays on Women's Art*, New York: Dutton, 1976.

Lippard, Lucy, *Mixed Blessings: New Art in Multicultural America*, New York: Pantheon Books, 1990.

Lipton, Eunice, *Alias Olympia: A Woman's Search for Manet's Notorious Model and Her Own Desire*, New York: Charles Scribner's Sons, 1992.

Livingstone, Marco, *David Hockney*, London: Thames and Hudson, 1996.

Lloyd, Jill, 'L'Expressionisme Autrichien' in *La Verité nue: Gerstl, Kokoschka, Schiele, Boeckl*, exh. cat., Paris: Fondation Dina Vierny-Musée Maillol, 2001, pp. 21–37.

López, Yolanda M. and Moira Roth, 'Social Protest: Racism and Sexism' in *The Power of Feminist Art*, eds. Norma Broude and Mary D. Garrard, New York: Harry N. Abrams, 1994, pp. 140–57.

Lucas, Sarah, 'A Nod's as Good as a Wink', interview with Carl Freedman, *Frieze*, no. 17, June–July–August 1994, p. 31.

Lucie-Smith, Edward, *Sexuality in Western Art*, London: Thames and Hudson, 1991 (1972).

Lyotard, Jean-François, *The Postmodern Condition*, Manchester: Manchester University Press, 1984.

MacKinnon, Catharine A., 'Pornography: Not a Moral Issue', *Women's Studies International Forum*, vol. 9, no. 1, 1986, pp. 63–78.

MacKinnon, Catharine A., *Only Words*, Cambridge MA: Harvard University Press, 1993.

Madoff, Steven Henry (ed.), *Pop Art: A Critical History*, Berkeley CA: University of California Press, 1997.

Magritte, René, *Écrits complets*, ed. André Blavier, Paris: Flammarion, 2001.

Mahon, Alyce, 'Outrage aux bonnes mœurs: Jean-Jacques Lebel and the Marquis de Sade' in *Jean-Jacques Lebel: Paintings, Sculptures, Installations*, exh. cat., eds. Uli Todoroff and Sophie Haaser, Vienna: Museum Moderner Kunst, Stiftung Ludwig Wien, 1998, pp. 93–112.

Mahon, Alyce, 'Staging Desire' in *Surrealism: Desire Unbound*, eds. Jennifer Mundy and Dawn Ades, London: Tate Publishing, 2001, pp. 277–91.

Mahon, Alyce, 'Pierre Klossowski, Theo-Pornologer', critical introduction to Sarah Wilson (ed.), *Pierre Klossowski: Decadence of the Nude/La Décadence du nu*, London: Black Dog Publishing, Revisions Series, 2002, pp. 33–101.

Mahon, Alyce, 'Hans Bellmer's Libidinal Politics' in *Surrealism, Politics and Culture*, eds. Raymond Spiteri and Donald LaCoss, London: Ashgate Publishers, 2003, pp. 246–66.

Mahon, Alyce, *Surrealism and the Politics of Eros 1938–1968*, London: Thames and Hudson, 2005.

Maloney, Martin, 'Everyone a Winner! Selected British Art from the Saatchi Collection 1987–97' in Norman Rosenthal et al., *Sensation: Young British Artists from the Saatchi Collection*, exh. cat., London: Royal Academy of Arts, 1997, pp. 26–34.

Mangan, J. A. (ed.), *Superman Supreme: Fascist Body as Political Icon – Global Fascism*, London: Frank Cass, 2000.

Marcuse, Herbert, *Eros and Civilization: A Philosophical Inquiry into Freud* (1956), London: Routledge, 1998.

Marinetti, F. T., 'Futurist "Founding Manifesto"' (1909) in *Art in Theory 1900–1990: An Anthology of Changing Ideas*, eds. Charles Harrison and Paul Wood, Oxford: Blackwell, 1992, pp. 145–9.

Mark, Lisa Gabrielle (ed.), *Mike Kelley and Paul McCarthy: Collaborative Works*, exh. cat., Toronto: The Power Plant Contemporary Art Gallery, 2000.

Marsh, Jan *The Pre-Raphaelite Sisterhood*, London and New York: Quartet Books 1985.

Marsh, Jan and Pamela Gerrish Nunn, *Pre-Raphaelite Women Artists*, exh. cat., Manchester: Manchester City Art Galleries 1998.

Marta, Karen (ed.), *Robert Gober*, exh. cat., New York: DIA Center for the Arts, 1992.

Martin, Timothy, 'Fresh Acconci, Beautiful Acconci' in *Mike Kelley and Paul McCarthy: Collaborative Works*, ed. Lisa Gabrielle Mark, exh. cat., Toronto: The Power Plant Contemporary Art Gallery, 2000, pp. 30–7.

Mavor, Carol, *Pleasure Taken: Performances of Sexuality and Loss in Victorian Photographs*, Durham NC and London: Duke University Press, 1995.

McCauley, Anne, 'Alfred Stieglitz et le nu féminin', *4814 La revue du Musée d'Orsay*, no. 19, Autumn 2004, pp. 78–92.

McCorquodale, Duncan (ed.), *Orlan: This Is My Body ... This Is My Software*, London: Black Dog Publishing, 1996.

Mekas, Jonas, 'Movie Journal' (1966) in *Jean-Jacques Lebel, retour d'exil: Peintures, dessins, collages 1954–1988*, exh. cat., Paris: Galerie 1900–2000, 1988, p. 73.

Mel Ramos, A Twenty-Year Survey, exh. cat., Waltham MA: Rose Art Museum, Brandeis University, 1980.

Merck, Mandy, 'Bedtime' in *The Art of Tracey Emin*, eds. Mandy Merck and Chris Townsend, London: Thames and Hudson, 2002, pp. 119–33.

Merck, Mandy and Chris Townsend (eds.), *The Art of Tracey Emin*, London: Thames and Hudson, 2002.

Merleau-Ponty, Maurice, 'Cézanne's Doubt' in *Sense and Non-sense*, trans. Herbert L. Dreyfus and Patricia Allen Dreyfus, Evanston IL: Northwestern University Press, 1964, pp. 9–25.

Meyer, Richard, *Outlaw Representation: Censorship and Homosexuality in Twentieth-Century American Art*, Boston MA: Beacon Press, 2004.

Michel, Alice, 'Degas et son modèle', *Mercure de France*, 16 February 1919, pp. 457–8.

Millet, Catherine, 'Jean-Jacques Lebel, oppositionnel', *Art Press*, May 1996, no. 213, pp. 20–7.

Monk, Philip, 'A Twisted Pedagogy', *Mike Kelley and Paul McCarthy: Collaborative Works*, ed. Lisa Gabrielle Mark, exh. cat., Toronto: The Power Plant Contemporary Art Gallery, 2000, pp. 8–19.

Monneret, Sophie, *Renoir*, Paris: Éditions du Chêne, 1989.

Montgomery, John, *The Fifties*, London: Allen and Unwin, 1965.

Morgan, Stuart, 'Behaviour', interview with Nayland Blake, *Frieze*, no. 5, June–August 1992, pp. 39–43.

Morgan, Stuart, 'Of Goats and Men', *Frieze*, no. 20, January–February 1995, pp. 34–8.

Morgan, Stuart, 'The Illustrated Man: Franko B' in Lois Keidan and Stuart Morgan, *Franko B*, London: Black Dog Publishing, 1998, n.p.

Morris, Frances (ed.), *Paris Post War: Art and Existentialism 1945–55*, exh. cat., London: Tate Gallery, 1993.

Morrisroe, Patricia, *Mapplethorpe, A Biography*, New York: Random House, 1995.

Mulvey, Laura, 'Visual Pleasure and Narrative Cinema', *Screen*, vol. 16, no. 3, Autumn 1975, pp. 6–18.

Mulvey, Laura, *Fetishism and Curiosity*, London: British Film Institute, 1996.

Mundy, Jennifer and Dawn Ades (eds.), *Surrealism: Desire Unbound*, London: Tate Publishing, 2001.

Munroe, Alexandra, 'Obsession, Fantasy and Outrage: The Art of Yayoi Kusama' in *Yayoi Kusama: A Retrospective*, ed. Bhupendra Karia, exh. cat., New York: Center for International Contemporary Arts, 1989, pp. 11–35.

Nead, Lynda, 'Representation, Sexuality and the Female Nude', *Art History*, vol. 6, no. 2, June 1983, pp. 227–336.

Nead, Lynda, *Myths of Sexuality: Representations of Women in Victorian Britain*, Oxford: Basil Blackwell, 1988.

Nead, Lynda, *The Female Nude, Art, Obscenity and Sexuality*, London and New York: Routledge, 1992.

Néret, Gilles, *Twentieth-Century Erotic Art*, Cologne: Taschen, 1993.

Néret, Gilles, *Balthus*, Cologne: Taschen, 2003.

Nezval, Vítězslav and Jindřich Štyrský, *Edition 69*, trans. Jed Slast, Prague: Twisted Spoon Press, 2004.

Nietzsche, Friedrich, *The Will to Power*, trans. Walter Kaufmann and R. J. Hollingdale, New York: Vintage, 1968.

Nixon, Mignon, 'Louise Bourgeois' *Fillette*', *Parkett*, no. 27, 1991, pp. 49–51.

Nochlin, Linda, 'The Origin without an Original', *October*, no. 37, Summer 1986, pp. 77–86.

Nochlin, Linda, *Women, Art and Power and Other Essays*, London: Thames and Hudson, 1989.

Nochlin, Linda, *The Politics of Vision, Essays on Nineteenth-Century Art and Society* (1989), London: Thames and Hudson, 1991.

O'Sullivan, Anna, 'Irish Art in New York', *Circa*, no. 64, Summer 1993, p. 22.

O'Grady, Loraine, 'Olympia's Maid: Reclaiming Black Female Sexuality', *Afterimage*, vol. 20, no. 1, Summer 1992, pp. 14–15.

Obrist, Hans Ulrich, interview with Matthew Barney, *Tate Magazine*, no. 2, 2002, online edition, http://www.tate.org.uk/magazine/issue2/barney.htm.

Ockman, Carol, *Ingres' Eroticized Bodies: Retracing the Serpentine Line*, New Haven CT: Yale University Press, 1995.

Ofili, Chris, interview with Marco Spinelli in *'Brilliant!': New Art from London*, exh. cat., Minneapolis MN: Walker Art Center, 1995, pp. 66–7.

Oldenburg, Claes, 'I Am for an Art . . .', first published in *Environments, Situations and Spaces*, Martha Jackson Gallery, exh. cat., May–June 1961; reprinted in *Art in Theory 1900–1990*, eds. Charles Harrison and Paul Wood, Oxford: Blackwell, 1992, pp. 728–30.

Ono, Yoko, *Grapefruit*, New York: Simon and Schuster, 1970.

Ono, Yoko, 'What Is the Relationship between the Artist and the World?', written for the Cannes Film Festival, 1971; reprinted in Barbara Haskell and John G. Hanhardt, *Yoko Ono: Arias and Objects*, Salt Lake City UT: Peregrine Smith Books, 1991, p. 109.

Orlan, 'Conférence' in *Orlan: This Is My Body . . . This Is My Software*, ed. Duncan McCorquodale, London: Black Dog Publishing, 1996, pp. 82–93.

Orlan, 'Virtuel et réel: dialectique et complexité' in Dominique Baqué, Marek Bartelik, and Orlan, *Orlan: Refiguration Self-Hybridations, Série Précolombienne*, Lyon: Galerie de Bellecour, and Paris: Éditions Al Dante, 2001, pp. 42–57.

Ormond, Léonée and Richard Ormond, *Lord Leighton*, New Haven CT: Yale University Press 1975.

Otto, Walter F., *Dionysus: Myth and Cult*, Bloomington IN and London: Indiana University Press, 1965.

Pagé, Suzanne et al., *Francis Picabia: Singuliér idéal*, exh. cat., Paris: Musée d'Art Moderne de la Ville de Paris, 2002.

Parker, Rosika and Griselda Pollock, *Old Mistresses: Women Art and Ideology*, London: Routledge and Kegan Paul, 1981.

Pater, Walter, *Greek Studies* (1895), Oxford: Blackwell, and New York: Johnson Reprint Corp., 1967.

Perry, Gill, 'Primitivism and the Modern' in *Primitivism, Cubism, Abstraction: The Early Twentieth Century*, eds. Charles Harrison, Francis Frascina, and Gill Perry, New Haven CT and London: Yale University Press in association with the Open University, 1993, pp. 3–85.

Petropoulos, Jonathan, *Art as Politics in the Third Reich*, Chapel Hill NC: University of North Carolina Press, 1996.

Petry, Michael, *Hidden Histories: 20th-century Male Same-Sex Lovers in the Visual Arts*, London: ArtMedia Press, 2004.

Phillips, Lisa, *The American Century: Art and Culture 1950–2000*, exh. cat., New York: Whitney Museum of American Art and W. W. Norton and Company, 1999.

Picabia et la Côte d'Azur, exh. cat., Nice: Musée d'Art Moderne et d'art Contemporain, 1991.

Picasso érotique, exh. cat., Paris: Galerie Nationale du Jeu de Paume/Réunion des Musées Nationaux, 2001.

Pierre, José (ed.), *Investigating Sex: Surrealist Discussion 1928–1932*, trans. Malcolm Imrie, London and New York: Verso, 1992.

Pietz, William, 'The Problem of the Fetish I', *Res*, vol. 9, Spring 1985, pp. 5–17.

Pietz, William, 'The Problem of the Fetish II', *Res*, vol. 13, 1987, pp. 23–45.

Plato, *The Republic*, ed. G. R. F. Ferrari, trans. Tom Griffith, Cambridge: Cambridge University Press, 2004.

Plato, *The Symposium*, trans. with introduction by Christopher Gill, London: Penguin Books, 2003.

Platt, Susan, *Art and Politics in the 1930s: Modernism—Marxism—Americanism: A History of Cultural Activism during the Depression Years*, New York: Midmarch Arts Press, 1999.

Poggioli, Renato, *The Theory of the Avant-Garde* (1962), trans. Gerald Fitzgerald, Cambridge MA: Harvard University Press, 1968.

Pollock, Griselda, *Avant Garde Gambits 1888–1893: Gender and the Colour of Art History*, London: Thames and Hudson, 1992.

Pollock, Griselda, *Mary Cassatt: Painter of Modern Woman*, London: Thames and Hudson, 1998.

Pollock, Griselda, *Vision and Difference: Femininity, Feminism and the Histories of Art*, London and New York: Routledge, 1988.

Powell, Richard J., *Black Art: A Cultural History*, London: Thames and Hudson, 2002.

Prettejohn, Elizabeth, 'The Modernism of Frederic Leighton' in *English Art 1860–1914: Modern Artists and Identity*, eds. David Peters Corbett and Lara Perry, Manchester: Manchester University Press, 2000, pp. 31–48.

Quinn, Billy, *A Plague of Angels*, exh. cat., Chicago: Mindy Oh Gallery, 1993.

Rahmani, Aviva, 'A Conversation on Censorship with Carolee Schneemann', *M/E/A/N/I/N/G*, no. 6, 1989, pp. 3–7.

Ramos, Mel, *The Girls of Mel Ramos*, Chicago: Playboy Press, and New York: Simon and Schuster, 1975.

Ratnam, Niru, 'Chris Ofili and the Limits of Hybridity', *New Left Review*, no. 235, May–June 1999, pp. 153–9.

Ray, Man *Self Portrait* (1986), with afterword by Juliet Man Ray and foreword by Merry A. Foresta, Boston MA: Bullfinch Press, 1998.

Rewald, John (ed.), *Paul Cézanne, Letters*, trans. Marguerite Kay, Oxford: B. Cassirer, 1976.

Reynolds, Joshua, *Discourses on Art*, New Haven CT: Yale University Press, 1981.

Rhodes, Colin, *Primitivism and Modern Art*, London: Thames and Hudson, 1994.

Rice, Shelley (ed.), *Inverted Odysseys: Claude Cahun, Maya Deren, Cindy Sherman*, Cambridge MA: MIT Press, 1999.

Riviere, Joan, 'Womanliness as a Masquerade', *International Journal of Psycho-Analysis* (1929), reprinted in *The Inner World and Joan Riviere: Collected Papers, 1920–1958*, London: Karnac Books, 1991, pp. 90–101.

Rizk, Mysoon, 'Constructing Histories: David Wojnarowicz's *Arthur Rimbaud in New York*' in *The Passionate Camera: Photography and Bodies of Desire*, ed. Deborah Bright, London: Routledge, 1998, pp. 178–9.

Roberts, Mary, 'Contested Terrains: Women Orientalists and the Colonial Harem' in *Orientalism's Interlocutors: Painting, Architecture, Photography*, eds. Jill Beaulieu and Mary Roberts, Durham NC and London: Duke University Press, 2002, pp. 179–203.

Robinson, Hilary (ed.), *Feminism—Art—Theory: An Anthology 1968–2000*, Oxford: Blackwell, 2001.

Roessler, Arthur, *Egon Schiele en Prison* (1922), Lyon: La Fosse aux ours, 2000.

Rose, Barbara, 'Is It Art? Orlan and the Transgressive Act', *Art in America*, vol. 2, February 1993, pp. 82–7 and p. 125.

Rosenberg, Harold, *The Tradition of the New*, Chicago and London: University of Chicago Press, 1960.

Rosenblum, Robert, *On Modern American Art, Selected Essays*, New York: Harry N. Abrams, 1999.

Rosenblum, Robert, '*Les Demoiselles d'Avignon* et le théâtre érotique de Picasso' in *Picasso érotique*, exh. cat., Paris: Galerie Nationale du Jeu de Paume/Réunion des Musées Nationaux, 2001, pp. 94–9.

Rosenthal, Nan, 'Assisted Levitation: The Art of Yves Klein' in *Yves Klein 1928–1962, A Retrospective*, exh. cat., Houston TX: Institute of the Arts, Rice University, 1982.

Rosenthal, Norman et al., *Apocalypse: Beauty and Horror*, exh. cat., London: Royal College of Art, 2002.

Rosenthal, Norman et al., *Sensation: Young British Artists from the Saatchi Collection*, exh. cat., London: Royal Academy of Arts, 1997.

Rubin, William (ed.), *'Primitivism' in 20th-Century Art: Affinity of the Tribal and Modern*, exh. cat., 2 vols., New York: Museum of Modern Art, 1984.

Rubin, William, 'Modernist Primitivism: An Introduction' in *'Primitivism' in 20th-Century Art: Affinity of the Tribal and Modern*, exh. cat., 2 vols., New York: Museum of Modern Art, 1984, vol. I, pp. 1–81.

Rubin, William, *Les Demoiselles d'Avignon, Studies in Modern Art 3*, New York: Museum of Modern Art, 1994.

de Sade, D. A. F., *Justine, Philosophy in the Boudoir, Eugénie de Franval and Other Writings*, eds. Richard Seaver and Austryn Wainhouse, London: Arrow Books, 1965.

Said, Edward, *Orientalism: Western Conceptions of the Orient* (1978), Harmondsworth: Penguin Books, 1995.

de Saint-Simon, Henri, *Literary, Philosophical and Industrial Opinion* (1825) in *Art in Theory, 1815–1900: An Anthology of Changing Ideas*, eds. Charles Harrison and Paul Wood, Oxford: Blackwell, 1998, pp. 37–40.

Sandler, Irving, *American Art of the 1960s*, New York: Harper and Row, 1988.

Sartre, Jean-Paul, *Essays in Existentialism*, ed. and foreword by Wade Baskin, New York: Citadel Press, 1993.

Saslow, James, *Ganymede in the Renaissance: Homosexuality in Art and Society*, New Haven CT and London: Yale University Press, 1986.

Schaffner, Ingrid, with photographs by Eric Schaal, *Salvador Dalí's Dream of Venus: The Surrealist Funhouse from the 1939 World's Fair*, New York: Princeton Architectural Press, 2002.

Schimmel, Paul, 'Into the Maelstrom: L.A. Art at the End of the Century' in *Helter Skelter: L.A. Art in the 90s*, ed. Catherine Gudis, exh. cat., Los Angeles CA: Museum of Contemporary Art, 1992, pp. 19–22.

Schneemann, Carolee, *Imaging Her Erotics: Essays, Interviews, Projects*, Cambridge MA: MIT Press, 2002.

Scruton, Roger, *Sexual Desire, A Philosophical Investigation*, London: Weidenfeld and Nicolson, 1986.

Seckel, Hélène (ed.), *Les Demoiselles d'Avignon*, exh. cat., Paris: Musée Picasso, 1988.

Seitz, William, 'What's Happened to Art? An Interview with Marcel Duchamp on Present Consequences of New York's 1913 Armory Show', *Vogue* (New York), 15 February 1963, p. 113.

Selz, Peter, 'Variety: Pop Goes the Artist', *Partisan Review*, Summer 1963, pp. 314–16.

Shiel, Mark and Tony Fitzmaurice (eds.), *Cinema and the City: Film and Urban Societies in a Global Context*, Oxford: Blackwell Publishers, 2001.

Short, Robert, *The Age of Gold: Surrealist Cinema*, New York: Creation Books, 2003.

Showalter, Elaine (ed.), *The New Feminist Criticism: Essays on Women, Literature and Theory*, London: Virago Press, 1986.

Showalter, Elaine, *The Female Malady: Women, Madness and English Culture, 1830–1980*, London: Virago Press, 1987.

Simmons, Sherwin, 'Ernst Kirchner's Streetwalkers: Art, Luxury, and Immorality in Berlin, 1913–16', *The Art Bulletin*, vol. 82, no. 1, March 2000, pp. 117–48.

Simpson, Marc, 'Thomas Eakins and His Arcadian Works', *Smithsonian Studies in American Art*, vol. 1, no. 2, Fall 1987, pp. 71–95.

Simpson, Marc, '*Swimming* through Time: An Introduction' in *Thomas Eakins and the Swimming Picture*, eds. Doreen Bolger and Sarah Cash, Fort Worth TX: Amon Carter Museum, 1996, pp. 1–12.

Sims, Lowery, 'Hannah Wilke: The Body Politic of the Adventures of a Good-Looking Feminist' in Benjamin H. Buchloh, Lucy Lippard, and Donald B. Kuspit, *Art and Ideology*, exh. cat., New York: The New Museum of Contemporary Art, 1984, p. 48.

Sinclair, John, *Guitar Army: Street Writings/Prison Writings*, New York: Douglas, 1972.

Smith, Alison, *The Victorian Nude: Sexuality, Morality and Art*, Manchester: Manchester University Press, 1996.

Kiki Smith: Silent Work, exh. cat., Vienna: MAK (Austrian Museum of Applied Arts), 1992.

Solomon-Godeau, Abigail, 'Going Native', *Art in America*, vol. 77, July 1989, pp. 119–28.

Solomon-Godeau, Abigail, *Male Trouble: A Crisis in Representation*, London: Thames and Hudson 1997.

Solomon-Godeau, Abigail, 'The Equivocal "I": Claude Cahun as Lesbian Subject' in *Inverted Odysseys: Claude Cahun, Maya Deren, Cindy Sherman*, ed. Shelley Rice, Cambridge MA: MIT Press, 1999, pp. 111–25.

Sontag, Susan, *Under the Sign of Saturn*, New York: Farrar, Straus, and Giroux, 1980.

Sontag, Susan, *Against Interpretation*, London: André Deutsch, 1987.

Spector, Jack, *The Aesthetics of Freud*, London: Allen Lane, 1972.

Spector, Jack, *Delacroix: The Death of Sardanapalus*, New York: Viking Press, 1974.

Spector, Nancy, *Matthew Barney: The Cremaster Cycle*, exh. cat., New York: Guggenheim Museum, 2002.

Spiteri, Raymond and Donald LaCoss (eds.), *Surrealism, Politics and Culture*, London: Ashgate Publishers, 2003.

Spivak, Gayatri C., 'Can the Subaltern Speak?' in *The Postcolonial Studies Reader*, eds. Bill Ashcroft, Garther Griffiths, and Helen Tiffin, New York: Routledge, 1995, pp. 24–8.

Sprinkle, Annie, *Post Porn Modernist*, Amsterdam: Torch Books, 1991.

Stallabrass, Julian, *High Art Lite: British Art in the 1990s*, London and New York: Verso, 1999.

Steinberg, Leo, 'The Philosophical Brothel', *Art News*, Part I, vol. 71, no. 5, September 1972, pp. 22–9 and Part II, vol. 71, no. 6, October 1972, pp. 38–47.

Steinem, Gloria, *Outrageous Acts and Everyday Rebellions*, London: Fontana, 1984.

Stich, Sidra, *Made in USA: An Americanization in Modern Art, the '50s and '60s*, Berkeley CA: University of California Press, 1987.

Stich, Sidra, *Yves Klein*, exh. cat., London: Hayward Gallery and Cantz, 1995.

Stoos, Toni and Patrick Elliott, *Alberto Giacometti, 1901–1966*, exh. cat., Vienna: Kunsthalle, and Edinburgh: National Galleries of Scotland, 1996.

Suleiman, Susan Rubin, 'Leonora Carrington and Max Ernst' in *Significant Others: Creativity and Intimate Partnership*, eds. Whitney Chadwick and Isabelle de Courtivron, London: Thames and Hudson, 1993, pp. 97–117.

Swenson, G. R., 'What Is Pop Art?', *Art News*, February 1964, pp. 40–1.

Alina Szapocznikow, exh. cat., Paris: Musée d'Art Moderne de la Ville de Paris, 1973.

Takemoto, Tina, 'The Melancholia of AIDS: Interview with Douglas Crimp', *Art Journal*, Winter 2003, pp. 80–90.

Tannenbaum, Judith, *Glenn Ligon, Unbecoming*, exh. cat., Philadelphia PA: Institute of Contemporary Art, University of Pennsylvania, 1997.

Tanning, Dorothea, *Between Lives: An Artist and Her World*, New York and London: W. W. Norton and Company, 2001.

Taylor, Simon, 'The Phobic Object: Abjection in Contemporary Art' in *Abject Art: Repulsion and Desire in American Art*, exh. cat., New York: Whitney Museum, 1993, pp. 59–83.

Temkin, Ann (ed.), *Alice Neel*, exh. cat., New York: Whitney Museum of American Art, 2000.

Temkin, Ann, 'Alice Neel: Self and Others' in *Alice Neel*, exh. cat., ed. Temkin, New York: Whitney Museum of American Art, 2000, pp. 13–31.

Saint Teresa, *The Life of St Teresa of Avila by Herself*, Harmondsworth: Penguin Books, 1957.

Theweleit, Klaus, *Male Fantasies, vol. I: Women, Floods, Bodies, History* (1977), trans. Stephen Conway, Erica Carter, and Chris Turner, Minneapolis MN: University of Minnesota Press, 1987.

Thomson, Belinda, *Gauguin*, London: Thames and Hudson, 1987.

Todoroff, Uli and Sophie Haaser (eds.), *Jean-Jacques Lebel: Paintings, Sculptures, Installations*, exh. cat., Vienna: Museum Moderner Kunst, Stiftung Ludwig Wien, 1998.

Tomii, Reiko and Kathleen M. Friello (eds.), *Yes Yoko Ono*, New York: Japan Society New York and Harry N. Abrams, 2001.

Tomkins, Calvin, *The Bride and the Bachelors*, New York: Penguin Books, 1965.

Tomkins, Calvin, *Duchamp: A Biography*, London 1997.

Trachtenberg, Alan (ed.), *Classic Essays on Photography*, New Haven CT: Leete's Island Books, 1980.

Varnedoe, Kirk, *Vienna 1900*, exh. cat., New York: Museum of Modern Art, 1986.

Varnedoe, Kirk and Adam Gopnik, *High and Low: Modern Art and Popular Culture*, exh. cat., New York: Museum of Modern Art, 1991.

Vasari, Giorgio, *Lives of the Artists*, vol. 1 (1568), trans. George Bull, Harmondsworth: Penguin Books, 1965.

La Vérité Nu: Gerstl, Kokoschka, Schiele, Boeckl, exh. cat., Paris: Fondation Dina Vierny-Musée Maillol, 2001.

Walker, Gerry, *Micheal Farrell*, Cork: Gandon Editions, 1998.

Walsh, John (ed.), *Bill Viola: The Passions*, exh. cat., Los Angeles CA: J. Paul Getty Museum, 2003.

Warhol, Andy, *The Philosophy of Andy Warhol (From A to B and Back Again)*, New York: Harcourt Brace Jovanovich, 1975.

Watney, Simon, *Policing Desire: Aids, Pornography and the Media*, London: Comedia, 1987.

Wavelet, Christophe, 'Vito Acconci, Yvonne Rainer, interviewed by Christophe Wavelet, at Acconci Studio, Brooklyn, 24 August 2003' in *Vito Hannibal Acconci Studio*, ed. Corinne Diserens, exh. cat., Barcelona: Museu d'Art Contemporani de Barcelona, 2004, pp. 12–45.

Webb, Peter, *The Erotic Arts*, London: Secker and Warburg, 1983 (1975).

Webb, Peter and Robert Short, *Hans Bellmer*, New York: Quartet Books, 1985.

Weiermair, Peter (ed.), *Erotic Art from the Seventeenth Century to the Twentieth Century*, exh. cat., Frankfurt: Frankfurter Kunstverein and Edition Stemmle, 1995.

Weisberg, Gabriel P. and Jane R. Becker (eds.), *Overcoming All Obstacles: The Women of the Académie Julian*, exh. cat., New York: The Dahesh Museum, and New Brunswick NJ and London: Rutgers University Press, 1999.

Weiss, Allen S., 'Between the Sign of the Scorpion and the Sign of the Cross: *L'Age d'or*' in *Dada and Surrealist Film*, ed. Rudolf E. Kuenzli, Cambridge MA and London: MIT Press, 1987, pp. 159–75.

West, Shearer, *The Visual Arts in Germany 1890–1937: Utopia and Despair*, Manchester: Manchester University Press, 2000.

White, Edmund, 'Altars: The Radicalism of Simplicity' in Robert Mapplethorpe, *Altars*, London: Jonathan Cape, pp. 128–34.

Whitford, Frank, 'The Many Faces of George Grosz' in *The Berlin of George Grosz: Drawings, Watercolours and Prints, 1912–1930*, exh. cat., London: Royal Academy of Arts, 1997, pp. 1–27.

Whiting, Cécile, *A Taste for Pop, Pop Art, Gender and Consumer Culture*, New York and Cambridge: Cambridge University Press, 1997.

Wilke, Hannah, 'Intercourse with…', text used in videotape performance and lecture at the London Art Gallery, London, Ontario, Canada, 17 February 1977; reprinted in *Hannah Wilke, A Retrospective*, ed. Thomas H. Kochheiser, Columbia MO and London: University of Missouri Press, 1989, p. 140.

Williams, Linda, *Hard Core, Power, Pleasure, and the 'Frenzy of the Visible'*, Berkeley and Los Angeles CA: University of California Press, 1998 (1989).

Williams, Linda, *Figures of Desire: A Theory and Analysis of Surrealist Film*, Berkeley CA and Oxford: University of California Press, 1992.

Wilson, Julia-Bryan, 'Remembering Yoko Ono's *Cut Piece*', *Oxford Art Journal*, vol. 26, no. 1, 2003, pp. 99–123.

Wilson, Sarah (ed.), *Pierre Klossowski: Decadence of the Nude/La Décadence du nu*, London: Black Dog Publishing, Revisions Series, 2002.

Wilson, Sarah, '*L'Histoire d'O*, Sacred and Profane' in *Orlan, This Is My Body… This Is My Software*, ed. Duncan McCorquodale, London: Black Dog Publishing, 1996, pp. 8–17.

Wilson, Sarah, 'Paris Post War: In Search of the Absolute' in *Paris Post War: Art and Existentialism 1945–55*, ed. Frances Morris, exh. cat., London: Tate Gallery, 1993, pp. 25–52.

David Wojnarowicz: In the Garden, exh. cat., New York: PPOW Gallery, 1990.

Wollen, Peter, *Raiding the Icebox: Reflections on Twentieth-century Culture*, London and New York: Verso, 1993.

Wollen, Peter, 'Little Stabs at Happiness', *Frieze*, no. 16, May 1994, pp. 44–5.

Yeats, William Butler, 'The Censorship and St. Thomas Acquinas', *Irish Statesman*, 11, 1928, pp. 47–8; reprinted in *Banned in Ireland: Censorship and the Irish Writer*, ed. Julia Carson, London: Routledge, 1990, pp. 130–2.

Yeldham, Charlotte, *Women Artists in Nineteenth-century France and England*, 2 vols., New York and London: Garland Publishing, 1984.

Zelevansky, Lynn, 'Dricing Image: Yayoi Kusama in New York' in Zelevansky et al., *Love Forever: Yayoi Kusama, 1958–1968*, exh. cat., Los Angeles CA: Los Angeles County Museum of Art, 1998, pp. 11–41.

Zelevansky, Lynn et al., *Love Forever: Yayoi Kusama, 1958–1968*, exh. cat., Los Angeles CA: Los Angeles County Museum of Art, 1998.

Zola, Émile, 'Édouard Manet' (1867) in *Modern Art and Modernism: A Critical Anthology*, eds. Francis Frascina and Charles Harrison, London: Harper and Row, 1982, pp. 29–39.

Zola, Émile, *Nana* (1880), trans. and introduction by George Holden, Harmondsworth: Penguin Classics, 1972.

Zola, Émile, *The Masterpiece* (*L'Œuvre*, 1886), trans. Thomas Walton, London: Elek Books, 1950.

List of Illustrations

The publisher and author apologize for any errors or omissions in the above list. If contacted they will be pleased to rectify these at the earliest opportunity.

Index

Note: references in *italics* refer to illustrations and captions.